CAMBRIDGE STUDIES IN
ANGLO-SAXON ENGLAND
12

INTERACTIONS OF THOUGHT AND LANGUAGE IN OLD ENGLISH POETRY

CAMBRIDGE STUDIES IN ANGLO-SAXON ENGLAND

Cambridge Studies in Anglo-Saxon England is a series of scholarly texts and monographs intended to advance our knowledge of all aspects of the field of Anglo-Saxon studies. The scope of the series, like that of *Anglo-Saxon England*, its periodical counterpart, embraces original scholarship in various disciplines: literary, historical, archaeological, philological, art historical, palaeographical, architectural, liturgical and numismatic.

Volumes published

1 *Anglo-Saxon Crucifixion Iconography and the Art of the Monastic Revival* by BARBARA C. RAW
2 *The Cult of the Virgin Mary in Anglo-Saxon England* by MARY CLAYTON
3 *Religion and Literature in Western England, 600–800* by PATRICK SIMS-WILLIAMS
4 *Visible Song: Transitional Literacy in Old English Verse* by KATHERINE O'BRIEN O'KEEFFE
5 *The Metrical Grammar of* Beowulf by CALVIN B. KENDALL
6 *The Irish Tradition in Old English Literature* by CHARLES D. WRIGHT
7 *Anglo-Saxon Medicine* by M. L. CAMERON
8 *The Poetic Art of Aldhelm* by ANDY ORCHARD
9 *The Old English Lives of St Margaret* by MARY CLAYTON and HUGH MAGENNIS
10 *Biblical Commentaries from the Canterbury School of Theodore and Hadrian* by BERNHARD BISCHOFF and MICHAEL LAPIDGE
11 *Archbishop Theodore* by MICHAEL LAPIDGE

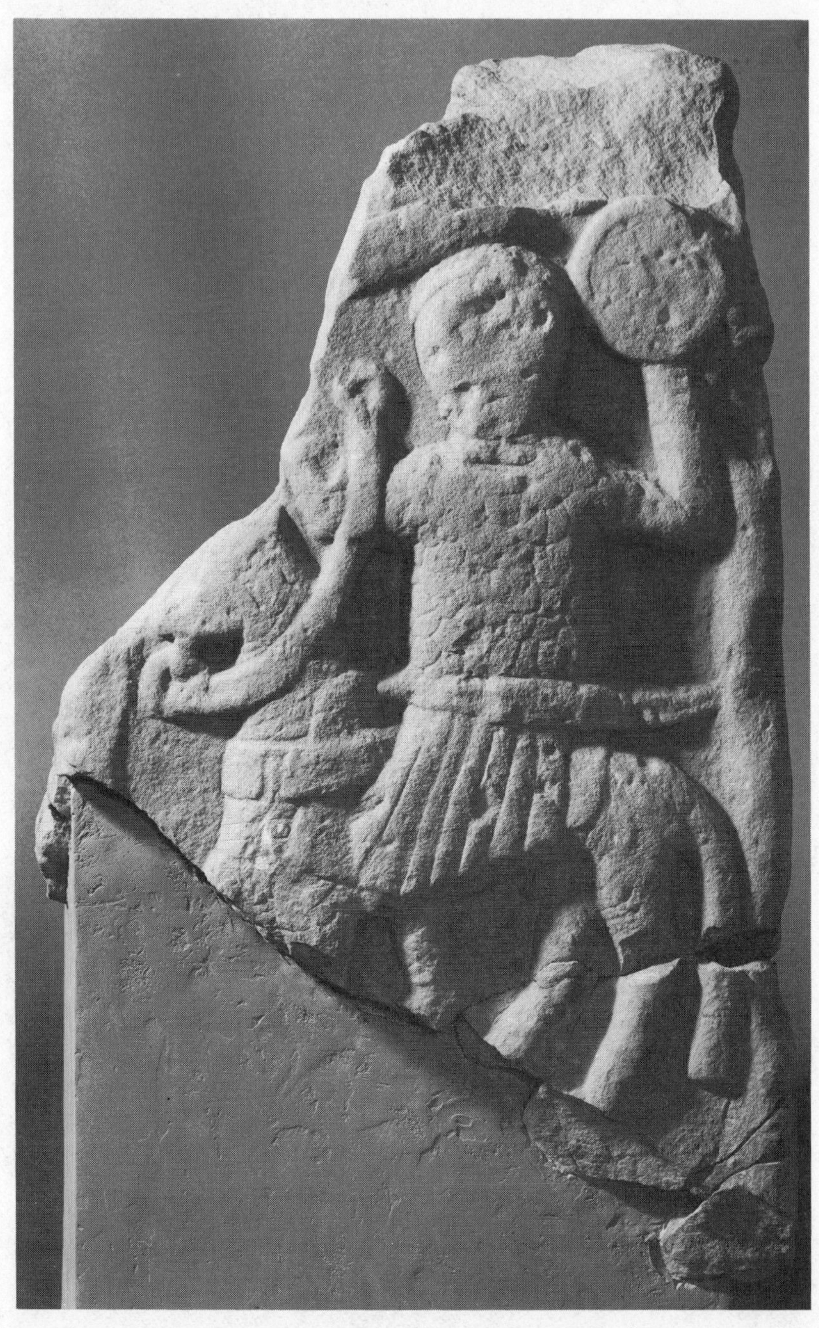

The rider face of the Repton Stone (scale 1:6)
('þæt wæs hildesetl heahcyninges, ðonne sweorda gelac . . . efnan wolde',
Beowulf 1039–41a)

INTERACTIONS OF THOUGHT AND LANGUAGE IN OLD ENGLISH POETRY

PETER CLEMOES
Life Fellow of Emmanuel College, Cambridge
Emeritus Elrington and Bosworth Professor of Anglo-Saxon, University of Cambridge

Published by the Press Syndicate of the University of Cambridge
The Pitt Building, Trumpington Street, Cambridge CB2 1RP
40 West 20th Street, New York, NY 10011-4211, USA
10 Stamford Road, Oakleigh, Melbourne 3166, Australia

First published 1995

Printed in Great Britain at the University Press, Cambridge

A catalogue record for this book is available from the British Library

Library of Congress cataloguing in publication data

Clemoes, Peter.
Interactions of thought and language
in Old English poetry / Peter Clemoes.
p. cm. – (Cambridge Studies in Anglo-Saxon England)
Includes bibliographical references and index.
ISBN 0 521 30711 2 (hardback)
1. English poetry – Old English, ca. 450–1100 – History and criticism.
2. Christian poetry, English (Old) – History and criticism.
3. Epic poetry, English (Old) – History and criticism.
4. Literature and society – England. 5. Beowulf.
I. Title. II. Series
PR201.C57 1995
829'.1–dc20 94–32005 CIP

ISBN 0 521 30711 2 hardback

CE

For my wife,
my family
and my college

Contents

Illustrations

PLATE

FIGURES

Preface

At the heart of this book is my conception of Old English poems as what the French call *lieux de mémoire*, by which I mean that they furnished society in the present with memorable images, sometimes unforgettable, typifying the past. In their case, the community was aristocratic warrior society and the images consisted of narrative, orally transmitted in a distinctive combination of traditional thought and customary form. The business of this poetry was social continuity. It placed social action of the past in a general perspective in order to show its relevance in the present. It dealt with the basis of action at any time, past or present, by converting accepted perceptions of active being into narrative through language designed by convention for the purpose. The core of poetic tradition was established form which regularly implied interaction of two (or sometimes three) fundamental potentials inviting, and receiving, fulfilment in explicit narrative. Time-honoured social observation of the roots of action was exemplified in practice over a range of experience broadly corresponding to that covered by explicit maxims. Poetic narrative consistently tested accumulated wisdom about the foundations of society's integrity, and of what threatened them, in the stresses and strains of 'real' life. The conventions special to poetry served practical needs thematically, as distinct from the 'defining' function of standard formulations in other traditional oral media, such as legal processes and magical rituals. First and foremost, therefore, I concentrate on Old English poetry's primary store of generalized allusive language, working in the interests of communal stability in aristocratic warrior society.

A second preoccupation which looms large in this book is with the transformation undergone willy-nilly by poetry's inherently social system of expression after the advent of Christianity in Anglo-Saxon England.

Vernacular poetry, so important to native tradition, could not escape the consequences of the general sea-change from oral to written transmission initiated by the new religion and demanding linguistic adaptation as radical as any required of English subsequently – by, for instance, its transition from the handwritten word to the printed or its exposure to the range of new media created by modern technology. Accordingly, I devote much space to describing poets' gradual disengagement from unformatted records of social orality and their attachment instead to stylishly textual presentation of narrative examples of the spiritual life which they shared with their fellow citizens of the kingdom of Christ. Devotional contemplation of the fixed events of universal spiritual story, past, present and to come, framing individual choice, became the order of the day for these poets, now rubbing shoulders with preachers and liturgical petitioners.

The poetry of aristocratic warrior society occupies the first part of this book (chs. 1–6) and that of the new religion the second part (chs. 7–13). But there was no neat chronological division between the two kinds. The emergence of the second from the first involved differences of milieu as well as of time. For example, on the one hand, I regard distinct cultural contexts as probably responsible for the dissimilarities of three such different poems as *Beowulf*, *Guthlac A* and the verses inscribed in early Northumbrian on the Ruthwell Cross (corresponding to part (or parts) of the much later Vercelli text of *The Dream of the Rood)*, all three of which, in my opinion, could have been approximately contemporary compositions. On the other hand, I consider that the comprehensive poetic nomenclature for the deity which Cynewulf deployed with schematic artistry would have required a considerable time to develop semantically and formally. A chronological factor must lurk in our extant corpus, difficult as it is to establish what it was. On the religious side the task appears to have some relatively fixed points: Cædmon seems to mark a beginning in the north during the third quarter of the seventh century, with Aldhelm (known to us only by repute) slightly (if at all) later in the south, and with Cynewulf reaching an apogee probably in the ninth century. On the social side, however, *Beowulf*, in the hands of controversialists, has become something of a wild card. Surely, in the face of a poem as manifestly social in the indigenous idiom as this, our most reasonable procedure is to identify when and where its conceptions of society, in this case with an admixture of Christianity, find their closest match with what we know of actual society, and to regard that environment as most likely to have produced the poem, unless there is a compelling reason for us not to. My principle is that, if several key features of a poem of the synthesizing *Beowulf* type both agree with the practices of one period and disagree with practice thereafter, they can fairly be taken as evidence that the poem is more likely to have been composed in the former time than later, provided that there are no convincing signs that the poet was systematically archaizing. In ch. 1 I set out my case, based on a range of diverse correspondences, for attributing the composition of *Beowulf* probably to Mercian royal circles in the second quarter of the eighth century – in Æthelbald's reign rather than Offa's. I rule out systematic archaizing for this poem, partly in general, because that approach would stress a sense of the difference of the past from the present, which would have run counter to the composer's primary concern with an overriding 'timelessness' subsuming them both (see pp. 14–16 and 122–3), and partly in particular, because some of my correspondences, as I point out in my chapter, involve subtle distinctions which an archaizer would have been unlikely to draw. Absolute proof is not available, but a series of convergences, which add up to my probability, is. A different view ought to be preferred, I submit, only if supported by a stronger case than any I know of.

Ch. 2 deals with another fundamental topic, the principles governing the ancient system of thought conventionalized by poetry. First I describe the basic concept of inherited potentials, producing characteristic actions, grouping beings into types and shaping narrative living. The dominant environment of narrative living, I point out, was the continuum of time, rather than space, thus endowing actions with their own propensity to analogy. These two sources of analogy – actors and their actions – normally reinforced one another straightforwardly, but sometimes the latter was called on to engineer unusual transfers of, or between, actors, especially for humanizing effects (as when a non-human being was endowed with speech). Formally these transfers were either striking actor-for-actor substitutions (metaphor) or generic actor-and-actor amalgamations ('hybridization', a term I coin for the purpose), with or without metaphor, as I demonstrate, drawing comparisons with the visual arts. Lastly I review typical Anglo-Saxon reactions to this system – for instance, recognition of in-built conflict and a relish for paradox – and poets' appreciation of the many-sidedness of humanity's rôle in it.

In chs. 3–6 I explore poetry's dramatization of this traditional thinking. In the first two of these I develop my view that the language was intimately connected with this thought world in a highly characteristic way. Poetry's regular binary noun-based structures (of any of three types – compounds and two which I term 'genitive combinations' and 'adjective combinations' respectively) acted as symbols, in my opinion, by initiating narrative through implying binary interactions of basic potentials. Customary thought and customary language worked through each other in these conventional units to exemplify, without defining, enduring general truths in action. Hence my title for this book. Together they harnessed the potential of poetry to produce effects akin to that which was made physically when Grendel's severed head, carried triumphantly into Hrothgar's hall, implied to the assembled company Beowulf's glorious victory under water. We tend to underrate these interactive units of sound and sense as mere features of style. My definition of a poetic symbol as 'a distinctive binary piece of language which implied an interaction of two socially recognized potentials of active being and which possessed a potentially narrative form culturally designed to blend with explicit language' (cf. p. 129), goes deeper than that, and therefore differs sharply from the common notion of a verbal formula slotted in for stylistic variation. As against this primary tradition of symbolism through implication, unique to poetry, I hold that the frequent standard, explicit binary structures in poetry's 'definite' language, notably word pairs, were derived from oral tradition in general, shared by poetic and other registers, such as those of law and magic. Finally, in the last two chapters of part I, my account of the principal types of narrative which issued from the implications of poetic symbols turns on a distinction between 'narrative', which was authenticated by a speaker's claim to be relating personal experience or first-hand witness, and 'story', which was told by someone claiming to speak for tradition and which therefore required internal verification as it proceeded.

In part II (chs. 7–13) I survey the radical changes which were set in train when the symbolic interactive mode of vernacular poetry became a branch of a narrative system with its centre beyond vernacular tradition. My principal themes are poets' adaptation to a more schematic network of ideas, alterations in their conceptions of the natural world, redefinition of individuality and establishment of a new system of personal responsibilities interrelating human society and the spiritual realm of God. No further comment seems to be called for here, since the chapter headings indicate the main stages in my account, while the indexes are designed to lead the reader to the various topics, such as extended studies of particular poems, or of particular words or symbols or phrases, or of particular images, and identifications of influences from Jewish thought and expression or from Christian Latin poetry, and comparisons with vernacular prose or cults of Anglo-Saxon saints. Suffice it for me to add that throughout the book my quotations of Old English poetry, except *Beowulf*, are taken from ASPR, and those of *Beowulf* from Klaeber's third edition (whether I agree with these texts in every particular or not), unless they conflict with my interpretations. In such a case, the deviation is reported.

Acknowledgements are due to the University of California Press for permission to re-use a passage from my essay in *Old English Poetry*, ed. Calder; to Martin Biddle and Birthe Kjølbye-Biddle for kindly supplying me with a print of a new photograph of the rider face of the Repton Stone (by Malcolm Crowthers) and for their permission to use it for my frontispiece; to the Cambridge University Press for permission to reproduce *ASE* 14, figs. 3 and 4 (drawn by Judith Dobie), as my two figures. My warm personal thanks go to Michael Lapidge, Simon Keynes, Malcolm Godden and Andy Orchard for reading an early draft of the entire book and offering much help and encouragement. To the first three I owe a general debt for advice, improvements and corrections which I gratefully record here; Andy Orchard's valuable contributions are acknowledged where they occur. In addition others have given me similar help of special kinds which is acknowledged where relevant. To Alicia Corrêa I extend heartfelt thanks for the care, concentration and accuracy which she has unstintingly devoted to converting a messy manuscript of such length into clean electronic form, to compiling the list of works cited and to providing the indexes. Alyson Cox also has helped with the last mentioned. I have appreciated too Michael Lapidge's generous understanding and tolerance as an editor and the considerateness I have invariably received from the Cambridge University Press in the persons of Sarah Stanton and, before her, Michael Black and Peter Richards. I am responsible, of course, for all remaining deficiencies and errors.

Those to whom I feel the deepest gratitude for priceless support throughout the nine years which I have spent preparing this book are identified by my dedication. I have been fortunate enough to recognize in their beneficence the force of Jerome's adage, 'caritas non potest conparari; dilectio pretium non habet; amicitia, quae desinere potest, uera nunquam fuit' (see p. 361, n. 61).

PETER CLEMOES
Emmanuel College, Cambridge,
April 1994

Abbreviations

Ælfric, *CH* I (ed. Thorpe)	Ælfric's *Catholic Homilies*, ed. B. Thorpe, *The Homilies of the Anglo-Saxon Church: the First Part containing the Sermones Catholici, or Homilies of Ælfric*, 2 vols. (London, 1844–6), vol. I
Ælfric, *CH* II (ed. Godden)	*Ælfric's Catholic Homilies. The Second Series*, ed M.R. Godden, EETS ss 5 (Oxford, 1979)
Ælfric, *SupplHoms* (ed. Pope)	*Homilies of Ælfric: a Supplementary Collection*, ed. J.C. Pope, 2 vols., EETS os 259–60 (London, 1967–8)
AntJ	*Antiquaries Journal*
ASE	*Anglo-Saxon England*
ASNSL	*Archiv für das Studium der neueren Sprachen und Literaturen*
ASPR	The Anglo-Saxon Poetic Records, ed. G.P. Krapp and E.V.K. Dobbie, 6 vols. (New York, 1931–42)
BAR	British Archaeological Reports (Oxford)
Bede, *HE*	Bede, *Historia ecclesiastica gentis Anglorum*, ed. B. Colgrave and R.A.B. Mynors (Oxford, 1969)
BJRL	*Bulletin of the John Rylands University Library of Manchester*
CCSL	Corpus Christianorum, Series Latina (Turnhout)
CMCS	*Cambridge Medieval Celtic Studies*
CSASE	Cambridge Studies in Anglo-Saxon England
CSEL	Corpus Scriptorum Ecclesiasticorum Latinorum (Vienna)
EEMF	Early English Manuscripts in Fascimile (Copenhagen)
EETS	Early English Text Society
os	original series
ss	supplementary series

EHD	*English Historical Documents*, c. *500–1042*, ed. D. Whitelock, 2nd ed. (London, 1979)
ELN	*English Language Notes*
ES	*English Studies*
HBS	Henry Bradshaw Society
JEGP	*Journal of English and Germanic Philology*
MÆ	*Medium Ævum*
MGH	Monumenta Germaniae Historica
MLN	*Modern Language Notes*
MLQ	*Modern Language Quarterly*
MLR	*Modern Language Review*
NM	*Neuphilologische Mitteilungen*
N&Q	*Notes & Queries*
OEN	*Old English Newsletter*
OEN Subsidia	Old English Newsletter Subsidia
PBA	*Proceedings of the British Academy*
PMLA	*Publications of the Modern Language Association of America*
PL	Patrologia Latina, ed. J.-P. Migne, 221 vols. (Paris, 1844–64)
RES	*Review of English Studies*
RS	Rolls Series (London)
SBVS	*Saga-Book of the Viking Society for Northern Research*
SM	*Studi Medievali*
SP	*Studies in Philology*
TRHS	*Transactions of the Royal Historical Society*
WM, *GP*	William of Malmesbury, *De gestis pontificum Anglorum*, ed. N.E.S.A. Hamilton, RS 52 (London, 1870)

I

The poetry of an aristocratic warrior society

1

The chronological implications of the bond between kingship in *Beowulf* and kingship in practice

Hwæt, we Gardena   in geardagum,
þeodcyninga   þrym gefrunon,
hu ða æþelingas   ellen fremedon!

['Lo, we have learned of the power of the Spear-Danes, of the kings of the people, in days long ago, how those princes put their fighting spirit into action!', *Beowulf* 1–3].

Our finest long poem in Old English took as its starting-point the mighty kings of a warlike people far in the past. The glory this people had achieved was a matter of knowledge which was shared (or at any rate was alleged to be) by the 'we' of the narrator and those he addressed (or at least some of them).[1] A poem beginning in this way was not going to turn into an exercise in idiosyncratic self-expression. Nor was it going to issue from some unique inspiration. The narrator was speaking for common report. He was assuming the function of giving fresh impetus to existing general knowledge. Unrestrained fantasy would not have served this purpose; nor would mere fact have been enough. His business was to make a portion of tradition come alive to an audience in the present, to stir a contemporary response of a traditional sort.

His entry into tradition was by way of invoking a name, *Gardene*, 'Spear-Danes', and playing on its associations.[2] It was not to the point to place this name in time more specifically than in the long ago; and this tribal name was sufficient in itself to suggest a region. What mattered was to activate straightaway the name's associative potential by placing it in a

[1] Elsewhere in this poem the narrator invariably referred to himself as 'I'.

[2] On the rôle of names as linguistic nuclei for stories in Germanic tradition, see Robinson, 'The Significance of Names', esp. the discussion of 'Hygelac' in *Beowulf* at pp. 53–7.

narrative setting which was both applicable to the name itself and valid in the present and was also rich in suggestion: to link the Spear-Danes' prosperity with their leaders' martial vigour was to do just that. Through this coupling this people immediately came to exemplify a broad, general, truth, namely that to do well in war is to prosper. They were being introduced as an illustration of a process of (what we would call) cause and effect which operated in an audience's own society as much as it had in theirs. And the Danes' reward could be counted on to rouse any audience's emotions – glory. What marked this distant people off from the present was, of course, that they had been judged already by posterity: their glory possessed the authority of common repute; it had passed the test of time, as contemporary reputation necessarily had not. They provided an exemplary fulfilment of a primary need of a present-day society: these Danish kings had given their people the kind of fighting leadership which Anglo-Saxons wanted their own rulers to exert. What they had done, therefore, the story of their successes and failures, was of compelling interest to an Anglo-Saxon audience, not for escapism but for illumination of current experience. A comparison had been initiated between kingship in poetry and kingship in practice.

Set as it was in a remote past and a far-off place, this poem perforce depended on the general conception of traditional kingship prevailing in the poet's own time. But this in no way put a curb on his ambition. On the contrary it was precisely his strength. A lively sense of that tradition enabled him to mount impressive full-length royal portraits. Firstly, in the person of Hrothgar, presiding over the Danish court when Beowulf freed it from the ravages of the monster, Grendel, he presented a moving study of a king whose early years of glory had turned into later ones of dark despair; and then, in the person of the hero, Beowulf, he furnished an absorbing account of the critical actions of a man who when young was proving himself fit to rule his people, the Geats, and when old was doggedly carrying out this duty in the face of death after ruling them with steady success for fifty years. The confidence of this delineation argues for a close rapport between past and present kingship, and in this chapter I want to examine the nature and implications of this accord.

From an institutional point of view kings in *Beowulf* were regularly rulers of peoples (not countries), as conveyed by the generic compound noun *þeodcyning*, 'ruler of the people' (2a and six (or seven) other places), and less often by *fold-* and *leodcyning*, and as expressed by the simplex *þeoden*, 'leader of a people', nearly forty times. Through other expressions, notably 'son of . . .' epithets, they were repeatedly set in the perspective of their kin; Hrothgar, for instance, was called 'bearn/maga/mago/sunu Healfdenes' (or 'Healfdenes sunu') fifteen times. Other terms, most numerous of all, depicted them in their active personal capacity as leaders of their close followers, their comitatus: for example, *dryhten* (formed in the same way as *þeoden)*, 'leader of a *dryht*, a troop of active soldiers', occurs fifteen times, and its compounds, *frea-*, *freo-*, *gum-*, *mon-*, *sige-* and *winedryhten*, were used twenty times between them.

First and foremost in this poem a king in his own person was his people's proud leader in war. His authority depended directly on his individual prowess as a soldier. When Hrothgar, then old, honoured Beowulf with the most valuable gifts possible in reward for the young hero's victory over Grendel, they included the saddle which had been the king's own when he had gone into battle himself in his younger days:

þæt wæs hildesetl heahcyninges,
ðonne sweorda gelac sunu Healfdenes
efnan wolde, – næfre on ore læg
widcuþes wig, ðonne walu feollon

['that was the high king's battle-seat when the son of Healfdene wanted to perform the play of swords – never did the prowess of the widely famed one lie low in the forefront when the slain fell', 1039–42].

It was as brave leader when swords were wielded that Hrothgar had shown his pride in his lineage and earned his widespread renown.

Warfare was incessant. Dangerous neighbours posed an ever-present threat. Swedes and Geats were represented as perpetually feuding; whenever a king of the one people had the upper hand he raided the territory of the other. A ruler invariably took advantage of whatever political opportunities came his way: aid and comfort were given to any disaffected among the opposition; Hrothgar gained a debt of gratitude when he played the peacemaker by paying compensation after a man of another tribe, Beowulf's father, had killed a man of yet another people (457–72). There were always ancient scores to settle: many a time, when the chance came, a king was driven to take revenge; Hrothgar attempted a pact with old enemies by giving his daughter in marriage to the Heathobard prince, Ingeld, son of a king whom the Danes had killed, but this was seen as a vain hope (2020–31). A king's overriding duty was to protect his people against its enemies. Beowulf's first claim to have been a beneficial ruler over fifty years was

> næs se folccyning,
> ymbsittendra ænig ðara,
> þe mec guðwinum gretan dorste,
> egesan ðeon

['there has not been the king of a people, any ruler of the neighbouring peoples, who has dared to attack me with war-allies, threaten with terror', 2733b–6a].

All the principal rulers in *Beowulf* were celebrated as 'folces' or 'rices hyrde' ('guardian of the people or kingdom'), while Hrothgar and Beowulf (approaching the end of his long reign) were each honoured as *eþelweard*, 'guardian of the native land'.

The seat of a king's power was his hall. As soon as Hrothgar had established his royal authority by success in war,

> Him on mod bearn,
> þæt healreced hatan wolde
> medoærn micel men gewyrcean
> þonne yldo bearn æfre gefrunon

['It came to his mind that he would order a hall to be built, a mead-hall greater than the sons of men had ever heard of', 67b–70].

This *folcstede*, 'place of the people' (76a), was to be an intertribal status symbol: it was to outdo other halls as Hrothgar's reign was to outshine all others. He ordered men from many distant tribes to adorn it; he whose word held sway far and wide named it *Heorot*, 'Hart'. 'Sele hlifade / heah ond horngeap' ('The hall towered, high and wide-gabled', 81b–2a), the most famous building under the skies; 'geatolic ond goldfah' ('splendid and decorated with gold', 308a), it had a radiance which shone over many lands. In it Hrothgar was surrounded by wise counsellors and a well-armed and well-disciplined troop of loyal fighting men. There his gold-adorned queen, Wealhtheow, personified the virtues of an ideal consort which gnomic poetry proclaimed for all time:

> [sceal] wif geþeon,
> leof mid hyre leodum, leohtmod wesan,
> rune healdan, rumheort beon
> mearum ond maþmum, meodorædenne
> for siðmægen symle æghwær

eodor æþelinga ærest gegretan,
forman fulle to frean hond
ricene geræcan, ond him ræd witan
boldagendum bæm ætsomne

['a wife shall thrive beloved among her people; she shall be cheerful, keep secrets, be generous with horses and valuables; at mead-dispensing before the company of warriors she shall at all times and places approach the protector of princes first, quickly pass the first cup to her lord's hand, and know the advice to give him as master and mistress of the house both together', *Maxims I* 84b–92].

There, in his hall, Hrothgar kept a nephew in check and his sons in good company. As gnomic poetry, again, put it:

Geongne æþeling sceolan gode gesiðas
byldan to beaduwe and to beahgife

['Good companions shall encourage a young prince to battle and to ring-giving', *Maxims II* 14–15].

There his *scop*, 'poet', played the lyre, telling stories, and sometimes the king himself took the lyre. There comradeship was enjoyed, news exchanged, etiquette observed, visitors were welcomed, memories revived and good food and drink served. Beyond its doors hawks were trained, stags and boars hunted and horses raced.

Above all, the hall was where a king was in union with his close followers, both the *duguð*, the experienced among them, and the *geogoð*, the young. His primary obligation was ceremonially to bestow gifts on his assembled warriors – 'Cyning sceal on healle / beagas dælan' ('A king shall distribute rings in hall', *Maxims II* 28b–9a) – and theirs was to pledge, in the hearing of all, that they would resolutely use in his defence the wargear he gave them. The king on his ceremonial *gifstol*, 'gift-seat', was the dominant image of this vital bond between leader and follower. For the king himself the seat symbolized his very rule: when Heardred, ruler of the Geats, was killed, the narrator could economically express Beowulf's succession by simply stating that the victor 'let ðone bregostol Biowulf healdan / Geatum wealdan' ('let Beowulf hold the princely seat, rule the Geats', 2389–90a). For the follower it represented his membership of a social group which provided for his essential needs. The king's comitatus shared his hearth and his table; they served him as his *þegnas* in various capacities (such as *heal-* or *sele-* and *ombihtþegn*) and the wise among them, the *witan*, those with knowledge born of much experience, were his advisors; they were his dear companions in the field, his *eaxlgesteallan*, his 'shoulder-to-shoulder comrades-in-arms'. Emotional ties of kinship and thegnship were strong. When Hrothgar lost his *aldorþegn*, 'head thegn', his *þegnsorg*, 'sorrow for a thegn', knew no bounds. If a thegn lost his friendly patron he became the sort of exile whose troubled sleep is depicted so movingly in *The Wanderer*:

þinceð him on mode þæt he his mondryhten
clyppe ond cysse, ond on cneo lecge
honda ond heafod, swa he hwilum ær
in geardagum giefstolas breac

['It seems in his mind that he is embracing and kissing his liege lord, and laying hands and head on his knee, as when from time to time in days of old be used to receive gifts from the throne', 41–4].

Material possessions expressed the corporate identity of the group. The adornments of the conquered became the ornaments of the conquerors, emblems of their superiority. The king was both keeper and distributor of his warriors' treasure ('hordweard hæleþa' and 'sinces' or 'beaga brytta'). Wealth gained, guarded and given by the king was the index of his people's well-being. It was integral to their social life:

Gold geriseþ on guman sweorde,
sellic sigesceorp, sinc on cwene

['Gold is fitting on a man's sword, choice ornament of victory, treasure on a woman', *Maxims I* 125–6]

was the conventional wisdom, and Beowulf's victory over Grendel called for 'win of wunderfatum' ('wine from wonderful vessels') in Heorot (*Beowulf* 1162a). The war-equipment conferred and accepted in hall-ceremonial was the touchstone of good discipline. When, the night after Beowulf's defeat of Grendel, the Danes lay down to sleep in Heorot, their care in first disposing their weapons round them, although they believed that their hall was safe again, drew an expression of general approval from the narrator:

Wæs þeaw hyra,
þæt hie oft wæron an wig gearwe,
ge æt ham ge on herge, ge gehwæþer þara
efna swylce mæla, swylce hira mandryhtne
þearf gesealde; wæs seo þeod tilu

['Their custom was that they were often ready in war, both at home and on campaign, in either case on such occasions as need befell their liege lord; that people was good', 1246b–50].

Failure to live up to the obligation which the arms brought was a betrayal leading inevitably to irreparable disgrace, as, after Beowulf's death, his young kinsman, Wiglaf, scornfully made plain to the picked men who had accompanied their king to the dragon's mound only to desert him in his hour of need.[3]

Both strength of mind and strength of body were essential to the good king in the *Beowulf* poet's view. This was the combination which marked out the young Beowulf as an ideal future ruler in Hrothgar's eyes: 'þu eart mægenes strang, ond on mode frod, / wis wordcwida!' ('You are strong as regards might and experienced in mind, wise as regards words!', 1844–5a), he declared admiringly and went on,

Wen ic talige,
. . .
þæt þe Sæ-Geatas selran næbben
to geceosenne cyning ænigne,
hordweard hæleþa, gyf þu healdan wylt
maga rice

['I consider it likely . . . that the Sea-Geats will have no better king to choose, guardian of the treasure of warriors, if you are willing to rule the kingdom of your relatives', 1845b and 1850–3a].

The bad king squandered his abilities by becoming a violent, treacherous, mean tyrant, such as the Danish king Heremod. By contrast Beowulf, fifty years a king, could look back over his long reign with a clear conscience when near to death (2732b–43a): he had given his people security; he had not put them at risk; he had been a good steward; he had not been violent; he had been a just man of his word; he had been loyal to his kin. 'þæt wæs god cyning!'

Insecurity, however, was endemic in *Beowulf*ian kingship, strong though it might be: any ruler was vulnerable to forces he could not control. Mighty agents from outside society, such as Grendel or the dragon, could destroy his kingdom. Pride could corrupt him within; his abilities, his sway and all that he had came from God, a mightier ruler than he

[3] See below, pp. 415–16.

(1724b–61a). An inevitability in events had to be faced too – *wyrd*, which no man, only God, could control (477b–9 and 1056–7a). For King Beowulf on the dragon's mound *wyrd* meant his death (2419b–24). Spells could intervene unpredictably: the treasure in the dragon's mound paid for by King Beowulf's life was subject to one which God alone could vary (3069–75). Death was a journey for the spirit (2819b–20) which King Beowulf, for his part, did not relish (2419b–24). What survived was reputation. King Beowulf on the point of dying gave instructions for the building of a memorial mound in a prominent position on the sea coast to give his posthumous fame a local habitation and a name (2802–8).

The kingship in Anglo-Saxon practice itself was certainly of the same general character as that depicted in *Beowulf* in being fundamentally a personal leadership based on pedigree and exercised over a territorial people. This personal element would have gone right back to the farming communities newly settled in the river valleys of England in the fifth and sixth centuries: these freshly formed groups would have faced problems of security, trade and internal order in unfamiliar surroundings and to tackle them would naturally have turned for leadership to those capable of giving it. Those strongest in mind and body would have been at a premium then just as they were in the poetry; and, given the normal expectation of 'like father like son', it would not have been long before an aristocracy was reestablished in these settlement, and immediately post-settlement, conditions. The significance of poetry's patronymics would have been experienced with pristine force. New dynasties were being born out of the shake-up of tribal groupings caused by migration. The most common designation for an emergent ruler, *cyning*, related him to his kin. Royal status was being rebuilt on its general foundations. The close identity of leader and dynasty had begun again in circumstances which made it particularly vital. And so too had the root connection between personal authority and territory which was expressed in the poetic epithet *eþelweard*, 'guardian of the native land'. For the early Anglo-Saxon settlers nothing could have captured the essence of their experience of personal leadership more completely than the poetic term *þeodcyning* (7× in *Beowulf*[4]) signifying a man of a certain stock ruling over the people holding a certain territory. Nor did corporate self-awareness cease to be focused on the person of the king, as communities, at first local, became regional, and

[4] 8× if the usual amendment is made at 3086a.

then, by about the second half of the ninth century, partly under ecclesiastical influence and partly under threat from Danish invaders, operated countrywide. Anglo-Saxon society never lost a prevailing sense that its well-being depended directly on the deeds of the king.[5]

It was inherent in Anglo-Saxon practice too that the battlefield and the court were the vital twin settings for the operation of personal rule. King Alfred's reign in the late ninth century illustrates both these working conditions very clearly. There could be no more striking proof of a people's total reliance on their king's performance against their enemies in battle than Alfred's stubborn, stage-by-stage, ultimately successful, fight for survival against the Danes. And Bishop Asser's Latin *Life* of this king vividly reveals how much the business of Alfred's kingdom centred on his person at his peripatetic court.[6] He was involved in an endless round of 'gently instructing, cajoling, urging, commanding' and, when required, 'sharply chastising . . his bishops and ealdormen and nobles, and his thegns most dear to him, and reeves as well' (91); the king himself, Asser reports, sat at judicial hearings for the benefit of high and low and looked into many judgements passed in his absence, taking them up with those responsible where required, 'either in person or through one of his other trusted men' (106); he reorganized the attendance of his thegns at court by arranging them in three groups, each serving there for a month at a time in rotation; he welcomed visitors (as Hrothgar did Beowulf) 'of all races, showing immense and incomparable kindness and generosity to all men, as well as to the investigation of things unknown' (76), and receiving information, messages and gifts from places as distant as Jerusalem (91).

Planned payment for services rendered was a mainstay of Alfred's court, with the dues to his fighting men, as in tradition, having priority. He paid out the first sixth of his revenues every year to them 'and likewise to his noble thegns who lived at the royal court in turns, serving him in various capacities' (100). To his craftsmen, 'who were skilled in every earthly craft' (101), he paid out no less than another sixth. Like Hrothgar when building Heorot, he 'assembled and commissioned [them] in almost countless quantity from many races' (*ibid.*). He was a great builder, ordering new

[5] For a very helpful general account of the formation of Anglo-Saxon kingship, see Loyn, *The Governance of Anglo-Saxon England*, pp. 3–29.

[6] For an excellent translation of and commentary on Asser's *Life*, see *Alfred the Great*, trans. Keynes and Lapidge. The bracketed numbers below refer to the sections of this translation.

royal halls and chambers to be built in stone and wood and old ones to be improved. He himself gave instructions to his goldsmiths and other craftsmen and made to his own design 'wonderful and precious new treasures which far surpassed any tradition of his predecessors' (76). He was an enthusiastic and skilled huntsman and personally instructed his falconers, hawk-trainers and dog-keepers. He was a devoted performer of English poetry, as Hrothgar had sung to the lyre in his hall. While still a young boy, before he could read, Alfred memorized poems he heard recited (22), on occasion reciting in his turn what he had learned (23), and, after he had been taught to read English at about the age of twelve (22–3),[7] he continued to learn poems by heart (76). He composed poetry too, for some time in the 890s he versified his English prose rendering of the metres of Boethius. In spite of greater systematization demanded by a larger scale of operation, and in spite of other differences of organization, we see here still in Asser's pages a highly personal kingship characterized by much of the spirit and expressed through many of the activities typified by rulers in *Beowulf*.

Some standard practices of Anglo-Saxon royal government may have been hinted at in *Beowulf*. For instance, when Beowulf, about to plunge into the fearsome pool to tackle Grendel's mother, said to Hrothgar

Wes þu mundbora   minum magoþegnum,
hondgesellum,   gif mec hild nime

['Be protector to my young thegns, close comrades, if battle takes me', 1480–1],

was he appealing to the right of *mund*, the protection which Anglo-Saxon kings could formally confer? And, again, when the narrator stated that during Grendel's twelve-year-long ravages it had been one of the Danes' particular miseries that the monster

sibbe ne wolde
wið manna hwone   mægenes Deniga,
feorhbealo feorran,   fea þingian

['did not want peace with any man of the army of the Danes, would not do away with the destruction of life, settle with money', 154b–6],

was this a reference to *wergild*, the Anglo-Saxon legal obligation to compensate for murder by a fixed money payment? These practices, though never becoming clearcut, seem to lurk under the surface of these allusions.

[7] Cf. *ibid.*, p. 239, n. 46.

In other matters, however, there appears to have been inconsistency. For example, Hrothgar's sway seems to have been on a small scale. His court appears to have been sustained by only a single hall, without any supporting system of itineration to other royal estates and/or to the residences of underlords with an obligation to render him hospitality, as was general practice in Anglo-Saxon kingdoms;[8] and *folctogan*, 'leaders of the people' (839a), who travelled 'feorran ond nean / geond widwegas' ('from far and near, throughout extensive ways', 839b–40a) to marvel at Grendel's hand, arm and shoulder affixed to Heorot the morning after the monster's night-time defeat, must have lived no more than a few hours' journey away. Yet, when King Hygelac rewarded Beowulf munificently on his young nephew's return, victorious, from Denmark, his kingdom seems to have been extensive enough for him to give away lordship on a grand scale, no less than 'seofan þusendo, / bold ond bregostol' ('seven thousand, hall and princely seat', 2195b–6a). If, as has been generally understood, 'seven thousand' refers to hides, Beowulf was being presented with an area of about the size of north Mercia.[9] Probably we should conclude that in this poem small-scale rule was attributed to the past but in this instance was being conflated incongruously with the larger scale of the present.

In other respects, however, the differences between *Beowulf*ian kingship and the monarchy as it had changed, and was changing, in Alfred's time would have seemed irreconcilable. The poet's single-minded concentration on the warrior leader and the hall-life shared by leader and followers took no account of the elaboration of Alfred's rule as a king who governed a state including ecclesiastical landowning institutions, who was advised by churchmen, who codified the law, who issued coinage and charters and who controlled a large and varied administration in order to provide, and provide for, not only those who fought but those who prayed and those who worked as well.[10] In the crucial military sphere the increased scale of Alfred's campaigning produced features which had no counterpart in *Beowulf*, as when the king organized the building and garrisoning of defensive forts nationwide and provided a continuous army in the field by a system of rotation. Nor did the poem show any inkling of a kingship of Alfred's sort, increasingly looking back to biblical, classical and Christian

[8] On food renders and royal circuits as economic bases of early Anglo-Saxon kingship, see Charles-Edwards, 'Early Medieval Kingships'.

[9] See *Beowulf*, ed. Klaeber, n. on 2195 and refs. there cited.

[10] See below, pp. 334–6.

precedents[11] and receiving support from Christian ceremony.[12] In practice, already by the ninth century, we may say with Wallace-Hadrill, Germanic monarchy in Anglo-Saxon England, as elsewhere, though still Germanic, had been 'transformed into an office with duties and rights defined by churchmen'.[13] If *Beowulf* was composed even as late as that the kingship it portrayed would have started to reflect not so much the nature of contemporary rule as the ethos of a lost past recalled in an antiquarian spirit.

In some respects, of course, this would not have made any difference, for by and large the customs and manners of the poem's warrior court were of the timeless sort which would have remained unchanged whatever the poet's day. Most of his material did not call at all for a phrase such as 'on þæm dæge þysses lifes' to draw a distinction between the past in the story and the present; those words were merely a stereotyped means of emphasizing a unique degree in something – Beowulf's strength (196–8a and 788b–90) or the wretchedness of Grendel's death (805b–7a). On both the military and the domestic fronts activities were regularly described as simply the commonplaces of society as such. For instance, when it was related that on arrival outside Hrothgar's hall as armed strangers Beowulf and his companions lent their shields against the hall wall and stacked their spears (325–32a), these actions were doubtless accepted conduct in any period for indicating that newcomers had come to talk with a king, not to threaten him; and likewise another dateless procedure was clearly involved when the narrator reported

Ða him Hroþgar gewat   mid his hæleþa gedryht,
eodur Scyldinga   ut of healle;
wolde wigfruma   Wealhþeo secan,
cwen to gebeddan

['Then Hrothgar left the hall with his troop of warriors, protector of the Scyldings; the war-chief wanted to seek Wealhtheow, the queen, as his bedfellow', 662–5a].

A king's withdrawal from his hall for the night after taking a formal farewell of his principal guest (652–61), while all the company stood ('Werod eall aras' (651b)), would surely have been an automatic custom at

11 See below, pp. 419–20.

12 See cautious comments on royal unction, Wallace-Hadrill, *Early Germanic Kingship*, pp. 150–1.

13 *Ibid.*, p. 151.

any phase of Anglo-Saxon society. It was this very ordinariness which would have set off strikingly the abnormality that in this case a king and his comitatus were surrendering guardianship of their hall to comparative strangers.

The poem's emotional fabric was similarly true to 'real' society of any time. For example, the dramatic test of loyalty on the dragon's mound, which separated out the *hildlatan*, 'cowards' (2486a), the 'tydre treowlogan' ('weak traitors', 2488a), the *scamiende*, 'ashamed' (2850a), *unleofe*, 'unloved' (2863b), majority of King Beowulf's comitatus from Wiglaf, the only one in whom 'Ne gemealt him se modsefa' ('His spirit did not melt', 2428a), was in essence the same as that undergone by the bodyguard of Ecgfrith, king of Northumbria, who were killed around their lord by the Picts at Nechtansmere in 685,[14] while the *edwitlif*, 'life of disgrace' (2891b), incurred by most of Beowulf's men, was the shame which was merited even more grievously by the followers of Æthelbald, king of Mercia, and those of Oswulf, king of Northumbria, who killed their own lords in 757 and 759 respectively.[15] Nor was Wiglaf's devotion of a sort found only in poetry: in 625 Lilla, a thegn of Edwin, king of Northumbria, saved his lord's life but was killed himself when he thrust his body between the king and an assassin's blow.[16]

The poet wove strong 'normal' feelings into an artistic texture of a dramatic, personal and reflective kind. For instance, when, in 856, Æthelwulf, king of Wessex, Alfred's father, on returning from a year's visit to Rome, had to agree to yield the western part of his kingdom to his eldest son, Æthelbald, in order to avoid a civil war, and then had to keep this agreement for the remaining two years of his life,[17] his feelings might well have been tinged with the sadness Hrothgar expressed in his recitations when he feasted in his hall as an old king (*Beowulf* 2105b–14). Each of the two had suffered a setback to his rule which he could not cope with (in Æthelwulf's case after seventeen years). But Hrothgar's ruin, dramatized as a fall from unsurpassed glory to abject helplessness when faced with a monster's destruction of the life of his hall, had been no affair

[14] *Two Lives of St Cuthbert*, ed. Colgrave, pp. 242–8 (ch. 27).

[15] For both, see 'Continuations' to Bede *HE* (p. 574).

[16] Bede, *HE* II.9 (*ibid.*, p. 164).

[17] Asser's *Life of King Alfred*, chs. 11 and 12 (trans. Keynes and Lapidge, *Alfred the Great*, pp. 69–70).

of run-of-the-mill politics. In his case a situation conjured up in the poet's imagination was being interwoven with an audience's 'natural' responses to an old man's frustration, a young man's good nature, and thoughts about the changeableness of life. As a result Hrothgar's mood impresses us because we can contrast it for ourselves with the confident ambition which had spurred him on in the prime of life when his hall was to be the beacon of everything great and glorious in his reign. We sympathize with the old king's sadness partly because we know of the helpless frustration he had suffered through the long years of Grendel's depredation of his hall and partly because we know, as the king himself did not, that Heorot was shortly to be destroyed by fire in a war which was to break out between him and the young man who would by then be his son-in-law: we have been haunted by a sense of foreboding on this score ever since the narrator implanted it at the very outset when relating the building of the hall (82b–5), and we have just been reminded of this unhappy prospect by hearing Beowulf express his misgivings about Hrothgar's plans for his daughter's marriage (2024b–69a). We also think all the better of the young Beowulf, to whom we owe the description of Hrothgar's elegiac performance, for observing the 'rumheort cyning' ('large-hearted king', 2110b) sympathetically and respectfully while 'hreðer inne weoll, / þonne he wintrum frod worn gemunde' ('his breast surged within him, when wise in years he remembered many things', 2113b–14). And we recall how Hrothgar had regarded his reversal of fortune as a typical pattern when he delivered his moralizing 'sermon' after Beowulf's fight against Grendel's mother (1700–84, especially 1769–78a). Now that we have heard this report of the old king's expression of sorrow we assent to his earlier generalization emotionally as well as thoughtfully, because his feelings seem basically natural.

For all his timelessness, however, the poet did display a number of specific affinities with the philosophy, morality and images of pre-Alfredian kingship which would have been difficult to recreate once they had receded into the past. As a first stage let us examine the affinities in the images representing the critical tests of society-serving heroism in kingship and comparable spheres. To begin with, the poet's conception that fitness to rule and worthiness in rule were demonstrated most profoundly by combat against monstrous enemies of society and an implacable fifty-foot fiery dragon belonged to the same order of imagination as that displayed in a practical context by the embossed warrior scenes and dragon and boar figures on the helmet buried among the regalia at Sutton Hoo probably in the 620s.[18] These images, in their combination, proclaimed on the headpiece the fiercely elemental analogies which expressed the true nature of battling kingship and thereby implied to beholders that the wearer of the helmet was endowed with these fundamental attributes when in action.

Likewise the small gold and silver coinages produced in the last half of the seventh century and the first half of the eighth made observations on the nature of aristocratic warriorship comparable to the poem's and by similar means. For instance, the poet's epitome of royal defence of treasure (in a brief, general, reference to King Hygelac), 'siðþan he under segne sinc ealgode' ('when he defended treasure under his standard', 1204), was based on the same set of associations – between ruler, wealth and standard – as that portrayed on coins minted in Kent *c.* 665–700 bearing a bust on the obverse and a military standard on the reverse, designs derived from fourth-century Roman coins.[19] More significantly, coins before the mid-eighth century not uncommonly linked dragon-like figures on the obverse with warrior figures on the reverse: for example, fourteen silver *sceattas* (600–750?) in Keary's list have 'dragon' designs.[20] Coins of this sort belonged to a relatively short period of independence from continental models, during which Anglo-Saxon engravers adopted images from 'insular' sources other than coinage (from metalwork?), before, in the middle of the eighth century, they returned to 'straight' conformity with 'foreign' coinage. A range of beast and bird imagery, some with analogies in *Beowulf*, was thus associated with aristocratic warrior or ruler figures on these coins at this time. Wolves were especially frequent, as on some coins minted probably in Kent or London *c.* 720–30, which have a diademed bust on the obverse and a wolf on the reverse,[21] while some coins minted probably in London *c.* 685–700 serve to exemplify other types of beasts or birds: together with a diademed head or bust enclosed in a serpent-headed circle on the obverse, they enclose a bird in another serpent-headed circle on the reverse[22] and thus

[18] See Bruce-Mitford, *The Sutton Hoo Ship Burial: a Handbook*, pp. 48–51, and, for more detailed discussion, Bruce-Mitford *et al.*, *The Sutton Hoo Ship-Burial* II, 138–231.

[19] Grierson and Blackburn, *Medieval European Coinage*, nos. 668 and 672–81; Keynes and Blackburn, *Anglo-Saxon Coins*, nos. 6 and 8.

[20] Keary, *A Catalogue of English Coins in the British Museum*, nos. 111, 112, 147 (on the reverse), 171–9, 182 and 187 (with long wings).

[21] Grierson and Blackburn, *Medieval European Coinage*, nos. 697–9; Keynes and Blackburn, *Anglo-Saxon Coins*, no. 15.

[22] Grierson and Blackburn, *Medieval European Coinage*, nos. 682–4; Keynes and Blackburn, *Anglo-Saxon Coins*, no. 9.

call to mind the bird of prey mounted on the Sutton Hoo shield.[23] In *Beowulf* the raven, eager for the carrion of Beowulf's followers doomed to die at the hands of enemies after their king's death, was imagined boasting to the eagle that it had already devoured casualties in company with the wolf (3024b-7). Designers of coins in the seventh century and the first half of the eighth, contemporary designers of weapons and the *Beowulf* poet all seem to have been of one mind in regarding creatures such as dragons, wolves, ravens and eagles as symbols of the predatory forces outside society against which aristocratic warriorship was society's defence.

But that is not all that the poem shared with the coins. When King Beowulf learned that his hall, 'gifstol Geata' ('the gift-seat of the Geats', 2327a), had been destroyed by a dragon's fire, his first thoughts were

þæt he Wealdende
ofer ealde riht ecean Dryhtne
bitre gebulge

['that he had bitterly angered the ruler, the eternal Lord, contrary to old law', 2329b–31a];

and Christian elements appear on the coins as well: the figures on the reverse of the 'dragon' coins cited above are regularly accompanied by one or more crosses, the obverse of the 720s Kentish or London coins combines a cross with the bust and the reverse of the last-mentioned coins includes a cross as well as the bird in the encircled area. In this coinage, as in the poem, Christian elements intermingled with non-Christian ones in a lively, seemingly not highly synthesized, fashion. But from the middle of the eighth century the 'insular' beast imagery disappeared from coins.[24] Carolingian monetary orthodoxy swept it away. From then on coinage settled down to a uniform scheme of a pseudo-Roman bust on the obverse (occasionally a geometric design) and a cross, monogram or inscription across the field of the reverse. The *Beowulf* poet's supremely confident, and more than competent, portrait of a Germanic kingship integrated with 'real' emotion and indigenous dragon and other beast imagery, along with some, but only some, Christian motifs, implies that this was the

[23] Bruce-Mitford, *The Sutton Hoo Ship Burial: a Handbook*, pp. 32–4 and 37–9, and Bruce-Mitford *et al.*, *The Sutton Hoo Ship-Burial* II, 54–61 and 63.

[24] There was only the occasional serpent during Offa's reign in the second half of the century.

consensus of a vigorous culture around him. The evidence of the coinage suggests that in practice at about the middle of the eighth century a more 'abstract' systematization of royal authority began to squeeze out this ensemble of native imagery supported by genuine feeling.[25]

The personage of St Guthlac also exemplifies a Christian variant of Anglo-Saxon aristocratic warriorship conditioned by pre-750 imagery. As a young member of the royal dynasty of Mercia this holy man had first attempted to gain power for himself by recruiting a warband from far and wide to impose his will on neighbouring peoples but then withdrew, first to receive two years' instruction at the monastery of Repton, which was closely associated with the Mercian royal house, and then to pursue a life of spiritual struggle on an island in the midst of fens at Crowland.[26] He was no saint of some distant foreign clime. The Latin *Life* of him, which was written by a certain Felix for Ælfwald, king of East Anglia, probably in the 730s and certainly by 749, combined elements from Latin literary tradition, especially *Vitae*,[27] with others from early-eighth-century Mercian militarism itself. The second and third of the three hosts of evil spirits which, on the model of St Antony, Guthlac warded off in his solitary abode took the forms of fierce human, Celtic warriors[28] and of threatening beasts which included the characteristically native varieties of boar, wolf, horse, stag, serpent and raven.[29] Of particular interest to us, with our *Beowulf*ian concerns, are the ferocious *semen Cain*, 'seed of Cain',[30] who formed the first of the troops threatening the saint, for the *Beowulf* poet likewise, through his narrator, categorized his evil enemies of royal power, Grendel and his kin, as descendants of Cain, and, in fact, this *Life* and the poem furnish the only two extant references from Anglo-Saxon times to progeny of Cain active in exile.[31] More generally, the two works deployed similar ranges of beast imagery in a public, not private, perspective. Guthlac's mental contests, like Beowulf's physical ones, were not just of

[25] The imagery of seventh- to eighth-century coins has been ignored by art historians and other non-numismatists. I am most grateful to Mark Blackburn for help and advice in this area.

[26] *Felix's 'Life' of St Guthlac*, chs. 16–25 (ed. Colgrave, pp. 80–8).

[27] See *ibid.* (ed. Colgrave, pp. 16–17).

[28] *Ibid.*, ch. 34 (ed. Colgrave, pp. 108–10); Guthlac had been an exile among the Welsh at one time in his warlike youth.

[29] *Ibid.*, ch. 36 (ed. Colgrave, pp. 114–16).

[30] *Ibid.* (ed. Colgrave, p. 106).

[31] For a discussion, see Clemoes, 'Style as the Criterion for Dating . . . *Beowulf*', pp. 182–3.

consequence to him personally: in his hermitage the saint was frequently visited by, among others, Æthelbald, of Mercian royal stock, to whom, when exiled, he acted as close spiritual adviser, and on whose career, culminating in kingship from 716 to 757, he had much influence. The two royal heroes, Beowulf and Guthlac, were envisaged as operating, each in his own way, at the limits of current warrior kingship, the one in a remote people in the far past and the other in a contemporary realm of spirituality.[32]

The monumental work, *De virginitate*, composed in both a prose and a poetic version by Aldhelm, probably while he was abbot of Malmesbury,[33] shows that at that house late in the seventh century or at the beginning of the eighth the sort of imagery employed in *Beowulf* to depict battling kingship was in vogue as an essential element in learned, Christian, Anglo-Latin portrayal of the assertion of spiritual authority in general. Beast and monster images were Aldhelm's narrative stuff as much as they were the *Beowulf* poet's: whereas the desert occupied by Paul the Hermit had been a place of peaceful solitude and prayer according to St Jerome's *Vita S. Pauli*, Aldhelm turned it into a location where the saint 'fearlessly scorned the horrendous trumpetings of elephants and the savage roars of lions'.[34] In particular Aldhelm clearly felt that his vigorous champions of virtue ought to prove themselves against society-menacing dragons as their supreme test.[35] For instance, he passed over other miracles of St Hilarion, an anchorite in the Palestinian desert, listed in Jerome's *Vita S. Hilarionis*, his source, in order to concentrate exclusively on two mighty public acts, the slaying of a huge dragon which was terrorizing a district by swallowing up men, cattle and sheep, and the stemming of a tempestuous sea threatening to engulf a city. Aldhelm was like Felix and the *Beowulf* poet in holding with native tradition that individual resistance to beasts and monsters was the acid test of personal nobility in public life.

All three also shared certain characteristic ways of applying a dramatic imagination to this social theme. They all had a strong sense of the actual phenomena of monstrosity. Aldhelm shows it by giving the dragons in the distant past and distant places of his written sources a dynamic physicality

[32] Cf. the illuminating comparison of Guthlac's struggles and Beowulf's, Mayr-Harting, *The Coming of Christianity*, pp. 231–7.

[33] Lapidge, '*Beowulf*, Aldhelm, the *Liber monstrorum* and Wessex', pp. 178–9.

[34] *Aldhelm: the Prose Works*, trans. Lapidge and Herren, p. 87.

[35] Cf. Lapidge, '*Beowulf*, Aldhelm, the *Liber monstrorum* and Wessex', pp. 158–62.

equal to that with which the *Beowulf* poet invested his dragon in the Geatland of long ago. The fifty-foot *wyrm* King Beowulf faced had not only deadly fiery breath but also a hard bony body (2577b–8a) and poisonous teeth in its jaws (2691b–2a): it was an *attorsceaða*, 'poison-injurer' (2389a), whose bite implanted *attor*, fatal 'poison', in any victim's body (2715a; the fearsome set of teeth in the jaws of the dragon on the Sutton Hoo shield are worth noticing too[36]). And Aldhelm's immense *draco*, destroyed by St Hilarion, was no less 'real': so far as Jerome was concerned, it had simply swallowed its victims whole and had been undramatically incinerated after the saint ordered it to mount a pile of wood,[37] but, as Aldhelm imagined it, it had a horrendous scaly body, killed cattle with poisonous teeth in its jaws, gulped its victims down with the greedy appetite of its stomach, and on the pyre had its rib-cage and rigid curved spine burned up by roasting balls of fire-brands.[38]

Contemporary imagination made literary tradition just as graphic in Felix's *Life of St Guthlac.* The author brought a typically Anglo-Saxon feeling for dramatic narrative to the business of converting information from those who had known the saint into conformity with existing Latin literature of the relevant sort. Thus, for example, ch. 36 was based on an episode in Evagrius's *Vita Beati Antonii Abbatis*, a translation from the Greek of Athanasius,[39] but Felix suitably adapted it (substituting a boar, horse, stag, ox and raven for asps, scorpions and leopards) and made it much more vigorous: generalized description (for instance, of a bull threatening with bellowing and horns) was replaced by a confrontation of an unmistakably Anglo-Saxon sort when Guthlac, the true soldier of the true God, 'heard the noise as of a herd of beasts rushing together and approaching his dwelling with a mighty shaking of the earth. Straightway he saw manifold shapes of various monsters bursting into his house from all sides. Thus a roaring lion fiercely threatened to tear him with its bloody teeth: then a bellowing bull dug up the earth with its hoofs and drove its gory horn into the ground; or a bear, gnashing its teeth and striking violently with either paw alternately, threatened him with blows: a serpent, too, rearing its scaly neck, disclosed the threat of its black poison.'[40] Yet these were no physical opponents like Beowulf's or

[36] See Bruce-Mitford, *The Sutton Hoo Ship Burial: a Handbook*, ill. 22.

[37] PL 23, col. 50.

[38] *Aldhelm: the Prose Works*, trans. Lapidge and Herren, p. 88.

[39] PL 73, col. 132.

[40] *Felix's 'Life' of St Guthlac*, ch. 36 (ed. Colgrave, p. 115).

Hilarion's. As in the *Vita Antonii*, they were phantasms. They had to be conquered in the mind and by words. They required a challenge of the sort aristocratic Anglo-Saxon warriors knew so well how to deliver. Whereas Antony, distressed in body but calm in mind, had invoked his trust in God and had been rewarded by a shaft of heavenly radiance which banished the evil spirits, Guthlac, true to his soldierly upbringing, armed his breast with the sign of salvation, poured scorn on Satan as one who had once aimed at making himself God's equal but was now reduced to imitating 'the whinneying, the grunting and the croaking of miserable beasts', and commanded him, in the name of Jesus Christ who had banished him from heaven, to cease the tumult.[41] A merely subordinate metaphor in the Latin had been turned into a proud warrior, with the confidence of might on his side, cutting his enemy down to size and issuing an uncompromising demand.

As we have just seen, Aldhelm displayed in Latin literature a dramatic sense that public authority had to prevail against monstrous embodiments of destruction, and, in similar Latin literary surroundings, Felix's Guthlac stoutly personified the mental resolution which that defence demanded, but it is only the poem *Beowulf*, in society's traditional language, which sympathetically and thoughtfully laid bare the essential combination of mind and body being tested to the limit in these supremely demanding conditions. Here alone the monstrous dimension was exploited to expose the strengths and weaknesses of the central social institution of personal warrior kingship fighting for survival in mighty achievement and honourable defeat. In this poem, surely, we see in full spate the native creative mainstream which overflowed into written Anglo-Latin literary composition at the end of the seventh century and early in the eighth.

That, however, is not to say that in *Beowulf* vernacular purity was uninfiltrated by Latin influence. It was affected, although there was only limited percolation and it may well have been indirect. For instance, the landscape in which the poet set the lair of Grendel and his mother, and hence a vital piece of action by his hero, seems to me a sign that he was at least in touch with a sub-literary culture. A sensation of fearfulness is conveyed 'picturesquely' by the *mise-en-scène* – wolf-slopes, windswept headlands and a dangerous fen-path (1358–9a); a mountain stream plunging beneath misty headlands (1359b–60); joyless frosty trees above a

[41] *Ibid.* (ed. Colgrave, pp. 115 and 117).

grey rock on a cliff hanging over a bloodstained, turbulent, pool of monster-infested water, fiery by night.[42] The atmospheric effect of this scenery is quite different from that of the spare setting of the dragon's mound, which is as austere as the bare gnomic generalization, 'Draca sceal on hlæwe, / frod, frætwum wlanc' ('A dragon belongs in a mound, old and proud of treasures', *Maxims II* 26b–7a), and is disclosed only step by step as the narrative action proceeds – as in 'hiorosercean bær / under stancleofu' ('he bore his battle-shirt under the rocky cliffs', 2539b–40a). The descriptive technique applied to Grendel's and his mother's habitat seems exotic and the one applied to the dragon's thoroughly native; and the most probable explanation for this difference, I suggest, lies in the 'literary' affiliations of the former represented by an analogue in a vernacular prose homily which is extant only in the Blickling manuscript of *c.* 1000 but which could have been of much earlier composition.[43] The homiletic passage,[44] which purported to describe what St Paul saw when he 'wæs geseonde on norðanweardne þisne middangeard' ('was looking towards the northern region of this world'), and was intended to be a warning against injurious spirits, contains several features which correspond to items in the *Beowulf*ian scenery, including 'swiðe hrimige bearwas' ('very frosty trees') as a principal element:

> ⁊ he geseah þæt on ðæm clife hangodan on ðæm isigean bearwum manige swearte saula be heora handum gebundne; ⁊ þa fynd þara on nicra onlicnesse heora gripende wæron, swa swa grædig wulf; ⁊ þæt wæter wæs sweart under þæm clife neoðan. ⁊ betuh þæm clife on ðæm wætre wæron swylce twelf mila, ⁊ ðonne ða twigo forburston þonne gewitan þa saula niðer þa þe on ðæm twigum hangodan, ⁊ him onfengon ða nicras
>
> ['and he saw that on the cliff on the icy trees many black souls hung tied by their hands; and the fiends in the likeness of water-monsters were grasping them like a greedy wolf; and the water was black underneath the cliff. And between the cliff and the water there were about twelve miles, and, when the twigs broke, down went the souls who hung on them and the water-monsters seized them'].[45]

St Paul's vision in this homily manifestly belonged to a tradition of Christian ideas about the topography of hell, in which trees with

[42] 1362b–6a, 1414–17a, 1421a and 1425-7.

[43] The Blickling manuscript had access to material which was probably early; see, e.g., Scragg, 'The Corpus of Vernacular Homilies', p. 265, n. 2.

[44] *The Blickling Homilies*, ed. Morris, pp. 209, line 29 – 211, line 7.

[45] *Ibid.*, pp. 209, line 31 – 211, line 5.

suspended sinful souls featured distinctively: they are first known from a redaction which, at some time after a period bounded by the fourth and early sixth centuries according to T. Silverstein, marked a stage in the tradition of the 'Long' text of a *Visio S. Pauli*, a Latin translation of a Greek-Egyptian apocryphal *Apocalypse of St Paul* purportedly describing revelations which St Paul had refrained from making known in II Corinthians XII:[46]

Et postea Paulus ductus ad portas inferni. Et uidit ibi arbores igneas, in quarum ramis peccatores cruciati pendebant: quidam per capillos, alii per pedes, alii per manus, alii per linguas, alii per colla, alii per brachia, alii per membra diuersa

['And afterwards Paul was led to the gates of hell. And there he saw fiery trees, on the branches of which sinners hung tormented: some by their hair, others by their feet, others by their hands, others by their tongues, others by their necks, others by their arms, others by various limbs'].[47]

The Blickling passage could not have been totally unconnected with this redaction of the 'Long' *Visio*, although the homily does not exhibit suspension by different parts of the sinners' bodies and instead (in typically Anglo-Saxon dire dramatic fashion) tells how the breaking of mere twigs plunges the souls headlong twelve miles down into the grip of water-monsters. Nor could the Blickling and *Beowulf* descriptions have been entirely independent of one another, for, while the latter has no suspended sinners, both have in common – as against the positionless fiery trees of the *Visio* – a plunging torrent, mist and an association of frosty trees and grey rock high up on a cliff above monster-infested water.[48] The likelihood

[46] See Silverstein, *Visio Sancti Pauli*. The relevant redaction is Silverstein's (lost) b. For its position in the development of the text, see the diagram *ibid.*, p. 60, and for dating of previous stages to a period beginning not earlier than the fourth century (A) and ending not later than early in the sixth (L^1), see *ibid.*, p. 37.

[47] *Ibid.*, p. 156; for the particular characteristics of this version of hanging sinners, see *ibid.*, pp. 69–70. The Latin version used for the vernacular translation which is extant in Oxford, Bodleian Library, Junius 85–6 did not belong to the redaction concerned and so neither the Latin nor the Old English contained this item at all (see *The Old English Vision of St Paul*, ed. Healey, p. 52).

[48] In the Blickling homily the passage already cited is preceded by the following:
Swa Sanctus Paulus wæs geseonde on norðanweardne þisne middangeard, þær ealle wætero niðergewitað, ⁊ he þær geseah ofer ðæm wætere sumne harne stan; ⁊ wæron norð of ðæm stane awexene swiðe hrimige bearwas, ⁊ ðær wæron þystrogenipo, ⁊ under þæm stane wæs niccra eardung ⁊ wearga
['So St Paul was looking towards the northern region of this world where all waters descend, and he

seems to me to be that the poet did not invent for himself this 'exotic' scenery, but that he owed it to a probably non-textual connection with the homily: he might have heard this homily, or a similar one, preached; or he and the homilist concerned may both have adopted elements from a vernacular 'literary', scenic, description of hell, which belonged to a quasi-Latin, quasi-vernacular, tradition known to them alike and which the poet thought was apt for his monsters' refuge probably because he knew that it was already associated with eternal damnation. When he sent his hero diving into the depths of monster-infested waters to be clutched by Grendel's mother (1494b–1512a), he may have gone as far as imagining that he was testing fitness for warrior kingship in a region which had been previously identified as the environs of hell.

The latter sort of derivation cannot be ruled out. A loosely standardized vernacular sub-literary description of hell would have been a natural product of the mixed culture prevailing in the visionary mode during the early centuries. Several visions encompassing hell, which were claimed in early Anglo-Saxon England and which are recounted in extant Latin literary works partly deriving from the visionaries themselves and partly shaped by others, notably the authors, show influence both from the *Visio S. Pauli* (though the genre owed its basic authority to St Benedict's vision reported in Gregory the Great's *Dialogi*) and from one another: there are the visions which Fursa, an Irishman, related as he travelled in Ireland, Wales, England and France, and which were recorded on the Continent in the middle of the seventh century; there is the late-seventh-century vision of a Northumbrian, Dryhthelm, which Bede wrote about in the 730s; there is a vision by a monk at Wenlock (Shropshire) which St Boniface described in a Latin letter in the second decade of the eighth century after he heard the monk recount it; and there is the night-time vision of 'the abominable throat of hell' which was attributed to St Guthlac in ch. 31 of Felix's *Life* before the middle of the eighth century.[49] As Sims-Williams has observed, the samenesses of, and differences between, these texts witness to a visionary tradition in early Anglo-Saxon ascetic circles in which the Latin and literary and the ver-

saw there above the water a certain grey stone, and north of the stone had grown very frosty trees, and there were dark mists, and under the stone was the dwelling of water-monsters and wicked ones', *The Blickling Homilies*, ed. Morris, p. 209, lines 26–31].

49 I am much indebted to Sims-Williams's meticulous and illuminating discussion of these texts in his *Religion and Literature in Western England*, pp. 243–72.

nacular and oral intermingled.[50] Nor should we forget, as a manifestation of spiritual excitement in these early times, the night-time reception of the cross's account of the crucifixion, drawn on for the vernacular verse inscription on the Ruthwell Cross, perhaps in the second quarter of the eighth century, and narrated in the poem, *The Dream of the Rood*, extant in the Vercelli Book of the second half of the tenth century.[51] The *Beowulf* poet could easily have come across a description of his fearful scenery if he had been on the fringe of sub-literary reporting of visions. One can well imagine him picking up the 'atmospheric' features from vernacular talk of the sort which would have impressed the prince Æthelbald (even though his mind was on politics), if, on one of this exile's visits to Guthlac in the fens, the hermit had given him a graphic account of the vision in the dead of night in which he had imagined himself escaping dramatically from the clutches of demons at the very entry to hell, partly by his own strength of mind and partly by the intervention of St Bartholomew. In such matters the imaginative composer of the secular poem, *Beowulf*, and the religious visionary Guthlac were only on different sides of a not very high fence.[52]

Language can show traces of sub-literary contact too. The Latin loanword *gigant* is a case in point, especially since the poet's conception of man-eating giants, a fiery dragon and sea-monsters, attacking ships and swimmers, and his vocabulary for them were basically Anglo-Saxon.[53] Through the mouthpiece of his narrator the poet included *gigantas* among the evil progeny of Cain:

þanon untydras ealle onwocon,
eotenas ond ylfe ond orcneas,
swylce gigantas, þa wið Gode wunnon
lange þrage; he him ðæs lean forgeald

['From that source {i.e. Cain} all evil broods arose, monsters and elves and evil spirits, likewise giants who contended against God for a long time; he gave them a reward for that', 111–14];

and subsequently he had the narrator reuse the word to designate the giants God had destroyed in the flood:[54]

[50] *Ibid.*, pp. 248 and 267. [51] See further, below, p. 244 and nn. 29 and 30.

[52] On the *Visio-Beowulf*-Blickling homily nexus, see Wright, *The Irish Tradition in Old English Literature*, pp. 116–36.

[53] Cf. Sisam, *The Structure of 'Beowulf'*, p. 6.

[54] As pointed out by Bandy, 'Cain, Grendel, and the Giants of *Beowulf*', p. 240.

syðþan flod ofsloh,
gifen geotende giganta cyn,
frecne geferdon; þæt wæs fremde þeod
ecean Dryhtne; him þæs endelean
þurh wæteres wylm Waldend sealde

['after the flood, the pouring ocean killed the race of giants; they suffered terribly. That was a people estranged from the eternal Lord; the ruler gave them final retribution for that through the surging of water', 1689b–93].

On the other hand the narrator never called Grendel or his mother a *gigant* when reckoning them to be living descendants of Cain,[55] using instead, for Grendel, a Germanic term, *eoten* (761a), in conformity with Beowulf's equally Germanic word for him, *þyrs* (426a), and Hrothgar's neutral description of him, 'mara þonne ænig man oðer' ('greater than any other man', 1353).

The idea that a race of evil giants had descended from Cain derived from interpretation of Genesis VI.2 and 4 which had been given authority and sharp definition by St Augustine,[56] whereas the notion that some of this wicked progeny had survived the flood depended on uncanonical, fabulous tradition.[57] But we should not take the poet's use of a Latin-derived word for the giants who were drowned and Germanic words for descendants of the survivors to imply that he himself necessarily appreciated the distinction between the two sorts of authority (or even that he knew that it was involved) and deliberately chose his words accordingly. Only the most scholarly users of the mother tongue at any phase of Anglo-Saxon learning would have been able to exercise that type of discrimination.[58] More probably it was essentially a case of the one tradition having the Latin word *gigantes* or its Anglicized form *gigantas* attached to it when it came to the poet, and the other not having it. The idea that ante-diluvian giants were descended from Cain was associated with the Latin word *gigantes* as part and parcel of its expression from the very outset of its transmission through

[55] Cf. above, p. 19.

[56] Mellinkoff, 'Cain's Monstrous Progeny in *Beowulf*: Part I', pp. 146–7.

[57] For a survey of this tradition, see Mellinkoff, 'Cain's Monstrous Progeny in *Beowulf*: Part II'.

[58] Cf. Helmut Gneuss's observation that Anglo-Saxons never had any rules or handbooks for guidance on linguistic borrowing, whether loan-translation or semantic loans or loan syntax; Gneuss, *The Study of Language*, p. 32.

orthodox exegetical channels.[59] It is likely that the word *gigantas* in the poet's reference to God's destruction of the race of giants by flood was the automatic result of this respectable Old Testament textual and exegetical

[59] *Gigantes* is invariably the word in all known Vulgate and Old Latin texts of Genesis VI.4 and is the word St Augustine used when interpreting this verse (*De ciuitate Dei* XV.23). I am grateful to Dr Richard Marsden for confirming this. Isidore of Seville too, early in the seventh century, related this word specifically to the same context (*Isidori Hispalensis Episcopi Etymologiarum sive originum libri xx*, ed. Lindsay, XI.iii.14). In *Genesis A* these Genesis giants are designated by the unique compound 'gigantmæcgas' ('giant brood', 1268a). This and the three occurrences of the simplex in *Beowulf* (113a, 1562b and 1690b) are the only uses of *gigant* in extant Old English poetry. A genitive combination (see below, p. 137), 'enta ærgeweorc' ('ancient work of giants', *Beowulf* 1679a), and an adjective combination (see below, *ibid.*), 'ealdsweord eotenisc' ('ancient giant sword', 1558a), are relevant to our appreciation of the genitive combination, 'giganta geweorc' ('work of giants', 1562b). The combination at 1679a is clearly a variant of *enta geweorc*, 'work of giants', which was itself used by the *Beowulf* poet at 2717b and is well attested elsewhere. (It occurs twice more in its basic form, once more (in *Andreas*, see below, p. 260) in the variant form of *Beowulf* 1679a, and three times – including once at *Beowulf* 2774a – in another variant form, 'eald enta geweorc' ('ancient work of giants'); for a survey, see Frankis, 'Thematic Significance', pp. 253–6.) In all but two instances *enta geweorc* (or its variants) denotes a large stone structure (as in *Beowulf* 2717b) and hence shows that *entas* (etymology unknown) were being thought of as builders in stone. The two exceptions, both in *Beowulf*, signify a sword-hilt (1679a) and treasure (2774a) respectively, and so reveal that this poet thought of *entas* as craftmen in metal as well. (See Frankis, 'Thematic Significance', pp. 254–60.) The unique 'giganta geweorc' (1562b), signifying a sword, is therefore to be regarded as a variation of *enta geweorc*, with *giganta* substituted for *enta* in the latter's second category of meaning. Why then did the poet make this substitution when the whole sword was concerned (1562b), and yet did not when the referent was this sword's hilt (1679a), which was all that remained of it after the blade had melted? The answer must surely lie in chronological implications in the change of reference: at 1562b it was to the sword as originally manufactured, but at 1679a it was to the hilt bearing a record of the destruction of giants in the flood. The line the poet drew elsewhere between *gigant* and Germanic words suggests that here he was discriminating between the sword's manufacture as ante-diluvian and the hilt's record as post-diluvian and was registering this distinction by maintaining his customary classification. (Frankis ('Thematic Significance', p. 260, n. 3) did not draw any distinction between sword and hilt.) Nor need the apposition between 'ealdsweord eotenisc' (1558a) and 'giganta geweorc' (1562b) disturb this conclusion, for the former combination (used by this poet twice elsewhere of other swords (2616a and 2979a), but only by this poet) lacked any specific relationship to manufacture, the unique adjective *eotenisc* being, we may assume, merely indicative of great size (cf. 1560–1). (By contrast, in the combination 'entiscne helm' ('giant helmet', 2979b) the unique adjective probably did relate to (quality associated with) manufacture by giants, because of the customary understanding of *entas* as craftsmen.)

influence whether or not the poet fully understood the tradition and whether his contact with it had been textual, inscriptional or oral. His idea of the *semen Cain* as active evil beings, by contrast, is likely to have been far more nebulous. So far as Felix's *Life of St Guthlac* was concerned,[60] it did not involve giants or any post-diluvian survival, since those whom the saint so called were evil spirits which had come in their crowds straight out of hell.[61] The chances are that the poet's tradition was so vague that he did not consider that his application of it to Grendel and his mother raised any questions of inconsistency provided that he kept *gigantas* out of post-diluvian times.

What he undoubtedly did appreciate was the effect which God's destruction of *gigantas* would have on an audience of his story. It emphasized, in general, that Beowulf's eradication of Grendel – 'Godes andsaca' ('God's adversary', 1682b) – and his mother was in accordance with God's will, and it supplied, in particular, through the motif that the *gigantas* perished because they were alienated from God, the moral dimension of a divine restoration to the young hero's victorious return from the mere: the hilt he brought with him was from a mighty sword made by them (1562b), which, at God's prompting, Beowulf had seen in the underwater hall in time to use it to kill Grendel's mother, and which had melted from the heat of Grendel's blood, apart from the hilt, when Beowulf had used it again to decapitate Grendel's corpse; it was while looking at this hilt on which divine punishment of these rebels was recorded (either by illustration or by inscription) – 'hylt sceawode' ('he examined the hilt', 1687b) – that Hrothgar combined his eulogy of Beowulf with a warning against excessive pride in transient worldly prosperity. When 'hit on æht gehwearf / æfter deofla hryre Denigea frean' ('it passed into the possession of the lord of the Danes after the fall of devils', 1679b–80), this hilt was an emblem of a divine restoration of power 'woroldcyninga / ðæm selestan be sæm tweonum' ('to the finest of earthly kings between the seas', 1684b–5). It was a Germanic-type symbol which, by virtue of being placed in a perspective of defeated Old Testament *gigantas*, became a solemn token to warrior kingship of the greater authority of God.

'Literary' echoes such as these, however, did not for one moment compromise the native independence of the *Beowulf* poet's art. We

[60] See above, p. 19.

[61] *Felix's 'Life' of St Guthlac*, ch. 31 (ed. Colgrave, pp. 104–6).

encounter everywhere in his work, uncontaminated, the combination of evocative elemental, conventional, perception and psychological alertness to dramatic context,[62] which was the essence of oral composition at its finest. Practised here most expertly is a type of linguistic craftsmanship radically different from the exercise in a written literary style which composition became for a poet, such as the probably ninth-century Cynewulf,[63] engaged in converting into a high-quality vernacular verse text a story taken whole from a Latin text.[64] There is intact in the native language of *Beowulf* a unity of socially formed thought and conventionally formed expression[65] which, it is reasonable to conclude, could never have been reconstituted as a living medium for this poem's range of mainstream thinking and feeling, once it had lost as much ground to 'literature' as it did in the course of the ninth century.

But, if the traditional type of composition flourishing here implies pre-ninth-century authorship, how is it that our only copy, datable by the handwriting of its two scribes to very early in the eleventh century,[66] so consistently retains the concentrated relationship between primary social imagination and dramatic narrative context[67] which could have come only from a single, controlling originator? Why is there so little of the loss of quality which we would expect as a result of long exposure to oral transmission and/or to the subjective licence characteristic of pen-and-ink copyists of vernacular poetry?[68] To answer, we have to test whether what we find in our surviving copy can be considered compatible with what it would be likely to owe to an ultimate origin in an eighth-century sub-literary culture. In the first place, prolonged oral transmission simply has to be ruled out, if we take a loosening of precise concentration to be its likely outcome in the extant text. In the second place, we have to conclude that there has been little copying which was not of a strictly textual, visual kind, if we look for loss of control over alliteration – as against a failure to supply alliteration through some accidental omission – as clear evidence of

62 For these qualities, see below, esp. pp. 189–206.

63 For arguments in support of this dating, based on the spellings of the name in 'signatures' worked into epilogues to four extant poems, see Sisam, *Studies in the History of Old English Literature*, pp. 1–7

64 See below, pp. 239–41 and 244–5.

65 See below, pp. 134–42.

66 London, British Library, Cotton Vitellius A. xv, fols. 132–201. For this, the most recent, dating, see Dumville, 'Beowulf Come Lately'.

67 See below, e.g., pp. 412–16.

68 Concerning this latter, see below, p. 31.

copying which had been led by general expectation rather than by attention to the wording of an exemplar.[69] There are only two instances of this vagueness in the work of the first scribe (although, of course, he may not have introduced either of them himself): one is *hand gripe* instead of (as all editors agree) *mundgripe*, 'handgrip', at 965a, where m- alliteration is required, and the other is *hild plegan*, 'battle-play', at 1073b, instead of (again all editors agreeing) *lindplegan*, 'shield-play', tó supply the necessary l- alliteration. And there is one other in the second scribe's stint at 1981a, where, after originally writing *reced*, 'building', he added a preceding *side*, 'wide', above the line. Actually h- alliteration is required, and most editors have agreed to read *healreced*, 'hall-building'. At this point this scribe was either correcting his own omission of part of an already non-alliterating reading in his exemplar or (maybe) was carelessly supplying a word out of his own head to make good an omission which was already in his exemplar but which he had not spotted until after he had followed suit. And that is all.

What we are left with is a process of copying text as text, evidenced by a crop of errors, ranging from three omissions of whole *a* or *b* verses (403b, 1803a and 2792b) to numerous literals. On a conservative estimate there are well over 200 uncorrected mistakes in our extant copy[70] and a similar number has been corrected by the two scribes.[71] In 1981, K. S. Kiernan performed a genuine service by stressing the importance of these corrections for an assessment of the poem's transmission[72] but then, unfortunately, threw the advantage away by taking the scribes' 'careful proofreading' to mean that the uncorrected errors which have been perceived by modern critics and editors are just so much moonshine. His standpoint that 'it is highly suspicious that all of the "glaring errors" perceived by modern editors were not corrected by these Anglo-Saxon correctors whose proofreading seems to have been quite thorough'[73] is patently erroneous. Rather we should infer that our two scribes had a limited, 'professional', 'textual' brief to produce a fresh copy of an exemplar and that, accordingly, their corrections were directed to doing that job properly and not to eliminating defects in their exemplar root and branch. As Kiernan himself

69 For the primary importance of alliteration in Old English metre, see below, pp. 142–5.

70 See Kelly, 'The Formative Stages of *Beowulf* Textual Scholarship', categories III–VI and table 9.

71 For a very careful recent analysis of the former, see Gerritsen, 'Have With You to Lexington!', pp. 20–4.

72 *'Beowulf' and the 'Beowulf' Manuscript*, pp. 191–218.

73 *Ibid.*, p. 195.

has remarked, 'the corrections are mostly of common mechanical errors like dittography and haplography'.[74] Most grosser errors (such as the omission of the three *a* or *b* verses) remain. The evidence of the uncorrected mistakes is at least as important as that of the corrected ones. Both classes must be taken into account.

The scribes' corrections provide evidence for their conception of their job very early in the eleventh century and for their using an exemplar which they did not find altogether straightforward. Close scrutiny might reveal some particular difficulties it presented them with. The uncorrected errors point further back. They (or most of them) witness to uncorrected errors in the exemplar which the early-eleventh-century scribes allowed to stand and which, by their nature, may give hints about what preceded the exemplar. For instance, if the early-eleventh-century scribes were copying an exemplar of late-ninth-century, Alfredian, times or later, that exemplar might, in turn, have been a copy of an earlier text which had been produced at a time when different habits of orthography and script prevailed. In particular, it was not until about the middle of the ninth century that *þ* and *ð* became the only regular spellings for the voiceless and voiced consonants familiar today as the initial sounds of, for example, *thick* and *this*, and until about the same time *ƿ* had not become the standard spelling for the sound [w]: previously *th* and *d* had been used as well as *þ* and *ð* to represent the fricatives,[75] and *u* or *uu* had only gradually given way to *ƿ*.[76] As to script, an open-headed *a* (rather like a *u*), used, among other forms of the letter, in early current or cursive minuscule, could have been one source of difficulty for a later copyist: it seems not to have been employed in documents after the middle of the ninth-century and to have been killed off in non-documentary contexts south of the Humber by the creation of square minuscule as a new formal script early in the tenth century.[77] Substitution

[74] *Ibid.*, p. 193.

[75] For the first two, see *tha* and *modgidanc* in the version of *Cædmon's Hymn* entered at the end of the Moore Manuscript of Bede's Latin *Historia ecclesiastica* (Cambridge, University Library, Kk.5.16, 128v) in the first half of the eighth century (cf. below, pp. 242–3).

[76] The former was used, for instance, throughout the Moore *Hymn* (*uard* (2×), *uere*, *uuldurfadur*, *uundra* and *gihuaes*), and *uu* in an inscription of *c.* 700 (*Cuthsuuithae*; see Sims-Williams, 'Cuthswith, Seventh-Century Abbess of Inkberrow', p. 21).

[77] For an early example, see (among many) in the Epinal Glossary (Epinal, Bibliothèque Municipale, 72 (2), fols. 94–107), now dated palaeographically as early as late in the seventh century, the second and third *a*s in *aurata* (100r(d), bottom line), reproduced in the facsimile, *The Épinal, Erfurt, Werden, and Corpus Glossaries*, ed. Bischoff *et al.*; for the

of *þ* for *th* would not have been a problem for a post-mid-ninth-century scribe, but the other 'modernizations' would not have been so straightforward: alteration of *d* to *ð* when the sound-value was the fricative but not when it was the plosive [d] would have been quite tricky; substitution of *ƿ* for either *u* or *uu* would not have been without its snags either; and consistent differentiation between open-headed *a* and *u* would have demanded sustained concentration. A post-mid-ninth-century copy of a pre-mid-ninth-century exemplar might be expected to have shown some traces of these processes in its errors.

Uncorrected errors in the *Beowulf* manuscript may supply some examples. There are at least two instances of *d* instead of *ð*, one in the first scribe's work at 1837a and one in the second scribe's at 2959b,[78] and there are at least three of *ð* instead of *d*, one of them where the first scribe was writing (1107a) and two where it was the second scribe (1991a and 2064a).[79] The two scribes do not seem to have been particularly prone to producing this sort of error themselves. For one thing, the second would have been unlikely to produce *d* instead of *ð* by accidentally failing to cross the ascender, since he usually formed the two letters differently by curving the ascender of his *d* markedly to the left and keeping it low; and, for another thing, there seem to be, all told, only two instances of *ð* corrected to *d* by erasure, one in the work of the first scribe at 1939a[80] and one in the second scribe's at 2580b.[81] Thus there is a little evidence for confusion between *d* and *ð* at a stage earlier than our extant manuscript but almost none for the confusion taking place at the extant stage itself; and there is also one possible vestige of an antecedent faulty substitution of *ƿ* for *uu* in

dating, see *ibid.*, pp. 15–16. The latest document in which the letter form has been spotted is a charter of Æthelwulf, king of Wessex, of 847 (Sawyer, *Anglo-Saxon Charters*, no. 298); it appears frequently in both the Latin of this charter, and its English bounds. For a non-documentary occurrence in a current grade of minuscule as late as *c.* 900, see the first Latin interlinear addition reproduced in Dumville, 'English Square Minuscule Script', pl. I, and commented on, *ibid.*, n. 96. The form is also one of the old-fashioned, current traits of the handwriting of Aldred, the tenth-century Northumbrian glossator of the Lindisfarne Gospels and Durham Ritual, as pointed out by Keller (*Angelsächsische Palaeographie* I, 35). David Dumville has been extremely kind in giving me his advice on the distribution of this letter form and in supplying me with some of the above references.

78 Another may occur within the first scribe's stint at 985a.

79 3152b might be a third.

80 Is there another at 1373a? No one reports it.

81 Someone else may have made these erasures at any time, of course.

the second scribe's uncorrected reading *blæwu*, instead of *blæw*, at 2296b. As regards confusion between *a* and *u* the signs are similar. Gerritsen reports seven instances of it peculiar to *Beowulf* among the contents of the extant manuscript and suggests that especially the two mistakes (one in the work of each scribe) which involve the stem of the word concerned and lack any contextual feature to account for them might well have originated in previous confusion between open-headed *a* and *u*:[82] the one miswriting is *wudu* for *wadu* at 581a (the same scribe had already correctly written *wada* at 508b and *wado* at 546a) and the other is *strade* for *strude* at 3073b (the same scribe later copying *strude* correctly at 3126b). The former is particularly striking since the reference is to the 'wadu weallendu' ('surging waters') of a strongly flowing current of the sea; and mere scribal inattention, without the distraction of a *u*-like *a*, might seem insufficient to account for such a misconception. And, once again, there is only a slight indication of any confusion of *a* and *u* at the extant manuscript stage, namely the second scribe's correction of *-a* to *-um* in the course of writing *ofermaðmum* at 2993b.[83] The present state of knowledge, we may well think, hardly amounts to proof that a pre-mid-ninth-century text lay behind the extant one at one remove (or more). Only more systematic, comprehensive, investigation could determine the degree of probability or improbability that this was so. But meanwhile it seems to me that there is a *prima facie* case for supposing that our poem underwent a three-stage textual transmission, consisting of a pre-mid-ninth-century writing, a post-mid-ninth-century copying and lastly another, very early-eleventh-century, one.

We can speculate further. The simplest explanation for the poem's combination of compositional purity and textual impurity is to suppose that the author himself began the textualization. To adopt that view we would need to envisage a poet who followed a method of composing and then writing down his verse (or having it written down for him by dictation) in current or cursive minuscule, perhaps a run at a time – in a script, if he himself were responsible for it, doubtless less expert than the composition. So far as our evidence other than this poem goes, this procedure would have been unusual before the middle of the eighth century,[84] and it might

[82] 'Have With You to Lexington!', p. 24.

[83] This, on the other hand, might have been a rare flash of recognition of an error in the exemplar.

[84] See below, pp. 35–6.

involve the notion that the poet learned orthography in order to write in the vernacular without using it as a means to read Latin, for, in my opinion, the poem affords no certain evidence that he knew that language at first hand. At first sight the whole idea might seem improbable, but there is nothing impossible about it: the close connections which prevailed between noble families and religious institutions from the start[85] could have led to some aristocratic individuals before 850 learning to write as a way of furthering an abiding interest in Germanic antiquity when they saw others using it in the interests of the 'new' Latin learning: a vernacular poet adopting this technique would have been the 'secular' counterpart to the more ecclesiastically educated Aldhelm, who, late in the seventh century and early in the eighth, composed not only written Latin poetry with Anglo-Saxon traits[86] but also, according to an early-twelfth-century historian, vernacular verse which survived, presumably in writing, to be much admired by King Alfred late in the ninth.[87] A member of a high-born family either in contact with religious foundations or belonging to one would fill the bill admirably. Others who postulate an author of this sort at this time usually see him as a cleric, and certainly this view would account straightforwardly for the ability to write which otherwise would have been quite exceptional.[88] But, all the same, composition of a poem of the stature of *Beowulf* in a religious house would have stood out above more run-of-the-mill well-attested monkish enjoyment of secular poetry and yet did not capitalize as much as it might be expected to have done on the also well-attested capacity of the warrior nobility 'to throw its traditions, customs, tastes and loyalties into the articulation of the new faith' in the spirit which, as Wormald rightly stresses, was the basic contribution of aristocratic 'secularity' to early church life.[89] In my opinion *Beowulf* fails to represent systematic Christianity fully enough to qualify without question as a product of monastic life. Preferably, to my mind, whether its origin lay 'inside' or 'outside' a religious community should remain an open issue. Given the paucity of our evidence – *Beowulf* is after all unique – I

[85] See, e.g., Wormald, 'Bede, *Beowulf* and the Conversion', esp. pp. 54–5.

[86] See below, pp. 430–1.

[87] William of Malmesbury reports, on evidence now lost, that Alfred considered that Aldhelm had never been equalled as a vernacular poet; WM, *GP*, p. 336.

[88] Patrick Wormald, for instance, refers to 'a literate poet, who was probably, therefore, a cleric' ('Bede, *Beowulf* and the Conversion', p. 58).

[89] *Ibid.*, p. 57.

tentatively propose for the poem, on the grounds of the nature of its extant text, a pre-mid-ninth-century author who employed a perhaps not very expertly formed hand (either his own or another's) to write his poem down, as he composed it, in order to impose a hitherto unattainable degree of control over its orality.[90] This accessory technique could easily have been, like 'literary' scenery or a Latin loanword, a mere Latin scion grafted on to the native stock of oral composition during early contacts between Christian text and vernacular orality before the former had attained the dominance over the latter which it established during the ninth century.

The chief dimensions of the *Beowulf* poet's portrayal of kingship, which were not intrinsic to the social model of Germanic warrior rule as such, were 'folk' imagination, threats from Cain-descended monstrosity and Christian responsibility to God. These conceptual elements in the cultural environment of *Beowulf*ian kingship we must now review for pre-ninth-century characteristics. The poet's attitude to the first of them, 'folk' imagination, was to regard it as a proper ingredient of story-telling: for instance, seafarers had told Hrothgar that young Beowulf had the strength of thirty men in his grip (377–81a; thirty was the number of thegns Grendel had killed on his first raid into Hrothgar's hall too (120b–3a)), and later the narrator was to assert that Beowulf swam back from Hygelac's raid into the Rhineland with thirty sets of armour on his arm (2359b–62). The poet's standpoint was essentially the same as the respect for popular belief in the strange, abnormal and unusual, as against suspicion of literature as an authority shown by the learned author of a Latin work, known as the *Liber monstrorum*, emanating from Aldhelm's circle.[91] This writer, probably a colleague or pupil of Aldhelm at Malmesbury,[92] when culling a wide range of Latin writings, including Vergil's poems, to compile this list of some 120 classical, and other, monsters, beasts and serpents, constantly distanced himself from these sources by comments such as *ut ferunt*, 'according to report', or *ut fingitur*, 'as is supposed', or

[90] This authorial procedure would have been a striking confirmation of the truth of Alan Jabbour's statement that 'a memorial tradition can interact smoothly and even profitably with lettered tradition' ('Memorial Transmission', p. 190).

[91] *Liber monstrorum*, ed. Porsia, and *Liber monstrorum de diversis generibus*, ed. Bologna; also Butturff, 'The Monsters and the Scholar'.

[92] For this vital attribution, see Lapidge, '*Beowulf*, Aldhelm, the *Liber monstrorum* and Wessex', pp. 162–76, and Orchard, 'Some Aspects of Seventh-Century Hiberno-Latin Syntax', pp. 178–9.

occasionally by dismissal of items out of hand.[93] His policy he explained in a prologue thus: 'Et de his [mirabilibus] primum eloquar quae sunt aliquo modo credenda, et sequentem historiam sibi quisque discernat' ('And about these [marvels] I shall speak first of the things which are to be believed to some extent, and let each person discern the following history for himself').[94] Accordingly a bisexual man, whom he himself had known, opened the list, to be followed by King Hygelac, cited as a well-attested specimen of those who are monsters by virtue of hugeness ('Et fiunt monstra mirae magnitudinis, ut rex † Huncglacus †):[95] this *rex*, it is stated, ruled the *Getis*, was killed by the Franks and could not be carried by a horse from the age of twelve, his bones now being preserved on an island at the mouth of the Rhine and displayed as a wonder to travellers from afar. Only this text and *Beowulf* among our extant sources know of Hygelac as king of a tribe called the Geats and only they agree that his body remained in enemy hands after he had been killed on his raid into the Rhineland. Both represent an English (as against Frankish, written) tradition, which in the *Liber* was combined with popular imagination of the sort the poet applied to Beowulf. Poem and late-seventh-century *Liber* relied on the same admixture of oral folk-credence for their hold on kingship in the past.[96]

Both of them also drew a distinction between monsters which were a degradation of the human race and those which, living on land or in the sea or in the sky, frighten humanity by being (as the *Liber* put it) 'in horrendi corporis ignota et metuenda forma' ('in an unknown and fearful form of a

[93] E.g., when he observed of the Midas touch, 'Quod nemo nisi ueritatem spernans credit' ('This no one believes unless scorning truth', *Liber monstrorum*, ed. Bologna, p. 62).

[94] *Ibid.*, p. 36.

[95] *Ibid.*, p. 38. The best surviving manuscript reads *Higlac(us)* here, and in the related chapter-heading *Hyglac(o)*; Lapidge, '*Beowulf*, Aldhelm, the *Liber monstrorum* and Wessex', p. 165.

[96] Another specific folk motif shared by these two works, which has been pointed out by Ohlgren (*Anglo-Saxon Art: Texts and Contexts*, p. 32, n. 13), is represented by the melting of the swordblade after Beowulf had used it to decapitate Grendel (see above, p. 96). It melted because 'wæs þæt blod to þæs hat, / ættren ellorgæst se þær inne swealt' ('the blood was so hot, poisonous alien spirit, who perished in there', 1616b–17; see also 1615b–16a and cf. 1605b–7a and 1666b–8a): the heat of Grendel's poisonous blood was three times identified as the cause. Likewise the *Liber* reports a monster of an unspecified, seemingly folk, type, whose poison melts any sword which pierces it (*Liber monstrorum*, ed. Bologna, pp. 114–16).

terrifying body').[97] The former kind but not the latter – in *Beowulf* Grendel and his kin but not the dragon – usually constituted a conjunction of two opposites, the rational and the bestial. According to the *Liber*, centaurs which were half man and half wild-ass combined 'corpora hominum rationabilia' above the navel and 'onagrorum setosa turpitudo' ('the bristly foulness of asses')[98] below, while Grendel had both the out-size form of a man and steely claws with which, no doubt, he seized the victims of his cannibalism. Particularly, inability to speak marked the presence of the bestial: in the *Liber* centaurs which were half man and half horse stopped short of being able to form words out of the sounds they made,[99] and in the poem neither Grendel nor his mother ever spoke.

Both works recognized too that deformity could arise within the human race. The author of the *Liber* had learned of a man in Asia who had had a man's feet and stomach and yet two breasts and four hands and two heads *monstrosa conmixtione*, 'through a monstrous mingling', of his human parents.[100] And it was this principle of man's own responsibility for degradation which the *Beowulf* poet elevated on to an explicitly moral, religious plane by linking the depravity of Grendel and his kin with descent from Cain. This brings us to our second cultural factor. As compared with the *Liber* the poem introduced the comprehensive concept that all *untydras*, 'abnormal broods' (111a), were descended from Cain as a result of God exiling him from mankind in revenge for his murder of Abel (104b–14): in God's eyes Grendel and his kin were outlaws (106–7a) and they in turn were in a murderous state of feud with human society (151b–4a). Monstrous distortion of humankind had thus been given a root cause in the social pattern of feuding through a heinous crime against God, and an analogy of a murder occasioning a feud with God was provided by late-seventh-century Anglo-Saxon society itself on the evidence of the legend of St Mildthryth who was abbess of Minster in Thanet, Kent, by 696. Most versions of her legend describe how Egbert, king of Kent, after the dynastically motivated killing of his cousins, Æthelberht and Æthelred, offered their *wergild* to their sister, who elected to take it in the form of land. The abbey of Minster in Thanet was founded on this land. The *wergild* payment was not a normal one, since it was made within the family and resulted from a killing which had been deliberately concealed

97 *Ibid.*, p. 100. This particular distinction was not drawn by Isidore (*Etymologiae* XI.xiii) or his authorities, Pliny and Augustine.

98 *Ibid.*, p. 46. 99 *Ibid.*, p. 44. 100 *Ibid.*

from human eyes: it was made because the killing had not been kept hidden from God; it was God who revealed the corpses by a miraculous column of light, and it was God's anger which Egbert is said to have feared. The clear inference is that the foundation of Minster in Thanet was effectively a *wergild* paid to God to avert a feud.[101] Nor is there any need to doubt the historical veracity of this point. There is a strong presumption that the legend of St Mildthryth originated in Kent before that kingdom became dependent on Offa of Mercia and there is no reason to suppose that the *wergild* payment was not a feature of it from the beginning.[102] As to the *Beowulf* poet's application of the theme of feuding to the general category of *untydras*, that can be matched in social terms from Celtic literature: belief that the Jews were in feud with God because of their killing of his son was developed with a full use of legal terminology by the Irish poet Blathmac, son of Cú Brettan, in the third quarter of the eighth century.[103] We may assume that the idea that murder could initiate a supreme feud between God and a society as well as between God and an individual could have been known to the *Beowulf* poet probably by some time in the eighth century.

In his poem, however, he showed no inclination to exploit the social aspect of this notion. Instead attention was concentrated exclusively on the individual. The 'wiht unhælo' ('being of sickness', 120b), Grendel, fixed in 'fæhðe ond fyrene' ('feud and crime', 137a) because of the creator's outlawing of Cain (104b–10), could hardly wait for the dead of night to take his cannibalistic revenge when he heard the *scop*, 'poet', in Hrothgar's hall singing of the Almighty's creation of man and of the beautiful earth, the sun and the moon and all living creatures for the benefit of man (86–98). This 'Godes andsaca' ('adversary of God', 786b and 1682b), 'feond mancynnes' ('enemy of mankind', 164b and 1276a), 'feond on helle', 'helle hæfta' and *helle gast* ('enemy', 'captive' and 'spirit in hell'),[104] occupied Heorot night after night for twelve years (166b–7 and 147a), but the Danes, Hrothgar included, did not understand the underlying cause and resorted, in their desperation, to heathen practices instead of fortifying their relationship with God, the 'dæda Demend' and *Drihten God* ('judge of deeds' and 'Lord God', 180b–1), by praising him as the *heofena Helm* and 'wuldres Waldend' ('protector of the heavens' and 'ruler of glory', 182–3a).

101 Rollason, *The Mildrith Legend*, pp. 49–51, esp. p. 51.

102 *Ibid.*, pp. 15–17.

103 *The Poems of Blathmac*, ed. and trans. Carney. I owe this reference to David Dumville.

104 101b, 788a and 1274a.

It took Beowulf, coming from across the sea, although himself ignorant of the depths of the situation, to clear up the mess.

The Christian elements in the code of conduct which operated in this crisis were almost completely confined to a personal, not collective, ethos.[105] The narrator's report of the Danes' failure to praise God was followed up by a generalization about eternity in terms of the individual:

Wa bið þæm ðe sceal
þurh sliðne nið sawle bescufan
in fyres fæþm, frofre ne wenan,
wihte gewendan! Wel bið þæm þe mot
æfter deaðdæge Drihten secean
ond to Fæder fæþmum freoðo wilnian

['Ill will it be for him who through severe hostility shall thrust his soul into the embrace of fire, not expect consolation to change things in any way! Well will it be for him who is able to seek the Lord after his day of death and to ask for safety from the arms of the father', 183b–8].

And similarly, when giving advance notice of God's allotment of a favourable outcome to Beowulf's fight with Grendel, he dealt with the benefit for the Danes by concentrating on their indebtedness to one man:

Ac him Dryhten forgeaf
wigspeda gewiofu Wedera leodum,
frofor ond fultum, þæt hie feond heora
ðurh anes cræft ealle ofercomon,
selfes mihtum

['But the Lord had granted them, the men of the Weders, webs of victories, consolation and help, that they all overcame their enemy through the ability of one man, his own powers', 696b–700a].

Beowulf too, when proffering his help, presented the outcome of the fight from the point of view of the two protagonists rather than from that of the desperate people whose wrongs he had come to avenge: 'ðær gelyfan sceal / Dryhtnes dome se þe hine deað nimeð' ('there he whom death will take shall trust in the judgement of the lord', 440b–1). And, while showing no inkling that the Danes through their infidelity were sinning against God as

105 A partial exception in the poem as a whole was the pity which God showed the Danes after long lordlessness by sending to Scyld Scefing a renowned heir (12–19); and cf. below, p. 50 and n. 146.

a group, he could see that a linkage between personal crime in this life and eternal judgement was applicable to Grendel: after the monster had suffered fatal injury in the contest, he declared to Hrothgar

ðær abidan sceal
maga mane fah miclan domes,
hu him scir Metod scrifan wille

['the man stained with crime shall await there the great judgement, how resplendent God will sentence him', 977b–9].

Likewise in Unferth's case he could declare that as killer of his brothers this man was doomed to hell: 'þæs þu in helle scealt / werhðo dreogan' ('for that you shall endure punishment in hell', 588b–9a).

Primarily perception was focused on the working of God's relationship to the individual in this world. The narrator's view was that the divine will is in control of events here and now,[106] and Hrothgar[107] and Beowulf[108] agreed. God acted through pre-Christian *wyrd*[109] and controlled it: Beowulf swore that he would not flee a footstep from the deadly, fiery dragon but would face the outcome of his fight with it 'swa unc wyrd geteoð, / Metod manna gehwæs' ('as destiny assigns to us two, ruler of every man', 2526b–7a), and Grendel killed one of Beowulf's men in Heorot

swa he hyra ma wolde,
nefne him witig God wyrd forstode
ond ðæs monnes mod

['as he intended to more of them, if wise God and the man's mind had not prevented fate', 1055b–7a].

The individual's rôle was to cooperate with this divine will, as Beowulf (1661–4), in addition to the narrator,[110] appreciated. Those concerned in action regularly wished one another God's favour (316b–18a and 955b–6) and thanked or praised God for a happy outcome.[111] Hrothgar was quick to point out that a man owes his gifts to God;[112] the narrator emphasized that

[106] 665b–7a, 696b–702, 705b–7, 1055b–8 and 1550–6.
[107] 381b–4a and 478b–9.
[108] 685b–7, 967–8a, 1657b–8 and 1661–4. [109] See above, p. 10.
[110] 939b–42a, 1055b–7a and 1550–6.
[111] 227b–8, 625b–8a, 928–31, 1397b–8, 1626b–8, 1778b–81 and 1997b–8.
[112] 942b–6a, 1724b–39a and 1841–3.

the key is for him to exert them to good effect,[113] and, for Hrothgar, Heremod had been the supreme example of a king courting disaster by failing to do precisely that (1714b–18a).

To the elderly Hrothgar the exercise of individual responsibility in this world was a theme calling for philosophical treatment. Deeply impressed by the victorious Beowulf's qualities of mind and body, he articulated an antithesis between pride in temporal success and appreciation of eternity ahead which must be comprehended by every member 'mæran cynnes' ('of a famous family', 1729b) before forthrightly advising the young hero,

þe þæt selre geceos,
ece rædas; oferhyda ne gym,
mære cempa

['choose what is better, eternal counsels; pay no heed to considerations of pride, famous warrior', 1759b–61a].

First he cited the terrible example of Heremod's bloodthirstiness – 'Ðu þe lær be þon, / gumcyste ongit' ('Learn by that, understand manly virtue', 1722b–3a) – and then graphically described how the man who is blinded with pride in all the good things which he owes to God lays himself open to the arrows of the devil, so that he becomes mean and greedy until he dies and his possessions are squandered by another (1724b–57).

Churchmen delivered to eighth-century English kings admonitions which were correspondingly philosophical and concentrated on personal accountability to God. A Latin letter, which St Boniface and seven other bishops on the Continent sent to Æthelbald, king of Mercia, in 746–7 (the Æthelbald who, when in exile, had visited St Guthlac), urged him to mend his wicked ways basically because of their consequence for his soul, and dealt with their effects on his kingdom in order to emphasize that he would be held responsible everlastingly for the example he set to others.[114] 'Beware', they enjoined him, 'of the darts [*iacula*] of the ancient enemy, by which you have seen your own relations fall wounded in front of you . . . Do not follow the examples of such to perdition . . . In the day of Judgment they will say: ". . . What hath pride profited us or what advantage hath the boasting of riches brought us? All those things are passed away like a shadow, and like a post that runneth on, and as a ship that passeth through

[113] 669–70, 1270–4a and 2181–3a.

[114] *Bonifacii et Lullii Epistolae*, ed. Tangl, pp. 146–55 (no. 73). For a translation (from which I quote below), see *EHD*, pp. 816–22 (no. 177).

the waves; whereof the trace cannot be found, or as when a bird flieth through the air."'[115]

The poet focused less on the royal individual's fate in the hereafter than Boniface and his fellow bishops did and did not use biblical words to express his message as they did, but within this difference the two types of moralist, the secular and the ecclesiastic, clearly drew on a common stock of didactic topics, as Hrothgar's second theme bears out as well. After he had given Beowulf the blunt advice to shun pride in possessions which can never be rendered immune from waste, the grey-haired king sought to impress upon him how many forces of waste were ranged against his young self and how, sooner or later, one or another of them was bound to sap his strength – sickness or sword-cut, or fire, or flood, or sword-blow, or spear-flight, or dire old age, or blindness – until death finally overpowered him (1761b–8). Again this was a consideration which had become familiar to kings already in the eighth century, as we can see – with greater emphasis on its eternal implications – in the preamble with which Cynewulf, ruler of Wessex (757–86), prefaced a Latin charter granting land to the church of Wells, perhaps in 766: 'In the name of our Lord Jesus Christ. Since it is agreed by all catholics and true believers in the Lord that the times of this temporal life far and wide throughout the globe daily pass away by uncertain and divers causes, and also men, overcome by sudden sickness, immediately give up and end their lives and lose at the same time all transitory things; for that reason we here expend and bestow the Lord's benefits to the poor without any delay, in order that there we may receive the harvest of reward in the eternal country with the Lord happily without end.'[116]

With Hrothgar as his spokesman, the *Beowulf* poet brought to bear on traditional personal rule commonplaces of Christian morality which were part of the actual conduct of kingship in the eighth century. The poem and the practice both alike drew on a corpus of didactic themes, images and techniques of expression which was common to Latin and the vernacular. The devil's arrows are a case in point. As well as appearing in Hrothgar's 'sermon' and in the episcopal letter to Æthelwulf, the image occurs in, for instance, Felix's Latin *Life of St Guthlac*: the saint is conceived of as overcoming, with St Bartholomew's heavenly aid, a poisoned arrow of

115 These words attributed to the wicked come from Wisdom V.8–11.

116 Sawyer, *Anglo-Saxon Charters*, no. 262; for a translation (from which I quote), see *EHD*, pp. 497–8 (no. 70).

despair driven into his mind by the devil.[117] Hearing vernacular preaching might have given the poet his access to this hortatory repertoire. What suggests this possibility is Hrothgar's coupling of finite verbs which are synonyms or near-synonyms: this feature occurs three times in his 'sermon' – 'weaxeð ond wridað' (1741a), 'forgyteð ond forgymeð' (1751a) and 'forsiteð ond forsworceð' (1767a) – but only seven times in all the rest of the poem put together.[118] Iteration of this sort, especially of verbs, is unlikely to have owed its origin to poetry[119] but was a frequent feature of vernacular prose homilies which could be among the earliest to survive. It occurs commonly in, for instance, the group in the Vercelli Book (homilies XV–XVIII) for which Dr Scragg has postulated as exemplar a Mercian homiliary of unknown date (e.g. 'getyde ond gelærde').[120] Or again, *(ge)weaxan* and *(ge)wridan/-ian* are coupled, in the same relative order as in Hrothgar's 'sermon', in the Blickling homily which contains an analogue to the poem's landscape of Grendel's mere. This homily, like Vercelli XVIII, could have been composed early.[121] On present knowledge,

117 *Felix's 'Life' of St Guthlac*, ed. Colgrave, pp. 94–8.

118 'Seomade ond syrede' (161a), 'Wit þæt gecwædon cnihtwesende / ond gebeotedon' (535–6a), 'Hafa nu ond geheald' (658a), 'wanode ond wyrde' (1337a), 'Manað swa ond myndgað' (2057a), 'hatode ond hynde' (2319a) and 'heold mec ond hæfde' (2430a). Verbs which do not both express the same idea were coupled in 'swefeð ond snedeþ [MS *sendeþ*]' (600a) and once verbs were coupled to point a distinction: 'wiston ond ne wendon' (1604a).

119 See below, pp. 154–7.

120 For the proposed exemplar, see Scragg, 'The Compilation of the Vercelli Book', pp. 202–3 and 205; the four homilies form group Db in C. Sisam's analysis (*The Vercelli Book*, pp. 42–3). For the quoted coupling, see *The Vercelli Homilies*, ed. Scragg, XVIII, line 89.

121 See above, pp. 22–5, esp. 23 and n. 43. For the verb-pair in question, 'geweox ond gewridode', see *The Blickling Homilies*, ed. Morris, p. 199, line 2. Another coupling of these verbs – 'weox ond wridode' – is in the letter of Alexander the Great to Aristotle in the *Beowulf* manuscript (*Three Old English Prose Texts*, ed. Rypins, p. 12, line 7); for the probably ninth-century Anglian (perhaps east Mercian) composition of this letter, see Sisam, *Studies in the History of Old English Literature*, pp. 83–93, esp. p. 89. It is also worth noting that the Blickling homily begins 'Men ða leofestan, manaþ us ond myngaþ . . .' (*The Blickling Homilies*, ed. Morris, p. 197, line 1; cf. *Beowulf* 2057a). Likewise Blickling homily XIV (extant only in the Blickling manuscript) begins, 'Men þa leofestan, her us manaþ ond mynegaþ . . .' (*ibid.*, p. 161, line 1), and Blickling homily X (also unique except that its second half is combined with Ælfric material in CCCC 198) contains 'ic myngige ond manige' (*ibid.*, p. 109, line 11). Both these homilies, like the one already cited, could be early. Was Beowulf's 'Manað swa ond myndgað

however, we have no way of telling how early an extant 'early' vernacular homily may have been, and so the case for influence specifically from that genre should not be pressed too hard. Rather perhaps we ought to bear in mind that repetition of this sort is characteristic of expository discourse as such[122] and settle for inferring more generally that the poet acquired his knowledge of Christian personal morality, ultimately derived from Latin literature, from clerical didacticism which by his day used a recognizable manner of its own in the native tongue.

This didacticism, as the poet deployed it through Hrothgar, was concerned with the individual as a member of warrior society. It had to do with the quality of the service which, through the gifts he had received from God, the individual could render his community, and it did not enter into either the individual's own spirituality or any spiritual dimension of society itself. For instance, in the former of these respects, the *snyttru*, 'wisdom', which, to Hrothgar's wonder, God dispenses to mankind (1724b–6), was connected by him simply to the essentials of the individual's place in society, 'eard ond eorlscipe' ('land and warriorship', 1727a), and not to the diversity of mental and physical gifts by which, through God's grace, according to Cynewulf in his Ascension poem (*Christ* (*II*) 659–85), individuals differ from one another.[123] Nor did Hrothgar make any attempt to inculcate defence against the devil's arrows through the 'breastplate' of the protective praying which was institutionalized in the public Offices of the church in the form of the psalm verse, 'Deus in adiutorium meum intende; Domine ad adiuuandum me festina' ('O God, make speed to save me: O Lord, make haste to help me', LXIX.2 [AV LXX.1]), and which was given varied expression in the 'breastplate' tradition in the late-eighth- and early-ninth-century Latin private prayer books, seemingly an English (or at any rate an Insular) innovation for the benefit of those to whom Latin was a foreign language and who were not able to pray spontaneously.[124] In his rôle of 'eald eþelweard' ('old guardian of the native land', 1702a) Hrothgar did no more than exclaim (942b–6a)

mæla gehwylce / sarum wordum' (*Beowulf* 2057–8a) intended to impart to the incitement of a young Heathobard by the 'eald æscwiga' (2042a) an ironic echo of sermonizing?

122 Cf. Koskenniemi, *Repetitive Word Pairs*, esp. pp. 118–19.

123 Cf. below, pp. 342–3.

124 For the *lorica*, 'breastplate', tradition and the surviving early private prayer books written in Anglo-Saxon England, see Sims-Williams, *Religion and Literature in Western England*, pp. 275–327.

that God had blessed the birth of Beowulf, this 'secg betsta' ('best warrior', 947a), attribute this young man's wise speech to God (1841–4) and, after saluting this hero's quality of body, mind and speech (1844–5a), declare that if Hygelac, the present king of Beowulf's people, were to be killed,

Wen ic talige,
. . .
þæt þe Sæ-Geatas selran næbben
to geceosenne cyning ænigne,
hordweard hæleþa, gyf þu healdan wylt
maga rice (1845b and 1850–3a).[125]

The succession itself, in Hrothgar's eyes, was not something ordained by an overriding God but was subject entirely to normal social processes.

As regards our third *Beowulf*ian cultural factor, the conception of the relationship between king and God, direct comparison between the poem and actual practice in formal Anglo-Saxon kingship is now called for. A significant distinction between the two opened up in the course of the eighth century. In the two prophecies, which, according to Felix's *Life*, St Guthlac delivered to his kinsman, Æthelbald, when, in his early twenties, for long an exile, this young aspirant was impatiently waiting for his chance to wrest the Mercian kingship from his second-cousin, Ceolred, the traditional *Beowulf*ian heroic virtues of body, mind and speech were not to the point. Æthelbald's claim to rule resided in a combination of royal blood and ecclesiastical support. Barbarous though he was – Boniface and his seven fellow bishops were to reproach him when king for himself violating nuns and robbing churches and monasteries and for allowing his followers to do the same[126] – the church preferred him to the even more dissolute Ceolred, who, according to the same bishops, 'feasting in splendour amid his companions, was – as those who were present have testified – suddenly in his sin sent mad by a malign spirit, who had enticed him by his persuasion to the audacity of breaking the law of God; so that without repentance and confession, raging and distracted, conversing with devils and cursing the priests of God, he departed from this light without a doubt to the torments of hell',[127] and who, in a prophetic vision before he died, was seen in hell by a monk at Wenlock, Shropshire.[128] Guthlac's first prophecy promised Æthelbald (drawing on wording from two psalms –

[125] See above, p. 9. [126] *EHD*, pp. 817–20 (no. 177). [127] *Ibid.*, p. 820.
[128] Sims-Williams, *Religion and Literature in Western England*, p. 243; cf. above, p. 25.

LXXXIX.9 and CXLIII.4 (AV XC and CXLIV) – and I John V.19), 'Not as booty nor as spoil shall the kingdom be granted you, but you shall obtain it from the hand of God [*de manu Domini*]; wait for him whose life has been shortened, because the hand of the Lord oppresses him whose hope lies in wickedness, and whose days shall pass away like a shadow',[129] and his second prediction delivered after the saint's death in a vision vouchsafed to Æthelbald at the shrine which he himself had provided, conveyed the message (first paraphrasing ps. LXXVII.35 (AV LXXVIII)), 'Fear not, be strong, for God is your helper . . . before the sun has passed through its yearly course in twelve revolutions you shall be given the sceptre of your kingdom.'[130] Æthelbald's succession was produced by a political partnership between an institutional church and hereditary royalty, and Guthlac's rôle, very different from Hrothgar's, was to voice the divine ordination of this procedure on the authoritative basis of holy scripture.

When Æthelbald became king, the ecclesiastical draftsmen of his charters formalized this ordination in the titles with which they glorified him for both factual and propagandist purposes. Whereas earlier kings by and large had been termed merely 'rex Merciorum' and the like (in the tradition to which the *Beowulf* poet's *Geata cyning* (2356a) etc. belonged), and Æthelbald's contemporaries in other kingdoms had been treated, *mutatis mutandis*, much the same, the first surviving authentic charter of his reign (716 × 717) proclaimed him as 'Ego Aethilbald ex diuina dispensatione Mercensium rex' ('I Æthelbald from divine dispensation king of the Mercians').[131] In the politics of early-eighth-century Mercia a move was evidently afoot to institutionalize kingship as a divinely disposed office, a movement which was continued in the reign of Æthelbald's successor, Offa, in the second half of the century and was developed to its logical conclusion in one of that king's latest charters (793 × 796) which assigned him an absolute divine basis of power in the words 'ego Offa rex a rege regum constitutus' ('I Offa established king by the king of kings').[132] Of this formulation of a divinely sanctioned Christian office *Beowulf*ian kingship shows no trace at all. The poet never used a 'king of kings' term

[129] *Felix's 'Life' of St Guthlac*, ch. 50 (ed. Colgrave, p. 151).

[130] *Ibid.*, ch. 52 (*ibid.*, pp. 165–7).

[131] Sawyer, *Anglo-Saxon Charters*, no. 102; trans. *EHD*, p. 489 (no. 64).

[132] Sawyer, *Anglo-Saxon Charters*, no. 139. For this process of innovation, see Scharer, 'Die Intitulationes der angelsächsischen Könige', pp. 48–70.

for God,[133] although the probably ninth-century Cynewulf did for Christ,[134] and so did the composer of the Advent lyrics probably well before the middle of the tenth century[135] among other poets.[136]

In the same, eighth-century, period another, related, distinction, this one with more than formal implications, was starting to develop between two conceptions of the leadership required of a king. On the one hand, King Beowulf believed that the divine judgement which awaited him after his death[137] would relate entirely to the traditional social standards of the warrior king:

> . . . me witan ne ðearf Waldend fira
> morðorbealo maga, þonne min sceaceð
> lif of lice

[' . . . the ruler of men will not need to charge me with murder of kinsmen when my life departs from my body', 2741–3a].[138]

On the other, Boniface and his fellow bishops in their letter to King Æthelbald based their warnings about his responsibility for his subjects' morals on the principle that he would be held to eternal account as a pastor of his people on God's behalf: 'For as many as we either by good examples bring to the life in the heavenly fatherland or by bad examples lead to perdition, for so many, without a doubt, we shall receive from the eternal Judge either punishments or rewards.'[139] As time went on even the poem's core conception of warrior leadership, comprising personal prowess and the

[133] For him, God the ruler (*W(e)aldend* (1693b, 2292b, 2329b, 2857a and 3109a), 'wuldres Waldend' (17a, 183a and 1752a), 'sigora Waldend' (2875a), *Alw(e)alda* (316b, 928b, 955b and ?1314a) and 'ylda/fira Waldend' (1661b and 2741b)) held sway as king primarily in heaven (*heofena Helm* (182a), 'wuldres Hyrde' (931b), 'rodera Rædend' (1555a), *Wuldurcyning* (2795a) and 'sigora Soðcyning' (3055a)). The nearest he came to relating God's kingship to earthly kings was in the expression (unique in extant poetry) *Kyningwuldor*, 'glory of kings(?)' (665b).

[134] 'ealra cyninga cyning' (*Juliana* 289a).

[135] 'ealra cyninga cyning' (*Christ* (*I*) 136a and 215a). For this dating, see below, p. 276, n. 6, and ref. there cited.

[136] '(ealra) cyninga cyning' (*Christ and Satan* 203b, *Andreas* 978a and 1192a, *Guthlac* (*A*) 17a and *The Judgement Day I* 95a). For the distribution, see Crépin, 'Poétique Vieil-Anglaise', p. 207.

[137] The narrator's words on that score were 'him of hræðre gewat / sawol secean soðfæstra dom' ('his soul went from his breast to seek the judgement of the righteous', 2819b–20).

[138] See also above, p. 6.

[139] *EHD*, p. 819 (no. 177).

blood royal, did not survive in practice unchanged. By the beginning of the eleventh century, according to the vernacular prose writer, Abbot Ælfric, a ruler's defence of his realm had itself become a pastoral duty: in one of his homilies he stated, 'the king is Christ's own representative over the Christian people whom Christ himself redeemed, hallowed as their shepherd, that he may protect them, with the people's help, against an attacking army and may pray for them to the true saviour who has given him that authority under himself'.[140] Personally responsible for the defence of society the king still was, and, in dire necessity, might have to give his life for his people in battle on the model of Christ, but normally he ought to rely on an able field commander and ensure this general's victory by praying, as Moses had secured Joshua's triumph over Amalek.[141] A portrayal of martial strength of body and mind, touched but not taken over by Christianity, would have seemed in the eighth century, and doubtless later too, in general a natural way to idealize the essence of earlier kingship, but as time passed the *Beowulf* poet's particular combination of native and Christian would have become more and more unlikely to be hit on and difficult to sustain consistently.

The poet's conception of God acting in a direct relationship to a ruler as a person but not to a whole people as a group also represented a distinction which Anglo-Saxons would have found increasingly artificial in the course of time. How firmly the poet maintained this demarcation is clearly demonstrated by his handling of the second part of his poem, the fight with the dragon (2200–3182). All references to God, whether by the narrator[142] or Beowulf[143] or Wiglaf,[144] applied to the individual and were often highly personal, as in Beowulf's emotional allusion to Hrethel's death (2468–9) and in Wiglaf's to the dead Beowulf in God's safe keeping (3107–9) and when forming an integral part of Wiglaf's passionate expressions of loyalty to his generous benefactor (2650b–2 and 2873–6) and of the dying Beowulf's intimate words to his young kinsman (2741–3a and 2794–8). At the critical moment when Beowulf learned that a dragon had destroyed by fire the 'gifstol Geata' ('gift-seat of the Geats', 2327a), his reaction as this people's *guðkyning*, 'war-king'

[140] Ælfric, *SupplHoms*, IX (ed. Pope, lines 48–53).

[141] *Ibid.*, XXII (ed. Pope, lines 80–90).

[142] 2292b, 2329b–30b, 2857a, 2858a, 3054b–5a, 3056a and 3075a.

[143] 2469b, 2527a, 2741b and 2794b–6a.

[144] 2650b, 2874b–5a and 3109a.

(2335b), was to think that God was showing anger directed against him, not them:

wende se wisa, þæt he Wealdende
ofer ealde riht ecean Dryhtne
bitre gebulge

['the wise one thought that he had bitterly angered the ruler, the eternal Lord, contrary to old law', 2329–31a];

and when it became a question of the Geats' bleak outlook after Beowulf, their king, had been killed by the dragon, that was to be entirely in the arena of their long-standing feuds against the Franks and Swedes in which God played no part. The general ideas which the poet displayed about God's operations towards men were that he was ruler of each and every person,[145] that he was the creator of humanity's natural setting (90b–8) and that he controls the sun (570a) and the seasons (1609–11). The Danes or Geats, or any of the tribes with which they dealt, were singled out only exceptionally to receive significant divine favour or disfavour of the sort meted out to the giants and monsters descended from Cain.[146]

In Anglo-Saxon society, on the other hand, the Old Testament idea that God rewarded or punished entire peoples gained much ground. Boniface and his bishops used the notion to drive home to Æthelbald the magnitude of his responsibility for corrupting his subjects by his sinful example of sexual debauchery:

For if the race of the English . . . spurning lawful marriage, lives a foul life in adultery and lasciviousness after the pattern of the people of Sodom, it is to be expected that . . . in the end the whole people, sinking to lower and baser things, will finally neither be strong in secular warfare nor stable in faith, neither honoured by man nor loved by God. Just as it has happened to other races of Spain and Provence, and to the Burgundian peoples; who thus, turning from God, committed fornication, until the omnipotent Judge allowed avenging punishments for such crimes to come and destroy them, through ignorance of the law of God, and through the Saracens.[147]

145 700b–2a, 1057b–8, 1661b, 1725–7, 2526b–7a, 2741b, 2858–9 and 3056a.

146 For the only two exceptions, both with otherwise pagan associations, see above, p. 40 (the advance notice that God had granted 'webs of victories' to the Danes through the ability of one man (Beowulf)), and *ibid.*, n. 105.

147 *EHD*, pp. 819–20 (no. 177).

Later, in the ninth century, King Alfred regarded it as a mere commonplace of vernacular thought that the ravages of the Danes had been a punishment for his kingdom's neglect of the wisdom which is the gift of God: 'Geðenc', he exclaimed to each of the bishops receiving his prose translation of Gregory the Great's *Regula pastoralis*, 'hwelc witu us ða becomon for ðisse worulde, ða ða we hit nohwæðer ne selfe ne lufodon ne eac oðrum monnum ne lefdon' ('Think what punishments befell us as regards this world, when we neither loved it [i.e. God-given wisdom] ourselves nor also allowed it to other men').[148] And early in the eleventh century Archbishop Wulfstan devoted his very considerable oratorical talents to elevating the nation's sins into a full-scale eschatological theme in his vernacular prose *Sermo Lupi ad Anglos*.[149] The grievous sins pervading the whole of English society at the instigation of the devil were seen here as no less than a perversion of the divinely appointed moral order foreshadowing the imminent rule of Antichrist: repent, the archbishop warned his fellow countrymen, as the only way of warding off the terrors of Antichrist's reign of which the degradations currently inflicted by the country's enemies are but a foretaste.[150] For us, pursuing our present inquiry, this powerful apocalyptic vision has other implications too, namely that Wulfstan was preaching long after it would have occurred to anyone (as it did to the *Beowulf* poet) to Christianize the past by adopting a concept of personal responsibility to God unaccompanied by an equivalent national responsibility. The likelihood is that, by portraying Hrothgar's court both listening to Cædmon-type Christian poetry *(Beowulf* 89b–98)[151] and resorting to heathen rites when under pressure (171b–8a), and by roundly condemning the devil worship this involved (178b–88) without invoking God's curse upon the Danes as a race, the poet was describing an inconsistency and applying to it a less than full logic, both of which would have been common Anglo-Saxon attitudes during the last third or quarter of the seventh century and the early eighth and would have remained in

[148] *Gregory's Pastoral Care*, ed. Sweet, p. 5, lines 5–6. The well-known preface in which these words occur has often been printed elsewhere.

[149] *Sermo Lupi ad Anglos*, ed. Whitelock. For Wulfstan's eschatological train of thought, see Hollis, 'The Thematic Structure of the *Sermo Lupi*'.

[150] For a summary of the Anglo-Saxon tradition of God's punishment of a people's sins, harking back to Gildas's early- or mid-sixth-century denunciation of the sins of the British and running up to Wulfstan's *Sermo*, see *EHD*, pp. 26–7.

[151] For Cædmon's compositions, see below, pp. 231–2.

living memory for only a while after that. His stance was probably a not-later-than-eighth-century one.

In any case it is highly doubtful whether anyone at all would have sought to Christianize – in terms of personal or public morality – a narrative of Germanic antiquity on the *Beowulf*ian scale anywhere near as late as Wulfstan's time. We have no reason to suppose that a florescence of vernacular narrative poetry of the *Beowulf* type coincided with the decay in the ability to read Latin, which had reached an advanced stage by the middle of the ninth century, according to King Alfred's preface cited above,[152] and should be antedated another fifty years, and probably more, on Professor Gneuss's evidence for a steep decline in Latin book production in England from at least the beginning of the century.[153] Rather, our limited evidence suggests that in the late eighth and the ninth centuries among those who could still read Latin there were some who aimed at putting long vernacular narrative poetry on to a new footing as a direct substitute for the written Christian Latin narratives to which fewer of their fellow countrymen by then had access. Cynewulf's composition of *Elene*, *Juliana* and his Ascension poem (*Christ II*) could well have owed something to this intention; and so perhaps did the anonymous production of poems such as *Andreas*, *Exodus* and *Christ III*, each transposing a major Latin narrative into a distinctively applied vernacular poetic medium. All the poets concerned, in their various ways, successfully converted traditional, public, didactic, poetic narrative of the *Beowulf* sort into a vehicle for implying, or stating explicitly, doctrine necessary for the salvation of the souls of those who read (or heard read) their poems in the native tongue.[154] In the ninth century this poetic textual initiative would not have been

[152] *Gregory's Pastoral Care*, ed. Sweet, p. 5, lines 8–13.

[153] Gneuss, 'King Alfred and the History of Anglo-Saxon Libraries', p. 37 and nn. 43 and 44. If the ten manuscripts which Gneuss considers were 'products of Anglo-Saxon scriptoria in the ninth century before Alfred', the further nine 'which', as he says, 'according to the paleographers, are datable at the turn of the eighth and ninth centuries' and two more which are dated to the first half of the ninth century by Jennifer Morrish (Morrish, 'King Alfred's Letter as a Source on Learning', nos. 11 and 13; Dr Morrish considers that Alfred exaggerated the decay in Latin learning), the grand total is only twenty-one books, extant as a whole or in part, which are English products of the period in question (Gneuss, 'A Preliminary List of Manuscripts', nos. 28, 45, 88, 126, 327, 377, 385, 432, 443, 448, 450, 456, 576, 611, 635, 646, 780, 857, 885, 898 and 911).

[154] See below, esp. ch. 8.

misdirected enthusiasm, judging by Alfred's statement in his *Pastoral Care* preface that, when the teaching of Latin had fallen off, 'ðeah monige cuðon Englisc gewrit arædan' ('many, however, could read English writings').[155] Certainly, when Alfred got a grip on this situation in the 890s, after it had been made much worse by wholesale destruction of the Latin books themselves in the course of his wars against the Danish incursors,[156] his ambition in turning to vernacular prose as the most effective means of cultural revival was not to restore the Germanic past as a prime model for public probity but to draw inspiration from the traditions of Christianity and – when choosing to compose his vernacular prose version of Boethius's *De consolatione Philosophiae* – from Christian interpretation of the ancient classical world. In Professor Bately's words, 'Through the activities and enterprise of the king and his colleagues, a not insubstantial glimpse of the brave new [i.e. classical] world which excited Alfred so much . . . was afforded to the literate if not latinate Anglo-Saxon of the late ninth century.'[157]

From the eighth century, royal rule was engaged in progressively redefining the past which formed its power base. In 736 Æthelbald of Mercia issued the first unquestionably original extant charter to use AD dating.[158] On the written pages of manuscripts of the *Anglo-Saxon Chronicle* circulated *c.* 890 an unbroken succession of AD year numbers formed an indissoluble tie between the beginning of redemptive history, Christ's birth, and the events of Alfred's reign.[159] As lawgiver Alfred placed his written vernacular code in a tradition stretching back to Moses. The genealogy of Alfred's father, Æthelwulf, entered in the *Chronicle* under the year 855, traced his ancestry back ultimately to Adam, but on its way to this eventual source, when it went beyond historical West Saxon times, the descent passed (via Woden) through a succession of legendary Germanic names, which, as Sisam aptly put it, though old themselves, 'were not attached to the ancestry of the West Saxon kings by old tradition'.[160] Up to a point these names had already formed part of genealogical materials, but evidently, either in Æthelwulf's reign (839–58)[161] or in Alfred's before

[155] *Gregory's Pastoral Care*, ed. Sweet, p. 7, lines 16–17. [156] *Ibid.*, p. 5, lines 8–10.

[157] Bately, 'Those Books that are Most Necessary for All Men to Know', p. 65.

[158] Sawyer, *Anglo-Saxon Charters*, no. 89; Scharer, 'Die Intitulationes der angelsächsischen Könige', pp. 58–9.

[159] See below, p. 117. [160] Sisam, 'Anglo-Saxon Royal Genealogies', p. 322.

[161] Cf. above, p. 15.

about 890, an enthusiastic genealogist had gone further by drawing in others, including some – Beaw, Scyld(wa), Heremod and Sceaf – which figure also in *Beowulf*. It appears that the spirit of *Beowulf* was still sufficiently alive in the ninth century for remaining Germanic traditions, however muddled, to be laid under contribution for the glorification of present-day kingship, but only eclectically within an overarching biblicism. Germanic antiquity was fast becoming, or had already become, a subordinate member of an organized Christian culture, which would have respected the less Christianized *Beowulf*ian one as doubtless an authentic earlier compromise but would not itself have invented it. Still less, by the same token, would any later period have managed to turn the clock back to the distinctive balanced complexity of *Beowulf*. For instance, early-eleventh-century nostalgia for a lost Anglo-Danish past might well have resulted in a renewed interest in any surviving text of such a poem, and hence in a wish to recopy it, but could never have recreated that vanished environment in the functional, unsentimentalized, unselfconscious manner of our poem.

When a learned West Saxon in Alfred's reign incorporated information about northern Europe in bk I of his English prose version of Orosius's Latin Christian history of the world, he did not know of the Geats as a currently existing independent people. Anyone who, doubtless well before this late-ninth-century time, was in the same position and was aware, as the latest piece of tradition about this tribe, that Heardred, Hygelac's son and successor to the kingship, had been killed while still young and heirless in a fight against his people's arch enemies, the Swedes (cf. *Beowulf* 2379b–88), would have been likely to wonder whether this king's premature death had been enough in itself to cause the disappearance of his people or whether further, unknown, events had led to their loss of identity. Unsatisfied curiosity would have opened up a space in his mental landscape of antiquity, and what better way would there have been to fill it than by supposing that there had been a King Beowulf, by no means a weed to be pulled up as soon as detected in the hard light of fact, but a plant to be cultivated in the sunshine and shadow of story? A royal personage, such as he, would have provided an organic space-filler in antique narrative, as Woden did in genealogy purporting to chart the origins of the Anglo-Saxon dynasties in the uncertainly remembered armed settlement of England. Created thus, Beowulf would have served a dual purpose richly: as a king triumphant in achievement and calamitous in death, he would have satisfied the historical imagination by supplying the vanished Geats with a truly impressive *edwenden*, 'reversal', in their national fortunes, and, as a royal monster- and dragon-slayer, accepting the tragic necessity of death in defence of his people, he would have furnished contemporary kingship with an awe-inspiring example.

Functioning in these ways, King Beowulf would not have been first and foremost an archaizing concept. Primarily his rôle would have been to represent continuity between the past and the present by symbolizing the essentials of warrior kingship underlying both. To do that convincingly he would have had to be true to the present in certain vital respects. One of these, we may infer, would have been the intensely practical matter of weaponry. Against the dragon Beowulf was equipped with a sword, broad *seax* (a short cutting weapon[162]), shield, helmet and corslet of ring mail. This weapon-set of sword and broad *seax* seems to have been in vogue for a limited period: according to the Biddles, it was adopted by English aristocracy at the earliest in the second half of the seventh century and probably not before the eighth, it was no longer in evidence in the tenth century and it was possibly already out of fashion in the ninth.[163] In the sentiment of his memorialization, likewise, Beowulf would have needed to be in tune with the present, however pagan the actual burial rites described, and here again datable agreement is available. The dying Beowulf's instruction to Wiglaf was to see that a mound in his memory was built on *Hronesnæss*, a promontory by the sea, so that sailors might be continually impressed (2802–8), and his wish was duly carried out (3156–8). Just so, though in a Christian context, kings of Mercia, as early as Æthelbald's murder in 757,[164] were buried at Repton, overlooking the flood-plain of the River Trent, and a magnificent mausoleum was built there to house their remains at least by 840.[165] Significantly, in the vernacular list of saints' resting-places in England, extant in two copies, Cambridge, Corpus Christi College 201 and London, British Library,

162 For its broadness, cf. *Beowulf* 1545b–6a.

163 Biddle and Kjølbye-Biddle, 'The Repton Stone', pp. 269–71 and 281–2.

164 On which, see above, p. 15.

165 For the latest published account, see Taylor, *St Wystan's Church Repton*, and for the latest published analysis of the architectural evidence, see Taylor, *Repton Studies 2*. We should not, of course, take it for granted that this memorial site was chosen because of its conspicuousness, for there had been a monastery there since at least the last years of the seventh century (when the young Guthlac entered it), but the conspicuousness was certainly part of the effect.

Stowe 944,[166] the items specifying places at which the relics arrived in the ninth century or earlier almost invariably relate the named site to nearby river, sea or fen, whereas the entries containing later information hardly ever do.[167] Characteristic of the former is 'Đonne resteð sancte Wigstan on þam mynstre Hreopedune neah þære ea Treonte' ('Then rests St Wigstan in the monastery at Repton near the River Trent').[168] This was not a matter of practical identification, for sometimes small streams were cited. As a memorial site Repton overlooking the Trent was a Christianized Sutton Hoo overlooking the Deben. Repton and Beowulf's *Hronesnæss*, both representing a feeling that a riparian setting was especially appropriate for commemoration, shared a tradition which seems not to have outlasted the ninth century.

Nor is it likely that that was the only congruity eighth-century Mercian aristocrats would have sensed between the antique heroic Scandinavian locations celebrated in *Beowulf* and their own contemporary Christian sites, far apart as the two were in time and space. Both were settings for personal adventurism, albeit in two different spheres of life. Repton, the mid-eighth-century burial place of King Æthelbald, whom Sir Frank Stenton characterized as 'the barbarian master of a military household',[169] was also the monastery which had nurtured the formerly militaristic young Guthlac towards the end of the seventh century before his victorious expedition to overcome evil spirits in the fens, just as the Geatish court had fostered the once sluggish prince Beowulf *(Beowulf* 2183b–8a) before his triumphant expedition to Denmark to extirpate Grendel (without knowledge of the monster's biblical affiliations). Any Mercian warriors who knew both *Beowulf* and Repton in the first half of the eighth century, or thereabouts, would have thought of the Geatish court and the midland monastery as complementary nurseries of the confident boldness which they regarded as the essential of personal authority in both state and church. Beowulf and Guthlac would have seemed like two sides of a coin.

The *Beowulf* poet's lavish praise of Offa, fourth-century king of the continental Angles (1947b-60a), would have pleased this nobility too, for it was a compliment to the royal blood in their veins which they were proud to trace back to this illustrious ruler. The cachet attaching to his name is

166 *Die Heiligen Englands*, ed. Liebermann, pp. 9–19.

167 For a full discussion, see Rollason, 'Lists of Saints' Resting-Places'.

168 *Die Heiligen Englands*, ed. Liebermann, sect. 16.

169 Stenton, *Anglo-Saxon England*, p. 205.

illustrated by its use for the man who became the Mercians' mighty king in the second half of the eighth century, and another, earlier, bearer of the name was one of Æthelbald's companions in exile, who later witnessed as 'king's thegn' to some of that ruler's earliest charters[170] and later still became an ealdorman. But this ancestry was not just a personal advantage, it was a collective strength. In Stenton's view, 'the commanding position held in central England by the historic Mercian kings, and in particular their success in bringing the various peoples of the midlands into a single state' are not to be accounted for in terms of the importance of their hereditary kingdom but become intelligible only 'if, as their genealogy asserts, they were descended from the men who had ruled the whole Anglian race before its migration to Britain'.[171] This superiority which the Germanic past had bequeathed to the eighth-century Mercian present could hardly be exaggerated, and the *Beowulf* poet pitched his eulogy of the continental Offa correspondingly high: this ruler, he asserted, had been a *hæleþa brego*, 'chief of warriors' (1954b), who was

ealles moncynnes   mine gefrægе
þone selestan   bi sæm tweonum,
eormencynnes

['the finest of all mankind, as I have learned, between the seas, of the huge kin', 1955–7a].

This was comparable to the encomium the Danes bestowed on Beowulf after his victory over Grendel:

monig oft gecwæð,
þætte suð ne norð   be sæm tweonum
ofer eormengrund   oþer nænig
under swegles begong   selra nære
rondhæbbendra,   rices wyrðra

['many a one often declared that south or north between the seas throughout the immense earth no other shield-bearer under the circuit of the sky was better, more worthy of rule', 857b–61].

[170] Sawyer, *Anglo-Saxon Charters*, nos. 88, 89 and 102. The same individual also features in a charter of the same reign which Dr Keynes has recently found in a transcript of a lost charter-roll of St Paul's Cathedral, London; on this, see now, Keynes, 'A Lost Cartulary of St Albans Abbey'.

[171] Stenton, *Anglo-Saxon England*, pp. 39–40.

In the context of the poem the claim was no less than that the ancestral Offa of the Mercians was the supreme leader in all warrior social history stretching from the remote past right the way to the present. In the context of eighth-century politics this was exactly what the Mercian ruling family wanted to hear and – in the days before an *Anglo-Saxon Chronicle* had furnished a visible vernacular record of West Saxon history, since the settlements in England, against a biblical and Roman background – it was in the appropriate contemporary form. Offa was a name for a poet to conjure with in such circles, and for the *Beowulf* poet as a particular case, if he were addressing them, it would have had the specific advantage of forming a reassuring bridge between the Scandinavian marine-oriented kingship of his main story and his land- and river-based audience. At any rate he saw to it that attached to this venerated name came the attributes essential to the ideal warrior ruler, whatever his territory:

. . . Offa wæs
geofum ond guðum, garcene man,
wide geweorðod, wisdome heold
eðel sinne

['Offa was, for gifts and battles, spear-bold man, widely honoured, he guarded his native country with wisdom', 1957b–60a].

And attached to it too was identification of the son through whom (by implication) these qualities had been transmitted to Mercian descendants: 'þonon Eomer[172] woc / hæleðum to helpe' ('from him Eomer arose as a help to warriors', 1960b–1a). The poet, through his narrator, was associating in the same antique league of excellence Beowulf, who had no issue, and the personage who was the accepted source of eighth-century Mercian prestige. It is hard to imagine why he should have done this unless he himself were among, or at least connected with, the aristocrats who were the beneficiaries.

Sculpture affords an interesting parallel to this poet's mode of praise. Mercian kingship itself was depicted performing an act which traditionally represented the essence of personal leadership – riding spiritedly to battle – in a carving which originally formed the top panel of a broad face of a stone cross-shaft and now survives imperfectly on a portion of the shaft unearthed at Repton in 1979 just to the east of the eighth-century mausoleum which

[172] MS *geomor*, 'sad'.

later became a crypt (see frontispiece and fig. 1).[173] Displayed is a rider who sits astride a stallion, prancing from right to left, and who turns through ninety degrees to face the front. He wears a shirt of ringmail, carries a single-edged, short, broad *seax* in a scabbard at his waist, and holds aloft a broad, two-edged sword in his right hand and a small round shield in his left. His mount's gear includes a saddle forming a raised area, which begins in front high against the horse's withers and ends flat behind the rider (or at any rate less high). A prominent feature of it is an ornamental broad, raised collar which passes round the horse's breast and runs over the saddle to disappear behind the folds of the rider's skirt. The rider does not wear a helmet, but instead has a 'crinkly band' across his head above the fringe of his hair, evidently the diadem which, derived from late Roman example, became the principal symbol of sovereignty in the version of the royal 'portrait' which was introduced on the coinage of Offa's reign in *c.* 787.[174] In other respects his weapon-set, lacking an axe and spear and based on the combination of sword and broad *seax* which was adopted in England at the earliest in the second half of the seventh century and more probably in the eighth,[175] constitutes the typical equipment of an aristocratic, Germanic warrior of eighth-century date. More personal are his long moustache, cleanshaven chin and corpulence – his body is wider above the top of his skirt than below it – which, in accordance with the conventions of early medieval portraiture, are likely to reflect actual features of the subject. A specific individual has been subsumed in an impressively dramatic image of royal warriorship. As regards the identity of this individual, the Biddles consider that the carving probably represented, at the height of his power, a middle-aged King Æthelbald, who was at least sixty by the time he was murdered in 757, and that the cross on which it was conspicuous probably was erected by Offa in memory of his kinsman at his burial-place. As regards the iconography, they perceive a

[173] For a full description and careful discussion, to which I am indebted at every turn, see Biddle and Kjølbye-Biddle, 'The Repton Stone', *passim*.

[174] See, e.g., Grierson and Blackburn, *Medieval European Coinage*, no. 1124A; Keynes and Blackburn, *Anglo-Saxon Coins*, no. 26. Another version of Offa's 'portrait', which forms a nice contrast, is reproduced on the cover of the present book as the symbol of CSASE (cf. Grierson and Blackburn, *Medieval European Coinage*, no. 1126; Keynes and Blackburn, *Anglo-Saxon Coins*, no. 25): this time Offa appears in 'Germanic', rather than 'Roman', guise with an extraordinary hair-do. Coinage and carving display the same ambivalence.

[175] Cf. above, p. 55 and n. 163.

Fig. 1 The rider face of the Repton Stone (scale 1:6)

mutation of a late Roman image of an *adventus* of the emperor on the field of battle: 'the unarmoured, helmetless emperor, in theory always victorious, has become a mail-clad warrior brandishing the weapons of his own Germanic race and age, triumphant not of right but from personal prowess, yet validated still by imperial style and an imperial diadem'.[176] A contemporary Mercian king, acting in a key behavioural pattern of his Germanic ancestors, has been given an organized visual form by a borrowing from Roman imperial iconography.

If the medium had been vernacular language, no looking beyond native resources would have been necessary. Poetic tradition provided time-honoured conventional means not only to describe conventional actions but also to relate them to states of mind in the doers.[177] For instance, the carver's depiction of the brandishing of the rider's sword calls to mind the *sweorda/ecga gelac*, 'play of swords/blades', at *Beowulf* 1040a and 1168a, the former instance associated with courage – 'næfre on ore læg / widcuþes wig, ðonne walu feollen' ('never did the prowess of the widely famed one lie low in the forefront when the slain fell', 1041b–2) – and the latter with murder – 'þeah þe he his magum nære / arfæst æt ecga gelacum' ('although he had not been merciful to his kinsmen in plays of swords', 1167b–8a).[178] In the first of these two occasions we are brought very close indeed to the ensemble and spirit of the carving. The topic at issue is the gift of eight richly furnished horses among the handsome presents which Hrothgar bestowed on Beowulf in reward for the young hero's victory over Grendel:

Heht ða eorla hleo   eahta mearas   1035
fætedhleore   on flet teon,
in under eoderas;   þara anum stod   1037
sadol searwum fah,   since gewurþad;
þæt wæs hildesetl   heahcyninges,   1039
ðonne sweorda gelac   sunu Healfdenes
efnan wolde, –   næfre on ore læg   1041
widcuþes wig,   ðonne walu feollon

['Then the protector of warriors ordered eight horses with gold-plated cheeks to be led on to the hall-floor, inside the precincts; on one of them stood a saddle skilfully decorated, adorned with treasure; that was the high king's battle-seat when the son

176 Biddle and Kjølbye-Biddle, 'The Repton Stone', p. 271.

177 See below, pp. 126–32.

178 Cf. *Beowulf* 587–8a.

of Healfdene wanted to perform the play of swords – never did the prowess of the widely famed one lie low in the forefront when the slain fell'].

Mention of the saddle was enough to conjure up in the poet's mind the same image of valorous leadership as that portrayed in the carving, and all the traditional terms he needed – *hildesetl*, *heahcyning*, *sweorda gelac*, 'sunu Healfdenes' and 'widcuþes wig' – were available to enable him to marshal this image in pithy praise of Hrothgar as archetypal *eorla hleo* (1035a): twenty words were enough to epitomize battling kingship as cooperation between saddle and royal stature (1039) and between swordplay and lineage (1040) and to attribute to this particular king the supreme personal quality of famed prowess amid carnage (1042). Crafting a compliment to an individual ruler out of traditional aristocratic, military attributes involved the carver in recourse to an outside, imperial tradition; the *Beowulf* poet required only the inherited terminology of native kingship.

Agreement about the elements of this kingship is not all that this carving and this poem had in common; they also placed them in similar narrative contexts. At the top of the narrow face of the cross-shaft round the corner behind the rider[179] a coiled serpent with a huge, ugly human head was depicted in the act of swallowing the smaller heads of two human beings embracing across its neck (see fig. 2). The cannibalism of the monstrous Grendel and his kin immediately comes to mind. Beowulf, on arrival in Heorot, Hrothgar's hall, immediately introduced a graphic sense of this barbarism – 'etan unforhte' ('eat fearlessly', 444a), 'eteð . . . unmurnlice' ('eats ruthlessly', 449) and 'swefeð ond snedeþ'[180] ('kills and feasts', 600a) – which the narrator was to more than match when it came to Grendel actually devouring human flesh:

Ne þæt se aglæca yldan þohte,
ac he gefeng hraðe forman siðe
slæpendne rinc, slat unwearnum,
bat banlocan, blod edrum dranc,
synsnædum swealh; sona hæfde
unlyfigendes eal gefeormod,
fet ond folma

[179] No more has been made out on the other two faces of the surviving portion than that they too were once carved.

[180] MS *sendeþ*.

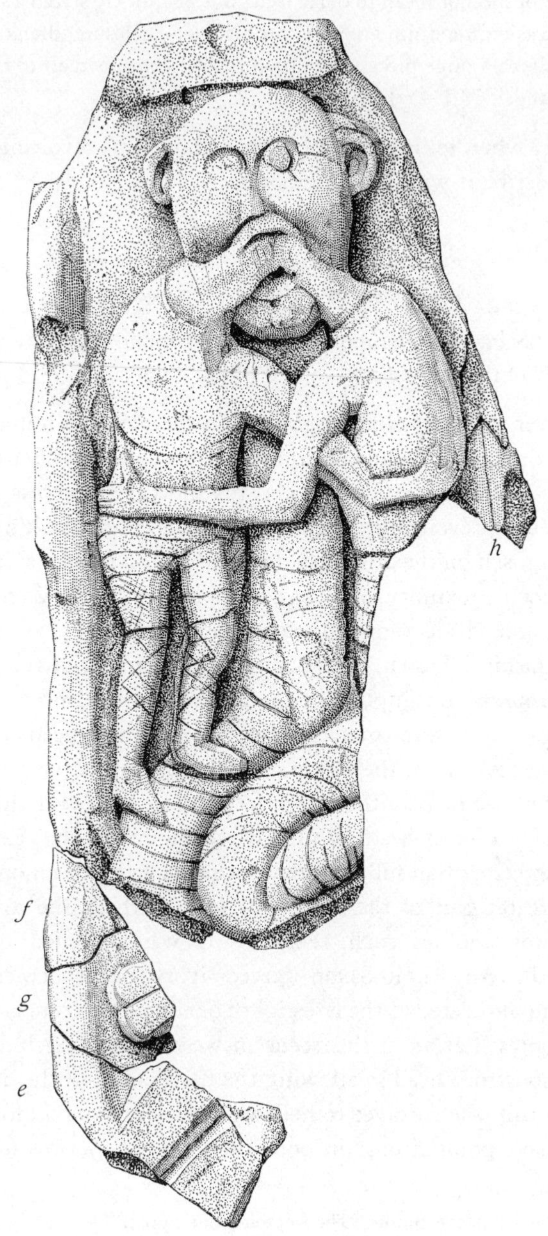

Fig. 2 The serpent face of the Repton Stone (scale 1:6)

['The warrior did not mean to delay that, but he quickly seized a sleeping man on the first occasion, rent him greedily, bit his bone-enclosure, drank the blood in his veins, swallowed huge pieces; very soon he had consumed all of the lifeless man, feet and hands', 739–45a].

And later, when telling King Hygelac about this revolting act, Beowulf was to describe it with strong emotion:

him Grendel wearð,
mærum maguþegne to muðbonan,
leofes mannes lic eal forswealg

['Grendel became the glorious young thegn's mouth-slayer, swallowed up the whole body of the beloved man', 2078b-80].

Stone carver and poet alike responded to the idea of a human-swallowing monster dramatically and feelingly. But, whereas Beowulf straightforwardly fought with Grendel and his mother, the cross-shaft does not seem to set the devouring serpent on the one face and the king self-reliantly proving himself on the other in a direct dramatic relationship. The general effect of their proximity is to suggest an antipathy between noble warrior kingship and crude cannibalistic monstrosity, akin to the distinction between 'rational' human nature and bestial degradations of it drawn in the *Liber monstrorum* and implied in the *Beowulf* poet's conception of Grendel and his kin as descendants of Cain.[181] A human-headed, man-eating, serpent, we feel, is just the sort of monster that might have found a place in the pages of the *Liber*, although in fact it does not occur there.

Probably a cross-head originally surmounted the Repton upright shaft[182] and Christian subjects may once have featured among the carvings on the greater part of the shaft now lost. Perhaps the man-swallowing serpent was another such. Possibly it was intended to represent a hell-mouth. An Anglo-Saxon carved ivory panel depicting the Last Judgement and dated to the late eighth or early ninth century – the earliest known representation of this scene in western art – includes in profile a similar monstrous head swallowing the head of one of the damned as they huddle within the entrance to hell, which itself is not a mouth.[183] As the Biddles have pointed out, in both carvings the victims (clothed on the

[181] See above, pp. 36–8.

[182] Biddle and Kjølbye-Biddle, 'The Repton Stone', pp. 240–1 and fig. 2.

[183] The ivory is in the Victoria and Albert Museum; see Beckwith, *Ivory Carvings*, pp. 22–4 and 118–19 (catalogue no. 4) and ills. 1 and 16.

Repton Stone, naked on the ivory) are not being forced into their fate, as was regularly the case in later representations.[184] And a devouring mouth was probably a familiar image of hell in Reptonian circles in the first half of the eighth century, for in Guthlac's vision which Felix related in ch. 31 of the saint's *Life*[185] the saint was carried 'ad nefandas tartari fauces' ('to the abominable throat of hell') and the threats he there received of punishment in the depths below included 'nunc Stigiae fibrae te vorare malunt, tibi quoque aestivi Acherontis voragines horrendis faucibus hiscunt' ('now the bowels of Styx long to devour you and the hot gulfs of Acheron gape for you with fearful throat').[186] The idea that hell was a man-swallower would have come naturally to Anglo-Saxons, who used their native verb *swelgan*, 'to swallow', to signify the action of fire, as the *Beowulf* narrator did apropos of the bodies of Hnæf and his nephew on one and the same funeral pyre after they had fought on opposite sides:

Lig ealle forswealg,
gæsta gifrost, þara ðe þær guð fornam
bega folces

['Flame, the greediest of spirits, swallowed up all those of both people whom battle had taken off there', 1122b–4a].

A further step would have come naturally to them too – to invent, by a process of metaphorical substitution,[187] a hybrid being, such as a man-headed serpent, to do the swallowing. The result would have been something that was not quite the mouth of hell nor quite other, but in between. 'A hellish mouth' might not be far from the mark as a modern caption for the Repton carving, rather as Grendel operating in this world was termed 'feond on helle' (*Beowulf* 101b).[188]

Early in the eighth century the monk of Wenlock in his vision, already referred to,[189] beheld prophetically the fates of several living sinners, including the Ceolred whom Æthelbald was to succeed as Mercian king: hordes of demons were torturing him.[190] This sort of retribution for sins

184 'The Repton Stone', p. 278. 185 See above, p. 25.

186 *Felix's 'Life' of St Guthlac*, ch. 31 (ed. Colgrave, pp. 104 and 106); cf. Biddle and Kjølbye-Biddle, 'The Repton Stone', p. 279.

187 See below, pp. 96–8.

188 For a discussion of this expression, see Andrew, 'Grendel in Hell'.

189 Above, p. 25.

190 Sims-Williams, *Religion and Literature in Western England*, pp. 269–70.

was commonplace in this period. Æthelbald, when he died in 757, was, according to the 'Continuations' of Bede's *Ecclesiastical History*, murdered by his own men.[191] Did the Repton carving of the man-eating monster depict hell seizing his murderers in the way it did Grendel when he died ('þær him hel onfeng', 852b), so that there they might endure the sort of punishment which Beowulf prophesied Unferth would receive for killing his brothers: 'þæs þu in helle scealt / werhðe dreogan' (588b–9a)[192]

Early-seventh-century weapons at Sutton Hoo, mid-seventh- to mid-eighth-century coins, the Repton cross-shaft fragment, carved probably soon after 757, and *Beowulf* all in their various ways proclaimed that in a partly Christianized environment self-reliant, resolute, warrior kingship had to prove itself by analogy with, or in combat against, beasts and monsters; the *Liber monstrorum*, probably early in the eighth century, surveyed the range of debased human monsters and frightening beasts reported to be in the world; and Aldhelm's writings, late in the seventh century or at the beginning of the eighth, and Felix's *Life of St Guthlac*, probably in the 730s and certainly by 749, demonstrated that public well-being demanded spiritual confrontation of monstrous embodiments of destruction too. In particular the close affinities between the celebrations of traditional military kingship on the Repton Stone and in *Beowulf* imply that in all likelihood a viable vernacular poetic medium of the sort exemplified at its civilized best in *Beowulf* was flourishing among Mercian and Mercian-related aristocracy in their eighth-century hey-day. Accordingly I regard this great work as our sole substantial specimen of vernacular poetry which was composed, in probably a Mercian milieu, at a time when an ancient Germanic conception of personal martial rule still remained essentially unaffected by the radical redefinition, bringing kingship more into line with Christian terms and continental, Carolingian, practices, and beginning in earnest during the second half of the eighth century – for example, when Offa formally associated his son, Ecgfrith, with his rule by having him consecrated king in 787. More Anglo-Saxon social traditions were preserved by this poem, however, than its central notion of kingship – more even than society's view of itself. The linguistic system was based also on an inherited way of perceiving and understanding the make-up of the individual and of the outside world which I believe to have been just as ancient. This wider thought-world I want to explore in the next chapter.

[191] See above, p. 15 and n. 15. [192] See above, p. 41.

The present one I will conclude by emphasizing my opinion that fortunately *Beowulf* provides us with unique testimony to the achievements in large-scale oral poetic narrative which this age-old conceptual and verbal tradition was still capable of in the eighth century in spite of the emergent Latin-, Christian-, classical-based literacy promoted most notably in the Northumbria of Bede and in the Canterbury school of Archbishop Theodore and Hadrian.[193] Other surviving poetry – maxims, elegies and riddles in particular[194] – drew on the same indigenous tradition of thought and language, but this poem alone affords us its extensive access to the accumulated intelligence, wisdom, sympathies and values which eighth-century secular aristocracy regarded as the ethos they shared with Germanic forerunners of centuries past and which even then was relatively untouched by the 'new' intellectual learning of the church.

[193] For the former of these, see Hunter Blair, *The World of Bede*, and for the latter, Lapidge, 'The School of Theodore and Hadrian'.

[194] See further, below, chs. 2 and 3.

2

Society's ancient conceptions of active being and narrative living

Old English poetry's transmission from its Germanic past of not only society's collective wisdom about itself but also its established perception of both the environment it needed to control and its human resources for doing so was the basis of the *Beowulf* poet's narrative authority. A monster- and dragon-slayer of his hero's sort was contending with forces in the world at large. Grendel represented a degraded form of human life and the dragon was a threat from outside mankind altogether. The dangers these enemies posed were based not just within society. Beowulf's representativeness of social values was being tested beyond its usual range. It was being exposed to antagonisms involving society's conception of its habitat. The story's dimensions were those of humanity in its total surroundings. A poem of this sort deployed an ancient system of expression which included non-human (or partly human) as well as human active beings.

The *Beowulf* poet's core vocabulary for the nature of his main protagonists exemplifies both the conceptual principles of this system and its antiquity. Beowulf and Wiglaf, who jointly killed the dragon, and the dragon, which they killed and which killed Beowulf, all possessed the same fighting spirit, *ellen* (*Beowulf* 2706b and 2348–9a).[1] It was the ingredient fundamental to the fighting capability of any being, whether human or otherwise. A sword, for example, could perform an *ellenweorc*, 'deed of fighting mettle' (1457–64). By exercising this power a combatant could kill his enemies (2706b and 2916–19a) and attain the material rewards for doing so (660b–1, 892b–5a and 2535b-6a). It constituted his claim to fame (340–1a, 358a, 827b–8a, 1470b–1a, 1787–9a, 3062b–4a and 3173–4a). It gave a human warrior his means of asserting his will to

[1] This word, and *eafoð*, *mægen*, *strengo*, *miht* and *cræft*, discussed below, are among those surveyed in Mincoff, *Die Bedeutungsentwicklung der ags. Ausdrücke*.

survive: 'Wyrd oft nereð / unfægne eorl, þonne his ellen deah!' ('Fate often protects the warrior not doomed to die, when his fighting spirit avails', 572b–3), as Beowulf declared. If a warrior failed to employ this capacity he forfeited it (2861b). It was the vital force which was extinguished by his death (2505–6a and 2814b–16a).

To the *Beowulf* poet it was a sort of kinetic energy, functioning, as we would put it, through the nervous system, and, in humans, cooperating with, but not originating in, willpower and mental functions generally, as is clear from such contexts as

Eft wæs anræd, nalas elnes læt,
mærða gemyndig mæg Hylaces

['Again the kinsman of Hygelac was resolute, not at all sluggish in fighting spirit, mindful of glorious deeds', 1529–30].

It was a bare, natural force, in itself devoid of moral implications: the admired dragon-slayer Sigemund and the hated tyrant Heremod both had it (893–5a and 901–2a). Distinctions between right and wrong arose only in the ways human beings applied it. It was simply an ingredient in natural conflict as such. Absence of it was significant: although his mother could kill *ellenlice* when put to it (2121b–2a), Grendel in his debasement seems to have been destitute of it.[2] In the twenty occurrences of the simplex in *Beowulf* its connotations are exclusively martial.[3]

In the make-up of the fighter *ellen* allied itself with *eafoð*, 'eafoð ond ellen' together constituting the being's fighting capability.[4] Cognate with *(ge)æfnan*, 'to perform, do, carry out',[5] a verb occurring only in poetry, the noun *eafoð*, also occurring only in poetry and, unlike *ellen*, not used to form compounds, denotes in its eight occurrences in *Beowulf*[6] a physical ability to fight. As in the case of *ellen*, in each of these instances the connotations are martial, and, again like *ellen*, this word signifies an ability which can be

[2] Since the MS reading *ellengæst* at 86a would represent the sole exception to this otherwise conspicuous lack, probably we would be well advised to accept the emendation *ellorgæst* which has been proposed but has not found favour. At 1617a the same scribe wrote *ellengæst* before altering *ellen-* to *ellor-*.

[3] With the single possible exception of its use in the obscure phrase 'elne unflitme' (1097a). *Ellen-* compounds also occur seventeen times and there is the one instance of the adverb *ellenlice* already mentioned.

[4] *Guð* (601b–3a) or *hild* (901–2a) or *wig* (2348–9a). (901–2a, assuming that MS *earfoð* at 902a is amended, as it surely should be.)

[5] As in 'ellenweorc æfnan' (1464).

[6] Counting the amended form at 902a.

possessed by a fighter that may be human or non-human and of any moral persuasion or none (Beowulf, Unferth, Heremod, Grendel and the dragon). The physicality of the attribute is not in doubt in, for example, 'eft sona bið, / þæt þec adl oððe ecg eafoþes getwæfeð' ('in turn it will soon come about that sickness or swordblade will deprive you of physical capability', 1762b-3). The word pair 'eafoð ond ellen', we may infer, summed up warriorship's essential combination of physical and mental power. Grendel's distinction was to have the one (*eafoð*, 960a) without the other.

It is likely to have been an ancient formulation. 'Eafoð ond ellen' seems to have been an Old English verbalization of a pre-English, Germanic epitome of warriorship, for a closely similar, but not identical, word-pairing, 'afl ok eljun', is recorded in three Old Norse verse texts. The oldest of these, *Rigsþula*, though extant only in a fourteenth-century manuscript, embodies very archaic Germanic traditions about the divine inheritance of man. The poem's hero, the first man to bear the title 'king', possesses, among the archetypal virtues of kingliness, the 'afl ok eljun' ('strength and vigour') of eight men. In all three Norse instances the phrase rings like an old heroic formula, in which a word of common usage, *afl*, is linked with a much rarer term, *eljun*, carrying emotive and moral overtones.[7] The lack of exact equivalence between *eafoð* and *afl* – both deriving from the same stem (cf. Latin *opus*) but employing different suffixes – makes direct borrowing from either language to the other unlikely.[8] More probably Old English and Old Norse each expressed in its own way a conceptual pairing which they both inherited from their Germanic ancestry.[9]

[7] For *Rigsþula*, see *Edda*, ed. Neckel I, 280–7; 'afl ok eljun' occurs in stanza 44. For the other two instances, see *Hugsvinnsmál*, stanza 116, and verse sequence III ('The Waking of Angantyr'), stanza 22, in *Hervarar Saga*, *Skjaldedigtning*, ed. Jónsson II, 205 and 269 respectively. I am most grateful to Ursula Dronke for advice on these Old Norse matters.

[8] Old Saxon probably had the word *abal*, for it occurs uniquely in the Old English *Genesis B*, a rendering of a poem in that language: the devil, alleging to Adam that God had ordered him to eat the apple, added, by way of justification, 'cwæð þæt þin abal and cræft / and þin modsefa mara wurde' ('said that your strength and skill and your mind would become greater', 500b–1). For the semantic range of *afl*, different from that of *eafoð*, see Cleasby and Vigfusson, *An Icelandic-English Dictionary*, s.v., and de Vries, *Altnordisches Etymologisches Wörterbuch*, s.v.

[9] In contrast to the direct verbal borrowing evidenced by Wulfstan's substitution of 'on woruldafelum' for Ælfric's 'on woruldlicum geþincðum' ('dignities', 'offices') at *Homilies of Wulfstan*, ed. Bethurum, XII, line 38 (p. 222).

Eafoð and *ellen* form a word pair only in *Beowulf* among our extant poems, but each word occurs elsewhere separately, in the case of *eafoð* no more than twice.[10] Apparently it became rare.[11] In the former instance it seems to have meant 'physical violence' and in the latter clearly signified 'spiritual strength'. As to *ellen*, the changed mental and emotional environment of its more numerous occurrences in Christian poetry is well illustrated by the gnomic generalization at *Andreas* 458–60:

Forþan ic eow to soðe   secgan wille,
þæt næfre forlæteð   lifgende god
eorl on eorðan,   gif his ellen deah

['Therefore I will say to you as a truth that the living God never forsakes a man on earth if his strength of spirit avails!'],

in comparison with that at *Beowulf* 572b–3, already quoted. *Ellen* had ceased to be the instrument of an individual's will to live in the face of an indifferent fate and had become instead his means of counting on protection from a personal God while he faced up to the perils of this life. Spiritual zeal or steadfastness in faith became uppermost in the meaning of the word.[12] Indeed, 'eagerly' could have been the operative meaning in at least one of the semi-adverbial uses of the dative, *elne*, in the military contexts of *Beowulf*, namely at 1967a, and *The Battle of Maldon* shows that the word still held its own at the end of the tenth century in verse, or at any rate in battle poetry, at this semi-adverbial level, if not necessarily at that of fully nominal signification, for Ælfwine is said to have spoken *on ellen* (211b) when declaring with the utmost sincerity, 'nu mæg cunnian hwa cene sy' ('now whoever is bold can prove it', 215), and pledging for his part, 'Ic wylle mine æþelo eallum gecyþan' ('I mean to show my noble descent to all', 216). *Beowulf*, however, stands alone in regularly using

[10] At *Andreas* 30a and *Juliana* 601b.

[11] It is to be noted also that the first scribe of the *Beowulf* manuscript once (902a) wrote *earfoð* (cf. *earfeþo*, 'hardships', 'difficulties', 534a) instead (and may have done at 534a also), and, since the error (or errors) remained uncorrected, we should infer that probably it was (or they were) already in the exemplar which was being copied (see above, pp. 31–4): the implication is therefore that *eafoð* was an unfamiliar word to the scribe who wrote that exemplar probably at some time after the middle of the ninth century (see above, *ibid.*).

[12] See, further, my 'King Alfred's Debt to Vernacular Poetry', p. 218.

eafoð and *ellen* to render components basic to warriorship in a line of descent from antique Germanic tradition.[13]

Eafoð has no history of prose usage at all, for it is confined to *Beowulf* and only two other poems (once each), as has been pointed out already. *Ellen*, however, was used sporadically in prose up to at any rate the end of the ninth century,[14] but only once, in King Alfred's version of Boethius's *De consolatione Philosophiae*, made any contribution to fundamental definition of the individual's resources for confronting issues of Christian living and dying. Alfred's unique exception was to choose the word for naming the third of the four cardinal, natural, virtues, prudence, temperance, fortitude and justice (as distinct from St Paul's three theological virtues of faith, hope and charity), on the first of the two occasions on which he enumerated these items without any equivalent in Boethius's Latin (but probably taking his cue from an available Latin gloss). From the context and from his other naming of the same virtue (*geþyld*) it is evident that 'steadfastness', 'endurance' (rather than 'eagerness', 'zeal') was the meaning he intended primarily to convey.[15] Elsewhere in prose the word seems to have gone into steady decline, and it is hard to detect any sign that it even survived outside verse, except as a fossil, after about the middle of the tenth century.[16] Two inferences concerning the chronology of Old English poetry may in passing be drawn from these considerations: one is that the *Beowulf*ian use of *eafoð* and *ellen* to designate primary elements in Germanic warriorship is unlikely to have continued at full strength alongside the changed meanings of the former word and the new Christian meanings of the latter, because, if it had, these words would probably have proved less susceptible to change than they did; the other conclusion is that once the usage preserved in *Beowulf* had been lost or seriously undermined, it could not have been reconstituted from either the altered usage in verse or the weakened usage in prose.

At 1716b–17a *eafeþum* (dat. pl.) is in apposition to 'mægenes wynnum'.

[13] This fundamental usage characterizes all eight occurrences of the former simplex and at least fifteen (3b, 573b, 602a, 637a, 902a, 1493a, 1529b, 2349a, 2506a, 2535b, 2695b, 2706b, 2816a, 2861b and 2876b) of the twenty occurrences of the latter.

[14] For complete refs., see *A Microfiche Concordance to Old English*, compiled by Healey and Venezky; for a summary, see my 'King Alfred's Debt to Vernacular Poetry', pp. 219–21.

[15] *King Alfred's Old English Version of Boethius 'De consolatione Philosophiae'*, ed. Sedgefield, pp. 62, lines 24–9, and 87, lines 7–8; see, further, my 'King Alfred's Debt to Vernacular Poetry', pp. 222–3.

[16] E.g., in a psalter gloss derived from an earlier gloss; see *ibid.*, pp. 221–2.

Derived from the Germanic base *mag*, 'to have power',[17] and with cognates in other Germanic languages,[18] *mægen* occurs in *Beowulf* nineteen times as a simplex and once in *ofermægen* and provides the first element in eight compounds (9×). That it denoted, like *eafoð*, a primarily physical might and vigour is plentifully demonstrated by context.[19] But, unlike *eafoð*, *mægen* was attributed by this poet specifically to humans: indeed, at 2836b–7a, *manna* (gen. pl.) were characterized collectively as 'mægen-agendra' ('might-possessing').[20] Another noun derived, like *mægen*, from Germanic *mag*, namely *miht*, occurring twice, signified God's power at 940a and probably at 700a as well,[21] while the related adjective, *mihtig*, was applied to God in four out of seven instances (701a, 1398b, 1716a and 1725a), to Grendel's mother in two out of the other three (1339a and 1519a) and to a sea-monster in the remaining case (558a), just as *æl-* and *foremihtig*, each occurring once, were applied to God and Grendel's mother respectively (92a and 969b). It seems that the poet's choice between *mægen* and *miht* turned on a distinction between human might and another, extra-human, kind of power. *Eafoð* and *miht* between them indicate that when Beowulf was challenging other beings he was putting his *ellen* at risk among elemental components of which some were like and some were unlike his own. But, whether it was a sameness or a difference in a particular instance, this poet was evidently drawing on a time-honoured vocabulary which registered a common system of observation. His usage rendered in conventionally accepted language ancestral identifications embracing the fundamental potentials from which the actions of beings sprang, the types into which beings were grouped by virtue of potentials in common and the consequences which potentials had for narrative living.

In the rest of this chapter I want to trace some of the concepts which

[17] Cf. Latin *magnus*, 'great'.

[18] In Old English cf. *magan*, 'to be able, to have the capability (to do something)'.

[19] At 196b ('mægenes strengest'), 517b–18a, 789b, 1270b, 1533b–4a, 1706a, 1761b–3, 1844a, 1886b–7a and 2084–5a. The physicality of the strength signified by *strengo* (n.), and hence by the compounds *hilde-*, *mægen-* and *merestrengo*, and by the related adjective, *strang*, in *Beowulf* is beyond question in such contexts as 'strenge getruwode, / mundgripe mægenes' ('he trusted his strength, the hand-grip of his might', 1533b–4a), and so I include in this list all collocations of *mægen* and *strengo*/*strang*.

[20] I take it that the *mægen-* in *mægenwudu* (236a, a spear), in *mægenfultum* (1455b, a sword) and in *mægenbyrþen(n)* (1625a, Grendel's head and a sword hilt, and 3091b, treasure) expressed the human might required in the user or carrier.

[21] If the latter's reference were to human might it would be unique.

constituted this traditional view of active being and resultant narrative living. Mainly I shall look to vernacular poetry itself, especially *Beowulf*, for there the language preserved inherited ideas most grandly and eloquently. But these ideas were not exclusive to poetry. They moulded Anglo-Saxon art of the Germanic zoomorphic sort; they guided Anglo-Saxon adaptation of Christian/classical ideas and Latin/Greek modes of expression, whether verbal or visual. They were not confined to any one phase of Anglo-Saxon culture: they persisted as underlying assumptions and were liable to show up at any time. And so I shall seek this web of native thought in contexts and times other than those of the most traditional vernacular poetry whenever it seems feasible and profitable to do so.

It will be best, though, to begin with poetry's display of the nature of active being and of its dynamic relationship to narrative living. When young Wiglaf, Beowulf's nephew, plunged into the desperate conflict with the dragon in support of his fatally wounded kinsman, he drew on inborn qualities:

> Ða ic æt þearfe gefrægn   þeodcyninges
> andlongne eorl   ellen cyðan,
> cræft ond cenðu,   swa him gecynde wæs

['Then I learned that at the time of need for the king of the people the warrior standing upright showed fighting spirit, ability in action and boldness, as was natural to him by birth', 2694–6].

He possessed certain potentials for action by virtue of his *gecynd*, his inherent nature, and that was the central fact which needed stating about him at this supremely testing moment. By comparison, other (we might well think important) considerations, such as the training he had received, did not rank a mention. In Anglo-Saxon eyes what really mattered about any being at all – be it human or non-human, animate or inanimate, natural or manufactured according to our classifications – was the potential, or potentials, for action which he/she/it had received from his/her/its origin. This (or these) constituted its basic identity and therefore settled the accepted terms of reference for its representation. Thus in visual art Germanic convention was to represent a being as an ensemble (or selection) of its members for eating, hunting or moving – jaws, beak, eyes, ears, wings, tail, legs, joints or feet, as the case might be. Stylized form expressed standardized perception that an animal characterized itself by using its jaws, a bird its beak, a quadruped its fore- and hindlegs, and so on.[22] And verse language, reduced to its simplest, performed the same function in a string of gnomic statements, such as

Forst sceal freosan, fyr wudu meltan,
eorþe growan, is brycgian

['Frost freezes, fire dissolves wood, earth causes growth, ice bridges', *Maxims I* 71–2];

and likewise 'Brim sceal sealte weallan' ('A sea surges with salt', *Maxims II* 45b), 'Ea of dune sceal / flodgræg feran' ('A river runs downhill in a grey flood', 30b–1a), 'Fugel uppe sceal / lacan on lyfte' ('A bird plays up in the air', 38b–9a), 'Leax sceal on wæle / mid sceote scriðan' ('A salmon glides in a pool with a trout', 39b–40a), 'Ecg sceal wið hellme / hilde gebidan' ('A sword-blade experiences battle against a helmet', 16b–17a) and 'Gim sceal on hringe / standan steap and geap' ('A jewel stands high and broad on a ring', 22b–3a). Other maxims identified equally plainly the potentials characterizing specified types of doer: for example, 'Guð sceal in eorle, / wig geweaxan' ('Fighting capability, capacity for battle, grows in a warrior', *Maxims I* 83b–4a), whereas '. . . treow [sceal] weaxan, / sio geond bilwitra breost ariseð' ('good faith grows; it springs up throughout the breasts of the honest', 159b–60).

The function of human craftsmanship was to render a material's innate potentials operational: wood of a certain sort became *gomenwudu*, 'wood for mirth' (*Beowulf* 1065a and probably 2108a), when, made into a lyre, it provided entertainment; wood of another sort became *bordwudu*, 'shield-wood' (1243a), when, cut thin, it was still able to resist impact; yet another sort of wood became *þrecwudu*, 'thrusting wood' (1246a), when, fashioned into a spear-shaft, it was stout enough not to break; and wood of again another sort became *sæ-* (226a) or *sundwudu*, 'sea-wood' (208a and 1906b), because, when efficiently carpentered, it best exploited the material's ability to float there. Various aspects of a single usefulness were differentiated likewise: a man-made *stol*, 'seat', for example, became a *bregostol*, 'princely seat' (2196a, 2370a and 2389a), in its potential for its user, a *gifstol*, 'gift-seat' (168a and 2327a), in its use, and an *eþelstol*, 'seat of the native land' (2371b), for those whom its use benefited.

The root idea of OE *gecynd*, 'nature', was the act of begetting or

[22] For a visual analysis of sixth- and seventh-century Anglo-Saxon animal art, see Speake, *Anglo-Saxon Animal Art*.

producing.[23] The potentials which a being (human or otherwise) possessed by virtue of his/her/its *gecynd* were transmitted at birth to that being's *feorh*, 'life'. A standard association between *feorh* and action is shown when an act's duration was expressed by a commonplace *feorh* phrase, such as 'þenden (*or* gif) feorh leofað (*or* wunað)' ('as long as (*or* if) life remains')[24] or 'to widan feore' ('ever').[25] *Feorh* was 'active life', but was not in a unique form in each individual: it was a group characteristic. A being belonged by birth to a *cynn*, 'kin',[26] and displayed the *feorh* common to that *cynn:* as *Maxims I* proclaimed, 'Feorhcynna fela fæþmeþ wide / eglond monig' ('Many an island, far and wide, contains numerous species of life', 14–15a). A *cynn* could be, in our terminology, a genus or a species, as the flexibility of *-cynn* compounds illustrates: *gumcynn* signifies 'mankind' at *Beowulf* 2765b but 'a kind of men' at 260. But, whatever the size of the group, identification of it was of first importance for foreknowledge of the behaviour of its members; the Danish coastguard, urgently needing to know how Beowulf and his men would act as newly arrived strangers, could not afford to lose time on this point: 'Nu ic eower sceal / frumcyn witan', he warned ('I must know your origin immediately', 251b–2a).

A *cynn*'s inherited nature which determined its actions was its *æþelu:* putting first things first, the *Exodus* poet defined the duties of genealogists as getting to know 'frumcyn feora, fæderæðelo gehwæs' ('the origin of living men, the paternal nature of each one', 361). Over the world at large the diverse *æþelu* of all beings amounted to a huge fruitfulness which was quite beyond calculation:

Monge sindon geond middangeard
unrimu cynn, þe we æþelu ne magon
ryhte areccan

['Many are the countless kinds throughout the world, whose inherited natures we cannot rightly reckon', *The Panther* 1–3a].

An *æþelu* in essence was an inherited capacity for action: in *The Battle of Maldon*, when his leader Byrhtnoth had been killed, Ælfwine declared

[23] Skeat, *An Etymological Dictionary of the English Language*, s.v. *kind*, and App. III (List of Aryan Roots), GA (or GAN).

[24] *Andreas* 1288–9a, *Juliana* 119 and *Genesis* (*A*) 906–9a.

[25] At *Beowulf* 932–4a and *Christ* (*I*) 275–7; mostly 'for ever' in Christian use, e.g., 'ond þæs to widan feore willum neotan' ('and joyfully possess that for ever', *Andreas* 810 and *Christ* (*III*) 1343).

[26] Ultimately derived from the same Indo-European root as *gecynd*; cf. Latin *genus*.

proudly before plunging into the fray again ('he on ellen spræc' ('he spoke with fighting spirit',[27] 211b)),

> Ic wylle mine æþelo eallum gecyþan,
> þæt ic wæs on Myrcon miccles cynnes

['I mean to reveal my noble descent to all, that I was of a great kin among the Mercians', 216–17].

Likewise Hrothgar welcomed Beowulf to his hall as a champion against Grendel because, having known Beowulf's father in action, he knew the son's *æþelu* (391–2). When Beowulf had vanquished Grendel, Hrothgar addressed him approvingly as *æþeling*, 'prince' (1225a), and when Grendel's mother had been defeated as well and Beowulf and his men were returning home, their mission accomplished, the narrator refers to them consistently as *æþelingas*.[28] They had successfully reactivated the honour transmitted to them by their ancestors. More particularly Beowulf and Wiglaf together destroyed the dragon as *sibæðelingas*, 'related nobles' (2708a); they honourably obeyed the promptings they shared through their kinship.

Æþelu, however, was certainly not just an inner state. Narratively it was linked to a certain environment. In a warrior's case that was notably the battlefield, but the connection differed from *cynn* to *cynn*. For instance, according to King Alfred's vernacular prose version of Boethius's *De consolatione Philosophiae*, at a point without exact counterpart in the Latin, a plant's *æþelu* determined that it would grow in one place but not in another.[29] The business of gnomic statements such as the following was to iterate these organic links with location:

> Wulf sceal on bearowe,
> earm anhaga, eofor sceal on holte,
> toþmægenes trum

['A wolf is a lone dweller in a wood, a boar lives in a wood vigorous in the strength of its tusks', *Maxims II* 18b-20a].

Similarly 'Draca sceal on hlæwe, / frod, frætwum wlanc' ('A dragon lives in a barrow, old and proud of treasures', 26b–7a), 'Bera sceal on hæðe, / eald and egesfull' ('A bear lives on a heath, old and terrifying', 29b–30a), 'þyrs

[27] Cf. above, p. 71. [28] 1804a, 1815a and 1920b.

[29] *King Alfred's Version of Boethius 'De consolatione Philosophiae'*, ed. Sedgefield, p. 91, lines 19–24.

sceal on fenne gewunian / ana innan lande' ('A monster lives in a fen, alone in the land', 42b–3a), 'Daroð sceal on handa, / gar golde fah' ('A javelin belongs in the hand, a spear decorated with gold', 21b–2a) and 'Duru sceal on healle, / rum recedes muð' ('A door belongs in a hall, a wide mouth for the building', 36b–7a). According to Anglo-Saxon ways of thinking, inheritance gathers beings into kinships, each of which shares a potential (or potentials) for action in a given environment and is marked by a consistent pattern of narrative living.

Cræft denoted an innate talent which spanned both active being and narrative living. It signified an ability to control action from potential to performance, and so combined the generality of the former with the latter's particularity. Occurring 125 times in the extant poetry as a simplex, it clearly afforded poets freedom to express insights right across the spectrum of action from inception to accomplishment, from mental to physical and from good to bad: the *cræft* Wiglaf showed in the dragon fight was a wholly admirable potential, but the double *cræft* of the devil tormenting hermits in their loneliness provides him with an abominable technique:

eaweð him egsan, hwilum idel wuldor,
brægdwis bona hafað bega cræft,
eahteð anbuendra

['He [i.e. 'he who begrudges them life', 85b] displays terror to them, at other times empty glory, the killer cunning in deceit has the skill for both, persecutes solitary-dwellers', *Guthlac (A)* 86–8a].

The word supplied linguistic malleability which a skilful poet could endow with sharp definition through context, especially by compounding. In the poetic corpus as a whole, whereas, say, *mægen*, a much less flexible word, was used as either a first or a second element almost equally[30] and there is only a single (adjectival) compound in *cræft-* (*cræftgleaw*, 1x), we find a large number of *-cræft*, *-cræftig* and *-cræftega* compounds with diversely defining first elements (forty-one of them occurring altogether ninety-six times).[31] An ability to control action in progress was at issue

[30] There are twenty-six *mægen-* nominal compounds occurring sixty-one times altogether and twenty-two *-mægen* ones (41×).

[31] *aglæc-*, *æ-*, *æl-*, *beadu-*, *bealu-*, *boc-*, *dry-*, *dwol-*, *eacen-*, *ellen-*, *firen-*, *galdor-*, *guð-*, *heah-*, *hell-*, *hyge-*, *lagu-*, *lar-*, *leornung-*, *leoð-*, *leoðu-*, *ma-*, *mægen-*, *mod-*, *morðor-*, *mund-*, *nearo-*, *rim-*, *run-*, *searo-*, *smið-*, *snyttru-*, *song-*, *sundor-*, *wæl-*, *wicg-*, *wig-*, *word-*, *woruld-*, *woð-* and *wundor-*. For the distribution of *cræft* and its compounds, see *Concordance to the*

here: active intelligence was involved. *Cræft* signified an innate, distinctively human, personal, faculty of organizing mental and physical activity[32] and therefore served preeminently both to distinguish the genus of *moncynn*, 'mankind', from other *cynn* and to delineate the species formed out of mankind's various potentials. Cynewulf, for instance, used this word when showing his lively sense of this variety, divinely disposed according to orderly principles, by changing a list (by Gregory the Great) of six spiritual endowments distributed by the Holy Spirit into a selection of ten discrete *cræftas* implanted by God in different people, five primarily in the mind and five mainly in the body (*Christ (II)* 662–88a).

Emotions, thoughts and words were important determinants of human performance. They were active beings in their own right. Either feeler or feeling might seize the initiative. A distressful longing had gripped the speaker in *The Wife's Lament*; she could not rest '. . . ealles þæs longaþes þe mec on þissum life begeat' ('for all the longing which has taken hold of me in this life', 41). But the speaker in *The Seafarer* courted the same unrest as a positive state of mind: '. . . a hafað longunge se þe on lagu fundað' ('he who sets out eagerly on the sea always has longing', 47). Wayward beings such as this longing lodged in the breast and needed firm control:

Hyge sceal gehealden, . . .
. . . snyttro [sceal] in breostum,
þær bið þæs monnes modgeþoncas

['The mind must be restrained, . . . wisdom shall be in the breast, where the man's thoughts are', *Maxims I* 121a and 122b-3];

and, as for words,

Wærwyrde sceal wisfæst hæle
breostum hycgan, nales breahtme hlud

['The sagacious man thinks in his breast, cautious of speech, not at all loud in noise', *Precepts* 57–8].

States of mind took charge: when Hrothgar bade Beowulf an emotional farewell,

Anglo-Saxon Poetic Records, ed. Bessinger, a work to which I am much indebted in this book; for *cræft*, see also *Dictionary of Old English, Fascicle C*, ed. Amos *et al.*, s.v.

32 See, further, my 'King Alfred's Debt to Vernacular Poetry', pp. 223–38.

. . . he þone breostwylm forberan ne mehte;
ac him on hreþre hygebendum fæst
æfter deorum men dyrne langað
beorn wið blode

['he could not restrain the surging of his breast; but fixed by the heartstrings hidden longing for the dear man burned within his blood', *Beowulf* 1877–80a].

Strong feelings without an outlet could be unbearable, as King Hrethel's grief was when his eldest son had been killed by one of the other two:

He ða mid þære sorhge, þe him to sar belamp,
gumdream ofgeaf, Godes leoht geceas

['Then with that sorrow which was too grievous for him, he gave up the joys of men, chose God's light', 2468–9].

A human being's relations with these entities was like carrying (*wegan*) weapons (2252b and 2703b–4) or ornaments (3015b–16): it was to Unferth's lasting shame, Beowulf declared, that Grendel 'lust wigeð' ('feels pleasure', 599b); looking back at his sufferings at the hands of Grendel, Hrothgar reflected, 'ic þære socne singales weg / modceare micle' ('I felt continually the great sorrow of mind of that persecution', 1777–8a); and Hrethel, overwhelmed by his intolerable anguish, 'heortan sorge / weallinde wæg' ('felt sorrow of the heart surging', 2463b–4a). Words could burst out of a man's breast, as when Beowulf was dying: '. . . wordes ord / breosthord þurhbræc' ('the point of a word broke through his breast-hoard', 2791b–2a).

Speech was very special to man; there is no sign that it was part of the sub-humanity of Grendel or his mother, and the dragon certainly had no such faculty. Feeling and thinking, however, were not clearly distinguished from one another and were not exclusively human. Man's mental processes consisted of both:[33] when Beowulf, confronted by the dragon's destruction of his royal hall, was filled with forebodings, 'breost innan weoll / þeostrum geþoncum' ('his breast surged within with gloomy thoughts', 2331b–2); when the *eardstapa* in *The Wanderer* said

. . . ic geþencan ne mæg geond þas woruld
for hwan modsefa min ne gesweorce

['I cannot think for what reason throughout this world my mind should not grow dark', 58–9],

[33] See Godden, 'Anglo-Saxons on the Mind', pp. 285–95.

he was thinking of his mind as the seat of both emotions and thoughts, not of either alone. Beings less than, or not at all, human had similar unitary experiences: Grendel clearly had – 'Hyge wæs him hinfus' ('His mind was eager to get away', *Beowulf* 755a)[34] – and so did his mother (1259b) and the dragon.[35] Where man pulled away from the rest was in the level and range of his consciousness allied to his use of words. For instance, although Grendel, and so presumably his mother, could 'know' (*witan*, 715b, 764b, 821b and perhaps 169b[36]), neither these monsters nor the dragon seemingly possessed human powers of perception: *ongitan*, the most commonly used word in poetry (including *Beowulf*) and in prose up to and including the reign of Alfred (but not later) to express the human act of understanding,[37] was not applied to any of them,[38] whereas the verb *onfindan*, 'to find out', regularly was.[39] The distinction at issue is well exemplified at 1495b–1500:

Ða wæs hwil dæges,
ær he þone grundwong ongytan mehte.
Sona þæt onfunde se ðe floda begong
heorogifre beheold hund missera,
grim ond grædig, þæt þær gumena sum
ælwihta eard ufan cunnode

['Then it was daytime[40] before he [i.e. Beowulf] could recognize the bottom. Immediately the one who had occupied the expanse of waters, fiercely ravenous, for

[34] Cf. 712a, 715b, 730b, 731a, 739b, 762a and 821b, and also 448b and 475b.

[35] 2565a, 2581b and 2689d.

[36] The verb *cunnan*, however, in either of its senses, 'to know' and 'to know how to (do something)', was never applied to Grendel or his mother or the dragon; on *witan* and *cunnan* as the chief Old English verbs meaning 'to know', see Ono, *On Early English Syntax and Vocabulary*, pp. 139–67.

[37] See Ono, *On Early English Syntax and Vocabulary*, pp. 169–214.

[38] Sea monsters (*nicras*) *ongeaton* noise, however, at 1431b, and the dragon *oncneow* a human voice at 2554b (*oncnawan*). *Ongitan* signifies human cognition ten times in all (308b, 1484b, 1496b, 1512b, 1518a, 1723a, 1911b, 2748a, 2770b and 2944a); at 14b God is probably the subject of *ongeat*. At 1291b the verb signifies terror's action of seizing someone ('þa hine se broga angeat' ('when the terror seized him')).

[39] Grendel 595a, 750a and 809a; Grendel's mother 1497a; and the dragon 2288b, 2300b and 2629b. *Onfindan* was applied to humans also (Beowulf at 1522b and 2713b, the coastguard at 1890b and anyone in general at 1293b and 2841b).

[40] For this translation, see Robinson, 'Elements of the Marvellous', pp. 121–4; cf. lines 1311b–13, 1600a and 1789b–90a. But for doubts, see Greenfield, 'A Touch of the Monstrous', pp. 294–300 (repr. Greenfield, *Hero and Exile*, pp. 67–73).

fifty years [i.e. Grendel's mother], grim and greedy, found out that some man was exploring the land of alien beings from above'].

An inherited potential expressed itself as actions in a cluster or series. For example, human command of language assumed various forms – 'Ræd sceal mon secgan, rune writan, / leoþ gesingan' ('Counsel shall be spoken, a secret written, a lay sung', *Maxims I* 138–9a) – while individuality consisted of the series of actions a doer performed by virtue of innate potential. The swimming contest Beowulf had had with Breca was evidence of his competitiveness when he presented himself in Hrothgar's hall to fight Grendel (*Beowulf* 499–606) – 'Eart þu se Beowulf, se þe wið Brecan wunne?' ('Are you the Beowulf who contended with Breca?', 506), Unferth demanded of him – and similarly his survival by swimming back alone from King Hygelac's ill-fated expedition to the Rhineland witnessed to his capacity for independent endurance, according to the narrator's assessment of him, when he determined to undertake single-handed his fatal encounter with the dragon (2345–68). A characteristic action was repeated. Conversely an action which was repeated was characteristic: when Grendel made a second murderous raid on Heorot the Danes were convinced of his malignance (134b–43). The *Beowulf* poet had a stock of commonplace tags to call attention to reiteration, such as *eft swa ær* (642a and 1787a), 'swa he ær dyde' (1891b), 'swa hie oft ær dydon' (1238b) and 'swa nu gyt deð' (1134b). Once an action became a habit it got a grip on its doer, as in Grendel's case:

. . . ymbe ane niht   eft gefremede
morðbeala mare,   ond no mearn fore,
fæhðe ond fyrene;   wæs to fæst on þam

['after one night he again performed more murderous destruction, and did not shrink from it at all on that account, feud and crime; he was too fixed in that', 135–7].

One of poetry's most interesting explicit bridges between innate potential and narrative living was the *se þe* . . ., 'the one who . . .', formulation of an active being. It used it quite often to epitomize an actor's characteristic or habitual action(s) at the moment when he/she/it was performing a critical action, as Grendel's mother was at *Beowulf* 1497b–9a just quoted, or as Beowulf was when, with all the odds against him, he peered into the barrow containing the fiery dragon:

Geseah ða be wealle se ðe worna fela
gumcystum god guða gedigde,
hildehlemma, þonne hnitan feðan,
stondan stanbogan

['Then he who had survived a great many fights, brave with manly virtues, many battle-crashes when foot troops clashed, saw stone arches standing by the wall', 2542–5a].[41]

The dragon too was characterized early on by the same means and in a similar context of carrying out an important action:

Hordwynne fond
eald uhtsceaða opene standan,
se ðe byrnende biorgas seceð,
nacod niðdraca, nihtes fleogeð
fyre befangen; hyne foldbuend
swiðe ondrædað. He gesecean sceall
hord on hrusan, þær he hæðen gold
warað wintrum frod; ne byð him wihte ðy sel

['An old dawn-time injurer found the hoard-joy standing open, the being which, burning, seeks mounds, bare hostile dragon, flies at night enveloped in fire; earth-dwellers fear it greatly. It seeks treasure hidden in the ground, where, old in years, it guards heathen gold; it is not the better for that at all', 2270b-7].

Usually the consistency of the characteristic action was intensified contextually by a feature such as 'hund missera', *worna fela* and *eald* in these examples or *wide* in Hrothgar's naming of his magnificent new hall ('scop him Heort naman / se þe his wordes geweald wide hæfde' ('he who exercised widely the authority of his word created the name Heorot for it', 78b–9)). That the most meaningful associations for a critical action, whether by a human or a non-human, was its doer's habitual action(s) shows how important a factor consistency was in estimating narrative action issuing from potential.

The *se þe* . . . formula always conveyed the representative nature of the potential concerned. Contextual wording such as *heorogifre* (1498a) or

[41] See also 78b–9, 90b–1, 788b–90, 809–12, 825–7a, 1618–19, 1977–8a, 2221–2, 2594b–5, 2777b–82, 2897b–8 and 3058–60a, and cf. 86–7, 102–4a, 229–32a, 494b–6a, 867b–71a, 1258b–63a, 1343b–4, 1448–50, 1742b–4, 1755b–7a, 1882b–3, 1886b–7, 1914–16, 2210b–13a, 2214b–16a, 2270b–7, 2684b–7a and 3124b–5.

'hildehlemma, þonne hnitan feðan' (2544) or the indefinite present verbs, *seceð* and *fleogeð*, in 2272b and 2273b regularly made clear the *se þe* . . . actor's representativeness. The formula was never without a dimension of generalization: 'the one who . . .' at 2542b was only a degree away from the more indefinite identification 'one who . . .' in 'Sægde se þe cuþe / frumsceaft fira feorran reccan' ('One who could narrate from far back the creation of men spoke', 90b-1); and this in turn was only a step from the completely indefinite 'anyone who . . .' in

Þæt, la, mæg secgan se þe soð ond riht
fremeð on folce, feor eal gemon,
eald eþelweard, þæt ðes eorl wære
geboren betera

['Anyone who does truth and right in the people, remembers all from far back, an old guardian of the native land, will indeed be able to say that this warrior was born superior', 1700–3a].[42]

An assertion, such as this, placing an indefinite identification in an indefinite present, alleged an inevitable linkage of a general kind, so that, if the consequential action was as free from specific contextual ties as the indefinite identification was, a full-blown gnomic generalization resulted, such as

Fela sceal gebidan
leofes ond laþes se þe longe her
on ðyssum windagum worulde bruceð

['Anyone who makes use of the world for long here in these days of strife, experiences much to love and much to hate', 1060b-2].[43]

The *se þe* . . . construction was regularly employed to formulate a collective truth to the effect that 'anyone who does so-and-so must or may or will do such-and-such'. Indeed, it provided society with one of its standard means of making legal pronouncements, as in the fiftieth decree of our earliest extant law code, which Æthelberht, king of Kent, issued in perhaps 602–3: 'Se þe cinban forslæhð, mid XX scillingum forgelde' ('Anyone who smashes a chin bone is to pay for it with twenty shil-

[42] See also 2864–72 and cf. 1048b–9, 2006–9a and 2041–3.

[43] See also 440b–1, 603b–6, 1002b–8a, 1386–9, 2291–3a, 2600b–1 and 2764b–6, and cf. 287b–9 and 1341–3a.

lings').[44] For poetry, we may say, the *se þe . . .* frame constituted a classic, succinct, instrument of insight into a doer's vital combination of active being and narrative living.

Narrative living, however, was not thought of as resulting exclusively from the potentials of active beings: it was conditioned by environmental factors in its environment, to which we should now turn. For one thing, an act was not perceived with the kind of separateness which it has to our minds. It was regarded as part of a continuum in a time and a space which were not differentiated from each other as clearly as in our thinking: *þær* often did not register an absolute distinction between the meanings 'there' and 'then'[45] or between 'where' and 'when'; the distance from place A to place B was reckoned in travelling time – so many days' walking or riding or sailing. Moreover the time thus employed was not so much an objective formal concept as a psychological set of linear periods, such as a day running from sunrise to sunset and therefore shorter in winter than in summer. The environment of action was perceived as a single psychological, basically temporal, linearity, which in visual narrative was reflected by the horizontal 'playing space' of an artifact such as the Bayeux Tapestry and in verbal narrative was registered by a frequent use of temporal connectives (*þa*, *syððan*, *oð þæt* and so on). The result, however, was no vacuum in either medium. What was presented to the imagination was potential 'space' free of any necessity to be described completely. For instance, the phrase 'fotes trem' in Beowulf's declaration before his fight with the dragon, 'Nelle ic beorges weard / oferfleon fotes trem' ('I do not mean to flee from the guardian of the mound the space of a foot!', 2524b–5a),[46] had an absolute force it would have lacked if measured by physical detail; and likewise the momentum of time as an uncluttered background rendered Beowulf's physical arrest of Grendel's flight memorably dramatic:

> Gemunde þa se goda,   mæg Higelaces,
> æfenspræce,   uplang astod
> ond him fæste wiðfeng;   fingras burston;
> eoten wæs utweard,   eorl furþur stop

['Then the brave man, kinsman of Hygelac, bore in mind his evening speech,

[44] *Die Gesetze der Angelsachsen*, ed. Liebermann I, 6. I am grateful for an interesting conversation with Jürg Schwyter, of Emmanuel College, Cambridge, about this formula in the laws.

[45] As at 157a, 271b etc.

[46] Cf. *The Battle of Maldon* 246b–7a.

stood upright and laid hold on him firmly; fingers burst; the giant was making outwards, the warrior stepped further', 758–61].

The temporal impetus of mental challenge produced a contrasting physical impact of stoppage. The interaction of primary time and secondary space generated a sustained potential for dramatic narrative.

The principle that space was subordinate to time led the composer of extended narrative, verbal or visual, to represent temporal continuity as a series of minimal, self-sufficient ensembles of salient features selected for their physical and psychological relevance. The language of poetic narrative carried out essentially the same operation of identifying salient features as the language of place-names did, and the technique remained the same whether the setting was out- or indoors: before Beowulf vowed not to yield a single footstep to the dragon, he had sat down on a headland ('Gesæt ða on næsse' (2417a)) and in that position had taken farewell of his close comrades one by one ('Gegrette ða gumena gehwylcne / . . . hindeman siðe' (2516–17)), and then, after finishing speaking, he had stood up armed for action ('Aras ða bi ronde rof oretta' (2538)); and likewise, before Beowulf prevented Grendel from escaping unscathed, the monster had swung open the hall door ('onbræd þa bealohydig, ða he gebolgen wæs, / recedes muþan' (723–4a)), had stepped on to the floor ('Raþe æfter þon / on fagne flor feond treddode' (724b–5)) which was covered with sleeping men ('Geseah he in recede rinca manige, / swefan sibbegedriht' (728–9a)), had devoured his first victim ('ac he gefeng hraðe forman siðe / slæpendne rinc' (740–1a)) and, advancing ('Forð near ætstop' (745b)), had grabbed the watching hero ('nam þa mid handa higeþihtigne / rinc on ræste' (746–7a)), who in his turn had seized the marauder ('he onfeng hraþe / inwitþancum' (748b–9a)), sat up ('and wið earm gesæt' (749b)) and then, mindful of the vow he had made earlier, stood up ('Gemunde þa se goda . . . / æfenspræce, uplang astod' (758–9)). The headland and the listeners at close quarters in the first sequence, and the hall door, the hall floor and the sleeping men in the second, associated in both with extensive references to states of mind, contributed physical and psychological accessories to the temporal linear action ('*ða*, *ða* and *ða*' and '*þa*, *raþe æfter þon*, *hraðe*, *þa*, *hraþe* and *þa*' *respectively) without establishing for them independent rights of their own.*[47]

[47] For a recent study of 'the very selective spatial information encoded in Old English discourse', see Waterhouse, 'Spatial Perception and Conceptions', pp. 87–102; the

The intervention of a single adverbial reference to space in the latter temporal series ('Forð near ætstop' (745b)) is intensely dramatic. Spatial relationships internal to narrative time were always deeply significant.[48] But they do not make us, the audience, part of that narrative space ourselves; we are not allotted a particular on-the-spot position to which description is directed.[49] We are separated from the story by a portion of time between its 'then' and our 'now', each with its own 'space'. In the case of a visual artifact, the object in front of the observer was conceived of as having an 'actual' space in the observer's present distinct from the in-time, psychological, 'space' represented on it. This, I believe, accounts for the *Hic*, 'here', combinations of present place and past time, which are typical of captions on the Bayeux Tapestry, such as 'Hic Harold mare navigavit' ('Here Harold sailed on the sea'), and which are regular, in the vernacular form, 'Her . . .', on the pages of the *Anglo-Saxon Chronicle* of *c.* 890 next to the columnar written year numbers, as in the entry, '607 Her Ceolwulf gefeaht wið Suð Seaxe' ('Here Ceolwulf fought against the South Saxons').[50] Indeed, when artists or carvers filled panels or borders with, say, artificially extended interlacing animal bodies, as they often did, the space of the physical object in an observer's 'now' took over entirely from any 'space' rightful to the creatures in the indefinite present to which they representationally belonged. The beholder's act of observation could exert as much psychological pressure on representation as the artist's act of creation. Each was a separate stage in a continuum which was both psychological and temporal. Time itself was inseparable from psychological interpretation of it (as in a painful dawn, a day's journey, a winter and so on) and therefore the successiveness of time was just as inseparable from interpretation. All sequential living was necessarily narrative because it could not be thought about as anything else.

quoted words are at 102. Professor Waterhouse observes (*ibid.*) that 'spatial detail seems subordinated to action and symbolism, rather than encouraging sensory appeal and visualisation in its own right. The non-elaboration of spatiality plays down the signifieds in themselves to focus more upon action and symbolism as they help to build up the thematic message.'

48 See, e.g., my analysis of the developing relationships between boat and sea initiated by 'Fyrst forð gewat; flota wæs on yþum, / bat under beorge' ('Time passed; the floater was on the waves, the boat under the cliff', 210–11a), 'Action in *Beowulf*', pp. 148–52; for a summary, see below, pp. 172–3.

49 Clemoes, 'Action in *Beowulf*', pp. 148 and 150.

50 See my 'Language in Context'; and see, further, below, p. 117.

Structure for this narrative of continuity was frequently derived from the same principle as that responsible for maxims – such as 'Wulf sceal on bearowe'[51] – proclaiming kinships based on potentials for action in certain physical environments: a narrative unit was regularly based on a link between progressive action and physical location. This was the case when, for instance, a thumb-nail consecutive narrative established the function of the look-out who spotted Beowulf and his companions landing in Denmark. He presented himself in terms of firstly where he had been stationed and secondly what he had done there, and, by doing so, associated himself with the primary boundary-relationship between land and sea: 'Hwæt, ic hwile wæs / endesæta, ægwearde heold' ('Lo, I have been on duty at the end of the land for a long time, have kept watch by the sea', 240b–1). And he encapsulated the newcomers in a correspondingly brief progression in the opposite direction as 'feorbuend, mereliðende' ('far-dwellers, seafarers', 254b-5a). But equally often a doer was only one party in an interaction which produced a preponderantly mental environment for what he did, as was the case when Beowulf's answer to the coastguard was announced as a reply to the question just put to him combined with disclosure of his own thoughts as leader:

Him se yldesta   andswarode,
werodes wisa   wordhord onleac

['The oldest answered him, the leader of the troop unlocked his store of words', 258–9].

The two-member interplay which was structural here was psychological. And so was one in the Bayeux Tapestry's depiction of, for example, Harold returning from Normandy: he was portrayed walking with outstretched arms and bowed head towards the pointing finger of the seated King Edward. And likewise, separate, but psychologically related, consecutive actions readily formed linear clusters:

Gewat him þa to waroðe   wicge ridan
þegn Hroðgares,   þrymmum cwehte
mægenwudu mundum,   meþelwordum frægn

['Hrothgar's thegn went riding then on his horse to the shore, brandished his mighty wooden spear forcefully in his hands, asked in formal words', 234–6].

[51] See above, p. 77.

Similarly the inscription on the Bayeux Tapestry, 'Iste nuntiat Haroldum regem de exercitu Wilelmi ducis' ('That man informs King Harold about the army of Duke William'), referred to depiction of a soldier watching the Normans and of (the same?) one reporting to Harold.

The continuity intrinsic to time itself, regarded psychologically, gave narrative its main character. A single course of action might be maintained for a long time. Grendel's conflict with Hrothgar was, for instance:

heteniðas wæg,
fyrene ond fæhðe   fela missera,
singale sæce

['he carried on violent hostilities, crime and feud for many years, continual strife', 152b–4a].

And so was Hrothgar's resultant suffering: 'Swa ða mælceare maga Healfdenes / singala seað' ('So the son of Healfdene continually caused the sorrow of the time to seethe', 189–90a). A line of action, however long, was perceived as continuing until another took its place:

Swa se ðeodsceaða   þreo hund wintra
heold on hrusan   hordærna sum
eacencræftig,   oð ðæt hyne an abealch
mon on mode

['So the injurer of the people watched over a certain treasure-house in the ground, hugely powerful, for three hundred years, until a certain man angered it in its mind', 2278–81a].

Or, again:

Swa he niða gehwane   genesen hæfde,
sliðra geslyhta,   sunu Ecgðiowes,
ellenweorca,   oð ðone anne dæg,
þe he wið þam wyrme   gewegan sceolde

['So he had survived every hostility, dangerous conflict, the son of Ecgtheow, every deed of fighting spirit, until the particular day on which he had to fight against the dragon', 2397–400].

Attention was sharply focused therefore on the junction between one action and a differing one. An actor might well serve to mark this replacement. For example, the mounted coastguard, guiding the newly arrived Beowulf and his companions to Hrothgar's hall, performed this function:

Him þa hildedeor hof modigra
torht getæhte, þæt hie him to mihton
gegnum gangan; guðbeorna sum
wicg gewende, word æfter cwæð:
'Mæl is me to feran; Fæder alwalda
mid arstafum eowic gehealde
siða gesunde! Ic to sæ wille,
wið wrað werod wearde healdan'

['Then the man fierce in battle pointed out the dwelling of proud men, resplendent, so that they could go straight to it; the warrior concerned turned his horse, and then spoke: "It is time for me to go; may the father, ruler of all, with his favours keep you safe on your journeys! I will make for the sea to keep watch against a hostile band"', 312–19].

The coastguard's carefully constructed sequence of pointing out the way ahead, turning his horse, taking his farewell and announcing his return to the shore furnished a clearcut staging post between the arrival of Beowulf and his troop on the coast and their arrival at the hall. Similar signals are given in the Bayeux Tapestry: for instance, Guy, count of Ponthieu, riding ahead of Harold, whom he had captured in his province and was to hand over to his overlord Duke William, turned his body in the saddle on coming face-to-face with William, also mounted, so that he both looked ahead at William and pointed back to Harold; and, again, Vital, a vassal of Odo, bishop of Bayeux, riding full tilt towards William as the duke rode at the head of the Normans advancing from Hastings to engage Harold and his army, pointed back towards the English in the direction from which he was coming. The coastguard, Guy and Vital, each in his way, embodied the dramatically contrastive two-directional movement which was so beloved of visual artists portraying the standard motif of an animal looking backwards against the direction of its moving body.[52]

The term *edwenden* conceptualized the pivotal experience of going into reverse, of passing from one course of events to its opposite, of changing from bad to good or from good to bad (*Beowulf* 2188b, probably 1774b and

[52] The backward-looking dog-like animals on the ninth-century Strickland Brooch in the British Museum are striking examples; see Wilson, *Anglo-Saxon Art*, p. 110 and pl. 115.

perhaps 280a). Hrothgar used the word (1774b) to docket his transition from security to insecurity on Grendel's advent. *The Fortunes of Men* and *The Riming Poem* hinge on the contrast between bad and good or good and bad fortune. In *Deor* five examples of misfortune culled from Germanic tradition support the comparativist, compensatory, refrain, 'þæs ofereode, þisses swa mæg!' ('From that it passed over, so it can from this'[53]), and lead to the realization 'þæt geond þas woruld / witig dryhten wendeþ geneahhe' ('that throughout this world the wise Lord goes his way constantly', 31b–2). In this poem a power outside events actively controls their changes of direction, as, in *Beowulf*, God operates the regular reversals from season to season:

ðonne forstes bend Fæder onlæteð,
onwindeð wælrapas, se geweald hafað
sæla ond mæla; þæt is soð Metod

['when the father loosens the bond of frost, undoes water-fetters, he who has control over times and seasons; that is the true God', 1609–11].[54]

Yet it was the momentum inherent in time itself which imposed overriding consecutiveness on all doers willy-nilly. The coherence of this imperious force, ominous to men, because of its impenetrability, was conceptualized as *wyrd*.[55] Zoomorphic art too represented the flowingness fundamental to all action by prolonging moveable members – jaws, tongues, ears, tails, limb-joints, legs, feet and ribbon-like bodies – into patterns of extended movement, curling, coiling, twining or whatever.[56] One also thinks of the inexorable progression embodied in a chain of coordinate clauses in early sections of the *Anglo-Saxon Chronicle*, such as, '⁊ on his dagum cuomon ærest .iii. scipu, ⁊ þa se gerefa þærto rad, ⁊ hie wolde drifan to þæs cyninges tune þy he nyste hwæt hie wæron; ⁊ hiene mon ofslog' ('And in his days there came for the first time three ships, and then the reeve rode to them and wished to force them to the king's residence for he did not know what they were, and they slew him').[57] Continuity was an

[53] For translating *þæs* and *þysses* as 'from that' and 'from this' respectively (i.e. as genitives of point of time from which) instead of Kemp Malone's 'as regards that' and 'as regards this', see Mitchell, *Old English Syntax*, sects. 1404–5, where it is claimed that there is no convincing evidence that Old English ever had genitives of respect.

[54] For further discussion of *Deor*, see below, pp. 110–11.

[55] See above, p. 10.

[56] See Speake, *Anglo-Saxon Animal Art*, *passim*.

[57] *The Anglo-Saxon Chronicle*, trans. Whitelock *et al.*, s.a. 787 (*recte* 789).

awesome condition from which narrative living was never free, and society felt a fundamental need to keep track of it, as annals, genealogies, regnal lists, the *Menologium* and the like testify in their various ways. The language of poetry, steadily maintaining forward movement through a chain of segments semantically overlapping or linked by mainly temporal connectives, the interweaving patterns of Germanic art and the catenated clauses of the *Chronicle* all alike registered the feeling for it. Native art, verbal or visual, primarily represented organic sequence.

Events, however, were not merely conceived of as an onward rush. Their temporal linearity was tempered by a lateral dimension which they owed to their common derivation from active being. Customary observation appreciated that each action when performed possessed a breadth of inherent analogy with other occurrences of that action, performed by the same actor or by other members of the same kin. This comparability was built into perception of narrative living, and must now be considered.

First, however, for purposes of elimination, it may be helpful to mention a deleterious effect which this connotational spread might, but did not, have: it did not lead to use of vague 'blanket' verbs. We are not told that men just 'used' a ship or a horse or a sword; they 'sailed' it or 'rode' it or 'wielded' it. The generality did not render action itself indistinct, as the range of verbs in *Beowulf* signifying basic actions testifies – for instance, those expressing locomotion on land or sea (*(ge)faran*, *feran*, *gewitan*, *gangan*, *gengan*, *(ge)gan*, *glidan*, *(ge-* or *æt-)steppan*, *wadan*, *liðan*, *scriðan*, *wendan*, *(ge-* or *æt-)windan*, *(æt)hweorfan* and *hwyrfan*, apart from those specifying speed[58]), or those meaning 'to look' (*locian*, *(ofer)seon*, *starian* and *wlitan)*. What it did result in was that distinctions in the action performed were ignored if not of general import. For example, in *Beowulf*, the verb *scufan*, 'to push', was enough in itself to identify satisfactorily both the action of those who launched Beowulf's ship for its voyage to Denmark (215b) and the action of those who heaved the dragon's carcass over the clifftop into the waves below (3131b): if the former pushing entailed poling off from the beach (as Harold's embarkation did in the depiction of this action near the beginning of the Bayeux Tapestry) and the latter involved levering up the fifty-foot-long dead weight, it was immaterial to say so. Psychological distinctions in the doer, if significant, were conveyed by means other than the verb. For example, *folgian*, 'to follow', *gretan*, 'to approach', and *secan*,

[58] Cf. Weman, *Old English Semantic Theory*.

'to seek', did not in themselves distinguish between different intentions in 'following', 'approaching' and 'seeking', and their contexts had to fill this gap, as in 'guðbilla nan gretan nolde' ('no war-sword would attack', 803), or 'mid hearme . . . / . . . grette' ('attacked . . . with harm', 1892–3a), or 'þe mec guðwinum gretan dorste' ('who dared attack me with his allies', 2735).

How near this generalized conception of action was to the forefront of observation is illustrated by ready invention of a single doer to represent multiple doers of a shared action – for instance, 'heold hyne syðþan / fyr ond fæstor se þæm feonde ætwand' ('from then on he kept himself further away and more secure who escaped from the enemy', 142b–3), when many did[59] – or, conversely, of a single action to represent that of many doers: when the Danes, sleeping in their hall, were surprised by Grendel's mother seeking revenge,

Ða wæs on healle heardecg togen
sweord ofer setlum, sidrand manig
hafen handa fæst; helm ne gemunde,
byrnan side, þa hine se broga angeat

['The hard-edged sword was drawn in the hall above the seats, many a broad shield raised firm in the hand; no one thought of the helmet, the spacious corslet, when the terror seized him', 1288–91].

More significantly, spontaneity was invariably represented by action typical of the kinship to which the doer(s) belonged. Horses, for example, acted in their natural way when allowed: 'hleapan leton, / on geflit faran fealwe mearas' ('they let bay horses leap, gallop in competition', 864b–5). So did swords: 'Let . . . / bradne mecne . . . / . . . entiscne helm / brecan ofer bordweall' ('He let the broad sword break the helmet made by giants over the protecting shield', 2977–80a). Likewise thoughts: 'læteð hworfan / monnes modgeþonc' ('he lets the man's thoughts turn', 1728b–9a). And spoken words: 'Let ða of breostum . . . / . . . word ut faran' ('Then he let words issue from his breast', 2550–1). Action typical of armour represented the life which was put to an end when it was buried:

ge swylce seo herepad, sio æt hilde gebad
ofer borda gebræc bite irena,

[59] Cf. 907–13a, 1460b–3a and 2860–1, and for discussion of the connotational range of the binary linkage conventionally expressed in a *se þe* . . . form, see above, pp. 84–5.

brosnað æfter beorne. Ne mæg byrnan hring
æfter wigfruman wide feran,
hæleðum be healfe

['likewise the war-garment, which has endured the bite of iron blades in battle above the crashing of shields, decays after the warrior. The ring[60] of the corslet cannot travel widely with the war-chief, by the side of heroes', 2258–62a].

The deep-set function of comparison is exemplified by Hrothgar's conception of his hall, Heorot: relativity was explicit from the start. This king aspired to make it greater 'þonne yldo bearn æfre gefrunon' ('than sons of men had ever learned of', 70). According to the narrator, and likewise to Beowulf and Hrothgar himself, the ambition was fulfilled: this was 'healærna mæst' ('greatest of hall-buildings', 78a), 'husa selest' ('best of houses', 146a, (Beowulf) 285b, (Hrothgar) 658b and (Hrothgar) 935a) and 'reced selesta' ('the finest hall', (Beowulf) 412a); to Beowulf and his companions on first catching sight of it, 'þæt wæs foremærost foldbuendum / receda under roderum' ('that was to dwellers on earth the most illustrious of halls under the sky', 309–10a). The claim was not that this building was essentially different from others. It performed as a *medo-* and *winærn*, 'mead- and winehall' (69a and 654a), a *gif-* and *medoheal(l)*, 'gift- and meadhall' (3×),[61] a *winreced*, 'winehall' (714b and 993b), and a *beah-*, *beor-*, *dryht-*, *gest-*, *gold-*, *guð-*, *hring-* and *winsele*, 'ring-, beer-, retainer-, guest-, gold-, battle-, ring- and winehall',[62] just as Finn's hall and Beowulf's own hall, when he was king, each operated as a *beorsele* (1094a and 2635a), and just as the hall, left empty by a young man who had been hanged, grieved his father intensely because it no longer acted as his son's *winsele* (2456a). Heorot achieved its purpose as typically as the *beorsele* in *The Rune Poem*'s general evocation of hall-life, 'ðar wigan sittaþ / on beorsele bliþe ætsomne' ('where warriors sit in the beerhall happy together', 39b–40), or as the *meoduheall* in *The Gifts of Men*'s exemplification of a thegn, 'Sum bið þegn gehweorf / on meoduhealle' ('One is the (?)active thegn in the meadhall', 68b–9a). From beginning to end its excellence lay in surpassing all others at being a typical member of its class.

As a consequence of this pervasive sense of analogy a likeness could

[60] For this translation, see the commentary by Brady, '"Weapons" in *Beowulf*', p. 112.

[61] 484a, 638a and 838a.

[62] 443a, 482a, 485a, 492a, 695a, 715a, 767a, 771b, 994a, 1177a, 1253a, 1639a, 2010a and 2083a.

remain implicit as long as a normal possession of the same inherent potential by the beings concerned was by common consent enough to account for it. It needed to be expressed openly only when it was exceptional in degree or kind. No more than four involving kind were stated in *Beowulf*, all employing the copulative *gelicost*, 'very like' (218b, 727a, 985b and 1608b). Probably it was specifically because a likeness between fire and eyes, presumably of burning, was thought unnatural in itself that in Grendel's case the comparison was drawn as a sign of his unnaturalness at the moment when he was stepping on to the hall floor covered with sleeping men: 'him of eagum stod / ligge gelicost leoht unfæger' ('a horrible light very like a flame shone from his eyes', 726b–7). And at 985 there was a one-off comparison between Grendel's fingernails and steel and at 1608 another between a melting sword-blade and ice.

At 218b perhaps the bird-likeness in the description of Beowulf's ship scudding across the sea to Denmark on its *wilsið*, 'willingly undertaken journey' (216a),

Gewat þa ofer wægholm   winde gefysed
flota famiheals   fugle gelicost

['then the foamy-necked floater, driven by the wind, went over the sea of waves very like a bird', *Beowulf* 217–18],

was made explicit because without that particularity the neck analogy in itself was not specific enough to the foamy wind-driven skimming of a shallow-draught sailing vessel running before the wind. This poet used either *-heals* or *-stefna* compounds eight times in all to signify prowed ships, two of the former type accounting for three of these occasions (*famigheals* (2×) and *wundenheals* (1×)) and three of the latter type for the other five times (*bundenstefna* (1×), *hringedstefna* (3×) and *wundenstefna* (1×)), and all these formations being unique to this poem except for *famigheals*, which occurs once elsewhere, in *Andreas*. The *-heals* sort the *Beowulf* poet seems to have associated exclusively with free movement across the sea (218a, 298a and 1909a),[63] but the *-stefna* kind with either that movement (*wundenstefna* 220a and *bundenstefna* 1910a) or stoppage (*hringedstefna* denotes a boat moored or beached at 32b, 1131a and 1897a[64]). Of the two *-heals*

63 This is true also at *Andreas* 497a.

64 Does *hringed-* refer to a ring for attachment of mooring ropes? One of the ships which the Bayeux Tapestry shows prepared for Duke William's fleet has a hole for a painter in its stem post.

compounds, the *wunden-* one, 'curved-necked', signifies a ship bearing a load across sea-currents (probably smoothly) at 298a, but the context of *famigheals* is wind-driven floating over waves at both 218a and 1909a.[65] Evidently foam was the natural concomitant specifically of wind-impelled, rapid skimming over waves in this poet's mind.[66] As to the neck, *-heals*, foamy or curved, an animal- or beast-headed prow would seem to be its most likely association – there are several depicted in the Bayeux Tapestry – but an animal or beast in general would not have provided the specific suggestion of wind-driven skimming which, we know, the poet saw in 'foamy'. To introduce that connotation into his first element perhaps he envisaged Beowulf's ship precisely as bird-headed, for then his image would have been unified at least to the extent that birds with a wind behind them are foamy-necked when they alight on the sea.[67] Discrimination of this order would have been entirely characteristic of him, but might well have needed the explicit 'very like a bird' to make it evident to others on the first occasion, at 218, but not when the same ship was described again under the same conditions at 1909.[68] In my opinion 218b calls for some such explanation as this to match the special reasons which can be readily adduced for the other three *gelicost* comparisons.

Under normal conditions implicit affinity between actors was free to trigger the substitution which we call metaphor: one doer could replace another if it was common knowledge that the action concerned sprang from an inherent capability which both shared. Action-for-action substitution, on the other hand, was ruled out because that would have abolished the very signal of sameness on which metaphor depended. Whereas we can feel

[65] At *Andreas* 497a the association is with a gliding motion (*glideð* 498a) maintained in spite of surging water (495b–6a).

[66] Wind does not seem to have played the same part in the *Andreas* poet's imagination. In the only other occurrence of a *famig-* compound, at *Exodus* 494a, *famigbosma*, 'foamy-bosomed', apparently referring to the walls of water falling on to Pharoah's host, exemplifies that poet's unusual, often eccentric, imagination.

[67] Actual bird-headed boats could have led the artists of the Carolingian Utrecht Psalter to include three in their illustrations of the text. (The ships concerned are the two going on the great and wide sea of ps. CIV.25–6 on 59v and, most notably, one of the two ships of Tarshish shown on 27v being blown across the sea by personifications of the winds in accordance with ps. XLVIII.7.)

[68] The *Andreas* poet, without such refinement, would seem to have picked up the collocation 'famigheals, fugole gelicost' as a whole from somewhere (some would say from *Beowulf* itself).

relatively confident that *heals*, 'neck', when applied to a (foamy or curved) prow, was an authentic actor-for-actor metaphor, we must be on our guard against considering that there is metaphor when Anglo-Saxons themselves were merely denoting an action which they regarded straightforwardly as natural to the doer in the doer's own right – for example, when a sword bit, or fire swallowed. For instance, we can be reasonably certain that the *Beowulf* poet used the verb *bewindan* free of actor-for-actor metaphor when it expressed the act of encirclement of hands grasping a sword (1457–61) or spear (3021b–2), of silver wire inlays spiralling round the iron crest of a helmet (1030–1),[69] of a man's body enclosing his *feorh*, 'life' (2424), of human grief enveloping the roaring fire of a funeral pyre (3143–6a) and of a magical spell governing a hoard (3051–2). Each of these agents, regardless of their differences, possessed the principle of active containment which showed itself in this encircling movement, and we may infer that language was simply directed to recognizing this primary testimony.

Metaphorical substitution of actor for actor was engaged in to enhance vernacular poetry's preoccupation with perceiving like actions as signs of kinship, as is exemplified by the substitution of 'feower wellan' ('four springs') for the teats of a mother ox suckling her young in *Riddle* 38 (3b) in the collection of poems in the Exeter Book, a manuscript of the second half of the tenth century.[70] This image had occurred before as 'four fountains' in Aldhelm's Latin *enigma* on the same subject and again as 'twice two streams proceeding from one source' in a Latin *enigma*, also on the same subject, by another Anglo-Saxon, Eusebius,[71] but the Old English riddler was the only poet of the three to express the gushing of the springs distinctly; in his poem the mother '. . . forlet / . . . feower wellan / scire sceotan' ('let . . . four springs shoot brightly', 2b–4a), whereas Aldhelm did not use any verb at all and Eusebius's verb (*progredientes*) is only vaguely general. Evidently the vernacular poet's imagination focused sharply on the action common to teat and spring and his medium expressed that appreciation graphically. Native vision, verb and adverb, acting together, gave to this natural borrowed metaphor the same freshness as that

[69] See Bruce-Mitford, 'A Note on the Word *wala* in *Beowulf*', in his *Aspects of Anglo-Saxon Archaeology*, pp. 210–13.

[70] For a complete facsimile of this manuscript, see *The Exeter Book of Old English Poetry*, ed. Cambers, Förster and Flower.

[71] For a text, translation and further discussion of these three riddles, see below, pp. 103–5.

which, for instance, indigenous imagination imparted to a numerical correspondence when a ship's four oars moving in the water[72] were called 'feowere fet under wombe' ('four feet below the belly') in another riddle (*Riddle* 36, 3).[73]

Another commonly practised imaginative process similar to that of metaphor was transference of an active capability from one actor possessing it naturally to another who/which could absorb it artificially, as when, in *Riddle* 63 beginning 'Oft ic . . .' ('Often I . . .'), an inanimate object, a glass beaker, employed the distinctively human attribute of speech. Since the result – in this case a talking beaker – was a combination of a receiving actor and a received potential, a hybrid was created, and accordingly I call this process 'hybridization'. Fundamentally it was an exercise in the same spirit of human understanding for the other-than-human as we find when a sword which was valued as a tried and trusted partner in danger, was assigned its own name and fame. That Hrunting, the sword which Unferth lent to Beowulf, failed to penetrate the head of Grendel's mother, was a matter to be noted in its own right, even at the height of a fight: 'ða wæs forma sið / deorum madme, þæt his dom alæg' ('that was the first occasion for the precious treasure that its reputation failed', *Beowulf* 1527b–8). The most intimate possible sign of this regard, however, from a human point of view, was to endow an artifact with the power to speak for itself, and the most direct response an artifact could make was to testify to its place in human society. Thus the prose legend on the Alfred jewel, '✠ AELFRED MEC HEHT GEWYRCAN' ('Alfred ordered me to be made'), enabled this beautifully crafted object to proclaim the social prestige which it owed to its august originating patron.

When a non-human acquired the 'voice' of a poetic first-person narrator and thereby described its way of living, it commanded a much wider range of expression. As an anomalous being it could puzzle its audience about its identity, for instance: 'Saga hwæt ic hatte' ('Say what I am called'), or something like it, was the oft-repeated challenge.[74] Or it could tease by, for example, employing metaphor in its account of itself, as this (in fact, inanimate) speaker does in robust fashion to give a misleading impression

[72] According to the most likely interpretation; see below, p. 185.

[73] For a commentary on the 'four feet' and the other elements in the intriguing *mélange* of which they were part, see *The Old English Riddles of the 'Exeter Book'*, ed. Williamson, pp. 251–2 (his riddle 34).

[74] See further, below, p. 184.

that it is a tailed animal when it describes the elemental contest which makes its life representative:[75]

> Oft ic sceal wiþ wæge winnan   ond wiþ winde feohtan,
> somod wið þam sæcce,   þonne ic secan gewite
> eorþan yþum þeaht;   me biþ se eþel fremde.
> Ic beom strong þæs gewinnes,   gif ic stille weorþe;
> gif me þæs tosæleð,   hi beoð swiþran þonne ic,
> ond mec slitende   sona flymað,
> willað oþfergan   þæt ic friþian sceal.
> Ic him þæt forstonde,   gif min steort þolað
> ond mec stiþne wiþ   stanas moton
> fæste gehabban.   Frige hwæt ic hatte

['Often I have to contend with the wave and fight with the wind, strive against them together, when I seek the earth covered with waves; that land is foreign to me. I am strong in the fight if I become still; if I fail in that, they are stronger than I, and tearing me soon put me to flight; they want to carry off what I must protect. I prevent them if my tail endures and stones can hold me fast, keep me firm. Ask what I am called', *Riddle* 16].

A talent for intriguing humankind with paradox and metaphor has brought an anchor out into the open to call attention to the hidden life of struggle its kind leads at the bottom of the sea.

Granting speech to a being which did not possess it naturally was, however, an example of only one kind of hybridization – that in which an additional potential was grafted on to a being who/which otherwise remained the same. There was another kind, in which the addition was grafted on to a being who/which was substituted for another metaphorically, as when a sword was termed *hilde-* or *beadoleoma*, 'a battle flame' (only at *Beowulf* 1143b and 1523a respectively). In this instance flame replaced sword by straightforward metaphor, because both can flash, but, by virtue of the first element, *hilde-* or *beado-*, flame was explicitly assigned the environment of battle natural to the sword.[76] Or, again, when a ship was

[75] Symphosius's Latin 'Ancora' riddle, the Old English poet's source, did not give the anchor a tail; see the commentary, *The Old English Riddles of the 'Exeter Book'*, ed. Williamson, p. 178 (his riddle 14).

[76] A compound, *gunnlogi*, denoting a sword like *hilde-* and *beadoleoma*, occurs fairly frequently in Old Norse poetry (and thence in prose), even as a proper name for particular swords. A much closer parallel, however, is *gunnljómi*, which occurs in the verses in *Eyrbyggja saga*; cf., further, Sveinbjorn Egilsson, *Lexicon Poeticum*, s.v. I am grateful to

termed *yðmearh*, 'a wave horse' (*Christ (II)* 863a and *The Whale* 49a), in addition to the metaphorical substitution of horse for ship, straightforward because both can carry men on them with a riding motion, the horse's natural land environment was explicitly replaced by that of the sea natural to a ship.[77] Each of these transformations resulted in a hybrid representing a measured increase in the normal range of an implied underlying maxim – in the first an extension of 'a sword belongs in battle'[78] into a supposed 'a flame, which is like a sword, belongs in battle'. A melting sword-blade, on the other hand, was too specialized a concept for a maxim, 'a melting sword-blade belongs in battle', to be supposed as an underlying starting-point for the hybrid, *hildegicelas*, when the blade of a sword which Beowulf was holding in the monsters' underwater home began to dissolve *hildegicelum*, 'into battle icicles' (*Beowulf* 1605b–7a), and an explanation was called for: 'þæt wæs wundra sum, / þæt hit eal gemealt ise gelicost' ('it was a particular marvel that it all melted very like ice', 1607b–8).[79] Narrative analogy – one being acting like another – was society's traditional basis not only for classifying the foundations of narrative living in all its variety but also for exploring them, and poetry consolidated and enriched both these enterprises by providing metaphors, hybrids and combinations of the two in prestigious language.

Hybrid beings were common in eighth- and ninth-century Anglo-Saxon visual art too. As in poetry, amalgamations cut across 'normal' distinctions between discrete doers, but, whereas in the verbal medium an actor was augmented with a potential – such as power of speech – which did not belong naturally to him/her/it, or underwent change when being substituted metaphorically for another actor, in the visual version active members of usually discrete actors were combined. The plant-scroll of Mediterranean origin, inhabited by separate birds, animals, monsters or men eating or picking its fruit, in Anglo-Saxon imagination sometimes became merged with the creatures within its coils, so that perhaps only a

Andy Orchard for pointing this out to me. At *Beowulf* 2583a *hildeleoman*, signifying the dragon's fire, are actual battle flames; presumably the compound was taken over for this relatively unusual use from its more common metaphorical-cum-hybrid application.

77 Cf. some creatures' ability to move, or be transformed, from one element to another as one of the principal types of 'mystery' which Aldhelm introduced into the 'riddle' genre (e.g., the aquatic salamander (*Enigma* XV) which can also inhabit fire, and salt (XIX) which, once (sea)water, can both undergo fire and become earth); see *Aldhelm: the Poetic Works*, trans. Lapidge and Rosier, pp. 63–4.

78 Cf. above, pp. 94–5.

79 See above, pp. 77–8.

head of the once separate creature remained and all the rest of it became plant; and from about the late eighth century some animals or birds not in vine-scrolls were given vegetal tails or bodies.[80] At much the same time, in the Anglo-Saxon carving on the ends of the walrus-ivory Gondersheim (or Brunswick) Casket, long curling tails of dragon- and lizard-like bipeds, intricately enmeshed in plant-branches, were depicted indistinguishable from the intertwining branches: tails and branches interweave alike in unified, symmetrical patterns, which, as a hybrid of the two, seem to proclaim that beasts and plants belong to a single order of being;[81] and the same union seems to be conveyed in the ninth century on, for instance, the lower guard of the Abingdon sword in the Ashmolean Museum, Oxford, by the fusion of animal- and plant-life in the long-bodied quadruped enmeshed in its long foliate tail which passes through its neck[82] – and much later too, for that matter, in the late eleventh century, by the balanced animal and plant components of a free-standing feline with a tail ending in an acanthus leaf, together making up the loop of a buckle, which was found in Leicester and illustrates the persistence of pre-Conquest features into Romanesque times.[83]

Creation of hybrid beings, part man, bird, animal or beast and part plant, was undoubtedly widespread in these visual terms, but was this by augmentation of an otherwise unchanged actor or did it involve substitution of the sort which in the verbal medium I have called metaphorical? I think the latter. For example, an animal actor, which was partly replaced by a portion of a plant actor – a curling (or coiling) tendril instead of a curling (or coiling) tail, for instance – could be validated by supposing an acceptable extension of a maxim, 'a tail belongs on an animal' into 'a tendril, which is like a tail, belongs on an animal'. However this may be, what can be accepted, surely, is that hybridization would not have been such a characteristic practice in two such different main art forms, the verbal and the visual, unless they both reflected the same fundamental mode of thinking about non-human nature.[84] Broadly the same relative

80 Wilson, *Anglo-Saxon Art*, p. 64.

81 Beckwith, *Ivory Carvings*, pls. 11–12, and Wilson, *Anglo-Saxon Art*, ills. 58–9.

82 Hinton, *A Catalogue of the Anglo-Saxon Ornamental Metalwork*, pl. 1(*d*), panel 26.

83 *The Golden Age of Anglo-Saxon Art*, ed. Backhouse, Turner and Webster, ill. on p. 207.

84 Leigh makes a similar observation concerning ambiguities in the earlier Anglo-Saxon and north Germanic art represented by square-headed brooches of the sort produced in Kent during the last years of the fifth century and well into the first half of the sixth,

chronology may apply to the process in both media too, for, while man- or bird- or animal- or beast-plant amalgamations became common visually only in the course of the eighth century, the linguistic 'sea horse' for 'ship' hybrids do not occur in *Beowulf* but are plentiful in, for instance, Cynewulf's probably ninth-century poems.

Anglo-Saxons had a keen appreciation of any incongruity in the connections of innate potential with being, kinship, inheritance and environment and in the influence of these factors on analogy-bearing narrative living. For instance, much satisfaction was taken in noting disparate or contrasting potentials in a single being. A vernacular riddle (no. 14) dwelt on the concentration of diverse functions in a horn, now in warfare, now as treasure, now for drinking. Aldhelm, around the year 700 (himself no mean poet in the vernacular[85]), was impressed, apparently at first hand, by a bivalve mollusc, *Pinna nobilis*, providing both food and clothing:

> E geminis nascor per ponti caerula concis
> Vellera setigero producens corpore fulva;
> En clamidem pepli necnon et pabula pulpae
> Confero: sic duplex fati persolvo tributum

['I am born in the blue waters of the sea from twin shells, producing tawny fleeces from my spiky body. Notice that I provide the wool of cloaks as well as food from my flesh: thus in two ways I pay my debt to fate', *Enigma* XVII].[86]

And he was impressed too, again apparently on his own experience, by hornets producing food that tasted so sweet to their kind and yet so nasty to humans:

whereby an animal's head and ears when turned through a right-angle appear to be a human profile mask, or whereby the eyes and nostrils of a full-face animal-head mask are converted into the nostrils and eyes respectively of a human mask when turned upside down ('Ambiguity in Anglo-Saxon Style I Art'). He refers to the kinship these phenomena have to Old English 'metaphors, kennings and riddles' and also to their possible relationships to religious and/or protective beliefs and practices. I am grateful to Rosemary Cramp for drawing my attention to this article and to David Hinton for much help and advice.

85 See above, p. 35 and n. 87.

86 My quotations of Aldhelm's *Enigmata* are from *Aldhelmi Opera*, ed. Ehwald, pp. 97–149, and my translations are those of Lapidge (*Aldhelm: the Poetic Works*, trans. Lapidge and Rosier, pp. 70–94 and 247–55). For the interpretation of *Enigma* XVII, see Cameron, 'Aldhelm as Naturalist', pp. 119–20.

Dulcia conficiens propriis alimenta catervis,
Et tamen humanis horrent haec pabula buccis

['[We amass] sweet food for our own throngs – and yet these comestibles are rebarbative to human taste', *Enigma* LXXV, 4–5].[87]

Paradox was particularly relished. That an anchor should win a fight by remaining still was an observation which the Old English riddler did not owe to Symphosius's 'Ancora' riddle.[88] Pliny's and Isidore's unsubstantiated claim that squids have flown out of the sea in such numbers that they can sink ships Aldhelm turned into a sober paradox, based probably on personal observation:

Cum volucrum turma quoque scando per aethera pennis
Et tamen aethereo non possum vivere flatu

['With flocks of feathery birds I likewise climb through the air; nevertheless, I cannot live by breathing air', *Enigma* XVI, 3–4].[89]

On another occasion Aldhelm spotted for himself the paradox in a pond-skater walking dry-foot on the surface of quiet waters:

Pergo super latices plantis suffulta quaternis
Nec tamen in limphas vereor quod mergar aquosas,
Sed pariter terras et flumina calco pedestris;
Nec natura sinit celerem natare per amnem,
Pontibus aut ratibus fluvios transire feroces;
Quin potius pedibus gradior super nequora siccis

['I walk on the waters borne up by my four feet, yet I do not fear that I shall drown in the watery main. Rather, I tread on foot equally on land and sea. Nature does not allow me to swim in the fast-moving beck nor to cross turbulent streams by bridge or by boat; instead, I walk with dry feet over still waters', *Enigma* XXXVIII].[90]

The three Englishmen, Aldhelm in his Latin *Enigma*, 'Iuvencus', Eusebius in his, 'De vitulo', and the anonymous author of the vernacular *Riddle* 38, already cited,[91] were all attracted to the paradox that one and the same animal should when alive (as a plough animal) break the soil and

87 For the interpretation, see *ibid.*, pp. 127–8.
88 See above, p. 99, and n. 75.
89 See Cameron, 'Aldhelm as Naturalist', p. 119.
90 See *ibid.*, pp. 121–2.
91 Above, pp. 97–8

when dead (as leather thongs) bind men, and each of them produced a version in his own way.

Probably the earliest of them, Aldhelm, using the most fundamental binary time-frame of all, that of living and then dying, created a powerful impression of an animal which when alive exerts massive strength to break up but, remarkably, when dead retains strength to bind:

Arida spumosis dissolvens faucibus ora
Bis binis bibulus potum de fontibus hausi.
Vivens sam terrae glebas cum stirpibus imis
Nisu virtutis validae disrumpo feraces;
At vero linquit dum spiritus algida membra,
Nexibus horrendis homines constringere possum

['Easing my parched mouth with foaming jaws, I thirstily drank up liquid from four fountains. While alive I break up the fertile sods of earth with its deep roots through the efforts of my mighty strength. But when the breath leaves my cold limbs, I am able to bind men with fearsome fetters', *Enigma* LXXXIII].

Aldhelm's steer, breaking roots deep in the earth through its natural strength in a generalized present (*disrumpo*) and recalling its vigorous sucking in its infancy (*hausi*), knew that, against all the odds, it would be able to impose force even after it had ceased to breathe. It was being treated as a primary type in the Anglo-Saxon world of active potentials.

Eusebius's time sequence consisted of birth, an indefinite present of suckling and a future of either living or dying:

Post genetrix me quam peperit mea, sepe solesco
Inter ab uno fonte rivos bis bibere binos
Progredientes; et si vixero, rumpere colles
Incipiam; vivos moriens aut alligo multos

['After my mother has borne me, I often become accustomed to drink among twice two streams proceeding from one source; and if I live I shall begin to break up hills; or dying I bind many living men', *Aenigma* XXXVII].[92]

With living and dying reduced to mere alternatives, the antithesis between breaking (*rumpere*) and binding (*alligo*) becomes more prominent and, with it, most prominently of all, the paradox of one dead binding many living compactly pointed up by 'vivos moriens'.

The vernacular riddler's treatment was different again in both technique

[92] For the text, see *Collectiones aenigmatum*, ed. Glorie I, 247.

and content. It presented an unnamed being within a dramatic situation: a first-person speaker had watched this being greedily sucking its mother's teats and had heard someone make a penetrating observation about the alternative courses of action that opened up before it:

> Ic þa wiht geseah   wæpnedcynnes,
> geoguðmyrþe grædig;   him on gafol forlet
> ferðfriþende   feower wellan
> scire sceotan,   on gesceap þeotan.
> Mon maþelade,   se þe me gesægde:
> 'Seo wiht, gif hio gedygeð,   duna briceð;
> gif he tobirsteð,   bindeð cwice'

['I saw the being of a weaponed kind, greedy for the pleasure of youth;[93] the life-sustaining one let four fountains shoot brightly as tribute to it, murmur to its delight. Someone spoke, who said to me: "That being, if it survives, will break up hills; if it bursts apart, will bind the living"' (*Riddle* 38)].

The presentation of living and dying as alternatives corresponded to Eusebius's but was turned into an antithesis between an endurance (*gedygeð*) which breaks other beings (*briceð*) and a bursting of oneself (*tobirsteð*) which (paradoxically) binds (*bindeð*) others. When alive this being had a fundamental potential to break others if it did not itself break up in the process. It was analogous to Beowulf grappling with Grendel.[94] When dead it paradoxically had the ability to bind together. It was a lesson in the quirkiness to which a systematic relationship between potential and performance could be subject.

Contradiction was, in fact, an inherent principle in the constitution of active beings. For instance, even while Heorot, King Hrothgar's timber hall, towered high and wide-gabled, it awaited the battle-surgings of fire (81b–3a): alongside its potential to house Hrothgar's treasure-giving (71–3) it embodied the same propensity to burn as that which the prose writer Ælfric perceived in a stick of wood when he wrote, 'nimm ænne sticcan. ⁊ gnid to sumum ðince. hit hatað þærrihte of ðam fyre þe him on lutað' ('take a stick and rub it on something: it gets hot straightaway from

[93] I follow ASPR *geoguðmyrþe* for MS *geoguð myrwe*, an emendation originating with Holthausen in 1907, but see Eric Stanley's warning that the rareness of the *myrgð* group before late West Saxon does not favour it (Stanley, 'Studies in the Prosaic Vocabulary of Old English Verse', pp. 410–11).

[94] *Beowulf* 745b–53a, 758–65a and 809–18a.

the fire which lurks within it').[95] And conflict between beings was equally prevalent. It was a regular part of the operation of the sun, overcoming (*oferswiðan*) the light of the stars and moon at dawn and driving away (*todrifan*) the cold of winter in the spring, as Ælfric put it in his *De temporibus anni*.[96] In *Riddle* 29 the moon was regarded as a plundering warrior and the sun as an avenger:

Ic wiht geseah wundorlice
hornum bitweonum huþe lædan,
lyftfæt leohtlic, listum gegierwed,
huþe to þam ham of þam heresiþe;
walde hyre on þære byrig bur atimbran,
searwum asettan, gif hit swa meahte.
Ða cwom wundorlicu wiht ofer wealles hrof,
seo is eallum cuð eorðbuendum,
ahredde þa þa huþe ond to ham bedraf
wreccan ofer willan, gewat hyre west þonan
fæhþum feran, forð onette

['I saw a remarkable creature carry booty between its horns, a shining air-vessel, skilfully prepared, booty home from the raid; it wanted to build a chamber in the dwelling, set it up with art, if that could be so. Then a marvellous creature, which is known to all inhabitants of the earth, came over the top of the wall, recaptured the booty and drove home the exile against its will – it journeyed west from there with hostility, hurried onward', 1–11].

A thunderstorm revealed the warring forces of nature in all their might: when the sky is filled with heat above and moisture lower down, Ælfric explained (following Bede), 'þonne winnað hi him betwynan mid egeslicum swege' ('then they fight one another with a terrible noise').[97] The consequences for the earth below could be dire: the sudden storm vividly described in Aldhelm's *Carmen rhythmicum* attacked the earth (*grassari*) with a deluge of hailstones, while the winds invaded the shore (*irruere*) and the sea pounded the coast (*pulsare*), with victory on its side (*suffragante victoria*).[98] The thread of violence, inward or outward, running throughout

95 *Ælfric's 'De temporibus anni'*, ed. Henel, p. 74; no source is known.

96 *Ibid.*, pp. 14 and 38; no source is known at either point.

97 *Ibid.*, p. 82; for Bede's words, see p. 83.

98 *Aldhelmi Opera*, ed. Ehwald, pp. 525, line 52, and 526, lines 101, 109 and 110. Cf. opposition between the elements as a recurring theme in Aldhelm's *Enigmata*; see *Aldhelm: the Poetic Works*, trans. Lapidge and Rosier, p. 64.

nature was standardized in Germanic animal art as the persistent motif of a beast biting itself or another.

Powerful sympathies, as well as rivalries, were perceived at work in nature. The moon's relationship to life is a notable example. When Ælfric, single-minded Christian that he was, roundly condemned heathen pagan practices as diabolical *wiglunga*, 'sorceries', in particular he corrected common misconceptions of the moon's rôle which they perpetuated.[99] But he was far from dismissing the whole business of the moon's influence; it was integral, in his view, to an all-embracing cycle: 'Hit is gecyndelic', he explained (following Bede and in turn himself followed by Byrhtferth[100]) 'þæt ealle eorðlice lichaman. beoð fulran on weaxendum monan. þonne on wanigendum' ('It is natural that all earthly bodies are fuller when the moon is waxing than when it is waning').[101] Full moon, Ælfric agreed, was the time to cut down trees for timber.[102] Particularly striking was the intimate relationship between sea and moon: 'Seo sæ ⁊ se mona geðwærlæcað him betweonan. æfre hi beoð geferan on wæstme. ⁊ on wanunge' ('The sea and the moon agree between them; they are always companions in growth and in decrease').[103]

Nature as a system depended on fecund collaboration of matching potentials. It was in these terms that King Alfred clothed Boethius's statement, 'dat cuique natura, quod convenit, et ne, dum manere possunt, intereant, elaborat' ('nature gives to each [plant and tree] what suits it, and as long as they can remain toils to prevent them dying'):[104] 'ælces landes gecynd is þæt hit him gelica wyrta ⁊ gelicne wudu tydre, ⁊ hit swa deð. Friðað ⁊ fyrðrað swiðe georne, swa lange swa hiora gecynd bið ꝥ hi growan moton' ('the nature of each land is that it engenders plants similar to it and wood like it, and it does so. It protects and helps them on very carefully as long as it is their nature that they may grow').[105]

99 See, e.g., Ælfric, *CH* I.vi (ed. Thorpe I, 100, lines 19–27, and 102, lines 10–19), and *De temporibus anni*, ed. Henel, p. 60.

100 See *De temporibus anni*, ed. Henel, p. 65.

101 *Ibid.*, p. 64, and cf. Ælfric, *CH* I.vi (ed. Thorpe I, 102, lines 20–2).

102 *De temporibus anni*, ed. Henel, p. 64, and Ælfric, *CH* I.vi (ed. Thorpe I, 102, lines 22–6).

103 *De temporibus anni*, ed. Henel, p. 66, and cf. Ælfric, *CH* I.vi (ed. Thorpe I, 102, lines 26–30).

104 Bk III, pr. xi.

105 *King Alfred's Version of Boethius 'De consolatione Philosophiae'*, ed. Sedgefield, p. 91, lines 22–5. Boethius had already stated that each plant and tree grows only in its natural habitat but had not explained what the naturalness consists of; see above, p. 77.

Man's agriculture and stock farming were designed to exploit this system. His ritual was aimed at harnessing it or interfering with it according to motive. For instance, the *Æcerbot* charm,[106] on three leaves in London, British Library, Cotton Caligula A. vii, written in the first half of the eleventh century, was introduced as 'seo bot, hu ðu meaht þine æceras betan gif hi nellaþ wel wexan oþþe þær hwilc ungedefe þing on gedon bið on dry oððe on lyblace' ('the remedy by which you can improve your fields if they will not yield well or where anything harmful has been done to them in sorcery or witchcraft', 1–3), and what followed was intended to restore the fertility system. Four sods were to be cut before dawn, one from each side of the land, and were to be replaced before sunset, the farmer being instructed to treat them meanwhile thus:

Nim þonne ele and hunig and beorman, and ælces feos meolc þe on þæm lande sy, and ælces treowcynnes dæl þe on þæm lande sy gewexen, butan heardan beaman, and ælcre namcuþre wyrte dæl, butan glappan anon, and do þonne haligwæter ðær on, and drype þonne þriwa on þone staðol þara turfa, and cweþe ðonne ðas word: Crescite, wexe, et multiplicamini, and gemænigfealda, et replete, and gefylle, terre, þas eorðan

['Then take oil and honey and yeast and milk of every cattle which is on the land and part of every kind of tree which is grown on the land, except a hard tree, and part of every well-known plant, except only *glappe*, and then pour the holy water on them, and then drip three times on the bottom of the sods, and then say these words, "Grow and multiply and fill this earth"', 5–12].

The ritual was meant to return fertility to the land from the animals and vegetation which had fed on it.

Active analogy between being and being could be induced by the one imitating the characteristic action(s) of the other, as a further ceremony in the same charm shows. The farmer was enjoined, after uttering a (Christianized) petition to the sun (26–38), facing east before sundown, 'Wende þe þonne III sunganges, astrece þonne on andlang and arim þær letanias' ('Then turn three times moving with the sun, then stretch yourself along the ground and say there the litany', 39–40). Turning about in the same direction as the sun seems clearly to have been designed to transfer the sun's fructifying power to the farmer – or at least to transmit it through

106 Cited here from ASPR 6.

him – and prostration to pass it on from him to the ground (on another communicative principle, that of contiguity).[107] Imitation of the sun's movement was apparently the Anglo-Saxons' way of creating a sunshine-conductor.

Ritualistic control over the analogic system could be exerted through linguistic or non-linguistic means or through a combination of both as in the recitation of the incantation just cited.[108] The function of language was by no means confined to docketing and exploring the elements of active being and the processes of narrative living; it had an extensive and complex part to play in mastering them as well. For one thing, it could set up powerful analogies of its own, as when the words 'Crescite, multiplicamini et replete terram', prescribed in the *Æcerbot* charm, echoed God's blessing of his creations in Genesis I.22 (sea creatures) and 28 (man and woman). For another, it could penetrate the animistic order of spirits believed to cause such symptoms as sudden pain and could produce there an effect which had an analogous beneficial result in the material world. For instance, in the metrical charm *Wið færstice* in London, BL, Harley 585 (of tenth- to eleventh-century date), it enabled the performer to issue orders directly to the non-material agent of pain by repeatedly uttering 'Ut, lytel spere, . . .' as well as to exhort the patient to shield himself against the onslaught which was imperceptibly assaulting him and to reassure him by

[107] Nöth has distinguished three types of relationship between a magic act and the process it was intended to induce (e.g. disappearance of a headache) – similarity, contiguity and symbolism ('Semiotics of the Old English Charm', pp. 66–7); his third type is also represented in this charm by the instruction to the farmer: 'And hæbbe him gæworht of cwicbeame feower Cristes mælo and awrite on ælcon ende: Matheus and Marcus, Lucas and Iohannes. Lege þæt Cristes mæl on þone pyt neoþeweardne . . . Nim ðonne þa turf and sete ðær ufon on . . .', which I take to mean that, when replacing his four sods, he was to bury underneath each of them a freshly made aspen(?) cross with an evangelist's name (different on each one) inscribed on its outwardmost extremity, so that between them the four crosses would define the area to be reinvigorated. For a commentary on the whole charm, see Storms, *Anglo-Saxon Magic*, pp. 178–87. I am grateful to Laurence Cameron for drawing my attention to Nöth's article.

[108] So far as a charm as a whole is concerned, the actions performed in magic, according to Storms, 'are at least as old as the words that are spoken. Among all primitive peoples actions are performed and words spoken, and not until the time that magic is declining and its practice largely disappears are the words given by themselves. Before that time we may meet with magical actions only but never with words only' (*Anglo-Saxon Magic*, pp. 143–4).

claiming that the speaker had actually heard and seen the fierce intruders previously and so knew how to counter them effectively:[109]

Hlude wæran hy, la, hlude, ða hy ofer þone hlæw ridan,
wæran anmode, ða hy ofer land ridan.
Scyld ðu ðe nu, þu ðysne nið genesan mote.
Ut, lytel spere, gif her inne sie!
Stod under linde, under leohtum scylde,
þær ða mihtigan wif hyra mægen beræddon
and hy gyllende garas sændan;
ic him oðerne eft wille sændan,
fleogende flane forane togeanes.
Ut, lytel spere, gif hit her inne sy!

['Loud were they, loud indeed, when they rode over the mound, they were fierce when they rode over the land. Shield yourself now you can survive this hatred. Out little spear, if it is in here! I stood under my shield of lime, under my light shield, where the mighty women betrayed their power and screaming sent their spears; I will send them another back, a flying arrow forward against them. Out little spear, if it is in here!', 3–12].

Language played a full part in the incremental, additive, cumulative principle of magic too.[110] After the farmer had turned about with the sun three times in the *Æcerbot* charm he was to recite, among other things, the Lord's Prayer three times (41–2), and in *Wið færstice* 'Ut, lytel spere, . . .' was said three times in all.[111] Formal verbal repetition, as such, was never quite free of ritualistic associations. Such was the case in, for instance, the refrain in *Deor*.[112] 'Þæs ofereode, þisses swa mæg!' was no vague 'There, there, never mind! Things are bound to get better.' Referring back to an example of misfortune in Germanic tradition and forward to another, unidentified, situation in the present, it asserted both the passing of the one and a corresponding potential for passing in the other. The refrain's appeal was to analogy between the two, reinforced by the balance of its binary form; and its reiteration, with a specifically changing, though

[109] For this distinction between the two types of addressee, demonic and human, and for three further degrees of deviation from normality in respect of addressees in charms, see Nöth, 'Semiotics of the Old English Charm', pp. 72–3, and, more generally, see Storms's discussion of this charm, *Anglo-Saxon Magic*, pp. 142–51.

[110] For this, see Nöth, 'Semiotics of the Old English Charm', pp. 70–1.

[111] 6, 12 and 15 and cf. 'Ut, spere, næs in, spere!' ('Out spear, not in, spear!', 17).

[112] See above, p. 91.

consistent, first referent and a constantly inexplicit second one, built up a cumulative series of analogies between analogies (1–27). An inclusive narrative ensued (28–34): a representative figure, *sorgcearig*, 'sorrowful' (28a), sits brooding over seemingly endless troubles but then is able to realize that a knowing (Christian?) power moves repeatedly throughout this world (31b-2), showing favour to some, disfavour to others. The recurrent refrain stayed well short of providing a charm to induce this ever-journeying *dryhten* to intervene favourably, but it did introduce a new potential state of mind: under its influence the *sorgcearig* becomes able to acknowledge that a volatile source of change prevails permanently, a reason for general hope to which the (fictitious) poet finally attested personally by applying the same refrain to the disaster he himself had experienced (35–42): 'From that it passed over' too. Repeated language could suggest persuasively the universally beneficial potential of narrative analogy.

Another creative principle of active living was struggle. In a fish's case it was struggle against the moving element it lived in. Ælfric, following St Augustine in treating the fish as an emblem of faith, converted his authority's point that the creature is not destroyed by the waves it inhabits into the positive claim that by its very nature (*gecynd*) it becomes stronger and healthier the more the waves toss it.[113] A being depending on this salutary struggle languished and died if its link with its proper habitat was broken. On the Franks Casket, a carved whale-bone box of *c.* 700, the verse inscription which runs round the front panel states,

fisc flodu ahof   on fergenberig
warþ gasric grorn   þær he on greut giswom.

Whatever the exact meaning of these phrases[114] (my own preference is 'the flood cast up the fish on to the rocky shore; the king of the ocean became wretched when he swam on to the shingle'), it is generally agreed that they refer to the stranding of a whale as the origin of whale-bone, for the front panel also bears the isolated words *hronæs ban* ('whale-bone') in apparent allusion to the material from which the box was made. Swimming out of its element, the mighty being was instantly rendered *grorn*, a word used in

[113] Ælfric, *CH* I.xviii (ed. Thorpe I, 250, lines 16–18); T. H. Leinbaugh kindly drew my attention to this passage. In Symphosius's *Aenigma* XII ('Flumen et piscis', in *Collectiones aenigmatum*, ed. Glorie II, 611–721, at 633), there is no struggle between river and fish; on the contrary 'Ambo . . . currunt' ('They both run on together', 3).

[114] See Page's discussion (*English Runes*, pp. 176–7).

another poem to describe the experience of the sinful when confronted with Christ's wounds on the day of judgement (*Christ* (*III*) 1204a). To the *Beowulf* poet a water-monster's *yðgewinn*, 'wave-strife', was equivalent to its active life (*feorh*, 'the active life characteristic of its kin'[115]):

Sumne Geata leod
of flanbogan feores getwæfde,
yðgewinnes, þæt him on aldre stod
herestræl hearda

['A man of the Geats deprived one of active life, of wave-strife, with a shot from his bow, so that a hard war-arrow transfixed its vitals', 1432b–5a].

For a human being, struggle in his/her multifarious circumstances was a more complex affair: it involved consciousness of his/her personal 'history'[116] and of analogy relevant to him/her personally too. For example, in *The Seafarer* it was because the speaker recollected his endurance of the tension between physical cold and hot feeling during past voyaging (8b–11a) that he keenly desired to journey again in the present (33b–5) and was thereby marked off from the man living placidly on land (12b-13). But it was not just this individual awareness which was concerned: a human was also inseparably part of a collective tradition. In King Alfred's transformation of Boethius's analytic dialogue with Philosophy, the mind (*Mod*) increasingly understood (*ongitan*) the more it grappled with what representative wisdom (*Wisdom*) taught. The wisdom which the mind sought, narrative in kind and rooted in analogy, was a harmony between private effort and public estimation: 'Ic wilnode', *Mod* declared, 'weorðfullice to libbanne þa hwile þe ic lifde, ⁊ æfter minum life þæm monnum to læfenne þe æfter me wæren min gemyndig on godum weorcum' ('I have desired to live worthily as long as I lived, and to leave after my life to the men who should come after remembrance of me in good works').[117]

On the personal side wisdom was not to be attained in linear temporal living without prolonged struggle: 'ne mæg weorþan wis wer, ær he age / wintra dæl in woruldrice' ('a man cannot become wise before he has his share of years in the kingdom of the world'), *The Wanderer* proclaimed

[115] See above, p. 76.
[116] For the concept of past-present personal 'history', see below, pp. 204–8.
[117] *King Alfred's Version of Boethius 'De consolatione Philosophiae'*, ed. Sedgefield, p. 1, lines 3–6.

(64–5a).[118] An individual, as he/she strove year after year, learned to face weal and woe, pleasure and pain:

Fela sceal gebidan
leofes ond laþes se þe longe her
on ðyssum windagum worulde bruceð

['Anyone who makes use of the world for long here in these days of strife, experiences much to love and much to hate', *Beowulf* 1060b–2].

Hrothgar, *wintrum frod* ('wise from his years', *Beowulf* 1724a and 2114a), had gone through the whole gamut. On the collective side wise persons absorbed the wisdom of others and in their turn contributed wisdom to society:

Þing sceal gehegan
frod wiþ frodne; biþ hyra ferð gelic.
. . .
Ræd sceal mid snyttro, ryht mid wisum

['Wise men hold meetings together. Their minds are similar. . . . Good advice goes with wisdom, justice with the wise', *Maxims I* 18b–19 and 22].

An individual grew to think and act wisely by participating to the full in customary perception and practice, by involving him/herself in an active tradition of social responsibility. He/she cumulatively underwent a personal training in a collective system of analogies which inculcated narrative virtues conducive to a stable society. Self-control is an example:

Wita sceal geþyldig,
ne sceal no to hatheort, ne to hrædwyrde,
ne to wac wiga ne to wanhydig,
ne to forht ne to fægen, ne to feohgifre
ne næfre gielpes to georn, ær he geare cunne

['A wise man is patient: he is not at all angry, or hasty of speech, or unreliable, or reckless, or timid or servile, or greedy for possessions, or ever eager for self-glorification before he is fully able', *The Wanderer* 65b-9].[119]

118 Note the choice of *winter* rather than the open term *gear* here and in the *Beowulf* quotation below. The distinction between the two words is shown up by the *Beowulf* poet's discrimination between them in conventional use: *wintrum frod* ('wise in years', 1724a, 2114a and 2277a), but *geara* (2664b) and *in/on geardagum* (1b, 1354a and 2233a), 'long ago', *ungeara* ('recently', 932a), 'ungeara nu' ('shortly', 602b) and 'hund missera' ('a hundred half-years', 1498b and 1769b). *Winter* represented the sequential time men experienced, *gear* its intrinsic linearity.

119 Cf. the discussion in *The Wanderer*, ed. Dunning and Bliss, pp. 117–18.

A list such as this did not record an individual's original discoveries; it delineated a figure who was representative through having learned the lessons of society's accumulated experience. It was through civilizing intercourse in the all-embracing, wisdom-laden medium of language that a human being attuned his/her personal effort to the narrative processes of society set in the collective perspective of traditional analogy.

The moral for the individual was that self-indulgence and self-deception had no place. His/her plain duty before acting was to marry personal powers of curiosity and discrimination with the correct conventional knowledge and wisdom. Circumstances determined the appropriate mix. A look-out coping with strangers, for example, had to rely primarily on his own trained judgement: the Danish coastguard, who spotted the arrival of Beowulf and his men ('hine fyrwyt bræc / modgehygdum, hwæt þa men wæron' ('curiosity urged him in his thoughts as to who the men were', *Beowulf* 232b–3)), squared up to the situation by declaring,

Æghwæþres sceal
scearp scyldwiga gescad witan
worda ond worca, se þe wel þenceð

['A sharp defensive warrior who thinks well discriminates regarding both words and deeds', 287b–9].

Forecasting the weather, however, depended on the right knowledge more than anything else: after explaining that the position of the round part of the moon, as seen, depends solely on the direction from which the sun 'kindles' it, Ælfric went on (following Bede[120]),

Nu cweðað sume men þe ðis gescead ne cunnon þæt se mona hine wende be ðan ðe hit wedrian sceall on ðam monðe . ac hine ne went næfre naðor . ne weder . ne unweder . of ðam ðe his gecynde is; Men magon swa ðeah . þa ðe fyrwite beoð cepan be his bleo . ⁊ be ðære sunnan . oððe þæs roderes . hwilc weder toweard bið

['Now some people who do not know this distinction say that the moon alters according to what the weather will be in the month, but neither good weather nor bad ever alters it from what its nature is. People who are curious, however, can observe what weather is coming by the moon's colour and by the sun's or the sky's'[121]].

When a kinsman desperately needed another's help, on the other hand, it was understanding of traditional fundamentals that was decisive: as the *Beowulf* narrator enunciated the principle, 'sibb æfre ne mæg / wiht

[120] See *De temporibus anni*, ed. Henel, p. 63. [121] *Ibid.*, pp. 62–4.

onwendan þam ðe wel þenceð' ('nothing can ever alter ties of kinship for him who thinks well', 2600b–1).

No matter the particular circumstances the individual's golden rule – part personal, part public, reached through language – remained the same: 'Andgit bið æghwær selest, / ferhðes foreþanc' ('Understanding is always best, foreknowledge of mind', 1059–60a). Only thereby could he/she integrate individual and collective experience in various situations. Only by that means could proper collaboration be established with surrounding forces and unnecessary confrontation avoided. Only thus could he/she accept inevitable conflict with sureness of mind. The narrative past was the store to go to for good examples: 'Wella, wisan men, wel; gað ealle on þone weg ðe eow lærað þa foremæran bisna þara godena gumena ⁊ þara weorðgeornena wera þe ær eow wæron', declared King Alfred ('Well, wise men, well; go all of you on the way which you are taught by the illustrious examples of the good men and of those eager for honour who have been before you';[122] Boethius had written, more abstractly, 'Ite nunc, fortes, ubi celsa magni / ducit exempli via' ('Go now, you strong, where the exalted way of great example leads'[123])).

Vernacular narrative poetry, rooted in an ancient tradition of social observation and expression, gave the surest guide to this illuminating past, for the concepts and attitudes of mind constituting the native inheritance of narrative thinking were preserved in it more fully, authentically and vitally than anywhere else. Here were displayed intrinsic mental and physical potentials constituting active being, by their distribution grouping actor with actor in kinships and distinguishing kin from kin, and, in the environments proper to them, producing distinctive performance; displayed also was the narrative living which these potentials consistently resulted in, conditioned psychologically more by the consecutiveness of time than by dictates of space and replete with the analogies born of common origins in shared potentials; so too were exuberant testing of the system through imaginative metaphor and hybridization, keenness to identify inherent contrast and paradox in the regular relationship between potential and performance, recognition of the inescapability of contradiction, conflict and violence and realization of the fruitful collaborations which could temper them; and here too the essential naturalness and

[122] *King Alfred's Version of Boethius 'De consolatione Philosophiae'*, ed. Sedgefield, p. 139, lines 5–7.

[123] Bk IV, met. vii, lines 32–3.

beneficial effects of struggle were demonstrated, and the maturity which could be developed over time by learning wisdom from one's own and others' experience. Verse was uniquely well equipped to manifest the whole system in action because its frequent use of compound nouns – the semantic feature most obviously marking this medium off from any other form of social transmission, such as legal prose – was directed specifically to the key process of inherent being becoming narrative living. The *Beowulf* poet's employment of the three characterizing compounds, *bæl-*, *heaðo-* and *wælfyr*, 'funeral-', 'battle-' and 'slaughter-fire', when set against the gnomic generalization, 'fyr [sceal] wudu meltan' ('fire dissolves wood', *Maxims I* 71b), makes this point. The maxim, with its finite structure, stands self-sufficient as an absolute statement, but the first element of each compound associates with fire an implication which requires a narrative context to draw it out: the association which was introduced by *bæl-* at 3143b was that of noble veneration, for the compound denoted Beowulf's funeral fire when his loyal followers lit it; *heaðo-* at 2522a and 2547a and *wæl-* at 2582a all had to do with the physical destructiveness of the dragon's fire as Beowulf estimated it when he was resolutely sizing up the dragon in advance and as it proved to be when he bravely confronted it; and *wæl-* at 1119b referred to the anguish Queen Hildeburh suffered when flames consumed both her brother and her son on the same pyre after they had tragically fought and died as enemies in a feud. This type of linguistic construction, and others like it, linked human involvement and elemental being time and time again and will be examined more systematically in the ensuing chapters. It opened up the continuous interplay of potentials in narrative living. It turned vernacular verse into a tappable reservoir of accumulated understanding and control of narrative living. It gave poetry the capacity to record past or present experience not only 'factually' but also with a transcendent vision of society's deepest experiential truths. The *Beowulf* poet's triumph was to exercise this ancestral authority superbly by laying bare how a wise and honoured champion of community values had behaved exemplarily when confronting forces of nature at the limits of human capability.[124] A noble specimen of active being was held up to general approbation and reflection about his make-up, motives and consequences for narrative living.

[124] For Beowulf's wisdom throughout his long life (*snotor*, *wis* and *frod*), see 826a, 1842b–5a, 2209b, 2329a, 2513a and 2800a.

3

Poetry's tradition of symbolic expression

Poetry's function was not only to register the progression from active being to narrative living but also to impart form to that key process. It shared society's instinct to see in the experience conditioned by the continuum of time a pattern leading up to and including the present. The simplest treatment society could give to this continuity was to plot it by listing like following like, as in genealogies or regnal lists,[1] but the urge to go further by using a more sophisticated method was strong, as we can see from the brilliant innovation in graphic presentation introduced in the manuscripts of the *Anglo-Saxon Chronicle* circulated *c.* 890. Thanks to new scribal technique their continuous series of year numbers, most of them each glossed with its related event or events, formed a visible chain, at one end connected to Christ's birth in the reign of Octavian but at the other still being forged in the fiery dangers of the reign of Alfred. A strong impression was given that the actions of the present, however perilous, were anchored in a secure and illustrious origin. The numerical cable stretching out from the past into the present offered social and political reassurance; it was a token of underlying stability. Written record was meeting an ancient need in a modern way.[2]

Vernacular poetry's tradition of eliciting pattern, however, was to set events in an indefinite environment of all time and space, whether the occurrences belonged to the past or the present, were far away or near at hand, as can readily be illustrated from verse's shaping of narrative itself. For instance, the blow-by-blow account in *Beowulf* of Ongentheow's death in the Battle of Ravenswood in early-sixth-century Sweden and the similarly staged account in *The Battle of Maldon* of Byrhtnoth's death late in

[1] Cf. above, pp. 91–2. [2] See ref. above, p. 87, n. 50.

the tenth century seem to have been constructed on a common model.[3] In each case the death marked the end of an old and respected leader – Ongentheow, terrible king of the Swedes, fighting invading enemies, the Geats, at Ravenswood, and Byrhtnoth, determined ealdorman of Essex, fighting invading Danes at Maldon. Both died bravely.

Ongentheow dealt Wulf, young son of Wonred, the first Geat who wounded him, a near fatal blow in retaliation, before receiving in return a mortal injury from Eofor, Wulf's brother:

> Þær wearð Ongenðiow   ecgum sweorda,
> blondenfexa,   on bid wrecen,
> þæt se þeodcyning   ðafian sceolde
> Eafores anne dom.   Hyne yrringa
> Wulf Wonreding   wæpne geræhte,
> þæt him for swenge   swat ædrum sprong
> forð under fexe.   Næs he forht swa ðeh,
> gomela Scilfing,   ac forgeald hraðe
> wyrsan wrixle   wælhlem þone,
> syððan ðeodcyning   þyder oncirde.
> Ne meahte se snella   sunu Wonredes
> ealdum ceorle   ondslyht giofan,
> ac he him on heafde   helm ær gescer,
> þæt he blode fah   bugan sceolde,
> feoll on foldan;   næs he fæge þa git,
> ac he hyne gewyrpte,   þeah ðe him wund hrine.
> Let se hearda   Higelaces þegn
> bradne mece,   þa his broðor læg,
> ealdsweord eotonisc,   entiscne helm
> brecan ofer bordweal;   ða gebeah cyning,
> folces hyrde,   wæs in feorh dropen

['There Ongentheow, grey-haired, was brought to bay by sword-blades, so that the king of the people had to submit to the sole authority of Eofor. Wulf, son of Wonred, angrily reached him with his weapon, so that because of the blow blood sprang from his veins out under his hair. He was not afraid though, old Scilfing, but he quickly repaid the onslaught with a worse exchange, after the king of the people had turned in that direction. The active son of Wonred could not deal a counterblow to the old man, who had cut through the helmet on his head, so that bloodstained he had to sink down, he fell to the ground; he was still not doomed, but he recovered, although the wound hurt him. The determined thegn of

[3] The likeness was pointed out by Scragg, ed., *Battle of Maldon*, introduction, n. 166.

Hygelac, when his brother lay on the ground, caused the broad sword, the ancient sword made by giants, to shatter the giant helmet above the protecting shield; then the king sank down, guardian of the people, he was mortally wounded'].

A succession of three mighty blows led to Ongentheow's death – dealt by Wulf (2964b–5), Ongentheow himself (2973) and Eofor (2977–80a) respectively. Increasingly graphic description conveys that each stroke was more damaging than the last, until we realize what a massive blow laid Ongentheow low: 'Let . . . / bradne mece, . . . / eald sweord eotonisc, entiscne helm / brecan ofer bordweal' (2977–80a). Byrhtnoth likewise killed the first young assailant who wounded him (*The Battle of Maldon* 130–48) and, even after being more severely wounded by another foe (149–58), was fighting off a third (159–63) when a fourth brought him down by disabling his sword arm (164–71). Each death took the form of an elderly hero succumbing to more than one assailant in the three phases of a blow or blows received, returned and received again. The same stylized simplification of the hurly-burly of battle appears to have been applied to both. In this 'empty' frame, formalizing actuality, the commanding sense of climax would have banished an Anglo-Saxon audience's awareness of distance between them and Ongentheow's situation, just as, with opposite tendency, time-honoured appellations[4] placed the embattled Byrhtnoth in an antique perspective. In the one narrative the past was brought forward into the present and in the other the present was taken back into the past. Or rather, treating a matching sequence of events with a similar blend of dramatic immediacy and traditional language in both narratives set them side by side in a time span which embraced both present and past.

And as with time, so with space. The wood to which the Geats, marauding in Sweden, just managed to escape after their leader, Hæthcyn, had been killed, and where they suffered Ongentheow's dire threats of destruction until desperately needed help arrived, was designated only by a name, *Hrefnawudu* (2925b) or *Hrefnesholt* (2935a), and the wood to which some of Byrhtnoth's followers fled to save their skins after his death was but a *wudu* (*The Battle of Maldon* 193b) or *holt* (8a). It was enough in each context to use a general term which evoked from an audience or reader a standard, instinctive sense that a wood was a place where enemies on the

[4] *Beorn*, *eorl*, *þeoden*, *fyrd-*, *guð-* and *hilderinc*, *modi man*, *wigena hlaford* and *æþela Æþelredes þegen*.

rampage could not easily get at you. In both instances the appeal was exclusively to unchanging, collective, ingrained, practical experience.

The same indefinite reference characterized poetry's explicit statements of general narrative truths. Two assemblages of such 'gnomes' or 'maxims', as modern readers call them, have come down to us in late Old English manuscripts (the Exeter Book and London, British Library, Cotton Tiberius B. i, their collections usually being designated *Maxims I* and *Maxims II* respectively). They range over abiding preoccupations such as the operations of society, the natural world, God, fate and death. Many are of ethical import, having to do with positive qualities such as physical courage or wisdom (or the lack of them). For instance, it is stated 'A sceal snotor hycgean / ymb þysse worulde gewinn' ('A wise man shall always consider this world's conflicts', *Maxims II* 54b–5a). Some pass forthright value judgements, such as 'Dom biþ selast' ('Glory is best', *Maxims I* 80b). But, whatever the signification, the formal signals of all alike are indefinite pronouns, such as *mon*, *gehwa*/*æghwa*, *gehwylc*/*æghwylc* and *ænig*, verbs in the indefinite present, such as *sceal*, *bið*, *mæg* and *deð*, and adverbs, such as *a*, *æfre*, *oft* and *gehwær*/*æghwær*.

Some maxims generated descriptive, explanatory or didactic narrative (especially in *Maxims I*), as in this case:

Scip sceal genægled, scyld gebunden,
leoht linden bord, leof wilcuma
Frysan wife, þonne flota stondeð;
biþ his ceol cumen ond hyre ceorl to ham,
agen ætgeofa, ond heo hine in laðaþ,
wæsceð his warig hrægl ond him syleþ wæde niwe,
liþ him on londe þæs his lufu bædeð

['A ship is nailed, a shield, light limewood, bound, a loved one welcome to a Frisian woman when a ship is moored; his boat has arrived and her man, her own breadwinner, has come home, and she invites him in, washes his dirty clothes and gives him fresh ones, yields to him on land what his love demands', *Maxims I* 93–9].

Just as easily the traffic could be from narrative to maxim, a situation in a story eliciting a pertinent general observation; for instance, Beowulf, confronted with Hrothgar's hopeless grief at the death of his beloved thegn, Æschere, countered with a whole string of received formulations:

Ne sorga, snotor guma! Selre bið æghwæm,

þæt he his freond wrece, þonne he fela murne.
Ure æghwylc sceal ende gebidan
worulde lifes, wyrce se þe mote
domes ær deaþe; þæt bið drihtguman
unlifgendum æfter selest

['Do not grieve, wise man! It is better for everyone that he should avenge his friend than that he should mourn much. Each of us experiences an end of life in the world; let him who is allowed achieve glory before death: that is best afterwards for a lifeless warrior', *Beowulf* 1384–9].

Much poetry was, in fact, an interplay of two forms of social generalization, the one explicit, the other implied by narrative. *The Wanderer* is an instance. In his monologue an *eardstapa* (6a) moves to and fro between his own experience and that of society as a whole:

Oft ic sceolde ana uhtna gehwylce
mine ceare cwiþan. . . .
. . . Ic to soþe wat
þæt biþ in eorle indryhten þeaw,
þæt he his ferðlocan fæste binde,
. . .
Ne mæg werig mod wyrde wiðstondan,
. . .
Forðon domgeorne dreorigne oft
in hyra breostcofan bindað fæste;
swa ic modsefan minne sceolde,
. . . feterum sælan

['Often, alone, I have lamented my trouble each dawn . . . I know for a fact that a noble custom in a warrior is that he should bind fast his breast, . . . An exhausted mind cannot stand up to its lot, . . . And so those eager for glory often bind fast a sad mind in the chamber of their breast; as I have tied my mind with fetters', 8–9a, 11b–13, 15, 17–19 and 21b].

The *eardstapa* was not speaking of himself just as an individual. His past bears the hallmarks of generalization.[5] He has the manner of someone who is representative by virtue of having found out for himself the truth of the maxims he utters: he knew from direct experience the solitude on which

[5] '*Oft . . . sceolde . . . uhtna gehwylce* (8) and *sceolde* (19b); 8–9a could easily be rephrased as a maxim: 'Oft sceal anhaga uhtna gehwylce / his ceare cwiþan' ('Often a solitary man laments his trouble each dawn').

they pronounced. He vouched for the generalizations ('Ic to soþe wat' (11b)) and they vouched for him (*swa ic* (19a)). He symbolized their indefinite generalization in action.

Poetry's language regularly effected the same symbolization by virtue of implication alone. Its syntactic procedures, for instance, were heavily charged with implied social generalization. Consider, for instance, the *Beowulf* poet's use of apposition in conjunction with the epithet 'mære þeoden' ('glorious leader of a people'). In nine out of the fourteen occasions on which he conferred this accolade on the Dane Hrothgar, on the Geat Beowulf and on the Swede Onela he accompanied it with one or more other terms each indicating an attribute or function of the king concerned: the illustrious monarch was high born (129b–30a); he fought for and protected his people (199b–201a and 2381b–4a) and was their friendly lord (350b–3a); he guarded and distributed his warriors' treasure (3×);[6] and he was a leader of his close followers (796-7a) and their dear personal friend (3×).[7] A semantic relationship of cause and effect was implied – but only implied – by the syntactic juxtaposition: the inference was that the leader referred to had become illustrious *because* he had employed the attribute or performed the function indicated. The poet paralleled 'mære þeoden' with, for example, 'beaga brytta' ('dispenser of rings', 352–3a) to create an association which was more semantic than verbal: his choice of wording was not designed primarily to supply, let us say, an *aide mémoire* for someone learning his poem by heart. Moreover, since the connection between 'mære þeoden' and related attribute or function was recognizably applicable to more than one ruler, an associated generalization was suggested too – along the lines of 'In every tribe a king earns praise by generous deeds.' But no such overt maxims were adduced: the evocative power of the poetic language would have rendered them nugatory. The appellations possessed plenty of general force of their own – 'mære þeoden' in conjunction with 'æþeling ærgod' ('excellent noble', 130a), *guðcyning*, 'war king' (199b), 'beaga brytta' (352a), *frea-* and *winedryhten*, 'lordly' and 'friendly leader of a noble troop' (796a and 2722a), and 'hordweard hæleþa' ('guardian of the treasure of warriors', 1047a). All that these expressions needed was to be set side by side for the story line to act as a fuse setting alight their smouldering relationship.

This is what happened when, for example, Hrothgar was called 'mære

[6] 350b–3a, 1046b–7a and 2381b–4a.

[7] 2720b–2a, 2788b–9a and 3141b–2b.

þeoden, / hordweard hæleþa' as he was rewarding Beowulf for his services against Grendel:

Swa manlice mære þeoden,
hordweard hæleþa heaþoræsas geald
mearum ond madmum, swa hy næfre man lyhð,
se þe secgan wile soð æfter rihte

['In such a manner becoming to a man the glorious leader, guardian of the treasure of warriors, repaid the onslaughts of battle with horses and valuables, that anyone who wants to speak the truth justly will never find fault with them', 1046–9].

The scale of Hrothgar's rewarding, the narrator affirmed, wholly satisfied universally accepted standards of manliness. More specifically, through the two epithets which were applied to the giver this estimate implied that his giving realized the potential for rewarding which society expected from leadership and guardianship. It was not said in an unfocused way that Hrothgar earned approval for what he did: the indefiniteness of *næfre* referring to an 'anyone' implies that he deserved favourable comparison with his peers past, present and to come for reenacting these traditional virtues to the full. As much as the *eardstapa* in *The Wanderer*, but wholly through analogy implicit in the language, he symbolized fulfilment of indefinite generalization.

Personal emotions no less than public acts were touched with indefinite analogies implied in the social terminology employed. Young Wiglaf's affecting ministrations to the dying Beowulf assumed impressive proportions through such means:

Hyne þa mid handa heorodreorigne,
þeoden mærne þegn ungemete till,
winedryhten his wætere gelafede
hilde sædne ond his helm onspeon

['Then with his hands the thegn immeasurably good washed the bloodstained glorious leader with water, his friendly lord wearied with battle, and unfastened his helmet,' 2720–3].

Wiglaf acted both as a nephew straightforwardly fond of his uncle and as a thegn totally loyal to the *mære þeoden* who was his *winedryhten*. Viewed in the social perspective of this wording his affections amounted to an ideal loyalty. In this poetry the touchstone of thought and feeling, as of time and place, was the general experience society had accumulated and established.

The language codified this inheritance. It converted implied analogy into implied generalization. But not in a constricting, pinning-down, pigeon-holing way. Like the words which signalled gnomic statement, poetic language had an open, expansive character. For any given generation it signalled society's traditional recognition of potential untrammelled by circumstances. Epithets such as *beaga brytta*, 'distributor of rings', or *beahgifa*, 'ring-giver', did not impose intellectual definition; they had not been arrived at by analytic thinking; they did not deal in abstract ideas; they did not impart new information. These time-honoured expressions simply identified familiar focal points in social perception. To view a warrior-leader as *beahgifa* was to see him as a practitioner in one of the two complementary functions which society had traditionally recognized in personal leadership. *Maxims II* declared

Geongne æþeling sceolan gode gesiðas
byldan to beaduwe and to beahgife

['Good companions shall encourage a young prince to battle and to ring-giving', 14–15].

Beahgifu, 'ring-giving', was the acting out of a potential of leadership classified by conventional wisdom. And just as the general force of the maxim was evident from the verb *sceolan*, so too the authority of the social experience enshrined in the term *beahgifu* was guaranteed by its conventional form: while 'ring-giving' traditionally stood for all bestowal of benefits by a leader, the compound noun *beahgifu* provided the nucleus of a standard unit of Old English verse. Such expressions crystallized conventional wisdom in conventional form. A cultural process produced the form itself. For instance, the words *eodor*, 'an enclosure, precinct', *helm*, 'a cover', and *hleo*, 'a shelter' were used (combined with an appropriate genitive plural) with reference to a king as protector of a social group only in poetry (as in *Beowulf*). Appellations such as *eorla hleo* or *wigendra hleo*, 'protector of warriors', resulted from the exercise of poetic artifice.

At the heart of the traditional diction of poetry was a stock of culturally invented linguistic signals inviting the same kind of social perception as that elicited by non-linguistic means in several episodes in *Beowulf*. For instance, the Danes reacted to Grendel's raiding Heorot on a second, successive night by giving up sleeping in the hall

ða him gebeacnod wæs,
gesægd soðlice sweotolan tacne
healðegnes hete

['when the hall-thegn's hate was signalled to them, told unmistakably by a clear token', 140b–2a].

The reiterated raid made plain to them the intruder's underlying malevolence. Grendel's cast of mind was thereby *gebeacnod*; his patterned action was recognized as a *tacen* of this attitude. In the same way the physical object of Grendel's torn-off hand, arm and shoulder gave the Danes the clear sign they longed for that Beowulf had put an end to their misery:

Hæfde East-Denum
Geatmecga leod gilp gelæsted,
swylce oncyþðe ealle gebette,
inwidsorge, þe hie ær drugon
ond for þreanydum þolian scoldon,
torn unlytel. Þæt wæs tacen sweotol,
syþðan hildedeor hond alegde,
earm ond eaxle – þær wæs eal geador
Grendles grape – under geapne hrof

['The man of the Geats had fulfilled his boast to the East Danes, likewise had completely remedied distress, grief caused by malice, which they had endured and had had to suffer out of sad necessity, no small affliction. That was a clear sign, after the man brave in battle laid down the hand, arm and shoulder – there all together was Grendel's grasp – under the spacious roof', 828b–36].

Grendel's mother, panic-stricken though she was, made sure she removed the shameful symbol when she raided the hall to take her revenge. And likewise, after his further victory at the bottom of the pool, Beowulf dramatically brought Grendel's head into Hrothgar's hall 'tires to tacne' ('as a token of glory', 1654a):

Þa wæs be feaxe on flet boren
Grendles heafod, þær guman druncon,
egeslic for eorlum ond þære idese mid,
wliteseon wrætlic; weras on sawon

['Then Grendel's head was carried by the hair on to the floor of the hall where men were drinking, terrible in front of warriors and the lady with them, an amazing spectacle; men gazed at it', 1647–50].

Fittingly, at the end of his long life, when he had succumbed to the dragon, Beowulf was commemorated by a mound designed by the most experienced men and skilfully constructed, high and broad, on a clifftop. There it was to stand as an enduring landmark which seafarers would call 'Biowulfes biorh' ('Beowulf's barrow') and would perceive as 'beadurofes becn' ('a sign of one famed for battle', 3160a). The barrow was to symbolize, and thus promote, Beowulf's posthumous social reputation over the years. Correspondingly, in my opinion, the most meaningful conventional expressions of Old English poetry, those, such as *beahgifa*, 'ring-giver', which focused on active potentials operating in narrative living, functioned as linguistic social symbols by transmitting nuclei of fundamental experience from generation to generation and recreating perception of them over and over again.

Much modern criticism would see these expressions as no more than 'formulas'. As Milman Parry defined the 'formula' in relation to Homeric verse, and as A. B. Lord, F. P. Magoun, Jr, and others have applied the term to Old English poetry, it refers to 'a group of words which is regularly employed under the same metrical conditions to express a given essential idea'.[8] Others before me have felt dissatisfied with wholesale application of this definition to Old English verse.[9] Formulas, in Parry's sense, there certainly were in this poetry,[10] but in my view, not all its traditional language was of this sort. Indeed, I am convinced, the most fundamental was not. I believe that at the deepest level a traditional thought and a traditional form were inherited by a poet, such as the *Beowulf* one, as an indivisible whole: for him and his like 'a given essential idea' in their core vocabulary was not a meaning to which some wording was regularly attached; it was no abstracted idea, defined as an item in a body of systematic thought. It was semantic potential in a received form of wording. The meaning existed through the wording. It was an inseparable part of a linguistic organism. It became active when its customary expression was used in a narrative context, just as the significance of Grendel's severed head came to life when the grisly object was carried into

[8] Parry, 'Homer and Homeric Style', p. 80. For a survey of the scholarship in the field, see Foley, *Oral-Formulaic Theory and Research*, esp., on Old English, pp. 41–7.

[9] Much has been written practising or refining or opposing this procedure; see Olsen, 'Oral-Formulaic Research: I' and 'II', and, for a highly sceptical view, Watts, *The Lyre and the Harp*.

[10] See further, below, pp. 154–5.

the midst of the company in Hrothgar's hall.[11] For example, when Beowulf and his men, returning triumphantly from Denmark, hurried eagerly to meet King Hygelac (it was this king's first entry into the action),

Hi sið drugon,
elne geeodon, to ðæs ðe eorla hleo,
bonan Ongenþeoes burgum in innan,
geongne guðcyning godne gefrunon
hringas dælan

['They journeyed, went on spiritedly, until they learned that the protector of noble warriors, slayer of Ongentheow, brave young battle-king, was distributing rings in the palace', 1966b–70a].

The person they were hastening to greet was designated not by his name but, in the first place, by the epithet *eorla hleo*. He was *eorla hleo* indeed: young as he was, he was 'bona Ongenþeoes' – responsible for the killing of his people's 'old and terrible' (2929a) enemy – and here he was, caught in the act (so to speak) – the symbolic act – of dispensing largesse. Beowulf and his men, we can still feel, were right to want to meet once again this young ruler fulfilling the traditional twin functions of kingship. With their eagerness we can correlate our own reaction to a doughty, liberal, youthful *eorla hleo* and find a match. Our response, so confirmed, reinforces the age-old authority of the term *eorla hleo* and that authority in turn validates our response. The story has effected a fusion between an ancient impulse and a contemporary reaction. The poet did not just have an old-fashioned idea and find old-fashioned words to fit it and leave the result to look after itself. By activating the expression *eorla hleo* mentally and emotionally in his story, he released in any audience some of the imaginative potential this epithet possessed as a token of experience which had been endorsed by society time out of mind. A new event took place – and can still take place – in the cultural tradition of which the linguistic symbol was a component.

A linguistic symbol as abstract form can be described as a frame for (usually binary) interaction at the primary level of being. In practice it identified and combined at least (and usually) two potentials of active being so as to imply an interaction of a general sort requiring a contextually

[11] Cf. an interesting observation that the epithets applied to an individual in *Beowulf* were less distinctive to him or her and more variable than Homeric epithets because the former were more generic and more related to context than the latter: see Whallon, *Formula, Character, and Context*, pp. 71–116.

defining narrative to activate it. Whether the linked potentials belonged to a single being (as in *feorhbora*, 'bearer of life') or to separate ones (as the man and instrument in *hornbora*, 'horn-bearer') was of no matter. What was essential was that each potential retained its own field of active indefinite reference so that the combination of them introduced an indefinite implication of narrative action: a *hornbora* carried a horn in order to play it from time to time; a *rædbora* carried counsel so as to give it to others as need arose. Each combination contained within it a seed of narrative thought, which, by virtue of its general character, constituted a unit of thinking in the epoch's basic appreciation of active being becoming narrative living.[12] The narrative generalization implied by the 'seed' acted in conjunction with a specific narrative which made it explicit. The definiteness of the latter needed the indefiniteness of the former just as much as the other way round. The implicit fructified the explicit. For instance, Cynewulf numbered *hornboran* (along with *frican*, 'heralds') among Constantine's army explicitly marching against a barbarian host (*Elene* 54a) doubtlessly to infer that these trumpeters sent out (as all trumpeters do) rallying calls as they went; when Æschere died, Hrothgar grieved for him as *rædbora* (*Beowulf* 1325b) surely because he loved this thegn for having given him sound advice (as is the nature of wise counsellors) many a time. The indefinite implication of the 'seed' impregnated the definite explicitness of the narrative.

Syntax was the mechanism through which this happened – a grammatical relationship between a symbolic subject or object and a narrative verb, for example, or an appositional relationship, as in Wulfgar's delivery of Hrothgar's welcome to the newly arrived Beowulf and his men:

[12] My view that these 'units of thinking' represent linguistic couplings is the reverse of that which supposes that they have arisen by a process of linguistic bifurcation, the opinion which underlies, for example, Meissner's broad definition of a *kenning* as 'ein zweigliedriger Ersatz für ein Substantivum der gewöhnlichen Rede' (Meissner, *Die Kenningar der Skalden*, p. 2), and Kemp Malone's variation of this, with reference to Old Germanic poetic diction, 'a two-member (or two-term) circumlocution for an ordinary noun' ('The Old English Period', p. 29). In this book I avoid all use of the term *kenning*, either in the broad sense just mentioned or in the more restricted meaning of 'Metapher mit Ablenkung' suggested by Andreas Heusler in 1922. Also it will be equally evident to the reader that my view that the binary expressions, which I term 'symbols', are consistently units of primary thought runs counter to the school of critical appreciation (represented at its best by Brodeur, *The Art of 'Beowulf'*) which interprets them as periphrastic embellishments seeking to vary meaning. Hence my avoidance of any reference to (semantic) 'variation' and preference for (syntactic) 'apposition'.

ond ge him syndon   ofer sæwylmas
heardhicgende   hider wilcuman

['and [that] you are to him, across sea-surgings brave thinking ones, welcome hither', 393–4].

'Heardhicgende' as a signifier in its own right – when it was without a narrative context – would have referred to any beings possessing a certain active mental attribute, and it retained this indefinite inclusiveness in this context so far as 'ofer sæwylmas' was concerned, which limited it only to the extent of relating the mental potential to an equally fundamental potential of the sea. But in the specific narrative context which was signalled by the personal pronoun, *ge*, the exclusive reference to a definite 'you' and 'him' and 'hither' supervened. As items of conventional language, the expressions 'heardhicgende' and *sæwylmas* were releasing their indefinite implications of narrative action into specific narrative without undergoing any change of form themselves or causing it in any feature of their context: they were simply transferring some of their own inherent indefinite analogy to the plain narrative force of the personal pronoun inferentially. They initiated a conversion which worked through implication alone formally as well as semantically. They themselves were linguistic symbols of the universal organic principle that active being has an inherent potential to become narrative living, because each of them contributed to the narrative experience a combination of form and thought both of which were potentially active.

Linguistic symbols, in my view, were poetry's inferential equivalents to maxims. *Rædsnottor*, 'one wise in counsel' (*Andreas* 473b), for instance, implied the interaction of potentials which a maxim, 'Ræd sceal mid snyttro' ('Counsel belongs with wisdom', *Maxims I* 22a), made explicit. The two formations referred to the interaction with the same general indefiniteness: the difference was that the one expressed it symbolically and the other explicitly. By a linguistic symbol in this poetry I mean therefore a piece of language through which an interaction of socially recognized potentials of active being was implied in a potentially narrative form culturally designed for blending with definite language.[13] These symbolic

[13] The operative principle of these two-element symbols in poetry was essentially the same as that of 'dithematic' names (e.g., *Cyneheard* and *Cynewulf* with variation in the second element, and *Æthelstan* and *Wulfstan* with variation in the first element) in the West Germanic social tradition of personal naming principally concerned with kinship-marking; for a recent brief summary of this tradition, see Clark, 'Onomastics', pp. 456–62.

pieces of language will be studied more particularly in the next chapter, but meanwhile it should be noted that my conception of them involves the corollary that tradition handed them on to a poet, such as the composer of *Beowulf*, as parts of a working system rather than as just the wording of some particular poems which happened to be known.[14]

A traditional poet's creative skill was to manipulate the structure of verse so as to institute meaningful relationships between symbolic expressions and specific narrative. A simple instance is the *Beowulf* poet's economy in establishing that the officer who was on duty when the hero and his men arrived as strangers at Hrothgar's hall was an authoritative speaker. When replying to Beowulf's identification of himself by name and of himself and his companions as 'Higelaces / beodgeneatas' ('Hygelac's table-companions', 342b–3a), this official was given a matching standing by means of an alliterative coupling between his name and symbolic membership of a people ('Wulfgar maþelode – þæt wæs Wendla leod' ('Wulfgar spoke – that was of a man of the (?)Vandals', 348)) and then, when approaching Hrothgar on the visitors' behalf, he was assigned the requisite close relationship to his king by the same structural means ('Wulfgar maðelode to his winedrihtne' ('Wulfgar spoke to his friendly leader', 360)).

Style was essentially variation in the relationship between linguistic symbol and narrative. The answer given by Wulfgar when Beowulf requested the favour of an audience with Hrothgar serves as an example:

Ic þæs wine Deniga,
frean Scildinga frinan wille,
beaga bryttan, swa þu bena eart,
þeoden mærne ymb þinne sið

['I shall ask the friend of the Danes, the noble lord of the Scyldings, about that, the distributor of rings, as you request, the glorious leader of the people, about your expedition', 350b–3].

There is a three-line-long main clause enfolding a half-line subordinate one (352b). No less than four symbols in apposition to one another in the main statement reflect the elaborate formality of the court. In particular, the alliterative link between the third symbol, 'beaga bryttan', and *bena* in the subordinate clause conveys that Wulfgar courteously associated Hrothgar's

[14] Cf. Sisam's unitary view that there could have been a common language of verse, 'a general Old English poetic dialect, artificial, archaic, and perhaps mixed in its vocabulary' (*Studies in the History of Old English Literature*, p. 138).

benevolent aspect with Beowulf's petition.[15] When Beowulf was departing for home again, however, his offer of future help for Hrothgar was couched in a warmer manner appropriate to the mutual respect which had by then developed between the men:

Gif ic þonne on eorþan owihte mæg
þinre modlufan maran tilian,
gumena dryhten, ðonne ic gyt dyde,
guðgeweorca, ic beo gearo sona

['If then anywhere on earth I can earn your affection, leader of noble warriors, more than I have yet done, in anything that has to do with deeds in battle, I shall be ready at once', 1822–5].

This time a three-and-a-half-line conditional clause precedes a half-line main one. Three well-spaced symbols – *modlufan*, 'gumena dryhten' and 'guðgeweorca' – stand self-sufficiently free of variation in the subordinate clause. Identifying the basic concepts of affection, respect and warfare respectively, they expansively and comprehensively condition the main statement of commitment, which, when it comes, accordingly needs only a single, simple, word, *gearo*, 'ready', to make it effective. As in Wulfgar's words, the junction between the main and subordinate clauses was carefully crafted: the substantial compound 'guðgeweorca', constituting a half-line in its own right at the conclusion of the conditional clause and alliterating with *gearo*, not only makes clear the kind of readiness Beowulf was offering but also points an effective formal contrast to the simplex *gearo* and thereby to the whole crisp sequence of short words forming the main statement. As a result we sense that Beowulf's pledge was delivered with a sincerity that was both ample and straightforward. Symbolism acted in the interests of court ceremony in enlarging Wulfgar's statement of intent and in the interests of personal regard in enlarging Beowulf's hypothetical formulation of circumstance.

The highest art was to sustain a powerfully dramatic narrative through integration of this kind. Once again, the *Beowulf* poet was a past-master. A good example is his narrator's presentation of the hero's state of mind when his life-and-death struggle with Grendel had reached a critical stage:

[15] For discussion of alliterative collocations, complementary or contrastive, especially those extending beyond the single *a* or *b* verse, see Quirk, 'Poetic Language and Old English Metre', and for a systematic study of those linking *a* and *b* verses in *Beowulf*, see Reinhard, *Semantic Relevance*.

Nolde eorla hleo   ænige þinga
þone cwealmcuman   cwicne forlætan

['The protector of warriors did not mean on any account to leave the slaughter-comer alive', 791–2].

The symbolic compound agent noun *cwealmcuma* expressed the essence of Grendel as a destructive being: in this raid on Heorot he had already been characterized as *scynscaþa*, 'phantom-injurer' (707a; MS *syn-*), *manscaða*, 'crime-injurer' (712a and 737b), and *hearmscaþa*, 'harm-injurer' (766a). The symbolic social force of Beowulf as *eorla hleo* was pitted against a creature whose very existence was a threat to organized society. Grendel embodied an anti-social contradiction between killing and living. *Cwealmcuman* and its adjective *cwicne*, agreeing grammatically, and jointly fulfilling the alliterative structure of the verse 'line', together culturally formalized this contradiction and thus epitomized the intolerable paradox which the *eorla hleo* resolved to end: the anti-social killer was to live no more; society was going to restore its normal relationships. The adjective partook of the symbolic status of the noun and the whole statement of resolve, as a narrative fulfilment of *eorla hleo*, acquired symbolic proportions. This was not just a use of structure to make a narrative pattern out of actor-symbols: symbols and story had become one. The result, at once deep and dramatic, was Old English poetry at its finest.

The narrative expectations aroused by symbols were partly social and partly cultural. For example, on the social side, when the *Beowulf* poet used the compound noun *wigheafola*, 'war-head' (2661b), he brought to bear the assumption that the wearer of the helmet – Wiglaf, Beowulf's young kinsman about to enter the fray against the dragon – would fulfil the standards of behaviour which society looked for in the sort of aristocratic warrior who would possess such equipment; and, on the cultural side, in matters of language, it would have been reasonable to assume that any compound which was encountered using the *-bora* element, special to poetry, was related to the verb *beran*, 'to bear',[16] even if the particular specimen was unfamiliar. Whatever the mix in a given instance, the explicit narrative always supplied the acid test. A *wigheafola*, for instance – if we are to judge from the stylized, complete head-covering at Sutton Hoo – was an elaborate image, but in practice it was effective only in so far as its wearer's actions were. Or again, what exactly might be the referent of

[16] Cf. above, p. 128.

guðfloga, 'war-flier'? An arrow perhaps? Or a predatory bird? Context alone determined that it was in fact applied at *Beowulf* 2528a to a dragon. Furthermore, sometimes a symbol was ambiguous in its internal make-up. The compound noun, *yðgewinn*, for example, associating wave-movement in water (*yð*) with struggle (*gewinn*), needed a narrative setting, such as

Sumne [nicor] Geata leod
of flanbogan feores getwæfde,
yðgewinnes, þæt him on aldre stod
herestræl hearda

['A man of the Geats deprived one [of the water-monsters] of active life, of wave-strife, with a shot from his bow, so that a hard war-arrow transfixed its vitals', *Beowulf* 1432b–5a],

to show when the struggle was that of a creature other than water *against* the water's movement, and another setting, such as 'hlæw under hrusan holmwylme neh, / yðgewinne' ('a barrow underground near the surge of the sea, the struggle of the waves', 2411–12a), to show when the movement and the struggle combined *in* the water as its turbulence. Or, similarly, was *merestrengo* the strength *of* the sea or strength exerted by another creature *against* it, as was the case in

Soð ic talige,
þæt ic merestrengo maran ahte,
earfeþo on yþum, ðonne ænig oþer man

['I claim as a fact that I possessed greater strength against the sea, endured greater hardships in the waves, than anyone else', 532b–4]?

The symbols and the story-line were inextricably interdependent. Different narrative settings reveal collectively that, in fact, the basic associations of potentials within *yðgewinn* and *merestrengo* were between the (moving) sea and a primary attribute (struggle or strength) which it possessed and which therefore had to be matched by any creature inhabiting it or venturing into it. In return, thanks to these symbols, Beowulf's swimming, the monster's swimming and the mighty sea's own turbulence were all perceived in their common fundamental nature. This was indeed narrative delineating the pattern produced by recurrent underlying forces. Through symbols and narrative working together events were converted into symbolic action.

4

The language of symbolic expression

Old English poetry's primary concentration on the inherent attributes of doers, which accounted for what they did, produced inevitably a preponderantly noun-based vocabulary. This was not a stock of words signifying thoughts and things as such, as we moderns expect from nouns, but more a register of the principal potentials responsible for the actions which society had learned to recognize from long experience. For instance, the sea was traditionally perceived as a mighty, encircling, tumultuous force perpetually to be reckoned with. Maxims formulated the agreed observations that it surrounds all land with its surging mass ('Brim sceal sealte weallan, / lyfthelm and laguflod ymb ealra landa gehwylc' ('The sea surges with salt, a sky-covering and ocean flood around every land', *Maxims II* 45b–6)), that it imposes its own terms on those who venture into it ('Werig sceal se wiþ winde roweþ' ('Exhausted is he who rows against the wind', *Maxims I* 185a)[1]), that it is dangerously fickle ('Storm oft holm gebringeþ, / geofen in grimmum sælum' ('The sea, the ocean, often brings a storm in fierce conditions', *Maxims I* 50b–1a)). Sizing up this formidable, contradictory power depended on practical experience and poets used a basic vocabulary which identified the main constituents of the phenomenon thus encountered. For example, the fifteen simplex nouns in *Beowulf*, referring to the sea – *brim*, *faroð*, *flod*, *geofon*, *hæf*, *holm*, *lagu*, *mere*, *sæ*, *stream*, *sund*, *wæd*, *wæg*, *wæter* and *yð* – designated between them its water, its volume and its vertical and horizontal movements.[2]

More distinctively, poetry's symbols, which were concerned allusively (as maxims were explicitly) with the vital process whereby active being

[1] Krapp and Dobbie (like some editors before them) amended MS *sceal se* to *scealc*.
[2] See Brady, 'The Synonyms for "Sea" in *Beowulf*'.

became narrative living,[3] engendered numerous noun-based binary structures designating interactive states of potential which, in the case of the sea, constituted either sea-related actors or the sea itself (such as *lyfthelm* and *laguflod* in the above quotation from *Maxims II)* or sea-related actions which themselves constituted agents (such as *cearsið*, 'a journey occasioned by, or involving, or causing, sorrow', which applied to an overseas expedition to obtain revenge at *Beowulf* 2396a). On all topics in *Beowulf* the frequent compound nouns[4] which occur (or have meanings which occur) only in extant poetry (or merely incidentally elsewhere) are the readiest testimony to this poetic fertility. On a conservative estimate there are more than 950 of them, used approximately 1,350 times between them – that is, not far short of once every two-and-a-half 'lines'. Selection among this plenty remained strictly functional. For instance, of the two poetic compounds, *hordburh*, 'treasure stronghold', and *hleoburh*, 'sheltering stronghold', indistinguishable alliteratively and metrically, why did the *Beowulf* poet use the former at 467a and the latter at 912a and 1731b, on all three occasions as an object of the verb *(ge)healdan*?[5] Was it because of a stylistic urge to vary meaning? I hardly think so. At 466–7a the theme was the young Hrothgar's justifiably confident sway; but at 909–13a it was the Danes' misplaced hopes in the young Heremod and at 1728–34 it was a young man's false pride in the welfare which God grants only for a while. *Hordburh* represented a justification of Hrothgar's confidence and *hleoburh* pointedly emphasized the security which was at risk. The choice between them was not dictated by style for style's sake, but by the distinctions of meaning called for by the differing narrative contexts.

As regards the sea's known capabilities the art of the navigator was to appreciate which of them applied to his own situation. The art of the poet was to appreciate which of them was psychologically appropriate to the circumstances in his narrative.[6] For as good a poet as the composer of *Beowulf* every sea-crossing demanded discrimination of a high order,

[3] See above, p. 117.

[4] And to a lesser extent compound adjectives, often used nominally or quasi-nominally; see below, p. 149.

[5] 'ond on geogoðe heold ginne rice, / hordburh hæleþa' ('and in my youth ruled a spacious kingdom, the treasure stronghold of heroes', 466–7a), 'folc gehealdan, / hord ond hleoburh' ('to guard the people, treasure and sheltering stronghold', 911b–12a) and 'to healdenne hleoburh wera' ('to preserve the sheltering stronghold of men', 1731)

[6] On the psychological determination of descriptions of nature in Old English poetry, cf. Stanley, 'Old English Poetic Diction', pp. 433–4.

however briefly alluded to. On the seventeen occasions when he expressed the meaning 'over the sea' by a phrase which occupied a complete *a* or *b* verse and consisted of the preposition *ofer* and a term denoting the sea[7] he never once repeated himself. Each phrase was adopted for its relevance to the context it was to occupy. For example, 'ofer lagustræte' aptly suggested the openness of the sea as a means of access in 'þe þus brontne ceol / ofer lagustræte lædan cwomon' ('who have come thus guiding the keel ridge over the water-street', 238b–9), whereas 'ofer geofenes begang' equally suitably indicated the sea's great extent in

Her syndon geferede,   feorran cumene
ofer geofenes begang   Geata leode

['Men of the Geats have journeyed here, have come from afar across the expanse of the sea', 361–2].

In the first case the circumstance was that the Geats had arrived unexpectedly; in the second it was that their long journey gave Hrothgar grounds for granting them an audience. Or, again, the metaphorical *ful* in 'ofer yða ful' enhanced the reference to transport of treasure in 'He þa frætwe wæg, / eorclanstanas ofer yða ful' ('He carried the valuables, precious stones, across the cup of the waves', 1207b–8). And likewise 'ofer floda genipu' provided the right atmospheric setting for the sailors who would apply Beowulf's name to the mound which, in accordance with his wish, was to memorialize him at a high point on the coast:

Hatað heaðomære   hlæw gewyrcean
beorhtne æfter bæle   æt brimes nosan;
se scel to gemyndum   minum leodum
heah hlifian   on Hronesnæsse,
þæt hit sæliðend   syððan hatan
Biowulfes biorh,   ða ðe brentingas
ofer floda genipu   feorran drifað

['Order men renowned in battle to construct a mound, bright after the funeral fire, on a promontory by the sea; it shall tower high on Hronesness as a memorial for my people, so that seafarers, who drive tall ships from afar across the mists of the floods, will thenceforth call it Beowulf's barrow', 2802–8].

[7] 10a, 200a, 239a, 297a, 362a, 393b, 464a, 471b, 1208b, 1826b, 1861b, 1910b, 1950a, 1989b, 2394a, 2473a and 2808a.

One is given a mental picture of ships looming out of the mist as their crews catch sight of the landmark they have been making for from afar.

Crossing the sea was exactly the sort of action to bring into full play poetry's unique store of expressions symbolizing the universal process of active being becoming narrative living. The interplay which verse contrived linguistically between potentials implicitly interactive and particular action(s) narratively explicit had an affinity with the cooperation of past experience and present action on which actual seafaring depended. For instance, in the passage just quoted, the interrelationship of the symbolically awesome *floda genipu* and the explicitly positive 'brentingas . . . drifað' was analogous to the real-life combination of skill, based on experience, and acts of sailing a ship safely through misty seas. Both conditioned the same narrative deed with a general factor. I consider it likely *a priori* that each of the terms which were combined with the preposition *ofer* in the seventeen phrases in *Beowulf* specified above was symbolic: each coupled two evocative semantic potentials in a state of implied interaction; in each case the general meaning of the term was applied to a narrative act of 'crossing'; each term (or phrase including it) fulfilled the metrical needs of an *a* or *b* verse. It would seem to me surprising if a poet had not consistently adopted a symbolic unit of language under such regular conditions.

In form, the term in six instances consists of a compound noun with a single, initial alliterating stress (*hron*-, 'whale-', and *swanrade* (10a and 200a), *lagustræte* (239a), *lagu*- and *brimstreamas* (297a and 1910b) and *sæwylmas*, 'sea-surgings' (393b)); in seven instances it is a genitive combination, comprising, that is, a simplex noun and a preceding noun in the genitive case (*geofenes* and *floda begang* (362a and 1826b), *floda genipu* (2808a), *yða gewealc*, 'the rolling of the waves', and *yða ful* (464a and 1208b), *wæteres hrycg*, 'the ridge of the water' (471b) and *ganotes bæð*, 'the gannet's bath' (1861b)); and in three of the remaining four it is an adjective combination, made up, that is, of a simplex noun and a preceding adjective (*fealone*, 'yellow', *flod* (1950a) and *sealt* and *wid wæter* (1989b and 2473a)),[8] while the fourth consists of a simplex noun and a following adjective (*sæ side*, 'spacious' (2394a)). Semantically the preposition *ofer* was not essential to these terms as such; they could be used in other (metrically fulfilling) ways: for example, *Beowulf* 1497b consists of 'se ðe floda begong' while 'garsecges begang' constitutes an entire verse at *Andreas* 530a. I take it that

[8] For more comprehensive definitions of the terms 'genitive combination' and 'adjective combination', see below, pp. 141–2.

both semantically and formally we have in these seventeen designations a representative handful of linguistic symbols.

Fourteen of the seventeen include a general 'sea' component, which is always in initial, alliterating, position in the nominal compounds and genitive combinations, but is second in three of the four adjective combinations (the exception being *sæ side)* and does not alliterate in one of these three. In some of these fourteen the 'sea' component denoted its referent more unequivocally, and hence made the symbol more independent of its narrative context, than it did in the others. *Sæ* or *geofon*, when present (362a, 393b and 2394a), left little room for doubt, but *brim*, *flod*, *lagu*, *wæter* or *yð* constituted less certain reference to open sea: the poet applied all these words also to the pool Beowulf dived into in order to settle accounts with Grendel's mother. Nor did the other component in any of these uncertainly 'sea' symbols decide the matter: for instance (perhaps surprisingly), the word *begang* in *floda begang* (1826b) did not, for at 1497b the same genitive combination referred just to the pool, and, again – obviously this time – there was nothing in the adjective *sealt* in *sealt wæter* (1989b) to prevent this combination being used in another context to denote, say, tidal water in an estuary, marsh or pool.

In each of the fourteen the contribution of the element which was compounded or combined with the 'sea' component was, above all, to stimulate the imagination in a certain way. Twice – in the compound *lagustræt* (239a) and the genitive combination *yða ful* (1208b), and maybe a third time in another genitive combination, *wæteres hrycg* (471b) – this imaginative contribution was effected by means of poetry's characteristic combination of metaphor and 'hybridization',[9] whereby one actor (say, 'street') not merely replaced another (say, 'sea') sharing a main potential with it, but also substituted for its own natural environment (say, 'land') that (say, 'water') which properly belonged only to the replaced actor, so that a third being, 'water-street', which was partly the one actor and partly the other, was created. The linguistic constructions of these composite symbols, by uniting 'sea' and 'non-sea' concepts in an equilibrium, authentically spanned the divide between sea and human life on land. In nine of the other eleven symbols, the 'sea' component retained absolute primacy, which was enhanced by the associated designation. The accompanying component invariably invoked a principal attribute of the sea –

[9] See above, pp. 96–102, esp. 99–100.

not an incidental, 'picturesque' feature but a part of the inherent nature which all other actors encountered in the sea and which the sea had in common with some other actors in the natural order of things – an attribute such as surging (*-wylmas* or *gewealc*) or great width (*wid* or *side*). In the remaining two instances the sea was subsidiary to a potential even greater than its own: a sense of boundless space dominated the symbols *geofenes* and *floda begang* (362b and 1826b) – a space stretching all round as far as an eye could see and filled by sea, as it could sometimes be by sky (*swegles begang* (860a and 1773a)). Most of the fourteen symbols straightforwardly presented the sea as a whole – street, circuit, ridge or cup of water or yellowish, salt, wide water – while the others combined its generality with emphasis on characteristic components – currents or surgings in the sea or mists on it. Symbolically, however, the result was the same in all fourteen cases, namely an interactive pairing of living potentials with which man might well contend whenever he intruded into the sea from outside and which was codified in a linguistic form signifying that society had recognized this interaction from time out of mind. Human participants in any narrative for which these expressions were employed were reenacting this stored experience.

In the three cases of symbols which did not include an explicit 'sea' component – *hronrad* (10a), *swanrad* (200a) and *ganotes bæð* (1861b) – the relationship between symbol and narrative was rather different. The scene which these expressions depicted was the sea right enough: *hron-* and *ganotes* made that plain in themselves and *swanrad* did so by virtue of a wholly unambiguous context.[10] But this sea did not directly manifest the active potentials men tackled in their voyagings: rather it presented itself as a natural habitat in its own right. Man was present in this environment, by implication, as spectator, observing the life the sea supported – the riding motion of swan and whale carried along its surface by undercurrents and the gannet's plunge into its depths for prey. Man felt sympathy with what he saw, as the familiar designations *rad* and *bæð* conveyed.[11] The age-old message of these three symbols (and of others like them) was that human beings could take heart from the stimulating sights of the sea to

[10] The same is true of the three other extant occurrences of this symbol (*Andreas* 196b, *Elene* 996b and *Juliana* 675a).

[11] On the meanings of the Old English noun *rad*, related to the verb *ridan*, 'to ride', and occurring in extant materials as a simplex and as an element in twelve compounds, only five of which refer to water, see Brady, 'Old English Nominal Compounds in *-rád*'.

harness its potentials for their own benefit. At 10a, 200a and 1861b the motives for crossing the sea were the positive ones of respectively asserting royal authority, undertaking an heroic enterprise and restoring regular friendly intercourse between two peoples. The link between symbol and story on these occasions was psychological.

The three symbols just discussed were more completely controlled by convention than the other fourteen. *Hronrad* here (10a) is one of five occurrences of this term in surviving Old English poetry,[12] *swanrad* (200a) is one of four[13] and *ganotes bæð* (1861b) one of three.[14] There is no other extant compound that couples any other beast or bird with the particular movement implied by *-rad*, and in our five examples *hran-/hron-* was consistently preferred to *hwæl-*. *Ganotes bæð* is the only extant genitive combination yoking a bird or other creature with the act of bathing except for *fisces bæð*, once (*Andreas* 293b). Neither the *-rad* nor the *-bæð* usage has any equivalent in extant Old Norse: there is no known *-reið* compound denoting the sea; *hran/hron* has no recorded Norse cognate (come to that, no Germanic cognate at all); *svanr* as an element in surviving Norse designations of the sea usually involves an idea of rest; *bað* does not occur in extant Norse poetry; and no notion of bathing enters into any known Norse 'sea' expression. The conceptual and linguistic conventions operating so strictly in the three symbols in question seem to have been formed entirely within Old English poetic tradition.

The influence of poetic convention in the other genitive combinations also extended to selection of words, though less rigorously. For example, *yða gewealc* (464a) is one of thirty-two extant instances in verse of a 'sea' word in the genitive case, and in initial, alliterating position, combined with a word signifying a rolling, surging or tossing movement. *Yða* is the 'sea' word in nineteen of these thirty-two (twice as *sealtyða)*, the other thirteen words being (in descending order of frequency) *wæteres* (4×), *wætera* and *flodes* (2× each) and *lagufloda*, *wæges*, *wæga*, *holma* and *waroðfaruða*, 'shore-currents' (1× each). *Gewealc* is the 'rolling', 'surging' or 'tossing' word in six of the thirty-two examples, the others being *wylm* (8×), *gelac* and *geþring* (4× each), *geswing*, *geþræc* and *gewin* (3× each) and *gewyrc* (?1×). The impression given by these statistics that at least *yða* was basically standard is encouraged by four occurrences of the seemingly

[12] The others are at *Genesis* (*A*) 205a and *Andreas* 266a, 634a and 821a.

[13] See above, p. 139, n. 10.

[14] The others are at *The Rune Poem* 79a and *The Death of Edgar* 26a.

conventional extension *atol*, 'terrible', *yða* . . . (*Beowulf* 848a (*geswing*), *Exodus* 456a and *The Seafarer* 6a (*gewealc*) and *Riddle* 22, 7a (*geþræc*)). *Gewealc* too was probably standard, since it occurs in extant poetry only in combination with preceding *yða*.[15] It looks as though the core symbol was *yða gewealc*, with variation acceptable in either word or both, especially, perhaps, out of a wish for a second alliterating syllable in an *a* verse (created in nine of the thirteen variations of *yða*).

We can infer too that a coupling of an alliterating simplex noun in the genitive case and a following non-alliterating simplex noun constituted the definitive form of genitive combinations as a symbolic type. The single initial alliterating stress, rendering the combination suitable for positioning in either *a* or *b* verses, was the primary formal feature, as in the case of compounds; and, again like compounds, these combinations offered, in *a* verses, the opportunity for self-alliteration as an optional extra – as in **w***æteres* **w***ylm* (*Beowulf* 1693a) alongside **s***æ***s***iðe* (1149a). As two ways of symbolically coupling a pair of simplex nouns, compounds and genitive combinations were alternative formations in principle. It would be interesting to know what conventions of meaning and metrical grammar[16] applied to a given pair of words either to rule out the one form or the other completely or to govern the choice between them. For instance, the *Beowulf* poet evidently felt free to couple *beag*, 'ring', and *hord*, 'hoard', by either process: compare 'onboren beaga hord' (2284a) with 'þæt he beahhordes' (894a), 'beahhorda weard' (921b) and 'Beahhordum leng' (2826b), the different choice at 2284a seeming, so far as meaning was concerned, to be due to a reference (to the particular hoard violated by a thief) more definite than those in the other instances.

In 'sea' symbols consisting of an adjective combination (that is, a simplex noun and preceding adjective) the rôle of convention seems to have been less specific. The three examples in 'over the sea' phrases in *Beowulf* (1950a, 1989b and 2473a) are among twenty-seven in these phrases in extant verse altogether. *Wæter* is the noun in twelve of them, the other nouns being *sæ* (4×), *holm* (3×), *brimu*, *flod* and *mere* (2× each) and *hofu* and *wæg* (1× each). The adjectives combined with *wæter* are *cald* (3×), *deop* (2×) and *brad*, *heah*, *scir*, 'bright', *sealt*, *sid*, *strang* and *wid* (1× each); those combined with the other nouns are *heah* and *sealt* (3× each), *brad*, *gealo*,

15 *Beowulf* 464a, *Exodus* 456a, *Andreas* 259a, *The Seafarer* 6a and 46b and *The Death of Edgar* 25b.

16 For a recent definition of metrical grammar, see below, p. 143, n. 18.

'yellow', *sid* and *wid* (2× each) and *won*, 'dark' (1×). *Wæter* emerges as the leading noun, but the adjective seems to have been a matter of choice. Evidently the only requirements for it were that it should identify a main attribute of the sea and normally be in initial, alliterating, position: exceptionally a noun with a following alliterating adjective, *sæ side* (*Beowulf* 2394a), indicates that a transposed word order could be an acceptable variation, however. There was, apparently, no tendency to standardize *wid* to form a self-alliterating combination with *wæter:* this noun occurs six times in *a* verses preceded by other adjectives. Desire for self-alliteration appears, however, to have been mainly responsible for choice of another noun: in all but one of the thirteen *a* verses in which this preference was exercised adjective and noun form a self-alliterating unit, whereas *wæter* was used in all but two of seven *b* verses, where, of course, self-alliteration was not acceptable.[17] The adjective evidently had the leading rôle metrically. Thus the core symbol seems to have comprised an inherently significant adjective with alliterating stress and a following noun *wæter*, and, as in the case of genitive combinations and for the same reason, we can infer that the basic unit of adjective combinations as a symbolic formation consisted of a generic adjective, bearing alliterating stress, and a following non-alliterating simplex noun; in addition, as in both the other types of symbol, self-alliteration was freely available as an optional extra in *a* verses.

My identification of symbolic units in semantic, grammatical and alliterative terms, as above, harmonizes satisfactorily with recent studies emphasizing the metrical importance of alliteration. Calvin B. Kendall has enunciated as a rule of the metrical grammar of *Beowulf* that the first element of a compound comprising two fully meaningful elements had to alliterate, and has pointed out that, in consequence, when following an alliterating word such a compound produced double alliteration and hence was normally excluded from second position in a *b* verse.[18] More radical

[17] The combination in an *a* verse without *wæter* and without self-alliteration is *sealtne mere* at *The Menologium* 103a.

[18] 'The Prefix *un-* and the Metrical Grammar of *Beowulf*', p. 52. In Kendall's view (*ibid.*, p. 51) the only two, certainly non-alliterating, compounds in second position in a *b* verse are at 164b ('feond mancynnes') and 495b ('hroden ealowæge'). More recently (since the present chapter was written) Kendall has published a book-length study entitled *The Metrical Grammar of 'Beowulf'*, in which he has developed his conception that a poet composed with verse units (whether traditional or original or a mixture of the two), each of which (*a* or *b*, as the case might be) conformed to one of the patterns

still is David L. Hoover's opinion that alliteration is primary in Old English metre.[19] On the premise that only alliterating stresses are metrically significant, he finds, in logic and practice, that two patterns, each containing a single alliterating stress, are fundamental to *a* and *b* verses alike and that six further patterns, each containing two alliterating stresses, can, and do, occur in *a* verses alone.[20] His theory, which 'defines the possible patterns with single alliteration and shows that verses with double alliteration are formed simply by adding an alliterating stress in any possible position',[21] is at one with the view which I have advanced here that a single, initial, alliterating stress was primary to the unity of two-element symbols and that any alliteration between their two elements was secondary.[22] Indeed there are indications that the option, exclusive to an *a* verse, of adding a second alliterating stress to the basic single alliterating stress, which was common to *a* and *b* verses, derived significant momentum from the capacity which the language obviously possessed to form a three-element symbol by modifying a simplex noun with both an adjective and a noun in the genitive or by introducing a compound into an adjective or genitive combination.[23]

Sure enough, we find signs that the procedure of modifying a simplex noun with both a pre-positioned adjective and a pre-positioned genitive noun was thought of as a conflation of two symbolic forms – those of adjective and genitive combinations – and hence that it implied that the adjective and the genitive noun should each rank as an alliterating stress: so much may be inferred from, for instance, the complete absence of a singly alliterating form of this construction from the first thousand 'lines' of *Beowulf*, *a* and *b* verses alike (the latter, of course, ruling out the possibility of two alliterations). But this absence is not all that striking. A self-

provided by his 'metrical grammar', i.e., by the set of 'rules' governing alliteration, metre and syntax which he had adopted (*ibid.*, p. 206).

[19] 'Evidence for Primacy of Alliteration'.

[20] *Ibid.*, pp. 94–5. [21] *Ibid.*, p. 95.

[22] For a full statement of Hoover's argument and conclusions, see his *A New Theory of Old English Meter*, esp. pp. 149–66.

[23] Very occasionally a quadruple symbol was formed: the first thousand 'lines' of *Beowulf* yield three ('nydwracu niþgrim' (193a), 'æscholt ufan græg' (330a), where *ufan græg* should perhaps be regarded as a compound, and 'drihtsele dreorfah' (485a)). When presenting, below, figures based on these thousand 'lines', for the sake of simplicity I leave out of account all instances involving special features, especially proper names, numbers, possessives and pronouns such as *ænig*.

alliterating three-element symbol of this type seems to have been sparely used anyway: the *a* verses of these 'lines' yield only two straightforward instances ('þryðlic þegna heap' (400a) and 'atol yða geswing' (848a)) and two more with inversion in their genitive combinations ('swutol sang scopes' (90a) and 'beorht beacen Godes' (570a)). It was the second amplifying procedure, inclusion of a compound in a genitive or adjective combination, which made the running.

Once again there are indications, this time clear ones, that this triple unit was felt to be a conflation of two symbolic forms and therefore normally to require two alliterating stresses. In the first place, singly alliterating specimens in *b* verses are few and far between: the first thousand 'lines' of *Beowulf* furnish only 'sidfæþmed scip' (302b), 'fæstrædne geþoht' (610b), 'sigerof kyning' (619b), 'beaghroden cwen' (623b), 'hringiren scir' and 'guðrinc monig' (322b and 838b, both with inversion of noun and adjective), 'hroden ealowæge' (495b, involving a breach of Kendall's rule about obligatory alliteration of compounds[24]), 'fifelcynnes eard' (104b), 'beahhorda weard' (921b) and (with an inversion involving another breach of Kendall's rule) 'feond mancynnes' (164b). In the second place, in the *a* verses of the same thousand 'lines' there is self-alliteration in all but one of the twenty occurrences of genitive combinations with a compound noun[25] and in forty-five of the forty-nine occurrences of adjective combinations[26] with either a compound noun (33×)[27] or a compound adjective (16×).[28] In all (including the three quadruple symbols), out of eighty-two combinations (adjective or genitive) containing compounds in *a* and *b* verses in these thousand 'lines' sixty-seven are self-alliterating, a proportion

24 See above, p. 142 and n. 18.

25 Either as the genitive (10×; 142a, 329a, 335a, 644a, 650a, 654a, 697a, 740a, 745a and 908a), invariably in initial position, or as the non-genitive (10×) in either initial (6×; 91a, 120a, 328a, 430a, 467a and 715a) or second position (4×; 65a, 823a, 938a and 986a). The sole exception is 'magorinca heap' (730a)

26 This total excludes the three quadruple symbols at 193a, 330a and 485a, cited above, p. 143, n. 23.

27 In either second position (23×; 21a, 31a, 54a, 103a, 129a, 160a, 165a, 223a, 263a, 275a, 288a, 502a, 554a, 558a, 592a, 596a, 641a, 690a, 732a, 770a, 773a, 816a and 890a) or first (10×; 67a, 69a, 136a, 215a, 232a, 406a, 522a, 552a, 753a and 776a).

28 In either first position (8×; 93a, 105a, 167a, 209a, 390a, 528a, 629a and 973a) or second (8×; 130a, 218a, 298a, 326a, 606a, 868a, 936a and 989a). The four exceptions are 'lagucræftig mon' (209a), 'widcuð hæleð' (390a), 'nihtlongne fyrst' (528a) and 'feasceaft guma' (973a), amounting to half the combinations with a compound adjective in initial position.

of approximately 82 per cent. In *a* verses the proportion is 93 per cent (sixty-seven out of seventy-two). The corresponding proportions for self-alliteration in combinations (adjective and genitive) comprising only simplexes are much lower: in *a* and *b* verses together only 30 per cent self-alliterate (forty-one out of 135 occurrences of adjective combinations and thirty-four out of 112 in the case of genitive combinations), and when only *a* verses are considered the proportion becomes 56 per cent of the total of 134 occurrences of combinations of either sort, a not very different frequency from the 51 per cent of *a* verses which have two alliterating stresses for all reasons. The rise from this general 51 per cent level of *a* verse double alliteration to the 93 per cent special to combinations containing compounds suggests that the compound-led conflation of binary symbolic forms was itself the cause. An organic relationship between symbolic thought and alliteration at the deepest levels of Old English verse composition seems likely.

What, at any rate, is clear here and now, in my opinion, is that three binary conventions, all paratactic and all full of implication, constituted poetry's main linguistic controls for all manner of narrative, namely two-potential symbols, alliteratively paired single stresses binding *a* and *b* verses together, and two-member appositional syntax (the most usual, although it could be three-membered or more for contextual reasons). By these means, whatever the variables and whatever the possible expansions, the poetic mode was formally bonded into binary thought.

Another point concerning the symbols in 'over the sea' phrases in *Beowulf* deserves comment. The genitive combinations *yða ful* (1208b) and *floda genipu* (2808a) are unique in our extant remains. They could well have been inventions of the *Beowulf* poet himself. *Yða ful*, for one consideration, is the only known *yða* (or *yða* type) genitive combination involving metaphor[29] and, for a second, has no Old Norse analogue. Probably a sense that the word *ful* signified essentially something full (of liquid) prompted the originator (whoever he was) to conceive of the idea that the seabed full of waves was like a cup (*ful*) full of wine. If so, it strikingly exemplifies how verbalization of potential could elicit imagination. *Floda genipu* too stands out from its fellows, differing somewhat from other extant *floda* genitive combinations in its degree of particularity: 'mists' were not as inevitable, as general, a component of 'floods' as was, for example, 'extent' in *floda begang*

[29] Unless *yða / sæs / wæteres hrycg*, occurring five times, including once in *Beowulf* (at 471b), is another.

(*Beowulf* 1497b and 1826b). *Genipu*, introducing a dramatic element into the sighting of Beowulf's clifftop memorial (as discussed above)[30], shows psychological insight into the very processes by which a coastline is perceived from an approaching ship and thereby suggests that it may have been devised specifically for this context. Both kinds of imagination – the linguistic in *yða ful* and the psychological in *floda genipu* – are plentifully displayed elsewhere by this gifted poet; as personal creations on his part both symbols would have been entirely characteristic of his art. But, whether or not they were original to him, we can safely see these expressions as clear signs that innovation as well as selection played a formative part in the symbolic vocabulary which a poet deployed. Traditional symbols were not created once and for all by a 'big bang'; the concepts they represented changed as society itself changed, and poets, no doubt as a matter of course, would have discarded some items and introduced others, some of which would then pass into wider currency longlastingly, some for but a short while and others not at all. The corpus of symbols was an evolving organism, shifting with the tides of cultural change and varying under the impact of individual imaginations.

Seafaring fascinated poets as a recurrent test, or demonstration, of human endurance and skill. They entered into it with zest whenever occasion offered. Thanks to their medium they could go straight to the heart of the matter: the symbolic vocabulary they inherited had staked out the essential elements of the challenge from time immemorial. Non-metaphorical compound nouns which were formed with the common 'sea' terms, *brim-*, *flod-*, *holm-*, *lagu-*, *mere-*, *sæ-*, *sund-*, *wæg-*, *wæter-* and *yð-*, provide a representative sample: the watery element these compounds portrayed had depth (*-grund*); it had mass and forceful, turbulent, violent movement (*-geblond*, *-fæsten*, *-fæðm*, *-faru*, *-faroð*, *-stream*, *-þracu*, *-gewinn* and *-wylm*); various creatures lived in or on it (*-hora*, *-deor*, 'beast', *-draca*, *-fisc*, *-fugol* and *-swimmend*); a shore with diverse features bounded it (*-beorg*, *-clif*, *-laf*, 'leaving' (i.e., 'sand'), *-næss*, *-stæð*, 'bank', *-waroð* and *-wong*, 'plain'); in its capacity to support travel it was *-rad*, *-stræt* and *-weg*, but human journeying on it (*-for*, *-lad* and *-sið*) required both an expertly made wooden vessel, which could float, glide, speed, cleave and thrust (*-bat*, *-bord*, *-flota*, *-genga*, *-lida*, *-naca*, *-þel*, *-þyssa* and *-wudu*), and navigational ability in the voyager (*-fara*, *-lida*, *-liðend*, *-mann*, *-rinc* or *-wisa*). This

[30] At pp. 136–7.

comprehensive vocabulary was a tribute to organized exploitation of the sea over centuries as a prime means of communication and transport. It celebrated society's mastery of the sea. It introduced a sense of social pride into any particular voyage in the present. Seafaring was symbolic in evoking both social and natural forces. Voyagers in narrative poetry pitted traditional resources against nature at its most magisterial, whether conditions were bad, as when a storm gathered alarmingly in *Andreas* during the apostle's ignorance of the divinity of the ship's pilot (369b–76a, owing only a hint to the poet's Latin source), or good, as when Beowulf and his companions were returning home from Denmark laden with Hrothgar's gifts (including eight horses).

In narrative terms symbols, through their binary make-up, provided the initial interactions from which all else derived. Their couplings furnished the fundamental impulses for narrative progression. For Beowulf's voyage home they offer a combination of a beneficent wind and sea and confident human expertise to match the triumph of the occasion:

Gewat him on naca[31]
drefan deop wæter,   Dena land ofgeaf.
þa wæs be mæste   merehrægla sum,
segl sale fæst;   sundwudu þunede;
no þær wegflotan   wind ofer yðum
siþes getwæfde;   sægenga for,
fleat famigheals   forð ofer yðe,
bundenstefna   ofer brimstreamas,
þæt hie Geata clifu   ongitan meahton,
cuþe næssas;   ceol up geþrang
lyftgeswenced,   on lande stod

['The vessel advanced stirring up the deep water, left the land of the Danes. Then a sea-garment was by the mast, the sail fastened by rope; the sea-wood resounded; not at all there did the wind above the waves hinder the wave-floater from its journey; the sea-mover travelled, the foamy-necked one floated ahead over the wave, the bound prow across the sea-currents, until they could perceive the cliffs of the Geats, the familiar headlands; the keel pressed up driven by the wind, stood on the land'].

The symbolic expressions in this passage pick out the four elements of sea, land, sky and ship. Twelve in all, they comprise seven references to the sea (*deop wæter*, *mere-*, *sund-*, *weg-*, *sæ-*, *famig-* and *brimstreamas*), three to the

[31] MS *nacan*; emendation to *naca* has been generally favoured.

land (*Dena land*, *Geata clifu* and 'cuþe næssas'), one to the sky (*lyft-*) and seven to the ship or its parts (*-hrægl*, *-wudu*, *-flota*, *-genga*, *-heals*, 'bundenstefna' and *-geswenced)*. A genitive combination, making the root connection between *land* and the name of a people, is a well-attested symbol (twenty extant occurrences, including six in *Beowulf*). The name of the people in the genitive plural could come first (13×), as here, or second (7×). *Geata clifu* I take to be a deliberate variation on the basic *land* form (a unique one so far as our remaining materials go). An adjective combination comprising an inflected form of *cuþ* plus noun seems also to have been an established symbol: there are ten examples extant, including two others in *Beowulf* (1303a and 1634a). Four of the symbols referring to the ship or its parts are unique among our survivals (*merehrægl*, *sægenga*, 'bundenstefna' and 'lyftgeswenced'); any or all of them could have been the poet's innovation. Eight of the nine nouns occurring outside the symbolic expressions also designate sea, land, sky, ship or part of the ship (*yð*, *land*, *wind*, and *naca*, *mæst*, *segl*, *sal* and *ceol*), the ninth (*sið*) signifying the journey as a whole.

Departure is marked by a symbolic reference to each of the relevant elements, sea and land (*deop wæter* and *Dena land)*. Five symbols then follow, each combining reference to sea and ship (*merehrægl*, *sundwudu*, *wegflota*, *sægenga* and *famigheals*). The relationship between the two elements varies as the series proceeds. A (metaphorical and hybrid) garment for travelling on the sea together with wood that copes with the sea's depth make up a creature that floats on the waves and moves over the sea, its (metaphorical) neck covered with foam as it goes: this well-made artifact ('bundenstefna') and the sea's currents (*brimstreamas*) independently work together. When the ship arrives the sea takes no further part: symbols now present the coastline recognized by the men (*Geata clifu*, 'cuþe næssas') and register that the boat was propelled by the wind ('lyftgeswenced') when it was beached in a direct, decisive final movement. The voyage, as the symbols present it, was essentially a successful collaboration of sea and man-made ship.

As narrative the voyage occupies in characteristic fashion, a continuum in time, one phase simply issuing into the next: the ship was rowed (I assume from *drefan)* into deep water; then (*þa* (1905a)) the sail was hoisted; never there (*no þær* (1907a)) did the wind fail to catch it and the ship sped on; until (*þæt* (1911a)) the men sighted land and the ship was beached. The three connectives (*þa*, *no þær* and *þæt*) join four stages in the action

(1903b–4, 1905–6, 1907–10 and 1911–13). Syntactically each stage consists of one or more sets of subject + finite verb (not necessarily in that relative order). The first stage comprises only one, made up of a single subject (*naca*) and two verbs in apposition to one another; the second stage comprises two sets (1905–6a and 1906b), the first of them having two subjects in apposition; the third stage comprises three sets (1907–8a, 1908b and 1909–10), the last with two subjects in apposition; while the fourth stage comprises two sets (1911–12a and 1912b–13), the second having two verbs in apposition. Continuity across the boundaries between the units within stages two, three and four, unmarked by connectives, is implied in various ways: the sail when in place and the rope holding it, by implication, against the wind (1905–6a) *caused* the ship's timbers to thunder (1906b); that the wind was no hindrance to the ship's movement (1907–8a) and that the ship moved on its way (1908b) were negative and positive forms of the same statement, while 1909–10 provide yet another statement that the ship moved freely; and lastly, given the following wind, the perception of the coast (1911–12a) was necessarily followed quickly by the unimpeded beaching of the boat (1912b–13). Again in absolutely typical fashion, the two verbs complementing one another in 1903b–4 separate out the two essential components of the single act of setting forth – entry into the sea and departure from the land; and likewise the two verbs in 1912b–13 distinguish between thrusting up and standing still as the two essential constituents of the single act of beaching.

The symbols fit into this structure intimately and elegantly. *Deop wæter* and *Dena land* are paired in alliterative balance as the twin formative elements in departure; *merehrægl* and *sundwudu* between them represent the equipment vital for the open sea; *wegflota* and *sægenga*, semantically in tandem, emphasize the essential identity of the negative and positive references to movement in 1907–8a and 1908b; the adjective *famigheals* (1909a, acting as a noun) and 'bundenstefna' (1910a) are felt to refer back to *sægenga* (1908b); the balanced alliterative coupling of the full-bodied compound nouns' 'bundenstefna' (the ship) and *brimstreamas* (the sea) – reinforced, probably intentionally, by crossed, **st**, alliteration in their second elements – formally confirms the cooperation of ship and sea that has been implied throughout the five preceding symbols; *Geata clifu* and 'cuþe næssas', the one before the verb of perception in 1911b and the other after it, identify the two aspects of the perceived – what it actually was and how it seemed to those sighting it; and 'lyftgeswenced', placed between the complementary verbs of 'thrusting' and 'standing', signifies the power that underlay both parts of the culmination.

The symbols were as practical as the rest of the language; only the compound, *merehrægl*, paralleled by an ordinary, everyday word (*segl*), was rather fancy. Even so, the symbolic expressions as a class had a style all their own: they exerted a powerful attraction, while their modest surroundings remained uniformly self-effacing. It would have been an act of folly for the poet to follow a subject such as *sægenga* with a verb that did anything else but fulfil the noun's special potency simply, directly and economically (as *for* does); the last thing he would have wanted to do was to disperse the concentrated energy of the symbol. The symbols dominated; and with their domination came a measure of abstraction: their primary concern with sea and land in the departure had the result of eliminating any reference to the men rowing off out; the focus on the sail ready to receive the wind out on the open sea excluded any mention of the men hoisting it; and so on. The symbols turned the voyage into an emblematic interaction of ship, sea, land and wind. But not dehumanizingly. In 1911a a pronoun sufficed to identify the men on board although they had been mentioned last eighteen 'lines' earlier. By implication these men were active throughout: they would have used the names which specify the country they left and the country they reached; they would have watched for the land to give way to open sea so that they could use the sail; they would have observed the prow like a neck frothy with foam as a sign that all was going well as they sailed ahead; they would have lowered the sail so that the wind gave them just enough force to carry the loaded boat cleanly up and on to the shore. Our impression of the journey, we feel, was theirs too: like us, they experienced it primarily as a continuous action through time regulated and brought to its proper conclusion by symbolic impulses at psychologically critical stages. The symbols mediate between the voyagers and us.

Symbols, of course, were not wholly different from all other use of language in poetry. The medium's pursuit of implication through language could operate in other ways too, though to a lesser degree. Poetry's simplexes for the basic constituents of social being could be exploited in their own right for their implications of potential in explicit narrative or in explicit pithy statements, such as gnomic generalizations, without necessarily first joining forces with one another to create purely implicative binary symbols. For instance, both *ellen*, 'fighting spirit', and *dom*, 'doom', 'judgement', 'decree', 'choice', 'authority', 'glory', 'honour', participated in all these three processes. The resonance of these words in open narrative is exemplified in

Æfter þæm wordum Weder-Geata leod
efste mid elne, – nalas andsware
bidan wolde

['After those words the man of the Weder-Geats hastened with fighting spirit – not at all would he wait for an answer', 1492–4a],

and in 'Ða wæs to ðam dome Daniel haten, / godes spelboda' ('Then Daniel, messenger of God, was summoned for the interpretation', *Daniel* 531–2a); the depth they gave to overt generalization is clear in 'Ellen sceal on eorle' (*Maxims II* 16a) and 'Dom biþ selast' (*Maxims I* 80b); and their capacity for symbolic formation is evident in compounds.[32] Use of both words, especially *dom*, in the first two, explicit, processes often shows some, but not all, of the implicative characteristics of their use in the third.

For example, at *Beowulf* 2694–6 in pure narrative a relationship of 'cause and effect' was implied by apposition involving *ellen*, as it was sometimes by appositional juxtaposition of symbols:[33]

Ða ic æt þearfe gefrægn þeodcyninges
andlongne eorl ellen cyðan,
cræft ond cenðu, swa him gecynde wæs.[34]

Ellen, *cræft* and *cenðu* do not seem to me to have been intended as three discrete objects of *cyðan*; their arrangement suggests that *cræft* and *cenðu* were jointly in apposition to *ellen* and hence that there was a narrative association between the first attribute taken singly and the other two taken together, which, if we were to make it explicit, we would express as 'and so' – 'fighting spirit *and so* ability and boldness in action'.[35] Moreover the explicit sequence, 'ellen cyðan, / cræft ond cenðu', was fulfilling the implications of the symbolic terminology, 'þeodcyninges / andlongne eorl', in a cooperation between the two types of language which could be illustrated again and again. For instance, when the narrator was commenting on the sword with which Beowulf delivered a mighty blow to Grendel's

[32] E.g., *ellendæd*, *-mærðu*, *-spræc*, *-weorc*, *-heard*, *-rof* and *-sioc*, and *domagend*, *-setl*, *-eadig*, *-fæst*, *-georn* and *-hwæt*.

[33] See above, p. 74. [34] See *ibid*.

[35] For reasons to regard the pairing, 'cræft and cenðu', as a standard *a* verse unit, see my 'King Alfred's Debt to Vernacular Poetry', pp. 215–16.

mother only to find that it did not harm her, symbols and explicit language, which included *dom*, collaborated semantically and formally to produce a single sequence of association:

ðolode ær fela
hondgemota, helm oft gescær,
fæges fyrdhrægl; ða wæs forma sið
deorum madme, þæt his dom alæg

['it had endured many hand-to-hand encounters, had often cut through a helmet, the war-garment of a doomed man; then was the first occasion for the precious treasure that its glory failed', 1525b–8].

Both 'hondgemota' and *fyrdhrægl* expressed symbolically the combination of human and non-human factors in the sword's past actions and in a similar vein the two words *deorum* and *dom* introduced social regard for the sword into the statement of what had now happened to it. Additionally, just as the two symbols together built human participation into the sword's history of action, so the alliterative link between *deorum* and *dom* in the second statement imparted an underlying implication that men valued the sword for the glory which it had achieved in their eyes in the course of that history.

As to the depth of implication which pithy statements could receive non-symbolically, the pronouncement about *ellen*, 'ferh ellen wræc', among the narrator's solemn reflections – half narrative, half comment – on Wiglaf's and Beowulf's killing of the dragon is a powerful example:

Feond gefyldan – ferh ellen wræc –,
ond hi hyne ða begen abroten hæfdon,
sibæðelingas; swylc sceolde secg wesan,
þegn æt ðearfe! Þæt ðam þeodne wæs
siðast sigehwile sylfes dædum,
worlde geweorces

['They felled the enemy – fighting spirit drove life out – and then they both had destroyed it, related nobles; such ought a man to be, a thegn at a time of need! For the leader of the people that was the last time of victory through his own deeds, the last achievement in the world', 2706–11a].

The story-teller's thoughts went to the heart of the action and the terse 'ferh ellen wræc' was no exception: in this brief shaft of light, as penetrating as his symbolic[36] and didactic[37] illumination of the social factors, the narrator

[36] 2708a, 2710a and b and 2711a. [37] 2708b-9a.

saw the killing as a victory of one mighty elemental force over another in the world of nature. Two active potentials collided within this 'half-line' as dramatically as they could in any symbol, but lucidly, intellectually, explicitly, in a complete object-subject-verb clause, not in the inferential manner of a symbol. Here the match with symbolism was in the profundity and the rhythmic unit.

The difference between symbolic and non-symbolic implicative use of poetry's vocabulary for potentials is brought out if we compare the functions of *ellen* or *dom* in the three pledges which Beowulf made before his fights with Grendel, Grendel's mother and the dragon respectively:

Ic gefremman sceal
eorlic ellen, oþðe endedæg
on þisse meoduhealle minne gebidan

['I shall perform a deed of fighting spirit worthy of a warrior, or experience my last day in this meadhall', 636b–8];

ic me mid Hruntinge
dom gewyrce, oþðe mec deað nimeð

['I shall achieve glory for myself with Hrunting, or death will take me', 1490b–1];

Ic mid elne sceall
gold gegangan, oððe guð nimeð,
feorhbealu frecne frean eowerne

['I shall attain the gold with my fighting spirit, or battle, deadly evil, will take your lord terribly', 2535b–7].

The framing convention common to all three utterances came from outside poetry, as *The Battle of Maldon* shows:

Raðe wearð æt hilde Offa forheawen;
he hæfde ðeah geforþod þæt he his frean gehet,
swa he beotode ær wið his beahgifan
þæt hi sceoldon begen on burh ridan,
hale to hame, oððe on here crincgan,
on wælstowe wundum sweltan;
he læg ðegenlice ðeodne gehende

['Quickly Offa was cut to pieces in the battle; he had carried out, however, what he had promised his lord, as he had vowed to his ring-giver that they would both ride home into the burh safe and sound or perish in the army, die of wounds on the battlefield; he lay like a true thegn close to the leader of his people', 288–94].

We are in the social setting of a *beot* or *gylp*, the vow recognizable and recollectable from its customary binary opposition between honour and death. In this context *ellen* and *dom*[38] stood at the same pole of a standard explicit 'either/or' declaration, which as a whole implied fundamentally that an individual's will would proceed from public utterance to the type of public action made explicit in uncompromising gnomic terms by the clear-minded Dunnere at Maldon:

Ne mæg na wandian   se þe wrecan þenceð
frean on folce,   ne for feore murnan

['He who means to avenge a lord on an army in battle can never flinch or care about life', 258–9].

What we are seeking to recognize for our present purposes is the difference made to the connotations of this conventional polarization by the presence or absence of symbolic language. When, we observe, vows and symbols straightforwardly collaborated, as they did in the alliterative confrontation of 'eorlic ellen' and *endedæg*, reinforced physically by 'on þisse meoduhealle', in Beowulf's first boast, a deep-seated commitment was expressed with the utmost conviction; when no symbol was employed, a smooth, business-like practicality prevailed, as in the second boast's crisp opposition between *dom* and *deað;* and when neither of the opposed goals was designated by either of our two words or a symbol, as in the third vow, these verbal resources could be redirected elsewhere, *ellen*, down-graded to mere instrumentality, unobtrusively leaving the way clear for 'feorhbealu frecne' to arouse full sympathetic expectation of a grievous outcome. Symbols, and symbols alone, imparted to the first vow the confident vitality of Beowulf's youth and to the third the melancholy limitation of his old age.[39]

The fundamental difference in kind, not just in degree, which ran right through poetry's conventional language was a distinction between aiming at activating potential implicitly, through symbolic interaction *par*

[38] *Dom*, however, unlike *ellen*, was not lost to death: as Beowulf urged when encouraging Hrothgar,

wyrce se þe mote
domes ær deaþe;   þæt bið drihtguman
unlifgendum   æfter selest   (*Beowulf* 1387b–9).

See above, p. 121.

[39] Cf., more generally, Pope, 'Beowulf's Old Age'.

excellence, and aiming at explicitly articulating narrative living. It was predominantly the second of these aims which was served by syntactic structures conforming to Parry's definition of a 'formula' – a 'group of words which is regularly employed under the same metrical conditions to express a given essential idea'.[40] The set 'So-and-so maþelode' ('So-and-so spoke'), used twenty-six times in *Beowulf*, always forming a complete *a* verse, with the alliteration provided by the speaker's name[41] or his or her designation (*weard* 1×), is an obvious example. Standard explicit phrases, such as this, often verb based,[42] evoked the dignity of both social and cultural convention but belonged to the story-line more than to its underlying patterns of potential. Fixed form in their case acted not so much to codify interaction of fundamental forces as to regularize recurrent actions. Set collocations had a widespread value in oral preservation of traditionally organized narrative living, and poetry was no exception to this rule. Verse abounds in binary collocations marked off from their contexts by self-alliteration or other internal correspondences of sound and employing explicit connectives, such as prepositions[43] or coordinating conjunctions, especially *and*.[44]

Explicit coupling of nouns or adjectives or verbs or adverbs by means of *and* was particularly frequent.[45] The extant poems contain some 1,200 instances featuring many recurrent pairs and always forming a unit which is not linked by a connective to any other word or words and which is contained in a single *a* or *b* verse. Thus on average there is one pair to about

40 See above, p. 126 and n. 8.

41 Beowulf 12×, Hrothgar 6×, Wiglaf 3×, Wulfgar 2× and Unferth and Wealhtheow 1× each.

42 Of the twenty-five main syntactic patterns identified by O'Neil and applied by him to elegiac verse in 'Oral-Formulaic Structure in Old English Elegiac Poetry' and (with some small differences) by Gattiker to *Beowulf* in 'The Syntactic Basis of the Poetic Formula in *Beowulf*', the most frequently occurring are fifteen, of which six are noun-centred and nine verb-centred. The less common ten divide five and five between adjective-based and adverb-based. (There are also five other minor types.) See Cassidy, 'How Free was the Anglo-Saxon Scop?', p. 78 and nn. 11 and 15.

43 E.g., 'secg on searwum' ('man in armour', *Beowulf* 249a, 2530a and 2700a).

44 E.g., 'ord and ecg' ('point and blade', *The Battle of Maldon* 60a); cf. 'wið ord ond wið ecge' (*Beowulf* 1549a).

45 The conjunction might also be (*oþþe* . . .) *oþþe* or the negative (*ne* . . .) *ne* (cf. *ær ond siþ* (*Juliana* 496b), *ær oþþe sið* (*Riddle* 60 8a) and *ær ne sið* (*Juliana* 548a); occasionally it was (*ge* . . .) *ge* ('leofum ge laðum' (*Christ* (*II*) 846a) and 'soðfæst ge synnig' (*The Phoenix* 523a)).

twenty-seven 'lines' (one to about twenty-three in *Beowulf*), approximately half of them being noun pairs, a quarter adjective pairs and the remainder verb or adverb pairs (the latter accounting for less than a third of this quarter).[46] In meaning, the two linked terms are sometimes close or even hardly distinguishable;[47] more often their meanings are readily distinguishable but together standardize an active whole;[48] not infrequently, by presenting two contrasting meanings, a pair of nouns, adjectives or adverbs states an inclusive whole;[49] and occasionally each of the paired meanings is seminal in its own right.[50] Words found only, or mainly, in poetry do not figure largely in this type of formulation, and still less do symbolic words. The vocabulary is prevailingly ordinary and prosaic, and internal correspondences in sound – alliteration (in *a* verses) or rhyme (either partial or complete) or assonance – act as a preservative. Stereotypes abound; indeed adverb pairs are almost always tags.[51] Primarily we can recognize in this structure an ancient type of formulaic unit serving a need which had been common to all oral transmission of traditional thought from time immemorial and was not peculiar to any single mode of transmission, such as poetry. Stated in general terms this conventional unit performed the valuable service of providing society with a uniform means of expressing commonplace inclusive 'definitions' of various sorts conforming to basic binary thought and usable in any traditional process which depended on

[46] In *Beowulf* nouns (55 per cent) and adjectives (22 per cent) represent about 87 per cent of the total.

[47] E.g., 'frofor ond fultum' ('consolation and help', *Beowulf* 2×), 'reoc ond reþe' ('savage and fierce', 122a), 'forgyteð ond forgymeð' ('forgets and neglects', 1751a) and 'oft ond gelome' ('often and often', 8× in seven poems).

[48] E.g., *hond ond rond*, 'hand and shield' (*Beowulf* 656a and *Andreas* 412b and the reverse 9b), *frod ond god*, 'wise and good' (*Beowulf* 279a, *Widsith* 114a and *Elene* 637a), 'habban and healdan' ('have and hold', *The Battle of Maldon* 236a; cf. *Daniel* 198a and *Christ* (*III*) 1648a) and 'grimme ond sare' ('grimly and grieviously', *Genesis* (*A*) 1275b and the reverse 2417b).

[49] E.g., *wer ond wif*, 'man and woman' (8× in as many poems and the reverse 1×, plus *wif oððe wer* 1×), *leof ond laþ*, 'loved and hated' (*Beowulf* 1061a and 2910a, plus 'ne leof ne laþ' 511a, and *leof ge laþ Christ* (*II*) 846a), and *feor ond neah*, 'far and near' (1+, plus *(oþþe) feor oððe neah* 4× and 'feorran ond nean' ('from far and near' 2× and the reverse 3×) in seven poems).

[50] E.g., 'wig ond wisdom' ('fighting force and wisdom', *Beowulf* 350a).

[51] *Dæges ond nihtes* etc., *iu ond nu þa*, *ær ond sið* or *sið ond ær*, *oft ond gelome*; *side ond wide* or *wide ond side*, *feor ond neah*, *feorran ond nean* or *nean ond feorran*, *suðan ond norðan* or *norðan ond suðan* etc., *innan ond utan*, *ufan ond neoðone*; and *mæst ond swiðost*.

consistent speech. Recitation of poetry was one such process and legal procedures and magical rituals were others. Any one of these could give rise to a particular 'definition' which was then available for assimilation by any of the other processes, if apposite to it.

The coupling *word ond weorc*, occurring in all three media and always with the same internal order, is a case in point. It was obviously useful to them all as a unit of thought, but it also possessed an exactitude occasioning relevance which was not the same to each of them: in poetry it linked what was said and what was done in the course of inferentially symbolic narrative; in legal procedures it either linked what someone explicitly swore to (or not to) say (or have said) with what he/she swore to (or not to) do (or have done), or it linked what someone explicitly declared he/she had (or had not) heard someone else say with what he/she declared he/she had (or had not) seen the same person do; and in charms it linked what was said and what was done in ritual which was applied to bring about a desired result. A sure outcome of, say, either life or death makes legal proceedings the most likely begetter of this precise formula, and this probability is convincingly borne out by the surviving evidence, which we should now survey as briefly as possible.

The only extant charm pairing these words ('A Journey Charm', recorded in an eleventh-century script in some margins of a manuscript, Cambridge, Corpus Christi College 41) places this coupling in the context of a primarily antique, pagan, though partly Christianized, ritual, which stipulates that, after drawing a circle round himself with a rod (*gyrd)* and commending himself to God's grace in order to ward off a series of wholly pagan, magical evils,[52] the traveller shall cry out in triumph, 'Sygegealdor ic begale, sigegyrd ic me wege, / wordsige and worcsige' ('A victory charm I sing, a victory rod I carry, victorious in word and victorious in action', 6–7a). In view of the rough verse in which the whole charm was cast (corrupted in our copy), including symbolic compounds, *word* here acknowledged the ritual's practical employment of the language which was shared by poetry and magic, whereas *worc* signified the symbolic action unique to ritual.[53] The formula thus bridged the poetic and magical functions of verse.

Poetic symbols and the formulas of oral legal procedures, however, in spite of their common membership of oral tradition, were much more

[52] E.g., *þane grymma gryre*, 'the fierce horror' (*The Metrical Charms* 11, 3).

[53] Cf. above, pp. 108–11.

distinct from one another, both as modes of thought and as modes of expression. Nineteenth- and early-twentieth-century scholarship[54] played down this difference, emphasizing instead the sameness. Jacob Grimm (1816), the first to make a case for an ancient connection between oral law and poetry, pointed out that the basis of both was 'etwas Gegebenes, Zugebrachtes' ('something given, handed down').[55] Orally proclaimed law and poetry, he argued, being thus alike in deriving their authority from antiquity, depended on fundamentally the same appeal to an audience's faith in inherited custom and hence from ancient times had necessarily been closely similar in form and content. That the legal medium for this call to faith was a species of poetry he believed principally because he considered its abundant tautology intrinsically poetic.[56] Later on, towards the end of the century, Edward Sievers refined on this conception by postulating that the laws employed a type of Germanic verse which was less artistic than that of Old English poetry and which he called *Sagvers*. The principal difference between the two grades in his view was that in the poetic type form was an end in itself, serving a purely aesthetic purpose, whereas in *Sagvers* content was all-important and form served only to impress it on the memory.[57] In 1932 Dorothy Bethurum was still granting that 'it seems highly probable that the Old English laws had behind them in the Germanic *Urzeit* just such a poetic tradition as Grimm and Schröder describe', subject to her qualification that it is difficult to confirm from the laws themselves 'Grimm's contention that Germanic law was nearer poetry than prose'; the form of the laws as we have them she ascribed to subsequent influence from Latin prose.[58] These views were right, of course,

[54] For a survey, see Bethurum, 'Stylistic Features of the Old English Laws', pp. 266–70, with refs.

[55] For the meaning, 'handed down', cf. another use of *zugebracht* by Grimm, 'und wurzelte der monolog nicht schon in der natur der sprach . . ., er müste uns durch jene völker zugebracht worden sein' ('and was not the monologue rooted in the nature of the language . . ., it must have been handed down to us through those peoples'), which is cited (as kindly pointed out to me by Helmut Gneuss) Grimm and Grimm, *Deutsches Wörterbuch* XVI, col. 251.

[56] Bethurum, 'Stylistic Features of the Old English Laws', pp. 267–8.

[57] *Ibid.*, p. 269.

[58] *Ibid.*, p. 277. It is interesting to note (*ibid.*, p. 275) that, while classifying the pairing of *word ond weorc* as wholly Germanic in form, she regarded its use in early-eleventh-century laws, drafted by Archbishop Wulfstan, as a translation of a biblical opposition *verbo et factis* (as in Rom. XV.18) or *opere et sermone* (as in Luke XXIV and 2 Thes. II.15);

to distinguish Germanic legal procedure from modern practice for not relying primarily on logical deduction from evidence, but, in my opinion, they failed to draw sufficient distinction functionally between law and poetry. The starting-point should have been not a broadly emotive style which could be regarded as 'poetic' but the strict unity of customary thought and customary language which was central to any authentic act of oral tradition and which varied according to the particular practical need which was being addressed. For legal judgement, hinging on the degree of trust which a witness could command, explicit formulas were required to standardize the docketing of declarative statements about narrative living. Couplings which categorized this material, such as *word ond weorc*, were needed to regularize the processes of oath-swearing, bearing witness and the like, in contrast to poetry's need, as we have seen, for symbols implicitly associating paired potentials in such a way as to standardize suggestion of narrative possibilities which depended on context for definition. The one was a technique for narrowing down, the other a mechanism for opening up.

The extant occurrences of *word ond weorc* clearly reveal that it was of the former kind. Especially notable is its use, in adverbial genitive singular form, in an oath of loyalty – 'ic wille beon N. hold ⁊ getriwe . . . ⁊ næfre willes ne gewealdes, wordes ne weorces owiht don ðæs him laðre bið . . .' ('I will be loyal and faithful to N. . . . and never in will and intention, word and deed, do anything which will be hostile to him . . .') – forming the first item of a collection of model formulaic oaths, headed in the early-twelfth-century 'Textus Roffensis', 'Hu se man sceal swerie', and edited by Liebermann under the title, *Swerian*.[59] This oath, similar to one at the beginning of the third code of Edmund, king of Wessex (939–46),[60] and consisting, like the rest of the *Swerian* set, of traditional formulas, combined in this case[61] with the Christian practice of swearing on relics in an amalgamation of Germanic and Christian strongly reminiscent of King Alfred's practice, could easily date from that king's reign.[62]

but, for another explanation, keeping this particular coupling completely within the Germanic legal tradition, see below.

[59] *Die Gesetze der Angelsachsen*, ed. Liebermann I, 396–9.

[60] III Em 1 (*ibid.*, p. 190).

[61] As in one other *Swerian* item.

[62] I am grateful to Patrick Wormald for offering this opinion and for drawing my attention to the resemblance to III Em 1.

Noteworthy too are the legal connotations in two occurrences of this pairing in poetry, one in *Beowulf* and the other in the early-ninth-century Old Saxon epic, *Heliand*. In the former the context was the occasion when Fin swore to Hengest ('aðum benemde', 1097b) that he would rule over the Danish survivors of the fight in his hall according to the judgement of his *witan*, 'þæt ðær ænig mon / wordum ne worcum wære ne bræce' ('provided that no one there broke the agreement in words or deeds', 1099b–1100); and in the latter it was the situation in the Jewish assembly, seeking grounds for Jesus's death, when the high priest demanded that the prisoner should declare on oath whether he was the son of the living God and added,[63] 'Uui ni mugun is antkennian uuiht / ne an thinon uuordon ne an thinon uuercon' ('We cannot see this at all either in your words or in your deeds', 5087b–8a). The testimony of false witnesses having previously failed, the high priest, following a thoroughly Germanic method, was now trying to show up a contradiction between what the assembled council might hear Jesus say and what they had already witnessed in his words and deeds.[64] Likewise on another occasion in *Beowulf* there were quasi-legal connotations when, on departing from Denmark for home, the hero pledged his armed support for Hrothgar, if the need were to arise in the future, and claimed Hygelac's backing by saying 'Ic on Higelace wat, / . . . / . . . þæt he mec fremman wile / wordum ond weorcum' ('I know from Hygelac . . . that he will support me in words and deeds', 1830b–3a); and once in *Guthlac A* too there were legal echoes when St Bartholomew, proclaiming to the horde of devils who had carried Guthlac to the door of hell, that henceforth the saint was under his guardianship, pledged,

sceal ic his word ond his weorc   in gewitnesse
dryhtne lædon.   He his dæde conn

['I shall carry his words and his deeds to the Lord in testimony. He will know his actions', 720–1].

These contexts, spread across two languages, signal that the coupling of

[63] Without an equivalent in the Latin version of the second-century *Diatessaron* of Tatian which was the poet's source.

[64] For the Germanic emphasis throughout this episode on a distinction between false and true witness and on formal swearing, see Lagenpusch, *Das germanische Recht im 'Heliand'*, pp. 61–3.

word ond weorc originated in legal practices and had already passed from there into poetic usage in Germanic antiquity.[65]

Once received into verse, however, this pair adapted to poetry's ways. It came to mean speech as heard and actions as observed in any situation and was used whenever description called for a two-part definition of this kind. For instance, at *Beowulf* 287b–9 the coastguard utilized it when underpinning his instant judgement of the newly arrived Beowulf and his men by delivering himself sententiously of this maxim, as though repeating the instructions he had been given in his training:

Æghwæþres sceal
scearp scyldwiga gescad witan,
worda ond worca, se þe wel þenceð.[66]

In poetry's terms the coupling was here playing a key part in defining the applicability of the social concept, 'scearp scyldwiga', to the specific situation concerned. And likewise, but this time in support of full-blown Christian imagery, in *The Phoenix* it defined the adoration which is offered when the blessed in heaven present '. . . dryhtne to giefe / worda ond weorca wynsumne stenc' ('as a gift to the lord the pleasant scent of words and deeds', 658b–9). In particular, most characteristic of this word pair in Old English poetry is an adverbial use in a dative plural form, as at *Beowulf* 1100a and 1833a already discussed, and as occurring eight times in extant fully Christian poems,[67] mostly (6×) with reference to humans behaving on earth in the perspective of God's judgement and twice[68] to the blessed offering their praise in heaven. In *Heliand* the evidence is similar. The pairing occurs in this poem nineteen times altogether (including 5088a already quoted),[69] concerning, in about equal numbers, God's actions before men (such as teaching and miracles) or men's before God and, when adverbial (12×), employing the dative plural (8×) or the instrumental

65 This probability holds good even if the controversial possibility of direct Anglo-Saxon influence on the *Heliand* is taken into account, for any legal connotations different from a society's own, seem an unlikely borrowing.

66 See above, p. 114.

67 *Christ and Satan* 48a and 222a, *Christ (III)* 917a and 1236a, *Guthlac (A)* 581a and 793a, *The Whale* 84a and *The Seasons for Fasting* 74a.

68 In the *Christ and Satan* instances; cf. *The Phoenix* 659a, already quoted.

69 5a, 541a, 1551a, 1578a, 1737a, 1768a, 1830a, 2034a, 2107a, 2116a, 2231, 2429a, 2434a, 2612a, 3473a, 3945a, 4713a, 5088a and 5480a.

singular (4×).[70] It seems clear that, when taken into poetry, the coupling underwent a transition, both semantically and formally, to a tradition appropriate to its new home, and that this had begun in Germanic times. On the Old English evidence the cause of the shift from adverbial genitive singular, customary in legal use,[71] to an adverbial dative plural may have been due to an absence of an adverbial genitive singular of means or instrument in poetry's conventions.[72]

In late Old English prose we find that the adverbial use of this *word and weorc* pairing by the leading practitioners, Ælfric and Wulfstan, differed from the one author to the other along the lines of the semantic and formal distinction which had separated poetry and law way back in Germanic oral tradition.

Ælfric's usage echoed poetic tradition. Characteristically concerned with the whole scheme of things, and so viewing human conduct as an entirety in the eyes of God, he uniformly employed the dative for adverbial purposes, either in the plural with *mid* or in the singular with *on* in about equal numbers, as in these examples: 'Soðlic eal seo ealde gecyðnys wæs witegung and getacnung . . . and witegode oððe mid wordum. oððe mid weorcum cristes menniscnysse. and cristenra manna lif' ('Truly all the Old Testament was prophecy and symbolism . . . and prophesied either with words or with works the humanity of Christ and the life of Christian people');[73] and 'se ðeoda lareow cwæð, Paulus, "Swa hwæt swa ge doð on worde, oððe on weorce, doð symle on Drihtnes naman . . . " ' ('the teacher of peoples, Paul, said, "Whatever you do in word or in work, always do in the Lord's name . . ." ')[74] But his intellectual framework was significantly different. By his time, and well before, *wordum/worde and/oððe weorcum/weorce* had become thought of as an equivalent to biblical *verbis/verbo et operibus/opere* and, above all, was frequently expanded in prose into a triple rendering of the 'cogitatione, verbo et opere' formulation which had been not uncommon in patristic writings, especially in connection with the theme of God's judgement, and which, as a result of Irish influence,

[70] Half (6×) with prepositions (most commonly (4×) *mid . . . mid . . .* preceding dative plurals) and half without.

[71] See further, below.

[72] Cf. Mitchell, *Old English Syntax*, sects. 1391–4, where *wordes* ⁊ *dæde* (in Wulfstan's prose) is included in a category of 'genitive of means or instrument', which is regarded as an alternative name for some 'genitives of manner' and is exemplified only from prose.

[73] Ælfric, *CH* II.iv (ed. Godden, lines 311–15).

[74] Ælfric, *CH* I.vi (ed. Thorpe, p. 102, lines 11–13).

became widespread in exegetical, liturgical, devotional and penitential use throughout western Christendom, including Anglo-Saxon England, from the second half of the seventh century.[75] Ælfric exemplifies this amplification in this statement of his customary distinction between animals and humans: '. . . þæt nyten næfð nane sawle . . . . Ac we ðe sind to Godes anlicnysse gesceapene, and habbað unateorigendlice saule, we sceolon of deaðe arisan, and agyldan Gode gescead ealra ura geðohta, and worda, and weorca' ('the animal has no soul . . . But we who are created in God's image and have an imperishable soul, we shall arise from death and render to God a discriminating account of all our thoughts and words and deeds').[76] In antique legal practice, to judge from 'willes ne gewealdes, wordes ne weorces' in *Swerian*,[77] a genitive singular word pair, *willes ond gewealdes*, had been used adverbially alongside *wordes ond weorces* to signify 'intention', if desired; and in our extant early legal materials *willes ne gewealdes* occurs once more, this time not accompanied by *wordes ne weorces*.[78] But Old English poetry, not taking a hint either from this legal tradition or from its own resources,[79] never developed, on our surviving evidence, a standard tripartite formula. The triple motif as such does occur occasionally in verse,[80] but in the only poem in which an adverbial formula

[75] Sims-Williams, 'Thought, Word and Deed'.

[76] Ælfric, *CH* I.vi (ed. Thorpe, p. 96, lines 16–20). Ælfric is not known to have been following any particular source at this point. For the notion of discrimination, which he probably would have understood as an essential semantic component of *gescead*, cf. his statement, 'Heo [*i.e.* Seo sawul] is ratio . þæt is gescead . þonne heo toscæt' ('It is *ratio*, that is "discrimination", when it separates', *Ælfric's Lives of Saints* I, ed. Skeat, no. I, lines 186–7). [77] See above, p. 159.

[78] In the second code of King Edward the Elder (899–924): 'ne ful nawar friðian ne feormian willes ne gewealdes' ('nor shall they anywhere shield or harbour [criminals] willingly and deliberately', ed. Liebermann, *Die Gesetze der Angelsachsen* I, 142). In legal usage a century later this coupling was made much of to draw an important distinction in Æthelred's sixth code, drafted by Wulfstan (on whom see further, below): '7 gif hit geweorþeð, þæt man unwilles oþþe ungewealdes ænig þing misdeð, na bið þæt na gelic þam þe willes 7 gewealdes sylfwilles misdeð' ('and if it happens that a man commits a misdeed involuntarily or unintentionally the offence is never the same as that done of a man's own will, voluntarily and deliberately', VI Atr 52, 1 (*ibid.*, p. 258).

[79] E.g., the wording of *Beowulf* 289, 'worda ond worca, . . . wel þenceð', cited above.

[80] Wright, 'The Irish "Enumerative Style" in Old English Homiletic Literature', esp. n. 143. The relevant two of the three seem to be represented in *Cædmon's Hymn* ('metudæs maecti end his modgidanc, / uerc uuldurfadur', 2–3a. 3a is also an early illustration of transposed word order, admissible as a variation of the genitive combination, as it was of the adjective combination (see above, p. 142)).

was adopted for it, *A Prayer*, a late composition,[81] the wording – 'hwile mid weorce, hwile mid worde, / hwile mid geþohte' (64–5a) – looks very much as though it was owed to prose. The only adverbial formula in Christian vernacular verse's own tradition remained seemingly the binary *wordum ond weorcum* ultimately adapted from Germanic oral legal practice.

By contrast, Archbishop Wulfstan's prose, in its frequent exploitation of the genitive singular adverbial form, *wordes ond/ne/oððe weorces*, to point up the direct connection between human behaviour and the approaching end of the world, and in its lack of any interest in the tripartite formulation, witnesses to the vitality still retained at this late period by the verbal tradition stemming ultimately from the oral legal practices of the Germanic past alongside the conventions of poetry. The archbishop used this particular coupling repeatedly in the law codes he drafted, in *Polity* and in several of his homilies, as in this stern warning: 'eal þæt ænig man oðrum her on unriht to hearme gedeð wordes oððon weorces, eal hit sceal eft mænigfealdlice derian him sylfum, butan he hit ær gebete' ('everything which any man does here unlawfully to the harm of another in word or deed, it shall all damage himself in return many times over unless he has already made amends for it').[82]

Before Wulfstan's copious style of law drafting, this particular adverbial formula had had no place either in the terse statutes making up the earliest written codes or in the fuller manner subsequently developed, but it does occur in the so-called 'Laws of Edward and Guthrum', a series of mainly ecclesiastical regulations, which claim in a prologue to have been agreed between Alfred and Guthrum, then renewed by Edward and Guthrum (erroneously supposed to have been contemporary rulers) and subsequently from time to time confirmed and revised by councillors, but which were in fact a relatively early composition by Wulfstan (probably between 1002

81 See, e.g., Eric Stanley's discussion of the *myrgð* group (represented in this poem by *mirigðe* (13b)), rare until 'WS in the wake of the Benedictine Reform' ('Studies in the Prosaic Vocabulary of Old English Verse', pp. 410–11).

82 *Homilies of Wulfstan*, ed. Bethurum, XIII, lines 60–2. Other homiletic instances are *ibid.*, IX, lines 102–3; XC, lines 41–4 and 152–4; and XVIII, lines 42–5 and 47–9. Wulfstan was also fond of the exhortation, 'utan word ⁊ weorc rihtlice fadian', which he included in the *Sermo Lupi*, in the laws he drafted and in *Polity*. Just occasionally he used an adverbial dative (singular or plural) with preposition, as in '[þe] nele forseon ne gescyndan oðerne ne mid worde ne mid weorce' ('(who) will not scorn and insult another with word or with deed', *Homilies of Wulfstan*, ed. Bethurum, IX, lines 47–8).

and 1008), as Dorothy Whitelock demonstrated,[83] subject to her proviso, 'It is more than probable that in general the code represents regulations of considerable antiquity, or otherwise the author's claim that they went back to Alfred and Guthrum would have been too demonstrably false.'[84] The regulation relevant to our present concern begins, '⁊ gif hwa Cristendom wyrde oððe hæþendom weorþige wordes oððe weorces, gylde . . .' ('And if anyone injures the Christian religion and honours heathen practices in word or deed, he shall pay . . .').[85] Because of the frequency of the *wordes/weorces* coupling elsewhere in the archbishop's works, Dorothy Whitelock thought that Wulfstan had introduced it here,[86] but if his written text had underlying it some traditional oral regulations which were thought to go back to the early days of the Danish colonization – which is highly probable – he might well have retained this pairing from those regulations, and, having liked it, gone on thenceforth to use it often in other writings.

He can certainly be observed doing just that in the instance of another very ancient legal coupling, *að ond wedd*, 'oath and pledge', which had last been used in a lawcode by Edward the Elder. Earlier than that Alfred had begun his code, 'Æt ærestan we lærað, þæt mæst ðearf is, þæt æghwelc mon his að ⁊ his wed wærlice healde' ('First of all we enjoin that the greatest need is that every man shall keep his oath and his pledge carefully'),[87] and there seems little doubt that Wulfstan was echoing this wording when stipulating in the fifth code of Æthelred, '⁊ æghwylc Cristen man do, swa him þearf is: gyme . . . ⁊ word ⁊ weorc fadige mid rihte ⁊ að ⁊ wedd wærlice healde' ('and let every Christian man do, as there is need for him: take heed . . . and order word and deed justly and keep oath and pledge carefully'),[88] and when exhorting in the *Sermo Lupi*, 'utan word ⁊ weorc rihtlice fadian ⁊ ure ingeþanc clænsian georne ⁊ að ⁊ wedd wærlice healdan . . .' ('let us order word and deed justly and purify our conscience eagerly and keep oath and pledge carefully').[89] I suggest that likewise oral traditions underlying

[83] Whitelock, 'Wulfstan and the So-Called Laws of Edward and Guthrum'.

[84] *Ibid.*, p. 18.

[85] E Gu 2 (ed. Liebermann, *Die Gesetze der Angelsachsen* I, 130).

[86] 'Wulfstan and the So-Called Laws of Edward and Guthrum', p. 7 and n. 2.

[87] Af 1 (ed. Liebermann, *Die Gesetze der Angelsachsen* I, 46).

[88] V Atr 22.2 (ed. *ibid.*, p. 242). Almost the same wording recurs in Æthelred's sixth code and Cnut's first.

[89] *Homilies of Wulfstan*, ed. Bethurum, XX(I), lines 123–5. I am grateful to Patrick Wormald for pointing out to me this source relationship.

the so-called 'Laws of Edward and Guthrum' probably drew the archbishop's attention to the efficacy of the *wordes ond weorces* pairing for his moral purposes and that in often using it he was conscious of giving a new lease of life to an ancient legal formula.

This short summary is enough to show that the coupling, *word ond weorc*, very probably originating in a non-poetic, legal, department of oral tradition, enjoyed more circulation outside poetry than within it. Evidently it met a widespread demand in Germanic oral tradition and could be employed whenever that need was felt, regardless of the particular usage which had given it birth. Not every coupling was so flexible. For example, 'eafoð and ellen', which, as we have seen,[90] probably represented a conceptual pairing stretching back into Germanic antiquity like *word and weorc* but in its case originating in poetry, failed to adapt to any other mode of expression in Old English outside verse and even in that medium did not outlive secular heroic narrative. Whatever the history of particular specimens, however, we can accept that explicit word pairing was a conventional structure common to Germanic orality in satisfying a general need for stable articulation of narrative living and that Old English poetry employed this formulaic type because it shared this requirement with other Germanic oral media. Its frequent use of the structure reflects the extent to which it felt this need, but what gave poetry its special character as a branch of oral tradition was its unique possession of a set of linguistic conventions to symbolize implications in the general perceptions which society often made explicit in maxims:[91] poetry alone actualized, for example, an 'egeslic eorðdraca' ('terrible earth-dragon', *Beowulf* 2825a) to represent the elemental terror underlying society's agreed conception that 'Draca sceal on hlæwe, / frod, frætwum wlanc' (*Maxims II* 26b–7a).[92] Symbolic language marked off poetry from any other branch of oral tradition because it was the sole register which methodically addressed the implications underlying narrative living.

The secret of its success did not lie in being constructed from vocabulary which was itself peculiar to poetry. For instance, of the twenty-four components making up the twelve symbols in the account of Beowulf's voyage home from Denmark, analysed above,[93] *brim* alone was confined mainly to verse and only a few others were special to verse either in meaning (*mere* and *sund*) or in form (*genga* and *stefna*). The key was

[90] Above, pp. 69–70. [91] See above, pp. 120–3. [92] See above, p. 77.
[93] At pp. 147–50.

symbolism's invaluable contribution to practical narrative living by imposing an order on powerful doers who/which, lacking it, would have been unpredictable: in essence, by this means doers regularly became classified as active beings. In *Beowulf*, for example, about 16 per cent of the 950 or so nominal compounds[94] are agent nouns,[95] while a great many more signify phenomena which are active by their very nature.[96] Genitive and adjective combinations regularly denote active agents too, although often less obviously: in 1903b–13 *Dena land* and *Geata clifu* invoke the life of the inhabitants, *deop wæter* buoys up a heavily laden sailing ship and 'cuþe næssas' command recognition. When action rather than actor is the referent, it is not 'action' in some abstract sense, but is what doers do: either it has basic implications for them[97] or it typifies all who do it.[98] Emotion, thought and imagination involved in action are regularly channelled through symbols free of exaggeration, sensationalism or sentimentality.

They instilled not only stability but discipline as well. They brought a constantly constructive attitude to society's need for a sense of proportion, for reliable personal relationships, for flourishing corporate institutions. *Guð-* ('battle-') compounds as a representative sample of war vocabulary registered a balanced acceptance of violence as a fact of life: they allowed for (royal) leadership (*-cyning*), natural ability (*-cræft*), boldness (*-freca* and *-hwæt*), resolution (*-heard* and *-mod*), fierceness (*-reow*), guardianship (*-weard*), comradeship (*-wine*), exhaustion (*-werig*), sorrow (*-cearu*), injury (*-sceaða*), slaughter (*-scearu*), death (*-deað*), survival (*-laf*), glory (*-hreð*) and fame (*-rof*). Compounds with *-gestealla* ('-one who stands in position') (*eaxl-*, *folc-*, *fyrd-*, *hand-*, *lind-*, *nyd-* and *will-*) testified to a leader's dependence on close, firm, active, loyalty from his retainers in battle. *Sele-*, *-sele*, *-seld*, *heal(l)-* and *-heal(l)* ('hall') compounds encouraged civilized appreciation of the hall as the centre of organized tribal life (*eðelseld*): they invited admiration of the complete building (*-ærn*, *-reced* and *heah-*) and of

94 See above, p. 135.

95 E.g., *wegflotan* and *sægenga* in 1903b–13 or 'heaðoliðendum' ('war-sailors', 2955a).

96 E.g., in 1903b–13, *merehrægla*, *sundwudu*, *famigheals*, 'bundenstefna', *brimstreamas* and 'lyftgeswenced'.

97 E.g., an expedition which is *wilsið* (216a) is willingly undertaken, one which is *gryresið* (1462a) strikes terror and one which is *cearsið* (2396a) causes sorrow, while *wræcsið* (338b and 2292a) is exile and *ellorsið*, 'a journey elsewhere' (2451a), is death.

98 E.g., *beorþegu*, 'taking of beer' (117a and 617b), and *beah-* or *sincþegu*, 'receiving of treasure' (2176a and 2884a).

its materials (*gold-* and *-wudu*) and parts (*horn-* and *hrof-*); they celebrated it as the proper site of social pleasures (*-dream* and *will-*), drinking (*-ful*, *beor-*, *medu-* and *win-*), entertainment (*-gamen*), bestowal of valuable gifts (*gif-*, *beah-*, *hring-* and *maððum-*), receiving of guests (*gest-*), rest (*-rest*) and protection (*burg-* and *-weard*): they projected it as the place where nobility (*dryht-*), service (*-þegn*) and good advice (*-rædende*) rightly belonged, but where comfortlessness (*wind-*), sorrow (*cear-* and *dreor-*), hostility (*nið-*), war (*guð-*) and death (*deað-*) could take over.[99] The wisdom which was signified in *gleaw-* and *-gleaw* ('shrewd, prudent, wise') compounds had to do not only with an individual foreseeing (*fore-*), thinking and feeling (*hyge-*, *-mod*, *ferhð-* and *hreðer-*), and speaking (*word-*), but also with the social processes of learning (*cræft-*) and nobility (*frea-*). Symbolic language supported the well-being, standards and values of aristocratic warrior society.

Explicit narrative providing symbols with their vehicle had its own generalizing conventions too, which will be analysed in the next two chapters, but meanwhile let us observe that symbols do not stay within the confines of a narrative through which they act. They do not even stay within the confines of the society which engendered them. They speak from society to society. They animate not only the time to which the story belonged, but also the time of the story's telling and the time of its reception, whenever that may be. They have a dramatic life of their own. They are an event in their own right whenever they occur. They deal in universals. They confront any generation, any social outlook, with the combination of aggression and protection (*guðreow* and *guðweard*), the blend of sorrow and triumph (*guðcearu* and *guðhreð*) and the clash of death and survival (*guðdeað* and *guðlaf*) which are at the heart of narrative living at any time, anywhere. They impart an intelligible cultural cohesion to the interplay of opposites inherent in human experience itself.

[99] Cf. Hume, 'The Concept of the Hall in Old English Poetry'.

5

Types of symbolic narrative

Having surveyed vernacular poetry's binary noun-based structures as a system for implying interactions of traditionally perceived basic potentials in active being, we should now turn our attention to the types of narrative which turned these implications into explicit active living, or – to put it in terms of the processes of poetry itself – produced active symbolization by converting symbolic potential into symbolic narrative. The essential agent of this change was a narrator: a narrator as a 'voice' uttering a poem was a *persona* distinct not only from anyone (or anyone else) in the narrative which he/she/it was telling but also from the composing poet on the one hand and an audience (or readership) on the other. The 'voice' had an 'identity' which varied from poem to poem, firstly according to the relationship which he/she/it claimed to have to what was being told – a narrator might assert that he/she/it had heard what was being recounted or had witnessed it or was speaking about him/her/itself – and secondly according to whether there was an explicit addressee (and, if so, of what sort) or no addressee in particular. Different types of narrative resulted from these variables in narration.

The *Beowulf* narrator, for example, was defined by a 'having heard' relationship to his material and by an absence of any claim to be addressing anyone in particular. He assumed the 'hearing' stance when relating, for instance, that Beowulf had passed on to Hygelac gifts which he had received from Hrothgar:

> Hyrde ic þæt þam frætwum feower mearas
> lungre, gelice last weardode,
> æppelfealuwe

['I have heard that four swift, matching, bay horses followed those treasures', 2163–5a].

On this occasion, as on others in the poem, the narrator was giving an explicit assurance that the story he was telling was based on what had been told before. He was claiming to be acting as a mouthpiece of oral tradition, and, indeed, he never referred to himself except in 'I have heard/learned' set phrases (and once in a 'We have learned' phrase which included along with him those he addressed (or at any rate some of them)).[1] But this by no means amounted to an undertaking that he was repeating the words of a previous telling. For example, Hrothgar's thegn, 'se ðe ealfela ealdgesegena / worn gemunde' ('who remembered a very great many old traditions', 869–70a), did no such thing: when he sang praising Beowulf's successful exploit against Grendel and recalling the glorious deeds of Sigemund and the grievous crimes of Heremod, he 'word oþer fand / soðe gebunden' ('composed new words truly joined',[2] 871b–2a). A poet drawing on tradition was not duty bound to reuse existing wording mechanically. The expectation was that his inherited material would be reexpressed in newly chosen, although thoroughly traditional, terms.

Reproduction was conceived of in this general sense. The intrinsic duty of a poet as an instrument of tradition was to recreate an emblematic tale by means of a fresh draught on the analogizing, generalizing, symbolizing potential of conventional poetic language – a tale in which, let us say, a representative 'hordweard hæleða' ('guardian of the treasure of warriors'), performing customary duties ('hordweorðung' ('honouring with gifts from the hoard') and so on), was tested against an elemental *cwealmcuma*, 'slaughter-comer', or *niðgæst*, 'violence-stranger', in a dramatic confrontation issuing in *wigsped*, 'success in war', or *sorhwylmas*, 'sorrow-surgings', and bringing in its wake either *ellenmærðu*, 'fame for fighting spirit', or *edwitlif*, 'a life of disgrace'. The recomposer of a traditional tale had the essential function of once more making the all-embracing language of poetry interact organically with his story, of calling on linguistic symbols yet again to bring to bear society's age-old perceptions of active being on the particular specimen of narrative living with which he was dealing. And his narrator had the function of reinforcing that bond between story and tradition – by formulating a general rule perhaps, or by making an

[1] On these formulas in general, see Parks, 'The Traditional Narrator', and, for the single 'we . . .', form in *Beowulf*, see above, p. 3, n. 1. For two important studies of the *Beowulf* narrator, see Greenfield, 'The Authenticating Voice' and Niles, *'Beowulf': the Poem and its Tradition*, pp. 197–204.

[2] On this translation, see *Beowulf*, ed. Klaeber, n. to 870 f.

underlying generalization explicit, or by pointing a universally applicable moral or by assigning praise or blame with which all would agree. For instance, the *Beowulf* narrator spoke up for this common experience at the outset of the poem, when he identified and sententiously approved of the behaviour which, on society's normal assumptions, would have accounted for the *woruldar*, 'honour in the world' (17b), which Scyld's young son had been granted:

Swa sceal geong guma gode gewyrcean,
fromum feohgiftum on fæder bearme,
þæt hine on ylde eft gewunigen
wilgesiþas, þonne wig cume,
leode gelæsten

['Thus a young man in the bosom of his father brings it about by generosity, by bold, rich gifts, that in turn willing companions remain with him in manhood, that his fellow-countryman do service when war comes', 20–4a].

And, again, when Beowulf presented to his *heafodmæg*, 'close relative' (2151a), Hygelac, the *hildesceorp*, 'battle-garment' (2155a), with which Hrothgar had rewarded him for his exploits in Denmark, the narrator offered a graphic generalization making the point that this was loyalty of the sort which is vital for the well-being of all kinsmen everywhere:

Swa sceal mæg don,
nealles inwitnet oðrum bregdon
dyrnum cræfte, deað renian
hondgesteallan. Hygelace wæs
niða heardum nefa swyðe hold,
ond gehwæðer oðrum hroþra gemyndig

['So a kinsman ought to do, not at all weave a net of malice for the other with hidden cunning, prepare death for his comrade. The nephew was very loyal to Hygelac, strong in battles, and each was mindful of benefits for the other', 2166b–71].

The narrator was giving voice to the time-honoured conceptions of propriety which the symbols implied.

As the *Beowulf* narrator's relationship to his material was rooted in social tradition, so too was his relationship to the audience which he never acknowledged explicitly but which nevertheless was always implied by the language he uttered. Like all narrators not speaking to a *þu* or *þe*, he never addressed a group in terms which were applicable only to them in a particular place at a particular time. His sole audience was the comprehensive one common to all poetry and therefore only generally conceived and not subject to particularized address. A narrator never identified a collective audience in front of him as 'you'. He never flattered them in this thirteenth- (or early-fourteenth-)century manner:

> Herken, lordyngys þat ben trewe,
> And y wol ȝou telle of Syr Orphewe.[3]

Nor did he ever invite them to imagine that they themselves were on the scene of action in their own right and were direct spectators of what had happened. Events were not angled towards their mind's eye as such. For instance, when Beowulf was about to embark for his *wilsið* to Denmark, it is stated 'flota wæs on yðum, / bat under beorge' ('the floater was on the waves, the boat under a cliff', 210b–11a). Beowulf had ordered an *yðlida*, 'wave-traveller' (198b), to be prepared and had led his picked men towards the 'landgemyrcu' ('shore', 209b). Then his *yðlida* materializes, so to say: 'Fyrst forð gewat; flota wæs on yðum, / bat under beorge' ('Time passed; the floater was on the waves, the boat under a cliff', 210–11a). But we, as an audience, are not assigned a physical standpoint from which to view the scene. We are not thought of as anywhere in particular, either specifically inside the action – on the shore beside the boat or on the clifftop, for example – or specifically outside it. Instead, set in sequential time, and in space only within that flow, a process is going on with which we have a general connection.[4] Symbolic *sundwudu* (208a) and 'landgemyrcu' (209b), towards which Beowulf, symbolized as 'lagucræftig mon' (209a), was heading with his men, have already been introduced, and the interaction involved has been rendered emblematic by insertion of 'lagucræftig mon' between *sundwudu* and 'landgemyrcu':

> fiftyna sum
> sundwudu sohte, secg wisade,
> lagucræftig mon landgemyrcu

['One of fifteen he sought the sea-wood, the man, one skilled on water, led the way to the margins of the land', 207b–9].

Sundwudu and 'landgemyrcu' have signalled the twin concepts underlying

[3] *Sir Orfeo*, ed. Bliss, lines 23–4 (MS London, BL, Harley 3810).
[4] See above, p. 87, n. 49.

the act of embarkation on the *yðlida*, namely that this vessel was the means both of voyaging on the deep sea and of leaving the land; and then the two functions of the *yðlida* materialize as *flota* and *bat* respectively, the one associated with the sea (*on yðum*) and the other with the land's edge (*under beorge*). We, like the narrator, are sharing in the interactions initiated by the symbols. His involvement and ours are equally parts of the total span of narrative implication in symbolic language. When the *Beowulf* narrator began his recital as a spokesman of traditional knowledge (1–3), those whom he associated with himself in the corporate *we* (1a) comprised, in respect of language, all who were inheritors of, and all who ever will inherit, the symbolic tradition.

That is not to say that we (today), as members of that unlimited audience, necessarily become remote from events or are in any way indifferent to them. Indeed, the reference to the boat both on the waves and under the cliff, coming when it does, proves the exact opposite. Our attention has been concentrated on Beowulf (so far unnamed) since he was introduced, some fourteen lines before, as 'Higelaces þegn' (194b), noble, mighty and intent on crossing the sea to free King Hrothgar from the misery of Grendel's depredations (196–8a and 199b–201). We have heard how he ordered a good ship to be made ready (198b–9a), how the wise among his countrymen encouraged him (202–4) and how he chose the boldest champions he could find to accompany him (205–7a). His preparations have moved on apace, as uncomplicated language conveys: he himself is *god* ('good', 195a and 205a) and so is the boat he orders (199b); apposition of nouns is employed only to stress the stature which the undertaking had in relation to Hrothgar as both *guðcyning* (199b) and 'mærne þeoden' (201a); finite verbs follow one another, without recourse to their subject, to indicate the speed with which Beowulf acted (*gefrægn* (194a), *het* (198b), *cwæð* (199b)) and the eagerness with which the wise urged him on ('lythwon logon' (203a), *hwetton* (204a), *sceawedon* (204b)). Our interest and anticipation are increasingly caught up in this personal initiative. Our confidence in the competence of 'Higelaces þegn' grows steadily until it is confirmed by the first symbolic epithet applied to him since he sprang into action: 'lagucræftig mon' (209a) reveals that he had just the sort of skill which the job immediately in hand demanded. The boat on the shore gave him his opportunity. We apprehend this ship, poised at a boundary between waves and cliff, as an embodiment of the hero's aspirations. It is a clearcut image of his irreversible commitment.

The interplay of symbolic implication and explicit narrative generates a psychological interest which engages and holds our sympathy throughout.

The narrator's audience-directed function was consistently to strengthen this interest by calling attention to the psychological elements in the story. For example, when about a quarter of the 120–line account of Beowulf's fight against Grendel (702b–823a) is devoted to the protagonists' thoughts and feelings, expressed in poetic, especially symbolic, terms, he regularly comments on them. Grendel's realization that he could not loosen his enemy's grip on his fingers evokes from the narrator the exclamation, 'þæt wæs geocor sið, / þæt se hearmscaþa to Heorute ateah!' ('That was a grievous journey that the harm-injurer took to Heorot!', 765b–6).[5] The Danes' terror at the noise of the fight and at the damage which the hall was sustaining is glossed by the narrator thus:

Þæs ne wendon ær witan Scyldinga,
þæt hit a mid gemete manna ænig
betlic ond banfag tobrecan meahte,
listum tolucan, nymþe liges fæþm
swulge on swaþule

['Wise men of the Scyldings had not expected that any man could ever by any means break it up, splendid and decorated with bone, cleverly pull it apart, unless the embrace of fire should swallow it in flame', 778–82a].[6]

When Beowulf's men drew their swords to defend their leader, the narrator supplies the information they lacked:

þone synscaðan
ænig ofer eorþan irenna cyst,
guðbilla nan gretan nolde;
ac he sigewæpnum forsworen hæfde,
ecga gehwylcre

[5] *Sið*, 'journey', with preceding adjective was a well-established symbol. Cf., e.g., in *Beowulf* alone, *eðe sið* ('ne wæs þæt eðe sið', 2586b), 'sorhfullne sið' (512a, 1278a and 1429a) and 'wide siðas' (877b); cf. also 'geocrostne sið' (*Daniel* 616a). (*Hearmscaþa* is, of course, a second symbol in this exclamation.)

[6] 'Witan Scyldinga' (cf. in other poems *Greca*, 'Romana' and 'Filistina witan') and *liges fæþm* (cf. *banan*, *bates*, *brimes*, *dracan*, *engla*, *eorðan*, *fæder*, *fæmnan*, *feondes*, *flodes*, *foldan*, *Francna*, *fremdes*, *fyres*, *godes*, *greotes*, *lifes* and *lufan fæðm*) are two symbols in this observation.

['no choice iron anywhere in the world, no battle-sword, would approach the wicked injurer; but he had rendered victory-weapons, every blade, useless by a spell', 801b–5a].[7]

The narrator's 'voice' sets the emotional and mental experiences of all the participants – Beowulf, Grendel, Geats and Danes – in more extensive perspectives of time, space, magic, fate or religion than the protagonists could perceive for themselves. Regularly, specifically and explicitly he bestows universal affiliations on the individual thoughts and feelings with which we directly sympathize.

When someone was relating events in his (or her) own experience to someone whom he/she knew, the scale was altogether different: then the account usually reflected only the points of view of the teller and the listener. This was the case when, for instance, Beowulf told Hygelac how he had fared in his encounter with Grendel (2069b–100). Gone are the *Beowulf* narrator's preoccupations with society, religion, fate and magic, with insights into Grendel's nature and states of mind, with a balanced view of two counterpoised combatants locked in elemental struggle (indeed there is no account of the fight at all), with reactions of Danes and Geats, with description as such. Instead we have just the hero's own painful memories of one of his beloved companions (now named for the first time) falling immediate victim to Grendel's rapacity (2076–80); of the ruthless killer, having once tasted blood and wanting more, advancing and grabbing hold of Beowulf himself (2081–5a); of the view he had had of Grendel's gaping pouch (not previously mentioned) into which he would have been pushed, like so many others, had he not resisted (2085b–92). And we have too his personal insistence that all had been done for the glory of Hygelac's people (2093–6a). This is a vivid, dramatic, account which began symbolically enough as 'hondræs hæleða' ('a hand-to-hand onslaught of warriors', 2072a),[8] but which never went outside the purview of the 'we' (2074b–5a), among whom the 'I', the teller (Beowulf (2069b, 2084b, 2089a, 2092a, 2093b and 2095a), had waited for Grendel to arrive in the hall (2072b–5), and of the 'you' (Hygelac), who was being told (2070b and 2095).

[7] *Synscaða*, *guðbill* and *sigewæpen* furnish this comment with three symbols.

[8] Cf. *beadu-*, *deað-*, *feond-*, *gar-*, *guð-*, *heaðo-*, *hilde-*, *mægen-*, *sweord-* and *wælræs* elsewhere in extant poetry, half of them in *Beowulf*, and especially 'wælræs weora' (*Beowulf* 2947a), a battle between Swedes and Geats.

Symbolic narrative, using traditional language which implied analogy and generalization, was at root a formalization of the personal, direct passing of news or opinion or advice which was part of everyday life. Indeed, some extant poems present themselves directly as the words of an individual addressing an individual hearer, without benefit of a mediating narrator. In such cases the speaker appropriated to him/herself poetic expression, including symbols, and, in so doing, joined to his/her consciousness of his/her own narrative existence narrative implications which were traditionally perceived at large in society and in nature and hence were perceivable by any audience in the symbolic tradition. This was a coordination of individual thinking and feeling with collective experience, not the technique we moderns would desire for analysing the mechanisms of the human mind. What could vary, however, was whether, on the one hand, the personal point of view or, on the other, the public perspective predominated in the resulting narrative, as two examples will show.

In *Wulf and Eadwacer* the speaker has our undivided attention, for the named persons (or person) being addressed (13–15 and 16–17a) were not physically present. We are listening to thoughts shaped by strong emotion. The language, deceptively simple, has meaning for the speaker which we grasp only in a general way, as at the beginning:

Leodum is minum swylce him mon lac gife;
willað hy hine aþecgan, gif he on þreat cymeð.
Ungelic is us. (1–3)

To whom do the third-person pronouns refer? *Hy*, 'they', presumably has its antecedent in *leodum minum*, 'my people'; but does *him* also refer back to *leodum minum* or, along with *hine* and *he*, to some person as yet unidentified? And does *us* couple the speaker with his/her people or with one or more others now first mentioned? Does *lac* here bear the meaning 'gift', 'sacrificial offering', 'booty' or 'battle'? Does *aþecgan* mean 'to take (food)'? Is the *willað hy* clause a statement or a question? Does *on* (*þreat*) mean 'into' or 'in' ('a troop')?[9] As regards the essential situation, however, we feel no doubt: the speaker's thoughts are wholly on a personal relationship set in subjective contrast to outside forces.

Soon our sympathies are both deepened and broadened. The information

[9] Cf. Greenfield, '*Wulf and Eadwacer*: All Passion Pent', p. 11 (repr. Greenfield, *Hero and Exile*, p. 191).

that the speaker is a woman in a sexual conflict is complemented by bold general images:

> Wulfes ic mines widlastum wenum dogode;
> þonne hit wæs renig weder ond ic reotugu sæt,
> þonne mec se beaducafa bogum gelegde,
> wæs me wyn to þon, wæs me hwæþre eac lað

['I have endured my Wulf's wide wanderings with hopes; when it was rainy weather and I sat crying, when the battle-bold man covered me with his bent arms, there was some pleasure for me, and yet there was also pain', 9–12].

Symbolic language is playing its part. *Se beaducafa* (11a) in combination with the woman weeping in rainy weather, his arms like boughs or bows, acts as a symbol of masculinity free of any particularities of identity. Unnamed herself, and with nature providing its counterpart to her grief, the woman is as elemental as this lover. A woman divided has become capable of embodying the spirit of imaginative universals: 'þæt mon eaþe tosliteð', she declares in her extreme of scorn (or desperation), 'þætte næfre gesomnad wæs, / uncer giedd geador' ('It is easy to sever what has never been united, the song of us two together', 18–19). Only a human heart could divide something which has never been a unit and yet is a song sung together by two people.[10] A woman's frustrated passion has attained communion with the interactive world through metaphor and bitter paradox.

In *The Husband's Message* (or, as would be better I think, *A Lover's Message*), on the other hand, movement is in the opposite direction: a man very much in the public domain is seeking to resume a personal relationship. (I discuss the poem in the form which results from John Pope's meticulous reconstruction of lost readings – some of them important – and from his inclusion, at the beginning, of the seventeen lines which Krapp and Dobbie printed as *Riddle* 60.[11] As a consequence my line numbers start with a series 1–17 (corresponding to Krapp and Dobbie's riddle) before starting again with the numbers those editors apply to *The Husband's Message*.)

First a being speaks which, in its natural environment of elemental

[10] Cf. Renoir, '*Wulf and Eadwacer*: a Noninterpretation', p. 149.

[11] Pope, 'Palaeography and Poetry', pp. 42–63. It is worth pointing out that if these lines were an independent riddle they would be the only extant one whose narrative consists of direct speech to a 'you'.

solitude, had little dreamed that, mouthless as it was, it would ever discourse in human society:

Ic wæs be sonde, sæwealle neah,
æt merefaroþe, minum gewunade
frumstaþole fæst; fea ænig wæs
monna cynnes, þæt minne þær
on anæde eard beheolde,
ac mec uhtna gehwam yð sio brune
lagufæðme beleolc. Lyt ic wende
þæt ic ær oþþe sið æfre sceolde
ofer meodubence muðleas sprecan,
wordum wrixlan

['I was by water[12] near a seawall at the ocean shore, dwelt firmly attached to my original base; there was hardly anyone of the human race that beheld my dwelling-place in that solitude, but every dawn the gleaming wave played around me with watery embrace. Little did I expect that I should ever speak, mouthless, over the mead-bench, discourse with words', (*Riddle* 60) 1–10a].

Marvellously, this piece of elemental nature goes on to relate, a man's deep thought and knife-point working together ('eorles ingeþonc ond ord samod' ((*Riddle* 60) 13)) have enabled it boldly to deliver a message 'to you' (*wiþ þe* ((*Riddle* 60) 14b)) in private ('for unc anum twam' ((*Riddle* 60) 15a)) 'swa hit beorna ma / uncre wordcwidas widdor ne mænden' ('in such a way that other men would not repeat our words more widely', (*Riddle* 60) 16b–17). It is made of yew, the object confides, and has had to voyage overseas many times at its lord's behest.[13] 'Eom nu her cumen' (8b), it continues,

on ceolþele, ond nu cunnan scealt
hu þu ymb modlufan mines frean
on hyge hycge. Ic gehatan dear
þæt þu þær tirfæste treowe findest

['I have now come here on board ship, and now you must know how you think in

[12] See Pope's discussion, *ibid.*, p. 55.

[13] Pope has surmised (*ibid.*, n. 71) that these former voyages might have been occasioned by the stick bearing other messages which would have been shaved off when no longer wanted. But yew is too hard a wood to be readily reused in this way. More probably, I think, the stick had travelled widely because its master did not know where the intended recipient of its message was.

your heart about my lord's love. I dare promise that you will find there unalterable[14] faith', (*The Husband's Message*) 9–12].

At this point the inscription itself, I believe, takes over the talking: 'Hwæt, þec þonne biddan het se þisne beam agrof / þæt þu sinchroden . . .' ('Lo, he who inscribed this piece of wood then commanded me to ask that you, richly adorned, . . .', 13–14a) I interpret as marking the transition.[15] It reminds the lady (as we now know her to be) of the vows she and her lover had often exchanged until he was driven into exile (13–20a), and urges her to set sail as soon as spring comes and to journey south, where he eagerly awaits her (20b-9): he can think of no greater pleasure than that God should grant that she may join him in the princely life which he has rebuilt there for himself, lacking only the joy of possessing her (30–47 or 48). It adopts a suitably lyrical style. For instance it renders 'when spring comes' as

siþþan þu gehyrde on hliþes oran
galan geomorne geac on bearwe

['as soon as you have heard at the cliff's edge the mournful cuckoo sing in the wood', 22–3],

and dilates in similar vein upon her lover going into exile:

wineleas gewat of wicstede,
nyde gebæded nacan ut aþrong,
ond on yþa gebelg ana sceolde
faran on flotweg, forðsiþes georn,
mengan merestreamas

[14] I have followed Pope in translating *tirfæste* so, accepting his suggestion that the use of the word here is related to *tir* as the name of the T-rune and to the meaning, 'a guiding star (or constellation) which keeps unfailing faith (*trywa*) with princes (*æþelingas*)', which is attributed to this name in *The Rune Poem*; see 'Palaeography and Poetry', p. 60 n. But I would go further and propose that in the present instance *tirfæste* refers directly to a T-rune opening the inscription on the piece of wood; and *þær* (12a) I take to mean 'in front of you'. A paraphrase which would convey the correct sense of 12 would be, in my opinion, 'You will find that this inscription in front of you expresses my lord's unfailing faithfulness.'

[15] A new paragraph starts here in the manuscript, but that is not decisive, as there are similar breaks at (*The Husband's Message*) 1 and 26, where no change of speaker is involved.

['[he] set out friendless from his dwelling-place, driven by necessity pushed out his boat, and alone on the swelling of the waves had to travel the seaway, eager to journey ahead had to stir the ocean-streams', 39–43a].[16]

Finally it 'hears'[17] five specified runes confer authority on the message by swearing

þæt he þa wære ond þa winetreowe
be him lifgendum læstan wolde,
þe git on ærdagum oft gespræcon

['that he [her lover] would fulfil, as long as he lives, the covenant and the loving faith which you two often declared in former days', 51–3].

A 'þeodnes dohtor' ('daughter of a leader of a people', 47a), *sinchroden* (14a), has received an eloquent message of love composed probably in verse and committed to a rune-stave by a *þeoden*, 'leader of a people' (29a), who, after misfortune overcome, now knows no lack

ne meara ne maðma ne meododreama,
æniges ofer eorþan eorlgestreona

['of horses or treasures or mead-joys, or of any kind of warrior-possessions on earth', 45–6],

except for her (47b). She first takes in the stave as a whole and then reads its inscription. We 'hear' the stave and the inscription 'say' in turn what she comprehends. But we do not enter into her mind. We do not know how she responds. All takes place purely on a symbolic plane. Our mind's eye forms an image of an aristocratic lady receiving an elegant reaffirmation of steadfast love and offer of social fulfilment.

When someone 'uttering' a poem about his/her/itself was not directly addressing anyone but was speaking only for the benefit of the general audience implied by symbolic language, the individual concerned was blended completely with the socially based narrator of oral tradition. The speaker of *The Wife's Lament*, for example, acknowledged this duality at the outset: 'Ic þis giedd wrece bi me ful geomorre, / minre sylfre sið' ('I utter this poem about my very sad self, my own experience', 1–2a). She was telling her individual tale to the world at large and adopted straightaway a mode of expression combining personal and public generalization:

[16] On the readings in 39 and 41 (Pope's 40 and 42), see Pope, 'Palaeography and Poetry', pp. 61–3 nn.
[17] See *ibid.*, p. 63 n.

Ic þæt secgan mæg,
hwæt ic yrmþa gebad   siþþan ic up weox,
niwes oþþe ealdes,   no ma þonne nu.
A ic wite wonn   minra wræcsiþa

['I can tell what distress I have endured ever since I grew up, recently or long ago, never more than now. I have suffered the torment of my deprivations always', 2b–5].

The experiences which she was going to relate had been constant and, as she implied by using signals customary to gnomic utterance (*mæg*, *no* and *a*),[18] were of a type long known to society as a whole. Above all, through the term *wræcsiþ*, symbolizing the unhappiness of a state of exile, she showed that she was going to view her actions in their broad, general nature as well as for their impact on her as their doer.[19] Her narrative account of herself which followed, in the same vein of generality,[20] put these intentions into effect, and so did her imagining of the grief (*breost-* and *modcearu* (44b and 51a)) which her lover, she believed, must be feeling (*habban sceal* (43b)) at that very time, whatever his circumstances, haunted by recollections (*gemon to oft* (51b)) of the happiness he had lost by their separation and by his estrangement from her which others had engineered. Her thoughts of him took their starting point from a maxim, 'A scyle geong mon wesan geomormod, / heard heortan geþoht' ('A young person should always be sad of mind, the purpose in his heart be hard', 42–3a), and another maxim summed everything up: 'Wa bið þam þe sceal / of langoþe leofes abidan' ('Ill is it for one who has to await a beloved out of longing', 52b–3). The whole of her adult existence had been a living example of this general truth, so that symbolic expressions of grief applied equally, whether the suffering was her own[21] or her lover's[22] or was the subject of explicit generalization (*geomormod*). Her consistently unfulfilled longing had been a pronounced instance of the *wræcsiþas* which are an integral part of all human experience.[23]

[18] Cf. above, p. 120.   [19] Cf. below, p. 401, esp. n. 106.

[20] See, e.g., *uht-* and *modcearu* (7b and 40a), *wræcsiþas* (38b) and *Ful oft* (32b).

[21] *Uht-*, *modcearu* and *weaþearf* (10b).

[22] *Breost-*, *modcearu* and *hygegeomor* (19b) and *werigmod* (49a).

[23] Cf. Hill, '"Þæt wæs geomuru ides!"', esp. 'the stereotype of the woman-as-victim, as *geomuru ides*, was a dominant one in Old English and . . . carried considerable emotional weight, akin to that of the exile, to which it is often close in circumstance and language' (p. 242).

Ill-considered action, another tendency inherent in active being, is signified by the *unrædsiþas* thematic to *Riddle* 11. The 'voice' of this riddle claims that its anarchic nature is to encourage this inclination in others:

Hrægl is min hasofag, hyrste beorhte,
reade ond scire on reafe minum.
Ic dysge dwelle ond dole hwette
unrædsiþas, oþrum styre
nyttre fore. Ic þæs nowiht wat
þæt heo swa gemædde, mode bestolene,
dæde gedwolene, deoraþ mine
won wisan gehwam. Wa him þæs þeawes,
siþþan heah bringað horda deorast,
gif hi unrædes ær ne geswicaþ

['My garment is shiny grey, ornaments on my raiment are bright, red and brilliant. I lead silly men astray and incite fools to ill-advised behaviour; others I steer away from a useful course of action. I do not know at all that, thus maddened, deprived of their wits, led astray in deed, they praise my crooked way in any respect. Ill will it be for them on account of that conduct, after they bring high the dearest of treasures, if they have not abandoned folly'].

This speaker, like the estranged wife in the *Lament*, is addressing the world at large and is measuring what it tells about itself against the canons of general truth (*Wa him* . . .). It takes that relationship with generality significantly further than she does, however: what it recounts is not the experience it has had so far but the course of its life now and at all times. It recites the recurrent, habitual behaviour which constitutes its very nature. It is claiming not merely to have fulfilled a long-recognized general pattern but to be a pattern. It is presenting the pattern which is its inherent self. And that means adopting the general standpoint against itself: willy-nilly it warningly characterizes itself as disruptive and potentially destructive to all. In clear but general terms it reveals itself to be a treacherous combination of an attractive appearance and an ability to inject into others a deadly mixture of folly (*unræd*) and enterprise (*sið*) which has disastrous consequences for them unless they throw off its evil influence.

Less clear is what exactly this being is. It could be wine (or other intoxicating drink) in a jewelled cup, as most critics think. (Some have preferred 'night' or 'gold'.) But it is also partly human: it wears clothes as well as possessing faculties of thought and speech, though it lays no claim to any other human features. And what are we to make of the words, 'heah bringað [*MS* bringeð] horda deorast'? (Textual uncertainties have provoked a variety of emendations.[24]) To what particular point of no return do they allude? Is it some sort of formal oath-taking ceremony in hall, I wonder? Or is 'horda deorast' the wine at communion, or the soul 'raised high' at the last judgement, or the sun, as has been variously thought? Evidently, identifying a specific dangerpoint in our existence mattered less than warning against a kind of danger, *unrædsiþas*, a symbolic loss of mental control over our actions. Doubtless that is why no account was given of how this being exerts its evil influence. Instead the poet has used the self-authenticating voice teasingly to take us into a metaphorical world of surreal images, there to administer to us the shock, general but no less real for that, of hearing an ambiguous quasi-anthropomorphous agent of destruction paradoxically denouncing itself.

Phenomena of this imaginary order speak for all to hear in over half our extant riddles, thereby assuming the validity of speaking beings. In the rest they are spoken of to the world at large by an independent first-person narrator, who in rather more than two-thirds of these cases, claims to have been a direct witness: *Ic seah*, 'I have seen', such a riddle typically begins. (*Ic gefrægn*, 'I have learned', or *Ic wat*, 'I know', occurs only exceptionally.) A speaker of this 'I have seen' kind was reporting an act of witness which often had had a dramatic impact on him: epithets such as *sellic*, *wrætlic(e)* and *wundorlic*, 'strange', 'amazing', 'wonderful', were on the lips of these witnesses much more often than beings used them about themselves; and 'Dum starem et mirarem vidi gloriam magnam' ('While I was standing and wondering, I saw a great glory'), was how the speaker of the only Latin riddle in the Exeter Book (no. 90) described the experience he had had. An 'I have seen' speaker had been an actor in a dramatic situation, which could have included, for example, a second observer chipping in, as in *Riddle* 38: 'Mon maþelade, se þe me gesægde' (5).[25] But the quoted speaker also remained wholly anonymous. At the heart of this 'I have seen' drama had been a direct encounter with a being which was every bit as elemental as those that spoke for themselves: for instance, while the essential nature of the being uttering *Riddle* 11 was to instigate *unrædsiþas*, the *wiht* observed in *Riddle* 38 was 'wæpnedcynnes' ('of a weaponed kind'), 'geoguðmyrþe

[24] For a convenient summary and for an account of the various solutions proposed for this riddle, see *The Old English Riddles of the 'Exeter Book'*, ed. Williamson, pp. 163–4 and 165–6 (notes and commentary on his riddle 9).

[25] See above, p. 105.

grædig' ('greedy for the pleasure of youth') and joyfully exacting tribute (*gafol*) from 'ferðfriþende' ('the life-sustaining one').[26] This anonymous narrator was as representative as this being. Enigmatic beings were authenticated equally effectively as symbolic, if strange, inhabitants of the narrative world whether they spoke for themselves or persons with conventional credentials gave their word to have observed them in action.

The expanse of imaginative experience which these two narrative procedures opened up had four main components. The starting-point was an actual creature (a cuckoo, ox, plough, sword, bagpipe, bookworm, weathercock, onion, iceberg or whatever) or an ensemble of creatures acting together (a pen and three fingers, for example). Secondly there were the features attributed to this initial creature (or group) metaphorically, by analogy with another living being, which might be of an indeterminate kind, or animal, or, most often, human.[27] Thirdly there was the being which resulted from this combination. *Wiht* was the word regularly applied to this last. Related to the transitive verb *wegan*, 'to move, bear, carry, weigh',[28] this term conveyed a sense of inherent movement. (The common translation 'creature', it should be noted, introduces an erroneous implication of 'something created'.) Fourthly there was what this *wiht* (or part of it) should be called. Many a riddle led up to the challenge 'Saga hwæt ic hatte' ('Say what I am called') – or, if the speaker was not the being itself, 'Saga hwæt hio hatte' – or words to that effect. The demand took the form of 'Say what it *is*' comparatively rarely.[29]

Poets played all parts of this system boldly, uninhibitedly, provocatively. For one thing, the creature which was the starting-point could be a singular oddity indeed – a one-eyed seller of garlic in *Riddle* 86, for instance. (We could not realize this without the aid of the title of a related Latin riddle (no. 94) of Symphosius.) Then bizarre metaphor could be applied: as transformed in *Riddle* 31, a bagpipe had a beautiful voice in its foot and brothers on its neck. The information supplied about a being could be perversely chosen: the being of *Riddle* 33, for instance (identifiable

[26] See *ibid.*

[27] For a classification along these lines, see *Anglo-Saxon Riddle-Songs*, trans. Williamson, pp. 19–23.

[28] Cf. above, p. 80.

[29] In contrast to the standard use of 'Say to me who / what is / was / does / did so-and-so' in the vernacular prose wisdom tradition represented by *The 'Prose Solomon and Saturn'*, ed. Cross and Hill.

for other reasons as an iceberg or ice floe), declares that it has a mother who is also, paradoxically, its daughter (9–11a)).[30] Numbers could be used to render a being a grotesque assemblage: for example, some editors and critics have identified as a ship the starting-point of the being of *Riddle* 36, 1–8, travelling with four feet under its belly and eight on its back, two wings, twelve eyes and six heads, but, not surprisingly, by no means all have agreed that that was in fact so.[31] Sometimes attributes were described so broadly that it is hardly possible to give their possessor a single name to the exclusion of all others; sometimes they are so paradoxical that it seems impossible to name their possessor at all: for example, what name could apply to the being of *Riddle* 74, at once a woman, both young and old, and a good looking man, flying with birds as well as swimming in the sea, diving dead with fishes as well as stepping alive on land? Should we call it ship-figurehead, water, cuttlefish, siren, soul, swan, sea-eagle or quill pen, as at least one critic has proposed in each case,[32] or was it none of these, or all of them, or more? On some occasions *double entendre* was deliberately contrived: in *Riddle* 44, for instance, the being could be called equally well penis or key. Or, again, a being's name could depend on (to us, at least) obscure numbers: in *Riddle* 22 sixty men went riding to a shore with eleven horses and four *sceamas* ('bright ones'?).

As to a being's name, whenever any information was provided it was coded in a form which constituted a part, or the whole, of the puzzle. If runes were cited, their names, with their own semantic value, partici-

[30] The riddler did not invent this paradox. He was giving his own mystifying form to a 'mother and daughter' paradox which had been traditionally applied to ice: Pompeius had cited it in his grammatical commentary, in the hexametric form 'mater me genuit, eadem mox gignitur ex me' ('a mother bore me, that very same is soon born from me'), as a defining example of an enigma and had supplied the solution 'ice'; and Aldhelm repeated this wording, but without reference to ice, in the introduction to his own *Enigmata* (*Aldhelmi Opera*, ed. Ehwald, p. 77); cf. *The Old English Riddles of the 'Exeter Book'*, ed. Williamson, p. 238 (his riddle 31). The *mater et filia* paradox, applied to the Virgin Mary as both mother and daughter of Christ, had been given wide circulation by St Augustine, and this tradition too was known to Aldhelm (*De virginitate*, ed. Ehwald, *Aldhelmi Opera*, p. 292); for an account of this tradition, see Mayer, 'Mater et Filia', cited Breeze, 'The Virgin Mary, Daughter of her Son', at n. 1. I am grateful to Andy Orchard for pointing out to me this reference and for other help with this note.

[31] See *The Old English Riddles of the 'Exeter Book'*, ed. Williamson, pp. 248–52 (commentary on Williamson's riddle 34).

[32] See *ibid.*, pp. 349–52 (commentary on Williamson's riddle 72).

pated in the verse.[33] In these circumstances an audience had first to convert the names into letters and then to try and make those letters yield a word or words; not uncommonly the letters had to be rearranged (reversed order was the easiest possibility to test). But that was nothing as compared with being faced by only cryptic clues: for instance, *Riddle* 58, after describing a being which, one-footed, heavy-tailed, small-headed, long-tongued and toothless, carries water into the air but itself neither drinks nor eats, ends tantalizingly, 'þry sind in naman / ryhte runstafas, þara is Rad foran [*MS* furum]' ('There are three correct runes in its name, of which *rad* is in front', 14b–15). Is *rad* a rune (and, if it is, is it counted in the three or not), or is it a word forming the first element of a compound which has a second element spelled by the three runes?[34] I do not suppose contemporaries would have found it entirely straightforward to identify the intended name even if equipped with an authentic text.[35]

The sport of riddling poets was to interfere in various ways with the usual relationships between generalization and recognition. The game, when taken to its limits, was first to strip away from a creature all but essential features of its active identity – leaving only a bagpipe's chanter, say, or a ship's keel, or a nightingale's voice, or a writer's hand, – and then to disguise the feature as an unlikely occurrence of the same active potential in another creature, a chanter, for instance, becoming a voice in a foot, a keel a single foot, and so on. Riddling offered the possibility of exempting the principles of active being from the restraints of normal physical manifestation. The potential of the mode was not limited to hybrid beings which were partly the original creatures and partly others, as *yðmearh*, 'a wave horse', was part ship, part horse.[36] Poets who chose to could exploit metaphoric imagination to create an order of altogether new, enigmatic combinations of active features. An assemblage of one foot, many ribs and a

[33] A disparate combination of potentials (see above, pp. 105–6) was involved when a runic character functioned both as a symbol of a sound and as a name with a meaning of its own – a diversity rendered overtly paradoxical by the words, 'ond se torhta Æsc / an an linan' ('and the bright *æsc*, one on the line', *Riddle* 42, 9b–10a).

[34] For the various opinions which have been advanced and for a summary of the emendations which have been proposed for MS *furum*, see *The Old English Riddles of the 'Exeter Book'*, ed. Williamson, pp. 311–12 (notes on Williamson's riddle 56). Are some words, including rune names, missing between *Rad* and *furum*?

[35] For a chronological bibliographical guide to all the solutions which have been proposed for each of the Exeter Book riddles, see Fry, 'Exeter Book Riddle Solutions'.

[36] Cf. above, pp. 99–100.

mouth, though no eyes, hands, shoulders or arms (*Riddle* 32), is an example. This was a being which carried a wealth of food, yelling as it went. The poet who imagined this fantastic phenomenon was not thereby seeking to express the human subconscious, as a modern surrealist might, through an irrational juxtaposition of realistic images: the interest for him lay in the imagined being, not in the imagination which created it. He and other poets like him were intent on exploring the possibilities of the symbolic system – on taking liberties with its processes of perceiving, metaphorizing and naming. They were inventing a range of vigorous beings which were strikingly abnormal in form while performing genuine symbolic functions. These poets' imaginations were spawning a progeny, which, however strange, could yet claim an age-old right to exist by remaining true to the symbolic system in what they did, and which were thus properly eligible to be validated in society at large by either of the standard narrative procedures of self-proclamation or representative direct witness.

A first-person speaker framing a whole poem by uttering it was always a facilitator of the symbolic system. The 'I have heard/learned' type was the vehicle for conveying to the present a part of the past of which the present was but a continuation. The 'I have seen', 'I have done', 'I do' types spoke for social or natural or imagined elements in the living environment. The tone could be highly personal in content and address, as is the *Wulf and Eadwacer* speaker's

Wulf, min Wulf,   wena me þine
seoce gedydon,   þine seldcymas,
murnende mod,   nales meteliste

['Wulf, my Wulf, hopes for you have made me ill, your infrequent comings, a sorrowing heart, not at all a lack of food', 13–15],

or consistently impersonal in both regards, as is the self-effacing lyricism with which the 'I have seen' narrator of *Riddle* 29 voiced humanity's sense of wonder when confronted by one of the mighty processes of nature: he/she had seen the moon and sun execute their routine (1–11)[37] quite indifferent to observation, had grasped the essentials of the whole scene when the sun successfully counter-attacked after the moon's *heresiþ* ('Dust stonc to heofonum, deaw feol on eorþan, / niht forð gewat' ('Dust rose to heaven,

[37] See above, p. 106.

dew fell on earth, night went on its way', 12–13a)), and took for granted the presence of mankind, collectively watching ('Nænig siþþan / wera gewiste þære wihte sið' ('No man afterwards knew the being's journey', 13b–14)). But, whatever variation there was in the personal input, the constant was a speaker's mediation between symbolic experience and the general audience implied by symbolic language. A framing voice was the *sine qua non* of a narrative poem for that very reason. A poetic narrative could be no other than a fresh, linguistic, act of integration within the symbolic system and a 'voice' was the indispensable instrument of that act.

6

Basic characteristics of symbolic story

The 'I/we have heard/learned' narrator by definition was not himself contributing the essential dramatic ingredient of direct witness. By alleging that he was the mouthpiece of tradition he was distancing himself from the events themselves by at least one remove and often many more. I call narrative with this inbuilt element of transmission 'story'. Story, thus constituted, especially if it was dealing with happenings outside living memory, was in no position to enforce a hard-and-fast distinction between original 'fact' and later 'fiction'. Beowulf himself, for instance, probably never existed.[1] In all likelihood stories were attached to him which had been attached to others before: for example, as Campbell pointed out, Beowulf probably owed his youthful swimming contest with Breca (499–589) to taking over the adventures of another hero who competed with Breca in this way in a lay known to the *Beowulf* poet and who was perhaps a Finn, since the sea, for no apparent reason, is said to have carried Beowulf to Finland (579b–81a).[2] Story's way of validating itself was to incorporate authenticating processes of witness as part and parcel of its own narrative. To carry conviction such testimony had to be true to collective experience, just as poetic language was. Story was symbolic in the observation it included as well as in the words it used: it reported representative witness in representative language.

Men when gathered in hall or other assembly were society's basic means of establishing corporate witness. Their authenticating presence was something to be mentioned if a being could have been observed in these circumstances: *Riddle* 55, for instance, began

[1] Cf. above, pp. 54–5.

[2] Campbell, 'The Use in *Beowulf* of Earlier Heroic Verse', pp. 284–5.

Ic seah in healle, þær hæleð druncon,
on flet beran feower cynna

['I have seen in hall, where warriors were drinking, four kinds carried on to the floor', 1–2].

And *Riddle* 59 similarly: 'Ic seah in healle hring gyldenne / men sceawian' ('I have seen in hall men look intently at a golden ring', 1–2a). In those riddles which had neither a being speaking for itself nor an 'I have seen' narrator and which were thus 'free-standing' narratives – a dozen or so among our extant materials – corporate witness could become a strongly felt dramatic moment. *Riddle* 86 began, 'Wiht cwom gongan þær weras sæton / monige on mæðle', ('A being came moving where many men were sitting in assembly', 1–2a). It had one eye, two ears, two feet, twelve-hundred heads, a back, a belly, two hands, arms and shoulders, one neck and two sides: it was a one-eyed seller of garlic. Just so, when Beowulf and his men returned triumphant from the monsters' mere,

Þa wæs be feaxe on flet boren
Grendles heafod, þær guman druncon,
egeslic for eorlum ond þære idese mid,
wliteseon wrætlic; weras on sawon (1647–50).[3]

The impact on society of dramatic impressions such as this gave story its beginnings. Grendel's torn-off hand, arm and shoulder, displayed as token of Beowulf's victory, drew a large crowd of warriors from far and near to gaze and marvel. Behind the facade of the narrator's formal account we can hear the excited chatter of those who followed the trail of footprints the defeated monster had left as he fled dying:

No his lifgedal
sarlic þuhte secga ænegum
þara þe tirleases trode sceawode,
hu he werigmod on weg þanon,
niða ofercumen, on nicera mere
fæge ond geflymed feorhlastas bær.
Ðær wæs on blode brim weallende,
atol yða geswing eal gemenged,
haton heolfre, heorodreore weol;
deaðfæge deog, siððan dreama leas
in fenfreoðo feorh alegde,
hæþene sawle; þær him hel onfeng

[3] See above, p. 125.

['Not at all did his parting from life seem painful to any of the men who examined the footprints of the inglorious one, how he, exhausted in mind, overcome by force, had brought his life-tracks away from there into the water-monsters' pool, doomed and put to flight. There the water was surging in blood, the deadly swirl of waves, all stirred up, boiled with hot blood, with battle-gore; the one fated for death had been concealed after, joyless, he had laid down his life in his fen-refuge, his heathen soul; there hell had received him', 841b–52].

Everyone was elated by what he saw. 'Just look at that blood!', we can imagine them saying as they looked into the pool, 'He's died in there alright, and gone straight to hell the bastard!' No wonder a surge of admiration for Beowulf welled up as the men rode home again in high spirits:

monig oft gecwæð,
þætte suð ne norð be sæm tweonum
ofer eormengrund oþer nænig
under swegles begong selra nære
rondhæbbendra, rices wyrðra (857b–61).[4]

Their enthusiasm knew no bounds. He was a world beater, that man. They could not stop saying so. And, before long, one of their number was crystallizing their feelings in bursts of song:

Hwilum cyninges þegn,
guma gilphlæden, gidda gemyndig,
se ðe ealfela ealdgesegena
worn gemunde, word oþer fand
soðe gebunden; secg eft ongan
sið Beowulfes snyttrum styrian,
ond on sped wrecan spel gerade,
wordum wrixlan

['From time to time a thegn of the king, a boastful man, mindful of songs, who remembered a very great many old traditions, found other words truly bound; the man began again skilfully to rehearse Beowulf's venture, and successfully to tell a fitting tale, varying his words', 867b–74a].

Observation was being converted into memory. A dramatic achievement which had been borne in upon a group of men by what they had just seen was becoming part of traditional narrative and would soon pass into traditional story.

[4] See above, p. 57.

Collective tradition from which collective story sprang, was not, however, just transmission of information; it involved assessment and judgement. Collective tradition became symbolic narrative in order to provide society with a combination of psychological realism and concentration on potentials as the basis of understanding. In this form it tested events against the wisdom which had been established by such means before. For instance, on returning from Denmark Beowulf employed this technique when he both passed on to Hygelac, and interpreted for him, some information about Hrothgar's daughter. First of all, he reported that he had heard her called Freawaru by the men whom she was serving, when he joined them for dinner in Hrothgar's hall (2020–1a) and he filled in some of her background to the effect that

Sio gehaten is,
geong goldhroden, gladum suna Frodan;
hafað þæs geworden wine Scyldinga,
rices hyrde, ond þæt ræd talað,
þæt he mid þy wife wælfæhða dæl,
sæcca gesette

['Young and adorned with gold, she is betrothed to the well-disposed son of Froda; the friendly lord of the Scyldings, guardian of the kingdom, has agreed upon it, and thinks it well advised that he should settle a great deal of deadly feuds and conflicts through that wife', 2024b–9a].

In the second place, he cited a maxim full of dramatic import and fitting this case precisely, seeing that the Froda referred to had been killed by the Danes:

Oft seldan hwær
æfter leodhryre lytle hwile
bongar bugeð, þeah seo bryd duge

['Usually the deadly spear rests hardly anywhere even for a short time after the fall of a prince, though the bride is good', 2029b–31].

And thirdly, he used narrative to apply the maxim explicitly to Hrothgar's plan:

Mæg þæs þonne ofþyncan ðeodne Heaðo-Beardna
ond þegna gehwam þara leoda,
þonne . . .

['On that account it can be displeasing to the prince of the Heatho-Bards and to every thegn of that people when . . .', 2032–4a].

After that he was in a position to pass a confident opinion:

Þy ic Heaðo-Beardna hyldo ne telge,
dryhtsibbe dæl Denum unfæcne,
freondscipe fæstne

['Therefore I do not consider the Heatho-Bards' loyalty, much of their high alliance with the Danes, deceitless, their friendship firm', 2067–9a].

Exploration of the issue through narrative led him to an opinion different from Hrothgar's own.

Hygelac, like other rulers receiving news and views, would have been accustomed to such narrative vignettes, but he would have admired the cogency of this one:

Mæg þæs þonne ofþyncan ðeodne Heaðo-Beardna
ond þegna gehwam þara leoda,
þonne he mid fæmnan on flett gæð:
dryhtbearn Dena, duguða biwenede;
on him gladiað gomelra lafe,
heard ond hringmæl Heaða-Beardna gestreon,
þenden hie ðæm wæpnum wealdan moston, –
oð ðæt hie forlæddan to ðam lindplegan
swæse gesiðas ond hyra sylfra feorh.
Þonne cwið æt beore se ðe beah gesyhð,
eald æscwiga, se ðe eall geman,
garcwealm gumena – him bið grim sefa –,
onginneð geomormod geongum cempan
þurh hreðra gehygd higes cunnian,
wigbealu weccean, ond þæt word acwyð:
'Meaht ðu, min wine, mece gecnawan,
þone þin fæder to gefeohte bær
under heregriman hindeman siðe,
dyre iren, þær hyne Dene slogon,
weoldon wælstowe, syððan Wiðergyld læg,
æfter hæleþa hryre, hwate Scyldungas?
Nu her þara banena byre nathwylces
frætwum hremig on flet gæð,
morðres gylpeð, ond þone maðþum byreð,
þone þe ðu mid rihte rædan sceoldest.'

Manað swa ond myndgað   mæla gehwylce
sarum wordum,   oð ðæt sæl cymeð,
þæt se fæmnan þegn   fore fæder dædum
æfter billes bite   blodfag, swefeð,
ealdres scyldig;   him se oðer þonan
losað lifigende,   con him land geare.
Þonne bioð abrocene   on ba healfe
aðsweord eorla;   syððan Ingelde
weallað wælniðas,   ond him wiflufan
æfter cearwælmum   colran weorðað

['On that account it can be displeasing to the prince of the Heatho-Bards and to every thegn of that people when a noble son of the Danes goes on to the hall floor with the woman and the retainers are entertained:[5] ancestral heirlooms shine on him, hard and adorned with rings, treasures of the Heatho-Bards while they were able to wield the weapons – until they led their dear comrades and themselves to destruction in the clash of shields. Then he who sees the ring speaks at the beer drinking, an old spear-warrior, who remembers all, the spear-slaughter of men – his mind is grim; sad of mind, he begins to test the heart of a young warrior through the thoughts of his breast, to awake the destruction of war, speaking thus: "Can you, recognize, my friend, the sword which your father under his army-mask carried into battle for the very last time, beloved iron, where Danes killed him, bold Scyldings controlled the place of slaughter after Withergild lay dead, after the fall of heroes? Now, here, a son of one or another of the slayers goes on to the floor exulting in the trappings, boasts of killing, and wears the treasure which by right you ought to possess." Thus he urges and reminds him on every occasion with painful words, until the time comes that the woman's thegn for the deeds of his father sleeps stained with blood after the cut of the blade, having forfeited his life; the other escapes from there with his life, knowing the land well. Then the oaths of warriors are broken on both sides; afterwards deadly hatreds surge in Ingeld and love for his wife cools in him after the wellings of sorrow'].

The narrative by which Beowulf envisaged the 'when . . .' (2034–62), with its inevitable sequel 'Then . . .' (2063–6), was convincing both as a counterpart to the symbolic narrative in the maxim (2029b–31) and as a depiction of particular events. The same uncontrollable forces prevail in maxim and ensuing narrative: once the old warrior, working on the younger, begins 'wigbealu weccean' (2046a), 'aðsweord eorla' (2064a) give way and 'weallað wælniðas' (2065a). The same kind of imagery is shared by both too. The spear and bride in the maxim have their counterparts in the

[5] I am, of course, departing from Klaeber's punctuation in so translating.

narrative: a captured sword is a social symbol of injured pride,[6] and an old warrior (2041b–4a) and a young one (2044b and 2061b) are representative figures without any trait of private personality. All alike emerge from a nebulous background, signify a destabilizing transition and fade into the background again. But, if the symbolic authority of the veteran and youngster in the narrative is unquestionable, so too is their realism. Their relationship has depth. The old warrior is to the fore and does the thinking and speaking; the young one acts as his agent but is no mere cipher: it is, after all, he who embodies the motive and performs the critical deed, and his escape afterwards (2061b–2) implies Danish retribution in the future. Feelings link the two men, the old warrior's rooted in the past and the young one's quick-growing in the present. The actual words by which the former's emotions penetrate and disturb the latter's (2044–6a) are at the heart of the narrative. Two ingredients coalesce in this incitement: psychological drama, directly and intimately portrayed, and an ancient historical process of transmitting social passion from generation to generation. The narrative is at once specific and symbolic. The combination irresistibly urges the rightness of Beowulf's opinion.

On this occasion Beowulf reached understanding by converting a sequence of prospective events into a symbolic narrative. Sometimes the method was to compare or contrast events to an existing symbolic model. This is presumably how Hrothgar's thegn proceeded when he extolled Beowulf's triumph over Grendel and went on to relate the famous deeds of Sigemund and the notorious crimes of Heremod (867b–915). And it was certainly the procedure Beowulf followed when, about to tackle the dragon, sad, restless and prepared for death, he was reminiscing to his companions about his long life and wanted to convey how his beloved grandfather, King Hrethel, had felt when the second of his three sons had accidentally killed the eldest. Beowulf first described the emotional effect of this tragedy in completely general terms as 'hreðre hygemeðe' ('wearying to the heart', 2442a) and then continued:

Swa bið geomorlic *gomelum ceorle* 2444
to gebidanne, *þæt his byre ride*
giong on galgan; þonne he gyd wrece, 2446
sarigne sang, þonne his sunu hangað
hrefne to hroðre, ond he him helpe ne mæg 2448
eald ond infrod ænige gefremman.

[6] 2036–40, 2041b, 2047b–52, 2054, 2055b–6 and, perhaps, 2060a.

Symble bið gemyndgad   *morna gehwylce*
eaforan ellorsið;   oðres ne gymeð
to gebidanne   burgum in innan
yrfeweardas,   þonne se an hafað
þurh deaðes nyd   dæda gefondad.
Gesyhð sorhcearig   on his suna bure
winsele westne,   windge reste
reote berofene, –   ridend swefað,
hæleð in hoðman;   nis þær hearpan sweg,
gomen in geardum,   swylce ðær iu wæron.
Gewiteð þonne on sealman,   sorhleoð gæleð
an æfter anum;   þuhte him eall to rum,
wongas ond wicstede.   Swa Wedra helm
æfter Herebealde   heortan sorge
weallinde wæg;   wihte ne meahte
on ðam feorhbonan   fæghðe gebetan;
no ðy ær he þone heaðorinc   hatian ne meahte
laðum dædum,   þeah him leof ne wæs.
He ða mid þære sorhge,   þe him to sar belamp,
gumdream ofgeaf

['*So it is sad for an old man to experience that his young son swings on the gallows;* he utters a lament, a sad song, when his son hangs as an enjoyment for the raven, and he, old and very wise, cannot do anything about it. *Regularly every morning a son's death is remembered;* he does not care to wait for another heir in the dwellings, when the one has experienced evil deeds with the necessity of death. Afflicted by grief he sees a deserted wine-hall in his son's dwelling, a windswept resting place deprived of joy – horsemen sleep, heroes in the grave; there is no sound of the harp, entertainment in the courts, as there was in the past. Then he goes to his bed, sings a dirge, one after another; fields and dwelling-place have seemed to him all too spacious. So the guardian of the Weder-Geats felt surging grief in his heart for Herebeald; he could not exact any retribution from the slayer; none the sooner could he hate the warrior for his grievous deeds, although he was not dear to him. Then with the sorrow which, too bitter, had befallen him, he gave up the joys of men'].

Beowulf's initial account of the occasion of Hrethel's sorrow was precise in information – Hæthcyn, the second son, had missed the target in archery and had shot Herebeald, his elder brother, instead (2437–40) – and it made the point that, as a result, no expiation or revenge had been possible (2441–3). What followed, however, though comparable, was different – a narrative of another frustrated father mourning a dead son, which was vague about what had actually happened (2453b–4 and 2457b–8a) but graphic in its description of grieving. In this second case the father was a symbolic *sorhcearig* (2455a), old and very wise (2449a), whose sorrowing was generalized by gnomic wording (italicized above, 2444–6a and 2450–1b) and by a present tense applicable to any present. Facts, as such, are not germane to this portrayal. But elements of the old man's grief which are both direct and general are: that his young son is swinging on the gallows pecked at by ravens; that the boy was his only heir; that the wine-hall where the young man used to enjoy the harp is silent, empty and windswept. We see with our mind's eye what the father sees with his as he stands in his dead son's room (2455–9) and we identify with his thoughts as he lies in his bed singing one sad song after another. The images of a corpse left hanging on the gallows, a deserted wine-hall, young men sleeping in an untimely grave, and a silent harp, were familiar to Anglo-Saxon sorrow, as was the resort to song to relieve the pain. The feelings of public humiliation, of personal grief which does not fade, of hopelessness, of deprivation, belonged to common experience. The sympathetic analogy which this narrative provided for the intolerable sorrow which destroyed Beowulf's grandfather (2458–9a) was at once intimate, universal and clean removed from any involvement with blaming the younger son, Hæthcyn, for what he had done.[7] Evidently Beowulf wanted to steer clear of the resentment Hrethel had nursed against the son who subsequently ruled as his successor for several years and whose death, when he was fighting the Swedes, was promptly avenged by the third, surviving son, Hygelac, Beowulf's *Hygelac min* (2434b).

In the main line of a symbolic story itself its narrator might well call upon symbolic narrative of a general sort to set a major event of his tale in a symbolic perspective. A case in point is the information the *Beowulf* narrator gave about the treasure in a mound which was violated by a thief while the dragon guarding it slept and which brought about Beowulf's death after the dragon, enraged by the robbery, began to devastate the kingdom and had to be exterminated. The presence of these riches was attributed to their burial long before by an 'eorlgestreona / hringa hyrde' ('guardian of the treasures, rings, of warriors' 2244b–5a), who was sole survivor of a company of noble warriors: 'Ealle hie deað fornam / ærran

[7] Cf. 2435–6, 2441, 2464b–7 and 2470–1.

mælum' ('Death had carried them all off in earlier times', 2236b–7a). This lone symbolic figure, interring the heirlooms of his race, was conceived of speaking thus:

Heald þu nu, hruse,   nu hæleð ne mostan,
eorla æhte!   Hwæt, hyt ær on ðe
gode begeaton;   guðdeað fornam,
feorhbealo frecne   fyra gehwylcne
leoda minra   þara ðe þis lif ofgeaf,
gesawon seledream.   Nah, hwa sweord wege
oððe feormie   fæted wæge,
dryncfæt deore;   duguð ellor sceoc.
Sceal se hearda helm   hyrstedgolde,
fætum befeallen;   feormynd swefað,
þa ðe beadogriman   bywan sceoldon;
ge swylce seo herepad,   sio æt hilde gebad
ofer borda gebræc   bite irena,
brosnað æfter beorne.   Ne mæg byrnan hring
æfter wigfruman   wide feran,
hæleðum be healfe.   Næs hearpan wyn,
gomen gleobeames,   ne god hafoc
geond sæl swingeð,   ne se swifta mearh
burhstede beateð.   Bealocwealm hafað
fela feorhcynna   forð onsended!

['Hold now you earth, now that heroes cannot, the property of warriors! Lo, good men obtained it on you before; death in battle, terrible deadly destruction, has carried off every man of my people who has given up this life – they have seen the last of the joy of the hall. I do not have anyone who wears the sword or polishes the ornamented cup, precious drinking vessel; the host has departed elsewhere. The hard helmet shall become deprived of its wrought gold, its golden plates; the polishers sleep, who should prepare the battle-mask; and likewise the war-garment, which has endured the bite of iron blades in battle above the crashing of shields, decays after the warrior. The ring of the corslet cannot travel widely with the war-chief, by the side of heroes. There has been no joy of the harp, no mirth of the entertainment-wood, the good hawk does not swing through the hall, nor does the swift steed beat the courtyard. Destructive death has despatched many a living race!'].

Invoking the unchanging, indifferent, earth during a particular act of interment (2247a and 2248b), the lament placed the event in a perspective of permanence. Intertwining the death of warriors – represented as violent destruction (2249b–51a and 2265b), loss of living (2251b–2a), departure (2254b and 2265b–6) and sleep (2256b) – with consequent neglect of the accoutrements of aristocratic warriorship (sword, hall cup, helmet and armour, 2252b–62) and lack of the adjuncts of aristocratic pleasures (harp, hawk and horse, 2262b–5a), the address related the action it accompanied to the general feeling for transience inherent in all social groups and, pertinently, in the collaboration between warriors and their equipment on which societies depended. The speech did not contain any feature – petition or curse – to influence the future course of events, or any message – a maxim, for instance – for outside general consumption. Evidently it was not the poet's main story-telling purpose to elicit any specifically ominous implications in the treasure in advance of Beowulf's action. In their directness the speaker's words simply marked in graphic fashion the end of some phase in society. In their generality, cast in the present tense, they registered the experience of any 'þanchycgende', *winegeomor* man ('thoughtful in mind', 2235a, and 'mourning his friends', 2239a) on any equivalent occasion. In their thematic content they viewed human society in the broadest possible environment of material, natural and uncontrollable forces. In their place in the poem they furnished the treasure with a symbolic origin which engaged the imagination both movingly and grandly. In their context in the story they set a general tone and scale for King Beowulf's ensuing death, shortly to be announced in similar terms (2309–11).

In the telling of a story as such the actors' own psychology, consistently informing a narrator's description, selection and ordering of events, sustained the story's symbolic character. The account of landfall at the end of Beowulf's voyage to Denmark furnishes an example. The ship sailed before the wind until, on the second day,

wundenstefna gewaden hæfde,
þæt ða liðende land gesawon,
brimclifu blican, beorgas steape,
side sænæssas; þa wæs sund liden,
eoletes æt ende

['the curved prow had journeyed, so that the seafarers perceived land, seacliffs shining, steep hills, broad headlands; then the deep sea was crossed, at the end of the (?)voyage', 220–4a].

The crew perceived land by degrees – first generally, then as cliffs, then hills, then headlands.[8] Their sighting had the ring of actuality about it. But more than that: what they saw was registered symbolically – *brimclifu*, *sænæssas*. An assurance was conveyed that they had an experience which many had had before and many would have again. Their psychological process was an affirmation of representativeness. It exemplifies a kind of authentication that was built in throughout the story.

An episode which laid its claim to symbolic authority by drawing on the psychology of a single actor is the account of young Wiglaf, at the bidding of the dying Beowulf, hurrying inside the mound and surveying the treasure left undefended now that the dragon was dead:

Ða ic snude gefrægn   sunu Wihstanes
æfter wordcwydum   wundum dryhtne
hyran heaðosiocum,   hringnet beran,
brogdne beadusercean   under beorges hrof.
Geseah ða sigehreðig,   þa he bi sesse geong,
magoþegn modig   maððumsigla fealo,
gold glitinian   grunde getenge,
wundur on wealle,   ond þæs wyrmes denn,
ealdes uhtflogan,   orcas stondan,
fyrnmanna fatu,   feormendlease,
hyrstum behrorene;   þær wæs helm monig
eald ond omig,   earmbeaga fela
searwum gesæled. –   Sinc eaðe mæg,
gold on grunde   gumcynnes gehwone
oferhigian,   hyde se ðe wylle! –
Swylce he siomian geseah   segn eallgylden
heah ofer horde,   hondwundra mæst,
gelocen leoðocræftum;   of ðam leoma stod,
þæt he þone grundwong   ongitan meahte,
wræte giondwlitan.   Næs ðæs wyrmes þær
onsyn ænig,   ac hyne ecg fornam

['Then I have learned the son of Weohstan obeyed his wounded, battle-sick leader quickly after the speech, went wearing his coat of mail, woven battle-shirt, under the roof of the mound. When he went by the seat, the triumphant man, the brave young thegn, perceived many precious jewels, gold gleaming close to the ground, wonderful things on the wall, and the den of the dragon, the old dawn-flier, pitchers standing, cups of men of old, without men to polish them, deprived of

[8] Cf. Greenfield, '*Beowulf* 207b–228', pp. 88–9 (repr. Greenfield, *Hero and Exile*, pp. 29–30).

ornaments; there was many a helmet, old and rusty, many arm-rings skilfully twisted. – Treasure, gold on the ground, can easily get the better of each race, heed [*or* hide] who will! – Likewise he perceived a banner covered with gold hanging high above the hoard, the greatest of hand-made marvels, woven with finger-skills; a light shone from it, so that he could apprehend the surface of the floor, scan the works of art. There was no sign of the dragon, but the sword-edge had despatched it'].

As in the description of landfall just discussed, a realistic process of progressive observation took place. There was deep gloom in the chamber within the mound. When, later, Wiglaf took seven companions inside with him, the one in front carried a torch (3123–5) but now, in his anxiety to get out again before Beowulf expired (2783–7), he plunged straight in (2752a). First he got a general sense of what lay inside – jewels, gold, marvels and the dragon's lair (2757b–61a); then he distinguished various kinds of objects – pitchers, cups, helmets, arm-rings – all rusting and neglected (2760b–4a); and lastly he realized that there was a beautifully made golden standard above the rest emitting a glow which gave him a whole view of the interior and its contents (2767–71a). But the experience was not a private one, even though Wiglaf alone had it. The realism was symbolic as well as personal: it was a matter of a *sigehreðig*, 'magoþegn modig', gazing at *maððumsiglu* (2756–7), and the banner, looked at closely enough for its workmanship to be appreciated, was an outstanding *hondwundor* owing its quality to *leoðocræftum* (2768b–9a). Wiglaf was typical in the way he used his eyes.

He was typical too in the way he reacted to what he saw, as, I believe, two interjections show (2764b–6 and 2771b–2). The first is a maxim. This generalization, in my opinion, should not be dismissed as irrelevant – with Klaeber, who (in his note to these lines) dubbed it 'apparently uncalled-for'. Much more probably, I would say, we should understand it as a piece of folk wisdom occurring to Wiglaf when the sheer scale of the wealth in front of his eyes began to sink in. After all, the comments about Beowulf's death which this young man was to make to the Geats when they arrived on the spot (3077–86) show that he was of a reflective turn of thought. A maxim which warned against allowing oneself to be overwhelmed by the powerful impression which was being received at that very moment, as this one did, was not out of place, we may consider, in the thoughts of the person who combined a stern sense of discipline[9] with

[9] In keeping faith with Beowulf (2650b–60 and 2864–91).

strong emotions,[10] but who could not refrain from attempting the impossible of reviving Beowulf when the old man was already dead (2852b–9). This first interjection was certainly not intended to reveal the workings of Wiglaf's mind for their own sake: his attitude to it was not explicitly stated. Its purpose was rather to relate Wiglaf's responses to general experience. And the same was true, in my view, of the second interjection (2771b–2). At this late stage there could be no factual point in declaring the obvious that the dragon was not there but was already killed. This statement's *raison d'être* was surely an implication that Wiglaf had an acute sensation of dramatic contrast as he surveyed the interior of the den so intimately identified with the dragon, and the point of including it was not to call attention to that sensation as such but to indicate that Wiglaf's fraught entry into those surroundings involved feelings of a well-known, conventional sort – the kind typified by 'nis þær hearpan sweg' (2458b) among the images that haunted the old man as he grieved for the loss of his son. Both interjections confirmed Wiglaf as an authentic figure in the continuum of symbolic story through the ages. And both did so in terms thematically apt to the context: the maxim associated him with pervasive mistrust of treasure buried long ago in a forgotten past, and his sharp feeling for what was dramatically absent was soon to be repeated in bleak images of the Geats' lot after Beowulf's death: 'nalles hearpan sweg / wigend weccan' ('not at all shall the sound of the harp rouse warriors', 3023b–4a).

An 'I have heard/learned' narrator as the voice of tradition assiduously underpinned the representative psychology of his actors. The different selections which were applied to the *Beowulf* narrator's two references to a dynastic struggle between Onela, king of the Swedes, and his two nephews, Eanmund and Eadgils, illustrate this practice. The first allusion (2379b–96) was part of his account of the dangers which Beowulf had survived since his victory over Grendel's kin, rehearsed in order to show why the king in his old age had the determination to face the dragon alone: the narrator recounted how Onela had allowed Beowulf to succeed to the Geatish throne when the Swedish king raided Geatland and killed Beowulf's predecessor, Heardred, for giving shelter to the exiles, Eanmund and Eadgils, and went on to relate how Beowulf as king subsequently helped Eadgils to mount an expedition into his homeland and in his turn

[10] When he saw Beowulf in dire need (2604b–10), dying (2720–3 and 2790b–2) and dead (2821–4a, 2852b–7 and 2906b–10a).

kill Onela. Beowulf gave Eadgils this aid in order to revenge the killing of the young Heardred (2391–6), whose loyal guardian he had been while the king was still a boy (2373–9a). The fact that Eanmund, who was referred to but never named in this account, was killed during Onela's raid into Geatland received no mention because that death had nothing to do with Beowulf's self-reliance. By contrast the narrator's second allusion to this phase in Swedish royal rivalries picked out Eanmund's death and said nothing about the sequence of events to which it belonged. On this occasion the subject was the pedigree of the sword which Wiglaf, Beowulf's nephew, was about to use in support of his uncle for the first time when the old king was engulfed by the dragon's heat: the weapon, we are told, had been part of Eanmund's wargear which had been captured when Weohstan, Wiglaf's father, had killed the Swedish prince in exile; Onela had conferred the equipment on Weohstan as reward and Weohstan for his part had bequeathed it to his son for him to use in emulation of his father (2611–25a). Weohstan's pride in the sword as a result of how he had obtained it was important psychologically for the way Wiglaf was about to use it, but the background of the weapon's capture was not.

Symbolic story organized its narrative convincingly in patterns of habitual thought, for instance in terms of a dramatic contrast between two successive periods of time. Just as a poignant sense of difference between past and present characterized the inflammatory words of the old Heathobard warrior and the images haunting the grieving father and the lament of the last survivor, so the messenger taking the news of Beowulf's death to the Geats reached the climax of his grim forebodings with evocative early-morning images opposing future and present:

Forðon sceall gar wesan
monig morgenceald mundum bewunden,
hafen on handa, nalles hearpan sweg
wigend weccean, ac se wonna hrefn
fus ofer fægum fela reordian,
earne secgan, hu him æt æte speow,
þenden he wið wulf wæl reafode

['Therefore shall many a spear, cold in the morning, be grasped by hand, raised in the hand; not at all shall the sound of the harp rouse warriors, but the dark raven eager for the doomed shall speak much, tell the eagle how he ate well while he plundered the dead with the wolf', 3021b–7].

A patterned sequence of a past and a present was the conventional way of viewing the action which was engendered by the interactive potentials twinned in symbols. It was in this way that the same messenger portrayed the threat posed by the Franks 'now' in consequence of the *flothere*, 'naval expedition', which Hygelac had led into their country many years before. The present was filled by expectation of war after the death of a king:

Nu ys leodum wen
orleghwile, syððan underne
Froncum ond Frysum fyll cyninges
wide weorðeð

['Now there is expectation for the people of a time of war after the fall of the king becomes widely revealed to the Franks and Frisians', 2910b–13a].

The offence had been created after the death of another king in the past:

Wæs sio wroht scepen
heard wið Hugas, syððan Higelac cwom
faran flotherge on Fresna land,
þær hyne Hetware hilde genægdon,
elne geeodon mid ofermægene,
þæt se byrnwiga bugan sceolde,
feoll on feðan; nalles frætwe geaf
ealdor dugoðe

['The severe offence was created against the Hugas, after Hygelac came sailing with a naval expedition into the land of the Frisians, where the Hetware engaged him in battle, fiercely brought it about by superior force that the armoured warrior fell, dropped dead in the foot-troop; not at all did the prince give treasures to the retainers', 2913b-20a].

Implacable hostility had endured from that day to this: 'Us wæs a syððan / Merewioingas milts ungyfeðe' ('For us, ever since, the mercy of the Merovingian has not been granted', 2920b–1). 'Nu ys . . . syððan . . .', 'Wæs . . . syððan . . .', 'wæs a syððan': the *orleghwil* flowed from the *flothere* with the inevitability of time.

A narrative combination of a past and a present constituted the standard portrait of an actor in symbolic narrative generally, including symbolic story, whether the portraitist was a narrator, another actor or the subject him/her/itself. The narrative thus organized formed the subject's 'history'.[11] For instance, this is how the rune-stave in *The Husband's Message*

[11] Cf. above, p. 82.

introduced itself to the aristocratic lady for whom it bore a message: 'Ic wæs . . .' ((*Riddle* 60) 1a), 'Nu ic . . . secgan wille' ((*The Husband's Message*) 1), 'Ful oft ic . . . gesohte' (6), 'Eom nu . . . cumen' (8b).[12] And it is how the speaker in *The Wife's Lament* presented the unfulfilled longing she personified:[13] 1–23a rehearse the past with brief allusions to the present (4b and 17b); the remainder concentrates on the present with occasional backward reference (27–8, 32b–3a and 41). In *Riddle* 37 a being which has been observed as a grotesque – its stomach was distended behind with something that flew through its eye (1–4) – convolutes the normal past-present sequence by paradoxically creating a son who is its father (5–8). Whatever its course a past-present 'history' was never less than dramatic. *Riddle* 27, typically, presents a being that is a living contradiction: in terms of my past, it declares, 'Ic eom weorð werum . . .' ('I am valuable to men . . .', 1–6a), but 'Nu ic eom bindere ond swingere . . .' ('Now I am binder and beater . . .', 6b–17). Just so, in the picture of Hrothgar grieving for the thirty thegns Grendel had seized in his first raid on Heorot the night before –

Mære þeoden,
æþeling ærgod, unbliðe sæt,
þolode ðryðswyð þegnsorge dreah

['The glorious leader of the people, the noble one, good from old times, sat joyless, the mighty one endured, suffered sorrow for his thegns', 129b–31] –

the king's present misery contradicted starkly the potentials ('Mære þeoden', 'æþeling ærgod' and *ðryðswyð*) echoing the narrator's introductory account of his glorious ancestry and glittering career hitherto (1–85).

The 'I have heard/learned' narrator frequently brought the past-presentness of an actor explicitly to bear on a moment of action for dramatic effect. For instance, Beowulf, Grendel, the Danes and Beowulf's fellow Geats all came in for this treatment during Grendel's gradual approach to, and arrival at, Heorot and during Beowulf's fight with him and victory there (702b–833a). Beowulf triumphed as 'se þe ær feorran com, / snotor ond swyðferhð' ('he who had come from afar, wise and strong minded', 825b–6a). For Grendel, when he perceived the hall as he made his way to it, 'Ne wæs þæt forma sið, / þæt he Hroþgares ham gesohte' ('That was not the first time that he had sought Hrothgar's home', 716b–17a), but, when

[12] See above, p. 178. [13] Cf. above, pp. 180–1.

he was desperate to flee, 'ne wæs his drohtoð þær / swylce he on ealdordagum ær gemette' ('his experience there was not such as he had met in his days before', 756b–7), and, when he finally found his body could not endure the strain, the realization came as a complete reversal, since he was

se þe fela æror
modes myrðe manna cynne,
fyrene gefremede

['he who had perpetrated many afflictions of the mind, crimes, against mankind before', 809b–11a].

The Danes were terrified when they heard their hall resounding with the noise of the struggle (767–9a) because

Þæs ne wendon ær witan Scyldinga,
þæt hit a mid gemete manna ænig
betlic ond banfag tobrecan meahte,
listum tolucan, nymþe liges fæþm
swulge on swaþule

['Wise men of the Scyldings had not expected that any man could ever by any means break it up, splendid and decorated with bone, cleverly pull it apart, unless the embrace of fire should swallow it in flame', 778–82a].

It was out of ignorance of Grendel's past that Beowulf's companions drew their swords to defend their leader as he fought (794b–7), for they did not know that a spell had rendered the monster immune from weapons (798–805a).

A 'history' was not a constant: it depended on the observer as well as on the observed. For example, in *Beowulf* the amazement the assembled company felt at the grisly spectacle of Grendel's severed head suddenly carried into their midst (1647–50)[14] depended on their fearful memories of the living monster to which the head had so recently belonged, whereas for Beowulf himself the object was *sælac*, 'sea-booty' (1652a), betokening the glorious victory which he had been granted at the bottom of the pool in the dramatic fashion he thereupon recounted to Hrothgar (1651–76).

An observer lacking knowledge of the past of a phenomenon which he saw in the present drew on imagination to supply the deficiency.

[14] See above, p. 125.

Wrætlic is þes wealstan wyrde gebræcon;
burgstede burston, brosnað enta geweorc

['Amazing is this wall-stone, fateful events have shattered it; places of defence have broken into pieces, the work of giants crumbles'],

The Ruin begins; and for the rest of the poem the observer's thoughts play to and fro between the decay in front of him and the antiquity it intimated:[15] the edifice had been constructed with massive skill; it had endured through long ages until impaired by collapse; it had been the setting for the joys of abundant, resplendent, social life until desolation struck; it had offered its inhabitants the elegant amenity of hot baths. Cultural tradition was imagination's guide for such reflections: to the mind's eye the mighty ruins, when whole, had housed a society of a typical Germanic kind, albeit more luxurious. The *wealstan*, observed in the present, implied a former glory of 'meodoheall monig . ᛞ . dreama full' ('many a meadhall full of the joys of men',[16] 23). A phenomenon's continuum of past and present resided ultimately in the system of symbolic potentials.

'Story' beings, such as Grendel, Grendel's mother and the dragon, whose very existence was a product of collective oral tradition (cf. *Beowulf* 1345–57a) and who never spoke for themselves, belonged wholly to the symbolic system. Their past-presentness had to conform only to underlying symbolic truth and any conventions already established by tradition. As a result they gave their presenters unusual scope. The *Beowulf* narrator, for instance, was assigned in effect an 'I have seen' relationship to Grendel's kin, free of the 'I have heard/learned' formulas appropriate to, say, Wiglaf's doings.[17] He was better placed than anyone else to put past-present knowledge about these creatures to good effect dramatically or conceptually, as when, just at the moment the Geats were in action, he reported that Grendel was protected by a spell of which the Geats knew nothing (as mentioned above), or when, more fundamentally, he explained that the monster was descended from Cain, whereas the Danes were even left uncertain as to whether there was a father (1354–7a). He was ready with past-present-future comments on what these beings were doing, thinking and feeling – such as

[15] For a close analysis of 1–2 as part of a study of 1–9, stressing the verbal subtlety which was applied to this poem's structure hinging on the opposition of present/past, see Bately, 'Time and the Passing of Time in *The Wanderer*', pp. 9–11.

[16] The rune + *dreama* = *mondreama*.

[17] 2694–6, 2752–5 and 2773–6a.

næfre he on aldordagum ær ne siþðan
heardran hæle, healðegnas fand!

['never in his days before or since did he find harder luck, hall-thegns!', 718–19]

and

Ne wæs þæt wyrd þa gen,
þæt he ma moste manna cynnes
ðicgean ofer þa niht

['It was not still destined that he could partake of more of mankind after that night', 734b–6a].

Communal witness, assessment and judgement constituted the moral basis of symbolic story. The individual was the proper focal point of this attention. There was a prevailing belief that the individual was all-important to society, a general agreement that the common welfare depended on how individuals of aristocratic status operated the system of understanding and the code of practices which custom had long established. Story had to do with an individual as society saw him (or her), not an individual view of society. Interest was in a sequence of action which tested how an individual's endeavour to realize his inherited potential through interplay with surrounding forces benefited or harmed the corporate good.

As far as foreseeable action was concerned, society framed the test by the *beot* or *gylp*, the customary vow to undertake an absolute public obligation. The only acceptable outcome was total achievement or death in the attempt. For either of these society awarded the person concerned the accolade of *dom*, 'glory'; anything else brought him disgrace.[18] In essence the individual owed to the community integrity of word and deed,[19] and the community in return owed him uncorrupted judgement and record. In *The Battle of Maldon* both debts were paid. The theme was the personal trust which bonded individual and society together, and defence of the homeland under threat provided the testing circumstances. Byrhtnoth's followers on many occasions in his hall had vowed their loyalty to him in battle (212–14), and, more specifically, at a general assembly which he had held on the day of the battle itself, many had pledged they would fight

[18] See above, pp. 153–4.

[19] For the formula, *word ond weorc*, traditionally used in oral society for complementary pairing of these two, see above, pp. 157–66.

bravely (198–201). The critical occasion to put these pledges into effect had come for every warrior 'þe on Denon wolde dom gefeohtan' ('who meant to win glory from the Danes by fighting', 129). Offa, for one, as we have seen, kept his word to the full after Byrhtnoth was killed.[20] In him and in the others like him the narrator presents without fantastic exaggeration or false heroics an impressive array of persons in each of whom words and deeds were at one.

Mutual respect between individuals and society was not the only virtue esteemed in this code of conduct: it promoted largeness of will and generosity of spirit too. And it did so among young and old, inexperienced and experienced alike, in conditions of imaginative enterprise as well as in ordinary circumstances, in sophisticated society as well as within homely relationships. *The Battle of Maldon* is richly imbued with these qualities, and so too is *Beowulf*. Beowulf himself complied with the highest standards of behaviour in both form and spirit throughout his exploits against Grendel, Grendel's mother and the dragon. His *gilpcwide*, 'boasting speech' (640a), before his fight with Grendel was simultaneously correct and courageous:

Ic gefremman sceal
eorlic ellen, oþðe endedæg
on þisse meoduhealle minne gebidan! (636b–8),[21]

he declared. Compact but not restricted, his words were matched by what he did. He was a rounded, whole, person in both substance and style, and that was how society saw him. Hrothgar made the authentic response by acknowledging that Beowulf's outstanding worth resided in his combination of body, mind and speech: 'Þu eart mægenes strang, ond on mode frod, / wis wordcwida!' (1844–5a),[22] the old king averred warmly when he bade the young hero an affectionate farewell.

The testing sequence of action was on its largest scale when it embraced the whole of an individual's life. The life was viewed in a threefold public pattern of initial impression, performance and final reputation. Heremod, for example, excited high hopes when a young prince, but turned out to be a mean, murderous tyrant as king, and died deserted and despised (901–15 and 1709b–22a). Beowulf, on the other hand, was thought slothful and timid as a youth (2183b–8a),[23] but acted with conspicuous distinction in

[20] See above, p. 153. [21] See *ibid.* [22] See above, p. 9.
[23] Cf. (most recently) Tripp, 'Did Beowulf have an "Inglorious Youth"?'.

manhood and died much honoured. An individual's reputation, what society thought of him (or her), was that person's 'character'. According to circumstances it could be simply local: Leofsunu, in *The Battle of Maldon*, was determined not to incur the reproaches of his friends back home at Sturmer. Or it could be rather grander: Ælfwine did not intend to be reproached by his distinguished Mercian kindred. Or it might be transcendent:

Þu þe self hafast
dædum gefremed, þæt þin dom lyfað
awa to aldre

['You yourself have achieved by your deeds that your glory will live for ever', 953b–5a],[24]

Hrothgar eulogized Beowulf after his victory over Grendel, and Wealhtheow saluted the hero in similar vein:

Hafast þu gefered, þæt ðe feor ond neah
ealne wideferhþ weras ehtigað,
efne swa side swa sæ bebugeð,
windgeard weallas

['You have brought it about that far and near men will esteem you for ever, as widely as the sea, home of winds, surrounds seawalls', 1221–4a].

'Characterization' in symbolic story was progressive. It was a cumulative process within the continuum of narrative. For instance, the initial impression Beowulf made was built up of the successive reactions of wise Geats, the Danish coastguard, Wulfgar (Hrothgar's court official), Hrothgar himself, Unferth and Wealhtheow. An actor was synthesized by the combined dramatic responses of others, including the narrator. A story was a psychological specimen of nature's interactive system, registered on a symbolic level and thereby stably based on society's permanent values. In the rest of this chapter let us examine how in *Beowulf* a poet of exceptional imagination and consummate artistry employed the symbolic system to fashion out of these values an all-embracing hero in emblematic combat with all-consuming enemies.

The narrator, Hrothgar and his queen, Wealhtheow, between them applied to Beowulf before, during and immediately after his exploits in Denmark eighteen compound adjectives (20× in all), each forming the

[24] All editors supply *dom*, not in MS.

nucleus (or entirety) of its 'half line' and symbolically used (1) absolutely as a noun ('the strong-minded one' etc.), or (2) quasi-absolutely, in association with a noun separately situated in the structure of the verse, neither adjective nor noun requiring the other, or (3) in association with a pronoun (*he*, *þu)* or (4) in close conjunction with a 'man' or 'warrior' simplex (*mon*, *hæle*, *secg*, *wiga*).[25] All but one of these compounds[26] record a developing social estimation of this young warrior as he proved himself in action, progressively marshalling his evident capabilities to attain the joy, distinction and glory of victory. According to the narrator, Beowulf himself in later life looked back on this period as the time he had furnished public proof that he was *sigoreadig* (2345–54a). His triumph over Grendel and Grendel's mother had established his manhood's fame symbolically (2183b–9).

Story's interaction on the symbolic plane was vital to establishing the dimensions of the imagination. Those symbolic beings reacting to Grendel, and to other beings which, like him, were imagined, belonged to the 'real' world. We apprehend him as a monster through their 'real' apprehension. We appreciate him as a *dædhata*, 'one who shows hatred by deeds' (275a), because that is how Beowulf, 'werodes wisa' ('leader of the troop', 259a), straightforwardly thought of him, and as a *dolsceaða*, 'foolish injurer' (479a), before God, because that is how Hrothgar, 'helm Scyldinga' ('protector of the Scyldings', 456b), philosophically had come to regard him. The process of assimilation is the same as when we learn that each of Grendel's fingers had a terrible claw on it as hard as steel, because that is what impressed the men gazing in awe at his torn-off hand, or as when we learn that the dragon was fifty foot long while the Geats were looking at this 'syllicran wiht' ('more wonderful being', 3038b), stretched out dead beside their lifeless king.

[25] *Higerof*, 'strong in mind' (204a, assuming an emendation accepted by all editors), *ellenrof*, 'strong in martial spirit' (304a), *heaðorof*, 'strong in battle' (381a), *wælreow*, 'fierce in slaughter' (629a), *heaðodeor*, 'fierce in battle' (688a), *þryðswyð*, 'strong in might' (736b), *higeþihtig*, 'firm in mind' (746b), *hildedeor*, 'fierce in battle' (834a, 1646a and 1816a), *dreamhealdende*, 'possessing joy' (1227b), *sigoreadig*, 'blessed with victory' (1311a), *fyrdwyrðe*, 'distinguished in war' (1316b), *werigmod*, 'weary minded' (1543a), *sigehreðig*, 'exulting in victory' (1597a), *swiðmod*, 'strong minded' (1624a), *dædcene*, 'daring in deed' (1645a), *wiggeweorþad*, 'distinguished in battle' (1783a), *rumheort*, 'large hearted' (1799a) and *tireadig*, 'blessed with glory' (2189a).

[26] *Werigmod* at 1597a, when Beowulf was out of the range of observation at the bottom of the mere.

Grendel was conceived of as a 'wiht unhælo' ('being of destruction', 120b), like a *wiht* of a riddle.[27] But he was no ordinary *wiht*, owed to the perception of a single observer. He rendered a whole community helpless over a long period; he was 'news' far beyond the community he directly affected; he triggered a resort to religion and destroyed the orthodox faith of most in society; he excited a spontaneous, disinterested offer of outside help; he exposed to scorn anyone who had failed to resist him effectively and had not learned humility as a result. No wonder he was consistently viewed symbolically by all concerned. Some twelve symbolic epithets were applied to him, sixteen times in all, up to the time he made for Hrothgar's hall on the fateful occasion Beowulf was waiting for him (eight compound nouns, one genitive combination, three adjective combinations). The repeated symbols are *aglæca*, meaning perhaps 'a dangerous opponent, one who struggles fiercely'[28] (used once by the narrator (159a) and three times by Beowulf (425a, 433b and 592b)), and *angenga*, 'a being who walks alone' (used once each by the narrator (165a) and Beowulf (449a)). The other compound nouns are MS *ellengæst* (86a; probably *ellorgæst*, 'alien spirit'[29]), *mearcstapa*, 'boundary-stepper' (103a), *healðegn*, 'hall-thegn' (142a),[30] *deaþscua*, 'death shadow' (160a), *dædhata*, 'one who shows hatred by deeds' (275a), and *dolsceaða*, 'foolish injurer' (479a). The genitive combination, 'feond mancynnes' ('enemy of mankind', 164b), and one of the three adjective combinations, 'wonsæli wer' ('unhappy man', 105a), belonged to the Christian register, while both the other two, *grimma gæst*, 'grim spirit' (102a), and 'werga gast' ('accursed spirit', 133a; cf. 1747b), probably had ancient Germanic affiliations.[31]

27 See above, p. 184; cf. Barley, 'Structural Aspects of the Anglo-Saxon Riddle', p. 157. Cf. also the dragon as 'syllicran wiht' (3038b), as mentioned above, p. 211, and discussed below, pp. 219–20.

28 The cluster of meanings, 'a fighter, valiant warrior, dangerous opponent, one who struggles fiercely', was proposed by Kuhn, 'Old English *aglæca* – Middle Irish *óclach*', p. 218, and was based on his examination of the more than thirty contexts in which the word occurs in extant Old English poetry. To account for these meanings Kuhn posited a seventh-century Mercian noun reshaping a prehistoric form, meaning 'young-warrior', of Irish *óclach*, which is extant in Middle Irish manuscripts. I owe this reference to the kindness of Alfred Bammesberger.

29 See above, p. 69 and n. 2, and cf. 807b.

30 Used by the narrator in a mystifying fashion typical of riddles, when Grendel had, in effect, captured Hrothgar's hall; cf. *renweardas*, 770a.

31 For 'wonsæli wer', cf. *Andreas* 963a and *Elene* 478a and 977a, and concerning *grimma gæst* and 'werga gast', see below, pp. 442–3.

Any further description of this *wiht* was in extension of implications in these symbols. For instance, the narrator amplified *mearcstapa* first by 'se þe moras heold, / fen ond fæsten' ('who occupied moors, fen and fastness', 103b–4a), and then by an explanation that this 'wonsæli wer' had long lived in this region of monsters ever since God had condemned him among the race of Cain, a statement in turn briefly supplemented by an account of God's banishment of Cain after he had killed Abel and a summary of Cain's monstrous progeny (104b–14). No one observed this being in all his detail: it is only to be inferred that he had ears, legs, feet, hands and a mouth because he heard (88b), moved (115a), left a track (132b), seized (122b; cf. 158b) and ate (44a; cf. 125a). He was also considered by Beowulf and Hrothgar to have thoughts of a sort (448b and 475b). The narrative of his murderous crimes was equally unspecific about him: how, for instance, did he gain entry to Hrothgar's hall time and time again? We learn only (from Beowulf) that this *æglaca* (433b) recklessly did not use weapons (433–4 and 681–3a). A general impression is conveyed of a powerful, menacing, symbolic being who terrorized society in ways that were both more and less than human.[32]

Fittingly the actions of this being were equally symbolic. For instance, the narrator's, Beowulf's and Hrothgar's use of compound nouns in *-bealu*, 'malignant destruction', *fær-*, 'sudden attack', *hete-*, 'hate', *nið-/-nið*, 'hostility', and *nyd-/-nyd*, 'enforced distress'[33] gives eloquent testimony to the symbolic evil Grendel inflicted on Danish society without remission throughout the twelve long years from his first raid on Heorot to his fight there with Beowulf. For the protagonists, the narrator and us alike the symbolic terms classify Grendel as a dramatic cluster of menacing potentials acting out his malignity against society with deadly consistency.

The narrator had only to continue in the same vein symbolically when recounting Grendel's approach to Hrothgar's hall with Beowulf on the watch inside, his struggle there with the Geat and mortal wounding, his flight to his fen-retreat, Beowulf's exhilaration after the victory, and the Danes' joy at conclusive evidence that Grendel had indeed been destroyed

[32] Michael Lapidge ('*Beowulf* and the Psychology of Terror') argues that avoidance of any precise visual description of Grendel reflects a deliberate intention on the part of the poet to create a monster arousing instinctive, nightmarish terror of the unknown.

[33] *Morðbealu* (136a), *hetenið* (152b), *feorhbealu* (156a), *færgryre* (174a), *nydwracu* (193a), *nihtbealu* (193b), *þreanyd* (284a), *heteþanc* (475b), *færnið* (476a), *nydbad* (598a) and *niðgeweorc* (683a).

(702b–852). Fourteen symbolic epithets were applied to the *wiht* at this stage, seventeen times altogether. The terrible being was designated *aglæca* three times (732a, 739a and 816a) and *sceadugenga*, 'a being who walks in shadow' (703a), and *ellorgæst* (807b) once each, but he was most continuously identified by a live-piece series of four *-scaða*, '-injurer', compounds,[34] and, when critically confronted by Beowulf's total determination, he was *cwealmcuma*, 'slaughter-comer' (792a).[35] Three compound adjectives, used absolutely, also characterized him at particular stages: *bealohydig*, 'the one malignantly intent on destroying' (723a), when he was swinging open the hall door, *tirleas*, 'the one deprived of glory' (843a), when the footsteps he had left behind were being examined, and *deaðfæge*, 'the one doomed to death' (850a), when men gazed at the bloodstained, swirling water that concealed him. Three genitive combinations were all Christian: 'fyrene hyrde' ('guardian of crimes', 750b), 'Godes andsacan' ('adversary of God', 786b) and 'helle hæfton' ('captive of hell', 788a).

The *-scaða* and other compounds in this narrative, however, give us a more immediate sense of the menace of this being than those, such as *mearcstapa* and *deaþscua*, employed previously. And so too do explicit references to his hands (722b, 746a and 834b), eyes (726b), fingers (760b and 764b), body (812a), shoulder (816a and 835a), sinews (817b), joints (818a) and arm (835a). We know too that he had teeth and a voice, for he bit (742a) and wailed (785b–8a), and we are told explicitly that he had a mind (730b and 755a) and a soul (852a). A horrid light, like a flame, shone from his eyes as he stepped on to the hall floor (724b–7);[36] he suffered pain as his shoulder joint was giving way (815b–18a); his hand, arm and shoulder, when torn off, betokened Beowulf's victory (834b–6). He was by turns malevolent (712–13), angry (723b), exulting (730b–4a), greedily impatient (739–45a), afraid (753b–4a), wanting to run away (755–7 and 762–6), anguished (782b–90), aware that his body could not stand the strain (809–12) and that his end had come (821b–3a). We come close to Grendel during his life-and-death struggle with Beowulf because, with the narrator, we are sharing in the Geat's intense concentration on the being he was challenging with all his powers.

Only a symbolic opponent in a symbolic setting could defeat a being with Grendel's symbolic past. Beowulf confronted him as a resolute

[34] *Scyn-* (707a; MS *syn-*), *man-* (712a and 737b), *hearm-* (766a) and *synscaða* (801b), 'phantom-, crime-, harm- and sin-injurer'.

[35] See above, p. 132. [36] See above, p. 95.

(*þryðswyð* (736b), *higeþihtig* (746b) and *swyðferhð* (826a)) kinsman of Hygelac (737a), a brave (*hildedeor* (834a)) protector of warriors (*eorla hleo* (791a)[37]), a noble leader of his troop (*freadrihten* (796a)) and a glorious leader of his people ('mære þeoden' (797a)). And he did so in a hall celebrated for its splendour and strength as a centre of generous and noble living (*horn-* and *winreced* (704a and 714b), *gold-*, *dryht-* and *winsele* (715a, 767a and 771a), *foldbold* (773a) and *gifheall* (838a)). The 'mæg Higelaces' remembered his boast of the evening before and grappled with the intruder; the only thought of the *hearmscaþa* was to flee to his *fenhopu*, 'fen refuge',[38] if he but could; the *dryhtsele* resounded as the two fought it out hand-to-hand in fierce anger (758–67a). For an Anglo-Saxon audience of the poem symbolic expressions placed this action in the whole sweep of cultural tradition; the person of Beowulf, the mental and physical components of the combatants and the setting in a hall constituted the action's 'reality'; the being, Grendel, was the product of an unimpeded play of imagination. The narrative dramatically integrated all three dimensions. Beowulf, seeking out the menace of Grendel in Hrothgar's hall and there eradicating it by an exceptional exertion of mental and physical powers, confirmed collective faith in wisdom and strength of mind:[39]

Hæfde þa gefælsod se þe ær feorran com,
snotor ond swyðferhð, sele Hroðgares

['He who had come from afar, wise and strong-minded, had then purged Hrothgar's hall', 825–6].

His enterprise symbolized society's will actually to overcome its fears. His triumph established him once and for all as the complete symbolic hero.

A symbolic actor set in a context which, in society's perception, elicited, or unacceptably challenged, his/her/its potentials for action was an immediate growth point of story. For example, the weapons carefully disposed by the Danes, when once again they slept in Hrothgar's hall after Beowulf's victory over Grendel, were in this dynamic condition:

Setton him to heafdon hilderandas,
bordwudu beorhtan; þær on bence wæs

[37] See above, p. 132.

[38] Cf. *morhopu* (450a). On *-hopu*, see Jespersen, *Language: its Nature, Development and Origin*, pp. 309–10.

[39] Cf. above, p. 9.

ofer æþelinge   yþgesene
heaþosteapa helm,   hringed byrne,
þrecwudu þrymlic

['They placed at their heads battle-shields, bright board-wood; there on the bench above a noble warrior was easily seen the helmet that towered in battle, the corslet made of rings, the mighty thrusting wood', 1242–6a].

The several weapons, symbolically designated, grouped round their representative owner *(æþeling)* and viewed *(yþgesene)* in this essential relationship, were pregnant with the Danes' praiseworthy readiness to go into action wherever and whenever their leader required:

Wæs þeaw hyra,
þæt hie oft wæron   an wig gearwe,
ge æt ham ge on herge,   ge gehwæþer þara
efne swylce mæla,   swylce hira mandryhtne
þearf gesælde;   wæs seo þeod tilu (1246b–50).[40]

And, sure enough, when Grendel's mother suddenly irrupted,

Ða wæs on healle   heardecg togen
sweord ofer setlum,   sidrand manig
hafen handa fæst

['The hard-edged sword was drawn in the hall above the seats, many a broad shield raised firm in the hand', 1288–90a].

Beowulf's entire enterprise against Grendel sprang directly from a similar perception of symbolic potentials in a dynamic state:

Þæt fram ham gefrægn   Higelaces þegn
god mid Geatum,   Grendles dæda;
se wæs moncynnes   mægenes strengest
on þæm dæge   þysses lifes,
æþele ond eacen

['Hygelac's thegn learned that from home, brave among the Geats, Grendel's deeds; he was the strongest in power of mankind on that day of this life, noble and mighty', 194–8a].

It was sufficient that a previously unmentioned symbolic 'Higelaces þegn' should simply learn of Grendel's deeds, just characterized by the narrator as 'nihtbealwa mæst' ('the greatest of malignant destructions at night',

[40] See above, p. 8.

193b), for a confrontation of the two to be set in place (195) and all the ensuing action to be set going without more ado, in that this thegn's people knew him to be brave, noble and outstandingly mighty and thus to have exactly the attributes Grendel was affronting. The wise among his compatriots were quickly urging him on (202–4). So too, many years later, Beowulf's final conflict became inevitable the moment his symbolic standing as an old, experienced guardian of his people was compromised by an unrestrained dragon:

he geheold tela
fiftig wintra – wæs ða frod cyning,
eald eþelweard –, oð ðæt an ongan
deorcum nihtum draca ricsian

['he held it well for fifty years – he was an experienced king then, an old guardian of the native land –, until a certain dragon began to hold sway in dark nights', 2208b–11].

The implications of these words were enough in themselves to draw the battle lines. The people's recognition of, and reaction to, the situation followed from events (2316–22a).

No fresh appraisal of this seasoned warrior-king was called for by the time he fought the dragon: a couple of the symbolic compound adjectives so frequent earlier – *stearcheort*, 'the stout-hearted one' (2552a), and *stiðmod*, 'firm in mind' (2566a) – served as reminder enough now. His personal qualities in action had long ceased to be in question. Wiglaf, pledging his support to his uncle, hard-pressed by the dragon's fire, appealed to him only to exert his capabilities to the limit:

scealt nu dædum rof,
æðeling anhydig, ealle mægene
feorh ealgian; ic ðe fullæstu

['now you, renowned for your deeds, resolute noble warrior, shall defend your life with all your might; I will help you', 2666b–8].

Beowulf, when fighting the dragon, was basically his people's institutionalized ruler of fifty years' standing.[41]

The dragon which Beowulf faced, a symbolic *nið*-, *lig*-, *fyr*- and

[41] In the narrator's and Wiglaf's symbolic terms, 'Geata dryhten' (2560b and 2576a), *guðcyning* (2563a and 2677b), 'mærum þeodne' (2572a), *þeodcyning* (2579a and 2694b), 'goldwine Geata' (2584a), 'folces hyrde' (2644b) and 'Wedra ðeodnes' (2656a).

eorðdraca, 'hostility-, flame-, fire-, earth-dragon',[42] was, as the narrator, Beowulf himself, Wiglaf and the messenger conceived it between them, a *þeodsceaða*, 'injurer of the people' (2278a and 2688a), and an *uht-*, *guð-*, *man-* and *attorsceaða*, 'dawn-, battle-, crime- and poison-injurer',[43] which for 300 years (2278b) had guarded treasure buried in a mound.[44] It was a *lyft-*, *wid-*, *guð-* and *uhtfloga*, 'sky-, wide-, battle- and dawn-flyer',[45] which, as an adversary, was an *aglæca*, 'dangerous opponent' (5×),[46] *hringboga*, 'coiled creature' (2561a), *guðfreca*, 'battle-warrior' (2414a), *gryregiest* and *inwit-* and *niðgæst*, 'terror-, malice- and hostility-stranger' (2560a, 2670a and 2699a), *ferhðgeniðla*, 'deadly enemy' (2881a), and *ealdorgewinna*, 'fighter for life' (2903b). When keeping watch over its treasure it was *eacencræftig*, 'exceedingly powerful' (2280a), when roused it was *stearcheort*, 'stout-hearted' (2288b), and *nearofag*, 'cruelly hostile' (2317a), when fighting it was *bealohycgende*, 'intent on destroying' (2565a), and *gryrefah*, 'terribly hostile' (2576b).

The fight to the death between these two elemental beings was dramatic indeed. *Stearcheort* as both were (2288b and 2552a), they struck terror into each other as they met in implacable hostility, Beowulf standing ready, with his sword drawn and shield raised, the dragon, straight out of its lair and eager for the fray, coiling itself to make its first onslaught: 'æghwæðrum wæs / bealohycgendra broga fram oðrum' ('each intent on destroying felt terror at the other', 2564b–5). 'Geata dryhten' and *gryregiest* / *gryrefah* were directly opposed in their full symbolical might as Beowulf interposed his shield,

Biorn under beorge   bordrand onswaf
wið ðam gryregieste,   Geata dryhten

['The warrior at the foot of the mound turned the rim of his shield against the terrible stranger, leader of the noble warriors of the Geats', 2559–60],

and as he struck his first blow,

Hond up abræd
Geata dryhten,   gryrefahne sloh
icgelafe

[42] 2273a, 2333a, 2689a, 2713a, 2825a and 3040b.

[43] 2271a, 2318a, 2514b and 2839a.

[44] *Hord-* and *goldweard*, *beorges weard* and *beorges* and *frætwa hyrde*, 'guardian of a hoard, gold and a mound' and 'protector of a mound and treasure' (2293b, 2303b, 2304b, 2524b, 2554b, 2580b, 2593a, 3066b, 3081b and 3133b).

[45] 2315a, 2346a, 2528a, 2760a and 2830a.

[46] 2520a, 2534a, 2557a, 2592a and 2905a.

['The leader of the noble warriors of the Geats swung up his hand, struck the terror-hostile being with his ? ', 2575b–7a].

Only one outcome from the total confrontation of these two inexorable symbolic antagonists was to be expected. Both had to die:

Sceolde lændaga[47]
æþeling ærgod   ende gebidan,
worulde lifes,   ond se wyrm somod,
þeah ðe hordwelan   heolde lange

['The outstanding noble warrior had to experience the end of his transitory days, his life in the world, and the dragon also, although it had guarded the treasure-hoard for long', 2341b–4],

the narrator had warned in words tinged with feeling; while the messenger's picture of the grieving Wiglaf keeping 'head-watch' over friend and foe lying dead side-by-side ('heafodwearde / leofes ond laðes' (2909b–10a)) presented the Geats with an economically precise symbolic image of the 'Nu . . .' ('Now . . .', 2900a) to which the mighty clash had inevitably led and from which everything else was to flow (2910b).

The dragon had been an elemental force in the environment of mankind, flying by night enveloped in fire, motivated by blind compulsion, devoid of human thoughts and feelings, awesome in its sheer power and antiquity. Once angered, it had spewed flame far and wide, bent on destroying everything alive. On the ground it had moved by gliding, coiling itself up to attack; at close quarters its heat had been unbearable. When it lay dead the Geats perceived it as a strange being:

Ær hi þær gesegan   syllicran wiht,
wyrm on wonge   wiðerræhtes þær
laðne licgean

['They had already seen there a more strange being, the dragon on the ground opposite, lying hateful', 3038–40a].[48]

It was not its individual features that struck them – not, for instance, the eyes and wings it must have had (how many wings were there, and did it have feet at its tail-end, like the dragon on the Sutton Hoo shield?[49]).

[47] Restoration is required in 2341b for *þend daga* at the beginning of a MS line with probable loss of letters at the end of the preceding line. Malone proposed *liþenddaga,* 'of his seafarer-days' (*The Nowell Codex*, ed. Malone, p. 89, col. 1).

[48] Cf. above, p. 211.

[49] See Bruce-Mitford *et al.*, *The Sutton Hoo Ship-Burial* II, fig. 50.

What impressed them was the whole being – that it lay there, burnt, fifty foot long, its capability to range the sky by night ended (3040b–6). The dragon had represented a core of active being, and, once that had gone, what was left was of no account (3131b–3).

Beowulf, on the other hand, had lived at the very heart of civilized society, preeminent in the distinctively human area of existence where personal feeling and public action coalesced, the territory of language, the domain in which verbal, as against visual, narrative reigned supreme. The young Wiglaf's expression of unqualified loyalty to his lord and kinsman, during and after the action against the dragon, and the dying Beowulf's resigned, proud, practical, affectionate words to his nephew had had the combined dignity of absolute sincerity and public weight.[50] The dragon fight had indeed been a confrontation of absolutes. All of Beowulf, past and present, man and king, had been involved. He had gone into action against his terrible foe as

se ðe worna fela
gumcystum god guða gedigde,
hildehlemma, þonne hnitan feðan

['he who had survived a great many fights, brave with manly virtues, many battle-crashes when foot troops clashed', 2542b–4].

The narrator had already accounted for Beowulf's lack of fear before the encounter[51] by characterizing him as a warrior who had been a tried and trusty survivor ever since he had defeated Grendel and his kin (2349b–54a), notably when he had performed prodigious feats after Hygelac had been killed at the mouth of the Rhine, and when he had succeeded to the throne after Heardred, Hygelac's son, had also been killed, some years later, feuding with the Swedes (2354b–96). Likewise Beowulf himself, saddened by the certain prospect of death and speaking in the presence of his companions without explicitly addressing them (2426–2509), in the time-honoured manner of individuals viewing their experience as part of general existence –

Fela ic on geogoðe guðræsa genæs,
orleghwila; ic þæt eall gemon

[50] Cf. above, p. 80.

[51] Cf., however, the fear which he (and the dragon) felt when they actually came face to face (see above, p. 218).

['Many battle-onslaughts, times of war, I survived in my youth; I remember all that', 2426–7][52] –

had thought of himself as bringing to bear on the present action a whole lifetime of private-public involvement with two generations of Geatish kings ('Ic wæs . . .' (2428–71), 'Þa wæs . . .' (2472–96), 'symle ic . . .' (2497–8a), 'ond swa to ealdre sceall . . .' (2498b–508a) and 'Nu sceall . . .' (2508b–9)). Fittingly the twelve hearth-companions riding round Beowulf's memorial mound lamenting the death of their lord recalled with praise the virtues of valour and kindness he had shown as king and man (3169–82).

The societies which viewed Beowulf in his entirety and appraised and accepted him as a hero were not just the neutral, anonymous bodies which riddlers used in order to authenticate enigmatic beings with corporate witness.[53] The Danes who observed Beowulf in the flower of his early manhood had been ravaged by Grendel for twelve years and all their hopes of rescue lay with this newcomer from abroad. The Geats whose king was searchingly displayed in his old age were devastated by the dragon and had only gloom and deprivation to expect if their defender were to die. Witnessed hero and witnessing society were in a dynamic relationship. Yet each had its own distinct past-present identity. Beowulf's strength was beyond that of all other men; he came from outside the community he was to save from Grendel; and he was related to the Geatish royal line only through his mother: a Swedish invader let him succeed to the throne (2387–90a), he had no son to follow him as heir and he is never shown as king presiding over his followers in hall or leading them in battle. The champion was presented in some degree set apart from each of the communities in which he played a crucial rôle. It was in the symbolic action that he and they were inseparably united: the adversaries this super-endowed hero fought were enemies of the entire community; the settings of his struggles – in a hall, then in the unknown depths of a pool and finally on a bare hilltop by the sea – seem to image stages in his own development as well as suit the social foes he faced.

The bond between hero and society expressed itself emotionally. In *Beowulf* during the first, Grendel, phase this happened to only a limited extent: strong feelings there were in plenty, but they were essentially the sorrows common to a wounded community – the Danes – channelled

[52] Cf. above, pp. 195–7. [53] Cf. above, pp. 189–90.

especially through their king, Hrothgar, and became connected with Beowulf, as their rescuer from abroad, in so far as he brought relief. The champion and his fellow Geats, for their part, remained first and foremost men of action, getting on in a business-like way with what they had come to do and not going in for emotion for its own sake: for instance, the instinct of Beowulf's companions was simply to defend their leader when he was locked in combat with Grendel (794b–7). Beowulf's underwater struggle against Grendel's mother, however, brought out an emotional group attachment to the hero: whereas, at the sight of bloodstains on the surface of the pool into which Beowulf had plunged, the Danes speedily gave up hope and left, the Geats sat on in anguish, hoping against hope to see their friend and leader again, and in due course were rewarded by greeting him delightedly when he emerged in triumph (1591–1605a and 1623–30a). In the testing time of Beowulf's lone fight against the dragon, group spirit finally failed, leaving an individual, Wiglaf, to stand uniquely in unbounded fidelity to a solitary king, while society became a background mourning the loss of their ruler. Like the settings, the emotional relationships between witnessed hero and witnessing society changed as he evolved in the course of the poem.

In range the narrative union of hero and society in *Beowulf* was broad and expansive throughout. Everything concerned with the past and present of the one was deemed relevant to the other. The social canvas extended to persons and peoples over a wide area of the Baltic and North Sea in the fourth, fifth and sixth centuries. The deeds of the hero drew out all of his long life. The action itself was of impressive proportions. The elemental nature of the hero's primary foes lifted the story out of everyday concerns, past or present, into the realm of fundamentals. The sequence of first monsters and then a dragon basically represented for society a shift from debased humanity to blind, indifferent force in its enemies, while, for the hero, siting his struggles initially in the very centre of social living, then within a confined, unfamiliar, natural environment and finally against a non-committal background of space took him through a similar development: society and champion both underwent an intense process firstly of extension and then of isolation of their powers. Pattern, as in the shared death of Beowulf and the dragon, implied the operation of underlying forces such as fate. Hindsight directed at distant events lent a unitary view and tone to materials of ultimately diverse origins: the poet's knowledge of Hygelac's raid into Frankish territory, for instance, contained elements from both Scandinavia and the Continent.[54] He had absorbed too some main elements of Christianity, notably a sense of God's majestic control of the cyclic life of man and nature and the moral concept of offence against God on which Hrothgar discoursed eloquently and which Grendel personified so wretchedly. The symbolic theme of society's dependence on the individual was conceived on the grand scale of a Shakespeare.

This poem is a complex of various binary interactions – between fundamental symbolism and dramatic narrative, between witnessed individual and witnessing society, between human and other-than-human, between reality and imagination, between a symbolic actor and an enabling or challenging context, between past and present, between prime of life and old age. Exploiting masterfully the binary organization of language traditional to his mode,[55] the poet composed an ambitious tale integrated conceptually, dramatically, linguistically and metrically. The work of art he produced, at once bold in conception and subtle in execution, displays every sign that he was at the height of his powers, an assured practitioner who consistently brought a creative imagination to the established capabilities of his traditional craft. Short lays probably underlay particular episodes of his poem,[56] but he had adopted a spacious mode of story-telling requiring narrative technique on the grand scale. Here again he showed himself eclectic. He may have owed his main structure to an ancient northern tradition of hero-testing by a combination of human-monster slaying and dragon slaying.[57] Perhaps he took a hint from Vergil in having his hero recount his early adventures retrospectively. (If he did, he improved on his model in his dramatic integration of the device and stands almost alone among Vergil's imitators, including Milton, by using it in the spirit of the original to throw light on his hero's potential.[58]) He certainly incorporated into the sinister landscape of Grendel's mere (1357b–79 and 1414–17a) some graphic features suggested to him (probably indirectly) by the *Visio Pauli*.[59] He was a gifted teller of tales whose mature art testifies to his largeness of vision, wide-ranging empathy, active imagination, nobility of outlook and human warmth.

[54] Cf. my '"Symbolic" Language', pp. 3–4. [55] See above, p. 145.

[56] See Campbell, 'The Use in *Beowulf* of Earlier Heroic Verse', and cf. above, p. 189.

[57] As argued (rather tenuously) by Chadwick, 'The Monsters and Beowulf'. See also (supporting Chadwick) Opland, 'A *Beowulf*-Analogue in *Njáls saga*'.

[58] See Campbell, 'The Use in *Beowulf* of Earlier Heroic Verse', pp. 283–4.

[59] See above, pp. 22–5.

Concentrating on the critical actions by which a notable individual had served society in early manhood and old age, the poet created a token, public, assessment of this eminent person. It was not a 'prose' analysis of the sort that came to the fore in Alfredian vernacular writing. The estimate was intended to emerge gradually from the unfolding of a traditional story about a man initially impressing society and finally acting to the limit on his community's behalf out of his resources of accumulated experience. Each telling of the poet's tale renewed the standards of behaviour on which communities had relied time out of mind. The story provided a humane and civilized medium. It encompassed both incisive action in response to evident need and action arising from a sense of duty, born of gloomy self-questioning and of proper pride in past achievements; it admitted principles of moral rectitude as well as the more dubious force of circumstances; it accepted that there might be sufficient or insufficient foresight, sufficient or insufficient capability; it allowed for both confidence and fear, even despair; it recognized that success might be complete, but eventually corrupt, or might be partial, but long-lasting in reputation. It displayed a high regard for initiative, daring, courage, vigour of manhood, self-control and balance of mind, integrity of word and deed, sympathy, generosity and gratitude, an absence of vindictiveness, loyalty, a sense of social propriety and of obligations to society, and a proper sense of human limitations and of dependence on and faith in God. It showed understanding of those who act criminally, those who act recklessly, those who act out of strong feelings, those who delay acting, those who fail to act and those who cannot. It indicated the frail periphery of human action as well as its commanding centre. It acknowledged the deeply felt personal relationships involved in the motivation, performance and consequence of actions. It respected strong feelings engendered by factors such as age, status, lineage, memory, sense of analogy, material objects, ties of loyalty, loss, unforeseen circumstances, another's words, an adversary, uncontrollable forces. It generated powerful themes of responsibility, judgement and fame.

The poem put into effect Hrothgar's declaration to Beowulf,

Þu þe self hafast
dædum gefremed, ðæt ðin dom lyfað
awa to aldre (953b–5a).[60]

[60] See above, p. 210.

Assimilated into a longeval, collective, narrative culture, the reputation of Beowulf's active life took on a general existence. A skilful poet fashioned out of materials traditional to his craft a timelessly evocative symbolic story about this human actor and thereby created an articulate counterpart to the 'beadurofes becn' ('sign of one famed for battle', 3160a) which, it was averred, had been devised in wood and earth by *foresnotre*, 'very clever', men (3162a) to memorialize him high on a headland above the sea.[61]

[61] Cf. above, p. 136.

II

The poetry of a universal religion

7

Vernacular poetic narrative in a Christian world

The process of cultural change which was initiated by the coming of Christianity affected the Anglo-Saxons' tradition of socially based poetry in all its departments. The ideas, mode, language and transmission of vernacular verse were all subject irrevocably to radical alteration. Narrative thought still prevailed, but was basically reorientated. The arena of action was reconceived and peopled by new relationships: a spiritual Christ-centred world enveloped the earthly environs of social concerns. The communities which previously had been defined in terms of human kingship and its related institutions became subsumed into the rule of Christ, lord over all creation for ever, the son begotten true God from true God before time began, the being through whom sky, earth and sea and their inhabitants were created bearing the divine imprint, the incarnated redeemer of lapsed mankind, adored in heaven and praised on earth, the promised judge ahead. The perspectives of human life – its lines of communication, its morality, its conceptions of individuality, its loyalties – all underwent permanent transmutation. The environment was rearranged. Verticality took on a greater prominance in surroundings which had a heaven above and a hell beneath than it had had before in horizontal continuous time:[1] the old Germanic term *middangeard*, 'middle dwelling', began to signify the region between heaven and hell rather than

[1] Architecture illustrates this change. The tall, narrow, shape of some Anglo-Saxon churches surviving from the earliest days (e.g. at Escomb, County Durham, and (the original building) at Bradford-on-Avon, Wiltshire) is a sign of the new awareness, and the provision of internal space for use at more than one level indicated by some surviving lofty churches (e.g. at Brixworth, Northamptonshire, and Deerhurst, Gloucestershire) witnesses to the complex organization of worship which developed under these conditions; for these churches and other relevant examples, see Taylor and Taylor, *Anglo-Saxon Architecture* I and II, and, for discussion, *ibid.*, III (by H.M.T.), 1035.

the inhabited land surrounded by sea.[2] The connotations of language became increasingly complex dogmatically, ethically and materially. In principle, vernacular poetry's symbolic expression of inherited potentials had much to offer a body of thought, such as this, founded on spiritual unseens. But the new complexity demanded a more systematic structure of explicit thinking: freshly acquired thought had to wean symbols away from registering socially perceived innate potentials in action and redirect them to fashioning images of ecclesiastically proclaimed fundamentals conditioning every individual's spiritual membership of the kingdom of God. Christian intellect overtook Germanic instinct. Implicit symbols surrendered to explicit images. Instead of traditionally structured language, which chronicled actions taking place, and which elicited, as it did so, greater or less insight and sophistication from its practitioners, a set of stylish techniques for embellishing fixed truths started to hold sway. Words became more and more the instruments of self-aware artifice. Functional apposition assumed the tone of artfully varied celebration. Latin 'style' replaced Germanic 'expression'.[3] The mechanism of tradition altered

[2] Cf. the word's connotations of the newer sort in the blessing which God spoke from heaven for St Andrew's journey across land and (mostly) sea, 'Hafa bletsunge / ofer middangeard mine, þær ðu fere' ('Have my blessing when you travel over the world', *Andreas* 223b–4) and its connotations of the earlier sort in the praise which the bearer of the tidings of King Beowulf's death bestowed on the generosity shown by the earlier king, Hygelac, when rewarding two of his warriors, 'ne ðorfte him ða lean oðwitan / mon on middangearde, syððan hie ða mærða geslogon' ('no one in the inhabited world had reason to reproach him for those gifts after they had performed those glorious deeds', *Beowulf* 2995b–6).

[3] It is illuminating to observe how Aldhelm, as a Latin author, handled this distinction. Since his composition of Latin octosyllables clearly reflected his feeling for the structural rôle of alliteration in vernacular verse (see below, p. 430), it is reasonable to infer that his differentiation of 'plain' vocabulary in his Latin poetry from proliferated artificial vocabulary in his Latin prose likewise reflected vernacular poetic influence. He confined his use of all-pervading 'hermeneutic' words (defined by Michael Lapidge, in his study of a later phase of Anglo-Saxon culture, as 'the ostentatious parade of unusual, often very arcane and apparently learned vocabulary' ('Hermeneutic Style', p. 67)) almost entirely to his prose (where there was no apt vernacular model for him to follow), whereas in matters such as word placement his models were the devices of classical and late Latin (and perhaps Hiberno-Latin) poetry – for instance, the splitting of a noun and its modifying adjective by another word, such as a verb – whether he was writing poetry or prose. Probably he excluded the lexical embellishment from his poetry because there a continual failure to call a spade a spade would have gone too much against the grain of the functional vocabulary he was familiar with in native verse. For writing this note I have benefited from an illuminating conversation with Andy Orchard.

too. Authority became increasingly textual, and so did poetry itself. The first period of basic change in the history of the use of English, from oral to written, was under way. Some of the principal effects of this new Christian order and its more 'literary' ways will be surveyed in the following chapters. Here, in this chapter, some main implications for narrative itself will be considered.

First of all, it will be appropriate to recognize the changed status which vernacular poetic narrative acquired *qua* narrative: previously it had been responsible for preserving society's entire body of active principles; now it became an arm of a narrative system based far beyond the vernacular. The new rôle which was assigned to it by common consent, at least in Bede's Northumbria, was that it should play an acknowledged part in the church's evangelization, and in effect it received this commission within seventy or eighty years of the arrival of Augustine's mission in Kent in 597 and forty or fifty of the first baptism of a Northumbrian king in 627. To Bede and his contemporaries early in the eighth century this development was in itself a miracle of the Christian universe. In the *Ecclesiastical History*, which he finished in 731, Bede told simply and affectingly a by then established story of how at Whitby, some sixty or so years before, Cædmon, a cowman until then unskilled in poetry, had been divinely inspired in a dream to sing some verses in English praising God, creator of the world. From this beginning, Bede wrote, Cædmon had gone on to memorize and ruminate, piece by piece, the whole course of sacred history and to sing in English about the creation of the world and origin of the human race, and all the story of Genesis, about Israel's departure from Egypt and entry into the promised land, about many other stories of sacred scripture, about the incarnation, passion, resurrection and ascension of the Lord and about the coming of the holy spirit and teaching of the apostles; he also made many songs about the terror of future judgement and the horror of the pain of hell and the sweetness of the kingdom of heaven, as well as very many others about divine favours and judgements, in all of which he took care to draw men away from delight in sins and stimulate them to love and good practice. As a result, Bede affirmed, many had been inspired to despise the world and to long for the heavenly life, and after Cædmon other Englishmen had attempted to compose religious poems, though none had been his equal.[4]

Cædmon in one stride had taken vernacular poetry to centre stage in

[4] Bede, *HE*, IV.24 [22] (pp. 414–18).

Christian mission to the Anglo-Saxons. All catechetical instruction should begin, according to St Augustine of Hippo, with the *narratio* of Christian world history, and Cædmon had shown how to use native poetry to tell this basic narrative in a way that roused the hopes and fears inherent in every individual. He had begun in the proper way with praise of God as creator and had accompanied description of divine judgement ahead and its eternal consequences with the appropriate exhortations to avoid sin and act rightly.[5] He had demonstrated that the traditional techniques of English poetry offered the means to reveal that every human being's spiritual life depended on a fixed world narrative. He had brought within the common range the message that the everyone had to come to terms with being a part of that narrative him- or herself.

Vernacular poetry's point of entry into this world history in the person of this poet was held to have been a vision in which the sleeping Cædmon saw someone standing by him and commanding him to sing. Native verse itself had thereby become part of a narrative order in which spiritual phenomena manifested themselves freely and dramatically, just as the stories which poetry told featured interventions with similar spiritually generalizing effect. For instance, it was a voice from heaven that inspired St Juliana to prove the universal validity of her sanctity by turning the tables on the *gæstgeniðla*, 'enemy of the spirit' (*Juliana* 245b), an *aglæca*, 'dangerous opponent',[6] which had been sent from hell, 'lyftlacende' ('flying through the air', 281a) in the disguise of an angel, in order to corrupt her when she was imprisoned for her resolute defiance of her heathen suitor: this devil had committed, as the saint forced him to confess, countless heinous crimes against humanity 'mægnes cræfte' ('through the ability of his might', 392b) ever since he had first destroyed Adam and Eve in paradise. Spiritual entities, good or bad, constantly entered into narrative living, to engage it in world history.

Another change of dimension was that the narrative of a person's material existence did not end with physical death. According to another poem, extant in two variant versions which editors call *Soul and Body I* and *II* respectively, every soul facing damnation after separation from its sinful body has to return at night weekly for three hundred years (unless the end of the world comes sooner) to upbraid the rotting remains as they are devoured by the worm *gifer*, 'glutton', and its ravenous companions. (The

[5] Day, 'The Influence of the Catechetical *Narratio*', esp. pp. 54–5.

[6] 268b, 319a and 430a; for the translation, see above, p. 212, n. 28.

blessed soul has a corresponding duty to comfort its former partner at regular intervals.) The unbodied voice from eternity contrasts strikingly with the vile disintegration of the once active, now silent, body:

Biþ þæt heafod tohliden,   honda tohleoþode,
geaflas toginene,   goman toslitene,
seonwe beoð asogene,   sweora bicowen;
rib reafiað   reþe wyrmas,
drincað hloþum hra,   heolfres þurstge.
Bið seo tunge totogen   on tyn healfe
hungrum to hroþor

['The head has split, hands are dismembered, jaws opened wide, gums torn apart, sinews are sucked out, the neck is chewed up; cruel worms plunder the ribs, drink the carcass in crowds, thirsty for blood. The tongue is pulled apart into ten pieces as a joy for the hungry', *Soul and Body II* 103–9a].[7]

A good deal of schematic, book-based thought went into description of the natural world viewed *sub specie aeternitatis*. From now on Christian revelation joined forces with the potentials which Old English poetry customarily recognized – Christian explicitness with the implicitness traditional to poetry's symbolic language. An alliance was forged between Christian explication and Germanic implication. For example, by virtue of his book-reading the poet of *The Panther* believed that 'feorlondum on' ('in distant lands', *The Panther* 10b), among the countless, only half-known, kinds of birds and beasts 'foldhrerendra' ('moving on the earth', 5b) as widely as this radiant bosom extends to the surrounding 'brim grymetende, / sealtyþa geswing' ('roaring sea, swing of salt waves', 7b–8a), there existed a bright-coated, eating, sleeping, cave-dwelling, sound- and scent-emitting 'wrætlice gecynd wildra' ('marvellous species of wild beasts', 9), with characteristics symbolizing a central part of the Christian narrative of world redemption. It was a creature which owed its very name to what 'wisfæste weras on gewritum cyþað' ('learned men make known in writings', 14), that is, to a version of the Latin *Physiologus*, or Bestiary, but the vernacular poem which was composed about it employed both open explanation and traditional suggestion.

Presented as gentle, kind and loving to all creatures apart from one ancient adversary (the dragon), the panther, in having this nature, was stated explicitly to parallel Christ's beneficence to all creation with the sole

[7] 108–14a in the most recent edition (*The Old English 'Soul and Body'*, ed. Moffat).

exception of the devil; and more specifically there was similarly explicit equivalence in the aromatic scent which this *þeodwiga*, 'great warrior' (38a), was alleged to produce on standing up *ellenrof*, 'renowned for fighting spirit' (40a), after eating its fill and sleeping in its cave for three days: the fragrance, more delightful and sweeter and stronger, *æþelicra*, 'more innately noble' (48a), than any given off by plants and trees adorning the earth, was claimed to attract 'beornþreat monig' ('many a troop of men', 50b), 'dareðlacende' ('waving their spears', 53a) as they hastened eagerly 'of ceastrum ond cynestolum / ond of byrgsalum' ('from fortresses and palaces and from castle halls', 49–50a), and was thus held to match the drawing power which Christ has exerted on flocks of the faithful all over the world since he imprisoned the devil in hell and, after suffering death on our behalf for three days, rose again as 'þeoden engla, / sigora sellend' ('prince of angels, giver of victories', 63b–4a). The vigorous symbolic military terminology common to this beast and the risen Christ had the effect of implying that the animal's conformity to this pattern symbolized not merely a possession but also an exercise of the redeemer's spiritual leadership over men. It expressed the relationship dynamically.

The schematic significance of another feature of the panther, however, was not spelled out at all, namely its remarkably variegated coat, which, according to the poet's rendering of a statement in his version of the Latin Bestiary that the animal's skin 'varius est sicut tunica Joseph', shone yet more brightly than Joseph's multi-coloured tunic. In the poet's mind there seems to have been knowledge of the exegetical point which was included in a commentary on the Pentateuch printed in Patrologia Latina as Bede's but in reality a Carolingian compilation: this was that the coat of many colours which was made for Joseph by his father represents the variety of peoples, from all races, who are gathered into the body of Christ, the son of God,[8] but this supportive exegesis the poet did not see fit to cite. No analysis along these lines was offered. Instead, in this case, he chose to rely on the cumulative power of his language alone to enforce the single unitary point that the animal's radiance surpasses even that which 'gæsthalge guman' ('men holy in spirit', 21a) attribute to Joseph's tunic: as each dye in

[8] 'Tunica autem polymita, quam fecit illi pater, varietatem populorum ex omnibus gentibus in corpus Christi congregatam significat' (PL 91, col. 265), doubtless taken from a previous authority. For rejection of Bede's authorship of this compilation, see Glorieux, *Pour revaloriser Migne*, p. 52, and Laistner, 'Some Early Medieval Commentaries on the Old Testament', n. 16.

that garment, he declared, gleamed, according to these authorities, more brightly than the others,

swa þæs deores hiw,
blæc brigda gehwæs, beorhtra ond scynra
wundrum lixeð, þætte wrætlicra
æghwylc oþrum, ænlicra gien
ond fægerra frætwum bliceð,
symle sellicra

['so the hue of that animal, shining in every variety of colours, gleams wonderfully more brightly and glitteringly, so that each dazzles splendidly more marvellously than the others, yet more singularly and beautifully, always more choicely', 25b–30a].

This overwhelming, indescribable, splendour does indeed seem more than natural. Evidently the poet was intent above all on celebrating this animal's symbolic energy.

The panther was both a *deor*, 'beast', among other birds and beasts and an *anstapa*, 'solitary walker' (15a), incomparably brilliant and fragrant, and possessing *sundorgecynd*, 'a special nature' (30b). It emblematically acted out in created nature the redemptive glory of its creator. By eating and sleeping and so on, it proclaimed that nature bore the imprint of fundamental Christian cosmic narrative. But it was an animal only to the same extent as an evangelist's symbol was in Anglo-Saxon art. It was a symbolic creature not because it presented an elemental force which tested men's powers to the limit progressively in narrative, as the dragon in *Beowulf* did, but because it represented a living restatement of Christian universal narrative formalized in nature by text-borne ideas. In the process active nature acquired an exotic, 'created', 'romantic', dimension unknown to traditional Anglo-Saxon riddling, which, however much influenced by literary antecedents and however heavily Christianized, remained at heart an operation of curiosity about actually perceived phenomena. A less functional, more self-conscious, attitude to activity was evolving.

The conviction that corporeality as such had a narrative content which was related to Christian cosmic narrative made the physical world which was within the range of normal observation a ready store of standard images of spiritual realities. But it is improbable that a vernacular poet would have drawn such analogies directly from nature. He would have been more likely to reuse an image already established by the authority of Latin literature or of church worship, as when St Juliana triumphed over the hellish 'þystra stihtend' ('ordainer of darkness', *Juliana* 419b) as 'wuldres condel' ('candle of glory', 454b).

Nevertheless, physical images, which were formed according to the traditional native sense of active being, made their own distinctive contribution to spiritual concepts. Pre-Christian imagination mingled with Christian when, for example, a remarkable image of painfully entangling vegetation, nourished by the blood of the murdered Abel and entwining all the subsequent history of mankind, was introduced into *Genesis A*, a versification of Genesis as far as the sacrifice of Isaac, generally not notable for substantial departures from its source. Ultimately this growth may have been a derivative of the forbidden tree in paradise: on several occasions in his *Moralia* Gregory the Great employed a tree image with reference to our descent from Adam and our inheritance of sin from his fall,[9] and in the same spirit the *Genesis* poet concluded his treatment of his image by lamenting the injury Eve's first sin did us. But no clear line of descent from that direction has been traced and, instead of an image subordinated to abstract thought, as in, say, Gregory's 'Hinc[10] est quod huius erroris ramus in humano genere ex illa nunc usque radice protrahitur' ('It is hence that the branch of this sin is drawn out in the human race from that root right up to the present'),[11] the poet presented a dramatic image firmly located in the arena of action. It is *a priori* likely that a sprouting such as this, fed by the blood of a murdered brother, would have owed a main debt to Anglo-Saxon imagination.[12]

The Bible, of course, supplied the earth's swallowing of Abel's blood (Genesis IV.11) but nothing growing from it. The poet provided the rest:[13]

[9] See *Genesis A: a New Edition*, ed. Doane, p. 247 n.

[10] That is, because of Adam's attempt at self-justification, 'The woman whom thou gavest to be with me, she gave me of the tree, and I did eat' (Genesis III.12).

[11] Gregory, *Moralia in Iob*, ed. Adriaen I, 187.

[12] For a discussion of the poet's treatment of the whole Cain and Abel narrative, rightly arguing that it had a traditional Anglo-Saxon social ethic rather than an exegetic one, see Brockman, '"Heroic" and "Christian" in *Genesis A*'.

[13] In a paper read to the International Society of Anglo-Saxonists in 1991, Charles D. Wright of the University of Illinois at Champaign pointed out, apropos of *Genesis A*, that Aldhelm in his *Carmen de virginitate* represented human pride, disobedience and slander as a dense, rough, scrub growing from Cain's crime:

Hie [i.e. Cain and Abel] þa drihtne lac 975
begen brohton. Brego engla beseah
on Abeles gield eagum sinum, 977
cyning eallwihta, Caines ne wolde
tiber sceawian. Þæt wæs torn were 979
hefig æt heortan. Hygewælm asteah
beorne on breostum, blatende nið, 981
yrre for æfstum. He þa unræden
folmum gefremede, freomæg ofsloh, 983
broðor sinne, and his blod ageat,
Cain Abeles. Cwealmdreore swealh 985
þæs middangeard, monnes swate.
Æfter wælswenge wea wæs aræred, 987
tregena tuddor. Of ðam twige siððan
ludon laðwende leng swa swiðor 989
reðe wæstme. Ræhton wide
geond werþeoda wrohtes telgan, 991
hrinon hearmtanas hearde and sare
drihta bearnum, (doð gieta swa), 993
of þam brad blado bealwa gehwilces
sprytan ongunnon. We þæt spell magon, 995
wælgrimme wyrd, wope cwiðan,
nales holunge; ac us hearde sceod 997
freolecu fæmne þurh forman gylt
þe wið metod æfre men gefremeden, 999
eorðbuende, siððan Adam wearð
of godes muðe gaste eacen 1001

['They then both brought an offering to the Lord. The prince of angels looked upon Abel's gift with his eyes, the king of all creatures, Cain's offering he would not behold. That was bitter to the man, grievous at his heart. Surging thoughts arose in the man's breast, pale hatred, anger out of envy. Then he performed a deed of folly with his hands, killed his noble kinsman, his own brother, and shed his blood, Cain Abel's. This world swallowed the gore of slaughter, the blood of a

Inde prava seges glitibus densescet acerbis,
Sanguine purpureo dum scaevus rura cruentat,
Inde superbarum nascuntur murmura vocum . . .

['Thence [i.e. from Cain's murder of Abel] an evil crop grows densely with rough thorns [*or* thistles *or* brambles] when the miscreant stains the fields with purple blood. Thence the mutterings of proud voices are born . . .', 2725–7].
As well as acknowledging my debt to Wright for this significant analogue I am grateful to Andy Orchard for a helpful conversation on the matter.

man. After the deadly blow grief was established, an issue of misfortunes. From that shoot afterwards sprang malignant cruel growths, the longer the stronger. Branches of strife reached widely throughout peoples, shoots of harm seized the sons of men painfully and grievously (they do so still), from them broad leaves of every destruction began to sprout. We can lament that story, violent fate, with weeping by no means without reason; but the noble lady injured us painfully through the first sin which men, dwellers on earth, ever performed against God, since Adam was endowed with a soul from God's mouth'].

A potential for prolonged growth shared by grief (*wea* (987b)) issuing from fratricide, and a seedling (*twig* (988b)) springing from the earth,[14] gave the poet a genuine basis in the authentic tradition of Old English metaphor[15] for substituting the latter for the former and thereby producing vegetation which inflicts harm on men. He did not, however, ground this metaphor as such in traditional poetic symbols, but reserved them for underpinning a thematic sequence leading from crime (*hygewælm* (980b), *freomæg* (983b) and *wælsweng* (987a)) to vegetal growth (*hearmtanas* (992a)) by way of the blood (*cwealmdreor* (985b)) which owed its rôle as intermediary to the Lord's words to Cain, 'And now art thou cursed from the earth, which hath opened her mouth to receive thy brother's blood from thy hand' (Genesis IV.11; cf. *Genesis* (*A*) 1016b–17a). Crime and growth together constituted a 'wælgrimme wyrd' (996a). Expressed symbolically, these sequential elements accorded with the deep-seated Anglo-Saxon conviction that action was a continuum. But, as well as that, the symbols which expressed them had become absorbed into a spiritual system of universal proportions: Cain's fierce resentment which made him shed Abel's blood was against a judgement by *brego engla* (976b) and 'cyning eallwihta' (978a), the ruler of heaven and of earth, of the spiritual as well as of the physical; 'þæs middangeard' (986a) swallowed the blood; and the vegetation sent its branches of strife 'geond werþeoda' (991a).

Physically active vegetal growth gave the operative essentials of the crime a living form which, in the traditional vein of Old English poetry, dispensed both with the particulars of the Bible (what the offerings were, what the Lord said to Cain when he was angry and where the murder took place (Genesis IV.3–8), features of the sort beloved of Christian exegetes) and with moralizing about sin. (That came only later with reference to Eve, 998b.) But the hostility and grief originating from a spiritual crime took

[14] Cf. Boyd, 'Doctrine and Criticism', pp. 231–2.

[15] Cf. above, pp. 96–8.

the physicality in this union beyond the normal limits of material things. The vegetal growth, matter though it was, grew in the spiritual universe to which the initial crime belonged. It embodied the capability of spiritual sin, once committed in the person of Cain, to corrupt man's whole existence. A succession of terse, pithy, simple clauses recorded the massive spread of this being of spiritual contamination through unmeasured time and space. With relentless cruelty the vegetation sprouting from polluted earth entangled man's entire history in its outgrowths of grief and suffering. The sadness of our own inescapable involvement in this organic human lot was so self-evident that it needed nothing more than an interjection to convey it – 'doð gieta swa'. Non-human nature in the shape of this vegetation had become more a means of projecting mankind's fatally flawed experience of the spiritual cosmos than an object of attention in its own, material, right.

'Realism' changed accordingly, if by 'realism' we understand poetry's rendering of phenomena subject to direct observation. In the Cain and Abel episode, branches, shoots and broad leaves were enough to lend credence to growing vegetation. Signals of physical normality were all that was needed to provide convincing counterparts of spiritual truths, by contrast to the signs of the extraordinary which were the hallmarks of imagined beings: whereas rousing symbolic characterization as *lyft-*, *wid-*, *guð-* and *uhtfloga* made the dragon in *Beowulf* credible as a living 'syllicre wiht' menacing an entire people,[16] the panther was fitted to bear its exegetic load through possessing the most ordinary animal-characteristics of having a coat, of eating and sleeping, of living in a den and of emitting a sound and a smell.[17]

Artistic realism had been traditionally an exercise in dramatic imagination. For instance, a ship's inherent vitality had been expressed by giving the vessel an animal-headed stem-post with a fluent line continuing the sweep of the prow,[18] or by appreciating it running before the wind as 'flota famigheals fugle gelicost' (*Beowulf* 218),[19] or by exuberantly envisaging it

[16] See above, pp. 219–20. [17] See above, pp. 233–4.

[18] Two figureheads of the Migration Period found in Belgium and now in the British Museum are examples, the one, from Moerzeke-Mariekerke, carved with a dolphin-like head with wide-open mouth, the other, from Appels, carved with a savagely beaked, toothed head and long neck. The former is carbon-dated to *c.* 350 and the latter to *c.* 400. Anglo-Saxons presumably used this type of stem. See Bruce-Mitford, 'Ships' Figure-Heads of the Migration Period', in *Aspects of Anglo-Saxon Archaeology*, pp. 175–87.

[19] See above, pp. 95–6 and n. 65.

as a being with four feet under its belly and eight on its back, two wings, twelve eyes and six heads (if ship this be in *Riddle* 36);[20] but such freedom was pared down by 'literary' considerations when a ship became purely an instrument for Cynewulf's purpose of developing as the culmination of a voyage an image of an 'anchor of hope' which he owed to a homily of Gregory the Great.[21] The line of thought the poet chose was that knowledge of a harbour of salvation (*Christ* (*II*) 859) was a gift made for our turbulent voyage through this world (850–6a) by 'godes gæstsunu' ('God's spirit-son', 860a), when through his ascension he granted

þæt we oncnawan magun   ofer ceoles bord
hwær we sælan sceolon   sundhengestas,
ealde yðmearas,   ancrum fæste

['that we can perceive over the side of the keel where we shall make sea-horses, old wave-steeds, secure with anchors', 861–3].

The notion of confident tethering of seahorses was called on to provide a native idiom to actualize Gregory's implied dropping of an anchor of hope and obliged with disciplined elegance and economy.

Selecting and marshalling appropriate symbols of material norms became an exercise in literary style, as Cynewulf demonstrated in his preceding parallel between life and a sea-journey:

Nu is þon gelicost   swa we on laguflode
ofer cald wæter   ceolum liðan
geond sidne sæ,   sundhengestum,
flodwudu fergen.   Is þæt frecne stream
yða ofermæta   þe we her on lacað
geond þas wacan woruld,   windge holmas
ofer deop gelad

['Now therefore it is as if we are sailing in ships on an ocean flood, over cold water, throughout on open sea, in seahorses, are ferrying boats of wood. That is a dangerous current, the waves without measure on which we toss here throughout this changeable world, the waters windy along the deep way', 850–6a].

20 See above, pp. 97–8.

21 Gregory's words underlying Cynewulf's *Christ* (*II*) 850–6b were 'Quamvis adhuc rerum perturbationibus animus fluctuet, iam tamen spei vestræ anchoram in æternam patriam figite, intentionem mentis in vera luce solidate. Ecce ad cœlum ascendisse Dominum audivimus. Hoc ergo servemus in meditatione quod credimus' ('Although your soul may have floated hither and thither with the confusion of things so far, now fasten the anchor

As a true Anglo-Saxon, the poet could not resist expanding the mere hint of Gregory's 'floating hither and thither', but his treatment was firmly controlled to serve as a prelude to a version of Gregory's exhortation about the goal:

Utan us to þære hyðe   hyht staþelian,
ða us gerymde   rodera waldend,
halge on heahþu,   þa he heofonum astag

['Let us fix our hope on that harbour, holy on high, which the ruler of the skies opened up for us when he ascended in the heavens', 864–6].

His 'sundhengestas' of 852b and 862b and 'ealde yðmearas' of 863a had to function both as ships of practical sailing and, under Christ-given direction, as our means of transport to the anchorage of salvation.[22] They showed a liveliness appropriate to both registers and no more. Cynewulf was pruning the elements of native expression to a commonplace analogy which had stood Gregory (and has stood many another preacher) in good stead. He was naturalizing a Latin literary topos with discretion and discernment. Thought and expression were not, as they once had been, the inseparable parts of a single cultural organism transmitted by indigenous social tradition. Poetic resources from one tradition were being applied to thought and sensibility from another. A match was being consciously made between what was being said in the native medium and how it should be said according to assimilated canons of good taste.

What was being told was often a narrative from the Bible or other seminal written source and was thus a part of sacred cosmic history rooted in a text. Authority lay primarily with pieces of Latin writing rather than, as before, with oral vernacular precedents. In the case of *Genesis A*, for instance, the poet kept close enough to the biblical text to reveal remarkably consistently whether at any particular point he was rendering a distinctively Old Latin reading or a specifically Vulgate one or wording which was common to both versions.[23] Gradually this textualization of authority was to shift the balance away from native orality towards acquired literacy in English poetry itself, but the process took a long time.

of your hope in the eternal homeland, concentrate your mind on true light. Lo, we have heard that the Lord has ascended to heaven. Let us therefore keep in meditation this which we believe', PL 76, col. 1219).

22 See *us to hælo* (859a), and cf. Calder, *Cynewulf*, p. 73.

23 See Remley, 'The Latin Textual Basis of *Genesis A*'.

Back in the third quarter of the seventh century, when Cædmon composed and recited songs telling the stories which he learned from teachers and committed to memory, it had not even begun: Bede's early-eighth-century account gives no sign that anyone had ever thought of writing down any of this poet's many songs.[24] And Bede himself brought about only a small, though significant, beginning, when he included in his *Historia ecclesiastica* a Latin paraphrase of the particular verses by Cædmon which were attributed to direct divine inspiration: in a vernacular version of these verses, which was supplied in the 730s in early copies of the Latin as a marginal gloss or supplement, the English was written without any points to indicate metre or sense (in contrast to the well-pointed Latin paraphrase in the main text), thus clearly demonstrating the essentially oral nature of the vernacular record.[25] These verses, conventionally called *Cædmon's Hymn*, represent only the opening of a longer song, for the poet added more in the morning, after his dream, before he recited the whole to Abbess Hild. Recording just these verses in writing obviously owed nothing to any contemporary general notion that a complete English song was a visual text.[26] Like the *Hymn*, the brief *Bede's Death Song*, touchingly simple, was

[24] For Bede's summary of these compositions, see above, p. 231.

[25] See O'Keeffe, 'Orality and the Developing Text of Cædmon's *Hymn*', p. 19. Subsequently, after the present chapter had been written, this article has been reproduced, in a somewhat different form, as ch. 2 in Professor O'Keeffe's book-length study, *Visible Song*.

[26] What status these vernacular words had in relation to Bede's Latin paraphrase has recently emerged as a vexed question (see Kiernan, 'Reading Cædmon's "Hymn" with Someone Else's Glosses'). In my opinion the question which needs to be put first is 'How did Bede come by the vernacular verses which he paraphrased?' Kiernan comments 'Scholars have not inquired too deeply into the exact nature of Bede's source' (*ibid.*, p. 158) and then, unfortunately, proceeds to do the same; in fact he ignores the issue altogether and confines himself to considering Bede's paraphrase and the vernacular 'gloss' purely textually.

As I see it, the way to explaining Bede's knowledge was pointed to by Cyril Wright years ago, when he included 'the bestowal of the gift of song on Cædmon' in a list of twenty-one 'stories in the *Historia ecclesiastica* which have every appearance of being drawn from oral tradition' (Wright, *The Cultivation of Saga in Anglo-Saxon England*, pp. 41–2). Filled out in terms of the relevant circumstances, this amounts to an inference that an oral, vernacular prose narrative about Cædmon's 'inspiration' took a settled form within the monastery at Whitby – becoming an item in the oral 'archives' of this house, to put it another way – and was passed to Jarrow in this form through personal contact to become, in turn, part of the traditions of that house. Favouring this hypothesis are the well-organized range of circumstantial detail which surrounds the alleged inspiration and the substantial number of other stories of a similar type which Bede drew on. This is by no means a unique case in his *History*.

The story's core motif of poetic inspiration through a dream may well have been owed to literary tradition; this is to be expected in a learned community such as Whitby. Plummer pointed out that this motif had been applied to Hesiod *(Baedae Opera Historica*, ed. Plummer II, 254–5), and Andy Orchard has kindly suggested to me Persius's *Satires* as a possible source, because an allusion to an inspirational dream experienced by the epic poet, Ennius, which Persius included in the opening lines of his prologue, was known and quoted by Aldhelm *(Enigmata*, praef. (ed. Ehwald, *Aldhelmi Opera*, p. 98, lines 12–13), and *De metris* (ed. *ibid.*, p. 78, lines 12–14)); see Neil Wright's appendix to *Aldhelm: the Poetic Works*, trans. Lapidge and Rosier, p. 265, n. 3. For evidence of later knowledge of Persius in Anglo-Saxon England, see Gneuss, 'A Preliminary List of Manuscripts', nos. 195 and 534, and, concerning the former, Keynes, *Anglo-Saxon Manuscripts in the Library of Trinity College, Cambridge*, no. 5 and pl. Va, showing the Persius lines in question. Aldhelm alluded to Persius's prologue in the preface to his *Enigmata* in order to make the point that in his own case inspiration came not in a mere dream but from God himself 'freely breathing His holy gifts into my obtuse mind' (*Enigmata*, praef., ed. Ehwald, *Aldhelmi Opera*, p. 98, line 15; trans. Lapidge and Rosier, *Aldhelm: the Poetic Works*, p. 70)). Just so, the Cædmon story introduced into the dream an undescribed personage who, according to Bede, was only *quidam* ('someone') and 'ille qui cum eo loquebatur' ('he who was speaking to him') and played no further part in the dream once Cædmon had sung, and whose action was interpreted by learned men the next morning as representing a grant of heavenly grace by the Lord himself (Bede, *HE*, IV.24 [22] (pp. 416–18)). The Christian deficiency which Aldhelm perceived in the dream to which Persius referred was thereby made good in the Whitby tradition about Cædmon. Cædmon's story as Bede knew it from Whitby consisted of, we may infer, a central feature probably derived from augmented literary precedent and a narrative setting which had been wholly supplied by 'in-house' tradition.

If this is so, what could be more likely than that the 'divinely inspired' verses themselves should have been quoted in the story? It is altogether probable that this quotation should have been Bede's source for them and also, at much the same time, the source of the first individual who wrote them down either to be a 'gloss' for Bede's Latin or for some other purpose. (Kiernan's statement ('Reading Cædmon's "Hymn" with Someone Else's Glosses', p. 157) that the scribes who appended the gloss to our two extant eighth-century manuscripts of Bede's Latin did so at an unspecified 'later' time is misleading.) Anyone at Jarrow around Bede's time would have been as likely as Bede himself to draw on his (or her) own memory of the vernacular tale of Cædmon with the wondrous verses embedded in it rather than to reconstruct the verses from Bede's Latin. In my view the vernacular gloss's claim to authority is the same as that of Bede's Latin paraphrase, namely that it rests not on Cædmon's own words directly but on their memorial transmission in a 'standard' oral story. (For this type of transmission, see Jabbour, 'Memorial Transmission'.)

written down as a special case (quotation in a Latin letter), and so too, owing to different factors, was *The Leiden Riddle*, a close translation of Aldhelm's Latin 'Lorica' *enigma*, probably carried out as a literary exercise by a Northumbrian in about the time of Bede, which in our sole, later, copy – in Malcolm Parkes's opinion written at Fleury in the tenth century – has a lay-out imperfectly reproducing through arrangement and punctuation the translation's relationship to the lines of its Latin original.[27] Other early poetry is known to us because it was inscribed in Anglian on a whale-bone box (the Franks Casket) *c.* 700[28] or, in another instance, in the margins of a panelled stone cross (the Ruthwell Cross in Dumfriesshire), erected perhaps in the second quarter of the eighth century.[29] (We do not know when the verses in *The Dream of the Rood* corresponding to those on this cross were first committed to parchment; we can be certain only that this had happened by the period of our sole surviving written text of the poem, in the Vercelli Book, the second half of the tenth century.[30]) Writing down vernacular poetry on parchment with pen and ink, we may conclude, remained the exception rather than the rule during the second half of the seventh century and the first half of the eighth.

By the ninth century things had changed. In a retelling of the story of Cædmon in an English prose translation of Bede's *Historia* carried out probably towards the end of the century it was simply assumed as a matter of course that the poet's teachers had written down the poems they had heard him recite.[31] And at least some vernacular poets in this ninth century were composing their poems as texts. Cynewulf, active probably at this time, was one such. Composing vernacular verse was for him but a particular kind of literary creation. The four poems which are taken to be his compositions by virtue of their incorporation of his name in runes[32] and which respectively tell of St Juliana's struggles against temptation, St

27 Parkes, 'The Manuscript of the Leiden Riddle', esp. pp. 213–15, and pl. I.

28 Partly quoted above, p. 111. For spellings, see Page, *English Runes*, p. 220.

29 For recent discussions of the dating of this cross, see Maclean, 'The Date of the Ruthwell Cross', and Meyvaert, 'A New Perspective on the Ruthwell Cross', pp. 147–50.

30 On the relationship between the inscription and the Vercelli text, see Clemoes, 'King and Creation at the Cruxifixion', n. 2.

31 For Bede's 'doctores suos [i.e. Cædmon's] uicissim auditores sui faciebat' ('his teachers he made in turn his hearers') the translator substituted 'his lareowas æt his muðe wreoton ond leornodon' ('his teachers wrote and learnt at his mouth', *Old English Version of Bede's Ecclesiastical History*, ed. Miller I, 346, lines 4–5).

32 On the relationship between the poems and the namings, see below, pp. 392–3 and n. 87.

Helena's discovery of the true cross, Christ's ascension and, in a series of vignettes, the fates of the apostles, were based on Latin narrative texts similar to those used by the probably ninth-century compiler of the prose Old English Martyrology, and both authors drew on sources in broadly the same way.[33] For instance, just as the martyrologist normally composed one of his 200 (and more) short notices by selecting details from here and there in several full-length sources, so Cynewulf fashioned each of his abbreviated accounts of the apostles by culling telling details from a full life or passion.[34] The prose martyrologist and the poet each cast a keen eye for vivid detail on their Latin manuscript sources and applied this same ability to their vernacular medium. Then again, Cynewulf's riddling incorporations of his name engage the eye of a reader in an elegant tease reminiscent of Latin acrostics.[35] Educated ninth-century English ecclesiastics, such as he, firmly transplanted their ancient native art of poetic story-telling into the milieu of narrative texts, hitherto the domain of Latin (and Greek).[36]

The transferred narrative tradition, all the same, did not become fully acclimatized to its new textual environment. It never entirely shrugged off its oral origins. In the second half of the ninth century King Alfred seems to have valued the written forms of poems primarily as a means of learning them by heart.[37] Asser, the king's biographer, relates how, before Alfred had learned to read (at about the age of twelve) his mother showed him and his older brothers a book of English poetry and offered to give it to whichever of them could memorize its contents quickest. With the help of his teacher Alfred learned the poems by heart and recited them to his

33 The compiler of the Martyrology may have been working in Latin (in which case the Old English which we have was a translation of a now lost original) or directly in English. For his sources and working methods, see Cross, 'On the Library of the Old English Martyrologist'.

34 See Cross, 'Cynewulf's Traditions about the Apostles'.

35 Cf. the signatory acrostic which includes the author's name twice and constitutes the verse preface to Aldhelm's *Enigmata* (*Aldhelmi Opera*, ed. Ehwald, pp. 97–9). Cf. also the acrostic naming *Iohannes* (probably, as author, John the Old Saxon), discussed by Michael Lapidge ('Some Latin Poems as Evidence for the Reign of Athelstan', pp. 72–83).

36 For a suggestion that Cynewulf was probably one of a number of vernacular poets composing Christian narrative verse in his time to compensate for reduced access to the Latin originals, see Clemoes, 'King Alfred's Debt to Vernacular Poetry', pp. 213–14.

37 A documented instance of what has been called 'memorial tradition' (Jabbour, 'Memorial Transmission').

mother first and so won the prize.[38] Alfred's children, in their turn, 'attentively learned the psalms, and books in English, and especially English poems'.[39] And all through adult life, while he was fighting wars and directing the government of his realm, Alfred made time for 'reading aloud from books in English and above all learning English poems by heart'.[40] The persistence of 'I/we have heard/learned' formulas throughout extant Old English poetry, whether composition was actually oral or written, shows that the tradition did not completely discard the conception of the narrator 'as one who recreates, who reenacts, who remembers the sayings (utterances) of the past and through his own acts of poetic discourse makes them present again'.[41]

Normally written continuously along manuscript lines at any stage of the Anglo-Saxon period, Old English poetry was never given the lay-out standard to Latin verse, manifesting its structure spatially, except under exceptional conditions, such as those of *The Leiden Riddle*.[42] Nor were the other regular visual clues of written Latin poetry, capitalization and punctuation, ever adopted consistently to mark off lines or half-lines or grammatical divisions. Indeed the beginnings and endings of whole poems were not always clearly distinguished in the Exeter Book in the second half of the tenth century.[43] Even the very wording did not have a degree of fixity like that of a Latin verse text unless it was being copied in Latin-dominated circumstances. For instance, the text of *Cædmon's Hymn* shows little variation as a gloss to the Latin of Bede's *Historia*, but as an integral part of the probably late-ninth-century vernacular prose translation of the *History* it manifests a much more fluid type of transmission 'somewhere between the formula-defined process which is an oral poem and the graph-bound object which is a text', as Professor O'Keeffe has expressed it.[44] The seven variants these few verses display in the five manuscripts concerned, all grammatically and semantically appropriate, witness to a reading-process which did not embellish the message but allowed a copyist freedom to introduce subjective changes within the

38 Asser's *Life* of King Alfred, ch. 23 (trans. Keynes and Lapidge, *Alfred the Great*, pp. 75 and 239, n. 29).

39 *Ibid.*, ch. 75 (trans. Keynes and Lapidge, *Alfred the Great*, p. 91).

40 *Ibid.*, ch. 76 (trans. Keynes and Lapidge, *Alfred the Great*, p. 91).

41 Parks, 'The Traditional Narrator', esp. p. 47. 42 See above, p. 244.

43 For an example, see above, p. 177.

44 'Orality and the Developing Text of Cædmon's *Hymn*', pp. 19 and 15.

context of expectations and the constraints of alliteration and rhythm.[45] And the limited overlap between extant copies of other poems reveals a similar state of affairs.[46] It is true that, like vernacular prose, poetry in English could be accompanied on occasion by extensive visual illustration, as in the case of the Old Testament poems (*Genesis*, *Exodus* and *Daniel*) forming Oxford, Bodleian Library, Junius 11, pt I,[47] produced probably in the second quarter of the eleventh century for a pious clientèle similar to that for which an ambitiously illustrated vernacular prose version of the first six books of the Old Testament was provided at about the same time.[48] But, so far as we know, no portion of English verse was ever transferred bodily from one poem to another, lifted from text to text, as not uncommonly happened to prose in, say, written vernacular homilies, and certainly no poem would ever have combined enough weight and exactness as a text to warrant the kind of warning which Ælfric attached to his prose *Catholic Homilies* to the effect that any scribe who copied his exemplar carelessly would put his eternal soul at risk. The full potentials of visual text which systematic sectionalization, capitalization and punctuation made a prospect for vernacular literary prose by Alfred's time were necessarily denied to the unformatted records of the stubbornly oral activity of poetry.

In Cynewulf's case 'written poetry' meant suitably organized refurbishment of traditional elements of story-telling. The language of the oral past remained as ever the means to bring to life the dramatic actions of history with, as it were, a series of broad brush strokes. It is a real army of Huns and other barbarians which assembles noisily and eagerly with its weapons shining and its battle standards on high, which sets out as a mighty host, making the wolf howl in the wood and the eagle cry in the sky as it goes, and which marches at speed in formation until, resolute and well armed, it takes up position on the banks of the Danube threatening Roman territory with tumult and plundering (*Elene* 18b–41a); and, when it comes, the battle is a real battle, and Emperor Constantine's victory through the sign of the cross is a real victory. As in the old heroic tales, human will is

45 *Ibid.*, pp. 15–16.

46 See Sisam, *Studies in the History of Old English Literature*, pp. 31–6, and, more recently, Jabbour, 'Memorial Transmission', pp. 183–90.

47 For a complete facsimile, see *The Cædmon Manuscript*, ed. Gollancz. Attribution of any of this manuscript's contents to Cædmon has long been discarded. Not quite two-thirds of the intended illustration was actually executed in this copy.

48 For a facsimile and discussion of the surviving copy of this prose production, see *The Old English Illustrated Hexateuch*, ed. Dodwell and Clemoes.

centre-stage in the great drama of mankind's history: St Juliana's single-mindedness overpowers a devil which has led into evil all the wrongdoers of the Old and New Testaments and all the weak and vulnerable ever since; it is through sheer determination that St Helena overcomes the Jews' spokesman, Judas, 'gidda gearosnotor' ('readily wise in oral traditions', *Elene* 418a), and thereby replaces the blindness of the Jews with the light of Christianity in the Holy Land. Formal, dignified speech of a traditional sort consistently holds the main issues in dramatic focus. Emotions long familiar to traditional psychology are engendered by the Christian faith – Judas's joy, for instance, when he finds the buried cross:

Þa wæs modgemynd   myclum geblissod,
hige onhyrded,   þurh þæt halige treo,
inbryrded breostsefa,   syððan beacen geseh,
halig under hrusan

['His mind was greatly gladdened, his purpose fortified, through that holy tree, his breast inspired, when he had seen the emblem, holy under the earth', 839–42a].

Traditional psychology still leaves its own distinctive imprint, as when the devil's declaration to Juliana that he had made some 'end their lives violently',[49] was rendered

Sume ic larum geteah,
to geflite fremede,   þæt hy færinga
ealde æfþoncan   edniwedan,
beore druncne.   Ic him byrlade
wroht of wege,   þæt hi in winsele
þurh sweordgripe   sawle forletan
of flæschoman   fæge scyndan,
sarum gesohte

['Some I have led on by my teachings, urged on to strife, so that suddenly they have renewed old grudges, drunk with beer. I have served them crime from the cup, so that they have given up their souls in the winehall through seizure of swords, have hastened from their covering of flesh doomed, beset with sufferings', *Juliana* 483b–90a],

or as when the narrator comments grimly on Eleusius's order for Juliana to be decapitated, 'Hine se cwealm ne þeah, / siþþan he þone fintan furþor cuþe' ('The slaying did not profit him after he knew the consequence

[49] *Sources and Analogues*, trans. Allen and Calder, p. 128.

further', 605b–6). The kind of society the Anglo-Saxons knew for themselves animates the action. For example, Emperor Constantine when rendered invincible by the horse's bit, which was made from the newly discovered nails of the crucifixion, is portrayed much more dramatically as Cynewulf's warrior figure (*Elene* 1172b–86a) than he is in the Latin text which is regarded as the poet's source.

Some text-based stories, however, deriving from narrative traditions quite different from the Anglo-Saxons' own, demanded radical 'literary' imagination to assimilate them to native modes of thinking and feeling. One such was the legend which an anonymous poet transferred into vernacular verse as the composition we call *Andreas*, a retelling of the dangerous expedition undertaken by St Andrew when commanded by God to voyage from Achaia (where the apostle was preaching and was later to be martyred) to Mermedonia, there to risk his life rescuing St Matthew, who was doomed to die three days later at the hands of ruthless cannibals. Mermedonia was much too far from Achaia for Andrew to reach it soon enough by any but supernatural means: the story belonged to a genre of tales of fantastic voyages, known in western Europe in Latin retellings of Greek versions which had been composed originally in a highly rhetorical style.[50] It was of a kind which launched an Old English poet into a fabulous domain of spiritual adventure with only his native symbolic language to give him his bearings. More particularly, in the *Andreas* poet's case, it meant combining with this new-fangled type of narrative – not always easily – markedly old-fashioned ways of thinking.

The story was very different from the solemn account of the apostle's martyrdom impressively related by Ælfric in vernacular prose towards the end of the tenth century.[51] It was of a high-pitched sort to which a plain, flat telling could not possibly do justice, as a dull prose version in an anonymous Old English homily demonstrates only too clearly.[52] The challenge it presented to a vernacular poet intent on deploying the resources of his tradition to the full was to symbolize the nature of spiritual devotion in a peculiarly intense personal relationship with God exercised in extraordinary circumstances. This central relationship was similar to that

[50] *Die lateinischen Bearbeitungen der Acta Andreas et Matthiae*, ed. Blatt, pp. 16–17.

[51] Ælfric, *CH* I.xxxviii, *Passio* (ed. Thorpe I, 586–98).

[52] This homily, extant imperfectly in the Blickling manuscript and complete in Cambridge, Corpus Christi College 198, is printed from the former, with the missing parts supplied from the latter, *The Blickling Homilies*, ed. Morris, pp. 229–49.

which the author Felix, writing in Latin, attributed to St Guthlac after that saint abandoned secular life and took up his solitary abode in the fens. The fantastic events the apostle encountered on his trip were of the type Guthlac confronted when he was taken prisoner by hordes of evil spirits invading his cell, was tortured, was carried to the jaws of hell and was there rescued by the intervention of St Bartholomew.[53] In this class of imaginative literature far-away Mermedonia and near-at-hand fenland were but two locations for untrammelled narrative on an exotic, exclusively spiritual, plane.

To his credit, the *Andreas* poet (commonly underrated)[54] evidently grasped that the active principle in vernacular poetry was capable of generating its own brand of spiritual melodrama: his use of *leoðword*, 'poetry words' (1488b), was far from aimless. For one thing he recognized in this fanciful matter the traditionally congenial theme of personal loyalty – in this instance that of a chosen apostle to God the exerciser of absolute power – and deliberately presented this vital element in spiritual life far more tellingly than had been the case in the Latin prose version which we can infer was his source.[55]

But to fasten on the theme of loyalty was not entirely to dispose of the problem for an Old English narrative poet of traditional outlook. This story had the particular characteristic that its central personage was confronting God's enemies not in order to extablish his or her own sanctity (as Felix's Guthlac or Cynewulf's Juliana was), but by way of exercising an already possessed apostolic spirituality. The requirement was for portrayal of a hero not undergoing development but maintaining constant faith with a God whose any spoken word would never be annulled (1435b–40) and who exerted a continuously despotic control over immediate circumstances. The story was about a stable spiritual loyalty depending on a stable

[53] *Felix's 'Life' of St Guthlac*, ed. Colgrave, pp. 100–8 (chs. 31–3).

[54] Entanglement with the secondary issues of his identity (was he Cynewulf?), his possible knowledge of *Beowulf* and his use of typology has, over the years, with a few notable exceptions, interfered with open-minded consideration of his poem as a whole in its own right. The first question is now dead and I leave aside the second.

[55] This version has not itself been traced among surviving materials: *Andreas* has some features which are in the Greek version reprinted by Blatt (see above, p. 249, n. 50) but not in any known Latin version, and has others in common with now one selection of Latin texts and now another; for a summary, see Schaar, *Critical Studies in the Cynewulf Group*, pp. 15–20. Whenever feasible I refer, as 'the C analogue', to the translation of the 'Casanatensis' Latin text supplied by *Sources and Analogues*, trans. Allen and Calder, pp. 14–34.

verbal relationship played out in unstable action among violent physical forces which were subject to abrupt and complete reversals. The volatile dramatic element was consequently not part of the hero himself, as it was in social narrative verse, but was a constituent of outside happenings, and was thus relatively external to him. Dramatic demonstration of his fidelity depended on the machinery of surrounding events. Whereas a traditional Old English poetic story-teller devoted his conventional language to the single, unified, purpose of making a protagonist's progressive struggle against his natural environment symbolize the society to which he belonged, the *Andreas* poet was called on to use inherited language in two distinct ways, to portray on the one hand the indissoluble verbal ties between God and his apostle and on the other the violent cosmic upheavals which formed the apostle's setting. The mental stamina Andrew had to exert in reconciling these two levels of action was a state of mind which remained fairly and squarely within native tradition in being general[56] but which made a clean break from precedent in having its *raison d'être* outside the material world and thus utilizing its physical environment only for the revelation which all mental conditions required before the first attempts were made at internal psychological analysis (in the twelfth century). The events which Andrew faced in this story had their causation not in this world of the senses but in a spiritual region somewhere between God's word and the saint's consciousness. Vernacular symbolic language was called upon to perform its traditional function by representing the fulfilment of interactive potentials from this special source in a dramatic display of transcendent power operating through actors in a theatre of arbitrary this-worldly violence.[57]

With Christ in person as steersman,[58] although his true identity

[56] No author, vernacular or otherwise, composed with any conception of unique personality before the twelfth century; cf. below, pp. 388–92, esp. n. 70.

[57] Cf. Calder, 'Figurative Language and its Contexts in *Andreas*', pp. 119–20.

[58] The poet, little concerned with distinctions between the three persons of the Trinity, eliminated from his many references to God the regular naming of 'Jesus' or 'Christ' or 'Jesus Christ' which he would have found in his Latin and instead only occasionally specified 'Christ' (e.g., in the set phrase 'Cristes cempa' ('soldier of Christ', 991a) or 'the son of God' (e.g., *bearn godes* (1613b)), or *fæder*, 'father' (e.g., *beorht fæder*, 'radiant father', 937b), or *frofre gast*, 'spirit of consolation' (906b), or 'fæder ond sunu ond frofre gast / in þrinnesse' ('father and son and spirit of consolation in threeness' (1684–5a)). The implication remains, however, that throughout his dealings with his apostles God was acting essentially in his second person.

remained as yet unrevealed to the apostle and his companions, the sea-voyage from Achaia to Mermedonia became, in the poet's treatment, a linguistic journey into a realm of human intercourse with God. Of the direct speech which makes up just over half this poem (54 per cent) nearly three-quarters (71 per cent, or 39 per cent of the whole poem) is addressed by God to Andrew or vice versa and no less than two-thirds of this exchange (68 per cent) takes place during the embarkation and sail.[59] Customary language was taking a trip into a kind of supernatural outer space. The further it went, the more the physical became absorbed into the non-material.[60] At the outset the components of the action were predominantly the familiar ones of the natural world:

Gewat him þa on uhtan   mid ærdæge
ofer sandhleoðu   to sæs faruðe,
þriste on geþance,   ond his þegnas mid,
gangan on greote.   Garsecg hlynede,
beoton brimstreamas.   Se beorn wæs on hyhte,
syðþan he on waruðe   widfæðme scip
modig gemette.   Þa com morgentorht
beacna beorhtost   ofer breomo sneowan,
halig of heolstre.   Heofoncandel blac
ofer lagoflodas.   He ðær lidweardas,
þrymlice þry   þegnas gemette,
modiglice menn,   on merebate
sittan siðfrome,   swylce hie ofer sæ comon

['He then at dawn with the first light of day went over the sand-dunes to the sea's surf, bold in thought, and his thegns with him, walking on the shingle. The ocean roared, the sea's currents pounded. The man was in high hope when, brave-minded, he found a wide-bosomed ship on the shore. Then the brightest of beacons, morning-radiant, came hastening over the seas, holy from concealment. The candle of heaven shone over the water-floods. There he found[61] crewmen, three glorious thegns, men proud of mind, sitting in the sea-boat eager to journey, as if they had come across the sea'].

59 Forming just over a third of the poem (a little more than in the C analogue), the embarkation and voyage take up, by contrast, hardly a seventh of the Blickling Homily.

60 Cf. Calder, 'Figurative Language and its Contexts in *Andreas*', pp. 118–20.

61 *gemette* not in MS. Sievers suggested it in 1885; previously *gesceawode* had been supplied (by Kemble) or *geseah* (by Grimm and others following him). Trautmann suggested *funde* as another possibility in 1907. The most recent editor (Brooks in 1961) reads *mette*.

The C analogue reads much less dramatically, 'When the morning came, blessed Andrew went down with his disciples and began to walk along the seashore as the Lord had commanded him. While he was walking along looking intently across the waves, he saw a little boat riding through the middle of the waves. Only three men were sitting in it. The Lord provided it through His holy power.'[62] The ingredients in the Old English, by comparison, work on one another: Andrew and his companions walking on the shingle (238a) were in direct relationship to the dawn (235), the sand (236a), the surf (236b) and their own boldness (237a). With them we sense the roar and pounding of the waves (238b–9a). Andrew's hopes were raised by his catching sight of a ship. When the sun rose brightly over the sea, this heavenly symbol illuminating its natural surroundings (243b–4a) enabled Andrew to perceive three men on board eager to depart. In the C analogue no sun shines. Probably the *Andreas* poet owed this feature to an association of motifs – a hero and his men, a beach, the start or end of a voyage, and the sun shining – which had become traditional to his medium, for there is a scene with these elements in *Beowulf*, in this case a triumphant return (*Beowulf* 1963–6a). But in *Beowulf* the interrelationship of the parts remained an implication. Of the three versions – those in *Andreas*, the C analogue and *Beowulf* – only the *Andreas* one exploited dramatic integration.[63]

Symbolism, however, was integrating more than man and nature. In the C analogue a 'great light' had enveloped God's voice replying to St Matthew, when, blinded and incarcerated, that apostle had prayed for his sight again, so that he might see how his torturers tore his flesh. In *Andreas* the imprisoned Matthew, honouring 'wuldres aldor' ('the prince of glory', 55b) and praying for the grace of 'leoht on þissum life' ('light in this life', 77a), so that in his blindness he might endure the cruel scorn of his tormentors, had received the response of 'wuldres tacen / halig of heofenum, swylce hadre sigel'[64] ('a token of glory, holy from heaven, like the bright sun', 88b–9), and had heard 'heofoncyninges stefn / wrætlic under wolcnum' ('the voice of the heaven-king wondrous under the clouds', 92b–3a), promising him (without warrant, so far as the C analogue is

62 *Sources and Analogues*, trans. Allen and Calder, p. 17.

63 Cf. Shippey, *Old English Verse*, pp. 119–20. For an overview of critical discussion of 'the hero on the beach', including references more recent than those cited by Shippey, see Olsen, 'Oral-Formulaic Research: I', pp. 583–4.

64 MS *segl* kept in ASPR (cf. 50b and 1456b).

concerned) 'neorxnawang . . . torht ontyned' ('radiant paradise opened', 102b–5a).[65] Light was common to nature and the spirit here, just as it was in the radiance of the panther's coat.[66] By contrast, the devil (not mentioned at this point in the C analogue) had constantly afflicted the Mermedonians, Matthew's man-eating captors, with inner darkness: 'Oft hira mod onwod / under dimscuan deofles larum' ('Often their mind passed under a dark shadow because of the devil's teachings', 140b–1). Now that his new hero, Andrew, was setting out on the beach at dawn, the *Andreas* poet was continuing in the same vein, using the same primeval imagery of light and dark and the same traditional type of language. His cosmic coupling of spiritual symbol and natural symbol in the free-standing, unamplified clause, 'Heofoncandel blac / ofer lagoflodas' (243b–4a), heralded fresh communion between the spiritual on the one hand and the mental, emotional and physical on the other,[67] and accordingly the crew whom Andrew saw as a result of the symbolic sunshine were glorious thegns (245) as well as seamen proud and eager to go. We are being prepared for the imminent revelation, to us but not to Andrew, about the crew:

Þæt wæs drihten sylf, dugeða wealdend,
ece ælmihtig, mid his englum twam

['That was the Lord himself, ruler of hosts, eternal and almighty, with his two angels', 248–9].

Traditional language had been moved out of its old natural order into the new one of the spirit. The parameters of meaning had been altered.

For a while longer, language, thus transferred, still conformed to the everyday world. Material and practical considerations remained in force: a long opening parley conducted by Andrew and the Christ–skipper (254–348) is physically positioned more clearly in the poem than in the C analogue, the apostolic participant being 'se ðe on greote stod' ('he who stood on the shingle', 254b) and the other one, God, speaking from the ship's prow ('of nacan stefne', 291b) across the surf of the shore ('ofer waroða geweorp', 306a). Whereas in the C analogue Andrew simply asked the sailors where they were going, in the poem his first, prudent, step was

[65] Cf. Irving, 'A Reading of *Andreas*', pp. 217–18. [66] See above, pp. 234–5.

[67] Cf. *heofoncyning* (already noted, 5× altogether), *heofonhalig*, *heofonhwealf* (2×), *heofonleoht*, *heofonleoma*, *heofonrice* (3×), *heofontorht* (2×) and *heofonþrym* (2×), the second and fifth of them, so far as our evidence goes, *hapax legomena*.

to ask these strangers where they were from;[68] and, in a similar strain, Christ's initial invitation to come aboard was made subject to the proper payment. A matter-of-fact style prevailed, Andrew's lack of money and provisions for the voyage prompting an exchange of maxims, with Christ's 'Is se drohtað strang / þam þe lagolade lange cunnaþ' ('The lot of him who tests the waterway for long is hard', 313b–14) countered by Andrew's

Selre bið æghwam
þæt he eaðmedum ellorfusne
oncnawe cuðlice

['It is more fitting for everyone that he should acknowledge humbly and kindly the man eager to go elsewhere', 320b–2a].

The turning point was Andrew's eulogy of (the 'real') Christ,

He is cyning on riht,
wealdend ond wyrhta wuldorþrymmes,
an ece god eallra gesceafta,
swa he ealle befehð anes cræfte,
hefon ond eorðan, halgum mihtum,
sigora selost

['He is king by right, ruler and maker of glorious power, one eternal God of all creatures, who comprehends all things with the capability of one being, heaven and earth, with his holy powers, supreme in triumphs', 324b–9a],

and his ringing declaration that Christ's command to his apostles had been 'Bodiað æfter burgum beorhtne geleafan / ofer foldan fæðm' ('Announce through cities the radiant faith across the expanse of the earth', 335–6a) without regard for gold or silver (337–8a). And, once the apostolic passenger and his companions were aboard, all other factors receded into the background, as the dialogue got under way between 'þegn þeodenhold' ('thegn loyal to his leader', 384a) and *wæges weard*, 'guardian of the wave' (601a and 632a), who (unknown to Andrew) was 'hæleða scyppend' ('creator of men', 396b) as well as practical steersman[69] (396a). All that mattered from now on was that the boat had become loaded, as the poet eloquently expressed it, 'heahgestreonum' ('with high treasures', 362b) of the spiritual life.[70]

Language had entered a metaphysical region where, so to speak, the

[68] Cf. Irving, 'A Reading of *Andreas*', p. 220.
[69] Krapp *helman*, MS *holme*.
[70] Cf. Irving, 'A Reading of *Andreas*', pp. 222–3.

world's atmosphere was thinner. Material surroundings had lost their independent identity and had become mere instruments of verbal interchange. A case in point is the storm which suddenly arose from nowhere soon after the embarkation and which the poet dramatized as an itemized list:[71]

Þa gedrefed wearð,
onhrered hwælmere. Hornfisc plegode,
glad geond garsecg, ond se græga mæw
wælgifre wand. Wedercandel swearc,
windas weoxon, wægas grundon,
streamas styredon, strengas gurron,
wædo gewætte. Wæteregsa stod
þreata þryðum

['Then the whale-sea was stirred up, aroused. The whale moved rapidly, gliding along the ocean, and the grey mew circled greedy for carrion. The weather-candle grew dark, winds got up, waves ground together, currents swirled, ropes creaked, sails became drenched. Water-terror arose with the might of hosts', 369b–76a].

This tempest was not an interactive development occurring in its own right within substantial nature so much as a bundle of violent items impinging on the intercourse between (skipper) God and man. It immediately made Andrew feel confident that God would counter the terrifying upheaval with his protection:

Wæteregesa sceal,
geðyd ond geðreatod þurh þryðcining,
lagu lacende, liðra wyrðan

['The water-terror, restrained and rebuked by the mighty king, the tossing sea, will become calmer', 435b–7].

Just so, he recalled, long ago the *ælmihtig* (445b), 'meotud mancynnes' ('governor of mankind', 446a), *cyning* (450b), 'engla eadgifa' ('benefactor of angels', 451a), had once stilled a tempest frightening the apostles when they were on board ship. The present storm Andrew recognized as an analogy, and when, at the close of his words, the sea became calmer his spirit was gladdened (467b–8) and the skipper-Christ acknowledged to him that the terror of the waves had subsided 'seoðþan hie ongeton þæt ðe

[71] Brodeur pointed out that this enumeration is 'rather unusual in that both subjects and verbs participate' in its effect; Brodeur, 'A Study of Diction and Style', p. 104.

god hæfde / wære bewunden' ('after they understood that God had encompassed you with protection', 534–5a).

The tempest had been a pastiche of an Anglo-Saxon topos, 'storm at sea'; its impact had been on the mind and the apostle's way to cope with it had been a right use of language. Whereas traditional narrative, such as *Beowulf*, dealt with the socially symbolic experience of protagonists combating by physical action the potentials of indifferent, or implacably hostile, external forces, Christian narrative, such as *Andreas*, portrayed the spiritually 'treowe tacen' ('true token', 214b) of protagonists expressing by what they said the faithful allegiance which would carry them safely through all the dire physical events ordained for them by God. Beowulf declared 'Wyrd oft nereð / unfægne eorl, þonne his ellen deah!' ('Fate often preserves an undoomed warrior, when his fighting spirit avails', *Beowulf* 572b–3), but Andrew affirmed *to soðe*, 'as truth' (*Andreas* 458a),

þæt næfre forlæteð lifgende god
eorl on eorðan, gif his ellen deah

['that the living God never forsakes a man on earth, if his strength of spirit avails', 459–60].

As a result of the storm the apostle had verbally exercised his absolute faith and shared his success with the skipper-Christ. The disturbance in the sea had served him as a means of spiritual attainment and had thereby raised interlocution to a new level.

The style of discourse changed accordingly. Andrew addressed an elaborately courteous enquiry to the 'eorl unforcuð' ('honourable man', 475a) in whose company he felt himself to be:

Wolde ic freondscipe,
þeoden þrymfæst, þinne, gif ic mehte,
begitan godne.
. . .
Wolde ic anes to ðe,
cynerof hæleð, cræftes neosan,
ðæt ðu me getæhte, nu þe tir cyning
ond miht forgef, manna scyppend,
hu ðu wægflotan wære bestemdon,
sæhengeste, sund wisige

['I would like, glorious leader, to obtain, if I might, your good friendship . . . I would like, illustrious man, to find out a special skill from you, that you should teach me, now that the king, the creator of men, has given you the glory and power, how you steer the course of the wave-floater drenched by the ocean, the seahorse', 478b–80a and 483b–8].

And the skipper-Christ crowned a developing sequence of sententious maxims with an eloquent tribute to God as creator of heaven:

Flodwylm ne mæg
manna ænigne   ofer meotudes est
lungre gelettan;   ah him lifes geweald,
se ðe brimu bindeð,   brune yða
ðyð ond þreatað.   He þeodum sceal
racian mid rihte,   se ðe rodor ahof
ond gefæstnode   folmum sinum,
worhte ond wreðede,   wuldras fylde
beorhtne boldwelan,   swa gebledsod wearð
engla eðel   þurh his anes miht

['The sea-surge cannot soon hinder any man against the good will of the governor; he who binds the oceans, restrains and rebukes the dark waves, himself has power over life. He rules over peoples by right, who raised up and made secure the sky with his own hands, fashioned and maintained it, filled the radiant house-riches gloriously, so that the native land of angels became blessed through the might of him alone', 516b–25].

By the time the apostle had arrived in Mermedonia, wafted there by angels at Christ's command after much elevated discourse of this kind, all that was needed for language to cast off any remaining earthiness was an overt revelation of divinity:

Ða him fore eagum   onsyne wearð
æðeling oðywed   in þa ilcan tid,
cining cwicera gehwæs,   þurh cnihtes had

['Then before his eyes became visible, a being of inherent nobility revealed at that very time, the king of every creature, through the form of a youth', 910–12].[72]

The verbal medium which had served human society over the centuries had finally gone into free spiritual orbit. Andrew was ready to hear and carry out the full will of 'wuldres aldor' ('the prince of glory', 913b), declared to him in open manifestation: as

[72] In the C analogue (and in the Blickling Homily) Andrew asked to see Christ, but in the poem the manifestation resulted simply from the apostle's prayer for forgiveness for failing to recognize the true identity of the person to whom he had been speaking in the boat.

beorn gebledsod, swa þe beorht fæder
geweorðað wuldorgifum to widan aldre,
cræfte ond mihte

['blessed man, whom the radiant father will honour for ever with gifts of glory, ability and might', 937–9a],

he was to enter the Mermedonians' chief city, there to release Matthew and his fellow prisoners and faithfully to endure extreme bodily pain, keeping the *bysen*, 'example' (971b), of Christ's own passion and crucifixion ever before him, so that he might lead many to the light of heaven.[73]

The city which was to provide this symbolic experience was, as the poet conceived it, a cauldron seething with uncontrollable perverted passion and boundless violence. When the cannibalistic citizens were about to slaughter an old man for food and he begged them to kill his son instead, their raging appetite could brook not an instant's delay:

Hie ða lac hraðe
þegon to þance. Þeod wæs oflysted,
metes modgeomre, næs him to maðme wynn,
hyht to hordgestreonum. Hungre wæron
þearle geþreatod, swa se ðeodsceaða
reow ricsode. Þa wæs rinc manig,
guðfrec guma, ymb þæs geongan feorh
breostum onbryrded

['Then they quickly received the offering thankfully. The people were filled with desire, sorrowing for food; they had no delight in precious things, no joy in hoarded treasures. They were grievously harassed by hunger, as the cruel injurer of the people held sway. Then many a warrior, many a man eager for destruction, was excited in his breast about the life of that young man', 1111b–18a].

Their craving was of the bestial sort that had no place for the normal human joy of possession functioning in a healthy society (1113b–14a). And the torture they inflicted on Andrew, when they captured him, was of the same headlong excess:

þær wæs sec manig
on þam welwange wiges oflysted
leoda duguðe. Lyt sorgodon
hwylc him þæt edlean æfter wurde.

[73] Cf. Irving, 'A Reading of *Andreas*', pp. 227–8.

Heton þa lædan ofer landsceare,
ðragmælum teon, torngeniðlan,
swa hie hit frecnost findan meahton.
Drogon deormodne æfter dunscræfum,
ymb stanhleoðo, stærcedferþne,
efne swa wide swa wegas to lagon,
enta ærgeweorc, innan burgum,
stræte stanfage. Storm upp aras
æfter ceasterhofum, cirm unlytel
hæðnes heriges. Wæs þæs halgan lic
sarbennum soden, swate bestemed,
banhus abrocen. Blod yðum weoll,
hatan heolfre

['There was many a man in that host of people in that place of slaughter filled with a lust for strife. They cared little what the reward would be for them afterwards. Then they ordered the suffering enemy to be led across the countryside, pulled time and time again, in the most terrible way they could devise. They dragged the courageous man, the stout-hearted one, through hill-caves, across rocky slopes, as widely as ways reached, former works of giants, within the cities, streets paved with stones. A tumult arose through the dwellings of the stronghold, no little clamour of the heathen host. The body of the saint was sodden from grievous wounds, soaked in blood, the bone-house shattered. Blood surged in waves, in hot gore', 1225b–41a].

When his turn came, the saint, made whole again by divine intervention, meted out retribution just as violent. At his bidding a marble pillar gushed out a mighty flood engulfing the whole city:

Weox wæteres þrym. Weras cwanedon,
ealde æscberend. Wæs him ut myne
fleon fealone stream, woldon feore beorgan,
to dunscræfum drohtað secan,
eorðan edwist. Him þæt engel forstod,
se ða burh oferbrægd blacan lige,
hatan heaðowælme. Hreoh wæs þær inne
beatende brim. Ne meahte beorna hloð
of þam fæstenne fleame spowan.
Wægas weoxon, wadu hlynsodon,
flugon fyrgnastas, flod yðum weoll.
Ðær wæs yðfynde innan burgum
geomorgidd wrecen. Gehðo mændan

forhtferð manig, fusleoð golon.
Egeslic æled eagsyne wearð,
heardlic hereteam, hleoðor gryrelic.
Þurh lyftgelac leges blæstas
weallas ymbwurpon, wæter mycladon

['The force of the water increased. Men, old spear-bearers, lamented. They were eager to flee out from the gleaming flood, they wanted to save their lives, to seek survival in hill-caves, sustenance on earth. An angel prevented that for them by enveloping the city in blazing fire, a hot battle-surge. The sea beating inside was cruel. A throng of warriors could not succeed in escaping from the fortress. Waves grew, waters resounded, sparks of fire flew, the flood welled up in waves. There in the city a chanted dirge was easy to meet with. Many a frightened man lamented his grief, uttered a song of imminent death. Terrible fire was seen, grievous devastation, noise was horrible. Through the turbulence in the sky blasts of flame enveloped the walls, the waters grew greater', 1536–53].

Only a turmoil of this magnitude could call a halt to the Mermedonians' rampaging wickedness by convincing them that the *wyrd*, 'fate' (1561b), which they faced would utterly destroy them if they did not turn to the holy man and 'helpe biddan, / geoce ond frofre' ('beg him for help, comfort and consolation', 1566b–7a). The irresistible onrush of fire and flood (partly apostolic, partly angelic in operation) was the outward sign of the spiritual force Andrew had at his command as a young thegn of the Lord of hosts (1206b–7b). Like the storm on his voyage from Achaia, this concourse of waters was no part of organic nature but occurred specifically to produce an intended effect on its victims and could vanish as swiftly as it had appeared, swallowed up by a fissure in the earth as soon as the apostle recognized a change of heart in his hitherto obdurate tormentors.

Dramatic machinery such as this, however, was but a sign and a symptom. It did not reveal how spirituality actually operated at the deeper levels common to heaven and earth. That process belonged to the language of communication between God, the glorious ruler of angels, of men and of all creation, and Andrew, this divine ruler's chosen representative in Mermedonia in his capacity as one of the twelve 'tireadige hæleð, / þeodnes þegnas' ('renowned warriors, thegns of the ruler', 2b–3a) whom the poet had celebrated as a group in an 'opening trumpet-blast'[74] (1–11a), unmatched in his Latin source. Just as the imprisoned Matthew had

[74] *Ibid.*, p. 216.

combined personal directness with the sweep of universal praise when expressing his trust in his Lord –

ic beo sona gearu
to adreoganne þæt ðu, drihten min,
engla eadgifa, eðelleasum,
dugeða dædfruma, deman wille

['I shall be immediately ready to suffer what you, my lord, bestower of the blessings of angels, will ordain, originator of the deeds of warriors, for the homeless', 72b–5][75] –

so Andrew affectingly intermingled intimacy and grandeur:

Ic gelyfe to ðe, min liffruma,
þæt ðu mildheort me for þinum mægenspedum,
nerigend fira, næfre wille,
ece ælmihtig, anforlætan,
swa ic þæt gefremme, þenden feorh leofað,
min on moldan, þæt ic, meotud, þinum
larum leofwendum lyt geswice

['I have faith in you, my author of life, that you in your compassion will never, saviour of men, on account of your mighty powers, eternal and almighty one, abandon me, who, as long as my spirit lives on earth, will contrive that I fall little short, ordainer, of your loving commands', 1284–90].

The closeness between God and apostle was not, however, a private matter. Public rhetoric projected the relationship on to the world stage, as in this utterance, highlighted by rhyme in a pair of its phrases:

Næfre ic geferde mid frean willan
under heofonhwealfe heardran drohtnoð,
þær ic dryhtnes æ deman sceolde.
Sint me leoðu tolocen, lic sare gebrocen,
banhus blodfag, benne weallað,
seonodolg swatige

['Never under the vault of heaven have I experienced at the Lord's will a harder way of life, in which I have had to declare the gospel. My limbs are pulled apart, my body painfully broken, my bone-house bloodstained, wounds gush, gory sinew-gashes', 1401–6a].

[75] Cf. *ibid.*, p. 218.

Compassion forged the intimacy between universal divinity and the human heart. Andrew's ordinary feelings of pity when he saw a youth about to fall victim to rampant cannibalism were enough in themselves to procure God's miraculous intervention (1135–54) without the spoken petition of the C analogue.[76] And divine words sufficed to restore the apostle to wholeness after his sufferings (1462b–77), as against the action of the C analogue[77] or the combination of action and speech in a Greek version.[78]

Andrew, for his part, understood how to use language as a means of cooperating with God's will. He comprehended the power of speech to exploit analogy as an active principle of the spiritual universe,[79] as in his bidding to the pillar to emit a torrent that would drown the perverse Mermedonians. According to the poet's source, after God had restored Andrew to wholeness, the apostle, still in prison, saw a marble pillar with a statue on it, ordered that through the power of Jesus Christ this statue pour out the flood from its mouth, and exhorted it not to feel unworthy as mere stone, seeing that God had written the ten commandments on tablets of that material.[80] But the poet made the comparison with the tablets primary. In his version Andrew saw a row of massive, weather-beaten columns by a wall down below the building which he was in ('be wealle . . . / under sælwage'[81] (1492–3a)) and addressed ('mæðel gehede' (1496b)[82]) one of them (1492–7) without any reference to possible unworthiness. Instead, in a situation emphasizing the spoken word passing between an addresser and an addressee[83] in a clearly defined physical context, what was

[76] *Sources and Analogues*, trans. Allen and Calder, pp. 28–9. [77] *Ibid.*, p. 31.

[78] See *Apocryphal Gospels, Acts, and Revelations*, trans. Wilson, p. 365.

[79] Cf. application of this principle to control the material world in charms (above, p. 109).

[80] This exhortation is not in the C analogue (*Sources and Analogues*, trans. Allen and Calder, p. 31), but in the light of the *Andreas* poet's treatment (see below), it is probable that his Latin source had it in a form equivalent to the one summarized above, which occurs in a Greek version (see *Apocryphal Gospels, Acts, and Revelations*, trans. Walker, p. 365); cf. Schaar, *Critical Studies in the Cynewulf Group*, pp. 58–9. More particularly, from the reference to gold in the Old English quoted below we may infer that the poet's Latin source included wording like that in a Greek manuscript translated thus by Walker as a variant reading: 'Yea, for assuredly you [i.e. the pillar as stone] have been honoured; for God did not write the law for His people on plates of gold or silver, but on plates of stone. Now therefore, O statue, do this that I require of thee' (*ibid.*, n. 4).

[81] MS *sæl wange*. [82] Cf. Stanley, 'Two Old English Poetic Phrases', pp. 77–8.

[83] Cf. exploitation of language for addressing non-human addressees in charms (above, pp. 109–10 and n. 109).

uttered was not a direct order to the pillar, as in the source, but an appeal to the material, of which it was made, to heed ('Geher ðu, marmanstan' (1498a)), and to respond to, a command of God, which was alluded to by the speaker,[84] on the grounds of the honour God had done to it before as bearer of his commandments:

Hwæt, ðu golde eart,
sincgife, sylla! On ðe sylf cyning
wrat, wuldres god, wordum cyðde
recene geryno, ond ryhte æ
getacnode on tyn wordum,
meotud mihtum swið. Moyse sealde,
swa hit soðfæste syðþan heoldon,
modige magoþegnas, magas sine,
godfyrhte guman, Iosua ond Tobias.
Nu ðu miht gecnawan þæt þe cyning engla
gefrætwode furður mycle
giofum geardagum þonne eall gimma cynn.
Þurh his halige hæs þu scealt hræðe cyðan
gif ðu his ondgitan ænige hæbbe

['Lo, you are better than gold, than a rich gift! On you the king himself wrote, the God of glory, revealed in words awful mysteries, and symbolized just law in ten commandments, ordainer strong in his powers. He gave it to Moses, as those firm in the truth kept it from then on, proud thegns, Joshua and Tobias. Now you can know that the king of angels adorned you much further with gifts in days long ago than all kinds of gems. Through his holy command you must at once reveal if you have any understanding of him', 1508b–21].

The pillar was not just being encouraged to overcome the modesty it might owe to its stoniness, as in the Latin; instead the apostle was undertaking the vital process of harnessing the marble's access to active spiritual analogy: this substance had transmitted the law of God once; now God was calling on it again to be instrumental in manifesting his authority. For the poet, Andrew's verbal act of eliciting this spiritual potential belonged, like performing a charm, to sharply defined present actuality, whereas the resultant flood, when it came, was on the metaphysical plane of the ten

84 'Læt nu of þinum staþole streamas weallan, / . . . nu ðe ælmihtig / hateð . . . þæt ðu . . . / . . . forð onsende / wæter widrynig to wera cwealme, / . . .', ('Let streams well up from your base, . . . now the almighty is ordering . . . that you send forth far-flowing water for slaughter of men . . .', 1503–8a).

commandments; both events consisted of a revelation of awful mysteries, the one in waters as the other had been in words. The power of analogy inherent in stone gave the water its means of propulsion.

To the traditional mind of the vernacular poet, an effective analogy between an event in the present and a divine action in recorded history gave the apostle the means to tap the vast reservoir of Christ-centred power in the cosmos. In this instance the catalytic agent was language, Andrew's words to the stone. But equally well what the apostle did could create the vital link. He became God's instrument by actions which, in their pattern, imitated Christ's, just as a user of the *Æcerbot* charm was intended to acquire, or transmit, the energy of the sun by imitating that body's movement.[85] For example, by articulating the apostle's sufferings in a sequence of public torture day by day and solitary endurance in prison night by night until on the third night the saint arose once more whole and unblemished, the poet gave these afflictions a concord with Christ's passion more clearly than his source had done;[86] and elsewhere in his poem he introduced other modifications which developed this parallel at points where it was only latent in his source.[87] These, in my view, were episodic, though deeply significant, manifestations of a general principle of analogy with the divine, giving Andrew's saintliness its *modus operandi* in the spiritual universe, but do not constitute the elements of an all-controlling narrative strategy.

This sense of proportion, I believe, we should apply to the poet's use of 'typological' motifs too. For example, when the apostle, 'gleawmod, gode leof' ('wise in mind, dear to God', 1579a), stepped out after ordering the streaming waters to be still, his confidence – he was 'cene collenferð' ('bold, courageous', 1578a) – had its counterpart in the dry street which opened up ahead of him through the flood (1579b–87a), a phenomenon irresistibly reminiscent of the dry passage which divided the waters of the Red Sea for the Israelites when Moses raised his hand at God's command.[88] Moses

85 See above, pp. 108–9.

86 From the C analogue we learn of this time span only when Andrew prays for an end to his sufferings; *Sources and Analogues*, trans. Allen and Calder, p. 30. It is unfortunate that our sole surviving text of *Andreas*, in the Vercelli Book, contains the minor slip of referring to Andrew's third night in prison as his fourth (1458b).

87 For these, and for the belief that the sufferings of the faithful continued the redemptive act of Christ's passion, see Biggs, 'The Passion of Andreas'.

88 For this analogy, cf. Irving, 'A Reading of *Andreas*', p. 236, and, for others, *ibid.*, pp. 228 (the Harrowing of Hell) and 229 (the Israelites leaving Egypt). In the C

leading the children of Israel across the Red Sea was, of course, the foremost type of baptism in Old Testament exegesis,[89] but to my mind it does not follow that this and the other allusions of a similar kind amount to evidence that *Andreas* was systematically structured upon 'the various traditional images of conversion in the early Church, especially the imagery of baptism, the Harrowing of Hell, and the Last Judgment'.[90] Typology, in my opinion, did not exert that kind of control over the composition as a whole. The poet surely did not work out his narrative as a formal allegory. I prefer to attribute to him a less intellectualized belief that Andrew drew on spiritual power, and in his turn was himself validated, by acting in analogy with Christ-centred world history; the poet, as I conceive of him, was including narrative features that partook of this more general principle of imitation.

A running image which was deeply thematic to this poem, as it was to Old English Christian narrative poetry generally, and indeed to vernacular Christian poetry of any sort, was light, sun-centred conqueror of darkness and cold in our world and primary element in the God-centred glory of heaven. The poet had introduced it at the outset, as a prominent component of apostolic valour 'under tunglum' ('under the stars', 2a), of Matthew's imprisonment and of Andrew's embarkation,[91] and, throughout, it suffused the workings of apostolic sanctity to a degree quite unknown to the poet's source. It combined intimately with Andrew's *imitatio Christi*, as when, 'Cristes cempa' ('soldier of Christ', 991a), he rescued the imprisoned Matthew and that apostle's companions in an echo of the release of the 'populus in tenebris' by the 'rex gloriae' in the Harrowing of Hell, and (without counterpart in the C analogue) the holy comradeship of the fellow 'wuldres þegnas' ('thegns of glory', 1026b) shone out in a heavenly radiance as they embraced in the gloom of the gaol:

Criste wæron begen
leofe on mode. Hie leoht ymbscan
halig ond heofontorht. Hreðer innan wæs
wynnum awelled

analogue Andrew's invitation to the now repentant people to follow him and then, as he led them, the water 'opening up to the right and left before him' (*Sources and Analogues*, trans. Allen and Calder, p. 32) firmly suggest the Old Testament prototype, but the poet's smooth street drying out as the apostle stepped on it (1579b–82) and other, similar, features are far more dramatic.

89 Cf. Hill, 'Figural Narrative in *Andreas*', p. 268.

90 Earl, 'The Typological Structure of *Andreas*', p. 67.

91 See above, pp. 252–3.

['Both were dear to Christ's heart. Light shone around them, holy and of a heavenly radiance. The breast within was excited joyfully', 1016b–19a].[92]

Light, part spiritual, part physical, was an integral part of Andrew's steadfast relationship with God. All through the *storm* (1236b) of cruel tortures which the apostle endured on the first day[93] he remained *sigeltorht*,[94] 'sun-bright' (1246a), 'oðþæt beorht gewat / sunne swegeltorht to sete glidan' ('until the bright, sky-radiant sun went gliding to its setting', 1247b–8) and, dear to Christ (1250b–1a), he was led with *leoht sefa*, 'shining mind' (1251b), 'under heolstorscuwan' ('under the concealing darkness', 1253b) of prison, there to maintain unremitting glorification of God (1267–8a) throughout a night of intense winter-cold (1265a) while fierce frost stalked the land:

Snaw eorðan band
wintergeworpum. Weder coledon
heardum hægelscurum, swylce hrim ond forst,
hare hildstapan, hæleða eðel
lucon, leoda gesetu. Land wæron freorig
cealdum cylegicelum, clang wæteres þrym
ofer eastreamas, is brycgade
blæce brimrade

['Snow bound the earth with wintry blizzards. The skies grew cold with cruel hailstorms, and likewise rime and frost, hoary marching warriors, confined the country of warriors, the habitations of men. Lands were freezing with cold icicles, the might of water hardened above water-currents, ice bridged over the shining movement of the sea', 1255b–62a].

In the face of the powerful, conventional, association between winter weather and the misery of loss (as in *The Wanderer)*, Andrew's radiance of mind remained throughout undiminished 'oððæt wuldres gim / heofontorht onhlad' ('until the jewel of glory revealed itself heaven-bright', 1268b–9a).

Singlehandedly tackling the conversion of the Mermedonians as a young thegn of the Lord of hosts (1206b–7a) – Matthew and his fellow prisoners had left the city after their rescue and we hear no more of Andrew's companions once God had appeared openly to the apostle outside the city gates – Andrew confronted the devil 'wann ond wliteleas' ('dark and unbeautiful', 1169a), as his primary foe. When Satan came, deadly cruel

92 Cf. Irving, 'A Reading of *Andreas*', pp. 228–9.

93 See above, pp. 259–60.

94 Krapp emends to *sigetorht*.

lord of murder (1313a and 1314a) shrouded in gloom (1313b), with six fellow demons – his *þegnas þryðfulle*, 'powerful thegns' (1329a) – to taunt and threaten the saint, 'deor ond domgeorn' ('brave and eager for glory', 1308a) and *wærfæst*, 'faithful' (1310a), in the dim building (1308b) where he lay imprisoned for the second night running, the devil's thegns were terror-stricken by the 'mære tacen' ('glorious sign', 1338b) of Christ's cross with which God protected the apostle's face, but Satan himself took flight only when Andrew declared his conviction that the same God would free him as had imprisoned the fiend in an irrevocable exile where 'wuldres blunne, / syððan ðu forhogedes heofoncyninges word' ('you have forfeited glory, since you despised the word of the king of heaven', 1380b–1). Andrew owed his victory to language, the medium which, as used by God, had given strength of mind to him through his obedience but had destroyed the devil through his disobedience. Words gave the apostle the sort of superiority in the contest between light and dark that Guthlac displayed in breaking the power of the demons about to thrust him into hell by asserting 'with unshaken nerves, with steadfast heart and sober mind', 'Woe unto you, you sons of darkness, seed of Cain, you are but dust and ashes'.[95]

With the debased Mermedonians, however, Andreas had no linguistic relationship. Their reformation had to await a break-through of spiritual speech. Their unconverted existence was an enslaved physicality. For example, the poet conceived that Andrew's arrival at Matthew's prison initiated a chain-reaction based on blood. According to the C analogue, when the apostle reached the prison, he looked up to heaven, prayed and made the sign of the cross and thereupon 'all the prison guards died and fell down'.[96] But the poet imagined that when his 'Cristes cempa' (991a) merely saw (*geseh* (992a)) the heathen guards,

Ealle swylt fornam,
druron domlease. Deaðræs forfeng
hæleð heorodreorige

['Death took them all away, they fell inglorious. The rush of death seized the bloodstained warriors', 994b–6a].

Then, when the 'hæle hildedeor' ('battle-brave man', 1002a) went inside, 'Hæðene swæfon, / dreore druncne, deaðwang rudon' ('The heathens slept,

[95] *Felix's 'Life' of St Guthlac*, ed. Colgrave, p. 107.

[96] *Sources and Analogues*, trans. Allen and Calder, p. 25.

drunk with blood, reddened the place of death', 1002b–3). And when the dead guards were later discovered by their fellow-citizens, whereas in the C analogue the city's leaders after some thought decided that the corpses should be eaten,[97] in the poem the men's *hildbedd*, 'bed of violent death' (1092b), was disturbed 'þurh heard gelac' ('by brute force', 1092a) as soon as the compulsive cannibalistic chiefs learned that

. . . þær heorodreorige hyrdas lagan,
gæsne on greote, gaste berofene,
fægra flæschaman

['the bloodstained guards lay there, lifeless on the ground, robbed of spirit, flesh-coverings of doomed men', 1083–5a].

A semi-personified death reacted to the presence of the spiritual warrior by releasing blood to cannibalistic lust. With brutish obsession such as this the saint could have no communication.[98]

The Mermedonians' cannibalism was dramatically symbolized as a blow to the heart of normal living by the weapon threatening the youth about to be sacrificed while pleading for his life:[99]

Sceolde sweordes ecg,
scerp ond scurheard, of sceaðan folme,
fyrmælum fag, feorh acsigan

['The sword's edge, sharp and hard in the storm of battle, from the hand of the injurer, stained by marks of fire, was to demand life', 1132b–4].

Their depravity deserved and received the narrator's forthright condemnation: these people were *unlæde*, 'wicked' (30a), as devils were (142a), *fordene*, 'corrupt' (43a), and *hellfuse*, 'heading for hell' (50a). They were a whole society corrupted by a blood lust like Grendel's.

A strong streak of exaggeration in their behaviour[100] hinted, however, that their unnaturalness was an aberration rather than a root-and-branch

97 *Ibid.*, pp. 27–8.

98 Cf. Calder, 'Figurative Language and its Contexts in *Andreas*', pp. 121–2 and 127. For the poet's development of a conception (with which this chain-reaction of depravity would contrast starkly) that the blood which Andrew himself shed in his sufferings, in order to secure salvation for the Mermedonians, was in continuity with the blood which Christ shed in his passion to redeem all mankind, see Biggs, 'The Passion of Andreas', pp. 415–24.

99 Cf. above, pp. 259 and 263.

100 Cf. Calder, 'Figurative Language and its Contexts in *Andreas*', pp. 121–2.

distinction. For instance, throngs of enraged, fully armed warriors massed for a mere routine inspection to see which prisoner was next for eating, and their wargear yelled:[101]

Duguð samnade,
hæðne hildfrecan, heapum þrungon,
(guðsearo gullon, garas hrysedon),
bolgenmode, under bordhreoðan

['The host assembled, heathen fighting men, thronged in troops – their wargear yelled, spears rang – enraged, under cover of their shields', 125b–8].

The Mermedonians were a bizarre irregularity, as irony and parody effectively displayed: a father saying 'Eat my young son rather than me' was *collenferhð*, 'excited, elated, bold in spirit' (1108a), right enough, but hardly in the positive sense the word usually implied; and, in this 'hæleða eðel' ('native land of warriors', 21a) which was actually a 'mearcland morðre bewunden' ('a border region enveloped in murder', 19), the inhabitants' intention to kill Matthew

ond þonne todælan dugeðe ond geogoðe,
werum to wiste ond to wilþege,
fæges flæschoman

['and then share out between the seasoned and the young warriors, as sustenance and pleasant feasting for the men, the flesh-covering of the doomed man', 152–4a][102]

caricatured a Germanic hall-feast. The poet persistently engineered a connotative disparity between customary expectation and clearcut context which was similar, in a general way, to the ambiguity contrived between customary expectation and uncertain context in a *double entendre* riddle. And he came closer still to the riddler in attributing to the Mermedonians the sort of paradox which riddlers traditionally presented,[103] when he conceived of this people as *wælwulfas*, 'slaughter-wolves' (149a), able to write.[104] In his imagination they were an eccentric phenomenon as against customary norms.

Abnormality included the possibility of normality, like a derangement

101 At *Widsith* 127b–8a spears in flight whine and scream (*hwinende*, *giellende*).
102 Cf. Irving, 'A Reading of *Andreas*', p. 219.
103 See above, pp. 103–5.
104 Cf. Calder, 'Figurative Language and its Contexts in *Andreas*', p. 128.

giving way to sanity. There proved to be a chink in this people's moral darkness, which Andrew, *wuldres þegn*, 'thegn of glory' (1678b), could exploit *torhtlice*, 'radiantly' (1681a), bringing them to a beautiful joy which no savage spirit might assail any more (1693–4) and which inspired them all to cry out with one accord,

An is ece god eallra gesceafta!
Is his miht ond his æht ofer middangeard
breme gebledsod, ond his blæd ofer eall
in heofonþrymme halgum scineð,
wlitige on wuldre to widan ealdre,
ece mid englum. Þæt is æðele cyning!

['One is the eternal god of all creatures! His power and his possession over the world are famously blessed, and his splendour beyond all shines on the saints in heavenly majesty, radiantly in glory for ever and ever, the eternal one among angels. That is a noble king!', 1717–22].

With this outburst of language, at a stroke the city had become a *winburg*, a place where wine was drunk (1637a and 1672a), a *goldburg*, 'gold-city (1655a), and a *wederburg*, 'city of good weather' (1697a). The converted were baptized in *godes tempel*, 'a temple of God', built where the punished flood had gushed out (1632–41a). Men, nature and heaven were united in creative harmony;[105] the devil's sterile darkness had been dispelled. Illuminated by the apostle's radiant spirit the true interactive system of the cosmos compelled the heathens' immediate assent.

Intent on returning to Achaia, his mission accomplished, Andrew was accorded the sort of affectionate farewell which the Danish king Hrothgar had given Beowulf about to leave Denmark for home (*Beowulf* 1870–80a). But, whereas the journey of Beowulf, the warrior, was from one human community to another, Andrew, the saint, was setting off into undefined space and time; Hrothgar's emotional goodbyes were appropriately said in the midst of his hall, but, just as fittingly, the Mermedonians stood weeping on a headland for as long as they could catch a glimpse of their beloved teacher sailing away over the ocean (1710–14). The one parting was bounded by the relationship between two peoples; the other was without limit. Feeling in the one case had the ordinariness of belonging to long-recognized conventions of social intercourse but in the other to the extraordinariness of yearning for the partly unknowable. Beowulf had

[105] Cf. *ibid.*, p. 132.

cleansed a society, but Andrew a sector of eternity. The social analogies traditionally implied by the language of poetry were all that the former enterprise required, but the second enlarged the context: Andrew's mission challenged the language of poetry to bring society's modes of thought to bear on the universal theme of human response to God's absolute power. The behaviour of an élite in the face of life's high drama, not humdrum domesticity, was at stake in this story as before, but now in an arena of Christ-shared language, of Christ-centred analogy, of images common to heaven and earth, of physical manifestations of metaphysical forces. Whereas in *Beowulf* symbolic language of active being reached back into a human past in which socially accumulated generalizations mitigated absolute *wyrd*, in *Andreas* it reached out into a universe of spiritual light and conflicting darkness, susceptible to the operation of analogy and, whatever the extremes of experience, to a dialogue between Lord and follower based on divine compassion and human faith.

8

Poet, public petitioner and preacher

In this chapter I want to trace how vernacular poetry's narrative practice was affected by some comparable uses of non-poetic narrative in Christian devotion and teaching. As an operator of just one sort among others meeting Christianity's diverse needs, a vernacular poet rubbed shoulders with allied, though differing, practitioners as never before. A common attitude to their subject-matter was the bond between them all, but, since his tradition was the newcomer, a vernacular poet was especially open to suggestion from the rest. When treating New Testament and subsequent Christ-inspired events – or, indeed, Old Testament history regarded from a New Testament point of view – an Anglo-Saxon 'I/we have heard/learned' narrator was no longer a disinterested spokesman for tradition, relating, from a purely representative point of view, how a hero achieved what success he could in the face of predetermined death by exerting his will to do what society expected of him, as Beowulf did; he was now the voice of the poet himself, retelling the written record of the absolute triumph over death secured by Christ or the apostles or saints, or the absolute fulfilment of God's will by an Old Testament Moses, in ever-felt contrast to the uncertainty of his own standing with God and hence his eternal fate. Cynewulf, for instance, reviewed the fates of the apostles – 'hu þa æðelingas ellen cyðdon, / torhte ond tireadige' ('how the men noble by inherited nature showed their spirit, illustrious and glorious', *The Fates of the Apostles* 3–4a) – for the very reason that he himself was weary of journeying and sick at heart: 'Hwæt! Ic þysne sang siðgeomor fand / on seocum sefan', he began (1–2a). What he saw in these men 'dryhtne gecorene' ('chosen by the Lord', 5b) was not primarily a set of examples for him to follow in placing eternal reward before all other considerations; rather, by virtue of their glorious deaths (85–7), they represented a source of the help, protection and succour on which, as he movingly put it in his appended epilogue, his soul would depend, when, on leaving its body to become food for worms, it set out on its solitary journey to an unknown destination in eternity. Supplicate this holy company on my behalf in this great need, the poet entreated everyone enjoying his poem, and he revealed his name for that purpose. All alike are vulnerable, he declared: 'swa bið ælcum menn / nemþe he godcundes gastes bruce' ('so it is for each man unless he partake of a divine spirit', 113b–14). It was in sharing everyone's uncertainty of God's favour that he claimed to be representative.

Cynewulf's poems in their several ways all stemmed from the exemplary insecurity he felt as he journeyed through this dangerous world between Christ's two comings. He remembered all the wounds of sin he had inflicted on himself, weeping that he had been too tardy in repenting (*Juliana* 709b–15a). He declared that he wanted to teach each of his dear friends

þæt he ne agæle   gæstes þearfe,
ne on gylp geote,   þenden god wille
þæt he her in worulde   wunian mote,
somed siþian   sawel in lice,
in þam gæsthofe.   Scyle gumena gehwylc
on his geardagum   georne biþencan
þæt us milde bicwom   meahta waldend
æt ærestan   þurh þæs engles word.
Bið nu eorneste   þonne eft cymeð,
reðe ond ryhtwis

['that he should not neglect the need of his soul, or gush in boasting, while God wills that he may remain here in the world, and his soul journey in his body, in the spirit-dwelling. Every man must earnestly reflect during his lifetime that the ruler of powers came to us mercifully the first time through the angel's words. Now he will be stern, when he comes again, severe and strict', *Christ* (*II*) 816–25a].

In his epilogue to *Elene* Cynewulf saw himself, now old, as an example of the transitoriness of all wealth and all beauties of the earth, and, ultimately, the passing of the entire world (1269b–81a). Especially in the same epilogue and in the one concluding his poem on the ascension (*Christ II*) his imagination dwelt on the substance and drama of the irrevocable judgement that lies ahead for all humanity when this entire world will be terrifyingly destroyed and each man, bearing the burden of his sins, will stand in dread before God the judge. May everyone who observes the festival of the finding of the true cross attain everlasting joy (*Elene* 1228b–35); let us petition God that we may possess that supreme happiness (*The Fates of the Apostles* 115–20a); no one need fear the devil if God shields him (*Christ* (*II*) 779–82a); the praise of God stands now and always, great and glorious, and his power remains, eternal and ever young, over all creation (*Fates* 120b–2): in pronouncements such as these lay his and mankind's hopes. Cynewulf belonged to a new breed of 'Lo! We have heard through holy books' poet-narrators,[1] whose didactic concern was no longer the traditional social wisdom which they shared both with the protagonists in their stories and with their audiences but the spiritual need which they and their readers had for penitence, petition and praise.[2] Such poets started from the same position *vis-à-vis* eternity as that of liturgical worshippers and preachers, and so in this chapter I shall explore some of the influences which these two analogous activities had on vernacular poems.

A penitent poet-narrator relating a part of world history as a representative of all men between the two comings of Christ was like a reciter of the Latin liturgy in uttering words of both historical and more-than-historical import. For instance, during the season of Advent a chanter singing, before and after the *Magnificat* at Vespers, the 'O' antiphon, 'O clavis David, et sceptrum domus Israel, qui aperis et nemo claudit, claudis et nemo aperit: veni et educ vinctum de domo carceris, sedentem in tenebris et umbra mortis' ('O key of David and sceptre of the house of Israel, you who open and no one closes, close and no one opens: come and lead out from the prison house the fettered, sitting in darkness and the shadow of death'),[3] was associating himself with a dramatic petitioning voice which by implication belonged not only to the patriarchs and prophets waiting for the Harrowing of Hell but also to all men seeking access to eternal life through Christ the redeemer.[4] The three elements of a personal need in present time, a narrative event in the past and the whole sweep of world history appertained to poet-narrator and chanter alike.

[1] *The Fates of the Apostles* 63; cf. 23a and 25b, *Elene* 240b–2 and 1251b–6a and *Juliana* 1–8a.

[2] Cf. Rice, 'The Penitential Motif in Cynewulf's *Fates of the Apostles*'.

[3] For the liturgical function and particular characteristics of the group of great 'O' antiphons of which this is one, see Rankin, 'The Liturgical Background of the Old English Advent Lyrics', pp. 328–30; see also below, p. 371.

[4] Both these implications (especially the second) depend on interpretation of the 'clavis David' symbol as Christ's authority over entry into the heavenly Jerusalem, for which, see Burlin, *The Old English 'Advent'*, p. 71.

By virtue of the personal factor both of them were conscious of themselves at a distinct remove from the events to which their words alluded. Each of them reached out to a narrative situation by exercising his, or her, own imagination in a way which was not demanded of the traditional vernacular poet and his 'I/we have heard/learned' narrator: both a native poet recomposing a story handed down in his society and the narrator he refashioned in the process were essentially controlled by the linguistic community to which they belonged: they were responding to the dramatic potentials with which conventional symbolic language had already invested a given situation.[5] But a worshipping poet-narrator and liturgical singer were directing their own, albeit conventionally channelled, emotion to a dramatic situation of universal import enshrined in a received text. They functioned as Christian recreators releasing their imaginations through an emotional mind's eye fastened on what had happened.

The distinction is made clear by their recreative use of an on-the-spot participant invented solely to provide bridging experience. This technique was used in, for instance, the 'O' antiphon, which may have been an English composition,[6] 'O Iosep<h>, quomodo credidisti quod antea expauisti? Quid enim? In ea natum est de Spiritu Sancto ē [*sic*] quem Gabrihel annuncians Christum esse uenturum' ('O Joseph, why have you believed what you feared before? Why indeed? In her has been born from the Holy Spirit he whom Gabriel announced was the coming Christ'): the unidentified spokesman (or spokeswoman) for world-understanding in this antiphon, by referring to the Virgin Mary as 'ea' ('her') shows that he/she, the spokesperson, was in effect (in historical terms) participating in a dramatic scene between Mary and Joseph through exclaiming to Joseph on his new-found state of mind. A chanter of this text was thus associating him- or herself imaginatively with a far-sighted witness supposedly in place at the time. And in the same way Cynewulf created – as a wholly new development in Old English poetry, so far as we know[7] – some anonymous

[5] Cf. above, pp. 171–5.

[6] Rankin, 'The Liturgical Background of the Old English Advent Lyrics', p. 332. The antiphon is known in only two contexts, as an item in a collection of liturgical texts assembled by Alcuin at York *c.* 790 and as a source used by an anonymous Old English poet composing probably well before the middle of the tenth century; for the latter dating, see *ibid.*, p. 334. I quote Rankin's transcription of one of the two surviving copies of it (*ibid.*, p. 340).

[7] Cf. Clemoes, 'Style as the Criterion for Dating . . . *Beowulf*', p. 177. For the various ways of incorporating witness as an internal feature of traditional 'story', see above, pp. 208–10.

person directly present and yet outside the action whose only function was to evoke the exhilaration of St Helena's fleet speeding across the sea on its expedition to find the true cross (a description which owed nothing to the poet's source):

Þær meahte gesion, se ðone sið beheold,
brecan ofer bæðweg, brimwudu snyrgan
under swellingum, sæmearh plegean,
wadan wægflotan

['There he who beheld the expedition could see sea-wood cut across the bath-way, hasten under swelling sails, seahorse sport, wave-floaters advance', *Elene* 243–6a].

'Se ðone sið beheold' had no part in the story other than to be there to see. He had the fanciful sort of perception that pictured ships as sporting seahorses; he contributed a spectator's response to the excitement of the adventure.

More usually, however, chanter and poet-narrator spanned the divide between themselves and dramatic events by the single arch of their own imaginations. A singer of, for example, the 'O' antiphon, 'O virgo virginum, quomodo fiet istud, quia nec primam similem visa es nec habere sequentem? Filiae Hierusalem, quid me admiramini? Divinum est mysterium hoc quod cernitis' ('O virgin of virgins, how will that be done, because you are seen to have no like either before or since? Daughters of Jerusalem, why do you wonder at me? This mystery which you perceive is divine'), put firstly a question conceived of as posed to the Virgin Mary by the daughters of Jerusalem and then her reply, and thus supposed him- or herself to have been present, directly experiencing the combination of personal feeling and universal thought in the exchange as it could have occurred. And just so, the anonymous *Andreas* poet imagined God replying simply, 'Ic þe friðe healde' ('I will keep you in safety', 915b), when the apostle, finding himself outside the gates of the chief city of the cannibal Mermedonians, sought forgiveness for his former failure to recognize the divine identity of the skipper of the ship which had brought him there: God's answer, as the poet conceived it,[8] supplied a genuine response to the combination of personal devotion and general maxim with which Andrew, now for the first time, thankfully acknowledged that his benefactor had been

[8] Without any equivalent in his Latin source, so far as we know.

. . . frofre gast
hæleða cynne. Þær is help gearu,
milts æt mærum, manna gehwylcum,
sigorsped geseald, þam þe seceð to him

['the spirit of consolation for the race of men. There help is ready, mercy from the glorious one, triumphant success given to every man who looks to him', 906b–9].

The main difference between chanter and poet was, of course, that whereas the former was repeating an already fixed set of words the latter chose, and sometimes created, his own. The poet could exercise his imagination in composition. The striking personification of hunger holding sway as 'se ðeodsceaða / reow' ('the cruel injurer of the people', *Andreas* 1115b–16a[9]) and that of rime and frost imposing themselves as 'hare hildstapan' ('hoary marching warriors', 1258a[10]), neither of which was owed to the Latin source, are signs of this free play in the case of the *Andreas* poet, although he did not invent the first epithet itself[11] and probably not the second either.[12] And there was a similar distinction between poet and preacher too: the former's type of composition allowed more room for imagination then the latter's. For example, the story of how the Israelites, under Moses's leadership and God's protection, journeyed from Egypt to the Red Sea and there escaped from their enemies by crossing safely themselves, whereas the Egyptians in pursuit were engulfed in the waters, could hardly escape judgemental treatment, but the version of it presented by the anonymous poet-narrator of *Exodus* was very different from the plain telling to be expected from a prose preacher bent on didacticism.[13] For instance, to attach to the fiery pillar, guiding the Israelites by night, the idea (general to the Old Testament) that fire was God's means of punishing disobedience[14] was to employ a motif attractive for moralistic comment, but

[9] See above, p. 259. [10] See above, p. 267.

[11] The *Beowulf* poet applied the compound to the dragon twice (2278a and 2688a).

[12] It is interesting to compare his 'ondlange niht / . . . / . . . / . . . hrim ond forst, / hare hildstapan, hæleða eðel / lucon . . .' (1254b–9a) with 'fjúk ok frost gekk alla nóttina' ('rime and frost walked about all night', *Fóstbræðra saga*, ch. 4, ed. Þórólfsson and Jónsson, p. 136), as Andy Orchard has pointed out to me.

[13] See, e.g., the business-like summary of Exodus XIV.21–9, Ælfric, *CH* II.xii (ed. Godden, lines 88–100, pp. 112–13).

[14] For references to occurrences of this idea and to commentaries (perhaps or perhaps not known to the poet) in which the fiery pillar had been linked to it, see *The Old English 'Exodus'*, ed. Irving, n. on 123–4, and the further n. on the same lines in Irving, 'New Notes on the Old English *Exodus*', p. 302.

the poet used it only to animate a personification like those I have cited from *Andreas:*

Hæfde foregenga   fyrene loccas,
blace beamas;   bellegsan hweop
in þam hereþreate,   hatan lige,
þæt he on westenne   werod forbærnde,
nymðe hie modhwate   Moyses hyrde

['The forerunner had fiery locks, shining rays; he threatened the warband with fire-terror, hot flame, that he would burn up the host in the desert unless they, bold-minded, obeyed Moses', 120–4].

This poet, showing signs, as we shall see, of stimulation from a certain kind of preaching, held to his native tradition of freshly imagining retold tales,[15] exercising this freedom with remarkably graphic psychological independence. An examination of his poem as a striking example of Christian instruction of a sort which only poetry could give will be rewarding.[16]

The central figure for didactic implication was Moses, belonging both to the Old Testament events concerned and to the spiritual history of the world. He it is, we are reminded at the start, who has given to generation after generation, the world over, the counsel of everlasting salvation in the legacy of his laws (1–7). Wise and bold leader of his people and binder of the race of Pharaoh, God's adversary, it was he whom God had entrusted with the task of bringing his kinsmen into possession of their promised land and whom God had strengthened by revealing to him the wonders of the divine creation of the world and the secret of the divine name (8–32).[17] He it was who, the poet declared towards the close of his poem, brought

[15] He used the 'I have learned' formulas at 98–100a and 367–8 as well as the 'we' of all Christians at 1–7a ('We have learned'), 529–30a and 530b–2a.

[16] For much illuminating discussion of this poem, including the many defects in its sole surviving text (in the Junius manuscript), difficulties of interpreting unusual words and forms of words, the poet's use of sources, and general questions of structure and style, see *The Old English 'Exodus'*, ed. Irving, the same critic's 'New Notes on the Old English *Exodus*' and his further '*Exodus* Retraced'. I have been much indebted to these invaluable publications, as my many references to them show. More recently Lucas has reconsidered these matters in a new edition (*Exodus*). The emphasis of his treatment is on an allegorical dimension which is revealed or hinted at rather than fully developed.

[17] I prefer the view of 30–2 stated by Irving in his n. on these lines in *The Old English 'Exodus'* to the one he adopted in his n. on 30–9a in 'New Notes on the Old English *Exodus*'. Lucas (ed., *Exodus*, n. on 30–2) agrees.

the successful crossing of the Israelites and the destruction of Pharoah's host to their triumphant conclusion by enunciating 'ece rædas' ('eternal precepts', 516b) to the assembled multitude, laws which *drihten* (521b) commanded on that journey and which nations can still read (516–22). We Christians, the narrator points out, have God's merciful instruction and can use the keys of the holy spirit to unlock the meaning of this instruction, if we will (523–30a); scripture tells us that we, like the Old Testament Israelites, are on a divinely ordained journey, for *drihten* (542b and 547b), the very Lord who gave them their commandments, will come with universal power to judge mankind and lead the souls of the faithful from the wretched exile of this life into the kingdom of heaven, there to praise him joyfully for ever (530b–48).[18] The implication is clear that, when the poet thereupon quotes the peroration of Moses's *muðhæl*, 'salutary speech' (549–64), resembling in parts the Song of Moses (Exodus XV. 1–19, regularly used as an Old Testament canticle in liturgical worship), we, as much as the Israelites, should take to heart the message it proclaims: 'you will overcome every enemy and occupy the promised land if you keep God's holy precepts'.

This poet's dramatic story-telling was his means of implying, but only implying, a preaching communication to the effect that the virtues which his story demonstrated apply equally to our lives viewed as a voyage. It was not his way to make his narrative a systematic allegory of salvation. For example, his bold use of a sustained nautical metaphor which transformed the guiding pillar of cloud into a sail, the Israelites, following it, into sailors, and their journey through the desert and Red Sea into a voyage,[19] in my opinion psychologically suggested that his story is a parallel to man's life as a voyage,[20] but did not serve at all to apply a consistent typological train of thought (that the wilderness symbolized the church, that a ship commonly symbolized the church, and that therefore the Israelites journeying in the wilderness were figuratively sailors in the ship of the church).[21] The poet certainly alluded to such general considerations, as,

[18] With this account of the gist of 516–48, cf. Irving, '*Exodus* Retraced', pp. 211–12.

[19] 80b–4, 88b–9, 103b–6a, 132–3a, 221b–3a and 331–4a. No more than hinted at by source material; see Irving's nn. on 81 in *The Old English 'Exodus'* and 'New Notes on the Old English *Exodus*'.

[20] See Cross and Tucker, 'Allegorical Tradition and the OE *Exodus*', pp. 124–5.

[21] As proposed by Earl, 'Christian Traditions in the Old English *Exodus*', pp. 561–3. Lucas, while considering that 'the poem is not a consistent allegory, not even predominantly allegorical or figural', argues that two levels, the narrative and the

doubtless, when he celebrated as 'lifes latþeow' the pillar of cloud guiding the Israelites through the desert 'heahþegnunga haliges gastes' ('by high service of the holy spirit', 96):

Forð gesawon
lifes latþeow lifweg metan;
segl[22] siðe weold, sæmen æfter
foron flodwege

['They saw the guide of life measure the life-way; the sail controlled the journey, the seamen followed it on the sea-road', 103b–6a].

But most of all he was keen to exploit the dynamic relationship between 'seamen' and 'sail': they were amazed, overjoyed and puzzled as it led them, shielding them from the burning sun (75–85); the sight of it towering in the sky made them realize that the lord of hosts was signalling where they should camp (88b–92); they followed joyfully when they saw it indicating the way they should go (103b–7a); they were sailors as they swiftly pitched, or eagerly struck, their tents (129b–33a and 221b–3) and as they swept without fear across the salt marsh of the divided sea (331–5a). Their 'sailing', as Irving has well said, was a locomotion 'with its own strange and joyous power'; like seafarers they experienced what *landmen* (179b), the proud Egyptians, could not share.[23]

Nor, for all his implied 'preacher's' standpoint, did the poet ever resort to explicit moralizing in the telling of his tale – even a maxim. He concentrated exclusively on the active continuum of the Israelites marching, being pursued and escaping under the leadership of Moses, the man of God, and looked elsewhere only for props and stays of a world stage on which to mount this epic. He turned to biblical narrative and other materials for motifs in the drama of Israelite hopes and fears, rather as Shakespeare was to treat his sources centuries later. For instance, probably picking up from somewhere (a homily perhaps) the rhetorical formulation that the Israelites were trapped between warriors and waters when they

allegorical, neither of them fully coherent, were unified by the central theme of 'Salvation by Faith and Obedience' (*Exodus*, ed. Lucas, pp. 61–9). This seems to me to underestimate the subsuming dramatic force of the poem's language.

22 Krapp keeps MS *swegl*. In dealing with the many textual problems, I reproduce Krapp's readings whenever I can and limit myself to pointing out any significant respect in which I differ from him or he differs from the manuscript.

23 '*Exodus* Retraced', p. 214.

were encamped for the night before the sea miraculously divided in the morning,[24] the poet adopted it and gave to it his particular brand of theatricality:

> Hæfde nydfara   nihtlangne fyrst,
> þeah ðe him on healfa gehwam   hettend seomedon,
> mægen oððe merestream;   nahton maran hwyrft.
> Wæron orwenan   eðelrihtes,
> sæton æfter beorgum   in blacum reafum,
> wean on wenum

['The one compelled to travel had the space of a night, although enemies lay in wait for him on each side, soldiery or sea; they had no other way to turn. They despaired of their right to a country of their own, sat scattered over the hills in black clothes, in expectation of misery' (208–13a].

So they sat until at dawn Moses's trumpets of brass summoned them to have courage in their hearts and to don bright armour (215b–20a).

The extent to which the poet gave his graphic imagination scope to integrate his narrative is well illustrated by his treatment of the biblical *columna ignis*, 'pillar of fire' (already mentioned above), in which the Lord went before the Israelites by night to show them the way (Exodus XIII.21, *Exodus* 107b–33a).[25] As the poet conceived it, this was a strange and wonderful *heofonbeacen*, 'heaven-sign' (107b), which rose every evening as the sun set and shone brightly 'ofer sceotendum' ('over shooters', 112a), making their shield coverings gleam[26] and dissolving shadows so that no hiding place could be afforded to any enemy lurking nearby. It was a *heofoncandel*, 'heaven-candle' (115b), burning as an altogether new kind of *nihtweard*, 'night-guard' (116a), over the host,

> þy læs him westengryre,
> har hæðbroga,[27]   holmegum wederum
> on ferclamme[28]   ferhð getwæfde[29]

[24] See Irving, *The Old English 'Exodus'*, n. on 210, and 'New Notes on the Old English *Exodus*', n. on 209–10. In any case the Israelites were in a traditional Germanic heroic 'backs-to-the-wall' situation.

[25] For hints he probably received from sources, e.g. the psalms, see Irving, 'New Notes on the Old English *Exodus*', n. on 123–4.

[26] For 'shield covering' as the primary meaning of *scyldhreoða* (or *bordhreoða*, 159a), see *Cynewulf's 'Elene'*, ed. Gradon, n. on 122, and Irving, 'New Notes on the Old English *Exodus*', n. on *Exodus* 113.

[27] *broga* not in MS.   [28] MS *ofer clamme*.   [29] MS *getwæf*.

['lest wilderness-terror, grey heath-panic, by sea-storms should put an end to their lives in its panic-grip', 117b–19],

and shining as a fiery-haired forerunner warning the Israelites against disobedience to their leader (120–4).[30] The whole company, gleaming with the light from the sky,[31] saw the way stretching straight ahead until *sæfæsten*, 'the stronghold of the sea' (127b), obstructed them at the land's end, however eager they were to keep on moving:[32] 'fyrdwic aras' ('a camp arose', 129b); the men recovered from their tiredness; food-thegns served them; the sailors spread out over the hills with their tents (129b–33a). Similarly the Israelites reacted to the daytime pillar of cloud by more than just a seeing; they followed it joyfully and noisily:

sæmen æfter
foron flotwege.   Folc wæs on salum,
hlud herges cyrm

['the seamen followed it on the sea-road. The people was happy, the noise of the army loud', 105b–7a].

But in the case of the pillar of fire the host reflecting its light was identified with it so closely that the responses of seeing and of following were inseparable from one another: the very sight of the way ahead which it illuminated (126) propelled the Israelites in an irresistible forward movement, made explicit to us only as a fatigue which they consequently felt (130–1) and as an eagerness (129a) which, when they were thwarted by the sea, swept them up onto the hillsides, there to rest, eat and pitch their tents.[33] The poet imagined not so much a reaction as a highly dramatic, single, organic process.

The fear which the Israelites felt when they saw the Egyptians pursuing them brought out strongly the psychological strain in the poet's story-telling. In the Bible this fear is conveyed by a 'We told you so' reproach to

[30] See above, pp. 278–9.

[31] In spite of Irving's arguments in favour of *scirwerod* in 125a (in *The Old English 'Exodus'* and again in 'New Notes on the Old English *Exodus*') and Lucas's agreement with them (ed., *Exodus*, n. on 125), I prefer *scir werod*, as in Krapp's text.

[32] See Irving's nn. on 126–9a in *The Old English 'Exodus'* and 'New Notes on the Old English *Exodus*'.

[33] The Bible reports only God's instruction to Moses that his people should camp by the sea, so that Pharoah should conclude that they were trapped, and does not describe the Israelites' arrival there.

Moses (Exodus XIV. 10–12). Moses's reassurance of them follows (XIV. 13–14); then come God's instructions to Moses that the Israelites should strike camp and that Moses should raise his staff, stretch out his hand and divide the sea in two, so that the Israelites should pass safely through it and the Egyptians follow and be brought low (XIV. 15–18); and finally there is action by an angel of God resulting in the pillar of cloud moving between the Israelites and Egyptians so that neither could see the other throughout the night (XIV. 19–20). In the poem, however, the Israelites' fear became the single dominating motif right up to the angel's intervention and evoked the poet's full sense of melodrama. As he told the story, the news of pursuit came to the Israelites encamped by the Red Sea as *færspell*, 'sudden dangerous tidings' (1356), causing immediate 'wælgryre weroda' ('violent-death-terror of hosts', 137a).[34] Fear turned to despair when Pharoah's army was actually seen coming from the south with its spears, shields, trumpets and banners (154–60). In their hopelessness it seemed to the watchers as though the birds of prey which they could hear screaming and the wolves which they could hear howling were already picking the bones of the dead and exulting at midnight when the doomed spirit fled (162–9). All that these desperate beholders could do was observe with hostile eyes as Pharaoh rode in the lead exhorting his bold thegns (170–9). By the time they had comprehended the vastness of the Egyptian host, with its two thousand leaders, rank upon rank, they cried out in lamentation, enmeshed, as they now felt, in nets of violent death (180–203a).[35] Until an angel of God pushed away the proud Egyptians so that neither hostile force could see the other (204b–7), 'feond wæs anmod, / werud wæs wigblac' ('the enemy was resolute, the (Israelite) host was made pale by fear of war', 203b–4a).[36]

[34] An excursus on the previous relationship of the Israelites and Egyptians and how it bore on the present (140b–53) is interrupted by a loss of perhaps fifty lines between 141 and 142.

[35] For this figurative understanding of *wælnet* (202a), see Irving, *The Old English 'Exodus'*, n. on 201b–3a, and '*Exodus* Retraced', n. 50.

[36] I believe that the poet set up a terse, climactic contrast in this pair of clauses by using (and probably coining) the adjective *wigblac* in the sense I have attributed to it, just as he probably invented the compound *flodblac* in order to describe the Egyptians drowning in the Red Sea as 'flodblac here' ('an army made pale by fear of the flood', 498b); for the latter, see *The Old English 'Exodus'*, ed. Irving, n. on 498. Cf. also the probably metaphorical *herebleað*, 'intimidated by an army (of waves)' (454a), describing the Egyptians when terrified by the waters closing in behind them. On these three

Both the Israelites' mounting apprehension and the cause of it unfolding before their eyes were projected in vivid language. Compound nouns and adjectives which are found nowhere else in extant Old English are prominent, occurring on average once in every four lines.[37] *Wælgryre* (137a), *wælnet* (202a) and *wigblac* (204a) dramatize the fear (as quoted above), and *herefugolas*, 'birds that follow armies' (162a), *wælceasega*, 'carrion picker' (164a), and *cwyldrof*, 'bold to kill' (166b), contribute graphically to the nightmarish foreboding that there would be casualties before the night was out. *Cinberg* (175a) suggests the sharpness with which the Israelites observed Pharaoh,[38] while *mearcþreat*, 'border-troop' (173b), *herecist*, 'picked army' (177a), and *fyrdgetrum*,[39] 'warband' (178a), between them connote the threat, choiceness and strength of Pharoah's *comitatus*. And when it comes to the whole army, *heorowulfas*,[40] 'sword-wolves' (181a), *þræcwig* ('þurstige þræcwiges' ('thirsty for hard fighting', 182a)), *guðþreat*, 'battle troop' (193a), *mægenheapas*, 'powerful bands' (197b), and *broðorgyld*, 'vengeance for brothers' (199b), all convey its savage strength and fierce aggression. In this scene we participate in a prolonged interaction of witnesses and what they were witnessing. Our sympathies throughout lie firmly with the witnesses. Nor were these witnesses intended to function just as representative authenticators of traditional symbolic story,[41] or as a mere device to evoke eye-witness excitement, as was Cynewulf's anonymous observer of St Helena's fleet speeding across the sea to find the true cross.[42] Their anguish is primary. Their perception constitutes the main action. The description of their advancing enemies was organized as a stage-by-stage development in their psychology. The poet's language was directed first and foremost to dramatizing their feelings in response to what they saw.

In an even more striking departure from the Bible to the same effect, the

compounds, see further, below, pp. 291–2. Of the twenty-two other occurrences of *werod* in this poem (including 125a, on which see above, p. 283, n. 31, and a compound, *leodwerod* (77a)), fifteen refer to the Israelites, five (including one instance involving emendation at 8b) form part of the epithet 'Lord of hosts', and only two (170a and 194a) refer to the Egyptians.

37 Skaldic influence on this poet's unusual use of compounds has been suggested by Roberta Frank ('What Kind of Poetry is *Exodus?*').

38 'guðweard gumena grimhelm gespeon, / cyning cinberge' ('the war-guard of men fastened his mask-helmet, the king his chin-guard', 174–5a).

39 MS *syrd*. 40 MS *heora wulfas*. 41 See above, p. 189.

42 See above, pp. 276–7.

poet converted the crucial event in his story into an act of witness. After reporting the angel's separation of the two armies the Bible makes two discrete statements: firstly, that Moses (in obedience to God's command to him before the angel's intervention) stretched out his hand over the sea and the Lord drove the sea back all night by a strong wind, dividing it and leaving dry land in between (Exodus XIV.21); secondly, that the Israelites advanced on to the dry ground in the middle of the sea, the water forming a wall on each side of them (XIV.22). Regarded straightforwardly as the first two stages in the fulfilment of God's expressed plan,[43] the division of the waters and the Israelites' entry into the dry land needed no explicit circumstantial linkage. To the poet, however, concentrating on the Israelites' following of Moses's leadership, the psychological connection between these two stages was all-important. Dramatic presentation of how the one action led to the other was his first priority, and the bold solution he adopted was to recast radically the whole first stage as a traditional address by a leader to his troops before battle (256–98);[44] the fully described second stage (299–361) then became the response.

But that is not all. And this gives a clue to a likely form of influence from outside poetry: the exhortation which Moses gave his troops was, in effect, a brief but forceful 'sermon', with a divine, *færwundor*, 'sudden miracle' (279b – this is one of the poet's unique words), as its awe-inspiring testimony. 'Do not be afraid but trust in the Lord!' is the 'preacher's' message. The time of deliverance is at hand, he tells the Israelites (259–68a), but you forget God's teaching (268b–9a). Honour the prince of glory, he advocates, and ask the Lord of life for favour (269b–72). Your powerful defender is no less than the eternal God of Abraham, the Lord of all creation. And then the demonstration and exhortation follow in three stages. (1) See now ('Hwæt, ge nu eagum to on lociað . . .' ('Lo, look now with your eyes on . . .', 278)), most loved of peoples, a sudden miracle, how I have struck – this right hand of mine with its green token – the deep of the sea! The waves rise up, the water quickly forms defensive walls. Grey, flat paths open up for our army, where men have never trodden before and waves will extend ever afterwards. The south wind has divided the sea (278–91a). (2) I know very well the truth ('Ic wat soð gere' (291b)) that mighty God has shown you his mercy, long-fortunate warriors.

[43] For the content of the command which God gives to Moses in Exodus XIV.15–18 but which was omitted from the poem, see above, p. 284.

[44] Cf. Shippey, *Old English Verse*, pp. 138–40.

(3) Hurry to escape from the clutches of your enemies, now that the divine owner has raised up the red streams into a protecting shield ('Ofest is selost / þæt ge . . ., / nu se agend . . .' ('Haste is best that you . . . now the owner . . .', 293b–5a)). The bulwarks reach to the sky (291b–8)!

The sequence of the three phases which I have numbered above, consisting of (1) the speaker's recognition of a narrative situation, (2) his deduction from it and (3) his injunction to others to act quickly, was in itself no import from outside native tradition. We find it employed in similar calls to prompt action in other extant poems. *Beowulf* contains two examples. One is the coastguard's instruction to Beowulf and his companions newly arrived on the Danish shore: (1) 'No her cuðlicor cuman ongunnon / lindhæbbende, . . . / . . . / . . . Næfre ic maran geseah . . .' ('Never have shield-bearers arrived here more openly, . . . Never have I seen a greater . . .', 244–51a); (2) 'Nu ic eower sceal / frumcyn witan, . . .' ('Now I must know your lineage, . . .', 251b–4a); and (3) 'Nu . . . / . . . / . . . ofost is selest / to gecyðanne, . . .' ('Now . . . haste is best to make known, . . .', 254b–7). The other comes towards the end of the messenger's speech to the Geats after Beowulf's death: (1) 'Ne ic te Sweoðeode sibbe oððe treowe / wihte to wene, . . .' ('Nor do I at all expect peace or good faith from the Swedish people, . . .', 2922–98); (2) 'Þæt is sio fæhðo ond se feondscipe / . . . ðæs ðe ic wen hafo, . . .' ('That is the feud and enmity . . . which I expect, . . .', 2999–3007a); and (3) 'Nu is ofost betost, / þæt we . . .' ('Now haste is best that we . . .', 3007b–10a). A third instance occurs in *Andreas*, when a spokesman of the Mermedonians addresses his drowning fellow countrymen thus: (1) 'Us seo wyrd scyðeð, / heard ond hetegrim. Þæt is her swa cuð,' ('Our fate, hard and fierce, injures us. That is so evident here', 1561b–2); (2) 'is hit mycle selre, þæs þe ic soð talige, / þæt we . . .' ('it is much better, as I reckon the truth, that we . . .', 1563–5a and 1566–7a); and (3) '(ofost is selest)' '((haste is best)', 1565b). Evidently, so far as the frame of his 'sermon' is concerned, the *Exodus* poet was reproducing the pattern of the decision-forming process traditional to leadership by a recognized spokesman in Anglo-Saxon oral society and hence to representation of that type of leadership in vernacular poetry.

Unique in his case, among these others, however, is that the transition from (1) to (2) was between a seen phenomenon (a miraculous separation of the sea) and a spiritual unseen (God's mercy). With this we enter the domain of Christian didacticism, in particular that of homiletic narrative in vernacular prose. For example, in the second Vercelli Homily, which sets forth the whole panoply of mankind's fears on the day of judgement, the preacher makes one of his points by means of the same seen-to-unseen connection. After saying, 'La hwæt, we us ne ondrædaþ þæt we dæghwamlice geseoð beforan urum eagum, nu we þam oðrum ne gelyfað, ure þa neahstan sweltan, ⁊ þonne þam lichoman bið laðlic leger gegyrwed, in þære cealdan foldan gebrosnod, . . .' ('Lo, we are not afraid that we daily see before our eyes, now we do not believe the others [the mind's eyes], our nearest die, and then a loathsome place to lie is prepared for the body, decayed in the cold earth, . . .'), he continues, 'Hwæt, þæt þonne, la, bið sarlic sar ⁊ earmlic gedal þæs lichoman ⁊ þære sawle, gif þonne se earma innera man, . . . aslidan scile in þa ecean helle witu, . . .' ('Lo, that then is a grievous sorrow and a miserable separation of the body and the soul if then the wretched inner man, . . . shall slide down into the eternal torments of hell, . . .'). A parallel is being drawn between what we see daily and fail to fear and the fearful eternal reality which we do not see.[45] Poet and preacher alike were exploiting dramatically the relationship between what 'ge/we nu eagum to on lociað/geseoð beforan urum eagum' and the mightier unseen behind it. This poet chose to use a teaching technique to make the pivotal point of his narrative.

The effect this 'sermon' had on the Israelites was to make them respond as one man. But it is addressed to us as much as to them. The essence of God's dramatic deliverance of his chosen people has been distilled into direct speech by the principal protagonist for the benefit of our imagination, just as the mystery of the Virgin Birth is made devotionally accessible in the words of the Virgin Mary in the 'O' antiphon quoted above.[46] The immediate outcome of Moses's forthright words is in fact a clear picture which is not for Israelite perception but for our mind's eye:

Æfter þam wordum werod eall aras,
modigra mægen. Mere stille bad.
Hofon herecyste hwite linde,
segnas on sande. Sæweall astah,
uplang gestod wið Israhelum
andægne fyrst

['After those words the host, the force of proud men, all arose. The sea stayed still. The warbands of picked men raised their white shields, their banners on the sand. The wall of sea rose up, stood upright beside the Israelites for a whole day', 299–304a];

[45] *The Vercelli Homilies*, ed. Scragg, II, lines 56–68. [46] At p. 277.

and as the Israelites march on to the fresh ground tribe by tribe they show off in front of us:

Þracu[47] wæs on ore,
heard handplega, hægsteald modige,
wæpna wælslihtes, wigend unforhte,
bilswaðu blodige, beadumægnes ræs,
grimhelma gegrind, þær Iudas for

['Impetus was in the van, hard hand-play, proud young warriors, slaughter-strokes of weapons, warriors unafraid, bloody sword-swathes, onslaught of battle-force, grinding of mask-helmets, where Judah went', 326b–30].

This poem is a psychological depiction of one of God's great acts of mercy in human history equivalent in magisterial sweep to a similarly psychological depiction – as in the vernacular prose Vercelli II – of the trauma of Doomsday through which only the blessed will be allowed to pass into glory. The one actualizes in the present a drama of God's reward of salvation for obedience in the past, while the other actualizes in the present the drama of salvation as the final reward in the future for the same virtue.[48] The *Exodus* poet himself explicitly drew the parallel between the two subjects when, near the end of his poem, he alluded to the last

[47] MS *þraca*.

[48] The sequence of thought leading to a call to prompt action in Vercelli II is broadly similar to that of Moses's miniature 'sermon' in the poem, but, of course, on a grand scale. An opening section (ed. Scragg, lines 1–24) presents graphically the dire features of the judgement (the roaring fires, its utter darkness, the cross flowing with blood between clouds, the Lord's face in the terrible appearance it had when he was scourged and hanged and spat upon, the weeping of the sinful, the blowing of trumpets, the resurrection, our Lord sitting in glory, wounded in the eyes of the sinful but whole to the faithful, and finally the irrevocable judgement). A second section (24–68), equally dramatic, presents the various fears we ought to feel now, but do not – including the fear which death should instil in us – and a third (69–83) inculcates constructive principles of behaviour ('Ac utan we beon gemyndige . . .', 'wyrcen we . . .', 'forlætan we . . .', 'lufigen we . . .', 'syn we mildheorte . . .', 'geþrowigen we . . .'). Finally a fourth section (83–106), rehearsing our needs to be humble, to open our ears and hearts to the teachings of the gospel, and to repent, leads to a concluding, fifth, section of exhortations to swift avoidance of death ('Utan we nu for þam efstan to Gode, ær þan us se deað gegripe, . . .' ('Let us now hasten to God before the death seizes hold of us, . . .')) and to swift seeking of the eternal kingdom ('Utan we nu efstan to þan, þa hwile þe we ura wega wealdan moton' ('Let us hasten to that now, while we can control our paths')) – a state of unbroken, unending, light and bliss and glory and joy with our redeemer Lord.

judgement as the Lord's release of the faithful from exile into eternal life.[49] He is entirely likely to have found narrative inspiration in vernacular set-pieces on that great happening at the end of time, whether in prose or verse,[50] while eschewing their explicit didacticism and rhetorical structures.[51] For a poet of his exceptional gifts it would have been enough to feel their encouragement for his boldness in applying native poetic language with an extrovert sureness of psychological effect. The 'sermon' he attributed to Moses, grafting a spiritual dimension on to a native sequence of thought, was like his poem as a whole, which treated a subject of primary import by grafting on to 'pure' traditional, psychological, poetic narrative a rare intensity induced by spiritual uplift.

The linguistic boldness is everywhere apparent. The expression is consistently provoking. Unexpected images startle, as when the Egyptians, resenting the Israelites, 'wære fræton' ('devoured the treaty', 147b); or when Simeon's marching *garfaru*, 'spear-army' (343a), was 'deawig sceaftum' ('dewy with shafts', 344a); or when (in an excursus) Abraham's sword, drawn to sacrifice Isaac, *grymetode*, 'roared like a wild beast' (408b). One image presses on the heels of another, as in the mature plays of Shakespeare: the pillar of cloud becomes a canopy, a net, a storm cloud, a sail and a tent within thirteen 'lines' (73–85).[52] Symbolic genitive or adjective combinations signifying actors or actions, following one another in rapid succession, give an impression of intense vitality: in the display of *þracu* at the head of Judah's tribe, for instance, the sequence of seven combinations forming 327–30a, with its run of action/actor/action/actor/

[49] See above, p. 280.

[50] This awesome subject was open to poets as well as prose homilists. An extant poem, the anonymous *Christ III* (on which see, further, below, pp. 299–307) offers a full-scale treatment every bit as dramatic as the most graphic homily, and uses many of the same motifs, while, for example, a large part of a homily in Oxford, Bodleian Library, Hatton 113 (*Wulfstan*, ed. Napier, XXIX) is verbally dependent on a surviving poem, *The Judgement Day II* (ASPR 6).

[51] For instance, the sections of Vercelli II, described above, are staked out by rhetorical markers. In the first section, initial 'in/on þam dæge' (7×) and *þonne* (5×) are emphatically reiterated, occasionally in contrast to the *nu* of the present; in the second, the signal *Hwæt la/Eala hwæt/La hwæt*, *Hwæt* recurs (8×), gradually brought closer to home through being followed twice by 'men him (eallinga) ne ondrædaþ' and then twice by 'we us ne ondrædaþ'; the third section has its successive subjunctives, already mentioned; the fourth is marked principally by threefold 'Hwæt, we behofigað/gehyrað'; and the fifth has its twice-used *efstan* formula.

[52] Cf. *The Old English 'Exodus'*, ed. Irving, p. 32.

action/action/action referents and with a secondary 'actor' reference in each of its 'action' items, creates an energetic effect of a comitatus in the prime of life, resolute and proud, well armed with sword and helmet, fearless and powerful.

The sounds of words were pressed into service: when the waters closed in behind the Egyptians, *wæg*, 'wave' (458a), superseded *weg*, 'way' (458b);[53] when the Egyptians were struggling to escape from the waters closing in behind them, 'flod blod gewod' ('blood pervaded flood', 463b). A certain high-handedness with norms of meaning or syntax is not infrequently disconcerting – especially to modern critics.[54] Many unusual, often arresting, words occur. *Hapax legomena* amount to approximately 15 per cent of the total vocabulary: there is a fresh instance in about every three-and-a-half 'lines', a remarkably high frequency. Some of these must surely have been coinages. For instance, all eight denotations of fear in this poem, occurring ten times between them, are dramatic in character and are found nowhere else: five of them are symbolic compounds, each specifying in its first element the causal agent of the fear (*bellegsa* (121b),[55] *blodegesa* (478b),[56] *flodegsa* (447b), *wælgryre* (137a)[57] and *westengryre* (117b));[58] one is a symbolic genitive combination, *wraðra gryre*, 'terror caused by hostile men' (20b); another is a symbolic adjective combination, 'gyllende gryre' ('yelling terror', 490a); and the remaining one is the stark 'eg(e)san stodon' (3×).[59] *Herebleað* (454a), which I take to mean 'intimidated by an army',[60] and which is the only extant instance of a *-bleað* compound, was probably a bold metaphorical invention in the vein of the '-terror' compounds, for it was the waves closing in behind the Egyptians that were the intimidating army.[61] The poet's two '-pale' compounds, both unique (*flodblac* (498b)

[53] I take 458b to be the end of the sentence which includes 458a rather than the start of the next one.

[54] See Brodeur, 'A Study of Diction and Style', pp. 111–12.

[55] See above, pp. 278–9.

[56] See below, p. 295.

[57] See above, p. 284.

[58] See above, pp. 282–3. There are six compounds out of nine unique denotations if *hæðbroga* [MS only *hæð*] at 118a is counted; see above, *ibid.* Extant poetry shows a fair sprinkling of *-broga*, *-eg(e)sa* and *-gryre* compounds specifying the causal agent in the first element and all but four occur only once each. Evidently in the main they were nonce words in an established pattern.

[59] 136b, 201b and 491b.

[60] See also above, p. 284, n. 36.

[61] *Here-* means primarily 'army' rather than 'war' or 'battle' in probably all the other *here-* compounds in this poem, but if *herebleað* was intended to mean 'timid in battle' it would

and *wigblac* (204a)),[62] can be taken to indicate his keen sense of dramatic appearances, for only one other *-blac* compound is extant.[63] In *herewop*, 'army-cry' (461b), he seems to have invented a marvellously compact histrionic sign of corporate anguish, like a mighty dramatic gesture, for no other *-wop* compound is found. It is notable that all the three compounds he used to describe the Egyptian's terror and their expression of it in 447–67[64] (*flodegsa* (447b), *hereblead* (454a) and *herewop* (461b)) are extant only in this one place.

The outstanding gift of the *Exodus* poet was undoubtedly the peculiarly intense dramatic imagination with which he exploited language in this outwardly theatrical way, as in his description of the Red Sea waters finally receiving the signal to fall in upon the already struggling Egyptians. The biblical account merely relates that when Moses stretched forth his hand the sea returned to its former place and rushed upon the fleeing Egyptians (Exodus XIV.27), but, characteristically, the poet, engrossed in the dramatic *mise-en-scène*, identified this moment as a critical turning-point and turned his full imagination on to it:[65]

heah ofer hæleðum holmweall astah,[66]
merestream modig. Mægen wæs on cwealme
fæste gefeterod, forðganges nep,[67]
searwum æsæled, sand basnodon[68]
witodre fyrde, hwonne waðema stream,
sincalda sæ, sealtum yðum
æflastum gewuna ece staðulas,

still have been metaphorical (though less strongly), since the 'battle' concerned would have been against the waves.

[62] See above, p. 284, n. 36.

[63] *Heoro-* or *hildeblac* at *Beowulf* 2488a [MS only *blac*], according to which emendation is preferred.

[64] On this passage as a unit, see next n.

[65] It is usually said that he gives a confused account of the drowning of the Egyptians, but this is unfair to him. His description passes through three main stages: the Egyptians' fear as they struggled to escape the raging water cutting off their retreat and drowning many of them (447–67; for the vocabulary of 'terror' in this passage, see above); the actual caving in of the waters upon them (468–97a); and the total destruction of God's adversaries (497b–515). So much continuous action occupies the foreground of stages 1 and 2 and the beginning of stage 3 that the main transitions are not clearcut.

[66] I take *heah* to refer to *holmweall* and have emended Krapp's punctuation accordingly.

[67] Krapp changes MS *nep* to *weg* and has no comma.

[68] MS *barenodon;* Krapp has a comma after *basnodon*.

nacud nydboda, neosan come,
fah feðegast, se ðe feondum geneop.
Wæs seo hæwene lyft heolfre geblanden;
brim berstende blodegesan hweop,
sæmanna sið, oðþæt soð metod
þurh Moyses hand mod gerymde;[69]
wide wæðde, wælfæðmum sweop.
Flod famgode, fæge crungon,
lagu land gefeol, lyft wæs onhrered;[70]
wicon weallfæsten, wægas burston,
multon meretorras, þa se mihtiga sloh
mid halige hand, heofonrices weard,
on werbeamas.[71] Wlance ðeode
ne mihton forhabban helpendra pað,
merestreames mod, ac he manegum gesceod
gyllende gryre. Garsecg wedde,
up ateah, on sleap. Egesan stodon,
weollon wælbenna. Witrod gefeol
heah of heofonum handweorc godes,
famigbosma; flodweard gesloh[72]
unhleowan wæg alde mece,
þæt ðy deaðdrepe drihte swæfon,
synfullra sweot

['High above the warriors a wall of water rose up, a raging sea-current. The army was fettered fast in death, failing in their advance, bound in their wargear. Sands waited for the doomed host, until a stream of moving waters, the always cold sea, with salt waves, the one accustomed to wanderings, naked messenger of compulsion, would come seeking its eternal foundations, a hostile walking spirit, which overwhelmed enemies. The azure sky was mingled with blood; the bursting sea threatened the journey of seamen with blood-terror, until the true God through Moses's hand gave room to its anger; it ranged widely, swept with deadly embraces. The flood foamed, the doomed fell, sea fell on to the land, the sky was aroused; the bulwarks gave way, waves crashed, water-towers melted, when the mighty one struck the sea-pillars with the holy hand, the guardian of the kingdom of heaven. The proud peoples could not restrain the path of the helpers, the fury of

[69] Krapp changes to 'modge rymde' and follows with a comma.

[70] Krapp's punctuation is a comma.

[71] *on* not in MS.

[72] MS and Krapp *flodwearde sloh*; Krapp has no punctuation after *famigbosma* and a comma after *sloh*.

the sea-stream, but he destroyed many with a yelling terror. The sea raged, climbed up, slipped in; fears rose up, deadly wounds gushed. The handiwork of God fell high from heaven, foamy-bosomed, on the path of the army; the guardian of the flood struck the unsheltered wave with his ancient sword, so that the hosts slept with the deathblow, the company of the sinful'].

The main characteristics of the poet's vivid imagination are all here. A luridly personified sea keeps sand and crippled army alike waiting on the brink of inundation until, released, it hunts and sweeps its terrified victims in irresistible fury; some ten graphic metaphors follow one another in swift succession; unusual vocabulary (sixteen *hapax legomena*, fourteen of them compounds) keeps up a constant verbal pressure; sound effects strikingly match the ranging action of the sea (*geneop*, *hweop*, *sweop* (476b, 478b and 481b) its sudden sweeping; *mod*, *gesceod* (489) its purposeful fury; 'up ateah, on sleap' (491a) its once-for-all movement up and then down). During the psychologically tense period of suspense (468–79a) the four elements of the wall of water (468–9a), the trapped army (469b–71a), the waiting sands (471b–2a) and the half-obscured sky (477) are separately described, while the highly personalized, menacing, sea, denoted by four *nomina agentis* piled up on top of one another in the *a* verses of successive lines (473–6), looms overhead as an unstable mass. The moment its mighty pent-up forces have been released into an unstoppable hunting and sweeping (479b–81), all the elements crash together in a dramatic, compact series of four short, sharp, actor-action statements (482–3). God's control over the water, kept to subordinate clauses (479b–80 and 485b–7a) and thus leaving his wrathful, engulfing agent unlimited scope, is exercised as a freeing and a striking until he delivers the *coup de grâce* of complete destruction (495b–7a).

The poet's imagination sets the cataclysm before us not by means of clear-sighted direct observation – though realism of that sort was put to sharp effect in 482–3 – but as a psychological drama of tension and release – within a larger emotional and mental pattern. The poem as a whole oscillates between feelings of confidence and fear under changing conditions of confinement and liberation. This was the phase when the Israelites' resolve had been tested and not found wanting in a narrow, artificially produced, space between two towering walls of water, and when the worst fears of the Egyptians were about to be realized in the uncontrolled, exposed, unprotecting space of the open sea. A bizarre watery being of a sort which a riddler might conjure up, a wanderer by nature, a naked herald of compulsion, a hostile marching spirit, threatening any in its way with the terror of blood, was scarcely held at bay until it was set free to go on a pitiless rampage, hunting prey with embraces of violent death and, when catching any, destroying them with a terrible scream. The dramatic impact of the language – 'æflastum gewuna', 'nacud nydboda', 'fah feðegast', *blodegsan*, *wælfæðmum*, 'gyllende gryre' – convinces us of this beast's kinetic essence, its concentrated hostility, its aggression, its power to terrorize, its physical strength. Its nakedness and scream disturb us. We experience a horrifying sensation of limitless brute force unleashed. A series of invented surreal images,[73] expressed in extrovert language of intrinsic vitality, releases in our imaginations a chilling figure of nature's insatiable appetite for aggression let loose by God upon his enemies in the event itself. The poet achieved a *tour de force* of concentrated cosmic psychological theatre not matched elsewhere in extant Old English poetry and only rarely in literature at all.

Adoption of rhetorical methods was the most usual effect of Christian didactic tradition on vernacular poets telling the moral story of a world bound to a primary distinction between sin and obedience to God. Rhetorical techniques, in verse or prose, for presenting invented direct speech made a particular mark, for instance. A vernacular poet might have been impressed by, say, St Boniface's pointed use of such devices in a Latin prose letter which he wrote to a certain Eadburg 716 × 719, recounting graphically a vision by a monk at Wenlock of the horrendous testing each soul will have to endure when passing into eternity mobbed by its sins shouting at it in accusation while its virtues speak out in excuse.[74] In Boniface's description each vice and virtue identifies itself in person, and angels and purified souls make various comments too, such as this brief lament by angels when compelled by the sinner's own wickedness to relinquish to tormenting devils the soul of Ceolred, king of Mercia: 'Pro dolor, quod homo peccator iste semet ipsum plus defendere non permittit; et ob ipsius propria merita nullum ei adiutorium possumus prebere' ('Alas,

[73] The wall of water and the hand of Moses as God's instrument were already in the biblical narrative of the crossing of the Israelites and engulfing of the Egyptians (Exodus XIV.22 and 26–7), and so were motifs of the sea returning to its former place (XIV.27), of its waves rolling in on the Egyptians (*ibid.*), and, in the Song of Moses (XV.1–19), of flowing waves under God's control first standing (8) and then, when covering the Egyptians, violent (*vehemens*, 10). But introduction of all else seems to have been due to the poet.

[74] *S. Bonifacii et Lullii Epistolae*, ed. Tangl, pp. 8–15 (no. 10).

that this sinful man does not permit himself to defend himself any more; and on account of his very own deserts we can give him no help').[75] In the initial clause a first **p**, **d**, **p** sequence (**P***ro*, **d***olor*, **p***eccator*) and another (**p***lus*, **d***efendere*, **p***ermittit*) enclose between them a cluster of pronouns intensifying the king's individual responsibility for his plight,[76] and in the second clause another three-unit sequence, this time alliterating only on **p** (**p***ropria*, **p***ossumus*, **p***rebere*) emphasize the link between the king's own deserts and the angels' helplessness. Boniface was using alliteration in a Latin manner very effectively to reinforce the moral point. Knowledge of direct speech in moral Latin narratives such as this, it seems reasonable to suppose, encouraged another Englishman, the anonymous poet of *Genesis A*, telling in the vernacular with strict fidelity to the biblical text the story of God's purposes working themselves out, to take the licence (rare for him) of supposing that Hagar, Sarah's servant, gave a highly contrived account of her situation in reply to an angel's questioning of why she was alone in the wilderness. According to the Bible (Genesis XVI.8) the maid simply answered 'I flee from the face of my mistress Sarah', but according to *Genesis A* responded,

> Ic fleah wean, wana   wilna gehwilces,
> hlæfdigan hete,   hean of wicum,
> tregan and teonan.   Nu sceal tearighleor
> on westenne   witodes bidan,
> hwonne of heortan   hunger oððe wulf
> sawle and sorge   somed abregde

['I have fled from grief, deprived of every joy, from the hatred of my lady, wretched out of the dwellings, from pain and wrong. Now with tears on my cheeks I must await my fate in the desert until hunger or wolf has wrenched from my heart soul and sorrow together', 2274–9].

This is definitely a servant who has risen above her station. The well-contrived sound-play (*fleah wean*, *wana* . . . *hean*) concluding with an alliterative pairing ('tregan and teonan'), the stylish pictorial allusion to grief (*tearighleor*) and the dramatic image of the outcome elegantly presented with zeugma (hunger or wolf plucking soul and sorrow, the

[75] *Ibid.*, p. 14.

[76] *Semet ipsum* here may have conveyed the same notion of an inner thinking self as it did when (occasionally) translated by King Alfred as *ingeðonc* ('. . . does not permit his inner thought to . . .'); see below, p. 389.

second pairing enhanced by self-alliteration) all bespeak a delicate mastery of formal rhetoric which would have graced her mistress herself. One can appreciate how Sarah had come to feel that Hagar, now bearing Abraham's child at Sarah's own instigation, was upstaging her.

The main contribution which this tradition of imagined rhetorical speech made to vernacular poetry was to furnish the principal protagonists in the moral story of the world with set-piece declamations of their states of mind. There was, for instance, a tradition, traceable at least as far back as Gaul around the year 500 (in a Latin 'epic' poem by Avitus, bishop of Vienne), of assigning to Satan a formal lament declaimed from hell after his fall from heaven. Some 200 years later, Aldhelm showed signs that the tradition was known in England, for in one of his Latin *Enigmata* (LXXXI) he had Lucifer, the morning star, say 'Oh, happy I was in times past, when I obeyed the law of the Thunderer! Alas! I subsequently fell, proud in my impudent arrogance, wherefore punishment cast down the deadly enemy' (6–8).[77]

Emphasis varied in the use of this model, according to the circumstances an author envisaged: in *Genesis B* (an Old English version of an Old Saxon poem)[78] Satan, still smarting from his expulsion from heaven and intent on malicious vengeance at the expense of Adam and Eve, uttered self-righteous defiance and could still appeal successfully to a sense of gratitude in his comitatus of fallen angels, but in another Old English poem, *Christ and Satan*, Satan, imagined to be at some later stage between his fall and the harrowing of hell, launched into a series of plaints as *se werega gast*, 'the accursed spirit' (125a), and his comitatus reviled him. In this latter poem the fallen angels were represented as a greedy, rapacious crew ('gredige and gifre', 32a and 191a) and Satan was a leader with only limited understanding. He could recognize that he and his fellows had acted out of excessive pride (*oferhygd* (50a and 113a)) and could acknowledge that he was 'nið-synnum[79] fah' ('stained with sins of hostility' (179b)), but that was where his comprehension stopped. He had no inkling of what it was to have sinned against God and therefore no notion of repentance. He appreciated keenly his loss of status and of tangible possessions and the hatefulness of his present home, but the only lessons he had learned were that his loss was greater than he had had any reason to expect and that his forfeiture without

[77] *Aldhelmi Opera*, ed. Ehwald, p. 135.

[78] See further, below, pp. 363–4 and n. 2.

[79] MS *mid synnum*.

remission was the penalty which the king of heaven exacts from anyone failing to obey and please him.[80] He condemned his pride only for its consequences.[81] The hands with which he yearned to reach heaven were still possessive, not penitential,[82] when he lamented in words flying forth in sparks which were very like poison,[83]

Eala drihtenes þrym! Eala duguða helm!
Eala meotodes miht! Eala middaneard!
Eala dæg leohta! Eala dream godes!
Eala engla þreat! Eala upheofen!
Eala þæt ic eam ealles leas ecan dreames,
þæt ic mid handum ne mæg heofon geræcan,
ne mid eagum ne mot up locian,
ne huru mid earum ne sceal æfre geheran
þære byrhtestan beman stefne!
Ðæs ic wolde of selde sunu meotodes,
drihten adrifan, and agan me þæs dreames gewald,
wuldres and wynne, me þær wyrse gelamp
þonne ic to hihte agan moste.
Nu ic eom asceaden fram þære sciran driht,
alæded fram leohte in þone laðan ham.
Ne mæg ic þæt gehicgan hu ic in ðæm becwom,
in þis neowle genip, niðsynnum[84] fah,
aworpen of worulde. Wat ic nu þa
þæt bið alles leas ecan dreamas
se ðe heofencyninge heran ne þenceð,
meotode cweman

[80] Cf. Sleeth, *Studies in 'Christ and Satan'*, p. 53. The contrast with *Genesis B* in the treatment of the comitatus is pointed out *ibid.*, p. 12.

[81] Cf. *ibid.*, p. 22. [82] Cf. *ibid.*, p. 16.

[83] 161b–2; cf. 78–9a. For discussion and examples of the general background of this fiery image of Satan's pernicious speech, see the note on 78a, *Christ and Satan*, ed. Clubb, p. 65; Hill, 'Satan's Fiery Speech'; and Keenan, 'Satan Speaks in Sparks'. The 'sprungon spearcan of þam muðe', cited and discussed by Hill as a terrifying feature of the devil revealed by an angel in the entry on St Bartholomew in the Old English Martyrology, was a straight rendering of 'scintillas emicantes ex ore eius' in the full *passio* of St Bartholomew which the martyrologist was abbreviating. The late-tenth-century vernacular prose homilist Ælfric, following the same source, had the sparks coming from the devil's eyes and sulphurous flame from its mouth. For the latest account of the precise text used by the martyrologist and Ælfric, see Cross, 'The Apostles in the *Old English Martyrology*', pp. 19–20.

[84] See above, p. 297, n. 79.

['Alas the glory of the Lord! Alas the protector of hosts! Alas the might of God! Alas the world! Alas the bright day! Alas the joy of God! Alas the troop of angels! Alas the heaven above! Alas that I am altogether bereft of eternal joy, that I cannot reach heaven with my hands, nor am allowed to look up with my eyes, nor indeed shall ever with my ears obey the call of the clearest-sounding trumpet! Because I intended to drive the son of God, the Lord, out of his hall and possess for myself dominion over the joy, the glory and the pleasure, worse befell me there than I could expect. Now I am separated from the shining company, led away from light into the hateful home. I cannot understand how I came into this deep darkness, stained with sins of hostility, cast out of the world. Now I know that he who does not think to obey the king of heaven, to please God, will be entirely bereft of eternal joy', 163–83a].

The concern of the 'I have learned' narrator of this poem (224a) was not to analyse the *oferhygdu*, 'arrogance' (6×),[85] *anmedla*, 'presumption' (74a) and *womcwide*, 'evil words' (281b), of Satan, or to compare them with the sin of Adam and Eve in their fall, but was to exhort every man here and now to beware of the fallen angels' example and to live with well-disposed thoughts, a sense of kinship, and wisdom in his breast (205–6a), so that in due course he might pass to heaven shining with righteousness (210b–11 and 306–8a) and fragrant with good deeds rooted in the words of God (355–7), there to receive the embrace and blessing of the father of mankind and to be led into eternal light (358–61a). The advocated response to Satan's self-revealed sickness (274a) was cultivation of a 'healthy, sweet-smelling, luminous spirit'.[86] A maxim summed up the moral principle involved:

Blæd bið æghwæm
þæm ðe hælende heran þenceð,
and wel is þam ðe þæt wyrcan mot

['There will be splendour for everyone who thinks to obey the saviour, and well is it for him who can accomplish that', 362b–4].

Above all, Old English poetic narration of the moral story of the world was supplied by Latin rhetorical preaching in early-sixth-century southern Gaul with a striking climax in the form of a stern indictment by Christ the judge. According to one of the sermons of Caesarius, bishop of Arles, Christ will arraign mankind after their resurrection on the day of judgement by invoking the essence of all God-related human history

[85] 50a, 69a, 113a, 196a, 226a and 369a.

[86] Sleeth, *Studies in 'Christ and Satan'*, p. 23.

'adstante ad testimonium conscientia singulorum, positis in conspectu peccatorum poenis iustorumque praemiis' ('with the conscience of every single person present for evidence and with the punishments of sins and the rewards of just deeds placed in view').[87] The anonymous poet of the eschatological *Christ III* in the Exeter Book adopted this disturbing expectation (though not necessarily directly from Caesarius), as did several anonymous composers of vernacular prose homilies.[88] The Latin speech which the poet followed (most of the version in Caesarius's sermon) presented Christ as an expert prosecutor of a silent representative of all humanity, created, fallen and redeemed:

> I created you, man, from earth with my hands, I infused spirit into your earthen limbs, I deigned to confer on you our image and likeness, I placed you among the delights of paradise: you, despising the vital commands, preferred to comply with the deceiver rather than with the Lord. But I pass over ancient matters. Moved afterwards by pity, when expelled from paradise by the law of sin you were held in bondage by the chains of death, I entered a virgin womb to be born without loss of virginity, I lay exposed in a crib and wrapped in cloths, I bore the ignominies of infancy and human sorrows, so that by them I might be like you (that is to say, that I might make you like me) I received the palms and spittle of jeerers, I drank vinegar with gall: beaten with scourges, crowned with thorns, fixed to a cross, pierced with a wound, that you might escape death, I sent my soul among torments. Behold the prints of the nails with which I hung fastened: behold my side pierced with wounds. I incurred your sorrows that I might give you my glory, I incurred your death that you might live for ever. I lay buried in a tomb that you might reign in heaven. Why have you lost what I brought you? Why, ungrateful, have you refused the gifts of your redemption? I do not ask anything of you on account of my death: return to me your life for which I gave mine; return to me your life which you destroy constantly with wounds of sins. Why have you desecrated with defilements of luxury the habitation which I had consecrated for myself in you? Why have you disfigured the body which is already mine with the unsight-

87 *Sancti Caesarii Arelatensis Sermones*, ed. Morin, *Opera* I, 253.

88 The poet's debt to Caesarius was first pointed out in the edition of Cook (*The Christ of Cynewulf*, p. 210). *Christ III* is now regarded as not by Cynewulf, and it is not known whether Caesarius was the inventor of the speech. For a recent summary of the reuse by the vernacular homilists, see *Eleven Old English Rogationtide Homilies*, ed. Bazire and Cross, p. 129, n. 6. For use of Caesarius's sermons as sources in Old English literature generally, see Trahern, 'Caesarius of Arles and Old English Literature'.

> liness of shameful enticements? Why have you fastened me on a cross of your crimes heavier than the one on which I formerly hung? The cross of your sins on which I hang against my will is indeed heavier for me than that on which willingly, out of pity for you, I climbed to kill your death.'[89]

'I did this and this and this and this to you', Christ passionately avers in Caesarius's tightly controlled structure: 'You did that to me (1–5). Then, out of pity for you, I underwent this and this and this so that you might gain so-and-so, and I suffered this and this and this so that you might not do likewise (5–13). See . . .! See . . .! I did this so that you might do that and this so that you might do that and this so that you might do that (13–17). Why have you lost . . .? Why have you refused . . .? Why have you desecrated . . .? Why have you disfigured . . .? Why have you nailed . . .? (17–28).

The vernacular poet paraphrased the Latin step by step (*Christ (III)* 1379–1494), greatly altering its structure and tone in the process. Comparison of the first three 'I did so-and-so' statements of the Latin with their vernacular equivalents – firstly the wording in one of the prose

[89] 'Ego te, homo, de limo manibus meis feci, ego terrenis artubus infudi spiritum, ego tibi imaginem nostram similitudinemque conferre dignatus sum, ego te inter paradisi delicias conlocavi: tu vitalia mandata contemnens, deceptorem sequi quam dominum maluisti. Sed antiqua praetereo. Motus postea misericordia, cum expulsus de paradiso iure peccati mortis vinculis tenereris, virginalem uterum sine dispendio virginitatis pariendus introii, in praesepio expositus et pannis obvolutus iacui, infantiae contumelias humanosque dolores, quibus tibi similis fierem, ad hoc scilicet ut te mihi similem facerem, tuli, inridentium palmas et sputa suscepi, acetum cum felle bibi: flagellis caesus, vepribus coronatus, adfixus cruci, perfossus vulnere, ut te eripereris morti, animam meam inter tormenta dimisi. En clavorum vestigia, quibus adfixus pependi: en perfossum vulneribus latus. Suscepi dolores tuos, ut tibi gloriam meam darem: suscepi mortem tuam, ut tu in aeternum viveres. Conditus iacui in sepulcro, ut tu regnares in caelo. Quur quod pro te pertuli perdidisti? Quur, ingrate, redemptionis tuae munera rennuisti? Non tibi ego de morte mea quero: redde mihi vitam tuam, pro qua meam dedi: redde mihi vitam tuam, quam vulneribus peccatorum indesinenter occidis. Quur habitaculum, quod mihi in te sacraveram, luxuriae sordibus polluisti? Quur corpus iam meum inlecebrarum turpitudine maculasti? Quur me graviore criminum tuorum cruce, quam illa in qua quondam pependeram, adfixisti? Gravior enim aput me peccatorum tuorum crux est, in qua invitus pendeo, quam illa in qua volens tui misertus mortem tuam occisurus ascendi' (*Sancti Caesarii Arelatensis Sermones*, ed. Morin, *Opera* I, 253). I have incorporated two of Morin's minor variant readings which clearly were in the text used by the poet.

homilies[90] and secondly the wording in *Christ III* – is enough to show the change:

Ego te, homo, de limo manibus meis feci,

Eala man, hwæt, ic þe geworhte of eorþan lame mid minum handum,

> Hwæt, ic þec mon   minum hondum
> ærest geworhte,   ond þe ondgiet sealde.
> Of lame ic þe leoþo gesette

['Lo, I first made you man with my hands, and gave you understanding. I formed limbs for you from clay', 1379–81a];

ego terrenis artubus infudi spiritum,

7 þinum ðam eorðlicum limum ic sealde mine sawle,

> geaf ic ðe lifgendne gæst

['I gave you a living spirit', 1381b];

ego tibi imaginem nostram similitudinemque conferre dignatus sum,

7 ic þe hiwode to mines sylfes anlicnesse,

> arode þe ofer ealle gesceafte,   gedyde ic þæt þu onsyn hæfdest,
> mægwlite me gelicne.   Geaf ic þe meahta sped,
> welan ofer widlonda gehwylc,   nysses þu wean ænigne dæl,
> ðystra þæt þu þolian sceolde.   Þu þæs þonc ne wisses

['honoured you above all creatures, I saw to it that you had an appearance, a beauty, like me. I gave you an abundance of powers, riches over every spacious land, you knew no portion of sorrow, of darkness, that you had to suffer. You knew no gratitude for that', 1382–5].

The much more frequent explicit references to the human 'you' in the poem, as compared with the Latin and with the vernacular prose, signal the shift: the Latin has only two (*te* and *tibi*) and the vernacular prose only three (*þe*, *þinum* and *þe*), but the poem has no less than ten, outnumbering the seven references to the divine 'me'. Indeed the pronoun *ic* occurs (5×) only in close association with *þe*. The stark antithesis in the Latin between, on the one hand, reiterated *ego* . . ., *ego* . . ., *ego* . . ., *ego* . . . (the three I have quoted and one more after them) and, on the other hand, a single decisive *tu* . . . following them collectively has been wholly abandoned in the poem

[90] *The Vercelli Homilies*, ed. Scragg, VIII, lines 46–9.

(though not in the vernacular prose). Instead the listening human 'you' has become an integral part of what the divine 'I' says: the 'you' is still a silent one, but his/her feelings are within, not beyond, the speaker's purview. The contrast is no longer between a superior 'I' and a 'you' about to be declared disobedient but is between two emotional attitudes, expansive conferment of infinite bliss (1383b–5a) and restrictive absence of gratitude (1385b). An intimate relationship between creator and created runs through the alliteration like a thread: *mon-minum*, *ærest-ondgiet*, *lame-leoþo-lifgendne*, *arode-ealle-onsyn*, *mægwlite-me-meahta*, *welan-widlonda-wean* and *ðystra-þolian-þonc*. The peremptory utterances of an accuser have turned into an elegiac expression of reproach.

But, if the poet did not maintain the antitheses based on the formal sentence structure of his Latin prose source, he introduced others on the smaller scale of the binary phrasing of his vernacular verse. For example, he constructed on this principle, with little or no hint from Caesarius's Latin, a telling concluding formulation of what Christ had done for each individual member of the human race:

Ic wæs on worulde wædla þæt ðu wurde welig in heofonum,
earm ic wæs on eðle þinum þæt þu wurde eadig on minum

['I was poor in the world that you might become rich in heaven, I was wretched in your country that you might become fortunate in mine', 1495–6].

Combining three individually clearcut but mutually supportive conceptual contrasts between unhappiness and happiness, between the 'patria' of earth and that of heaven, and between 'I (Christ)' and 'you (human being)' gave considerable scope for subtlety. Set out as a group twice in a pair of parallel, plainly structured, two-clause sentences, which occupy a long 'line' of verse each and are linked to one another by rhyme (*heofonum-þinum-minum*), these distinctions are developed interactively by a blend of the 'old' traditional form and the 'new' rhetorical techniques. The basic opposition between wretchedness and bliss is firmly established in each sentence by an alliterative word pair (*wædla/welig* and *earm/eadig*) and the two terms for the leading concept of 'happiness' are rhymed (*welig-eadig*). In both sentences inverted word order correlates with 'unhappiness' in the main clause and normal order with 'happiness' in the subordinate clause. In the first sentence chiasmus marks a contrast between two associations of condition and place (*on worulde wædla / welig in heofonum*), while in the second sentence, by marking a contrast between two associations of condition and person (*earm ic wæs / þæt þu wurde eadig*), it balances this distinction with the third, completing one between two associations of place and person, pointed up this time by rhyme (*eðle þinum / minum*). The simple matter of the heart, that Christ's love was expressed in unselfish actions, is made explicit in unaffected vocabulary; the deliberate formulation of the utterance corresponds to the calculated operation of this love and to intellectual appreciation that failure to be grateful for it (a charge explicitly restated in the next sentence, 1497–8) has had incalculable consequences for the fate of humanity in all eternity. Universal thoughts and personal feelings are as inextricably entwined in this expression as they always are in the great events of world history themselves.

Narrative in a poem such as *Christ III* was concerned not with actions symbolizing the principles of society's military élite, as in native pre-Christian tradition, but with thoughts and feelings epitomizing the drama of living in a God-centred world. Feelings of sorrow, gratitude and devotion were every individual's bond with God because of – indeed, in spite of – all that had happened in the history of mankind; thoughts readily took the form of warnings to all of what lies ahead. Vocabulary was used less than before as a register of interactive potentials recognized by social tradition and more as a set of signs positioned in the verse to mark the flow of emotion or to point up the force of admonition. Vernacular verse was increasingly treated as a preexisting framework for rhetorical expression. A poet of the *Christ III* sort was regarding its structure more abstractly than had his predecessors.

Through this fondness for direct, narrative-conveyed, moral instruction of his fellow men a poet-narrator became first cousin to an Old English prose preacher and shared with him many a dramatic motif already enshrined in Latin didactic tradition. The idea that Christ will come to judge on Doomsday, appearing kind and gracious to the good but fearful and terrible to the bad is an instance[91] common to *Christ III* and an early-eleventh-century expanded version of approximately the first half of Vercelli Homily II.[92] Poet and sermonist were equally intent on emphasiz-

[91] For a recent summary of scholarly identifications of antecedents for the various features of this distinction, in Gregory the Great's *Moralia* and elsewhere, see Biggs, *The Sources of 'Christ III'*, pp. 9–11.

[92] *Wulfstan*, ed. Napier, XL, published again more recently Stanley, '*The Judgement of the Damned*', pp. 370–9, and *The Vercelli Homilies*, ed. Scragg, facing Vercelli II (each editor using a manuscript (not the same one) which supplied only variants to Napier). It is

ing that behaviour here and now is the critical factor in this ultimate distinction.

Each, however, went about putting the message across in terms of his own tradition. For the sermonist the moral principle came first: God's teaching, he proclaimed at the outset, is that only truthful and righteous conduct in this life can protect us 'on þam egeslican dæge' ('on that terrible day'); and to make the point he proceeded (as Vercelli II had begun) by declaiming stages in the great judgement representing its fearfulness and each heralded by 'In/on þam dæge . . .'. On the eighth occasion the declaration was 'In þam dæge ure drihten cymð in his þam miclan mægenþrymme mid þam nigon endebyrdnessum heofonwara þæt bið mærlic ⁊ wunderlic mægenþrym. ⁊ þonne bið he þam synfullum swiðe wrað æteowod, ⁊ þam soðfæstum he bið bliðe gesawen' ('On that day our Lord will come with his great retinue, with the nine orders of the inhabitants of heaven. That will be a glorious and wonderful retinue. And then he will be revealed to the sinful very angry and to the righteous he will appear well disposed').[93] The terror we ought to feel *now* at this awful prospect, but do not, was the sermonist's next point. For the poet, on the other hand, the appropriate procedure was to present a fully fledged dramatic narrative, with stark moral contrast its theme, so that the ability of the man who is wise here and now to participate in it fearlessly could be duly appreciated:

Þonne semninga   on Syne beorg
suþaneastan   sunnan leoma
cymeð of scyppende   scynan leohtor
þonne hit men mægen   modum ahycgan,
beorhte blican,   þonne bearn godes
þurh heofona gehleodu   hider oðyweð.
Cymeð wundorlic   Cristes onsyn,
æþelcyninges wlite,   eastan fram roderum,
on sefan swete   sinum folce,
biter bealofullum,   gebleod wundrum
eadgum ond earmum   ungelice.

extant in four manuscripts altogether and is longer in one of them (the one printed by Scragg) than in the other three. Scragg gives a clear account of their relationship to one another and to Vercelli II. For Vercelli II, see above, pp. 289–90, nn. 48 and 51.

93 *The Vercelli Homilies*, ed. Scragg, II, lines 27–31 (MS N). Vercelli II reads, 'On þam dæge siteð ure dryhten in his þam myclan mægenþrymme ⁊ his onsyne ætyweð . . . his lichoman; þonne bið seo wund gesewen þam firenfullum, ⁊ þam soðfæstan he bið hal gesewen' (ed. Scragg, lines 15–18).

He bið þam godum glædmod on gesihþe,
wlitig, wynsumlic, weorude þam halgan,
on gefean fæger, freond ond leoftæl,
lufsum ond liþe leofum monnum
to sceawianne þone scynan wlite,
weðne mid willum, waldendes cyme,
mægencyninges, þam þe him on mode ær
wordum ond weorcum wel gecwemdun.
He bið þam yflum egeslic ond grimlic
to geseonne, synnegum monnum,
þam þær mid firenum cumað, forð forworhte.
Þæt mæg wites to wearninga þam þe hafað wisne geþoht,
þæt se him eallunga owiht ne ondrædeð,
se for ðære onsyne egsan ne weorþeð
forht on ferðe, þonne he frean gesihð
ealra gesceafta ondweardne faran
mid mægenwundrum mongum to þinge,
ond him on healfa gehwone heofonengla þreat
ymbutan farað, ælbeorhtra scolu,
hergas haligra, heapum geneahhe

['Then suddenly on Mount Sion from the south-east the light of the sun will come from the creator shining more brilliantly than men can imagine it in their minds, gleaming brightly, when the son of God appears hither through the lids of the heavens. Christ's wonderful form will come from the east, the beauty of the noble king, from the skies, sweet in disposition to his own people, angry to the wicked, wondrously varied, differently to the blessed and the wretched. He will be joyful in appearance to the good, beautiful and gracious to the holy company, lovely in gladness, friendly and kind; it will be pleasant and serene for dear men to behold the radiant figure, delightfully benign, the coming of the ruler, of the king of power, for those who have well pleased his spirit in words and deeds. For evil men he will be terrible and fierce to see, for sinful men who come there with crimes, destroyed for evermore. It can be a defence against punishment for him who has wise thought, that he who has absolutely nothing to fear will not become afraid in his mind before the awe of that appearance, when he beholds the Lord of all creatures become present with mighty wonders for a meeting with many, and a throng of heavenly angels encircles him on every side, a host of radiant beings, armies of saints, in multitudes abundantly'].

Up to a point the poet was loyal to his conventional craft both as story-teller and as moralizer. His circumstantial, increasingly dramatic, narrative of Christ's manifestation[94] stood in the same broad tradition as did Grendel's advance on Heorot where Beowulf awaited him,[95] and his moral point was related to the time-honoured concept of 'he who is wise' (921b). But the circumstantial features of Christ's revelation ('on Syne beorg', 'suþaneastan', 'þurh heofona gehleodu' and 'eastan fram roderum'), culled from a variety of sources,[96] were not intended to develop psychological tension between watched and watchers, as similar details in *Beowulf* were. The progressive action of the watched and the two contrasting kinds of observation by the watchers were each set out separately and at length,[97] as was the fourth element, of the observers' fear of punishment, from which a wise man can protect himself by having a clear conscience (921–9). The story was being told in such a way as to display its moral components side by side for our benefit and its circumstantial features were meant to serve that end: the sunlight eradiating from the creator brighter 'þonne hit men mægen modum ahycgan' and the son of God's approach *hider* (904b) were explicit calls to our imagination. In his own way the poet was addressing his audience of the here-and-now as directly as was the preacher.[98]

Poetry of this kind, following the precepts of rhetoric as to how best to lay out eternal moral wares before the gaze of earthly watchers, lost its hold on the organically interactive narrative which had been the monopoly of vernacular poetic tradition from time immemorial. Rhetoric, in fact, proved something of a poisoned chalice to verse. Applicable to moral narrative in either prose or poetry, it combined with the former more strongly, partly because that medium made overt didacticism primary and partly because comprehensive prose teaching could be systematically parcelled up, as in Ælfric's two series of *Catholic Homilies*, each providing a year's preaching. As the stronger, prose could, and did, absorb the narrative strength of the weaker, poetry. It seized the initiative when poetry slackened its grip. The vernacular prose preacher, Ælfric, reinstated

94 'Þonne semninga on Syne beorg / suþaneastan sunnan leoma / cymeð of scyppende scynan . . . (899–901) . . . Cymeð wundorlic Cristes onsyn / . . . eastan fram roderum (905–6) . . .'

95 'Com on wanre niht / scriðan sceadugenga (*Beowulf* 702b–3a) . . . Ða com of more under misthleoþum / Grendel gongan (710–11a) . . . Com þa to recede rinc siðian (720) . . .'

96 See Biggs, *The Sources of 'Christ III'*, pp. 9–10.

97 899–909, 910–17 and 918–20.

98 It is worth noticing that he shares the pairing, 'egeslic ond grimlic' (918b), with Archbishop Wulfstan; see *Sermo Lupi ad Anglos*, ed. Whitelock, line 8 (referring to the coming of Antichrist).

interactive thought as the principle of didactic narrative. For him, imbued as he was with late-tenth-century/early-eleventh-century monasticism, the primary function of narrative was not to catch erring humanity's attention by dramatic display but to promote men's communion with God, and the task of explicit teaching was to furnish explanatory comment which would foster this relationship.[99] The day of judgement, for example, was in his view first and foremost a demonstration of the power that belongs to God alone, and accordingly, in treating its advent,[100] Ælfric, for testimony to this unique universal might, concentrated on two dicta of Christ's, to the effect that no one on earth or in heaven save the father knows when it will come (Mark XIII.32) and that the sun and moon will be darkened when the son of man comes (Matthew XXIV.29).[101]

The motif of Christ's two contrasting aspects, one for the good and one for the bad, Ælfric reserved for the moment when God's angels will have gathered all risen humanity before him, the elect standing on his right and the reprobates on his left:[102]

Þonne sitt se Hælend on his heofonlican ðrymsetle,
mihtig and wuldorful, and milde þam godum,
egeslic and andrysne þam earmum synfullum,
and ealle men geseoð swutollice þone Hælend
on ðære menniscnysse, ac ne moton swaðeah
ða earman synfullan geseon his godcundnysse;
ða godan ana geseoð þa godcundnysse

['Then the saviour will sit on his heavenly throne, mighty and glorious, and gentle to the good, terrible and dreadful to the wretched sinful, and all men will see clearly the saviour in his humanity, but yet the wretched sinful will not be able to see his divinity; the good alone will see the divinity', *ibid.*, lines 347–53].

Clearly, not only did this prose writer share with traditional poetry its conception of fundamental binary interaction but also, trained to analyse language, he appreciated the organic union of thought and language which was the essence of poetic tradition and sought to recreate this relationship

99 Cf. Clemoes, 'Ælfric', esp. pp. 191–2.

100 Ælfric, *SupplHoms*, XI (ed. Pope, lines 273–89, pp. 429–30).

101 *Ibid.*, lines 273–9 and 283–9.

102 Ælfric's source, his own Latin digest of a work in three books, *Prognosticon futuri sæculi*, by Julian, a late-seventh-century archbishop of Toledo, did not place the motif here, but in the usual way, when Christ was coming to judge; see the wording supplied as source for lines 348–9 (ed. Pope, p. 434).

in his prose as much as possible by transplanting verse's binary alliterative structure.[103] In this passage the first three pairs of alliterating phrases concern Christ's appearance outwards and the remaining four pairs humanity's returning vision of him. There is an emanation and a reaction. But the sequence is not conveyed pictorially: it is expressed as an interaction of four attributes – divinity and humanity in Christ, goodness and sinfulness in men – and alliteration emphasizes the words which plot this interaction. First, divinity and humanity are blended in Christ: *Hælend* and *heofonlican* chime together (347). But then goodness and badness in men separate out Christ's divinity from his humanity, and the final, enduring, coupling is between *godan* and *godcundnysse* (353). The old power of poetry to initiate elemental interaction had returned, but in a prose environment of balance and proportion designed to corroborate correspondences and contrasts in universal thought. Vernacular prose had been rendered fit intellectually and aesthetically to express human participation in divinely authorized principles.[104] Without the forerunner of poetry nothing of this sort would have been possible.

[103] For my purposes I have spaced the above excerpt as though it were verse, but, of course, this style is really rhythmical prose, as Pope has correctly shown by limiting his editorial treatment to lineation based, without sub-division, on what I have called 'pairs of phrases'. Ælfric's own practice was to run on continuously along manuscript lines, marking off each sentence as a unit by capitals and punctuation and using a point to divide phrase from phrase rhythmically within the sentence.

[104] Cf. Clemoes, '"Symbolic" Language', pp. 12–13, and Clemoes, *Rhythm and Cosmic Order*, pp. 16–21.

9

Symbolic language serving the company of Christ

Biblical ideas of society required relatively little adaptation from traditionally minded Anglo-Saxons, society for society. Especially they felt a natural affinity with the community which the Old Testament portrayed, living off their land, constantly protecting their patrimony by warfare, worshipping the one true God and obeying his anointed king. Converted Anglo-Saxons readily accepted Jewish society as an authentic model for their own. When consolidating a greater-than-West-Saxon authority in the late 880s and the 890s, King Alfred saw fit to preface his written body of vernacular laws with an introduction which set the code in a tradition stemming from Mosaic law, and, in a similar spirit, when supplying the brief *argumenta* for his vernacular prose translation of the first fifty psalms, he methodically related each psalm first of all to the historical David and then, by extension, to the user in the present.[1]

Furthermore Jewish society sustained its traditions by means of a system of expression which was in itself congenial to Anglo-Saxons. The binary parallelism which was its primary form was like Old English apposition both in having been conventionalized in oral composition of poetry and in being based on meaning. Indeed, the direct bond between parallelism and sense was even more clearcut in the Hebraic variety of verse than in the Old English one. In the latter tradition distinct meanings in apposed language were commonly separately linked to surrounding narrative through alliteration, as, for instance, in the double reference to Beowulf in the first *b* verse and the second *a* verse of

[1] See below, pp. 368–70 and n. 18. For other references, see *ibid.*, n. 14 and for the Davidic emphasis, O'Neill, 'The Old English Introductions to the Prose Psalms', pp. 31–5. For further examples of Alfred's Old Testament mentality in its depth and width, see Keynes, 'A Tale of Two Kings', pp. 209–10.

Þæt fram ham gefrægn Higelaces þegn
god mid Geatum Grendles dæda (*Beowulf* 194–5).

In the former tradition, however, parallelism was founded on straight synonymy alone, as in the Hebrew word pairs, without corresponding sounds, rendered by *habitabit* and *requiescet* and by *tabernaculo* and *monte sancto* in the Vulgate version of ps. XV. 1, 'Domine, quis habitabit in tabernaculo tuo? aut quis requiescet in monte sancto tuo?', and by *abide* and *dwell* and by *tabernacle* and *holy hill* in the Authorized Version of the same verse, 'Lord, who shall abide in thy tabernacle? who shall dwell in thy holy hill?'[2] There were no barriers at all for Anglo-Saxons in this mode of expression. They easily assimilated the social wisdom – akin to that of their own maxims – in wry observations such as 'The poor useth intreaties; but the rich answereth roughly' (Proverbs XVIII. 23).[3] There is, for instance, an easy blend of Germanic and Jewish wisdom in content, and maybe also in form, in this riposte by Solomon in the perhaps ninth-century poetic dialogue *Solomon and Saturn* (*II*):

Dol bið se ðe gæð on deop wæter,
se ðe sund nafað ne gesegled scip
ne fugles flyht, ne he mid fotum ne mæg
grund geræcan; huru se godes cunnað
full dyslice, dryhtnes meahta

['Foolish is he who goes into deep water, who has no swimming, no ship with a sail, no bird's flight, nor can he reach the bottom with his feet; indeed he puts to the test the powers of God, of the Lord, very foolishly', 225–9].

'Dol bið se ðe . . .' (225) was an orthodox Old English gnomic formula,[4] but the specification which follows (226–8a) produces more a proverb than a maxim, less a comprehensive general truth – such as, 'Dol biþ se þe his dryhten nat' ('Foolish is he who does not know his Lord', *Maxims I* 35; cf. *The Seafarer* 106a) – than a statement relying for its general force on a second, parallel, statement (228b–9a). Nor is the connection between the applied and the general left 'open', as it would be in a statement of the

[2] For examples of influence from Hebraic parallelism on Anglo-Latin, see Howlett, 'Biblical Style in Early Insular Latin', pp. 133–8.

[3] For a shrewd analysis of the use of language in Old Testament parallelism in comparison with Homeric, Old English and Old French poetic practice, see Whallon, *Formula, Character, and Context*, pp. 139–72.

[4] See *Maxims I* 35 and *The Seafarer* 106 and cf. 'Til biþ se þe . . .' (*The Wanderer* 112a).

type, 'It is foolish to get into deep water if you can't swim.' 'Ne fugles flyht' introduces an ironical reminder that what we are talking about here is a man, not a bird, and the man is finally cut right down to size by explication of what is implied by 'deep': 'He cannot reach the bottom with his feet.' We are not merely being invited to appreciate the relevance of this specific folly to our living in general but are also being prepared for regarding the connection from the characteristically Jewish point of view that God is great but man is small, and thereby for accepting the subsequent parallel statement (228b–9) in its full force. And likewise formally, whereas the Old English way of making the link between 225–8a and 228b–9 would have been purely alliterative and appositional, as in a sequence such as 'Foolish is he who goes into deep water . . .; he tests the Lord's might',[5] there seems to be a touch of Hebraic parallelism in the key word-for-word repetition *Dol*, *dyslice*, which, through its grammatical shift from noun (or adjective acting absolutely as a noun), *dol*, to adverb, *dyslice*, effects the thoroughly characteristic Anglo-Saxon transition from active being to narrative living within a sequence of fundamental alliterative collocations, *Dol . . . deop* (225), *grund . . . godes* (228) and *dyslice . . . dryhtnes* (229).

The warnings provided by Old Testament God-dependent society about communal sin – for instance, the concept of divine punishment of communities collectively for their wrong-doing – were left, however, for vernacular prose preachers to take up, as Archbishop Wulfstan did dramatically in his *Sermo Lupi*. For an Old English narrative poet, already equipped with his own inherited conventional language for personalized history, the natural tendency was to drain Old Testament society of its specifically Jewish character and to portray it instead in terms of his native aristocratic warrior traditions. This, as N. Boyd, has ably argued,[6] is what the *Genesis A* poet consistently did: in his poem God the creator became 'the epitome of the Anglo-Saxon king, wisely and liberally distributing gifts'; spiritual blessings were represented by the giving and receiving of treasure, and piety by the exercise of wisdom and *ellen;* the rôle of inherited attributes was duly stressed (for instance, in Isaac's case 'crevit igitur puer' became 'Cniht weox and þag, swa him cynde wæron / æðele from yldrum' ('The boy grew and thrived, as the qualities he had inherited from his ancestors determined', 2772–3a)); and God bestowed his *freondscipe* on

[5] Cf. 'Dol biþ se þe him his dryhten ne ondrædeþ; cymeð him . . .' (*The Seafarer* 106).

[6] 'Doctrine and Criticism', pp. 234–8.

Noah, Lot and Abraham because of what they did as men of *ellen*, wisdom and wealth.

But with the New Testament concept that a fresh phase in human history had been opened up by the incarnation and was due to come to an end once and for all for the whole of mankind on the day of judgement, corporate responsibility took on altogether greater dimensions which Old English poets could not ignore. They had to convert the loyalty of follower for leader, the primary structural unit of traditional warrior society, into the obligation of every individual to direct (or redirect) his, or her, behaviour towards eternal communion with the universal redeemer. As Cynewulf declared succinctly, dramatically and artistically at the end of his narrative of the ascension in *Christ II*,

Hwæt, we nu gehyrdan   hu þæt hælubearn
þurh his hydercyme   hals eft forgeaf,
gefreode ond gefreoþade   folc under wolcnum,
mære meotudes sunu,   þæt nu monna gehwylc
cwic þendan her wunað,   geceosan mot
swa helle hienþu   swa heofones mærþu,
swa þæt leohte leoht   swa ða laþan niht,
swa þrymmes þræce   swa þystra wræce,
swa mid dryhten dream   swa mid deoflum hream,
swa wite mid wraþum   swa wuldor mid arum,
swa lif swa deað,   swa him leofre bið
to gefremmane,   þenden flæsc ond gæst
wuniað in worulde.   Wuldor þæs age
þrynysse þrym,   þonc butan ende

['Lo, we have now heard how the healing child through his coming here has granted salvation again, has freed and made peace with people below the skies, the glorious son of God, so that now every living man while he remains here has to choose either the humiliation of hell or the glory of heaven, either the radiant light or the loathsome night, either the throng of glory or the misery of darkness, either joy with the Lord or clamour with devils, either punishment with enemies or glory with angels, either life or death, as it is more pleasing to him to do while flesh and spirit dwell in the world. May the might of the trinity have glory for that, gratitude without end!'].

Social warriorship had to typify the individual's universal lot of battling against the sin which would destroy him, if he let it, rather than, as hitherto, his defence of society until he was overtaken by a fate over which he had no control. The Christian individual was in a dynamic relationship with a narrative world of organized moral values. His/her overriding duty was not to stand firm before an implacable fate in the name of society but was to stand guard against the wiles of the devil in common with all his fellow humans. The emissary from hell confessing to St Juliana in Cynewulf's poem celebrating this holy virgin acknowledged that he was utterly defeated

Gif ic ænigne ellenrofne
gemete modigne metodes cempan
wið flanþræce, nele feor þonan
bugan from beaduwe, ac he bord ongean
hefeð hygesnottor, haligne scyld,
gæstlic guðreaf, nele gode swican,
ac he beald in gebede bidsteal gifeð
fæste on feðan

['If I meet any warrior of God vigorous in fighting spirit, brave against the force of arrows, one who will not flee from battle far from there, but, wise in mind, lifts his holy shield of wood, his spiritual armour, will not be a traitor to God, but, bold in prayer, makes a stand, firmly in the company on foot', *Juliana* 382–9a].

But, when he encountered

ellenleasran,
under cumbolhagan, cempan sænran,
þe ic onbryrdan mæge beorman mine,
agælan æt guþe

['a warrior less spirited in fighting, slower, beneath the banner-phalanx, whom I can excite with my barm, hinder in battle', 394b–7a],

he enjoyed more success:

Þeah he godes hwæt
onginne gæstlice, ic beo gearo sona,
þæt ic ingehygd eal geondwlite,
hu gefæstnad sy ferð innanweard,
wiðsteall geworht. Ic þæs wealles geat
ontyne þurh teonan; bið se torr þyrel,
ingong geopenad, þonne ic ærest him
þurh eargfare in onsende
in breostsefan bitre geþoncas
þurh mislice modes willan,

þæt him sylfum selle þynceð
leahtras to fremman ofer lof godes,
lices lustas

['although he begins spiritually bold in virtue, I am ready straightaway so that I may scan all his inner thought, how his mind is secured within, his defence made. I open the gate of the wall by means of iniquity; the tower is pierced, the entrance opened, when I first send forth bitter thoughts into him through a flight of arrows, into his breast through various desires of the mind, so that it seems to him better to commit sins contrary to praise of God, lusts of the body', 397b–409a].

Christian tradition itself had already created models for applying the language of warfare to moral battles which Old English poets readily accepted, as this image of planned assault on a fortress clearly exemplifies. It constituted a shift of customary, native, military vocabulary away from its normal field of physical battle into the 'literary' realm of Latin patristic metaphor for individual spiritual defence against sin. Protection of permanent walled and gate-towered defences was not the Anglo-Saxons' primary mode of warfare: as a vehicle for Christian metaphor of fundamental import it must have seemed to them of a decidedly literary turn. Indeed Cynewulf may not have found the image already used in the Latin source he was following for this poem, for it is not present in the nearest identified extant text; he may have introduced it himself, out of a general familiarity with patristic writings such as Gregory the Great's, where a besieged city several times serves as a figure for the Christian's resistance to the devil. If so, the ease with which he had assimilated the analogy in this literary spirit is all the more remarkable, as is his confidence that, given his step-by-step spiritual interpretations, his readers or hearers would readily receive it in accordance with this intention.[7]

This metaphor was, in fact, only a particular application of a developed tradition of analogy between warriorship and the struggles of an individual's spiritual life which had originated in very early Christian times and, as such, became thoroughly familiar to Anglo-Saxons. As their vernacular prose testifies extensively, they well understood that – as enshrined in the Benedictine Rule and commentaries on it – the service and obedience demanded of every member of military society were just as essential to organized monasticism, that the suffering of the martyr was

[7] See Hill, 'The Soldier of Christ in Old English Prose and Poetry', pp. 62 and 69–70, and nn. 31–3 and 62–3.

akin to that of the soldier, that solitary steadfastness against demons – such as St Guthlac's – was a form of single combat, and that every man's resistance to sin was spiritual warfare.[8] The *miles Christi*, 'soldier of Christ' – the individual Christian confronting and triumphing over spiritual enemies, or over human opponents when victory against them was owed to faith or divine intervention[9] – was a ubiquitous concept which became standardized in Old English prose and verse through a specialized application of the noun *cempa* – which had originally meant 'champion' in single combat and seems to have been used mostly as a simplex and only rarely to form compounds in symbolic 'warrior' tradition – and through related use of the verb *campian*.[10] When the devil confessing to Juliana called the Christian whom he could not suborn 'metodes cempan' (*Juliana* 383b),[11] Cynewulf was putting this noun to a use which was commonplace in the vernacular by some time in the ninth century, when the writer of the prose Old English Martyrology, without equivalents in the two relevant Latin *passiones* and without explanation or elaboration, used 'campode for Criste' as a stereotyped expression for 'was martyred' in his notices for St Vitus and St Mamas.[12]

Nor was it only the spiritual follower whom Christian tradition had already standardized in terms of the social warriorship congenial to vernacular poets: the concept of divine spiritual leadership had been given the same garb too. According to a verse paraphraser of ps. L in a mixture of Kentish and West Saxon, the psalmist David was 'cyninga cynost, Criste liofost' ('the bravest of kings, the dearest to Christ', *Psalm 50* 3): whether

8 *Ibid.*, pp. 57–63 and related nn.

9 *Ibid.*, pp. 63–4 and related nn.

10 *Ibid.*, pp. 59–61; Morison, 'OE *cempa* in Cynewulf's *Juliana*'; and Hill, 'On the Semantics of Old English *cempa* and *campian*'. For two examples of effective non-Christian symbolic use of *cempa* in genitive combinations in *Beowulf* ('Geata cempa' 1551b and 'Huga cempan' (dat. s. 2502b), the gen. pl. in each case being the name of a people), see Brady, '"Weapons" in *Beowulf*', pp. 237 and 241; the existence of this pattern, even if rather sparsely used, would have facilitated establishment of the 'Cristes cempa' formation. The only recorded *-cempa* compound in a non-Christian context is 'feþecempa' in *Beowulf* (1544a and 2853a), on which see *ibid.*, pp. 235 and 237.

11 Cf. Hill, 'The Soldier of Christ in Old English Prose and Poetry', pp. 69–70.

12 'he wæs seofon geara cniht ða he campode for Criste' and 'se wæs .xii. wintre cniht ða he for Criste campode' respectively; *Das altenglische Martyrologium*, ed. Kotzor II, 119 and 182. Cf. Hill, 'The Soldier of Christ in Old English Prose and Poetry', p. 61, and 'Old English *cempa* and *campian*', p. 275 and n. 17.

'soð sigecempa' ('true champion of victory', 10a) in war, or penitent, confessing his sins, as in this psalm, this mortal king was first and foremost *se dryhtnes ðiowa* (9a), the servant of a leader of a troop of active warriors, a leader who was the paramount Lord of hosts ('weorada dominus' (17b), and 'weoruda dryhten' (30a)). Christ, the eternal king of kings, the Lord of heaven and earth, the ruler of all, stood at the head of his universal retinue of faithful soldiers, among whom David was prominently numbered. The cult of Christ as king had been a dominant force in the church since the fourth century,[13] and was part and parcel of Anglo-Saxon devotion from the start. For instance, in a Latin Ascensiontide hymn by Bede[14] Christ was celebrated as *rex gloriae*, *rex saeculi*, *rex altithronus*, *rex regum* and *rex gloriae*, *virtutis atque gratiae*, and vernacular poets in the earliest days, as a matter of course, began to develop a suitably celebratory terminology: in the brief praise-verses which Cædmon was believed to have been inspired to sing in the third quarter of the seventh century,[15] no less than four of the seven different epithets for God were adaptations of aristocratic military 'leader' appellations ('hefaenricaes uard' ('guardian of the kingdom of heaven', 1b), 'eci dryctin' ('eternal leader of the warrior troop', 4a and 8a), 'moncynnæs uard' ('guardian of mankind', 7b) and 'frea allmectig' ('almighty Lord', 9b)). Christian Old English poets grafted on to Latin tradition their inherited system of symbolic 'leader' language to produce a rich crop of expressions proclaiming that Christ is king as well as creator, saviour and judge-to-be.[16]

A vernacular poet, steeped in the traditions of the bond between secular leader and comitatus, was well fitted to appreciate Christ's divine kingship as the source of spiritual potential in his loyal followers. As we have seen above,[17] it was through a controlled infusion of a wealth of terms extolling the God of absolute power during a prolonged interlocution between voyaging apostle and skipper-Christ that the *Andreas* poet gradually raised the physical, emotional and mental elements of human make-up on to the spiritual level at which a direct manifestation of 'cining cwicera gehwæs'[18] to the *hæleð*, 'fighter', Andrew (919a), became possible. The poet was

[13] For its origins, see Beskow, *Rex Gloriae*.

[14] Bede, 'hymnus Ascensionis', (ed. J. Fraipont, CCSL 122, 419–23). Concerning this hymn, see Gneuss, *Hymnar und Hymnen*, p. 53.

[15] See above, p. 231.

[16] For a study of the whole field of these terms, see Crépin, 'Poétique Vieil-Anglaise'.

[17] Pp. 255–8. [18] See *ibid.*, p. 258.

employing his ancient sense of symbolic potential actively to develop the spiritual relationship between lord and follower which was at the heart of his poem. In addition, the twenty-five different symbolic appellations of Christ used to similar effect in seventy-four-and-a-half 'lines' of another poet's, Cynewulf's, narrative of the ascension[19] testify to the fine discrimination possible in this spiritual application of social symbolism, including a keen sense of 'literary' metaphor: when Christ summons his apostles, he is *brega mæra*, 'renowned prince' (456a), and 'þeoden þrymfæst' ('glorious leader of a people', 457a); when he teaches them, he is a *sincgiefa*, 'giver of treasure' (460a), 'tires brytta' ('distributor of glory', 462b) and *wuldres helm*, 'protector of glory' (463a); when the apostles glorify him, he is 'lifes agend' ('owner of life', 471b) and 'fæder frumsceafta' ('father of original creatures', 472a); when he lays his commission on them to evangelize the world, he is 'waldend engla' ('ruler of angels', 474b) and *frea mihtig*, 'mighty Lord' (475a); and in his ascension, as they see and hear it, he is the son of God ('ancenned sunu' (464b), 'efenece bearn' (465a), *godbearn* (499a) and *frumbearn* (507a)), the eternal source of life, peoples, blessing and joy (*liffruma* (504a), 'ealra folca fruma' (516a), 'ece eadfruma' (532a) and *wilgifa* (537a)), the owner of victory and the sky ('sigores agend' (513b) and 'swegles agend' (543b)), guardian of glory and of men (*wuldres weard* (527a) and 'haligra helm' (529a)) and glory of kings, leader of princes, king of archangels and ruler of all ('cyninga wuldor' (508a), 'æþelinga ord' (515a), 'heahengla cyning' (528a) and 'ealles waldend' (544b)). The poet's symbolism serves to emphasize Christ's combination of divinity and manhood, crucial to the doctrine of the ascension, with impeccable regard for narrative relevance.

The apostles are presented as the comitatus of this great king, 'his þegna gedryht' ('his troop of thegns', 457b), his *hæleð*, 'fighters' (461a), his *gesiþas*, 'retainers' (473a). Christ and they behave towards one another in accordance with this relationship: he summons them as their *þeoden* (*gelaðode* (458a)); he is their distributor of treasure (*sincgiefa* and 'tires brytta'); they assemble in a *burh* (461b), a *þingstede*, 'meeting place' (497a); he rewards them ('lean æfter geaf' (473b)); he exhorts them to destroy enemy idols ('hergas breotaþ, / fyllað ond feogað, feondscype dwæscað' (485b–6)); they form a rearguard for him ('last weardedun' (496b)); and they depart grieving from the place where they have watched him ascend

[19] *Christ* (*II*) 456–545a, less Christ's own words to the apostles (476–90), in which, naturally, they do not occur.

(533–40a).[20] They and angels shared the same fellowship with their common leader. The ascending Christ in this poem passed from one *gedryht* or *weorud*, 'troop of active soldiers', that of his apostles (457b and 458a), to another, that of his angels (515b and 493a). Apostles and angels combined in a single Christocentric order. Likewise the visionary in *The Dream of the Rood* was left longing for the cross to fetch him from this transitory life and bring him to heaven 'þær is dryhtnes folc / geseted to symle' ('where the company of the leader of the troop is seated for the feast', 140b–1a). An individual's overwhelming sense of 'dryhtnes dreamas', the joys of the heavenly Lord, could make him despise the gratifications of society on earth, as in *The Seafarer*, but, more straightforwardly, appreciation of the ties which Christ's loyal followers enjoy collectively with their creative king in both this world and the next elevated traditional social relationships as a pattern of shared communion with God. Poetry's age-old symbolic denotation of human society not only offered to the new society of God and man a system for its symbolic representation but also provided human minds with a broad, familiar avenue of approach.

Nor did poetry stand alone in subsuming its traditional conceptions of earthly society in a glorious spiritual kingship of Christ. Anglo-Saxon society itself did the same. Some of the profound institutional changes which were wrought as a consequence have been indicated already.[21] It increasingly set its permissions and its sanctions in this perspective. For instance, in many a charter infringement of the document's provisions was portrayed as an act of disloyalty to Christ meriting eternal exile from his company, as in this wording in a formal grant of land by Æthelwulf, king of Wessex, in 847: 'If anyone, however, at any time or for any reason, and of whatever dignity, profession or order, shall with sacrilegious presumption attempt to pervert or to make invalid the conferment of this munificence, may he be separated from the community of the church of Christ and from the fellowship of the saints here and in the future, and may his part be set with misers and robbers and may he be associated with Judas Iscariot who betrayed the Lord.'[22]

[20] Cf. *The Dream of the Rood* 67b–9a. Their sadness contradicted Luke XXIV.52, but Bede's commentary on Acts I.11 implied sadness (Bede's *Expositio Actuum Apostolorum*, ed. Laistner, p. 9).

[21] E.g., Offa's claim in the 790s to have been 'established king by the king of kings' (see above, p. 47).

[22] *EHD*, no. 88, from which I take the above translation (p. 524).

In the same way society's narrative estimation of itself was refashioned under ecclesiastical influence – the sort of stories it told about itself. The account of Oswald, of the royal house of Bernicia and king of all Northumbria 634–42, given in Bede's *Historia ecclesiastica* rather less than a hundred years after Oswald's death, is an early example. The stories about him which Bede owed to Northumbrian oral tradition, moulded by the church, did not portray a king who, after a prosperous rule, died defending his people in the face of an implacable *wyrd*, but a *rex Christianissimus*, *rex pius*, *rex religiosus*, *rex sanctissimus ac uictoriosissimus* and *rex Deo dilectus*, whose power rested on spiritual as well as secular authority, who had attained his kingdom as a *miles Christi* through devotion to the cross, who had ruled in prayerful piety and humble charity, and who had met a Christian death at the hands of heathen foes, uttering as he fell a prayer for his enemies which had become proverbial ('people say as a proverb', Bede reported, 'Oswald, falling to the earth, said: God have mercy on their souls'). In the aristocratic milieu common to church and state in Northumbria and beyond, Oswald had become a cult figure responsible for many miracles of healing or preservation well before Bede's time.[23] Oswald's career in the pages of Bede is a politico-religious success-story. Single-minded and energetic in promoting and supporting the church, personally devout and active in alms-giving, brave as soldier of Christ, victorious on earth and rewarded in heaven, Bede's Oswald sanctified the beneficial collaboration between church and state by which alone society could thrive in the Christian era.[24] A new set of symbolic values essential to Christian kingship in Anglo-Saxon England – and, indeed, in all medieval Europe – was being promulgated.[25]

Another issue critical to the politico-religious nexus in Christian kingship, reconciliation of warrior leadership and unresisting self-sacrifice like Christ's, was thematic to the cult of the *rex et martyr* Edmund, ruler of the East Anglians, killed by the Danes in 869. The Edmund known to the earliest historical records after his death (the West Saxon *Anglo-Saxon Chronicle* and Asser's *Life of Alfred*) was no more than one of various kings

[23] Bede's account of Oswald's life and cult does not form a single, consecutive narrative but is dispersed through several chapters of his *HE*, III.1–3, 5–7 and 9–13 and IV.14 (pp. 212–21, 226–37, 240–55 and 376–81). For a rather fuller summary of it than I have given here, see Clemoes, *The Cult of St Oswald on the Continent*, pp. 1–4 and 5–6 and related nn.

[24] *Ibid.*, p. 6.

[25] For the continental dimension of the Oswald cult, see *ibid.*, pp. 4–24.

who lost their realms and their lives to the raiding armies.[26] Veneration of him as a saint probably had its origins in the local East Anglian community quite soon after the event and then (on the evidence of copious extant memorial coinage) assumed a larger political scale in the late ninth and early tenth centuries, when, apparently, it was taken up by the converted rulers of the Eastern Danelaw for their own governmental motives.[27] West Saxon involvement in the cult seems to have dated from the reign of Athelstan in the second quarter of the tenth century. It was then that a young Dunstan, later to be archbishop, listened as the story of Edmund's martyrdom was told to Athelstan by a very old man who claimed to have been Edmund's armour-bearer on the day the king died. No doubt the old man's story had become increasingly Christianized over the years. He must have dined out on it many times. Some sixty years later still, Dunstan, not long before his own death, recounted to a foreign visitor, Abbo of Fleury, a version containing some elements – in particular the saint's incorruption and a miracle of the first half of the tenth century – which he is more likely to have derived from the traditions of the community serving the saint's shrine at *Bedricesgueord* (Bury St Edmunds) than from the armour-bearer, and it was this visitor who, adding some further information of his own, gave the cult the full hagiographical treatment in his Latin *Passio sancti Eadmundi regis et martyris*, composed in the period 985 × 987.[28] The Edmund whom Abbo portrayed was a ruler of noble descent and Christian virtues who, famed as a doughty warrior, on being faced in the prime of life with pagan enemies he could not vanquish militarily, preferred a glorious martyr's death to ignominious capitulation. Here was a Christian warrior king whose reward in heaven symbolized the ultimate victory of all who refuse to give in to the forces of unbelief whatever the circumstances.

From the middle of the tenth century West Saxon rulers of England identified themselves with the cults of early non-West-Saxon royal saints, such as Oswald and Edmund, as valuable symbols of the national historical

[26] For the most recent summary, see Ridyard, *The Royal Saints of Anglo-Saxon England*, pp. 61–2.

[27] *Ibid.*, pp. 211–23. Edmund did not receive an entry in the probably ninth-century vernacular prose martyrology (as Oswald did), on which work, see above, pp. 244–5.

[28] Ridyard, *The Royal Saints of Anglo-Saxon England*, pp. 62–5. The most recent edition of the *Passio* is in *Three Lives of English Saints*, ed. Winterbottom. All the three earliest surviving copies, of late-eleventh-century date, may also contain some elements of post-Conquest Bury propaganda. For a discussion of the *Passio*, see Mostert, *The Political Theology of Abbo of Fleury*, pp. 40–5.

identity they were keen to foster.[29] To these late West Saxon kings, whose claims to national sovereignty rested on successful resistance to heathen enemies, antecedent native saintly royal defenders of the faith had an immediate pertinence which distant rulers in ancient non-Christian Germanic days, such as Beowulf, could never possess, however adapted. And the cults formed a national inheritance just as welcome to eleventh-century Danish kings of all England and Norman conquerors: they too could invoke these native protectors in heaven in the interests of the country's church and state. The English prose versions of the Latin texts basic for devotion to Oswald and Edmund (Bede's and Abbo's respectively) which the Winchester-trained author, Ælfric, included in the set of vernacular *Lives of Saints* he composed in the 990s at the request of Æthelweard, ealdorman of the western provinces, and his son Æthelmær, illustrate the influence these early royal exemplars of saintly values exerted on late Anglo-Saxon aristocracy. Not surprisingly, whereas Beowulf died thinking of his kin, Byrhtnoth (in 991) according to *The Battle of Maldon* sank to the ground with his eyes on heaven, thanking the 'ðeoda waldend' ('ruler of peoples', 173b) for all the joys he had experienced in the world and acknowledging his dependence on the *milde metod*, 'merciful God' (175a), to grant his soul the blessing of a peaceful passage into the power of the 'þeoden engla' ('leader of the angels', 178b), away from the clutches of *helsceaðan*, 'injurers from hell' (180a). For Christian military leaders, such as Byrhtnoth, both living and dying had as a matter of course a next-worldly as well as a this-worldly dimension under God's rule.

In this poem symbolic epithets for God were placed on the lips of a late-tenth-century English nobleman, fighting for his homeland. In *Andreas*, by contrast, they were confined almost entirely to the special relationship between chosen apostle and God: they played no part in 'ordinary' hopes and fears but operated on an exotic, exclusively spiritual plane of verbal interchange with Christ, from which 'ordinary' men and women were excluded as grotesque cannibals or, at best, mere recent converts.[30] It is in Cynewulf's poetry of the ninth century that we find

[29] Earlier, in 909, Oswald's principal relics had been translated from Bardney, in Lindsey, to a monastery founded at Gloucester by Æthelred, ealdorman of Mercia, and his wife Æthelflæd, daughter of King Alfred. In the twelfth century the chronicler, Hugh Candidus, referred to the presence of Oswald's right arm at Peterborough at the time of the Norman Conquest.

[30] See above, pp. 255–72.

symbolic appellations fully established in performing the service which they uniquely could provide for the company of Christ, that of integrating 'ordinary' thoughts and feelings in a spirit of communal worship which embraces the terrestrial and the celestial alike.

Cynewulf's narrative of the ascension as seen by the apostles watching on the ground demonstrates this union very pointedly:

Ða wearð semninga   sweg on lyfte
hlud gehyred.   Heofonengla þreat,
weorud wlitescyne,   wuldres aras,
cwomun on corðre.   Cyning ure gewat
þurh þæs temples hrof   þær hy to segun,
þa þe leofes þa gen   last weardedun
on þam þingstede,   þegnas gecorene.
Gesegon hi on heahþu   hlaford stigan,
godbearn of grundum.   Him wæs geomor sefa
hat æt heortan,   hyge murnende,
þæs þe hi swa leofne   leng ne mostun
geseon under swegle.   Song ahofun
aras ufancunde,   æþeling heredun,
lofedun liffruman,   leohte gefegun
þe of þæs hælendes   heafelan lixte.
Gesegon hy ælbeorhte   englas twegen
fægre ymb þæt frumbearn   frætwum blican,
cyninga wuldor.   Cleopedon of heahþu
wordum wrætlicum   ofer wera mengu
beorhtan reorde: 'Hwæt bidað ge,
Galilesce   guman on hwearfte?
Nu ge sweotule geseoð   soðne dryhten
on swegl faran;   sigores agend
wile up heonan   eard gestigan,
æþelinga ord,   mid þas engla gedryht,
ealra folca fruma,   fæder eþelstoll.
We mid þyslice   þreate willað
ofer heofona gehlidu   hlaford fergan
to þære beorhtan byrg   mid þas bliðan gedryht,
ealra sigebearna   þæt seleste
ond æþeleste,   þe ge her on stariað
ond in frofre geseoð   frætwum blican.
Wile eft swa þeah   eorðan mægðe
sylfa gesecan   side herge,

ond þonne gedeman   dæda gehwylce
þara ðe gefremedon   folc under roderum.'
Ða wæs wuldres weard   wolcnum bifongen,
heahengla cyning,   ofer hrofas upp,
haligra helm.   Hyht wæs geniwad,
blis in burgum,   þurh þæs beornes cyme.
Gesæt sigehremig   on þa swiþran hand
ece eadfruma   agnum fæder

['Then suddenly loud music in the sky was heard. A troop of heavenly angels, a company shining in beauty, messengers of glory, came in a throng. Our king departed through the roof of the temple where they were watching, those who still defended the footprint of the loved one in the meeting place, chosen thegns. They saw on high the Lord ascend, the son of God from the ground. Their mind was sorrowful, hot at heart, their thought grieving, because they could no longer see so dear a one beneath the sky. The messengers from above raised a song, praised the prince, hymned the author of life, rejoiced in the light which shone from the saviour's head. They saw two radiant angels shining with adornments, beautiful around the first-born child, the glory of kings. They called out from on high with wonderful words above the multitude of men in a clear voice: "What are you waiting for, Galilean men in a circle? Now you see clearly the true Lord go into the sky; the owner of victory will rise up from here to his home, foremost of princes, with this company of angels, the creator of all peoples, to the native throne of his father. We with such a troop will conduct the Lord above the lids of the heavens to the bright city, with this happy company – the best and noblest of all victorious sons – whom you gaze at here and consolingly see shine with adornments. He himself however will again seek the tribe on earth with a vast army and then judge every deed which people beneath the skies have performed." Then the guardian of glory was received by the clouds, the king of archangels, up above the roofs, the protector of saints. Hope was renewed, joy in the cities, through that warrior's coming. The eternal source of prosperity sat exulting in victory at the right hand of his own father'].

The poet did not present the apostolic witnesses as some company apart, exercising a spirituality inaccessible to the rest of us, but conflated them with contemporary visitors to the Holy Land.[31] They were placed specifically in a setting which belonged in actuality only to pilgrims-to-be looking up, as they prayed, through the unroofed centre of the circular church which was built in the fourth century on the top of the Mount of

[31] For a fuller discussion than I give here, see Clemoes, 'Cynewulf's Image of the Ascension', esp. pp. 300–4.

Olives round the alleged footprints left by Christ when he ascended (494b–7).[32] And they were presented as picked thegns (497b) who felt keenly the anguish of losing sight of their beloved lord (499b–502a).[33] It was this disappearance, as viewed by thegns from below (528b), which initiated the renewal of spiritual hope for all in heaven and on earth brought about by the return of the victorious king to sit by his father in heaven, an eternal source of blessing (527–32).

The Bible made the watching of the ascension by the apostles, standing in undescribed surroundings, the principal dramatic interest of the narrative: 'while they beheld, he was taken up; and a cloud received him out of their sight' (Acts I.9), 'they looked steadfastly toward heaven as he went up' (*ibid.*, 10), and two men standing by them in white apparel asked why they stood gazing up into heaven and declared that 'this same Jesus, which is taken up from you into heaven, shall so come in like manner as ye have seen him go into heaven' (*ibid.*, 11). In this account the disappearance, as such, was thus reported only once, early on, undramatically. Cynewulf's version, by contrast, changed the dramatic focus significantly. His concluding, summarizing,

Ða wæs wuldres weard   wolcnum bifongen,
heahengla cyning,   ofer hrofas upp (527–8)

turned the disappearance into the climax of a fully substantiated act of seeing from the viewpoint of the apostles/pilgrims/thegns looking up at their ascending Lord (*hlaford* (498b)), who was the son of God (499a), through the open centre of the church in which they stood round his footprint. The universal significance of the event was not worked out in

32 Adamnán's *De locis sanctis* (as first pointed out by Bright, 'Cynewulf's *Christ* 495 and 528', p. 14) could have been Cynewulf's source of knowledge of this building, but Adamnán gave the looking up as only one of two (if not three) reasons for the lack of roof and made much of the footprints. Perhaps the poet drew on an intermediate text, or on what he had seen for himself if he had been a pilgrim, or on word of mouth, or on some visual representation. Could he, by any chance, have thought that the building was already there when the ascension took place? The probably ninth-century vernacular prose martyrologist reproduced Adamnán's account fairly fully; *Das altenglische Martyrologium*, ed. Kotzor II, 84–91. Incidentally, did Cynewulf intend *on hwearfte* (511b) as another reference to the circular building in which the apostles were standing?

33 Similarly, but with noteworthy psychological differences, King Hrothgar, saying goodbye to Beowulf, wept because he thought he would never see him again, and the Mermedonians, seeing off St Andrew on a headland, wept as long as they could see him sailing away; see above, pp. 271–2.

terms of theological implications such as manifestation of the creator's power to elevate himself unaided by any of his creatures,[34] but, together with due regard for the essential tenet that the ascending Christ was both human and divine,[35] was directly tied to the historically real, and subsequently commemorated, psychological experience of observers on the ground. And what gripped the attention of these observers was the dramatic elevation of *cyning ure*, '*our* king' (494b): we as well as they are caught up in the devotion inherent in the symbolic epithets.[36]

Cynewulf's link between 'us' worshippers and the ascending king was not, however, just a general association with apostle/pilgrim/thegn witnesses. His narrative bore the imprint of liturgical practices. There was as much hearing in it as seeing: music, heard loud and sudden in the sky at the end of Christ's words to the apostles, heralded the ascension (491–2a); the joyful song of the angels hymning the ascending Christ (502b–4a) interrupted a sequence of references to the apostles seeing (494b–502a and 506–8a); and the speech addressed to the apostles by two angels rang out from on high (508b–10a). Probably in this last feature Cynewulf was reproducing an impression which he had gained specifically from the

[34] This point was made by Gregory the Great in his Latin Ascension Day homily which gave Cynewulf his underlying train of thought (ed. PL 76, col. 1216).

[35] See above, p. 318; *beorn* as well as 'ece eadfruma' (530b and 532a).

[36] Concentration on the disappearance of Christ as the crucial stage in the ascension was intellectualized and consolidated a century and more later in visual art of the late Anglo-Saxon Benedictine reform period, when English artists apparently introduced the convention of depicting the ascending Christ, not full-figure as in former tradition (this is how he is portrayed in, e.g., the two English carvings mentioned below, p. 327 and n. 39), but with just his feet showing beneath the clouds (see Schapiro, 'The Image of the Disappearing Christ'), a formula which, once thus begun, was to dominate the visual arts for the rest of the Middle Ages and beyond. Notable early-eleventh-century examples are a full-page picture in the Sacramentary of Robert of Jumièges (Rouen, Bibliothèque Municipale, Y.6 (274), of *c.* 1020, and a drawing in coloured outline disposed in the margins of a text page of the Bury Psalter (Vatican City, Biblioteca Apostolica Vaticana, Reg. lat. 12), of the second quarter of the century. In the psalter drawing the Virgin Mary (traditional to visual representations, though without biblical authority) and apostles receive the words of the two angels (see below) on scrolls and look up towards the disappearing Christ with an animation which is in the spirit of Cynewulf's dramatic narrative, but in the sacramentary the composition is more exclusively learned. In this version the Virgin Mary, Christ's human mother, stands prominently among the apostles, in a mandorla like that of her partly visible son above, whereas Cynewulf had seen no reason even to specify her as a member of his apostle/pilgrim/thegn audience.

liturgy. The words used by the angels in his poem were based on 'Viri Galilæi, quid statis aspicientes in cœlum? Hic Jesus, qui assumptus est a vobis in cœlum', which, according to Acts I. 11, was said to the apostles by the two men standing by them in white, and which furnished the text for several of the sung parts of the Mass and Offices at Ascensiontide. We do not know for a fact how this text was sung in ninth-century England, but, as a consequence of the assumption (as in Gregory's homily)[37] that the speakers of Acts were angels, it was sung from a height, we know, at Essen somewhat later, and there is good evidence that architectural conditions in Cynewulf's England could have given liturgical singers of the angels' words appropriate symbolic height.[38] Certainly the poet's 'ofer wera mengu' (509b) would apply to singers above a congregation in a sizeable church or cathedral better than to angels above the small group of apostles; and the sound of liturgical voices coming from above could have suggested to him the description 'beorhtan reorde' (510a). We may, I think, take it that probably liturgical usage led Cynewulf to position his speakers high up, in contrast to Acts and Gregory's homily which placed them on the ground, and in contrast to the two comparable eighth- and ninth-century English visual depictions,[39] which showed them down on a level with the apostles. And there are also more general signs that the poet was thinking of his image within the framework of the great liturgical sequence of Resurrection-Ascension-Pentecost, for he explicitly placed the ascension forty days after the resurrection – when Christ fulfilled the universal prophecies of the Old Testament through his passion (466–70a) – and ten days before Pentecost (542b). Ever since the fourth century Ascension Day had become increasingly prominent in the Easter season which formed the climax to the annual cycle of the cult of Christ the saviour. Taking part in the inspiring liturgical celebration of this festival, which included singing of the angels' words from on high, may well have given Cynewulf the initial impulse to compose his poem.

The poet followed his dramatic narrative of Christ's grieved-for departure from earth with another of his triumphantly welcomed arrival in

[37] See above, p. 326, n. 34. [38] See my 'Cynewulf's Image of the Ascension', p. 302.

[39] On an eighth-century stone slab preserved in Wirksworth church, Derbyshire, and on the upright of a ninth-century stone cross now, as a fragment, serving as the stem of a font in Rothbury church, Northumberland; see further, *ibid.*, pp. 296–9 and pls. I and II.

heaven (545b–85[40]), which was based on the Ascensiontide hymn by Bede already mentioned.[41] The combination of these complementary narratives was controlled by the unifying image of the two Jerusalems, the earthly and the heavenly. The former was the city which Christ had hallowed by his presence and to which the apostles went, sad at heart, after the ascension

> (Gewitan him þa gongan   to Hierusalem
> hæleð hygerofe,   in þa halgan burg,
> geomormode

['Then they went to Jerusalem, strong-minded heroes, into the holy city, sad at heart', 533–5a]),

there to await Pentecost ('in þære torhtan byrig' ('in the radiant city', 542a)). The latter was the city to which Christ went in glory ('to þære beorhtan byrg' ('to the bright city', 519a)), a *ceaster* (578a) with a throne (516b and 555a) from which gifts are dispensed (572a) and with gates (576b) and shining buildings (742a[42]). Both cities alike shared the joy of Christ's arrival in heaven ('blis in burgum' (530a)).

Cynewulf's portrayal of the arrival did not go beyond the contents of Bede's hymn, but his account of the departure integrated diverse elements into the apostles/pilgrims/thegns' act of seeing, terminated by Christ's disappearance up above roofs – a round church with a footprint open to the sky, the lord's ascension above the 'lids' of the heavens (518a)[43] to the bright city, his head luminous (504b–5), a glorious throng of angels singing as they descended to attend him and praising his radiance as they escorted him to his celestial destination, two of their number addressing the apostles from on high. The brightness of the ascending saviour's head seems to have been derived from a visual impression of a nimbed, haloed

[40] Some sixty-five to seventy lines are wanting between *frætwum* and *ealles waldend* in 556b owing to the loss of a leaf from the Exeter Book after fol. 15; see Pope, 'The Lacuna in the Text of Cynewulf's *Ascension*'

[41] Above, p. 317, and n. 14.

[42] Lines 740b–2a contain a further brief but graphic reference to the joy of the angelic citizens when they saw Christ approaching.

[43] Presumably the poet meant that Christ passed above the *cælum aereum*. The distinction between this layer and the upper *cælum aethereum* into which Christ ascended was explained by Gregory earlier in the homily (on which, see above, p. 326, n. 34) in his commentary on Mark XVI.19.

Christ;[44] and the curious word *gehlidu*, 'lids' (518a), may have been occasioned by a visual source too.[45] Writings other than the Bible or Gregory's homily were responsible for the large number of escorting angels.[46] Scripture, other texts, pilgrimage, the liturgy, visual artifacts, and motifs and symbolic language traditional to native poetry were all pressed into service to form Cynewulf's truly majestic devotional image of Christ's kingship in his ascension.

The sharing of symbolic language unites angels, apostles/pilgrims/ thegns and ourselves into a single worshipping community. The day on which the apostles gladly availed themselves of the *tacne fela*, 'many tokens' (462a), made known to them by their *sincgiefa*, 'tires brytta' and 'wuldres helm' (460a, 462b and 463a), before his ascension was our *wildæg*, 'day of joy' (459a), too. We, like the angels, praise Christ as the source of life (504a). *The Kentish Hymn* in a mid-tenth-century manuscript (London, BL, Cotton Vespasian D. vi) exhorts all Christians to adore the Lord of hosts in gratitude, just as Cynewulf's apostles did ('lufedun leofwendum lifes agend' ('gratefully worshipped the owner of life', 471)):

Wuton wuldrian weorada dryhten
halgan hlioðorcwidum, hiofenrices weard,
lufian liofwendum, lifes agend

['Let us glorify the Lord of hosts with holy speech, the guardian of the kingdom of heaven, gratefully worship the owner of life', *The Kentish Hymn* 1–3].

Cynewulf's devotional appellations were very close indeed to liturgical

[44] I do not know of any other text which located radiance in Christ's head as he ascended; Bede's hymn did not.

[45] Could it have been prompted by thin clouds representing the *cœlum aereum* (see above, n. 43) in, e.g., the seventh-century mosaic of the apse in the chapel of St Venantius in the baptistry of St John Lateran, Rome (see Oakeshott, *The Mosaics of Rome*, pl. 99)? *Gehlidu* occurs also, in the same sense and same plural form, at *Christ* (*III*) 904a and Genesis (*B*) 584a. The usual Latin words for the *cœlum aereum* in its full height were *arx* and *culmen*, both sometimes plural (e.g. Bede's Ascensiontide hymn has 'cuncta transiens caeli micantis culmina'), and the usual Old English word was *hrof* (see, e.g., *til hrofe*, *Cædmon's Hymn* 6a (in Bede's paraphrase of the 'hymn', 'pro culmine tecti'), and 'of heum heofnes hrofe''ex summa cæli arce', *The Durham Ritual*, ed. Brown *et al.*, 48v3, and cf. Cynewulf's use of *hrof* at *Christ* (*II*) 749b and *Elene* 89b). I do not know of any patristic comment which would account for *gehlidu*. Nor does alliteration depend on it in any of its three occurrences.

[46] See 'swa gewritu secgað', 547b. There are throngs in Bede's hymn. For a full comment, see my 'Cynewulf's Image of the Ascension', p. 297, n. 2.

invocations: 'sigores agend' (513b), for instance, is an exact equivalent of *triumphator* in the antiphon *in evangelio* for second vespers on Ascension Day in the Leofric and Wulfstan Collectars[47] and so is *wuldres cyning* (565b) of *rex gloriae* in Bede's Ascensiontide hymn. Copious draughts from the liturgy nourished poetry's symbolic system as a common language for the universal company of worshippers of Christ the king.

A uniform dramatic unity of light and song prevails too. The apostles saw the ascending Christ[48] and saw the two singing angels about to speak to them (506a); these two angels saw the apostles seeing the ascending lord clearly (512–13a) and seeing the joyous, radiant throng of angels as a whole (519b and 521b–2); and the singing angels adored the light shining from the saviour's head (502b–5). The loud song raised by the angelic host was suddenly heard (491–2a and 502b–3a), implicitly by the apostles, and its impact is imagined by us. The human speech used by the two angels made a distinct impression (510a), again implicitly on the apostles, and makes its mark on us by virtue of the narrator's description. A vitality and harmony pervade this Christ-centred domain combining earth and heaven. We experience the spirituality of it as participants in the lively praise which it offers its king in all its parts. Our involvement is not essentially different from that of other actors: the angels are visually described to the apostles (521b–2) and to us (492b–4a and 506–8a) only in terms of their brightness, the rest being left to the apostles/pilgrims/thegns', and our, general knowledge, and likewise the angelic song of joyous praise, apart from its loudness and suddenness (491–2a), is undescribed for both the apostles and ourselves. Liturgical worship doubtless provided the main impetus for this dramatic synthesis, just as it did for the language used, but an organized composition in the visual arts could have contributed architectonically as well.[49] Symbolic language had been absorbed into a self-contained, self-sufficient, ecclesiastical culture in which art, architecture, music and language interacted.

There is a hint that the spiritual space and time into which the

[47] *The Leofric Collectar*, ed. Dewick and Frere I, col. 175, and *The Portiforium of Saint Wulstan*, ed. Hughes I, 64 respectively.

[48] 495b, 498, 501–2a and 535b–6 (they left, grieving, for Jerusalem, 'þonan hy god nyhst / up stigende eagum segun' ('from where they had just seen with their eyes God rising up')).

[49] For exploration of this possibility, see my 'Cynewulf's Image of the Ascension', esp. pp. 299–304.

apostles/pilgrims/thegns and, by association, we ourselves look up at our king are not sequential as space and time are in this world. The angels, speaking to those below, insert between an antecedent (þas bliðan gedryht, i.e., the throng of angels (519b)) and its relative clause ('þe ge her on stariað . . .' (521b–2)) an interjection (520–1a), not explicitly amplifying this host's happiness, as we might expect it to, but expressing praise of Christ, which is in terms of the relationship between the nobility of the victorious son of God and that of all victorious sons (necessarily of men, and thus by implication relevant to angelic happiness), but which interrupts the relationship between angels seen and apostles seeing.[50] An underlying fundamental association between the joy of angels and Christ, who is at once divine and human, interferes with human narrative structure. A suggestion results that the heavenly part and the earthly part of this king's realm are not identical.

There were two ways in which this difference could be dealt with. One was to describe the earthly in terms of the heavenly by means of allegory, as in the Latin Bestiary, which gave an Old English poet a model of a panther as an animal with a gentleness, kindness and love towards all creatures except the dragon, paralleling Christ's beneficence to all creation other than the devil.[51] The other way was to describe the heavenly in terms of the earthly by means of metaphor. An instance of this occurs in Cynewulf's account of Christ's arrival at the gates of heaven (themselves metaphorical, of course), triumphantly leading the host he has redeemed by his harrowing of hell, when the poet envisaged one of the escorting angels declaring to those within,[52]

> Wile nu gesecan sawla nergend
> gæsta giefstol, godes agen bearn,
> æfter guðplegan

['Now the saviour of souls wishes to seek the giftseat of spirits, God's own son, after battle', 571–3a].

The statement that, after doing battle victoriously with the devil, the son of God will assume a *giefstol* in heaven was a narrative way of saying, in terms of terrestrial practice, that henceforth saving grace will always be

[50] Cf. *ibid.*, pp. 298–9 and p. 299, n. 1.

[51] See above, pp. 233–4.

[52] The speech (558–85) was based on the dramatic dialogue which Bede, in his Ascensiontide hymn, modelled on ps. XXIV.7–10.

available to all righteous souls.[53] The *giefstol* of earthly society was a metaphor for eternal divine beneficence. In metaphor the denotation of symbolic language was heavenly and the connotations were earthly, while in allegory the link was the other way round.

Cynewulf's metaphorical social symbolic language, however, was not confined to his narrative of the saviour's triumphant arrival in heaven. It was used as well in his narrative of the same Lord's departure from earth. Behind both phases lay a question and answer in the homily by Gregory: 'Why did the angels that appeared at Christ's nativity not wear white garments, whereas those appearing at his ascension did?', Gregory asked, and replied, 'Because the white garments signified joyous celebration in heaven when God returned there as man.'[54] The poet began with advice to 'mon se mæra' ('the illustrious man', 441a) to ponder this contrast between nativity and ascension, and amplified his reference to the former's absence of white clothing[55] with a brief narrative of that occasion (443b–6 and 448b–53a) and his reference to the latter's presence of white clothing (455b and 545b–50a) with the much longer narrative of Christ's last teaching of the apostles, his departure from earth and the apostles' ensuing wait in Jerusalem (456–545a). The wearing of white at the ascension was justified, Cynewulf went on to say (550b–4a), by the suitability of brightly dressed thegns at the immense, happy feast which followed 'in þæs þeodnes burg' ('in the city of that leader'), a reference to celebration which was then utilized to usher in the narrative of Christ's triumphant arrival in heaven bringing with it the prospect of peace between angels and men and of a sacred agreement between God and men for evermore (554b–85). The essential consequence of this redemptive act, the poet finally stressed, is that now every man has the opportunity, but not the certainty, of salvation (586–99).[56] All the preceding narrative, whether of departure or arrival, had been subordinate to the intention of stating this momentous outcome with the utmost clarity. There had been no fundamental difference between the disappearing *wuldres weard* (527a) and the *wuldres cyning* (565b) who, as announced by the angelic herald at the gates of heaven, had just rescued countless souls from hell: each appellation, whatever its state in the sequence of events, is equally related to the ultimate potential of

[53] Bede's hymn has only the co-eternal son sitting at his father's right hand.

[54] For Gregory's Latin in full, and a Modern English translation of it, see my 'Cynewulf's Image of the Ascension', p. 293 and n. 4.

[55] 443a, 447–8a and 453b–5a.

[56] See above, p. 313.

salvation emanating from the ruler of all. Each is a metaphor for the divine source of spiritual well-being in both this world and the next.

All symbolic epithets for God as creator and as redeemer and judge of men were ultimately metaphorical in that they combined divine potential, common to heaven and earth, with narrative thinking specific to humans. But for Anglo-Saxons, as represented by Cynewulf, that distinction would probably have been considered artificial, if it occurred to them at all. They would have found it relatively straightforward to accept that these terms, as expressions of praise for a triune God who had become partly human in the person of Christ, were as usable by angels as by themselves.

Sib sceal gemæne
englum ond ældum a forð heonan
wesan wideferh

['A relationship shall be common to angels and men henceforth for ever!', 581b–3a],

declared the angel announcing the ascended Christ at the gates of heaven in this poet's version, without any corresponding thought in Bede's hymn or Gregory's homily. Poetic symbolic language had become the medium of an everlasting community uniting heaven and earth in worship of a Christ who was both God and man. It had been transferred into the symbolic time of ecclesiastically inspired devotion to this eternal king. It had taken with it the ancient native ideal of social nobility into a realm of unending light and sound. Now it occupied a universe in which, for humans, time ultimately stood still in the sense that men were subordinated for ever to events which had occurred, and would continue to occur, once and for all, and about which they could ask only interpretative questions. This domain was already determined by all-commanding events, past and to come, on which human imagination, and hence the implications of language, played forwards as much as backwards. Devotional symbolic language now operated in an inclusive, dramatic, spiritual, time-frame which was radically different both from the practical, daily present of society outside the church and from the recurrent, socially symbolic past transmitted to the present by Germanic poetic tradition. Poetry's continued concern with the practical present in this new context will be taken up next.

10

Adaptation to a new material morality

The 'ordinariness' of day-to-day practical society, left behind by mainstream vernacular poetry when symbolic language was elevated into the spiritual realm, became increasingly subject in the vernacular to prose-led analysis and classification. Even in the areas in which traditional, poetry-led, modes of thinking and feeling would have been strongest, such as the shared obligations of king and followers,[1] new methodology was taking over. Alfred, for instance, clearly showed this trend when dealing with these mutual responsibilities in a passage he supplied on his own account in his vernacular prose version of the *De consolatione Philosophiae*. In connection with Boethius's assertion to 'Philosophy' that he had been little motivated by an ambition for mortal things but had desired material for action,[2] the king made his spokesman, 'Mind', specify the essential needs of someone who is called upon to rule, as Alfred himself had been: 'A king's material for ruling with', Mind says, 'is that he shall have his land fully manned: he must have men who pray, and soldiers and workmen . . . Also his material is that he shall have sustenance for those three orders; the sustenance consisting of land to dwell on, and gifts, and weapons, and food, and ale, and clothes, and everything those three orders require.'[3] Alfred no longer attempted to embed the practical needs of society in the emotive language of age-old human ties, as poetic symbolic expression did, but instead provided an itemized list. Nor did he turn to traditional poetic narrative for his model, but instead (for the first time known to surviving written record) he applied a tripartite classification of society, which the vernacular prose authors Ælfric and Wulfstan were to use again a century or so later,

[1] See above, pp. 7–8. [2] *Gerendis*, or in some manuscripts *regendis*, 'ruling'.

[3] *King Alfred's Old English Version of Boethius 'De consolatione Philosophiae'*, ed. Sedgefield, p. 40, lines 15–23.

but which (on internal evidence) Ælfric owed not to Alfred but to a written Latin source (Wulfstan, for his part, deriving the categorization from Ælfric). The earliest known reference outside England to a tripartite division specifying workers as a separate order in their own right alongside those who pray and those who fight (as against merely distinguishing those praying and those fighting from a general populace) is in the *Carmen ad Rotbertum regem* composed by Adalbero of Laon in the late 1020s:

> Triplex ergo Dei domus est quae creditur una.
> Nunc orant, alii pugnant aliique laborant

['Threefold therefore is the house of God which is believed one. Now they pray, others fight and others work'].[4]

This is slightly later than Ælfric's three treatments[5] (and that of Wulfstan, dependent on Ælfric[6]). Ælfric's source had *bellatores*, not the *pugnatores* which would have been the precise equivalent of Adalbero's *pugnant*. Adalbero and Ælfric, it seems, represent two minor variants of an enumeration[7] which had been defined at least as early as the late ninth century when Alfred made the first recorded use of it. The chances are that the king did not invent this enumeration himself but that it came to him from a spoken or written source in the tradition later known to Ælfric and Adalbero.[8] It represented a bold departure for him in that it meant stepping out of the binary mode of social thought, on which the poetry to which he was devoted[9] had been founded time out of mind, into a different

[4] *Adalbéron de Laon, 'Poème au roi Robert'*, ed. Carozzi, lines 295–6; for Carozzi's views on the early tradition of the tripartite classification, see his introduction, *ibid.*, pp. cxx-cxxvi.

[5] *Ælfric's Lives of Saints*, ed. Skeat, xxv, lines 812–62 (written before 1002); Ælfric's Latin Letter to Wulfstan, ed. Fehr, *Die Hirtenbriefe Ælfrics*, 'Brief 2a', sect. XIV (written 1002–5); and Ælfric's 'On the Old and New Testament', ed. Crawford, *The Old English Version of the Heptateuch*, lines 1204–20 (written 1005–6).

[6] Wulfstan's 'Institutes of Polity, Civil and Ecclesiastical', ed. Jost, *Die 'Institutes'*, pp. 55–7. Wulfstan's source was clearly Ælfric's 'On the Old and New Testament'.

[7] For Ælfric (and hence Wulfstan) the tradition depended on the key words *laboratores*, *oratores* and *bellatores* but not on any fixed order between them, for he varied his sequence according to the theme he was addressing on the particular occasion.

[8] Enumeration, as such, was an Irish characteristic which had considerable influence on Old English literature. For a recent study of this topic, see Wright, 'The Irish "Enumerative Style" in Old English Homiletic Literature', and for a possibility that the three orders were of Irish origin, see Dubuisson, 'L'Irlande et la théorie médiévale des "trois ordres"'.

[9] See above, p. 145.

trinary system. Alfred was willing to cross this threshold, we may assume, because by doing so he clarified the reality of his own situation.[10]

In vernacular treatment of this society of newly categorized practical responsibilities wisdom became less exclusively the generic attribute of aristocratic warriorship and warrior leadership, as it had been for centuries in poetry, and more a talent for a particular function or a qualification for a particular office, even in verse, as one or two examples readily show. For the *Beowulf* narrator the basis of the good fame of the *Wendla leod*, Wulfgar, was simply the 'wig ond wisdom' for which he was known to many (*Beowulf* 348b–50a), and likewise the lavish praise which tradition heaped on Offa, king of the continental Angles, was amply justified by saying, 'wisdome heold / eðel sinne' ('he protected his native land by wisdom', 1959b-60a). And, even in the late period, in the Bayeaux Tapestry William the Conqueror exhorted his soldiers to prepare themselves for battle against the army of the English 'viriliter et sapienter' ('manfully and wisely').[11] Evidently the old twinning of 'wig ond wisdom' still retained its force for fighting *per se*, although the late-tenth-century poet of *The Battle of Maldon* did not invoke this coupling and was content to cite wisdom along with prosperity to mark a successful tenure of an office, when Ælfwine expressed his pride in his lineage by declaring that his grandfather was 'wis ealdorman woruldgesælig' ('a wise ealdorman, prosperous in the world', 219).

It was not, however, that wisdom merely became more variously distributed. Different sections of society were being expected to contribute different kinds of wisdom to the common weal. While for King Alfred wisdom remained the essence of all good kingship he recognized that its availability depended on more than one resource. When, in his preface to his translation of Gregory's *Regula pastoralis*, he looked back at kings in

[10] The king's grasp of the distinct, but complementary, practical functions of *bellatores* and *laboratores* is well illustrated in the *Anglo-Saxon Chronicle* annal for 895: 'Then afterwards at harvest time the king encamped in the vicinity of the *burh* [London] while they [presumably men from the *burh*] reaped their corn, so that the Danes could not deny them the harvest' (Asser's *Life of King Alfred*, trans. Keynes and Lapidge, *Alfred the Great*, p. 118). Cf. also Alfred's division of his army into two, 'so that always half of its men were at home, half out on service, except for those men who were to garrison the *burhs*' (annal for 893), on which, see *ibid.*, pp. 285–6. Alfred's realization of the separate importance of *oratores* is exemplified by his foundation of a monastery at Athelney and a nunnery at Shaftesbury.

[11] *The Bayeux Tapestry*, ed. Wilson, pls. 57–61.

former times who had had more secure and expanding power than his own, he did not merely continue to use time-honoured words to recall 'hu him ðа speow ægðer ge mid wige ge mid wisdome' ('how they then prospered both with war and with wisdom')[12] but also specified that the wise men throughout England on whom those kings had depended had been both religious and lay,[13] thereby perceiving in the workings of society a distinction corresponding to that seen in kingship itself by an unknown member of his royal circle who differentiated in the vernacular prose version of Orosius's *Historiae adversum paganos* betweeen *onweald*, God-given authority, and *rice*, management of a kingdom.[14] Indeed the very idea that the function of wisdom was first and last to ensure good service to society was under threat. A conception of a primary spiritual wisdom was undermining desire for position in the world. For example, the statement by Boethius's 'Philosophy' that human souls, sharing with celestial and divine beings freedom to will or not to will, 'are necessarily more free when they keep themselves in examination of the divine mind and less when they descend to bodies, and even less when they are bound up in human limbs'[15] was converted by 'Wisdom', in King Alfred's vernacular prose, into an antithesis between concentration on divine matters and desire for worldly honour: 'The men always have the more freedom the nearer to divine things they set their minds, and have the less freedom the nearer they set their mind's desire to this-worldly honour (*þisse woruldare*).'[16] According to this view in the final analysis worldly ambition was no more than a barrier to spiritual wisdom.

Social living required a practical morality which united diversity in the community with a code of behaviour conforming coherently to the premises of spiritual wisdom. Promotion of a moral consensus of this sort was a fresh challenge which vernacular poetry could not avoid if it was to stay true to its traditions of social involvement. The *Beowulf* poet knew that mankind owed wisdom to God:

Wundor is to secganne,
hu mihtig God manna cynne
þurh sidne sefan snyttru bryttað,
eard ond eorlscipe

[12] *Gregory's Pastoral Care*, ed. Sweet, p. 3, lines 8–9. [13] *Ibid.*, lines 3–4.
[14] Kretzchmar, 'Adaptation and *anweald* in the Old English Orosius', pp. 137–45.
[15] Bk V, pr. 2.
[16] *King Alfred's Old English Version of Boethius 'De consolatione Philosophiae'*, ed. Sedgefield, pp. 140, line 31 – 141, line 3.

['It is a wonderful thing to relate how mighty God through his great mind distributes to mankind wisdom, land and warriorship', *Beowulf* 1724b–7a].

But he took this no further than warning against overweening pride and made no attempt to exploit a conception of *snyttru* as a God-given instrument for warding off the wiles of the devil (1740–68). There was no calling into question all the this-worldly objectives which poetry had honoured for so long. In the poet's eyes, after the Danes had suffered a long period of leaderlessness, the *woruldar* which God bestowed on their king, Beowulf, the son of Scyld (16b–17), was an unqualified blessing, subject to no moral scruples whatever. Poetry had to convert its symbolization of the modes of perception, classification and behaviour forming the ancient core of warrior society into representation of conduct based on the individual in the new Christian moral order.

A case in point is the Exeter Book poem of Christian instruction, known as *Precepts*, in which a symbolic father – *frod fæder*, *modsnottor* and 'maga cystum eald' ('a man old in virtues') – advised his son 'wordum wisfæstum' (1–3a).[17] As the maxim in *Beowulf*,

Æghwæþres sceal
scearp scyldwiga gescad witan,
worda ond worca, se þe wel þenceð (287b–9),[18]

defined the relevant acumen for the Danish coastguard when Beowulf and his men arrived as strangers on the shore over which he was keeping watch, so the father in *Precepts* instructed his son to draw a moral distinction thus:

Ongiet georne hwæt sy god oþþe yfel,
ond to scead simle scearpe mode
in sefan þinum ond þe a þæt selle geceos

['Recognize keenly what is good or evil, and constantly distinguish them sharply in your mind and always choose for yourself the better', 45–7].

In fact, old-fashioned maxims on occasion could still serve unchanged, as when the old adage 'think before you speak' was restated:

Wærwyrde sceal wisfæst hæle
breostum hycgan, nales breahtme hlud (57–8).[19]

[17] For a survey of parental instruction as a genre common to Sumerian, Babylonian, Egyptian, Israelite and Old Irish cultures, as well as in Old English, see Hansen, *The Solomon Complex*, pp. 12–67.

[18] See above, p. 114.

[19] See above, p. 79.

In general this symbolic sage aimed at recasting traditional gnomic wisdom in a moral hue.

But there are also signs of the times in what he said. He spoke for Hebrew wisdom when he assimilated the fifth commandment:

> Fæder ond modor   freo þu mid heortan,
> maga gehwylcne,   gif him sy meotud on lufan

['Honour your father and mother with your heart, every relative, if they love God', 9–10].

He made individual responsibility explicitly Christian when he enjoined,

> Ac læt þinne sefan healdan
> forð fyrngewritu   ond frean domas,
> þa þe her on mægðe gehwære   men forlætaþ
> swiþor asigan,   þonne him sy sylfum ryht

['But let your mind observe continually the old writings and the Lord's judgements, which men here in every people allow to decline more than would be good for themselves', 72b–5].

And the verb-reliant, rather than noun-reliant, pithiness of his 'Do a þætte duge, deag þin gewyrhtu' ('Always do what would be good: your deeds will be good', 4) seems closer to sententious prose than to gnomic verse.

Clearly this father was not intent on instructing his son on how to distinguish between the good and the bad in specific circumstances. His advice came as a collection of general principles signalled by traditional linguistic markers and set in a narrative framework of ten numbered occasions. His precepts, at once patriarchal and deeply conventional, placed essential items of practical Christian morality at the symbolic centre of orally transmitted, inherited experience, and thereby asserted that the traditional binary conceptualization of narrative thought in terms of a fundamental compatibility or incompatibility between primary forces[20] remained intact in the moral system. In the conservative mould of this poem the repetition of *dugan*, 'to avail', 'to be competent', 'to be good', in 'Do a þætte duge, deag þin gewyrhtu' imparted an internal, moral connotation to the same basic connection between a man's intention and action – a relationship we would call 'cause and effect' – as that enunciated in an extrovert, pagan environment of interacting doers (*wyrd*, *eorl* and *ellen)* in Beowulf's maxim to the effect that 'Fate often protects [*nerian*]

[20] See above, pp. 105–7.

when a man's fighting spirit is good [*dugan*]': 'Wyrd oft nereð / unfægne eorl, þonne his ellen deah' (*Beowulf* 572b–3).[21] And likewise the antithesis between *god oþþe yfel* (*Precepts* 45b) is the moral equivalent of the opposition between *leof* and *laþ* expressed in the *Beowulf* narrator's maxim,

Fela sceal gebidan
leofes ond laþes se þe longe her
on ðyssum windagum worulde bruceð (1060b–2).[22]

The *Precepts* father followed 'Do a þætte duge, deag þin gewyrhtu' with

god þe biþ symle goda gehwylces
frea ond fultum, feond þam oþrum
wyrsan gewyrhta. Wene þec þy betran

['God will always be a Lord and help to you as regards every good, an enemy to the other worse in deeds. Accustom yourself to do the better thing', 5–7].

Similarly on another occasion he warned, 'Ne gewuna wyrsan' ('Do not keep company with anyone worse', 23a), and on another coupled an injunction to shun defilement for fear of God with the warning, 'He þe mid wite gieldeð, / swylce þam oþrum mid eadwelan' ('He will repay you with punishment, as he will the others with happiness', 19b–20). In the face of the twin possibilities of friendship or enmity from the creator of men ('weoruda scyppend' (62b)) towards each of his creatures now (5–7) and for ever (19b–20), a system was being worked out which applied to moral behaviour the graduated scale of worst, worse, bad, good, better and best which traditionally had been directed to warrior action, as when Unferth tauntingly used the outcome of Beowulf's swimming contest against Breca to judge the newly arrived hero's prospects against Grendel –

Beot eal wið þe
sunu Beanstanes soðe gelæste.
Đonne wene ic to þe *wyrsan* geþingea,
ðeah þu heaðoræsa gehwær dohte,
grimre guðe, gif þu Grendles dearst
nihtlongne fyrst nean bidan

['The son of Beanstan truly carried out his entire boast against you. I then expect for you a *worse* result, although you have always been strong in battle-attacks, in fierce fighting, if you dare to wait for Grendel near at hand all night long', 523b–8] –

[21] See above, p. 69. [22] See above, p. 84.

and when the *Beowulf* narrator, philosophizing about the implications for warrior life of God's rule over men, concluded 'Forþan bið andgit æghwær *selest*, / ferhðes foreþanc' (1059–60a).[23]

The Christian ideas to which poetry adapted might be developments of themes already in verse's own inherited traditions or new concepts or wholesale reversals of its former values. An example of the first sort is the belief that all temporal, material existence was inherently transient as a mere prelude to eternity, for this added a fresh dimension of Christian intellectual absoluteness to traditional symbolic expression of the impressive death of the mighty, as employed by the *Beowulf* narrator when the Geats gazed at their king, Beowulf, killed in heroic combat against the dragon:

þa wæs endedæg
godum gegongen, þæt se guðcyning,
Wedra þeoden wundordeaðe swealt

['then the last day had been reached by the good man, that the battle-king, leader of the Weders, perished in a wondrous death', 3035b–7].

Various stages in this extension are exemplified in our extant poems. In *The Seafarer* the passing of the mighty represented a general decline in the quality of life:

næron nu cyningas ne caseras
ne goldgiefan swylce iu wæron,
þonne hi mæst mid him mærþa gefremedon
ond on dryhtlicestum dome lifdon

['There are now no kings, no emperors, no givers of gold as there were once, when they performed between them the greatest glorious deeds and lived in the noblest renown', 82–5].

Similarly the *Se* (*þe*) speaker in *The Wanderer*[24] exclaimed 'Eala beorht bune! Eala byrnwiga! / Eala þeodnes þrym!' about symbols of warrior glory which his predecessors too would have grieved to lose and then went on to reflect more far-reachingly than they would have done, 'Hu seo þrag gewat, / genap under nihthelm, swa heo no wære' ('O the bright cup! O the

[23] See above, p. 115. For an excellent analysis of *Precepts* along lines similar to those above, see the study by Hansen, *The Solomon Complex*, pp. 41–55 (first published as '*Precepts*: an Old English Instruction', *Speculum* 56 (1981), 1–16).

[24] See below, pp. 404–5.

armoured warrior! O the splendour of the leader of a people! How that time has passed away, grown dark beneath the cover of night, as though it had never been!', 94–6). This speaker's apocalyptic conclusion that 'eal þis eorþan gesteal idel weorþeð' ('this entire foundation of earth will become useless', 110) was felt to be by no means a remote possibility but to be an immediate reality certified by belief that the end of the world was at hand, as a teaching voice emphasized to the *þe* he was addressing in a poem we call *An Exhortation to Christian Living*, written in a script of the beginning of the eleventh century in Cambridge, Corpus Christi College 201:

Þeos woruld is æt ende, and we synd wædlan gyt
heofona rices; þæt is hefig byrden

['This world is at its end, and we are still beggars of the kingdom of heaven; that is a heavy burden', 20–1].

An idea which was new to poetry was that man's God-derived this-worldly wisdom in all its forms partakes of an organization and harmony which the deity has imparted to the whole of his creation – a proposition eloquently promoted in the vernacular prose of Alfred's reign, especially in the king's rendering of Boethius. That Cynewulf had thoroughly assimilated this principle is shown by his treatment of the God-given talents of men which he substituted for the list of six *dona*, 'gifts',[25] in the homily by Gregory the Great serving as his source.[26] First the poet's ten items were introduced collectively in relation to the creator's intention to provide humanity with eternal security in heaven:

Ða us geweorðade se þas world gescop,
godes gæstsunu, ond us giefe sealde,
uppe mid englum ece staþelas,
ond eac monigfealde modes snyttru
seow ond sette geond sefan monna

['Then he who created the world, God's spirit-son, honoured us and granted us gifts, eternal habitations above with angels, and also sowed and planted manifold wisdoms of the mind throughout men's understandings', *Christ* (*II*) 659–63].

Then (664–85) the active 'modes snyttru', the first five predominantly mental and the second five more physical, were carefully crafted as pieces in a single pattern. In each five the first word of the first item is *Sumum*, 'to one man [God gives such-and-such an ability]', whereas the other four items

[25] Based on St Paul's list in I Corinthians XII.8. [26] See above, p. 326, n. 34.

each begin with the word *Sum*, 'one man [can do such-and-such a thing]'. And in each five the description of the first item is markedly longer than that of any other; the second item comes next in length, consisting of a *b* verse, the following *a* and *b* verses and the *a* verse after that; and the third, fourth and fifth items each comprise just a *b* verse and the following *a* verse. By virtue of their liveliness and diversity these *cræftas* (687b), abilities of perception and expression, and skills in music, law, astronomy, writing, fighting, sailing, tree-climbing, weapon-making and travelling, reach right down into this world of multiple action and by a scattering of symbolic expressions ('gleobeam gretan', 'sundwudu drifan' etc.) suggest that they betoken it. But the dominant impression they give is of *snyttru* which, in their subordination to overall balanced listing and systematic proportions, reflect an orderliness owed to their divine source.

A Boethian chain between divine and human wisdom held fast in this poet's view of the world. But equally primary was the realization that man's present experience, governed by choice, differs radically from the fixed state which he believes is in store for him in eternity. The here-and-now has a split right down the middle of it. In a passage previously quoted from the same poem (*Christ II*),[27] Cynewulf exploited his consummate sense of binary verse structure to impart a rhetorical outward pattern to man's present absolute choice between two eternal destinations. Five rhymed pairs of *a* and *b* verses (591–5) form the referential 'envelope' pattern hell/heaven, heaven/hell, heaven/hell, heaven/hell, hell/heaven, clinched by the concluding, summarizing verse, 'swa lif swa deað' (596a). The syntax and word order also form a tightly controlled pattern (genitive combination : genitive combination (591); demonstrative + adjective + noun : demonstrative + adjective + noun (592); genitive combination : genitive combination (593); prepositional phrase + noun : prepositional phrase (employing the same preposition) + noun (594); noun + prepositional phrase (the same preposition) : noun + prepositional phrase (again the same preposition, 595); and noun : noun (596a). And so do the rhythm (/x/x : /x/x (591); x/x/ : x/x/ (592); /x/x : /x/x (593); x/x/ : x/x/ (594); /x/x : /x/x (595); and x/x/ (596a)) and the number of syllables (5 : 5 (591); 5 : 5 (592); 5 : 5 (593); 5 : 5 (594); 6 : 6 (595); and 4 (596a)). The system as such is simplicity itself. There can be no compromise between two possible outcomes, just as no third factor was

[27] Above, p. 313.

envisaged in the binary contrast of the customary vow[28] by which Beowulf committed himself to confronting Grendel:

Ic gefremman sceal
eorlic ellen, oþðe endedæg
on þisse meoduhealle minne gebidan (*Beowulf* 636b–8).[29]

But, whereas Beowulf was voluntarily applying to his particular circumstances a conventional declaration that he was pitting against death his own primary potential, and this basic binary conflict was thus appropriately implied in an alliterative set-off between 'eorlic ellen' and *endedæg*, Cynewulf was explicitly stating divinely ordained alternatives which apply willy-nilly in all circumstances to all men; he was not concerning himself with how the individual chooser is to call on his inner resources to make and apply his personal choice. This poet was therefore patterning descriptive language to give the divinely originated disjunction an external form which was worthy, in miniature, of the perfection of God's own total plan. For each individual down on the middle ground of experience, however, living with this dichotomy was another matter altogether and would have called for a different kind of expression. For one thing, to be wise down here was not merely to be simple. As the father in *Precepts* observed in a gnomic saying with echoes of the Old Testament,[30]

Seldan snottor guma sorgleas blissað,
swylce dol seldon drymeð sorgful
ymb his forðgesceaft, nefne he fæhþe wite

['Rarely is the wise man glad without sorrow, and likewise the fool seldom tempers joy with sorrow about his destiny, unless he knows of hostility', 54–6].

A notion which completely reversed the received poetic point of view was deliberate renunciation of this transitory, material existence in order to achieve spiritual communion with God. *The Seafarer*, for example, begins

[28] See above, pp. 153–4. [29] *Ibid.*, p. 153.

[30] See Hansen, *The Solomon Complex*, pp. 195–6, n. 33. A Norse analogue (first pointed out to me by Andy Orchard) can be added to the references there cited: 'Meðalsnotr / skyli manna hverr, / seva til snotr sé; / því at snotrs manns hjarta / verðr sjaldan glatt, / ef sá er alsnotr er á' ('Middling-wise must each man be, never too wise; for a wise man's heart rarely becomes glad, if he who owns it is completely wise', *Hávamál*, ed. Evans, stanza 55, the note in this edition comparing 'He that increaseth knowledge increaseth sorrow' (Ecclesiastes I. 18)). Recently Larrington has drawn attention to the thematic similarity between the Old English and Norse gnomes and their difference from the sentiment of Ecclesiastes ('*Hávamál* and Sources outside Scandinavia', pp. 143–4).

with an anonymous speaker recalling the night-time danger, the physical cold and the stress of mind he has often endured when seafaring in winter. His experience has been a state of exile from the social life of the hall: storms, waves and seabirds have accompanied him, not happy and generous friends. The antithesis between ease of life on land and the extreme demands which seafaring has made on his body and mind has enlarged his consciousness:

Þæt se mon ne wat
þe him on foldan fægrost limpeð,
hu ic earmcearig iscealdne sæ
winter wunade wræccan lastum,
winemægum bidroren,
bihongen hrimgicelum; hægl scurum fleag

['That the man for whom things fall very happily on land does not know, how, wretchedly sad, I dwelt for a winter in the ice-cold sea in the paths of exile, deprived of friendly kinsmen, hung with icicles; hail flew in showers', 12b–17].

The social deprivation of his seafaring has been symbolic ('winemægum bidroren'), and it is not long before his mind is filled with a conviction that confrontation of nature at its hardest by voluntary, passionate, laying of *wræclastas*, 'tracks of exile' (57), is the way to spiritual enlargement, of seeking 'dryhtnes dreamas' ('the joys of the Lord', 65a) in contrast to 'þis deade lif, / læne on londe' ('this dead life, temporary on land', 65b–6a). The social exile has become the spiritual hero.[31]

Total renunciation of material existence was for only the few, however. Society still had to work out its own salvation under God. Notably the social operation of wealth remained an important issue not to be ignored. Traditionally, material possessions were represented in poetry as integral to the giving and receiving which knitted together the warrior unit of leader and comitatus. Treasured possessions, actively shared in communal surroundings, symbolized the corporate identity of a group[32] and, more generally, social life itself. Received wisdom understood the link between *feohgifte* and 'wilgesiþas' to be symbolic of social health, as in these sequential maxims,

Swa sceal geong guma gode gewyrcean,
fromum feohgiftum on fæder bearme,
þæt hine on ylde eft gewunigen

[31] See further, below, pp. 475–9. [32] See above, pp. 8–9.

wilgesiþas, þonne wig cume,
leode gelæsten; lofdædum sceal
in mægþa gehwære man geþeon (*Beowulf* 20–5).[33]

To break this bond, as the cruel, mean, tyrant, Heremod, did, meant for the wrongdoer *sorhwylmas*, 'surgings of sorrow' (904b), in exile, and for his entire people *aldorcearu*, 'life-care', 'dire sorrow' (906b). Poetry could not readily abandon this symbolic concern for the welfare of society.

It had always faced up to the insecurity, instability, indeed impermanence, of material ownership. Poignant rupture of links with physical objects recurrently symbolized society's evanescence. For instance, in Beowulf's imagination an old father, rendered heirless when his only son has been hanged, gazes in helpless grief at the 'winsele westne' ('deserted wine-hall', *Beowulf* 2456a) left windswept and joyless without his young son to fill it with his horse-riding friends and harp playing.[34] Or again, the *Beowulf* narrator imagined the only survivor of a tribe, which had been cruelly wiped out by war, himself without long to live, addressing to the earth, as he buried his forebears' treasures, a heart-felt lament that *sweord* ('sword'), 'dryncfæt deore' ('beloved drinking-vessel'), *hearda helm* ('hard helmet'), *beadogrima* ('battle-mask') and *herepad* ('army-garment', 2252b–62a) no longer had anyone to value, care for and use them.[35] More abstractly, the 'speaker' of the Exeter Book poem we call *The Ruin*, faced with the majestic remains of a city (usually accepted as Bath), was roused by the antique might in front of him to imagine those who, until slaughtered, had wonderfully constructed and maintained these impressive structures generations ago, and to set before his mind's eye the joyous life the then radiant mead-halls had contained. Those who had seen these piles of stones in their heyday as a shining city, he reflected, had feasted their eyes on every sort of splendour: this was

þær iu beorn monig
glædmod ond goldbeorht gleoma gefrætwed,
wlonc ond wingal wighyrstum scan;
seah on sinc, on sylfor, on searogimmas,
on ead, on æht, on eorcanstan,
on þas beorhtan burg bradan rices

[33] See above, p. 171, to which needs to be added a translation of 24b–5: 'a man prospers in every people through praiseworthy deeds.'

[34] See above, pp. 195–6. [35] See above, p. 198.

['where long ago many a warrior, joyous and bright with gold, adorned in splendour, magnificent and flushed with wine, shone in wargear; he looked on treasure, on silver, on jewellery, on wealth, on property, on precious stone, on this shining city of a broad kingdom', 32b–7)].

Death was the relentless agent of destruction which (*deað* (*Beowulf* 2454a)) had sent the grieving father's son on his journey elsewhere (*ellorsið* (2451a)) and which (*deað* (2236b), *guðdeað* (2249b), *feorhbealo* (2250a) and *bealocwealm* (2265b)) had despatched ('forð onsended' (2266b)) the last survivor's tribe. In *The Ruin* the keynote was wonder at the destruction fate had brought upon the ancient massive walls: 'Wrætlic is þes wealstan, wyrde gebræcon' (1). The overriding inevitability in events ('wyrd seo swiþe' (24b)) had laid waste the shining mead-halls and banished the radiant life within them. Poetry was quite prepared emotionally to accept that material possessions, as such, will count for nothing ultimately. But that was not to gainsay that they remained a moral responsibility here and now. The interests of society, traditionally poetry's concern, were not to be served by turning one's back on riches. Wealth was not to be despised as in itself sinful. A collection of forty-one sententious statements in verse, mostly maxims and injunctions, known as *Instructions for Christians* and occurring in Cambridge, University Library, Ii. 1. 33,[36] proclaimed boldly,

Ne dereð mycel wela manna ænegum,
gif he to swiðe ne bið sylfe beleawen[37]
on þes feos lufan mid feondes larum

['Much wealth does no harm to anyone if he himself is not too strongly betrayed into love of the riches through the devil's teachings', 141–3].

As poetry saw it, the necessity was for a new moral wisdom of wealth which married the needs of society with the eternal needs of every man's soul before God.

Almsgiving combined both sorts of virtue, 'Beo þu . . . ælmesgeorn' ('be charitable'), the teacher of *An Exhortation to Christian Living* enjoined (3). Secret almsgiving was a sacrifice to God (32–4).

36 A manuscript of the second half of the twelfth century with saints' narratives in vernacular prose by Ælfric as its main contents; the verse was first edited and given its present title by Rosier ('*Instructions for Christians*'). For a most helpful analysis of it, see Hansen, *The Solomon Complex*, pp. 108–14.

37 As MS. Rosier incorrectly prints *beleapen*.

Ceapa þe mid æhtum eces leohtes,
þy læs þu forweorðe, þonne þu hyra geweald nafast
to syllanne

['Purchase eternal light with your possessions, lest you perish when you do not have the power over them to give', 35–7a].

Charitable giving of earthly possessions was a virtue on the eternal scale. But it did not amount to an automatic qualification for heavenly wealth:

And þeah þu æfter þinum ende eall gesylle
þæt þu on eorðan ær gestryndes
goda gehwylces, wylle gode cweman,
ne mihtu mid þæm eallum sauwle þine
ut alysan, gif heo inne wyrð
feondum befangen, frofre bedæled,
welena forwyrned

['And although after your end you give all that you have acquired on earth of every good, wishing to please God, you will not be able with all that to redeem your soul, if it is seized within by devils, separated from grace, deprived of blessings', 22–8a].

Almsgiving had to keep company with the practice of other virtues such as humility, love of God and men, prayerfulness and hope for God's forgiveness (3–11), and with avoidance of sins such as gluttony, drunkenness, fornication and sloth (41–5).

Composers of verse were sharing common ground with vernacular prose homilists in dealing with such matters as these. Indeed *An Exhortation to Christian Living*, *Instructions to Christians* and other poems like them survive in manuscripts which have mainly prose contents. Verse was continuing to serve a need for apophthegmatic wisdom, but changes in society had deprived it of its status as the symbolic organ of fundamental, comprehensive social homogeneity. The long-standing union of poetry and society was pulled apart by, for example, a marked increase in monetary wealth, as against bestowed ownership of land and military equipment, in the course of the tenth and eleventh centuries, resulting in a heightened public awareness of the distinction between commercially acquired monetary wealth and the traditional aristocratic power-base of noble birth and military prowess. Prose went further than poetry in recognizing this basic change: in the course of the tenth century it promoted a new meaning, 'rich', for the adjective, *rice*, whereas poetry retained the earlier 'powerful' meaning and was content to incorporate wealth alongside high birth as a component in the authority of the *rice*. The prose writer Ælfric, for instance, late in the tenth century, used *rice* and *welig* interchangeably to translate Latin *dives* and almost always showed that he had the idea of 'wealth' uppermost in employing *rice*, as when, in his rendering of the *Magnificat* ('he hath scattered the proud in the imagination of their hearts. He hath put down the *mighty* from their seats, and hath exalted the humble and meek. He hath filled the hungry with good things; and the *rich* he hath sent empty away'), he combined the two Latin categories of *potentes* and *divites* into a single group of *rice* consisting of, he explained, those who, through pride, prefer earthly wealth to the heavenly. The poet of *The Battle of Maldon* on the other hand, although composing contemporaneously with this prose author, still used *rice* in much the same way as Cynewulf had done more than a century before. The latter had taken for granted that the authority of the *rice* Heliseus, St Juliana's unwelcome suitor, termed a *senator* in the Latin source, was based on both wealth and noble birth – 'Sum wæs æhtwelig æþeles cynnes / rice gerefa' ('There was a certain wealthy man of a noble family, a powerful reeve', *Juliana* 18–19a) – and this seems to have been the combination which the *Maldon* poet also had in mind when alliteratively coupling *gerædest* and *ricost* in the words he attributed to the Viking messenger demanding tribute from the *eorl*, Byrhtnoth, standing on the opposite riverbank in the midst of his comitatus, in a high state of military preparedness:

Ne þurfe we us spillan,   gif ge spedaþ to þam;
we willað wið þam golde   grið fæstnian.
Gyf þu þæt gerædest,   þe her ricost eart
þæt þu þine leoda   lysan wille,
syllan sæmannum   on hyra sylfra dom
feoh wið freode,   and niman frið æt us,
we willaþ mid þam sceattum   us to scype gangan,
on flot feran,   and eow friþes healdan

['We need not destroy ourselves, if you are rich enough; we will establish a truce in return for the gold. If you, who are the most powerful here, decide that you will free your people, give to the seamen, at their own assessment, property in exchange for peace, and accept protection from us, we will embark with the money, put out to sea and leave you in peace', 34–41].[38]

[38] For the increase in coinage, the related semantic shift in *rice* and references for the Ælfric example cited above, see Godden, 'Money, Power and Morality in Late Anglo-Saxon England', pp. 41–4 and 52.

Prose also went further than poetry in applying received ideas about the morality of wealth directly to society as it actually was. For instance, in one of his homilies, Ælfric started from a passage in a Latin source which proclaimed the moral attitudes to material circumstances appropriate to (1) *sublimes et divites* (whom Ælfric classed collectively as *ða rican)*, (2) *mediocres* and (3) *pauperes*, and, following his source, warned the first group not to put their hope 'on ðam swicelum welum' ('in the deceitful wealth'), rendering thus 'in incerto diuitiarum' ('in the uncertainty of riches') in the Latin. Then, of his own accord, he appended to the 'rich' a category of merchants to whom he directed this advice: 'Cypmannum gedafenað. þæt hi soðfæstnysse healdon. and heora sawla ne syllon. ðurh swicele aðas. ac lofian heora ðing buton laðre forsworennysse' ('For merchants it is proper that they should preserve truth and not sell their souls through false oaths, but praise their goods without hateful perjury').[39]

Poetry was more concerned to present the complete range of general principles. *Wela*, 'wealth', was life's potential for abundance, for plenty. Cynewulf celebrated it as the bounty of the fruits of the earth nourishing men:

> Dreoseð deaw ond ren, duguðe weccaþ
> to feorhnere fira cynne,
> iecað eorðwelan

['Dew and rain fall, arouse fruitfulness as sustenance for the race of men, increase the wealth of the earth', *Christ (II)* 609–11a].

It is the gift of God the creator: 'He [dryhten] us æt giefeð ond æhta sped, / welan ofer widlond' ('He [the Lord] gives us food and abundance of goods, wealth over the spacious earth', 604–5a). Through God's beneficence there is *eadwela*, 'blessed wealth', in heaven (*Elene* 1316a) and on earth alike (in an anonymous poem, *The Fortunes of Men* 67a). In heaven it is eternal (*Elene* 1316a), in earth but transitory, as bleakly foreseen in the *eardstapa*'s apocalyptic 'þonne ealre þisse worulde wela weste standeð' ('when the riches of all this world stand desolate') in *The Wanderer*.[40] Some men, but not all, understand, through the gift of the holy spirit, that God's grace is infinitely superior to earthly wealth:

> Sum her geornlice gæstes þearfe
> mode bewindeþ, ond him metudes est
> ofer eorðwelan ealne geceoseð

[39] *Ibid.*, pp. 56–7 and references there cited.

[40] See below, pp. 403–4.

['One here zealously clasps the need of the spirit with his mind, and chooses all the grace of God for himself over earthly wealth', *The Gifts of Men* 86–8].

Æhtwela, 'wealth of material possessions' (*The Fates of the Apostles* 84a and *Guthlac A* 388a), was essentially a part of mankind's fallen state. In his prelapsarian perfection man could have avoided having any problems with it: to begin with, in paradise, Adam and Eve had been 'mid welan bewunden' ('surrounded with wealth', *Genesis* (*B*) 420a). It was by their own fatal mistake, when tempted by the devil, that they made the wrong choice between a tree of life and a tree of death, which the creator had set beside them so that

moste on ceosan
godes and yfeles, gumena æghwilc,
welan and wawan

['every man had to choose one of good and evil, happiness and woe', 464b–6a].

Distinctions between wealth and poverty of goods in this corrupted world were therefore in themselves ultimately of insignificance: at the terrifying last judgement 'þær hæfð ane lage earm and se welega' ('there the poor and the wealthy man will have a single law', *The Judgement Day II* 164). The real point was that in terms of heavenly wealth we are all beggars, as the teaching voice in *An Exhortation to Christian Living* urged:

Þeos woruld is æt ende, and we synd wædlan gyt
heofena rices; þæt is hefig byrden (20–1).[41]

Elegant paradoxes of immense import could be constructed on this theme, such as the biting one the poet of *Christ III* attributed to Christ the judge indicting the sinner:

Ic wæs on worulde wædla þæt ðu wurde welig in heofonum,
earm ic wæs on eðle þinum þæt þu wurde eadig on minum (1495–6).[42]

Christian vernacular poets, inheriting a long tradition of involvement with primary potentials, were interested in the ethics of the underlying relationship between human control over this world's wealth and eternal spiritual welfare more than in the morality pertaining to the particular material make-up of society.

[41] See above, p. 342. [42] See above, p. 303.

In story set at the interface of the material world and the life of the spirit vernacular poets by and large fixed their attention firmly on the latter. Viewed in this perspective worldly wealth became the marker of either God-fearing fulfilment or heathen blindness. It became the spirit's touchstone, as it had been for so long society's. For example, when Cynewulf composed his poem telling the story of St Juliana's martyrdom, he used a Latin source which,[43] after introducing two personages of the saint's fiancé as a senator and a friend of Maximianus, imperial persecutor of Christians, and the saint herself as an intelligent Christian, sensible in thought and speech, virtuous and diligent in praying and church-going, proceeded to open the action by relating that, when this fiancé wanted to celebrate the wedding, Juliana first demanded as a precondition that he had to become a prefect and next, when gifts to the emperor had brought that about, required that before she could agree he had to believe in and worship God the Father, Son and Holy Spirit. The vernacular poet, on the other hand, cut out any reference to the saint's characteristics and habits or to her insistence on the prefectship and instead set up straightaway a clearcut opposition between a determination on her part to preserve her virginity free of sin for the love of Christ (*Juliana* 29b–31) and an ostentatious ownership of worldly wealth by her pagan fiancé (22b–4a):

Hire wæs godes egsa
mara in gemyndum, þonne eall þæt maþþumgesteald
þe in þæs æþelinges æhtum wunade.
Þa wæs se weliga þæra wifgifta,
goldspedig guma, georn on mode,
þæt him mon fromlicast fæmnan gegyrede,
bryd to bolde. Heo þæs beornes lufan
fæste wiðhogde, þeah þe feohgestreon
under hordlocan, hyrsta unrim
æhte ofer eorþan. Heo þæt eal forseah

['For her, fear of God was more in her thoughts than all the treasure-hoard which resided in the nobleman's possessions. Then the wealthy man, the lord rich in gold, was eager in his mind for the dowry, that the woman should be made ready for him very quickly, the bride for his house. She firmly despised the warrior's love, although he owned riches in his treasure-chest, countless ornaments over the earth. She scorned all that', 35b–44].

[43] If, as most scholars accept, it was closely related to the text translated by Allen and Calder at *Sources and Analogues*, pp. 122–32.

In the ensuing confrontation the prefect's anger at his frustration (common to the Latin source and the English) is linked to his wealthy status in the vernacular but not the Latin: whereas the source merely reports that the prefect told Juliana's father exactly what she had said to him, the poem has him complaining to the father,

Me þa fraceðu sind
on modsefan   mæste weorce,
þæt heo mec swa torne   tæle gerahte
fore þissum folce

['The insults are most distressing to me in my mind, in that she has attacked me so grievously with blasphemy in front of this people', 71b–4a];

and when the source merely states, 'The prefect . . . wondered what punishment to inflict upon her',[44] the poem says,

Þæt þam weligan wæs   weorc to þolianne,
þær he hit for worulde   wendan meahte,
sohte synnum fah,   hu he sarlicast
þurh þa wyrrestan   witu meahte
feorhcwale findan

['That was distress for the wealthy man to endure, as to where he could change it before the world; stained with sins he sought how he could most painfully, through the worst torments, devise her slaughter', 569–73a].

Finally, when her soul was led away from her body to the long bliss through the stroke of a sword (669b–71a), and, to punish him (678a), her persecutor was drowned at sea along with thirty-four companions (675b–81a), her death and his are explicitly contrasted in the poem, though they are not in the Latin. For him and his men it meant everlasting frustration of their materialism:

hroþra bidæled,
hyhta lease   helle sohton.
Ne þorftan þa þegnas   in þam þystran ham,
seo geneatscolu   in þam neolan scræfe,
to þam frumgare   feohgestealda
witedra wenan,   þæt hy in winsele
ofer beorsetle   beagas þegon,
æpplede gold

44 *Ibid.*, p. 131.

['Deprived of joys, without hopes, they sought hell. Those thegns in that dark home, that band of retainers in that deep pit, had no reason to expect sure treasure-hoards from that leader, that they would receive in the wine-hall, upon the beer-bench, rings, round(?) gold', 681b–8a].

But her death meant that praise of God now prevails where materialism reigned before:

Ungelice wæs
læded lofsongum lic haligre
micle mægne to moldgræfe,
þæt hy hit gebrohton burgum in innan,
sidfolc micel. Þær siððan wæs
geara gongum godes lof hafen
þrymme micle oþ þisne dæg
mid þeodscipe

['Differently was the body of the saint led to her grave by a great throng with songs of praise, so that they, a huge multitude, brought it inside the city. There afterwards, through the passage of years, praise of God has been raised up with great splendour until this day with one accord', 688b–95a].

Her absolute rejection of the pagan materialism personified by the prefect served as preparation for her supreme spiritual triumph forming the middle half of the poem, namely the verbal defeat which, as 'wuldres condel' ('candle of glory', 454b),[45] she inflicted on 'feond moncynnes' ('the enemy of mankind', 317b and 630a), whose father is 'hellwarena cyning' ('king of the inhabitants of hell').[46] Her preliminary exercise of inviolate anti-worldliness provided the symbolic background against which we hear the devil declare that, of all mankind since the beginning of the world

Ne wæs ænig þara
þæt me þus þriste, swa þu nu þa,
halig mid hondum, hrinan dorste,
næs ænig þæs modig mon ofer eorþan
þurh halge meaht, heahfædra nan
ne witgena

['None of them has dared to touch me thus boldly, as you have now, holy one with your hands, nor has any person on earth been so brave through holy power, no patriarch, no prophet', 510b–15a].

[45] An image unknown to the Latin source.

[46] 437a and 543–6a; cf. 522b–3a.

A quite different point-of-view prevailed in some of the stories, both religious and secular, written in vernacular prose in the tenth and eleventh centuries. Deriving through Latin versions from the Greek tradition of adventure-story-telling from which the poem *Andreas* was also ultimately descended,[47] these tales were marked by a much more circumstantial, psychological, strain than any in symbolic stories such as that of *Juliana*. These prose stories proceeded from episode to episode set in the intimate experience of human beings on this side of the material/spiritual divide.

The surviving religious example of this type is a version of the legend of the Seven Sleepers of Ephesus which an unknown author composed in the vernacular probably in the last quarter of the tenth century[48] and is known to us as an item in the main surviving copy of Ælfric's *Lives of Saints* although it certainly was not by him. The account of a mass persecution of Christians which opens this story – just as there is one at the start of *Juliana* – shows us immediately that the focus is quite different from the latter's lofty, general view. In *Juliana*

Oft hi þræce rærdon,
dædum gedwolene, þa þe dryhtnes æ
feodon þurh firencræft. Feondscype rærdon,
hofon hæþengield, halge cwelmdon,
breotun boccræftige, bærndon gecorene,
gæston godes cempan gare ond lige

['Often they committed violence, led astray in their deeds, those who hated the law of the Lord through propensity for crime. They promoted enmity, raised up idols, killed the holy, destroyed the book-learned, burned the chosen, persecuted[49] God's soldiers with spear and flame', 12b–17].

This poem sets up a symbolic persecution of *halge*, *boccræftige*, *gecorene* and *godes cempan* by 'dædum gedwolene', 'þa þe dryhtnes æ / feodon', possessed by *firencræft* and intent on *hæþengield*. But the prose Seven Sleepers legend presents a reader with sharp visual images, such as this: 'and hi ða hæþenan men þonne hi cristene men ahwær fundon . hi hi ut drifon . and him beforan feredon swilce lytle gærstapan . and to ðam folce læddon ðær ealle men hæðengyld mid ðam casere wurðedon . and þa cristenan nyddon þæt hi

[47] See above, p. 249.

[48] See my opinion reported by Whitelock, in her 'The Numismatic Interest', p. 188 and n. 3.

[49] For the rare verb *gæstan*, see further, below, p. 449, n. 61.

mid heom deofle wurðedon' ('and the heathens, when they found Christians anywhere, drove them out and carried them in front of them like small grasshoppers, and led them to the people where all were worshipping idols with the emperor').[50]

This narrative, which was intended specifically to demonstrate that the resurrection of the body on the day of judgement is perfectly credible, takes place in this world of our own hopes and fears, where by rights belongs too the story of the finding of the true cross by the mother of Emperor Constantine, told by Cynewulf in his poem, *Elene*. But, whereas that poet, conveying the excitement of St Helena's embarkation at the start of her voyage to the Holy Land for her search, set about engaging our mind's eye only indirectly by way of an on-the-spot spectator invented for the purpose –

Þær meahte gesion, se ðone sið beheold,
brecan ofer bæðweg, brimwudu snyrgan
under swellingum, sæmearh plegean,
wadan wægflotan (243–6a)[51] –

this prose author so freely assumed empathy with the sufferings endured by martyrs for their inward love of God that he could claim that, had we been there, we would have supported him in hyperbole:

Swilc mihte campdom beon . swilce man ðær mihte geseon . ðæt hi god inweardlice lufedon þa hi for ðære lufe his naman yrmðe geþafedon . and þone sylfan deaþ to ðan swiðe þafedon . and na þæt an mænan mihton and heora eorfoða behreowsian . ac gif we ðær wæron we mihton gehyran swa swa ealle ða gehyrdon þe ðær æt wæron . þæt wæs onmang ðam mycclan geþryle . and on ðam egeslican geþryngce ða man þa martyras cwylmde . þe wolde þincean færunga swilce ealle ða anlicnyssa ðe on þære byrig to godon geond ealle gesette wæron ðæt hi ealle ætgædere oncwædon . and anre stemne clypedon . þæt hi mid ealle aweg ðanon woldon for þam mycclan yrmðum þe ða godes halgan for heora ðingan þolodon . and swilce þa stræta ealle eac oncwædon . for ðam halgan banum þe toworpene him onuppan geond ealle ða byrig lagon . Eac swilce þa burhweallas cwacedon and bifedon . swilce hi feallan woldon for þam halgum lichamum þe on heom geond þa birig on ælce healfe hangedon

['Such warfare took place that it was seen there that they loved God inwardly when they endured affliction for the love of his name and suffered death itself so severely; and not only did they lament and bewail their sufferings, but if we had been there

[50] *Ælfric's Lives of Saints*, ed. Skeat, XXIII, lines 55–9. [51] See above, p. 277.

we would have heard, as all those heard who were present among the great crowd and in the terrible throng when the martyrs were slain, that it suddenly seemed as though all the images which were set up as gods throughout the city spoke together, calling out with one voice that they wanted to leave there completely because of the great miseries which God's saints suffered on their account, and as though all the streets spoke too because of the holy bones which lay thrown on them throughout the city; moreover as though the city walls shook and trembled as if they would fall because of the holy bodies which hung upon them throughout the city on every side', 86–99].

The setting of *Elene* was a mighty imperial authority which was a Christianized, moralized, type of the successful warrior-kingship attributed to the Danish ruler of long ago, Scyld Scefing, at the beginning of *Beowulf*. The founder of the Danish royal line, to which Hrothgar belonged, reigned thus:

Oft Scyld Scefing sceaþena þreatum,
monegum mægþum meodosetla ofteah,
egsode eorlas, syððan ærest wearð
feasceaft funden; he þæs frofre gebad,
weox under wolcnum weorðmyndum þah,
oð þæt him æghwylc ymbsittendra
ofer hronrade hyran scolde,
gomban gyldan; þæt wæs god cyning

['Often Scyld Scefing deprived companies of harmful enemies, many tribes, of meadseats, struck terror into warriors, after he was first found destitute; he experienced consolation for that, grew under the skies, prospered in honours, until every neighbour across the whaleroad had to obey him, pay tribute; that was a good king!', *Beowulf* 4–11];

and Emperor Constantine, the initiator of the finding of the cross, characterized simply as 'a great man and reverent worshipper of God' in Allen and Calder's translation of the Latin text regarded as Cynewulf's source,[52] in the poem ruled in this way:

Wæs se leodhwata lindgeborga
eorlum arfæst. Æðelinges weox
rice under roderum. He wæs riht cyning,
guðweard gumena. Hine god trymede
mærðum ond mihtum, þæt he manegum wearð

[52] *Sources and Analogues*, p. 60.

geond middangeard   mannum to hroðer,
werþeodum to wræce,   syððan wæpen ahof
wið hetendum

['That courageous shield-protector was gracious to his warriors. The authority of the prince grew under the skies. He was a just king, battle-guardian of men. God strengthened him with glories and powers, so that he became throughout the world to many men a benefit, to many peoples an affliction, after he raised his weapon against haters', *Elene* 11–18a].

The miraculous in this story – the revelation of the whereabouts of the nails of the crucifixion by a divinely granted *tacen*, 'sign' (1104a), of a leaping flame, brighter than the sun (1109b–10a) – only served to enhance this massive power, for the iron of the nails was fashioned into a bit for the emperor's horse, thereby conferring invincibility on its rider. In the face of this symbolic universal *caserdom*, 'imperial power' (8b), we become mere spectators on the side-lines of history.

In the Seven Sleepers, however, a wholesale shift in our position has taken place. This story involves us at close range in the worries, fears and anguish of 'ordinary' vulnerable people faced with a relentless persecution of their faith. Even what is extraordinary – the streets crying out and the city walls shaking with horror at the sufferings of the martyrs – is a fanciful exaggeration of a sensation anyone might have of cobbled streets and stone walls shimmering in the heat of the day. The main episode, following God's awakening of the seven after a sleep of 372 years in a cave, is a visit to Ephesus by one of their number to buy bread. Occupying about a third of the total vernacular version (but only about a quarter of the Latin source), it concentrates on the puzzlement and mounting alarm of this emissary, unaware of any lapse of time, increasingly astounded at all the changes he saw and heard, and finally thrown into a panic when the coins which he offered to merchants for his bread were received as curiosities. Internal dialogue expresses the twists and turns of his confusion, as in the following:

Ða . cwæð . he eft to him sylfum . to soðan ne þincð me næfre þæt hit soð sy þæt þis sy efesa byrig . forðy eall heo is on oþre wisan gestaðelod . and eall mid oþrum botlum getimbred . ne her nan man ne spricþ on hæþenra manna wisan . ac ealle æfter cristenra manna gewunan; þa wiðgynde he eft his geðance . and him þus andwyrde; ac ic nat eftsona . ne ic næfre git nyste þæt ænig oþer byrig us wære gehende buton ephese anre her on em celian dune

['Then he said to himself again, "Really it doesn't seem to me at all that this in fact can be Ephesus, because it's all established in another way and all made with other buildings. Nor does anyone here speak like heathens, but everyone in the fashion of Christians." Then he changed his mind and replied to himself like this: "But then again I'm not so sure; I never knew before that any other city was near us except just Ephesus here on the Celian Hill"', 536–43].

This private language was a very far cry from the formal, public manner of direct speech in *Elene*. Some tenth- and eleventh-century prose intimately conveyed an ordinary, everyday, moment-to-moment, personal stream of consciousness which symbolic poetry was quite unsuited to register.[53]

A secular story with a similarly lively psychological content is the version of a romance, *Apollonius of Tyre*, put into vernacular prose probably early in the eleventh century and extant in a single, very defective copy[54] written in the middle of that century.[55] The Old English closely rendered a variant text of a perhaps fifth-century Latin version of a Greek tale of romantic adventure which had been composed probably some two centuries earlier.[56] Consisting of enticing features such as 'a storm and shipwreck, kidnapping by pirates, dreams and apparitions, separations and recognitions, remarkable constancy of affection, chastity almost incredibly preserved, and finally the reunion of long-suffering lovers',[57] this was a story which enjoyed widespread popularity and exerted considerable influence on other romances from its inception right through to the end of the Middle Ages and well beyond. (Shakespeare retold it in *Pericles, Prince of Tyre*.[58]) The Old English translator thus stood at (so far as we know) the beginning of a very long-lasting taste for romantic entertainment in English literature. More particularly, he seems to have pioneered in his own time use of light, lucid, vernacular prose for sensitive treatment of refined, sometimes intricate, emotional relationships as the very stuff of story. For instance, when the cultivated, winningly mannered, young

[53] I am grateful to Hugh Magennis for showing me in typescript parts of the introduction to his edition of the Old English *De septem dormientibus* in preparation for Durham and St Andrews Medieval Texts.

[54] Only about half of it survives.

[55] See *The Old English 'Apollonius of Tyre'*, ed. Goolden.

[56] For a recent summary account, see Archibald, *Apollonius of Tyre*, pp. 6–8.

[57] *The Old English 'Apollonius of Tyre'*, ed. Goolden, p. ix and, more generally, pp. ix-xiii.

[58] Archibald, *Apollonius of Tyre*, pt I.

prince, Apollonius, destitute from shipwreck on the coast of Cyrenaica, had been generously fitted out again by the local king, we hear this king's daughter, fearful of losing the company of such an attractive stranger, persuading her father thus (and next morning too, after a sleepless night, continuing in the same vein when getting her father to appoint Apollonius as her teacher):

Ða adred þæt mæden þæt heo næfre eft Apollonium ne gesawe swa raðe swa heo wolde, and eode þa to hire fæder and cwæð: 'Ðu goda cyningc, licað ðe wel þæt Apollonius þe þurh us todæg gegodod is þus heonan fare, and cuman yfele men and bereafian hine?' Se cyngc cwæð: 'Wel þu cwæde. Hat hine findan hwar he hine mæge wurðlicost gerestan'

['Then the girl was afraid that she would never see Apollonius again as soon as she wanted, and went to her father and said, "O good king, does it really please you that Apollonius who has been enriched by us today should leave here in this way and wicked men should come and rob him?" The king said, "Well said. Order that he be found a place where he can rest very worthily"'].[59]

From such delicate beginnings as these was to spring a life-long mutual fidelity between the two lovers strong enough to triumph ultimately over all manner of vicissitudes.

In spite of its ancient pedigree the story presents to a reader (whether Anglo-Saxon or present-day) a perennially fresh face. The good and the bad – a high-born, rich and wise, faithful, young lover on the one hand and an incestuous father on the other, for instance – do not require any particular cultural heritage to be seen for what they are. They are easily accepted as representatives of right and wrong. Virtue is not set in a perspective of inherited wisdom, as it is in traditional Old English maxims, but is something pure in itself because placed in clearcut, ever-'contemporary' contrast to 'ordinary', immediate, worldly interests. For instance, a 'cyrlisc man', a man of no social standing, refuses any reward for his loyalty to Apollonius 'forðon þe mid godum mannum nis naðer ne gold ne seolfor wið godes mannes freondscipe wiðmeten' ('because among good men neither gold nor silver is exchanged for the friendship of a good man').[60] The vernacular translator took over an aphorism from his Latin source, 'Apud bonos enim homines amicitia praemio non comparatur' ('Among good men

[59] *The Old English 'Apollonius of Tyre'*, ed. Goolden, p. 28, lines 11–17.
[60] *Ibid.*, p. 12, lines 22–3.

friendship is not exchanged for a reward'),[61] and allowed its antithesis to make the same 'pure' effect in his own language as in the original by retaining both its succinctness (apart from a mildly repetitious 'godes mannes') and its relationship to an actor who lacked the type of social background which conventionally would have accounted for such high-minded disinterestedness.

In literature such as the Seven Sleepers legend and *Apollonius of Tyre* men have to exercise personal responsibility when undergoing experience not wholly predicted by convention. The body of inherited wisdom at their disposal is more proverbial than gnomic. Appeal to general wisdom depends on individual initiative in whatever situations turn up; and the situations themselves, though standard, do not carry the necessity of any single, invariable outcome. For instance, the arrival in a city of a man under a complete misapprehension which puts him at cross-purposes with all the inhabitants could in principle give rise to several kinds of consequences, comedy among them. In the particular case of the Seven Sleepers legend the implications are overwhelmingly serious. Our close view of the state of mind of someone misunderstanding ordinary, rough, citizens as potentially ruthless religious persecutors is a dramatic prelude to a general revelation that God has overriding powers to resuscitate the human body whenever so minded, however long a time has elapsed. Man's immediate instinct for self-preservation as he goes about his daily business is intimately displayed at variance with divine transcendence of a totally different order. God directs events 'mid his ðære mæran fadunge' ('with his glorious arrangement') unknown to the participants: 'Eall hit wæs heom uncuð . ac hit wæs gode ful cuð' ('It was all unknown to them, but it was fully known to God', 256–7 and 258–9). In this prose story God's thinking and man's are set apart. Poets, on the other hand, preferred to concentrate on the relationship between man's consciousness and God's. In their eyes the primary condition of human thought and feeling, however 'ordinary' these might be, was the service which these faculties owed to the

61 Archibald, *Apollonius of Tyre*, p. 120. As Donald Bullough has kindly pointed out to me in a private communication, this saying had a long pedigree stretching back to Cicero and the Vulgate Ecclesiasticus with a few twists added by Sallust and Seneca. Jerome's conclusion to a letter to Rufinus is the version which most medieval writers adapted and which comes near to the *Apollonius* example: 'caritas non potest conparari; dilectio pretium non habet; amicitia, quae desinere potest, uera nunquam fuit' ('love cannot be exchanged; love has no price; friendship which can cease was never true', *Sancti Eusebii Hieronymi Opera*, ed. Hilberg I, 18).

transcendent lord- and leadership of Christ and through him to God, and thus the overriding theme of poetry remained the rendering of this service, through outright rejection of this-worldly materialism perhaps, or through virtuous conduct consonant with spiritual eternity, or through worship. The implications of this obligation for poetry's conception of the individual will be examined in the next chapter.

11

From social hero to individual *sub specie aeternitatis*

The starting-point for living according to the tenets of the spirit was the individual more than society as a whole. For the age-long view that individuality was determined by social values and that warrior aristocracy was the determining group the church substituted an individual ultimately answerable to Christ the Judge. A new sense of the make-up of the person began to assert itself and demand alterations in poetic expression.[1]

The changing character of the emotions expressed in poetry reflects this development. Progressively feelings became more the instrument of every human being's concern for the unending fate of his or her soul at the will of an absolute God and less a by-product of a hero's assertion of vigour and courage in the face of death in the prime of life, or of an old man's loss of his youthful powers, or of a person's sense of active oneness with his or her surroundings, or of a woman's loss of or separation from loved ones through social forces. Feelings which belong by right to every individual as a soul-bearer became his or her means of identifying with the common instinct for everlasting self-preservation. They formed the substance of personal relationships with God (or the devil), and 'natural' speech gave them outward expression, throughout the drama of human life on earth, past, present and future.

Emotion thus became the common currency for dramatic characterization of protagonists on the stage of world history. Contrasting feelings involved in the fall of man, for instance, could be confidently imagined and uninhibitedly expressed in speeches such as those which were attributed to the biblical personages in the emotional version of the successful tempta-

[1] Cf. discussion of God's rôle in shaping personal experience, below, beg. at p. 452.

tion of Eve in *Genesis B*.[2] The devil's messenger, laughing and skipping in triumph, exults to his master, '. . . is hearm gode, / modsorg gemacod' ('an injury, a heartfelt sorrow, has been caused for God', 754b–5a) and declares in satisfaction,

Forþon is min mod gehæled,
hyge ymb heortan gerume, ealle synt uncre hearmas gewrecene
laðes þæt wit lange þoledon

['Therefore my mind is healed, the thoughts around my heart are set free, all our injuries in respect of the enmity we two have long endured are avenged', 758b–60a];

Adam vents his despair and bitterness upon Eve ('You are seeing hell, dark and greedy, now our destiny', he cries out to her in words to this effect, 'You can hear it raging from here! What shall we do against hunger and thirst and cold and heat? What is to become of us now? It pains me that I asked God to create you! Now it will pain me to all eternity that I set eyes on you!' (791–820)); while Eve's contrition is almost too deep for words:

Ða spræc Eue eft, idesa scienost,
wifa wlitegost; hie wæs geweorc godes,
þeah heo þa on deofles cræft bedroren wurde:
'Þu meaht hit me witan, wine min Adam,
wordum þinum; hit þe þeah wyrs ne mæg
on þinum hyge hreowan þonne hit me æt heortan deð'

['Then Eve replied, most radiant of ladies, most beautiful of women; she was the work of God, though she had then been brought low into the devil's power: "You can reproach me for it, my lover, Adam, with your words; yet it cannot grieve you worse in your mind than it does me at heart"', 821–6].[3]

A woman's words were designed here to reflect strength of feeling in the human heart as another woman's were in *Wulf and Eadwacer*. But, whereas in that poem the speaker wrenched paradox intuitively from her bitter-

[2] A poem which consists of an excerpt from an otherwise lost, much longer, quasi-Anglo-Saxonized, derivative of a continental Saxon poetic *Genesis*, which is itself lost apart from some fragments overlapping only slightly with the Old English *Genesis B*. For a recent edition of the extant Old English and Old Saxon texts, stressing their combined witness to the otherwise lost Saxon composition, see *The Saxon Genesis*, ed. Doane.

[3] It has been argued that these lines probably originated with the Old English poet and were not owed to the Old Saxon poem which he was following; see *The Later Genesis*, ed. Timmer, p. 60.

ness,[4] Eve's emotional words were formally framed by the narrator's preceding paradox in terms of the common human lot. Her feelings not only sprang from her own sense of guilt but also appeal to ours. They express her identity and ours alike. They convert the past into a universal present. Her personal grief was a pure universal, acting on us through her simple recognition that it existed.

Native tradition, by contrast, had regarded passions as essentially a force outside the individual, acting on him (or her) of their own accord or cooperated with by him/her as an act of will.[5] They did not belong to an individual as a distinct personality. They were a raw material in his/her dramatic encounter with external forces. Their separateness from constant personality and their association with the flux of outside forces can both be readily seen in, for example, the *Beowulf* poet's presentation of his hero's declaration to Hrothgar's coastguard offering to rid the king of the scourge of Grendel:

Ic þæs Hroðgar mæg
þurh rumne sefan ræd gelæran,
hu he frod ond god feond oferswyðeþ –
gyf him edwenden æfre scolde
bealuwa bisigu bot eft cuman –,
ond þa cearwylmas colran wurðaþ

['I can through a roomy mind advise Hrothgar about that, how, wise and good, he will overcome his enemy – if reversal should ever come to him again, remedy against the affliction of evils – and the surgings of care will become cooler', 277b–82].

The advice Beowulf claimed to be able to give was aimed at affecting two agents, Hrothgar himself and the hot feelings which afflicted him, if *edwenden* would permit, that is, if ever a sudden reversal in fortune[6] should swing events back in his favour, as it had to if he was to succeed. Hrothgar, his feelings and *edwenden* were all acting independently in the same arena.

From the point of view of the individual, *edwenden* was experienced as a change in emotion: Hrothgar, looking back at the *edwenden* which had come to him when Grendel had become his invader, saw it as 'gyrn æfter gomene' ('grief after joy', 1775a), and the narrator's summing up of

[4] See above, pp. 176–7.

[5] See above, pp. 79–80, and cf. Godden, 'Anglo-Saxons on the Mind', p. 286.

[6] See above, pp. 90–1.

Beowulf's triumph of character over the Geats' poor opinion of him in his youth was 'Edwenden cwom / tireadigum menn torna gehwylces' ('Reversal of every affliction came to the man blessed with glory', 2188b–9). Emotion subject thus to outside forces was ready to join, in a general way, with a Christian sense of individual responsibility before God for sin, as we see in Beowulf's reaction to the terrible news that the dragon had burnt his royal hall down to the ground:

Þæt ðam godan wæs
hreow on hreðre, hygesorga mæst;
wende se wisa, þæt he Wealdende
ofer ealde riht ecean Dryhtne
bitre gebulge

['That was distress in the breast for the good man, the greatest of sorrows in the heart; the wise man thought that he had bitterly angered the ruler, the eternal Lord, contrary to old law', 2327b–31a].

But the broad categories of feeling recognized in poetic tradition were not well suited to the more personal sequence of shame, repentance, confession, penance and absolution through which a penitent was taken by a confessor under the practice of private penance assimilated by the English church by at least the eighth century.[7] Poetry resisted exchanging its usual public forum for this more psychological delving. For instance, no poem among our extant remains explores the function of personality hinted at by the Englishman, Alcuin, when he asserted in his *Liber de virtutibus et vitiis*, at the end of the eighth century, that God's forgiveness of a sin depended not on the scale of the penance performed but on the sincerity of the penitent's remorse.[8]

With its traditional emphasis on the representative individual, vernacular poetry, so far as our evidence goes, preferred prayer which asked God, as the 'I' speaker does in *Resignation A*,[9] to forgive not faults specific to the petitioner but the supplicant's sin in general. Unique communion with

[7] On this practice, originated by the Irish and used by them already in the sixth century, and on the headway it made in England in the absence of public penitential ritual in this country until after the Carolingian reforms on the Continent, see Frantzen, *The Literature of Penance in Anglo-Saxon England*.

[8] *Ibid*, p. 115 and n. 76.

[9] *Resignation* 1–69. On these lines as a fragment of one poem and the rest of *Resignation* (70–118) as a fragment of another, see Bliss and Frantzen, 'The Integrity of *Resignation*'; for an edition based on this distinction, see *Resignation*, ed. Malmberg.

God is not engendered by this speaker's 'Forgif me to lisse, lifgende god, / bitre bealodæde' ('Forgive as a kindness to me, living God, bitter evil deeds', 19–20a). With its social traditions, Old English poetry more easily converted an individual's private sense of shame into a desire to avoid public shame on Doomsday, as when, in *The Lord's Prayer II*, amplification of 'Et dimitte nobis debita nostra' begins

Forgif us ure synna, þæt us ne scamige eft
drihten ure, þonne þu on dome sitst
and ealle men up arisað

['Forgive us our sins, that they may not shame us again, our Lord, when you sit in judgement and all men rise up', 84–6]

and continues

þar we swutollice siððan oncnawað
eal þæt we geworhton on worldrice,
betere and wyrse, þar beoð buta geara.
Ne magon we hit na dyrnan, for ðam ðe hit drihten wat,
and þar gewitnesse beoð wuldormicele,
heofonwaru and eorðwaru, helwaru þridde

['there we will clearly disclose afterwards all that we did in the kingdom of the world, the better and the worse, both will be made ready there. We shall not be able to hide it at all, because the Lord knows it and the witnesses there will be gloriously great, the inhabitants of heaven and the inhabitants of earth, the inhabitants of hell third', 90–5].[10]

Poetry embraced the principle that each sinful soul stands alone before Christ its judge but preferred to dramatize this situation on the world stage at Doomsday.

Likewise traditional verse tended to lessen the individual voice of the psalmist in his one-to-one communion with God. The corpus of 150 psalms, learned by heart by every member of a religious order and sung repeatedly in a regular sequence in daily services – once a week in its entirety according to the advice of St Benedict – provided the primary medium for the individual's spiritual life within the organized commu-

[10] On the motif of preferring shame before one man now to shame before God and the three hosts on the day of judgement, occurring in English prose and poetry some fifteen times and in Latin only in the writings of two Englishmen, Boniface and Alcuin, see Godden, 'An Old English Penitential Motif'; see also below, p. 391.

nity. It was only during the second half of the eighth century that choral psalmody became the norm in monastic communities in place of the solo method whereby a single monk (chosen in rotation) sang while the others, listening intently, supplied the words with an interior exegesis.[11] Individual meditation on the psalms, developed within this practice and structured by established doctrinal, prophetic and moral interpretations, was well suited to yield poetic fruits, and probably did so in the English vernacular tradition although we do not have the evidence to prove it today: the meditations on antiphons in the Advent lyrics of the Exeter Book, discussed below, represent an analogous process. Nevertheless it remains true that the symbolic language of vernacular poetry, which for centuries had been intended to root narrative in the traditionally perceived foci of dramatic interaction within human society and between that society and its physical environment, and which was then adapted and augmented primarily to bring collective experience to bear on the drama of men's uncertain destiny in Christian world narrative, could not so easily render the plain psalm text without loosening the original's grip on individual emotion. Symbolic vocabulary of essentially 'public' feeling could certainly combine with intimate address to intensify a spiritual relationship in a highly dramatic situation displayed on the world stage, as it did to great effect in the interlocutions of God and apostle firmly channelling strong currents of spirituality through the lurid landscape of events in *Andreas*.[12] But, for instance, the epithets 'wuldres ealdor' and 'ece drihten' rendering simple *domine* in the first part of verse 1 of ps. V, 'Verba mea auribus percipe, domine; intellege clamorem meum',

Word þu min onfoh, wuldres ealdor,
and mid earum gehyr, ece drihten

['Receive my words, prince of glory, and hear with your ears, eternal Lord', *Fragments of Psalms*],[13]

float the psalmist's words off into the general domain of 'public' praise and do not contribute to appreciation of the individual base of personal feeling. The advantage is with King Alfred's prose rendering of the same Latin:

[11] For a recent summary, see Dyer, 'The Singing of Psalms', pp. 535–46.

[12] See above, pp. 255–72.

[13] The fragments concerned came from the complete metrical version of the psalter of which pss. LI.6–CL.3 survive in the Paris Psalter, a manuscript written towards the middle of the eleventh century.

'Drihten, onfoh min word mid þinum earum; and ongyt mine stemne and min gehrop' ('Lord, receive my words with your ears and understand my voice and my clamour').[14] The initial *Drihten* establishes the directness of the psalmist's address and the word pair 'mine stemne and min gehrop', of a type based primarily outside poetry,[15] effectively stresses the dramatic thrust of his emotional utterance. Much the same is true also in the case of the psalmist's plea, 'Pity me, O God', in the first verse of ps. L, 'Miserere mei, deus, secundum magnam misericordiam', where we have two vernacular metrical versions to compare with Alfred's one in prose. All three agree in rendering 'secundum magnam misericordiam' simply as 'æfter þinre [*or* ðinre þære] mycelan mildheortnesse', but, whereas Alfred also worded 'Miserere mei, deus' straightforwardly as 'Miltsa me, Drihten',[16] both versifiers diluted these words with lateral spread: *Fragments of Psalms* reads 'Mildsa me, mihtig drihten, swa ðu manegum dydest', and the other metrical text, a paraphrase of the psalm concerned already cited,[17]

> Miltsa ðu me, meahta walden,   nu ðu wast manna geðohtas,
> help ðu, hælend min,   handgeweorces
> þines anes,   ælmehtig god

['Pity me, ruler of powers, now you know the thoughts of men, O saviour, help me, the handiwork of you alone, almighty God', *Psalm 50* 31–3].

Admittedly here we are not comparing like with like: these two metrical practitioners were only mediocre versifiers, while Alfred wrote good prose. But, so far as our limited evidence goes, the primary bond of individual emotion between psalmist and God could be served in the vernacular better by prose than by verse. In Alfred's rendering at any rate, prose provided a compact core of strong, natural, personal feeling, which he placed in a framework of practical applications and, on occasion, locally glossed with a practical sense. For example, he introduced ps. V thus:

Ðe fifta sealm ys gecweden Dauides sealm; ðone he sang be his sylfes frofre, and be herenesse ealra ðæra rihtwisena ðe secað yrfeweardnesse on heofonrice mid Criste, se ys ende ealra ðinga. And ælc mann þe þisne sealm singð, he hine singð be his

[14] *Liber psalmorum: the West-Saxon Psalms*, ed. Bright and Ramsay, p. 7. For Alfred's authorship of this prose version of pss. I-L, see Bately, 'Lexical Evidence for the Authorship of the Prose Psalms'.

[15] See above, pp. 154–7.

[16] *Liber psalmorum: the West-Saxon Psalms*, ed. Bright and Ramsay, p. 121.

[17] Above, pp. 317–18.

sylfes frofre. And swa dyde Ezechias, þa he alysed wæs of his mettrumnesse. And swa dyde Crist, þa he alysed wæs fram Iudeum

['The fifth psalm is called David's psalm; which he sang about his own consolation, and about praise of all the righteous who seek their inheritance in the kingdom of heaven with Christ, who is the end of all things. And each man who sings this psalm, he sings it about his own consolation. And so did Ezechias, when he was freed from his infirmity. And so did Christ, when he was freed from the Jews'],[18]

and in the third verse he rendered 'Mane adstabo tibi et videbo' as 'Ic stande on ærmergen beforan ðe æt gebede, and seo þe; þæt is þæt ic ongite þinne willan butan tweon, and eac þone wyrce' ('I will stand before you in prayer at daybreak and behold you; that is, I will recognize your will free of doubt and carry it out as well', *ibid.*). A comparison of this firmly organized prose and the weak, monotonous, metrical version of the whole psalter, from which I have quoted twice,[19] which was composed in perhaps the middle of the tenth century[20] and which was still in use during the first half of the eleventh (presumably *faute de mieux*), persuades us that by the end of the ninth century, as a medium for an effective vernacular 'plain text' of the psalms, verse had finally lost out to prose, which, after all, enjoyed the advantage of long-standing psalter glossing in non-symbolic English behind it.

Liturgical worship, however, promoted individually steered meditation which is well represented in the surviving poetry. Indeed, the originality thus exercised probably had a more profound effect on the composition of vernacular verse than that of any other constituent of redefined individuality. It was a form of independence which opened up to the vernacular poet congenially fresh grounds for creativity. In the past his originality had shown in the degree of imagination with which he had recreated linguistically an already unitary social and cultural tradition embedded in the life

[18] *Liber psalmorum: the West-Saxon Psalms*, ed. Bright and Ramsay, p. 7. For the king's independent construction of fourfold *argumenta*, following a tradition which had been developed and used by Irish commentators on the psalms, and drawing his matter mainly from two Latin works which differed in their origins (one of them quite possibly by Bede) but which had circulated together for a hundred years or so by Alfred's time, see O'Neill, 'The Old English Introductions to the Prose Psalms'. O'Neill, however, writing before the publication of Bately, 'Lexical Evidence for the Authorship of the Prose Psalms', did not name Alfred as the author and, in fact, did not raise the question of the author's identity at all.

[19] See above, p. 368, n. 13.

[20] See Sisam and Sisam in *The Paris Psalter*, ed. Colgrave *et al.*, pp. 16–17.

around him. Now his new-found sense that his essential self was a soul destined for its own final judgement was given liberty of choice in personal communication with God within the controlled traditions of ecclesiastical learning. His art became one of expressing this inviting, but disciplined, freedom of the spirit in the symbolic narrative mode native to him and his fellow-countrymen.

A poet who availed himself of this new scope especially imaginatively was the anonymous composer of *Christ I* (*Christ* 1–438), a group of lyrics at the beginning of the Exeter Book composed in close sympathy with the range and disposition of the Latin antiphons which were used in the Roman liturgical tradition during the pre-Christmas waiting season of Advent and then at Christmas itself. Sung before and after the unvarying *Magnificat*, the variable antiphon was intended to arouse the devotional response to the *Magnificat* selected for the occasion concerned. Each opens with an invocation, usually of the Messiah under an appellation which is of biblical origin, and normally concludes with a petition issuing from the appellation concerned, as in 'O oriens, splendor lucis aeternae, et sol iustitiae: veni, et illumina sedentes in tenebris et umbra mortis' ('O orient, splendour of eternal light, and sun of justice: come, and illumine those sitting in darkness and the shadow of death'). Typically the vernacular lyric evolving from a given antiphon takes up an etymological, typological or theological idea, or ideas, embedded in the particular appellation and develops a narrative treatment of the relationship between God, thus understood, and human dependence.[21]

This poet's basic ability to exploit the potential for emotional generalization in symbolic language in these new creative circumstances is well illustrated by his expansion of the petitional, 'veni . . .', part of the great 'O' antiphon,[22] 'O Emmanuel, rex et legifer noster, expectatio gentium et

[21] Three of the antiphons have been cited above, pp. 275–7. The Old English lyrics are generally agreed to be the work of a single poet. Twelve survive (the first of them imperfectly) and it is likely that originally three more (now lost) preceded them. They have been edited on their own as *The Advent Lyrics of the Exeter Book* by Campbell and again, as a basis for extensive commentary, in Burlin, *The Old English 'Advent'*, but I cite the ASPR text and line numbers. For the poet's unmatched repertoire of antiphons and the pattern he created by his selection and cyclic arrangement of them, see Rankin, 'The Liturgical Background of the Old English Advent Lyrics', esp. pp. 334–7. On her evidence (for which, see below, p. 383, n. 46), he composed his set probably well before the middle of the tenth century (*ibid.*, pp. 333–4).

[22] Concerning the group of antiphons of this type, see the reference cited above, p. 275, n. 3.

salvator earum: veni ad salvandum nos, Dominus Deus noster' ('O Emmanuel, our king and lawgiver, expectation of peoples and their saviour: come to save us, O Lord, our God'):

Nu hie softe þæs
bidon in bendum hwonne bearn godes
cwome to cearigum. Forþon cwædon swa,
suslum geslæhte: 'Nu þu sylfa cum,
heofones heahcyning. Bring us hælolif,
werigum witeþeowum, wope forcymenum,
bitrum brynetearum. Is seo bot gelong
eal æt þe anum [. . . . . .] oferþearfum.
Hæftas hygegeomre hider [. . . . . .]es;
ne læt þe behindan, þonne þu heonan cyrre,
mænigo þus micle, ac þu miltse on us
gecyð cynelice, Crist nergende,
wuldres æþeling, ne læt awyrgde ofer us
onwald agan. Læf us ecne gefean
wuldres þines, þæt þec weorðien,
weoroda wuldorcyning, þa þu geworhtes ær
hondum þinum. Þu in heannissum
wunast wideferh mid waldend fæder'

['Now patiently they waited in chains for when the son of God would come to the anxious. And so, weakened by torments, they spoke thus: 'Come now yourself, high king of heaven. Bring a life of healing to us, weary, tortured slaves, overcome with weeping, with bitter burning tears. The remedy for our extreme needs depends entirely on you alone. You seek here prisoners sad in mind; when you go hence, do not leave behind you a multitude as great as this, but royally show mercy on us, saviour Christ, prince of glory, and do not let the accursed one hold sway over us. Leave us the eternal joy of your glory, that those whom you have created with your hands may worship you, glorious king of hosts. In the highest you dwell for ever with the ruling father'].

In the antiphon the *nos* of the petition is general, simply because it follows invocation of God as king and as the hope of peoples and because it is unattributed. In the poem, however, 'they' who were petitioning (146b–7a) become representative of more than themselves to the extent to which their words, spoken in their particular situation, satisfy the expectations of universal grandeur already aroused by the narrator's invocation (130–46a). The theme of that initial section has been the sublime truth enshrined in the etymology of the name Emmanuel, 'God is with us', and in the use of this name in the Bible story of the incarnation to signify fulfilment of the Old Testament (Isaiah XXXIII.22) in the New (Matthew I.23).[23] The 'now' of the vernacular speakers (146b) was thus the critical stage in the spiritual history of mankind which this name symbolizes so profoundly: they were the souls of Old Testament figures about to receive at long last the advent of the eternal ruler of all (140a), from whom they had received law and guidance and whose coming they had hoped for through ages,

swa him gehaten wæs,
þætte sunu meotudes   sylfa wolde
gefælsian   foldan mægðe,
swylce grundas eac   gæstes mægne
siþe gesecan

['as it had been promised to them that the son of God himself would cleanse the people of the earth, and likewise would seek out the depths also in a journey by the might of his spirit', 142b–6a].

Universality accrues to these souls in these circumstances because of the concentrated sensitivity of their moving imagery and language. These slaves to anguish were paradoxically appealing gently to their creator in his mercy not to abandon them to the devil but instead to grant that they might worship him for ever in the glory of his eternal royalty. Symbolic terms, of pre-Christian and Christian stock, establish the general nature of the three principal components of the appeal, the earthly, grief-stricken petitioners (*witeþeowum*, *brynetearum* and 'Hæftas hygegeomre'[24]), the heavenly addressee petitioned ('heofones heahcyning', 'Crist nergende', 'wuldres æþeling', 'weoroda wuldorcyning' and (indirectly) *waldend fæder*), and the objective of the petition (*hælolif* and *ecne gefean*). But the working out of this theme is a controlled flow of feeling: from the intensely human, compact cluster, 'werigum witeþeowum, wope focymenum, / bitrum brynetearum' (151–2a) the alliteration moves through 'opening up' adverbs of divine locomotion, 'hider . . . behindan, . . . heonan . . .' (154b–5), to the praise-laden, pithy 'gecyð cynelice, Crist nergende' (157) and thence into the culminating celebratory expansiveness of the mainly w-based 'wuldres æþeling . . . awyrgde . . . / onwald agan . . . ecne gefean / wuldres . . . weorðien, / weoroda wuldorcyning . . . geworhtes . . . / hondum . . . heannissum/ wunast wideferh . . . waldend fæder' (158–63).

[23] Cf. Burlin, *The Old English 'Advent'* pp. 108–9.

[24] Cf. *Beowulf* 2408a.

A plea for mercy thus penetratingly and beautifully expressed cannot but figure the ultimate hope of all created mankind. We readily associate ourselves with this heartfelt entreaty as members of the whole suffering community of sinners, alive or dead.[25]

That this poet's assimilation of ecclesiastically conditioned imagery was freely available to his independent imagination is well illustrated by his evocative recurrent use of the image of God-centred light, conqueror of darkness, profoundly characteristic of vernacular Christian poetry[26] and thematic to Advent as a contrast between divine light and human darkness. The lyric which pleads for the sun of the Lord of life to illumine our frail minds, just as the mystery of the incarnation made prophecies burgeon, is a leading example fully discussed below.[27] But no fewer than six other poems also exploit this powerfully suggestive image for various fundamental purposes. In one a plea for rescue is mounted by the victims of 'se swearta gæst ('the dark spirit', 269b) to the son of God, who is celebrated (239–40, without equivalence in the relevant Latin antiphon) for acting as the creative wisdom when God the ruler (*se waldend* (240a)) separated light and darkness (226b–8a) and commanded,

Nu sie geworden forþ   a to widan feore
leoht, lixende gefea,   lifgendra gehwam
þe in cneorissum   cende weorðen

['Now let there be henceforth for ever light, a shining joy to all living things which will be born in their generations', 230–2].

In another, Christ is hailed as *sigorbeorht*, 'radiant with victory' (10a),[28] in his redeeming truth. In a third, seraphim praise him for ever in the light of heaven (401–3), and on earth his praise is 'beorht mid beornum' ('clear-sounding among men', 411b–12a). In a fourth, the incarnation is conceived of as an emanation of light: in the Virgin Mary's words to Joseph, the archangel Gabriel

Sægde soðlice   þæt me swegles gæst
leoman onlyhte,   sceolde ic lifes þrym
geberan, beorhtne sunu,   bearn eacen godes,
torhtes tirfruman

[25] Cf. *The Advent Lyrics of the Exeter Book*, ed. Campbell, p. 21.

[26] Cf. above, pp. 266–8.

[27] At pp. 378–80.

[28] The word occurs only here, but cf. *sigetorht* at *Christ and Satan* 238b.

['said truthfully that heaven's spirit would shine on me with his light, that I was to bear the power of life, a radiant son, richly endowed offspring of God, glorious source of brightness', 203–6a].

In yet another, Mary is hailed as the only one among women who has sent the bright gift of her virginity to heaven (287–94a). In the lyric related to the 'O oriens' antiphon[29] the redeemer is eloquently hailed as the source of all light:

Eala earendel, engla beorhtast,
ofer middangeard monnum sended,
ond soðfæsta sunnan leoma,
torht ofer tunglas, þu tida gehwane
of sylfum þe symle inlihtes

['O rising light, brightest of angels sent to mankind over the earth, and true ray of the sun, brilliant beyond stars, you illumine from yourself all seasons always', 104–8].

The petition sent to this eternal radiance comes from those who by contrast are enveloped in dark mortality. They implore

þæt þu þa beorhtan us
sunnan onsende, ond þe sylf cyme
þæt ðu inleohte þa þe longe ær,
þrosme beþeahte ond in þeostrum her,
sæton sinneahtes; synnum bifealdne
deorc deaþes sceadu dreogan sceoldan

['that you send the bright sun to us, and come yourself so that you illumine those who for a long time past, covered with smoke and in darkness here, have sat in continual night; enfolded by sins we have had to endure the dark shadow of death', 113b–18].

The overriding reality which renders the darkness subservient to the light and thereby deserves our thanks for ever is that

somod eardedon
mihtig meotudes bearn ond se monnes sunu
geþwære on þeode

['the mighty offspring of God and the son of man have dwelt together in concord among people', 125b–7a].

[29] The Latin of this antiphon is given in full, above, p. 371.

The all-embracing conviction which this poet owed to native tradition was that a train of thought or feeling could be none other than a narrative sequence. Indeed, he allowed two of his poems to consist almost entirely of free-standing dramatic dialogue – in the one case between son and daughter of Jerusalem and the Virgin Mary (71–103), as in its related Latin antiphon (although that mentions only *filiae*),[30] and in the other case between Mary and Joseph (164–213), an invention of his own, drawing out into an explicit form a narrative implication in the related antiphon.[31] The narrator contributed no more to what was said than briefly to characterize the Virgin as a speaker 'symble sigores full' ('ever full of victory', 88a) in the one and to announce that what she was about to explain was 'ryhtgeryno' ('the true mysteries', 196a) in the other. In the 'O Emmanuel' antiphon, as we have just seen, his way of substantiating the implied relationship between the 'expectatio gentium' in the invocation and an ensuing universally applicable petition was to provide a sequential narrative (135b–46a) moving from a *gefyrn*, 'long ago' (135b), of prophecy and witness to a *Nu*, 'now' (146b), of direct utterance.

And so it was when the poet was dealing with a line of thought which in his Latin starting-point was governed by an overarching image. His primary concern with explicatory narrative is revealed clearly by, for example, his use of subordinate clauses in his treatment (18–49) of the 'O clavis' antiphon which presented him with a main image running right through from an invocation of a key that opens or closes irreversibly to a plea for release from the darkness of a prison foreshadowing death.[32] The poet's approach is revealed straightaway by the relative clause in his equivalent to the opening invocation of the Latin, 'O clavis David, et sceptrum domus Israel, qui aperis et nemo claudit, claudis et nemo aperit':

Eala þu reccend   ond þu riht cyning,
se þe locan healdeð,   lif ontyneð,
eadga[.] upwegas,   oþrum forwyrneð
wlitigan wilsiþes,   gif his weorc ne deag

['O judge and just king, who guard the lock, open life, the blessed ways upwards, refuse the radiant, wished-for journey to another, if his work is not worthy', 18–21].

[30] For the Latin, see above, p. 277. [31] For which, see above, p. 276.
[32] For this antiphon, see above, p. 275.

The 'key of David' image in the Latin and the royal personage who is substituted for it in the English are both alike related to antithetic finality by their attendant relative clauses, but, whereas the general narrative content of the Latin clause does no more than imply an underlying connection between the Old Testament key and Christ's absolute control over entry into the heavenly Jerusalem,[33] the more explicit narrative in the vernacular clause applies kingly function specifically to human aspirations to eternal life.

The ensuing petition, 'veni et educ vinctum de domo carceris, sedentem in tenebris, et umbra mortis', was also treated along the same lines: it has become a plea that God may not abandon

cearfulra þing, þe we in carcerne
sittað sorgende, sunnan wenað,
hwonne us liffrea leoht ontyne,
weorðe ussum mode to mundboran,
ond þæt tydre gewitt tire bewinde,
gedo usic þæs wyrðe, þe he to wuldre forlet,
þa þe[34] heanlice hweorfan sceoldan
to þis enge lond, eðle bescyrede

['the cause of the anxious, on which account we sit sorrowing in prison, hope for the sun, when the Lord of life will open up light for us, become protector of our mind, and envelop the frail understanding with honour, make us worthy of that, us whom he relinquished for glory and who had to turn abjectly to this confined land, cut off from our native country', 25–32].

Narrative amplification in this chain of subordinate clauses has turned an appeal for release of the prisoner from the shadow of death into an expression of the hope-against-hope which we cling to in our spiritual exile that the Lord of life will protect our weak minds with his heavenly glory. The implied general force of the Latin petition, like that of the preceding invocation, has been applied in the English explicitly to us. The plea in the vernacular once again exemplifies our kinship to the Old Testament souls awaiting the Harrowing of Hell by being expressed in terms which are similar to those used by those souls in the poet's version of the petition of the 'O Emmanuel' antiphon, although this time more sharply dramatic in calling for the divine sun (*sunne*) to overcome darkness

[33] Cf. Burlin, *The Old English 'Advent'*, p. 71.

[34] Krapp and Dobbie amend to *we*.

of mind, rather than, as in the other case, God's glory (*wuldor*) to overcome grief.[35]

There is also another, more significant, difference between the two vernacular poems: on this occasion, after the initial invocation 'we' are not heard addressing God directly, as the petitioners are in the other case, and as the unspecified petitioner of the Latin 'veni et educ vinctum' is. 'We' merely report that we '. . . m[. . .]giað þone þe mon gescop / þæt he ne . . .' ('exhort him who created man that he should not . . .', 23–4a). 'We' have become relaters of our experience, a relation and an experience with entirely general reference points: 'we' are reminding an indefinite audience that 'we' supplicate the Lord of life for the light of his grace out of necessity, since 'we' are those of his creation whom he has left behind when he departed to glory. 'We' are in a representative narrative situation which is both more circumstantial and more explicitly universal than its source. A Latin plea directed in general terms to an image in its lofty self-sufficiency – 'O clavis . . . qui aperis et nemo claudit, claudis et nemo aperit' – has been converted into a vernacular narrative of 'our own' psychology, here and now, down on the ground, hoping against hope that God may send from above the light of his glory to protect and dignify 'our' minds.

The basis of this hope of 'ours' lies in a further narrative about the redeemer, which, having no equivalent in the Latin, is validated by attribution to 'se ðe soð spriceð' ('he who speaks truth'), the authority conventional to native tradition, and is linked to the first by *forþon*, 'for':

Forþon secgan mæg,   se ðe soð spriceð,
þæt he ahredde,   þa forhwyrfed wæs,
frumcyn fira.   Wæs seo fæmne geong,
mægð manes leas,   þe he him to meder geceas;
þæt wæs geworden   butan weres frigum,
þæt þurh bearnes gebyrd   bryd eacen wearð.
Nænig efenlic þam,   ær ne siþþan,
in worlde gewearð   wifes gearnung;
þæt degol wæs,   dryhtnes geryne.
Eal giofu gæstlic   grundsceat geondspreot;
þær wisna fela   wearð inlihted
lare longsume   þurh lifes fruman

[35] See above, pp. 371–4. For the implication of application to both the Old Testament figures and ourselves, which was already in the 'veni et educ vinctum' of the Latin, see above, p. 275 and n. 4.

þe ær under hoðman   biholen lægon,
witgena woðsong,   þa se waldend cwom,
se þe reorda gehwæs   ryne gemiclað
ðara þe geneahhe   noman scyppendes
þurh horscne had   hergan willað

['For he who speaks truth can say that he rescued the race of men when it had been turned away. The woman was young, a virgin without sin, whom he chose for his mother; it had come about without the love of a man that the bride became pregnant through the carrying of a son. There has never been, before or since, any reward of a woman equal to that; that was hidden, the mystery of the Lord. Every spiritual gift sprouted throughout the earth; many shoots were illumined through the author of life, longstanding teachings which had previously lain concealed under darkness, eloquent songs of wise men, when the ruler came, who enlarges the mystery of every voice of those who through a wise nature wish to praise continually the name of the creator].

The Lord of life, the poet was affirming, has already rescued mankind once by the supremely mysterious act of his incarnation (33–41). As an effect of this action the spiritual sayings of the prophets were quickened like plants responding to sunshine. God, ruling then (46b) and now (18–21), always bestows his grace thus on those with the wisdom to praise him unstintingly (47–9). A conviction that analogy was a basic principle of divine action was being relied on in this sequence of thought, as it was by St Andrew when the ship in which he was sailing was endangered by a storm.[36] As Andrew asserted that the God who had once protected his apostles from a storm at sea would do so again this time, so the poet of the Advent lyric was asserting inferentially that the God who had once brought spiritual life to the words of the prophets could do the same to our petitions in the present; and just as Andrew concluded by declaring *to soðe*, 'as truth', a maxim which affirmed that God never abandons men who maintain their spiritual strength,[37] so the Advent poet's representative spokesman, 'se ðe soð spriceð', ended by a claim that his spiritual ruler unfailingly responds to those wise enough to maintain his praise (47–9), a generalization which could well have formed a main-clause maxim:

He reorda gehwæs   ryne gemiclað
ðara þe geneahhe   noman scyppendes
þurh horscne had   hergan willað.

[36] See above, pp. 256–7.   [37] See *ibid.*, p. 257.

Both poets, the author of *Andreas* and the lyricist, were employing narrative fortified by Christianized natural imagery to follow a train of universal thought based on the general principle of analogy.

This creative lyrical poet was certainly not just telling stories in his Advent compositions. Nor was he presenting formal essays in typology: for instance, on my reading of the lyric related to the 'O clavis' antiphon the Old Testament 'key' has itself disappeared and only its typological significance remains.[38] Nor again was he constructing formally logical arguments; his associations were through allusion and implication. Nor was his interest in original ideas; he dealt in images which had already flowed through many learned and devotional channels on their way to him and carried much deposit as a result. He was fashioning narrative sequences of a received kind and steering them along lyrical courses of his own choosing among the thoughts and feelings common to errant humanity as we praise and plead with God who has been our creator, has already come to us through birth, can come again to our hearts and minds in his grace, and ultimately will open up – to those of us found worthy of him – eternal life in heaven. The poet was exercising a form of identity which, he realized, belonged to him among the mass of worshipping humanity. He was deliberately applying the workings of his own mind to the cosmic ideas and images which mattered to him most as he followed his calling as a worshipping Christian here in this world. A sense that human personality primarily consists of a mental and emotional make-up gave him his creative principle in vernacular poetry. As a self-aware person in a universal situation he was contributing to the sum total of devotion the mix of narrative thought and feeling which belonged to him in his own right. He was offering to others his own inner, meditative, 'exegesis' of public, collective, liturgical text.

Independent handling of narrative thought as a mark of mental and emotional identity was not confined to poetry. King Alfred was another who struck out lines of narrative thought for himself, but, in his case, expressed them in vernacular prose. The preface which the king composed for his translation of Gregory the Great's *Regula pastoralis* affords a good example in the narrative sequence there presented as the basis for a new policy of translating major Latin works into English prose and of educating as many young men as possible to read English properly: first Alfred related

[38] Cf. Burlin, *The Old English 'Advent'*, pp. 70–1.

at some length that he had very often recollected how in England long ago kings and men of wisdom and learning had contributed to mutual prosperity, and how more recently it had come about through neglect that only a few could understand the many books they possessed, because they were not written in their own language; next, he said, he had recalled how the Greeks, the Romans and 'all other Christian peoples' had translated the Bible; and finally this narrative of his past thoughts led him to another one, this time of his present thinking, 'For ðy me ðyncð betre . . . ðæt we eac . . .' ('Therefore it seems to me better . . . that we also. . .').[39]

The king's basic conception of thought as a narrative sequence informed the whole of the two substantial vernacular prose treatises which he especially impregnated with his own experience, the first of them an adaptation of Boethius's Latin dialogue, *De consolatione Philosophiae*, turned into a dialogue between *Wisdom* and *Mod*, 'mind', and firmly placed in a preliminary narrative setting of Boethius's historical situation,[40] and the second a formulation of the immortality of the soul and its knowledge of God in this life and in the hereafter, organized as a dialogue between St Augustine of Hippo ('his mind very often turning over[41] and pondering various and strange matters') and *Gesceadwisnes*, 'discrimination' ('either himself or some other thing, either inside him or outside, he didn't know which').[42] This latter work the king culled from Boethius and various patristic works in addition to its main source, the *Soliloquia* which Augustine had composed as a dialogue between *Ratio* and himself. Alfred's demonstration of the doctrine of the immortality of the soul is typical of his total reliance on narrative. For him a man's recognition of this immortality depended not on the dialectical and metaphysical reasoning supplied by his Latin sources but on differing degrees of trustworthiness within worldwide narrative tradition. Are not Christ's saying, 'The unrighteous shall go into everlasting torment and the righteous into everlasting life', and his other sayings about the immortality of the soul, and those of his apostles and the patriarchs and prophets, infinitely more trustworthy, *Gesceadwisnes*

[39] *Gregory's Pastoral Care*, ed. Sweet, pp. 3–7. The preface has often been printed elsewhere too.

[40] *King Alfred's Old English Version of Boethius 'De consolatione Philosophiae'*, ed. Sedgefield.

[41] MS *gastende* (*gastande* with *e* written above the second *a*).

[42] *King Alfred's Version of St Augustine's 'Soliloquies'*, ed. Carnicelli, pp. 48, line 18 – 49, line 5. *King Alfred's Old English Version of St Augustine's Soliloquies*, ed. Hargrove, is also of value. For the rare verb *gæstan*, see further, below, p. 449, n. 61.

demands of 'Augustine', than anything the emperor Theodosius, Honorius his son, or their thegns have told you about something they have seen or heard, which you believe although you have not seen or heard for yourself what they report? And 'Augustine' caves in accordingly, 'Now I am ashamed that I ever had doubts about that.'[43] Not surprisingly, in these two works, representing Alfred's own contributions to the narrative of world thought, his *Mod* and 'Augustine' are much more lively than their stiff and formal Latin counterparts. For example, whereas in the Latin, after *Philosophia* has made the point that God rules all things by goodness, Boethius replies merely, 'I agree heartily; this is just what I thought you were going to say although I wasn't quite sure', in the Old English, after a similar point, *Mod* says, 'Now I confess to you that I have found a door where before I had seen only a little chink, so that I could hardly see a very small gleam of light from this darkness; and yet you had pointed out the door to me, but I could not find my way nearer to it unless I groped for it round about where I saw that little light twinkling. . . . Now you have explained it to me very clearly, as if you had pulled open the door which I had been looking for.'[44]

A further characteristic which Alfred shared with the Advent lyricist was an independent use of narrative images to impart spiritual understanding, especially when he found the arguments of Boethius or a patristic authority too abstract. For example, whereas Augustine had taken pleasure in having *Ratio* pose the question, 'Is it enough to know God as one knows line and sphere in geometry?' and in being guided himself to conclude elegantly that the knowledge is different because what is known is different, the king swept such ratiocination aside and instead had *Gesceadwisnes* offer some forthright advice by extending an already used ship simile: 'It is needful that you should look directly towards God with the mind's eyes, as directly as a ship's cable is stretched straight from the ship to the anchor; and fix the eyes of your mind in God as the anchor is fixed in the earth.' The eyes of the mind, *Gesceadwisnes* went on to explain (unaided by *Ratio*, of course), are discrimination and other virtues such as wisdom and humility.[45]

[43] *Ibid.*, pp. 88, line 9 – 89, line 22. Cf. Gatch, 'King Alfred's Version of the *Soliloquia*', pp. 34–5.

[44] *King Alfred's Old English Version of Boethius 'De consolatione Philosophiae'*, ed. Sedgefield, p. 97, lines 13–25.

[45] *King Alfred's Version of St Augustine's 'Soliloquies'*, ed. Carnicelli, pp. 61, line 23 – 62, line 10; Gatch, 'King Alfred's Version of the *Soliloquia*', pp. 29–30. For the list of virtues, cf. the twice-stated list of the four cardinal virtues in Alfred's *Boethius*, on which see Clemoes, 'King Alfred's Debt to Vernacular Poetry', pp. 222–3.

The poet of the Advent lyrics, composing 'probably well before the middle of the tenth century',[46] and King Alfred, writing his prose late in the ninth, also set the same limits on narrative thought. Both regarded it as part of present existence as distinct from eternity beyond. For instance, when treating the everlasting implications of the incarnation – as he did in more than half his extant lyrics – the poet invariably concentrated on the person of the Virgin Mary, to whom alone in this mystery mortal beings could relate, because the element of spiritual immortality in the virgin birth necessarily lay, as such, outside their understanding: as the poet/speaker affirmed in one poem, 'þæt degol wæs, dryhtnes geryne' ('that was hidden, a mystery of the Lord', 41),[47] and, as the Virgin herself declared in another, '. . . þæt monnum nis / cuð geryne' ('that to men is not a known mystery', 94b–5a). In yet another, taking a hint from an antiphon's apostrophe of Christ as 'tu ante saecula nate' ('you, born before the ages') to pursue the theme (natural to Anglo-Saxons) of the Messiah's *fædrencynn*, 'paternal kin' (248a), the poet/speaker addressed to the 'king of all kings' (215a) the acknowledgement (239–48) that humans can discern nothing about *þin fromcyn*, 'your origin' (242a), earlier than that

Þu eart seo snyttro   þe þas sidan gesceaft
mid þi waldende   worhtes ealle

['You are the wisdom who made this extensive creation with the ruler', 239–40].[48]

And likewise Alfred, in his belief that both the soul and God exist for ever, passionately wanted above all to understand how the former's knowledge of the latter in this life affected its equivalent knowing in eternity. Fundamentally poet and king alike were concerned with the drama of an individual's consciousness in this world within his total endless being and were intent on dramatic portrayal of representative narrative thought to give everyone living in this Christian world access to valid thinking and feeling and hence to proper control over his (or her) personal actions in

[46] See above, p. 371, n. 21. Susan Rankin infers this from the likelihood that the poet's repertoire of 'O' antiphons was available in England by the late eighth century, if not before, and from the fact that it was significantly larger than that of the Frankish tradition which exerted a fresh wave of influence at the time of the Anglo-Saxon Benedictine revival late in the tenth century. It should be noted that Gatch has recently (*Speculum* 68 (1993), 734–5) restated his preference for associating the lyrics with the monastic reform period itself (first argued Gatch, *Loyalties and Traditions*, p. 96).

[47] See above, p. 378.   [48] Cf. above, p. 333.

advance of eternity. Their common use – each in his own way – of invented on-the-spot direct speech shows this clearly.

The poet employed this technique to good effect in, for instance, his lyric, 'Eala þu mæra . . . / . . . cwen . . .', based on an antiphon invoking the Virgin Mary, 'O mundi domina . . .' ('O queen of the world . . .'). This was his means of bringing to a dramatic climax a quite lengthy story of a vision of massive locked golden gates which he introduced into 'our' address to the Virgin constituting the whole poem.[49] According to the story which 'we' say 'we' have learned ('Eac we þæt gefrugnon' (301a)), 'Isaiah' beheld the noble portal when he was taken to where he could see the whole dwelling-place (*gesteald*) of life (304–5). So firmly was it bolted and barred that he was thinking that no human could possibly undo it, when an angel of God brought joy to him by saying,

> Ic þe mæg secgan þæt soð geweard
> þæt ðas gyldnan gatu giet sume siþe
> god sylf wile gæstes mægne
> gefælsian, fæder ælmihtig,
> ond þurh þa fæstan locu foldan neosan,
> ond hio þonne æfter him ece stondað
> simle singales swa beclysed
> þæt nænig oþer, nymðe nergend god,
> hy æfre ma eft onluceð

['I can tell you that the truth has come out that on a certain occasion in the future God himself will purify these golden gates with the power of the spirit, almighty father, and visit the earth through the secure locks, and then after him they will stand closed up eternally, always, for ever, so that no other except God the saviour will evermore unlock them again', 317–25].

This divinely informed speaker, prophetically applying what was to become the standard interpretation of Ezekiel's gates, has the effect on us of making 'Isaiah's' already convincing direct impression a wholly authoritative dramatic experience which inevitably leads 'us' to salute the Virgin Mary as its fulfilment,

[49] The image of golden gates is not in the 'O mundi domina' antiphon, but it occurs in one invoking the Messiah, 'O rex pacifice . . .', and was alluded to briefly in the vernacular lyric related to that (251–3). The vision in the lyric now under discussion is attributed to the prophet Isaiah, but in fact clearly it was derived from one which the Bible assigned to Ezekiel (Ezekiel XLIV.1–2). On the switch to Isaiah and other matters, see Hill, 'A Sequence of Associations in the Composition of *Christ*', and references there cited.

Nu þæt is gefylled þæt se froda þa
mid eagum þær on wlatade.
Þu eart þæt wealldor, þurh þe waldend frea
æne on þas eorðan ut siðade

['Now is fulfilled that which the wise one then looked upon with his own eyes. You are that wall-door, through which the ruling lord once journeyed out on to this earth', 326–9];

and then, just as irresistibly, to address her, thus actively appreciated, in supplication:

Iowa us nu þa are þe se engel þe,
godes spelboda, Gabriel brohte.
Huru þæs biddað burgsittende
þæt ðu þa frofre folcum cyðe,
þinre sylfre sunu. Siþþan we motan
anmodlice ealle hyhtan
nu we on þæt bearn foran breostum stariað.
Geþinga us nu þristum wordum
þæt he us ne læte leng owihte
in þisse deaðdene gedwolan hyran,
ac þæt he usic geferge in fæder rice,
þær we sorglease siþþan motan
wunigan in wuldre mid weoroda god

['Show us now the grace which the angel, God's messenger, Gabriel, brought to you. Citizens pray especially that you may show forth to peoples the consolation, your own son. Henceforth we shall all be able to hope steadfastly, now we behold that child before your breast. Intercede for us now with bold words that he may not let us obey error in this valley of death at all longer, but that he may transport us into his father's kingdom, where we may thenceforward without sorrow dwell in glory with the God of hosts', 335–47].

The analogy of the dramatic revelation granted to 'Isaiah' gives 'us' promise of another for ourselves, which, when it comes with the special intimacy of a mother with her baby at her breast (341),[50] emboldens us to ask its source, the Virgin herself, for her advocacy (339b–47).

Alfred similarly, when he was setting out the basis for his new policy of

[50] Mary Clayton has been kind enough to inform me that she does not know of any other equally early verbal or visual portrayal of the Virgin and child explicitly expressing this particular relationship. More recently (since this chapter was written), see her *The Cult of the Virgin Mary in Anglo-Saxon England*, pp. 200–1.

translation and education in the prose preface to his translation of Gregory's *Regula pastoralis*,[51] was not content merely to report a chain of recollected circumstances. He was intent on pointing out the states of mind, which the situations had involved, in order to establish by reference to them the correct line of thought for the present; and, since he was (no doubt) dictating to a secretary[52] a letter which was addressed to his bishops individually[53] and which would have been read aloud by the recipients, his appropriate technique for conveying past thinking was to supply a series of typifying items of direct speech. When he stated that he had remembered seeing people who, before the pillaging by the Vikings, had plenty of books but had very little benefit from them because they were written in Latin which they could not understand, he had, he related, brought these frustrated people to mind as if they were saying, 'Our ancestors, who formerly held these places, they loved wisdom and through that they obtained wealth and left it to us. Their track can still be seen here, but we cannot follow them. We have now lost both the wealth and the wisdom because we have been unwilling to bend down to the track with our minds.'[54] And again, when he reported wondering very much why those who had earlier understood the books had not translated them while they could, he went on to relate that he had answered himself by saying, 'they did not expect that men would ever become so careless and the teaching would decline so: they left it undone on purpose, and intended that there would be the more wisdom here in this country the more languages we knew.'[55] As a result his 'voice' in the present, saying directly to an individual bishop, 'For ðy me ðyncð betere . . . ðæt we eac . . .'[56] was heard as a dramatic outcome of his version of what these spokesmen had said in the past.

Alfred's vernacular prose defined mental and emotional identity more clearly than Christian vernacular poetry did. The poems we have show little sign of the king's idea that the eternal soul is specifically a thinking self. Belonging to a cultural tradition of evaluating a person according to the standards and ideals of his peers, a vernacular poet was more likely to

[51] See above, pp. 380–1.

[52] There is no evidence that Alfred himself could ever write pen in hand, just as his new educational policy was to teach young men to read, without any mention of writing.

[53] Each copy of the preface began with the king's greetings to a named bishop.

[54] *Gregory's Pastoral Care*, ed. Sweet, p. 5, lines 13–18.

[55] *Ibid.*, lines 22–5.

[56] See above, p. 381.

view the individual's everlastingness as a prolongation of reputation. This was how, for example, the *Seafarer* poet saw it, when contemplating the impermanence of mortal life:

Forþon þæt bið eorla gehwam æftercweþendra
lof lifgendra lastworda betst,
þæt he gewyrce, ær he on weg scyle,
fremum on foldan wið feonda niþ,
deorum dædum deofle togeanes,
þæt hine ælda bearn æfter hergen,
ond his lof siþþan lifge mid englum
awa to ealdre, ecan lifes blæd,
dream mid dugeþum

['And so for every warrior the praise of the living commemorating him is the best memorial, which he may bring about before he has to depart, by good actions on earth against the malice of enemies, by bold deeds against the devil, so that the children of men may praise him afterwards, and his praise thenceforth may live among angels for ever, blessedness of eternal life, joy among the hosts', *The Seafarer* 72–80a].

Alfred, on the other hand, using the more recently established medium of written, literary, vernacular prose, was relatively free to adopt 'modern' ideas. He deployed the more analytic belief in an eternally intellectual soul which was inherited from Christian and classical antiquity through a Latin, mainly prose, tradition. For example, this notion of a self capable of transcendental thinking underlay the king's instruction to each of his bishops to avoid succumbing to worldly pressures: 'ic ðe bebiode ðæt ðu do swæ ic geliefe ðæt ðu wille, ðæt ðu ðe ðissa woruldðinga to ðæm geæmetige swæ ðu oftost mæge, ðæt ðu ðone wisdom ðe ðe God sealde ðær ðær ðu hiene befæstan mæge, befæste' ('I command you that you do as I believe you wish, that you disengage yourself as often as you can from these worldly affairs in order to apply the wisdom which God has entrusted to you wherever you can apply it').[57]

Alfred's two prose dialogues, in fact, amount to a thorough-going exposition of the operation of the thinking soul. This entity was for him an inner, unitary, conscious mind constituting an individual's rationality.[58] It was the individual's inner means of comprehending his physical

[57] *Gregory's Pastoral Care*, ed. Sweet, p. 5, lines 1–4.
[58] See Godden, 'Anglo-Saxons on the Mind', esp. pp. 274–7.

perceptions: 'It now seems to me', *Gesceadwisnes* declares to 'Augustine', 'that you do not trust your outer sense, neither the eyes, nor the ears, nor the smell, nor the taste, nor the touch, that through any of them you can as clearly understand [*ongytan*] what you wanted to know, unless you understand [*ongytæ*] it in your inner thought [*ingeþance*] through your intellect [*gesceadwisnesse*].' And 'Augustine' replies, 'That is true; I never trust them.'[59] The individual's supreme capability (*cræft*) with these powers of internal understanding was to search for (*spurige æfter*) God and behold (*hawie* and *geseo*) him[60] in spite of the bodily preoccupations which throughout this life keep the eyes of the mind (*þæs modes eagum*) from seeing God openly, just as clouds or distance prevent our physical eyes from seeing the sun as it really is.[61] Those who eagerly desire wisdom, Alfred declared, differ from each other in the extent to which they succeed in seeing the eternal sun of wisdom, although they can all live by its light, just as those attending a king's court vary from one another in the ways they reach it and in the sort of lodging they have there, although they all belong to the same household.[62] Each person's processes of understanding, he affirmed, continue to function in a partly moral, partly intellectual way through all eternity: 'Now I have heard', 'Augustine' declares towards the end of his dialogue with *Gesceadwisnes*, 'that my soul [*sawel*] is eternal and lives for ever, and all the virtues [*goodra crefta*] which my mind [*mod*] and my intellect [*gescadwisnesse*] gather they may have always; and I hear also that my understanding [*gewit*] is eternal.'[63] When, after the day of judgement, we all know God for ever as he knows us,[64] the good will behold him 'heom to frofran, and to gefean, and to are, and to eaðnesse, and to wuldre' ('as their consolation, and joy, and grace, and ease, and glory'),[65] while the bad will see him 'swa ylce swa þa godan, heom þeah to wite' ('just like the good, though as their torment').[66]

Ingeðonc, 'inner thought', is a frequently occurring word signifying an

[59] *King Alfred's Version of St Augustine's 'Soliloquies'*, ed. Carnicelli, p. 59, lines 5–9.

[60] *Ibid.*, p. 69, lines 9–11. For a comprehensive study of Alfred's thematic use of the word *cræft*, see my 'King Alfred's Debt to Vernacular Poetry', pp. 223–38.

[61] *King Alfred's Version of St Augustine's 'Soliloquies'*, ed. Carnicelli, pp. 92, line 22 – 93, line 6.

[62] *Ibid.*, pp. 77, line 4 – 78, line 8. [63] *Ibid.*, p. 91, lines 21–4.

[64] *Ibid.*, p. 93, lines 18–20.

[65] *Ibid.*, lines 24–5. [66] *Ibid.*, lines 25–6.

individual's internal personal state of mind in the king's translation of Gregory's *Regula pastoralis* and in his two prose dialogues.[67] It renders word for word a variety of Latin words in the *Regula pastoralis* – some seven in all – but in eleven of the twenty-one instances of these relationships the Latin equivalent is *intentio*.[68] In another thirteen instances the word was occasioned simply by an expression of 'inwardness' in the Latin (*interior*, *intimus*, *intus*, *interius* or *introrsus*) and in a further three or four by a reference to 'self' (*apud se*, *semetipsis* or *nobismetipsis*). Quite often nothing in the Latin required its use at all. Evidently it was a term which Alfred understood in its own right and was free to use independently of Latin whenever he chose to. The state of mind thus referred to could be good or bad (*arfæst* and *gesceadwislic* or *yfel* and *unryhtwis*), and was of a settled, long-term sort: as against hasty faults arising from heedlessness or weakness of mind or body, 'sio ðonne ðe longe gesired bið, sio cymð symle of yflum ingeðonce' ('that which is long designed, always comes from evil inner thought').[69] In the king's use the word evidently denoted an individual's disposition consisting of an inner set of mind (and occasionally denoted the thoughts produced by such a disposition).[70]

With this key denotation, *ingeðonc* naturally figures prominently in Alfred's statements about vital topics such as the soul's knowledge of God, as when 'Augustine' declares fervently, 'I would know about God in my intellect [*gesceadwisnesse*] and in my inner thought [*ingeþance*] so that

[67] It is found seventy-six times in the *Pastoral Care*, seventeen times in the Boethius and nine times in the *Soliloquies*. An alternative word, *ingehygd*, occurs twice in the *Pastoral Care* and once in Alfred's versification of his prose version of Boethius's metres. *Ingehygd* occurs a few times in the Old English Bede and (with a similarly occasional use of *ingeðonc)* in Werferth's translation of Gregory's *Dialogi*. *Ingehygd* was to be Ælfric's regular word (see Godden, 'Anglo-Saxons on the Mind', pp. 286–7), while Wulfstan was to use *ingeðanc* from time to time (as in the *Sermo Lupi)*. *Ingeðoht* is another, very occasionally occurring alternative, and in one of his versified metres Alfred used *incofa*. Expressions such as 'mid innewearde mode' also occur.

[68] The others are *mens* (3×), *cogitatio* (2×), *cor* (2×), *animus* (1×), *conscientia* (1×) and *consideratio* (1×).

[69] *Gregory's Pastoral Care*, ed. Sweet, p. 435, lines 14–17.

[70] Cf. Godden's account of Ælfric's similar use of *ingehyd*, 'Anglo-Saxons on the Mind', pp. 286–7. As Godden points out (*ibid.*, pp. 284–5 and 295), whereas for Alfred the inner thinking self was a preexistent soul-and-mind temporarily trapped in the body, Ælfric made it more personal to the individual by declaring emphatically that God creates each soul as a separate act of creation and implants it in the foetus.

nothing could disturb me or bring me in any doubt.'[71] The word features also in many pronouncements in the *Pastoral Care* about the character which a teacher ought to have and about the various mentalities – of rich and poor, of ealdormen and retainers, impatient and patient, silent and talkative, and so on – to which he will have to adapt his teaching. For instance, it is laid down that a man 'who mortifies his body with many sufferings, and lives spiritually, and does not dread any adversity in this world, but loves the will of God alone' has the sort of *ingeðonc* (Gregory *intentio*) that makes him especially suited to be a bishop;[72] and it is observed, by way of demonstrating how a person's habit of silence can easily nurture in him a false self-esteem, 'though the tongue stays humbly quiet, the mind [*mod*, Gregory *mentem*] is very exalted and the more freely he blames all other people in his inner thought [*ingeðonce*, Gregory *apud se*] the less he recognizes his own vices [*uncysta*]'.[73] *Ingeðonc*, the inner, thinking, conscious self, was apprehended as a dominant factor in psychological character.

In poetry, by contrast, *ingeðonc* (or one of the equivalent *in*-words) occurs only infrequently and then as part of the general vocabulary for thought. It is found a mere nine times.[74] It is almost always in an explicitly Christian context, the only exception being line 13 of *Riddle* 60 (the seventeen lines which, in agreement with Pope, I have taken to be the opening of *The Husband's Message*);[75] here 'eorles ingeþonc' refers to the thought a man has put into composing a carved inscription, just as Alfred says, in prose, that Augustine composed his *Soliloquia* 'be his agnum ingeþance'.[76] In the eight overtly Christian instances *ingeðonc* indicates the seat, or form, of holy

[71] *King Alfred's Version of St Augustine's 'Soliloquies'*, ed. Carnicelli, p. 58, lines 24–6. Cf. *ibid.*, p. 59, lines 5–9, cited above, p. 388. In both these cases *ingeþanc* has no direct equivalent in the Latin Alfred was following. Cf. also, e.g., *King Alfred's Old English Version of Boethius 'De consolatione Philosophiae'*, ed. Sedgefield, pp. 44, line 28 – 45, line 3; p. 54, lines 1–3; pp. 67, line 30 – 68, line 3; pp. 94, line 27 – 95, line 7; and p. 106, lines 23–6.

[72] *Gregory's Pastoral Care*, ed. Sweet, p. 61, lines 6–9.

[73] *Ibid.*, pp. 271, line 24 – 273, line 2.

[74] Counting *Daniel* 279b and *Azarias* 1b as one. *Ingehygd* occurs even more rarely – once in Cynewulf's *Juliana*, once in the metrical preface to Werferth's translation of Gregory's *Dialogi* and once in the metrical psalms in the Paris Psalter (ps. CXVIII. 145). On Cynewulf's use of *ingehygd* to signify the Christian's inner integrity, see above, pp. 314–15.

[75] Above, pp. 177–8.

[76] *King Alfred's Version of St Augustine's 'Soliloquies'*, ed. Carnicelli, p. 48, line 13.

praise (*Daniel* 279b/*Azarias* 1b), of terror (before God, *Christ* (*III*) 1013b), of humility (before God, *Psalm 50* 128b and 152b), of desire (to find Calvary, *Elene* 680b), of thinking (*Andreas* 35b), of sinful thoughts (*Christ* (*III*) 1315b) and of determination (to achieve social advancement, *Genesis* (*A*) 2184a). Clearly, in verse the word was involved in the traditional native association of 'mind' with, as Godden has put it, 'emotion and a kind of passionate volition and self-assertion'.[77] It signified an essential part of a personal mood, not an eternal thinking identity, as it did in Alfred's prose: for instance, Cynewulf did not use it to describe his spiritual self for which, as poet, he was so concerned.[78]

On every occasion its use in poetry contributed to the dramatic effect of a rhetorical narrative statement. For example, in *Christ III*, apropos of our need to repent now if on the day of judgement we are to avoid the misery of having our sins dramatically exposed to God and to the assembled hosts as stains on our souls seen through bodies rendered as transparent as glass,[79] it is exclaimed that no one can describe how zealous we would be to rid ourselves of our unclean inner thoughts (*ingeþoncas*) here and now in order to be free of reproach from those who are our neighbours for but a short while, if these thoughts were visible to bodily eyes (1312–26). *Ingeðonc* in verse was part of poetry's resources for emotive expression. But it was never a mainstream term. More evocative, symbolic alternatives were available. For example, whereas in prose Alfred employed *ingeðonc* when translating 'Totum spiritum suum profert stultus: sapiens differt, et reservat in posterum' (Proverbs XXIX. 11), as 'Se dysega ungeðyldega all his ingeðonc he geypt, ac se wisa hit ieldcað, ⁊ bitt timan' ('The impatient fool reveals all his inner thought, but the wise man delays and bides his time',[80] the poet of *The Wanderer* used *ferðloca* and *hordcofa*, quintessential products of his native craft, when expressing a similar thought:

Ic to soþe wat
þæt biþ in eorle indryhten þeaw,

77 'Anglo-Saxons on the Mind', p. 295. At *Psalm 50* 128b the *ingeþancas* are in the heart ('cor contritum et humiliatum' is rendered as 'hiorte geclænsod / ond geeadmeded ingeþancum' (127b–8)), at *Elene* 680b 'feores ingeþanc' is in apposition to 'willan minne' (681b) and at *Andreas* 35b 'wera ingeþanc' is in apposition to *gewit* (35a) and 'heortan on hreðre' (36a).

78 See above, pp. 273–5.

79 See Godden, 'An Old English Penitential Motif', pp. 232–3, and above, p. 367 and n. 10.

80 *Gregory's Pastoral Care*, ed. Sweet, p. 220, lines 9–10.

þæt he his ferðlocan fæste binde,
healde his hordcofan

['I know as a truth that it is a very noble custom in a man to bind fast the breast where his mind is shut in, keep control of the place where his thoughts are stored', 11b–14a].

King and poet were both restating folk-wisdom about mental discipline,[81] but the one was using the new manner of prose, the other the age-old mould of poetry.[82] Verse was unsuited in both vocabulary and syntax to articulate the elements of psychological personality.

The effect which the concept of a transcendent thinking self had on poetry was a general one: it produced not so much a sharper definition of identity as an increased emphasis on the individual's representative mental experience. Cynewulf's self-awareness as the only Old English poet (as against narrator) who refers to himself in our records is very much a case in point. He presented his self-consciousness as a foreboding common to all[83] and described his personal inspiration to compose his poem on the finding of the cross as a release from the burden of sinfulness known by all. As a poet he saw his relationship to his audience in terms of universal psychology.

He made no attempt to individualize himself more specifically than that. When he wanted to enable his readers to remember him in their prayers, he identified himself only to the extent of making his name an emblem of the human condition of mortality and fear of judgement. He spelt out his name cryptically in runes,[84] so that the letters either referred to him undergoing judgement (*Christ II* and *Juliana*) or applied to him by third-person reference,[85] while, at the same time, the letters themselves or their meanings formed part of elegiac statements about the transience of

[81] For this interpretation of the Wanderer's words and for association of 14b with what follows, see Clemoes, *'Mens absentia cogitans'*, p. 76 and n. 2.

[82] It is of interest to note that the dramatic, preaching, eschatological poet of *Christ III* (see above, pp. 300–7) used both *ingeþoncas* (1315b) and *hreþercofan* (1328a) as equivalents of *conscientia* in the sermon by Caesarius of Arles which he was following as his source; see Irving, 'Latin Prose Sources for Old English Verse', p. 591.

[83] See above, pp. 273–5.

[84] *The Fates of the Apostles* 98b–105a, *Elene* 1256b–70a, *Christ* (*II*) 797–807a and *Juliana* 703b–9a.

[85] *Secg*, *he* and *him* (*Elene* 1256b, 1258a and 1261b), 'hwa þas fitte fegde' ('who composed this short poem', *The Fates of the Apostles* 98a) and 'hwa on þam wordum wæs werum oncyðig' ('who has been revealed to men in those words', *ibid.*, 106).

earthly wealth and beauty, and ultimately of the whole world, and about everyone's terror on the day of judgement. That he felt the urge to present himself to his readers at all may well have been due to the influence of Latin literary tradition. But to become an object of their prayers was his declared motive for doing so, and in this perspective references to himself such as 'hwa þas fitte fegde' served merely as secondary, supplementary, linking information. The primary assemblage consisted of a poem on the apostles or a saint or the cross or Christ, in combination with the poet's name and a request for prayer. The whole, taken together, formed an emblematic memorializing artifact comparable to a stone grave marker carrying a cross and an inscription calling for prayer for a named person.[86] Cynewulf's naming of himself had a commemorative purpose very different from a modern author's (or publisher's) intention to promote this-worldly reputation (and therefore sales) by satisfying readers' curiosity.[87]

[86] For a mid-seventh- to mid-eighth-century example bearing a cross in relief and a carved Latin inscription which is to be translated 'Pray for Vermund [and] Torhtsuid', see Cramp, 'General Introduction', in *County Durham and Northumberland*, pp. 99–100 (Hartlepool 4) and pl. 84, 436.

[87] I cannot agree with Daniel Donoghue's contention that there is sufficient evidence (his own and others') to disturb the natural view that all the four poems which conclude with the epilogues naming Cynewulf were indeed his compositions (*Style in Old English Poetry*, pp. 106–16). For his finding that the behaviour of auxiliary verbs with a dependent verbal in *Elene* and *Juliana* 'is almost indistinguishable' but that in *Christ II* and *Fates* they 'follow entirely independent patterns' (*ibid.*, p. 116), the explanation he prefers is that, while 'it seems safe to say' that Cynewulf was the author of both *Elene* and *Juliana*, 'he was more likely a poetic reviser' of the other two texts (*ibid.*). In his discussion he rightly leaves *Fates* aside (until including it in his conclusion) as too short to provide meaningful comparisons and concentrates on the distinctions between (a) *Elene* and *Juliana* and (b) *Christ II*. Here, however, his case seems to me to suffer from a fundamental drawback. He starts his consideration of (b) by linking it with its written sources ('One's first instinct is to attribute the differences of *Christ II* to subject-matter (homiletic) and to the influence of Cynewulf's models, especially part of a sermon by Gregory the Great', *ibid.*, pp. 111–12), and from that restricted base fails to come up with a satisfactory reason for its differences from (a) ('One must also wonder what led Cynewulf to be bound by the structure of Gregory's homily, if he was so innovative in other respects', *ibid.*, p. 113). He never establishes (b) as the type of composition it was in its own right in contradistinction to the narratives of (a), namely construction of a devotional image which, on a basis in written sources, synthesized experience of liturgical worship, ecclesiastical art, architecture and music, and pilgrimage, as I have described above (pp. 323–9). Consequently Donoghue never asks what coherent strategy of revision by Cynewulf could have produced the unified poem we have while keeping a previous poet's usage of auxiliaries. For my part I cannot conceive of one.

Similarly he presented the coming of his poetic inspiration, personal though the experience itself had doubtless been for him, as a psychological process of a general sort. He thought of it as involving his own spiritual self, sure enough, for, as he explained in his epilogue to *Elene*, the narrative of the finding of the cross had come to him as a marvellous revelation only after prolonged meditation (*ingemynd*):[88]

Ic þæs wuldres treowes
oft, nales æne,   hæfde ingemynd
ær ic þæt wundor   onwrigen hæfde
ymb þone beorhtan beam,   swa ic on bocum fand,
wyrda gangum,   on gewritum cyðan
be ðam sigebeacne

['I had had inner remembrance of the tree of glory often, not once, before I uncovered the miracle about the bright wood, as I found revealed in books, in the course of events, in writings about the symbol of victory', 1251b–6a].

But God's grant of joyous eloquence to him had not been an experience of a kind unique to him either in matter or in manner, consisting, as it had done, not only of release from the common oppression of sin and grief but also of a traditional unlocking of his share of a communal poetic craft:

Ic wæs weorcum fah,
synnum asæled,   sorgum gewæled,
bitrum gebunden,   bisgum beþrungen,
ær me lare onlag   þurh leohtne had
gamelum to geoce,   gife unscynde
mægencyning amæt   ond on gemynd begeat,
torht ontynde,   tidum gerymde,
bancofan onband,   breostlocan onwand,
leoðucræft onleac.   Þæs ic lustum breac,
willum in worlde

['I was stained by deeds, fettered by sins, afflicted by sorrows, bound by bitternesses, encompassed by cares, before the king of might bestowed instruction on me gloriously as help for an old man, meted out a noble gift and poured it into my mind, disclosed brilliance, amplified it sometimes, unbound my body, opened the enclosure of my breast, unlocked the craft of poetry.[89] I have used that joyfully, willingly in the world'].

[88] Cf. King Alfred's frequent recollections, above, p. 381.

[89] It is by no means certain that *leoðucræft* means 'the craft of poetry'; see, e.g., *Cynewulf's 'Elene'*, ed. Gradon, n. on 522.

A single symbolic term, *mægencyning*, identifies the fount of mental change and, in its position at approximately mid-point, provides a pivot for the whole passage; a close sequence of appositional, dramatic, rhyming past participles – *asæled*, *gewæled*, *gebunden* and *beþrungen* – vividly convey the previously prevailing impairment of mind, tersely stated at the outset (1242b); three spacious 'lines' (1245–7) express the actual sympathetic giving of bountiful grace; five more finite active verbs, four of them sharing the prefix *on-*, the first four of the five linked to one another by rhyme and all in apposition to *begeat* (1247b) – *ontynde*, *gerymde*, *onband*, *onwand* and *onleac* – stress the freeing and relieving which this act involved; and lastly (1250b–1a) comes the beneficiary's full-hearted affirmation of acceptance, tied by rhyme to the giving (*onleac* and *breac* (1250a and b)). Attention is not diverted to eulogy of the divine bestower; it remains throughout focused on a dramatic, artistic, narrative of the individual human receiver's psychological experience. But that experience is related in entirely general terms.

This psychological strain in authorial generality differed too from writers' self-presentation in the Latin literature of the time and in the vernacular prose more closely modelled on the Latin than the poetry could ever be. The Latin tradition, with its stronger sense of the thinking self as a separate identity, regarded personal, biographical information as an essential means of establishing an author's credibility. For example, Bede's telling of the story of Cædmon, which was intended to show convincingly that the divine inspiration of this individual had in a crucial way begun the naturalization of the new religion in the Anglo-Saxon kingdoms,[90] had included the particulars of this man's occupation, his shyness, his lack of formal education, his piety, his humility and his innocence, but had not described the psychological process he underwent when he was receiving inspiration. Likewise Bede – with good European precedents behind him, such as Gregory the Great introducing his *Dialogi* and Gregory of Tours his *Historia Francorum* – had thought it proper and desirable to give an account of himself as author of his Latin ecclesiastical history, not only by giving his name, alluding to moral usefulness in his work and asking for the benefit of his readers' intercessions (all of which Cynewulf was to match), but also by backing up his history with information about the sources and principles he had applied in its composition and with a potted autobiography from

[90] See above, pp. 231–2.

birth to priesthood, followed by a complete list of his writings to date (the age of fifty-eight), which more than justified his claim that ever since he had entered his monastery at the age of seven his delight had been to learn or teach or write.[91] The view of authorship which Latin literature had introduced to Anglo-Saxons, as personified by Bede, was that the author's credentials for dealing with matters of general import lay not in his psychological representativeness of the human lot as such (as they did for Cynewulf) but, more specifically, in his own *curriculum vitae*.

Vernacular prose, not bound by the psychological type of generality traditional to poetry, adopted the autobiographical view freely. Just as King Alfred was the subject of Bishop Asser's Latin *Life* containing much biographical detail, so in his own vernacular prose he wove particulars about himself in and out of his general themes. For example, he expressed concern about deterioration in the knowledge of Latin in England not only by describing the thoughts about this lamentable state of affairs which had kept on coming into his mind[92] but also by tying a certain stage of the decline to the time 'when I succeeded to the kingdom',[93] and by identifying another stage as what 'I saw before everything was ravaged and burnt up' by the Vikings.[94] Like Bede, Alfred felt it right to identify himself with his general subject-matter through personal history.

Two contrasting conceptions of generalization were responsible for the distinction between vernacular poetry's validation of the individual through psychological representativeness and the autobiographical validation characteristic of Latin literature and vernacular prose. Poetry traditionally expressed a philosophy inherently of this world within continuous time and hence it viewed individual integrity as inescapably subject to the often tragic drama of forceful – in the last resort, indifferent – circumstances, whereas in the Christian system of thought generalizations were based intellectually on eternal spiritual constants beyond the pressures of this world, so that in principle an individual in this life was called on to apply to circumstances, as they occurred, an absolute code of conduct. General observations in poetry were relative to a this-worldly fatalism, but Christian ethics were affected only by mortality. Christianity's basic demand on an individual was to identify him- or herself with the right sort

[91] Bede, *HE*, *Praefatio* and V.24 (pp. 2–6 and 566–70).

[92] See above, p. 381.

[93] *Gregory's Pastoral Care*, ed. Sweet, p. 3, line 18.

[94] Cf. above, p. 386.

of cosmic invariable – primarily God as against the devil – and to stick to it for life.

The two thought processes – conceiving of generalization as immediately social, temporal and relative or as ultimately religious, eternal and absolute – employed personalization in different ways. The former tradition required that a general idea should issue from the wisdom of a representative person who had sized up a given situation. For instance, this intrinsic link was basic to the *Andreas* poet's treatment of the Mermedonians' reaction to the mighty flood engulfing them at the apostle's bidding:[95] whereas we read in the C analogue[96] 'They all cried out convulsively and said with great weeping, "Woe to us for all these things which have come upon us. This flood has occurred because of the pilgrim we imprisoned and all the evils we inflicted on him unjustly. . . . Whether we want to or not, let us believe in him . . ."',[97] the poet picked out one of the 'ealde æscberend' ('old spearbearers', 1537a), whom he had already vividly described crying out in desperation to stay alive in the flood,[98] and had him say to a crowd which he had gathered around him (1555b–6),

Nu ge magon sylfe soð gecnawan,
þæt we mid unrihte ellþeodigne
on carcerne clommum belegdon,
witebendum. . . .
is hit mycle selre, þæs þe ic soð talige,
þæt we hine alysan of leoðobendum

['Now you yourselves can recognize the truth, that we have unjustly afflicted the stranger in prison with fetters, cruel bonds . . . it is much better, as I reckon the truth, that we should release him from his bondage', 1558–61a and 1563–4].

In this example of Anglo-Saxon oral society's customary reliance on the words of a wise leader to bring about a collective decision[99] a representative individual established his credentials to lead by formulating a recognizable collective truth. In the 'absolute' tradition, on the other hand, abstraction itself was personified, as is strikingly exemplified by the rhetorical figure of prosopopœia introduced by the anonymous author of the Old English

95 See above, pp. 260–1.

96 On this Modern English translation of a Latin version related to the poem, see above, p. 250, n. 55.

97 *Sources and Analogues*, trans. Allen and Calder, p. 31.

98 1536b–40a; cf. 1543b–4, 1547–9 and 1554–5a.

99 See above, p. 287.

Orosius, in the time of Alfred, in order to convey that the city of Babylon had a moral message for mankind: this once finest of cities, the vernacular prose writer declared, is now as if it were an example to all men, saying, 'Nu ic þuss gehroren eam ⁊ aweg gewiten, hwæt, ge magan on me ongietan ⁊ oncnawan þæt ge nanuht mid eow nabbað fæstes ne stronges þætte þurhwunigean mæge' ('Now I have thus fallen and passed away, lo, you can realize and understand in me that you have nothing with you secure and strong so that it may remain').[100] Not as far along this road of personalized abstraction was the *Andreas* Latin C analogue's 'They all cried out . . ., "Woe to us . . ."', cited above, or Alfred's invocation of a collective voice when he supposed that those whom he had once seen surrounded by Latin books which they could not read had said together, 'Our ancestors, who formerly held these places, they loved wisdom and through that they obtained wealth and left it to us. . . . We have now lost . . .'[101] And not much further ahead, in Middle English literature, lay abstract concepts, such as virtues and vices, systematically allegorized in human forms. Whereas, we may say, the practice of relative generalization personalized the formulation of abstractions, under the system of absolute generalization abstractions already formed were personalized.

Two different conceptions of personal responsibility also resulted, as two versions of a generalization about action and posthumous reputation will illustrate. Beowulf, when encouraging Hrothgar not to sorrow overmuch at the loss of his favourite thegn, urged him to take revenge on this preceptual basis:

wyrce se þe mote
domes ær deaþe; þæt bið drihtguman
unlifgendum æfter selest

['let him who is allowed achieve glory before death; that is best afterwards for a lifeless warrior', *Beowulf* 1387b–9];

but King Alfred, claiming that he had never been governed by greed and ambition, summed up his moral record thus: 'Þæt is nu hraðost to secganne, þæt ic wilnode weorðfullice to libbanne þa hwile þe ic lifde, . . . æfter minum life þæm monnum to læfenne þe æfter me wæren min

100 *The Old English Orosius*, ed. Bately, p. 44, lines 3–6. The Latin original did not have the city speaking, but its wording may have put the idea into the Old English author's mind; see *ibid.*, n. on 43/34–44/6.

101 See above, p. 386.

gemyndig on godum weorcum.' ('That is now to say very briefly, that I have desired to live worthily as long as I have lived, and to leave after my life to the men who should come after me my memory in good works').[102] The king was restating poetry's age-old wisdom about reputation in terms of a moral will and, in a prose fashion, based on sentence structure. A coordinating '7' ('and') divided the complete statement of what was willed into two complementary members, with their interconnection marked by an assonantal sequence running through them both from *libbanne* and *lifde* in the first to *life* and *læfenne* in the second, together with **w**- alliteration throughout, and their difference indicated by **m**- alliteration in the second member alone. Beowulf presented as his model a man of action in progress, achieving what he can while he can; Alfred, by contrast, commended himself as a whole man who has consistently exercised the moral will in such a way as to produce a lifetime of good works. To Beowulf individual integrity was an ability to rise actively to each occasion; to Alfred it consisted of an entire life of moral thought and feeling.

Vernacular poetry, for long the medium of the former ethic, was able to portray profoundly and movingly the mental upheaval facing anyone intent on replacing the relative goals with the absolute one as the guiding principle of living. This is the turmoil which *The Wanderer* depicts with such impressive psychological force through a series of representative speakers,[103] whose emotional thinking leads them to develop rules of

[102] *King Alfred's Old English Version of Boethius 'De consolatione Philosophiae'*, ed. Sedgefield, p. 41, lines 3–6.

[103] There are various opinions as to whether a single personage speaks throughout this poem, or, if not, as to how many there are; and there are equally serious doubts as to whether *Swa cwæð* . . . (6a) or *Swa cwæð* . . . (111a), or both of them, is/are to be understood as applying to foregoing speech or to following speech or to both. Certainty in these choices is not possible and, fortunately, not essential: they pertain to dramatic narrative structure, not to theme. The working hypothesis I adopt here is that the two opening generalizations (1–5), which frame all that follows, are likely to have been uttered by a narrator and that all portions of subsequent direct speech are likely to be equally primary – in other words, I consider it less likely that any speaker, other than the narrator, quotes another. Hence I attribute to the narrator lines 1–7, 88–91 and 111. It then follows, so it seems to me, that key stages in the thought and feeling which develop the initial proposition of lines 1–5 are articulated most clearly if *Swa cwæð* (6a), *þas word acwið* (91b) and *Swa cwæð* (111a) are each regarded as signalling the beginning of a contribution by a separate, unnamed but described, authoritative speaker. (For two examples elsewhere in extant poems of *swa* used before a speech, see Mitchell, 'Some Syntactical Problems in *The Wanderer*', pp. 175–6 (repr. *Selected Papers*, pp. 101–2).

individual behaviour based on an increasingly abstract perception of an environment governed ultimately by absolutes. Between them these speakers gradually reach comprehension that society's traditional codes of conduct conducive to personal dignity – such as loyalty to a lord, self-discipline in the face of harsh adversity and thoughtful application of conventional remedies – are by themselves not enough for inhabitants of a divinely ordained system which is following a relentless course to final dissolution: in such a cosmic context an individual's perseverance is inevitably reliant on the mercy of God operating from beyond this world. The personal trauma of adjusting long-held this-worldly views to the thinking required by a transcendent Christian universe is tackled head-on.

Two opening, successive, gnomic-type generalizations (1–5) frame the ensuing, directly spoken testimonies: firstly, often a symbolic *anhaga* – that is, a man who is essentially on his own[104] – experiences (*gebideð*[105]) the grace, the mercy, of God, though he has long had to journey in exile, troubled in mind (*modcearig*) and icy cold (1–5a); and secondly, 'wyrd bið ful aræd' ('what comes to pass is fully determined', 5b). Heralded thus, the rest of the poem is not going to take an unforeseen course. A symbolic, personal, narrative connection between relentless suffering mentally and physically and receiving mercy from an all-controlling God has been announced, just as the *Beowulf* narrator defined a unit of his symbolic story when, having reported the night-time ravages of the dragon, he stated

Wæs se fruma egeslic
leodum on lande, swa hyt lungre wearð
on hyra sincgifan sare geendod

['The beginning was terrible for the people in the land, as it quickly was ended grievously in their treasure-giver', 2309b–11].

What is to be expected in each case is a filling-in, a working-out, of the narrative area which has been enunciated. But, whereas in *Beowulf* the proclaimed area is a linear span of action, beginning and ending finitely in a

I think it improbable that, as argued in *The Wanderer*, ed. Dunning and Bliss, at pp. 32–3, both these *swa* clauses are subordinate, not principal.) I see *Swa cwæð* . . . at 6a and 111a as meaning '. . . has spoken as follows (in connection with what has just been said in this poem)'.

104 For discussion of this word, see *ibid.*, pp. 37–40.

105 On preference for interpreting this word as 'experiences' rather than 'awaits' or 'expects', see *ibid.*, pp. 41–2.

people's history, in *The Wanderer* it comprises an implication of interaction between two fundamentally different types of individual experience in the divinely controlled continuum of time. The latter poem sets up an initial cosmic juxtaposition which invites a narrative exploration of its imperatives for individual behaviour.

As a first stage in this voyage of the mind the reality of personal suffering, endured continuously ('uhtna gehwylce' ('each dawn', 8b)), is vouched for by the testimony which, the narrator reports, has been given (*cwæð* (6a)) by a symbolic *eardstapa*, 'wanderer on the earth' (6a), a quintessential exile from society,[106] when he was looking back over his long, lonely years, mindful of his hardships ('earfeþa gemyndig' (6b)), the fierce battles in which his kinsmen had died (7). This man had been no political refugee such as the royal Eadgils, an honoured guest at Beowulf's court, biding his time to mount an expedition back into his home country with his host's help, in order to take his revenge on an uncle and thereby gain his native kingship for himself (*Beowulf* 2379b–97). On the contrary, he had experienced the sort of loneliness which intensifies an awareness of individuality outside society altogether. With no one to confide in (9b–11a), cut off from home and kindred (20b–1a), he had been thrown back on his own thoughts and feelings while searching far and wide for a friendly protector to replace the one he had lost through death (19–29a). He had been travelling *wintercearig*, 'as desolate as winter' (24a), 'ofer waþema gebind' ('across frozen waves', 24b). The words which the narrator passes on to us have issued from the heart and mind of a symbolic man utterly isolated from the warmth of society. They are the register of a vulnerable person, stripped of all communal security and totally alone in non-human surroundings. The speaker was not so much the traditional social man of action as someone whom psychological experience had fitted to question what it is to be human.

His experience of grief had been very personal indeed: for instance, it was not how his *goldwine*, 'generous lord' (22b), had died that he recalled, but the pain of covering this friend with the darkness of the earth. He had not been turned into a private introvert, however: the epithet *goldwine*, with which he lovingly recalled his dear lord, is repeated (35b) in his touching evocation of the cruel memories that haunt anyone who is separated from his loved ones (34–6a). Emotive symbolic language was

[106] For exile as a poetic convention, see Greenfield, 'The Formulaic Expression of the Theme of "Exile"'.

equally essential to his account of his own experience (8–11a and 19–29a) – *modsefan* (2×), *earmcearig*, 'eðle bidæled', 'freomægum feor', *goldwine*, *wintercearig*, *seledreorig*,[107] 'sinces bryttan' and *meoduhealle* – and to his generalized description (29b–57) of his kind of sorrow ('Wat se þe cunnað / hu . . .' ('He who tries knows how . . .')). His first- and third-person portrayals were alike typifying:[108] he himself had suffered in the heroic mould and in his turn he suffused the general with his own intimate affection, as when he described any wretched man who thinks alone ('earmne anhogan' (40a)) dreaming

þæt he his mondryhten
clyppe ond cysse, ond on cneo lecge
honda ond heafod, swa he hwilum ær
in geardagum giefstolas breac

['that he is embracing and kissing his liege lord, and laying hands and head on his knee, as when from time to time in days of old he used to receive gifts from the throne', 41b–4].

Personal as this *eardstapa*'s memories were, he had retained his socially representative outlook. He had not invented his own way of grappling with his anguish but had numbered himself among the *domgeorne*, 'those eager for glory' (17a), who, at the behest of social, gnomic precept (11b–14a),[109] 'dreorigne oft / in hyra breostcofan bindað fæste' ('often bind fast a sad mind in the chamber of their breast', 17b–18).

As he saw it, the general state of his mind was thoroughly symbolic: the adjectives *earmcearig*, 'wretched and troubled' (20a), and *wintercearig* (24a), with which he described himself, are members of an increasingly intense series initiated by *modcearig* in the poem's opening gnomic generalization (2b). But not all his thinking was in this native tradition. The more particular psychology he employed took him beyond the confines of social convention into a conception of mental activity derived from Christian patristic thought: when he stated that any solitary man who endures long years of suffering, such as his, is repeatedly driven by sorrow to send his thoughts far and wide through time and space (39–57), he was describing thinking in terms which the Fathers had used when demonstrating that it is in just this ability to escape from the enclosing body and to range widely that the human mind partly reflects the total power of the divine mind to

[107] Krapp and Dobbie prefer *sele dreorig*. [108] Cf. above, pp. 121–2.
[109] See above, p. 121 and n. 5.

keep all parts of the universe simultaneously and always present to it.[110] The *eardstapa* was echoing a tradition in which the boundaries of individual thought were set not within social custom but out in the universe itself. His mode of thinking had made a transition into a more extensive context for generalization.

In the situation which he and others like him confronted, however, practice was painfully at variance with this potential for mental freedom. The *eardstapa*'s personal anguish had consisted especially of being obsessed with a happy past quite unlike his desolate present. His memory had brought stretches of a model past into a long-endured present which they could do nothing to cure. His mind had remained imprisoned by his past. His only idea of a present had been a scarcely bearable contrast and his only idea of a future had been a restoration of the past. But now he related this personal constriction of outlook to the universal context of thought itself:

> Forþon ic geþencan ne mæg   geond þas woruld
> for hwan modsefa   min ne gesweorce,
> þonne ic eorla lif   eal geondþence,
> hu hi færlice   flet ofgeafon,
> modge maguþegnas

['And so I cannot think for what reason throughout this world my mind should not grow dark when I ponder every aspect of the life of warriors, how they have suddenly given up the hall, proud young thegns', 58–62a].

And a generalization embracing all space and time was the result: 'Swa þes middangeard / ealra dogra gehwam dreoseð ond fealleþ' ('So this world every single day fails and falls', 62b–3).[111]

The practical implications of this scale of understanding needed to be considered first: only long experience of this world can give a man wisdom, and the wisdom he thus acquires is above all that of patience and restraint (64–72). But such mundane thoughts were soon left behind by the *eardstapa*'s mind now alert to its setting in the universe. The *gleaw hæle*,

[110] For this patristic tradition and the use made of it in *The Wanderer*, see my '*Mens absentia cogitans*', esp. pp. 73–7.

[111] At 58b ('geond þas woruld') and again at 62b ('Swa þes middangeard') the compound demonstrative, *þes* etc., begins to signal a steadily deepening and widening implication that current time and space are relative to something beyond (58b, 62b, 74a, 75b, 85a, 88a, 89a and 101a), a connotation which finally, after 'weoruld under heofonum' (107b, reinforced by repeated *Her* (4×, 108–9)), becomes explicit at 110a ('eal þis eorþan gesteal').

'far-seeing man' (73a), he asserted, has to understand how terrifying[112] it will be 'þonne ealre þisse worulde wela weste stondeð' ('when the riches of all this world stand desolate', 74), as wind-swept, snow-swept, ruins now stand in various places the world over, deserted since the death of the warriors who once owned them (75–80a). The bodies of the slain have undergone many sorts of fates (80b–4). Clear vision converts the image of scattered ruins, prompted by a personal past, into a single symbol of all created, sequential time: 'Yþde swa þisne eardgeard ælda scyppend' ('The creator of men laid waste this city thus', 85).

The *eardstapa* had advanced a long way into extrovert intellectual perception from his original, self-absorbed, reliance on looking to society's precepts about the *ferðloca* (13a), *hordcofa* (14a) or *breostcofa* (18a), the locked chamber of the breast, for control of his *modsefa* (3×),[113] that is, his mind as agent of his emotion.[114] He had come to appreciate that the transience, which he himself had experienced so painfully in the life of warriors around him, formed part of a gradual, continuous, process of decay which had had its beginning in creation and would have its end in a final dissolution (73–4). But these ultimate limits remained for him means of explaining what he knew directly for himself rather than concepts which could be exploited to yield an understanding of all time as such. That further degree of intellectual development awaited another mind.

The speaker whom the narrator introduces to take this fresh initiative is characterized in open-ended terms appropriate to this extra potential. He is a *Se* ('He who', 88a), the *Se þe*, 'whoever', of gnomic statements of the 'He who does this, does that' type:[115] he is anyone who has thought wisely (*wise* (88b)) about this universal image of a wall-foundation left by the creator of men and who ponders every aspect of this dark life ('deope geondþenceð' (89b)); and accordingly he speaks in an indefinite present (*þas word acwið*

[112] I accept this sense of *gæstlic* (73b) adopted by Dunning and Bliss in their edition (p. 53), although I do not agree with all their particular lines of argument (on which, see below, p. 441 and n. 25). It should be pointed out here that in all the eleven other occurrences of *gæstlic* (adj.) or *gæstlice* (adv.) in poetry the meaning is '(positively) spiritual(ly)'.

[113] 10a, 19a and 59a.

[114] Godden, 'Anglo-Saxons on the Mind', pp. 291–3, esp. 292.

[115] Cf. the use of this form of generalization by the *eardstapa*, 'Wat se þe cunnað' (29b, cited above, p. 402). For a use of *se* (relative), rather than *se þe*, in a formulation of this kind, cf. 'heold hyne syðþan / fyr ond fæstor se þæm feonde ætwand' ('he who escaped from the enemy kept himself further away and more securely thereafter', *Beowulf* 142b–3).

(91b)).[116] Such a person, remembering often, from far back, a great many violent slaughters, is a symbolic 'frod in ferðe' ('one whose mind is charged with the experience advanced age brings', 90a).[117] He speaks for all those who have the requisite depth and range of thought and emotion to pronounce on transience as the ultimate condition of this world.[118]

The first concept with which this sage presents us is that the present, by its very nature, destroys the past. 'Where is the fabric of yesterday's society?', he asks rhetorically in a run of elegiac questions, at once heartfelt and formal, of the type, 'Where are the joys of the hall?' (93b).[119] As an immediate response comes a series of equally elegiac symbolic apostrophes, such as 'O the splendour of the leader of a people!' (94–5a), and then follows a final, inclusive exclamation, 'Hu seo þrag gewat, / genap under nihthelm, swa heo no wære' ('How that time has passed away, grown dark beneath the cover of night, as though it had never been!', 95b–6). By a moving reuse of the ancient, comprehensive image of day passing into night, this thinker has converted interpretation of sequential events from traditional, pre-Christian belief in an inflexible *wyrd* into recognition that the present continuously obliterates the past.

And so the effect of time will ever be, he realizes. A ruin, buffeted by the storms of winter as it stands a towering witness to slaughtered beloved warriors, becomes to his mind's eye a dramatic symbol of an all-embracing system of transience in full cry (97–105): grand symbolic language – 'leofre duguþe', 'wyrmlicum fah', 'æsca þryþe', 'wæpen wælgifru', *stanhleoþu*,

116 The different definition in 'ond þis deorce lif deope geondþenceð' (89) as against 'þonne ic eorla lif eal geondþence' (60) signals his more coordinated state of mind.

117 Occurrences of 'frod on ferhðe' (cf. *higefrod* (*Genesis* (*A*) 1953a) which are likely to be comparably symbolic, in that probably in their instances too the adjective functions nominally and the epithet as a whole expresses an interactive coupling of potentials implying narrative and generalization (see above, p. 129), are at *Exodus* 355a and *Elene* 1163a; 'on ferþe frod' at *Juliana* 553a and the plural 'ferþþum frode' at *Riddle* 59, 3a are likewise probably symbolic, and so too is *ferþum gleaw* at *Riddle* 84, 34a. *On ferþe* (or *ferþum*) epithets were formed also on adjectives outside the 'wisdom' group (*fægen*, *forht* (4×), *frecne*, *fus* and *unfrom*).

118 For a similarly portentous, dramatic, introduction of a representative speaker, but without any of the intellectual element so important in the present case, cf. Beowulf's presentation (*Beowulf* 2041–6) of a symbolic 'eald æscwiga' ('old spear-warrior') whom he envisages speaking (*þæt word acwyð*) as the advocate of revenge when stung by the sight of his own people's dearly prized weapons in the hands of their enemies.

119 On the derivation of questions in this conventional mould, see Cross, '"Ubi Sunt" Passages in Old English'.

'wintres woma', *nihtscua* and 'hreo hæglfare' – unites man, the man-made and nature into a single powerful emblem; the height of the wall, with its serpentine patterns, strikes wonder ('wundrum heah' (98a)) and it is the very slopes of stone in the forefront of the image (*þas stanhleoþu* (101a)) which the violent storms are battering; the weapons that deprived the dear warriors of life were greedy for slaughter (99–100a) and the tumult of winter directs fierce hail from the north in ill-will against men (103–5). This speaker's 'now' (*nu* (97a)) is not dispersed among many examples, as the *eardstapa*'s had been (*nu missenlice*, 'now in various places' (75a)), but is concentrated on a single mighty symbol of human relationships annihilated, of artifacts in decay or turned against their masters, of hostile nature unconstrained. He has attained the viewpoint of a last survivor. His vision is of the wastage that is in all time. Struggle and transience will ever be absolute twin principles of human experience in this world (106–9), and finally 'eal þis eorþan gesteal idel weorþeð' ('this entire foundation of earth will become useless', 110).[120] He has perceived that in the last analysis every man, always, is acting alone in a divinely ordained, finite totality of time heading for an apocalyptic conclusion which was already implicit in its creation.[121] The philosophical framework which includes both the individual's necessity to endure and his need for God's overriding mercy has been set in place mentally.

A *snottor on mode*, 'one wise in mind' (111a), the narrator reports, has already fulfilled his symbolic rôle[122] while communing with himself in private: personal virtue in the conditions envisaged, he has declared (*cwæð* (111a)), essentially consists of keeping one's faith, combining disciplined

[120] Cf. above, p. 342.

[121] For the apocalyptic theme in this poem, see Green, 'Man, Time and Apocalypse'.

[122] Comparable, probably symbolic, epithets occur at *Riddle* 84, 35a ('mon [*recte* on?] mode snottor'), *Riddle* 86, 2b (the plural, 'mode snottre'), *Beowulf* 1844b (*on mode frod*), and *Riddle* 59, 2b and *Azarias* 190a (the plural, 'modum gleawe'). In view of these I believe it more likely that the prepositional phrase *on mode* here combines with *snottor* to form a symbolic epithet (= *modsnottor* (*Soul and Body I* 126b and *II* 121b, *The Gifts of Men* 41b and *Precepts* 2a); and cf. *hygesnottor* (*Guthlac* (*A*) 1109a, *Juliana* 386a and *The Metres of Boethius* 10, 7b)) than that it should be construed adverbially with the *cwæð* preceding *snottor* and so be rendered 'inwardly', as some have thought. (For a recent statement of this latter view, see Richman, 'Speaker and Speech Boundaries in *The Wanderer*', pp. 469–73.) For 'frod in/on fer(h)ðe' with symbolic status, see above, p. 405 and n. 117. *On mode* epithets built on adjectives outside the 'wisdom' group are fairly frequent.

feeling with positive action, and seeking the assistance of grace (*ar* and *frofor* (114b–15a)) from the father in heaven, where, and nowhere else, we shall be secure (112–15).

The *eardstapa*'s mind had endured an unremitting binding, fastening and fettering: over and over again in his wretchedness he had had to restrain his *modsefan* with fetters ('feterum sælan' (19–21)), since he knew it to be an aristocratic virtue for a man to bind his *ferðlocan* fast ('fæste binde' (11b–14a) and 'bindað fæste' (17–18)); he and others like him had travelled *wintercearig* over frozen waves (*waþema gebind* (23b–4)), repeatedly sending their exhausted thoughts across the congealed mass of water (*waþema gebind* again (56–7)); sorrow and sleep together he knew only too well, often bind (*gebindað*) the destitute solitary thinker (39–40). And likewise in the second speaker's emblematic image of a storm-beaten ruin a driving snowstorm freezes (*bindeð*) the earth (102). Binding the mind, beset by cold (33a) and darkness (59b) in *þis deorce lif* (89a) of temporal and physical night and winter, is a valid defence so far as it goes, but keeping one's *treow*, 'faith, trust' (112a), within a divinely created and controlled cosmos is a larger, nobler, principle. Seeking assistance from the father in heaven is an essential first stage in permanent liberation from the insecurity endemic in this world: it brings the prospect of *eal seo fæstnung*, as the *snottor on mode* expressed it (115b), stable, eternal, security.[123]

Through progressive authentic emotion the poem redefines exemplary conduct. The lesson it draws from painful experience is that conversion of one's past-bound, this-worldly, thinking and feeling into forward-looking, disciplined, Christian trust is the prime obligation of every individual in this life. The successive contributions by the archetypal solitary figures of wanderer, 'last survivor' and wise man sitting apart symbolized the phased transformation which every person's mind has to undergo. By first assuming the authority of representative past experience, by next viewing the past as a vanished whole, and by finally looking forward into eternity, these three speakers, each in his own position in narrative time which is impregnated with God's mercy (1–5), gradually transferred the conceptual basis of individual living from the social, temporal, relative mode on to the religious, eternal, absolute plane.[124] By

[123] On the connotations of *fæstnung*, see the note on this word, *The Wanderer*, ed. Dunning and Bliss, p. 50.

[124] On the conversion of transitory time into the permanence of eternity, see Bately, 'Time and the Passing of Time in *The Wanderer*', esp. pp. 13–15.

virtue of this narrative evolution of representative psychology the age-old social patterns of this world's thought and emotion, preserved by vernacular poetry, were made to yield the Christian concept of the thinking self *sub specie aeternitatis*.

12

Loyalty as a responsibility of the individual

How did the ancient social bond of loyalty between leader and follower fare as a time-honoured theme of vernacular poetry when straightforward adherence to an ancestral set of aristocratic warrior values had become overlaid with an extended network of public relationships and an individual's concern for his spiritual fate? *The Battle of Maldon* may seem deceptively simple as our principal evidence. But its late-tenth-century character cannot be adequately appreciated without an understanding of the changed social outlook it was reflecting and without a recognition of its artistry as a branch of the 'mixed' state of verse which developed when, not later than the ninth century, the symbolic system was adapted to human existence redefined by Christ's redeeming incarnation and ascension. These twin lines of enquiry, then, will be followed in this chapter, including discussion of some features in the ninth-century poetic 'mix' which have not yet been pointed out in this book.

The declaration of heroism by Byrhtwold signals for us the new points of reference for behaviour in a crisis. A trusty retainer of probably relatively humble origins, his invocation was less a standard appeal to corporate aristocratic values than a call for his companions to exercise the virtue which he, as an individual, sensed was directly relevant to the predicament he and they were in after the death of their leader, Byrhtnoth.[1] His heroic antithesis, which still rings through the ages to us in its

[1] Byrhtwold was an *eald geneat* (310a; perhaps *ealdgeneat* on the analogy of *ealdgesiðas* (*Beowulf* 353b)), who might have been the servant (*cniht*) to whom Byrhtnoth's sister-in-law had bequeathed land at some date before the battle (*Anglo-Saxon Wills*, ed. Whitelock, p. 36, lines 24–5). At any rate in the poem he is of no named parentage and seems to have fought as an ordinary shield and spear warrior (309b and 310b), without the sword wielded by those of higher degree.

pointedness and dramatic relationship to his self-sacrifice in uttering it when he did,

> Hige sceal þe heardra, heorte þe cenre,
> mod sceal þe mare, þe ure mægen lytlað

['Thought shall be the more resolute, heart the bolder, mind shall be the greater, the more our strength lessens', 312–13],

came closer in spirit to the straightforward 'ordinariness' of Apollonius's humble friend-in-need[2] than a more sententious maxim would have done – such as 'Æfre sceal mod miclian þonne mægen lytlað!' ('Mind shall grow larger whenever strength grows less!'). Byrhtwold exerted leadership not by invoking an inherited code of experience through a generalizing word such as *æfre* or *a*, 'always', but by setting a personal example of applying to himself a precept directed to his 'us' in 'our' (*ure* 313b) particular desperate circumstances. And likewise, when he went on to echo a conventional maxim, 'A mæg gnornian / se ðe nu fram þis wigplegan wendan þenceð' ('Always will he have cause to mourn who now thinks of leaving this fighting', 315b–16), he subordinated the generalization of its *A* to a *nu* and a *þis*. The relevance of the maxim was not left to implication, in the manner of tradition, but was pinned down explicitly in the here and now.[3] *Maldon*, honouring a contemporary event in the spirit of ancient Germanic warriorship more faithfully than any other late Old English poem that we have, nevertheless portrayed a present which, far from being completely governed by the past, selected from it according to its own psychological needs. By this time the solemn truths of aristocratic warrior tradition in themselves did not command absolute authority. They had been absorbed into a more open body of thought out of which an individual fashioned his own destiny.[4]

[2] See above, p. 360.

[3] Probably a preexisting maxim was being adapted here, for 'A mæg gnornian / se ðe fram wigplegan wendan þenceð' would satisfactorily reduce the high number of unstressed syllables at the beginning of 316 pointed out in *The Battle of Maldon*, ed. Scragg, p. 84, n. on 316.

[4] Three of the four other quoted speakers after Byrhtnoth's death delivered personal exhortations without recourse to 'abstract' propositions. The other one, Dunnere, an 'unorne ceorl' ('simple peasant', and therefore, like Byrhtwold, not a man of rank), was the sole exception in citing an unadapted maxim in the old-fashioned way:

> Ne mæg na wandian se þe wrecan þenceð
> frean on folce, ne for feore murnan (258–9)

(see above, p. 154).

The old concept of a monolithic aristocratic warrior society, at one with the natural world, was still available in the middle of the tenth century to express uncomplicated patriotic triumphalism, as we know from the poem celebrating the English victory at *Brunanburh* in 937, and included in most of the surviving manuscripts of the *Anglo-Saxon Chronicle*. The opening of this poem invoked this ancient homogeneity straightaway:

Her Æþelstan cyning, eorla dryhten,
beorna beahgifa, and his broþor eac,
Eadmund æþeling, ealdorlangne tir
geslogon æt sæcce sweorda ecgum
ymbe Brunanburh. Bordweal clufan,
heowan heoþolinde hamora lafan,
afaran Eadweardes, swa him geæþele wæs
from cneomægum, þæt hi æt campe oft
wiþ laþra gehwæne land ealgodon,
hord and hamas. Hettend crungun,
Sceotta leoda and scipflotan
fæge feollan, feld dænnede
secga swate, siðþan sunne up
on morgentid, mære tungol,
glad ofer grundas, godes condel beorht,
eces drihtnes, oð sio æþele gesceaft
sah to setle

['Here King Athelstan, leader of warriors, ring-giver of men, and his brother also, Ætheling Edmund, gained life-long glory through the blows of their sword-blades in strife around *Brunanburh*. With the blades left by hammers the sons of Edward cleft the shield-wall, hewed battle-shields, as it was inborn in them from kinsmen that often in battle they would defend land, treasure and homes against every enemy. Antagonists perished, people of the Scots and sailors fell doomed, the field darkened with the blood of men, from the time the sun, glorious celestial body, up in the morning, glided above the lands, the bright candle of God, the eternal Lord, until the noble creature sank to its seat', 1–17a].

But when it came to treating personal responsibility, as *Maldon* did later in the century, the very sense of collective duty itself came under question.

When 'hæðene scealcas' ('heathen warriors') cut Byrhtnoth down (181), three named sons of Odda, followed by many more, fled to the safety of the nearby wood (185–201). But others reacted differently:

Þa wearð afeallen þæs folces ealdor,
Æþelredes eorl; ealle gesawon
heorðgeneatas þæt hyra heorra læg.
Þa ðær wendon forð wlance þegenas,
unearge men efston georne;
hi woldon þa ealle oðer twega,
lif forlætan oððe leofne gewrecan

['Then the leader of the army, Æthelred's noble warrior, had fallen; all the hearth-companions saw that their lord lay dead. Then bold thegns advanced, undaunted men hastened forward, they all then intended one of two things, to lose life or to avenge the loved one', 202–8].

The distinction was between those who stood by their word and those who did not:

Swa him Offa on dæg ær asæde
on þam meþelstede, þa he gemot hæfde,
þæt þær modiglice manega spræcon
þe eft æt þearfe þolian noldon

['So Offa had said to him [i.e. Byrhtnoth] earlier in the day in the meeting-place, when he held a council, that many spoke bravely there who afterwards, in time of need, would not endure', 198–201].

An indissoluble bond between land tenure and unqualified loyalty to a lord did not come into automatic operation, sufficient in itself to divide off the faithful from the unfaithful. The afraid and the unafraid separated out from one another by demonstrating an individual disregard or regard for a link between personal integrity and public behaviour. Fulfilment of the publicly shared *beot*, 'vow',[5] given to the *frea*, 'lord', at the *gemot*, 'meeting', earlier in the day, to fight to the death on his behalf if need be,[6] rested on individual considerations as diverse as pride in a grandfather's rank (218–19), fear of reproach from neighbours (249–52a) and dread of remorse (315b–16). The poet dwelt on the variety of feelings involved in sticking to one's word for members of a local ealdormanic society under stress within the more general background of Æthelred's kingdom.

Not so in *Beowulf*. The composer of that poem was interested in

[5] 15b and 213b; cf. 290a.

[6] 13b–16 and 289–93; cf. 81–3, 166–8a, 198–201, 205–8, 212–14, 232b–7a, 246–8, 271–2 and 274b–6.

typifying true fidelity and personified the type in Wiglaf when Beowulf, in the sight of eleven companions, was enveloped by the dragon's deadly fire:

Nealles him on heape handgesteallan,
æðelinga bearn ymbe gestodon
hildecystum, ac hy on holt bugon,
ealdre burgan. Hiora in anum weoll
sefa wið sorgum; sibb æfre ne mæg
wiht onwendan þam ðe wel þenceð

['Not at all did close comrades in a band, sons of nobles, take up their stand round him with battle-virtues, but they turned to a wood, protected life. In one of them a mind surged with sorrows; nothing can ever alter ties of kinship for him who thinks well', *Beowulf* 2596–601].

Wiglaf's heroism contrasted with a general rupture in the symbolic tie between 'se ðe ær folce weold' ('he who had ruled the people', 2595b) and 'handgesteallan', 'æðelinga bearn' and 'hildecystum', and his action was to restore the entire system by taking a stand on its deepest truth enunciated in the narrator's maxim. When Wiglaf 'geseah his mondryhten / under heregriman hat þrowian' ('saw his liege lord under his war-mask suffer heat', 2604b–5), he remembered the debt of gratitude he owed to his hard-pressed leader and immediately – this was the first time in his patron's defence – drew the sword which was part of the arms which his now dead father had won for himself by killing their former owner (2611–27):

Gemunde ða ða are, þe he him ær forgeaf,
wicstede weligne Wægmundinga,
folcrihta gehwylc, swa his fæder ahte;
ne mihte ða forhabban, hond rond gefeng,
geolwe linde, gomel swyrd geteah

['Then he remembered the patrimony which he had granted him, the wealthy dwelling place of the Wægmundings, every folk-right, as his father had possessed; then he could not hold himself back, hand seized shield, yellow wood, drew the ancient sword', 2606–10].

The crucial union between past experience and present behaviour was recreated in a creative partnership between firmness common to symbolic mind and symbolic weapon:

Ne gemealt him se modsefa, ne his mæges laf
gewac æt wige; þæt se wyrm onfand,
syððan hie togædre gegan hæfdon

['The thoughts of his mind did not melt, and his kinsman's legacy did not weaken in the fight; that the dragon discovered after they had joined battle', 2628–30].

From then on Wiglaf spoke and acted as representative of loyal warriorship. First the 'wordrihta fela' ('many just words', 2631b) which he addressed to the other ten men rooted their obligation to the lord 'ðe us ðas beagas geaf' ('who gave us these rings', 2635b) in the *guðgetawa*, 'war arms', symbolizing the promise which they had made to him 'in biorsele' ('in the beer-hall', 2635a)

þæt we him ða guðgetawa   gyldan woldon,
gif him þyslicu   þearf gelumpe,
helmas ond heard sweord

['that we would repay the war-arms to him if need like this befell him, the helmets and hard swords', 2636–8a].

Then came a reminder that Beowulf had picked them out for this expedition 'þe he usic garwigend gode tealde, / hwate helmberend' ('because he reckoned us good spear-fighters, valiant helmet-bearers', 2641–2a).

Nu is se dæg cumen,
þæt ure mandryhten   mægenes behofað,
godra guðrinca

['Now the day has come that our liege lord needs military strength, good battle-warriors', 2646b–8a],

Wiglaf continued bluntly. And finally came his own commitment:

God wat on mec,
þæt me is micle leofre,   þæt minne lichaman
mid minne goldgyfan   gled fæðmie.
Ne þynceð me gerysne,   þæt we rondas beren
eft to earde,   nemne we æror mægen
fane gefyllan,   feorh ealgian
Wedra ðeodnes.   Ic wat geare,
þæt næron ealdgewyrht,   þæt he ana scyle
Geata duguðe   gnorn þrowian,
gesigan æt sæcce;   urum sceal sweord ond helm,
byrne ond beaduscrud   bam gemæne

['God knows that as for me it is much more dear that flame should embrace my body with my giver of gold. It does not seem to me proper that we should bear spears back home unless we can first kill the enemy, defend the life of the leader of the Weders. I know for sure that his deeds of old have not deserved that he alone of the noble host of the Geats should suffer affliction, sink in battle; sword and helmet, corslet and battle-apparel, shall be common to us both', 2650b–60].

Guðgetawa, *garwigend*, *helmberend*, *mandryhten*, *guðrinca*, *goldgyfan*, *ealdgewyrht*, *beaduscrud* – to pick out only the compounds – symbolically integrated the essential elements of armed, fighting loyalty to a giving leader and concentrated them dramatically in the person of Wiglaf stepping forth as the same striking symbolic figure he had seen his lord to be (2604b–5): 'Wod þa þurh þone wælrec, wigheafolan bær / frean on fultum' ('Then he strode through the deadly fumes, bore the war-head in support of his lord', 2661–2a). And when, after it was all over, the *hildlatan*, 'sluggish in battle' (2846a), 'tydre treowlogan' ('weak traitors to their pledge', 2847a) emerged from their place of safety, Wiglaf, beside his dead lord, expressed his contempt for them in the same root-and-branch terms:

Þæt, la, mæg secgan se ðe wyle soð specan,
þæt se mondryhten, se eow ða maðmas geaf,
eoredgeatwe, þe ge þær on standað, –
þonne he on ealubence oft gesealde
healsittendum helm ond byrnan,
þeoden his þegnum, swylce he þrydlicost
ower feor oððe neah findan meahte –,
þæt he genunga guðgewædu
wraðe forwurpe, ða hyne wig beget

['That, indeed, he who will speak truth can say, that the liege lord who gave you the treasures, the gear of horse-riders, which you stand in there – when on the ale-bench he often gave to hall-sitters helmet and corslet, the leader of the people to his thegns, such as he could find mightiest anywhere far or near – grievously threw away the battle-garments directly when war befell him', 2864–72].

The whole social nexus of lord, hall life, thegns, weapons and fighting had been affronted, and entire families had to pay the comprehensive penalty of losing the rights and privileges of hereditary ownership of land:

Nu sceal sincþego ond swyrdgifu,
eall eðelwyn eowrum cynne,
lufen alicgean; londrihtes mot
þære mægburge monna æghwylc
idel hweorfan, syððan æðelingas

feorran gefricgean   fleam eowerne,
domleasan dæd.   Deað bið sella
eorla gehwylcum   þonne edwitlif

['Now receiving treasure and sword giving, all enjoyment of hereditary estate for your people, hope shall fail; every man will have to go deprived of the domain of the kindred, after nobles have learned from afar of your flight, inglorious deed. Death is better for every warrior than a life of disgrace!', 2884–91].

In *Maldon* this organic integration of society, warrior and weapons did not take place. Young Ælfwine recalled his kinship with Byrhtnoth: 'Me is þæt hearma mæst; / he wæs ægðer min mæg and min hlaford' ('For me that is the greatest of sorrows; he was both my kinsman and my lord', 223b–4). But no principle of right thinking was explicitly invoked thereby, as there was in Wiglaf's case. The ties between leader and followers in fact took a variety of forms. *Þa geearnunga*, the rewards 'þe he him to duguþe gedon hæfde' ('which he [Byrhtnoth] had given them [those he led in this battle] for their benefit') and which, according to the narrator, they should all have borne in mind (195–7), were of several kinds.[7] In the heat of the battle Byrhtnoth, as *ðeoden*, thanked one, Edward, as his *burþen*, 'chamberlain' (120–1a). The treachery of Godric (one of the sons of Odda), who fled from the battlefield on the horse of his dead *hlaford*, was especially reprehensible in that he 'þone godan forlet / þe him mænigne oft mear gesealde' ('left the good man who had often given him many a horse', 184–90). The loyalty which the *geneat* Byrhtwold felt so strongly for his good and beloved *ealdor* and *hlaford*,[8] may well have been that of a tenant for his lord of the manor.[9] And when it came to a functional relationship between fighters and their weapons, that was reduced to no more than an iterated formula ('gehealdan heardne mece, / wæpnes wealdan' (167b–8a), 'wæpen / habban and healdan' (235b–6a), 'wæpna wealdan' (272) and 'wæpna neotan' (308b)).

Action gave a clearcut outward sign of an attitude of mind, with little or

[7] There is clear documentary evidence approximately contemporary with the poem (*Anglo-Saxon Charters*, ed. Robertson, nos. LIX and LXIX, cited Bullough, *Friends, Neighbours and Fellow-Drinkers*, p. 23 and (with refs.) n. 43) that *duguð* when denoting a group of men had been generalized from its strictly military sense of 'a body of tried retainers' to that of 'the leading men of a shire'. The 'benefit' denoted by *duguð* in this poem is therefore probably to be understood with the various connotations applicable to the wider group.

[8] 314a, 315a, 318b and 319a.

[9] Cf. Gneuss, *Die 'Battle of Maldon'*, p. 41 and n. 112.

no symbolic underpinning. After Ælfwine had declared 'Ic wylle mine æþelo eallum gecyþan' ('I mean to make known to all my inherited nobility', 216), he single-mindedly did just that:

Þa he forð eode, fæhðe gemunde
þæt he mid orde, anne geræhte
flotan on þam folce, þæt se on foldan læg
forwegen mid his wæpne

['Then he advanced, remembered the feud, so that with his spear he got at a certain sailor in the army, so that he lay on the ground despatched by means of his weapon', 225–8a].

Behaviour projected mentality outwards in easily recognizable ways:

Þa þæt Offan mæg ærest onfunde,
þæt se eorl nolde yrhðo geþolian,
he let him þa of handon leofne fleogan
hafoc wið þæs holtes, and to þære hilde stop;
be þam man mihte oncnawan þæt se cniht nolde
wacian æt þam wige, þa he to wæpnum feng

['When the kinsman of Offa first realized that the noble warrior did not intend to endure cowardice, he let his beloved hawk fly from his hands towards the wood, and advanced to the battle; by that it could be understood that the youth did not mean to weaken in the fight when he took hold of his weapons', 5–10].

What made Godric's behaviour particularly odious was that it gave a fatally misleading impression:

Us Godric hæfð,
earh Oddan bearn, ealle beswicene.
Wende þæs formoni man, þa he on meare rad,
on wlancan þam wicge, þæt wære hit ure hlaford;
forþan wearð her on felda folc totwæmed,
scyldburh tobrocen. Abreoðe his angin,
þæt he her swa manigne man aflymde

['Godric, cowardly son of Odda, has deceived us all. Very many a man believed, when he rode on the horse, on the proud steed, that it was our lord; therefore here on the field the army was divided, the shield-wall broken up. May his action fail, that he put to flight so many a man here!', 237b–43].

Common perception focused on outward appearances.

The function of language too was to be open and plain. Old-fashioned, implicit, symbolism inevitably had a reduced rôle. It was subordinate to, rather than dominant in, narrative, as in 'Oft he gar forlet, / wælspere windan on þa wicingas' ('Often he let a spear fly, a slaughter-spear on to the Vikings', 321b–2): the *wælspere* had an authentic deadly image of its own as it flew, but there was no attempt to exploit it further. Symbolic expressions had been down-graded to becoming a resource for special effects. For example, the *Beowulf*ian compounds for setting swords in the whole tradition of warfare – *beado-*, *guð-*, *hilde-* and *wig-*, *-bill*, *-mece* and *-sweord* – do not occur and 'sword' genitive combinations do not either, while any 'sword' adjectival combinations involving an epithet less routinely utilitarian than *brad* (15 and 163a), *god* (237a) or *heard* (167b and 236b) – namely *bruneccg* (163a), *ealde* (47b), *fealohilte* (166b) and *gerenod* (161b) *bill* or *swurd* – were used exclusively to highlight Byrhtnoth's aristocratic leadership.[10] They contribute rhetoric to his retort to the Viking messenger:

Gehyrst þu, sælida, hwæt þis folc segeð?
Hi willað eow to gafole garas syllan,
ættryne ord and ealde swurd

['Do you hear, seaman, what this army says? They will give you spears as tribute, poisoned spear and ancient sword', 45–7].

They oppose the Vikings' naked lust for loot to the resolute blow-for-blow self-defence of the wounded *eorl* when he was coming under increasing pressure:

Eode þa gesyrwed secg to þam eorle;
he wolde þæs beornes beagas gefecgan,
reaf and hringas and gerenod swurd.
Þa Byrhtnoð bræd bill of sceðe,
brad and bruneccg, and on þa byrnan sloh

['Then an armed man advanced towards the noble warrior; he wanted to obtain the warrior's rings, clothing and rings and decorated sword. Then Byrhtnoth drew his sword from its sheath, broad and bright-bladed, and struck the corslet', 159–63].

Above all they symbolize the pathos of his death:

Feoll þa to foldan fealohilte swurd;
ne mihte he gehealdan heardne mece

[10] For a recent discussion of this poet's more frequent reference to the use of spears than to that of swords, see Brooks, 'Weapons and Armour', pp. 212–14.

['Then the yellow-hilted sword fell to the earth; he could not hold the hard sword', 166–7].

The unique *fealohilte* (cf. *gylden hilt* (*Beowulf* 1677a)) seems to have been chosen because of the associations of *fealo* with decay and sadness (as in 'Ne feallað þær on foldan fealwe blostman' ('Yellow flowers do not fall on to the earth there', *The Phoenix* 74)). The poet centred these symbols on Byrhtnoth not just because he saw him as an archetype but more particularly because he wanted to portray him as a personage of special refinement.

This leader's 'specialness' lay not in figuration of a revered past stretching into the mists of time so much as in his evident contemporary combination of wealth and nobility.[11] He was every inch the late-tenth-century Christian ealdorman and showed it in his feeling for his native country when he was rebuffing the Vikings' offer – 'eþel þysne, / Æþelredes eard' (52b–3a) – and in his trust in a God who is the 'ruler of peoples' (173b) when he was dying.[12] Probably he drew moral authority from the Christian concept of the 'just war'.[13] In life, receiving a grievous wound in battle, he was 'Æþelredes þegen' (149–51), dead on the battlefield he was 'Æþelredes eorl' (202–3a). It was only in this context of Christian patriotism that he called on more ancient motives when in the heat of battle

bæd þæt hyssa gehwylc hogode to wige
þe on Denon wolde dom gefeohtan

['[he] urged that each young warrior who meant to win glory from the Danes by fighting should concentrate on war', 128–9].[14]

Beyond the network of personal relationships in local ealdormanic society which he shared with his followers the perspectives which he alone brought into play were those of a national identity and a religious eternity.

His parameters were thus at once more narrowly and more broadly drawn than those of the antique symbolic bond between Beowulf and his (mostly disloyal) companions on the dragon's mound. Restrictively, a finite national history had supplanted the ranging vista of Germanic ancestry as the measure of present-day heroic action. Even that most

[11] For discussion of the meaning of *rice* (and its collocation *gerædest*) in 36, see above, p. 349.

[12] As against 'ruler of glory or men or victories' at *Beowulf* 17a, 183a, 1661b, 1752a, 2741b and 2875a; on *Maldon* 173–80, see above, p. 322.

[13] See Cross, 'The Ethic of War in Old English', p. 274.

[14] On *dom*, see above, pp. 150–4.

straightforwardly traditional of tenth-century poems, *The Battle of Brunanburh*, had regarded recorded history since the Anglo-Saxon conquest of England as the field of its patriotic vision:

Ne wearð wæl mare
on þis eiglande æfre gieta
folces gefylled beforan þissum
sweordes ecgum, þæs þe us secgað bec,
ealde uðwitan, siþþan eastan hider
Engle and Seaxe up becoman,
ofer brad brimu Brytene sohtan,
wlance wigsmiþas, Wealas ofercoman,
eorlas arhwate eard begeatan

['Never yet before this had a greater slaughter of an army been achieved by swordblades in this island, as books tell us, old sages, since the Angles and Saxons invaded here from the east, sought Britain across broad seas, bold battle-makers overcame the Welsh, glorious warriors conquered a country', 65b–73].

Expansively, the remote past from which political authority ultimately issued had become more than just Germanic. The Alfredian prose compilation of the *Anglo-Saxon Chronicle* provided its epitome of Anglo-Saxon, especially West Saxon, history with antecedents in the history of Britain from the landing of Julius Caesar in 60 BC, the life and passion of Christ, and Jewish, church and Roman imperial history, all organized within an overarching system of AD dating.[15] A poem such as *Widsith* could have been intended as a *fin d'époque*, personalized, digest of a Germanic heritage which was shrinking, and *Maxims I* and *II* might represent similarly antiquarian collections. *Beowulf* was recopied but could not have been reinvented.[16] The ultimate compass of national power had become Christological. The Christian concept of human individuality in an eternal relationship with God had become combined with Anglo-Saxon aristocratic, warrior, leadership from as far back as the cult of St Oswald, king of Northumbria, in the seventh century.[17] It had been deep-set in King Alfred's thinking late in the ninth.[18]

[15] For a survey of the relevant annals, see Bately, 'World History in the *Anglo-Saxon Chronicle*'.

[16] See above, p. 54.

[17] See above, pp. 319–20.

[18] See my study of his thematic use of the word *cræft* in his vernacular prose and the debt this usage owed to vernacular poetry, 'King Alfred's Debt to Vernacular Poetry', pp. 223–38.

Not surprisingly, narrative depiction of this changed style of leadership called for fewer symbols. *Maldon*, today consisting imperfectly of 325 lines, contains only about half as many as there are in the first 325 lines of *Beowulf*. The sharpest decrease is in the number of compounds: adjective combinations have more or less held their own and genitive combinations have not been quite halved, but compounds are scarcely more than a third as frequent. The ratio of compounds to all other symbols put together (slightly above parity in *Beowulf*) has dropped by nearly a half. Increased use of prepositions also represents a move away from implied relationships towards more explicit ones: there are about one-and-a-half times as many prepositional phrases of all sorts in *Maldon* as there are in *Beowulf* 1–325. Nouns have lost some of their dominance, with the result that connections between verb and verb are responsible for more onward movement than in *Beowulf*: there are about two-and-a-half times as many steps from verb to verb effected by coordination (*and*) or by apposition than there are in *Beowulf* 1–325. In the latter, characteristically, when the narrator reported that men (in particular Beowulf) learned through sad song the news

þætte Grendel wan
hwile wið Hroþgar, heteniðas wæg,
fyrene ond fæhðe fela missera,
singale sæce

['that Grendel had contended a long while with Hrothgar, carried on violent hostilities, crime and feud for many years, continual strife', *Beowulf* 151b–4a],

more narrative thrust is given by nouns (especially the compound *heteniðas* and adjective combination 'singale sæce' in symbolic apposition) than by verbs (*wan* and *wæg* in apposition). But it is the verbs which make the running in this typical passage of *Maldon*:

he gehleop þone eoh þe ahte his hlaford,
on þam gerædum þe hit riht ne wæs,
and his broðru mid him begen ærndon,
Godwine[19] and Godwig, guþe ne gymdon,
ac wendon fram þam wige and þone wudu sohton,
flugon on þæt fæsten and hyra feore burgon

['he leapt upon the horse which his lord owned, in the trappings in such a way that it was not right, and his brothers with him both ran away, Godwine and Godwig,

[19] ASPR retains the *Godrine* of Casley's transcript.

did not care about the battle, but turned away from the fight and sought the wood, fled into that place of safety and saved their life', 189–94].

Action had become much more articulated. The narrative sequence did not so much receive massive charges of symbolic electricity as conduct a freely flowing current.

We might be inclined to think that *Maldon* shared this plain articulation with a tradition of oral prose story-telling about contemporary heroic events, such as that which we have good reason to believe existed back in the late eighth century on the evidence of a written summary, which was interpolated in the *Anglo-Saxon Chronicle* a hundred years or so after the events concerned and which, with a severely factual tone and without a trace of poetic language, briefly but circumstantially described the killing of Cynewulf, king of Wessex, by a revengeful ætheling, Cyneheard, and the loyalty maintained to the death by followers of each of them. The essential ingredients for establishment of an oral prose narrative of this sort were firstly a core event and secondly an account of it conforming to a cultural consensus. In the Cynewulf and Cyneheard case this conformity was to the emotional fabric of customary relationships of the type portrayed in *Beowulf*: its protagonists belonged to this system as completely as Beowulf did. Ecclesiastical oral prose narratives also were based on the twin components of first-hand authority and cultural consensus, to judge by the already cited examples of Bede's telling of the story of Cædmon's inspiration,[20] by Boniface's epistolary write-up of the vision related to him by the monk of Wenlock who had had the original experience perhaps two or three years before,[21] and, in the 980s, not long before *Maldon*, by the narrative of an idealized St Edmund which Dunstan in old age recounted to Abbo of Fleury, embellishing the archbishop's recollection of a version which he had heard told some sixty years earlier by Edmund's armour-bearer, then an old man.[22] Our question therefore is: in what respects, *mutatis mutandis*, did *Maldon* rest on the same two foundations?

So far as first-hand knowledge in *Maldon* is concerned, we may feel reasonably confident that direct experience, possibly even by the poet himself, played a formative part in the poem's composition. At the least, we can perhaps agree about the poet's version that, as Scragg has said, 'it is perverse to assume that the main features of the battle strategy, the fight at the ford and the subsequent principal encounter away from the river, which

[20] See above, p. 242, n. 26. [21] See above, p. 25. [22] See above, p. 321.

do not appear to be dictated by artistic necessity, are not a reflection of contemporary reports of what happened'.[23] And a prevailing sober respect for plain narrative seems to imply only deliberate divergence from received report elsewhere too. For instance, the occasional use of rhyme, as in

> æfre embe stunde he sealde sume wunde
> þa hwile ðe he wæpna wealdan moste

['repeatedly he inflicted some wound as long as he could wield weapons', 271–2].[24]

never took rhetorical charge, as rhyme did in another example of late Old English verse on traditional subject-matter, the account of Earl Godwine's imprisonment of Alfred the ætheling, Æthelred II's youngest son, in manuscripts C and D of the *Anglo-Saxon Chronicle*, *s.a.* 1036:

> Ac Godwine hine þa gelette and hine on hæft sette,
> and his geferan he todraf, and sume mislice ofsloh;
> sume hi man wið feo sealde, sume hreowlice acwealde,
> sume hi man bende, sume hi man blende,
> sume hamelode, sume hættode.
> Ne wearð dreorlicre dæd gedon on þison earde,
> syþþan Dene comon and her frið namon.
> Nu is to gelyfenne to ðan leofan gode,
> þæt hi blission bliðe mid Criste
> þe wæron butan scylde swa earmlice acwealde

['But Godwine then stopped him and put him in prison, and his companions he scattered and some he killed in various ways; some of them were sold for money, some cruelly killed, some were fettered, some were blinded, some mutilated, some scalped. No more bloody deed was done in this country since the Danes came and made peace here. Now it is to be trusted to the beloved God that they rejoice happily with Christ who were without guilt so wretchedly killed', *The Death of Alfred* 6–15].

The age-old emotion which this ruthless treatment of a political rival stirred in this chronicler-poet's breast resulted in a verse cousin to a literary sentence such as this in the anonymous vernacular prose version of the Seven Sleepers legend, describing the treatment meted out to steadfast Christians by Decius's persecutors: 'þam man eac nan þingc ne

[23] *The Battle of Maldon*, ed. Scragg, p. 13 and n. 48.

[24] Cf., esp., 282 and 42 and 309.

wandode . ac hi to eallre yrmðe getucode . and heora lima man ealle tobræd ælc fram oþrum . eall swa windes blæd swæpð dust of eorðan . and hi man holdode and hi ealle hricode . swilce oðer wæterflod swa fleow heora blod' ('To them also no respect whatever was paid, but they were punished by every affliction, and their limbs were all pulled apart each from the other, just as a blast of wind sweeps dust from the earth, and they were disembowelled and all cut to pieces, and like a second deluge, so flowed their blood').[25] *Maldon* never became rhetorical in this hyperbolic fashion. The poet's narrative never altogether lost touch with living memory of what had actually happened.

Solid communal consensus, such as that from which the Cynewulf and Cyneheard story had been carved, in all probability was not available to the *Maldon* poet, however. Conflicting interpretations of Byrhtnoth's leadership, for instance, are likely to have been strongly canvassed in the society to which it belonged. The poet's attitude probably was not universally shared. Yet he did not fashion his poem in a spirit of propaganda. He stood firm on the inherited view of personal loyalty to an aristocratic leader common to the Cynewulf and Cyneheard piece and *Beowulf* in a narrative, which was like the former and unlike the latter in being given next to no support by judgemental comment,[26] but was unlike them both in consistently adhering to a conspicuous set of artistic canons which married narrative lucidity to pieces of explicit language not specially memorable individually and yet each contributing distinctly to a clearcut whole.[27] A linguistic exactness runs throughout whereby, for example, 'like the spear which Wulfmær later draws from Byrhtnoth's body and sends back to kill a Viking, the barbed words of the Viking's challenge are deftly caught, ironically accepted, and sent back in a notable display of heroic wit'.[28] Byrhtnoth cancelled out the Viking messenger's portentous pronouncement 'and eow betere is / þæt ge þisne garræs mid gafole forgyldon' ('and it is better for you that you should buy off this onslaught of spears with tribute', 31b–2) by retorting

Gehyrst þu, sælida, hwæt þis folc segeð?
Hi willað eow to gafole garas syllan

[25] *Ælfric's Lives of Saints*, ed. Skeat, XXIII, lines 70–4.

[26] Only 190b and 195–7; for the latter, see above, p. 416, and for the *Beowulf* narrator assiduously giving voice to society's point of view, see above, pp. 170–1.

[27] For a judicious account of the poet's style, see *The Battle of Maldon*, ed. Scragg, pp. 28–35.

[28] Irving, 'The Heroic Style in *The Battle of Maldon*', p. 460.

['Do you hear, seaman, what this army says? They will give you spears as tribute', 45–6].

His substitution of the alliterative sequence *gafole*, *garas* for the seaman's *garræs*, *gafole* was a play on words of a sort entirely absent from Beowulf's refutation of Unferth's taunt (*Beowulf* 499–609).[29] And again, the messenger's own smooth words, 'we willaþ mid þam sceattum us to scype gangan' ('we will embark with the money', 40) were turned against their user when Byrhtnoth repeated them, with the significant substitution of *urum* for *þam* ('þæt ge mid urum sceattum to scype gangon', 56), in order to say 'Ne sceole ge swa softe sinc gegangan' ('You shall not obtain treasure so gently', 59), this *swa softe* at the end of the reply contrastively echoing the *swa hearde* at the beginning of the Viking's haughty address (33a). Words could, and did, interact across the surface of this poem. For instance, a set collocation of a type which I have classified as non-symbolic[30] echoes from the messenger's arrogant lips through later events: his phrase 'beagas wið gebeorge' ('rings in return for protection', 31a) is revived twice in the contrasting form 'bord to gebeorge' ('a shield as protection', 131a and 245a), once when Byrhtnoth's death is imminent and once during the heroic stand after it. *Maldon* possessed a *gravitas* equal to that of the Cynewulf and Cyneheard story or *Beowulf*, but pursued it in an artistic environment all its own. It portrayed a psychological situation which was open and various; it articulated a root connection between personal integrity and public deed in direct language and uncomplicated action; it deployed a verbal confidence of a 'literary' type. This is the cultural organism which needs to be elucidated.

The increased use of physical space to define fundamental narrative action in *Maldon*, as against the traditional dominance of continuous time in poetry such as *Beowulf*,[31] can be illustrated by the different determinants when the verb *hatan*, 'to command', was used in precise situations to denote on the one hand Beowulf's exercise of authority and on the other Byrhtnoth's. When the former, in his native land, learned of Grendel's evil deeds abroad, in Denmark, first 'Het him yðlidan / godne gegyrwan' ('He ordered a good wave-traveller to be prepared', *Beowulf* 198b–9a) and then, having picked the companions whom he wanted,

[29] Anderson has seen Byrhtnoth's combination of similarity in sound and dissimilarity in sense as an instance of the Latin rhetorical figure of *paranomasia* ('"Flyting" in *The Battle of Maldon*', p. 199).

[30] Above, p. 155. [31] See above, pp. 85–6.

fiftyna sum
sundwudu sohte,   secg wisade,
lagucræftig mon   landgemyrcu (207b–9).[32]

Beowulf's command, expressed by *Het*, had only an indirect relationship to space: sequential time was of the essence. The order was for a general, unplaced action (preparing a boat), which, when carried out, provided a marker (a prepared boat) for Beowulf's first physical action ('sundwudu sohte'). In *Maldon*, however, both Byrhtnoth's command, expressed by *Het* (2a),

Het þa hyssa hwæne   hors forlætan,
feor afysan,   and forð gangan,
hicgan to handum   and to hige godum

['Then he ordered each warrior to leave his horse, to drive it far away and to move forward, to concentrate on his hands and on his good heart', 2–4],

and its sequel,

Þa þæt Offan mæg   ærest onfunde,
þæt se eorl nolde   yrhðo geþolian,
he let him þa of handon   leofne fleogan
hafoc wið þæs holtes,   and to þære hilde stop (5–8),[33]

were explicitly spatial. In this poem the mental command and the physical response were consecutively delimited in space.

The *Maldon* poet as a narrator maintained a 'reporter's' outward view of what happened within a spatial field of action, very different from the *Beowulf* narrator's primary involvement with actors' inherent states of mind within time. In *Maldon* the spectator's standpoint prevailed even when the narrative technique was at its most traditional, as in lines 96–101a:

Wodon þa wælwulfas   (for wætere ne murnon),
wicinga werod,   west ofer Pantan,
ofer scir wæter   scyldas wegon,
lidmen to lande   linde bæron.
Þær ongean gramum   gearowe stodon
Byrhtnoð mid beornum

['Then wolves of slaughter advanced, did not care about water, the band of Vikings, west across the Pant, across bright water, carried shields; sailors bore lime-shields to land. There[34] against the fierce ones stood ready Byrhtnoth with his warriors'].

The Vikings' act of crossing was being perceived in the ancient native way

32 See above, p. 172.   33 See above, p. 417.   34 Or conceivably 'land, where'.

as a continuum, developing dramatically from 'wading across' (96–7), through 'carrying shields across' (97–8), to 'carrying shields to land' (99), but not so as to produce explicit progressive mental interaction with their English antagonists. The confrontation, when it came at the conclusion of the process, was simply between *grame* and *gearwe* (100). The psychological build-up was not to the fore on this occasion as it was when, during Grendel's progressive advance on Hrothgar's hall, it is said of Beowulf waiting inside

> . . . he wæccende   wraþum on andan
> bad bolgenmod   beadwa geþinges

['. . . he who was awake in fierce anger awaited enraged the issue of battles', *Beowulf* 708–9],

and then, directly afterwards, of Grendel approaching

> Ða com of more   under misthleoþum
> Grendel gongan,   Godes yrre bær;
> mynte se manscaða   manna cynnes
> sumne besyrwan   in sele þam hean

['Then from the moor, beneath misty slopes, Grendel came moving, bearing God's anger; the criminal injurer meant to ensnare someone of the race of men in the lofty hall', 710–13].

Clashing *bolgenmod* and *manscaða* were instinctively opposed in their inmost beings; the readiness of Byrhtnoth and his men, on the other hand, was of a practical, public sort:

> he mid bordum het
> wyrcan þone wihagan,   and þæt werod healdan
> fæste wið feondum

['He ordered them to form the battle-hedge with their shields, and the troop to hold fast against the enemy', *Maldon* 101b–3a].

The *Maldon* poet-narrator's concept of a playing-space and his assumption of a spectator's viewpoint in it is reminiscent in miniature of how a Christian poet treated the world as the arena to which a divine saviour had descended from heaven in his incarnation and from which he had returned to heaven in his ascension,[35] and how his narrative imagination recalled

[35] E.g., Cynewulf stressing these cross-boundary journeys as a pair in his ascension poem, *Christ II*, in order to stress the culminating significance of the second for human salvation on earth; see above, p. 313.

action within that arena through a recreative mind's eye.[36] Abstract forces are not depicted constantly in play in the *Maldon* arena. God foresees (94b–5) and is thanked (1476–8) and prayed to (262b–4) in the heat of battle, but does not impose a rule and judgement over what happens, as he does in *Beowulf*.[37] An all-embracing fate does not preside (*wyrd* is never mentioned), although men have to die ('Wæs seo tid cumen / þæt þær fæge men feallan sceoldon' ('The time had come that doomed men had to fall there', 104b–5)[38] and a fatefulness may be implied in the poet's unusually frequent use of *weorðan*, as against *beon*, in combination with a past participle to report an eventful happening, such as Offa's death ('Raðe wearð æt hilde Offa forheawen' ('Soon Offa was cut down in battle', 288)) or the advent of uproar which attracted the traditional birds of prey:

Þær wearð hream ahafen,   hremmas wundon,
earn æses georn;   wæs on eorþan cyrm

['An outcry arose there, ravens circled, an eagle eager for carrion; there was uproar on earth', 106–7].[39]

This was not a narrative presenting active beings achieving as much as they could in the face of interposing uncontrollable outside forces, as *Beowulf* was, so much as a story in which actions, with their own implications and running along foregone lines, made their own impact, as in a poem such as *Exodus*. The ground was clear for conduct imbued with ethos to make its own impression within a 'spectator's' field of vision; and that is why, for example, modern readers, with different backgrounds, have produced such divergent interpretations of Byrhtnoth's *ofermod* when he allowed too much land to the hateful enemy (89–90): the poet did not supply the judgemental guidance we require; we are obliged to fall back on the word's extant use

[36] E.g., Cynewulf, in the same poem, conflating biblical apostles and contemporary pilgrims; see above, pp. 323–6.

[37] Cf. 94b-5 with, e.g., Beowulf's final words before lying down to await Grendel's arrival in Heorot:

ond siþðan witig God
on swa hwæþere hond   halig Dryhten
mærðo deme,   swa him gemet þince

['and afterwards let wise God, holy Lord, adjudge fame on whichever hand seems fit to him', *Beowulf* 685b–7].

[38] Cf. 119b, 125a and 297a.

[39] For the high frequency of *weorðan*, etymologically related to *wyrd*, and the above interpretation of it, see Donoghue, *Style in Old English Poetry*, pp. 122–5.

in other contexts as noun or adjective and on the use of its equivalents (noun and adjective) in other Germanic languages and do the best we can that way.[40]

That is not to say, however, that this poem casts us adrift rudderless among its community values. Outward form reflects the underlying principles of behaviour here on the battlefield of Maldon as consistently as was the case (more elaborately) in the limitlessness of God's redeemed world when Cynewulf declared that every individual has to choose between heaven and hell.[41] The earlier poet created a verbal emblem of the redeemer's all-embracing, once-for-all, eternal, relationship with all men (*Christ* (*II*) 586–9a and 598b–9) enfolding each individual's temporal dualism (589b–98a); the later one employed a sequence of word-and-deed vignettes to suggest that the bond between mind and body was the basic principle of integrity running through all personal variations.[42] In points of style too both poets exercised the same thematic binary control, exemplified in the *Maldon* poet's case by this passage:

He ne wandode na æt þam wigplegan,
ac he fysde forð flan genehe;
hwilon he on bord sceat, hwilon beorn tæsde,
æfre embe stunde he sealde sume wunde,
þa hwile ðe he wæpna wealdan moste

['He never flinched in the battle-game, but he shot an arrow forth frequently; sometimes he struck the shield, sometimes injured the man; repeatedly he inflicted some wound as long as he could wield weapons', 268–72].

The firm balance created by the coupled 'hwilon . . . hwilon . . .' (270) and by the rhyming '. . . stunde . . . wunde' (271) formalizes the bond between the underlying resolve (268) and the repeated action (269) which this mere Northumbrian hostage, Ashferth (265–7), never loosened as long as his strength lasted (272). We can detect clear signs that this poet's conception of style stood in a tradition which stemmed from the practice of vernacular poets, such as Cynewulf, who, when handling full-blown Christian narratives not later than the ninth century, had grafted on to their native

40 For a rebuke of past interpreters for ignoring this comparative evidence altogether or, at best, using it incompletely, and for a judicious assessment based on it, see Gneuss, 'Byrhtnoð's *ofermod* Once Again'.

41 See above, p. 313.

42 See above, p. 209; for the narrative structure, cf. *The Battle of Maldon*, ed. Scragg, p. 36.

stock a range of sentence structures and overt devices learned from Latin literature and specifically Latin poetry.[43]

We must now examine this sea-change, wrought on vernacular poetic composition by this cultural exposure. But first it will be as well to remind ourselves that, to begin with, the influence had been in the other direction, from vernacular to Latin, as is demonstrated particularly clearly by the way Englishmen fashioned Latin octosyllabic verse at the end of the seventh century and the beginning of the eighth. The earliest authors concerned were Aldhelm, abbot of Malmesbury and bishop of Sherborne, who died in 709 or 710, the pioneer in composing Latin verse as a non-native speaker (indeed the first-ever person in such circumstances to compose extensively in quantitative hexameters), and his pupil, Æthilwald.[44] Aldhelm owed his extraordinary proficiency in Latin mainly to his education by two masters at Canterbury, Theodore and Hadrian, but – unless King Alfred was mistaken, towards the end of the ninth century, or William of Malmesbury was, early in the twelfth – he was no mean poet in his native tongue either.[45] At any rate, as has been convincingly shown by A.P.M. Orchard,[46] Aldhelm, in his *Carmen rhythmicum*,[47] departed significantly from existing Latin tradition – classical or Irish – by pairing a considerable proportion of his octosyllabic lines in couplets by means not only of rhyme but also of alliteration which agreed specifically with vernacular practice in patterning and pronunciation: he alliterated at least two syllables in the first line of a couplet with the first (and only the first) syllable in the second line, he alliterated *f* and *v* and, in direct contradiction to classical Latin usage, he alliterated any vowel with any vowel and avoided alliterating *s* with any of the *s-* combinations, *sp-*, *st-* and *sc-*. Æthilwald displayed the same vernacular characteristics in one of his octosyllabic poems[48] and developed them much further in the three others which survive,[49] greatly increasing the proportion of couplets fashioned in this manner. Old

[43] As Campbell has rightly remarked, 'doubtless the educated poets learned as much about style by reading poems of Prudentius, Sedulius, Virgil and Persius as they did from theoretical techniques taught by the manuals of Donatus and Isidore' ('Adaptation of Classical Rhetoric in Old English Literature', p. 189).

[44] Lapidge has stated Aldhelm's unique position very pointedly ('Aldhelm's Latin Poetry and Old English Verse', pp. 209–11).

[45] For the reference, see above, p. 35, n. 87.

[46] *The Poetic Art of Aldhelm*, pp. 45–51.

[47] *Aldhelmi Opera*, ed. Ehwald, pp. 524–8.

[48] *Ibid.*, pp. 528–33.

[49] *Ibid.*, pp. 533–7.

English poetic composition and its newly introduced Anglo-Latin counterpart were not thought of in complete isolation from one another.

By the time the well-educated Cynewulf composed his vernacular poems, probably in the ninth century, the tide was flowing strongly his way from Latin. For instance, in the passage with which he concluded his narrative of the ascension and which I have quoted and discussed before,[50] the sentence structure, word order and combination of polysyndeton[51] and rhyme all witness to the extent of the Latin influence he had received. The single long sentence beginning with 586 and ending with 598a is a particularly illuminating specimen of a complex syntactic structure which could not have been built out of the customary native resources of mainly temporal connectives.[52] The object clause beginning *hu* (586b) and ending *in worulde* (598a) includes a result clause running from *þæt* (589b) to the end (*in worulde* (598a)), which in turn contains a temporal clause, *þendan her wunað* (590a), and a modal one, 'swa him leofre bið . . . in worulde' (596b–8a), the latter having within it yet another temporal clause, 'þenden flæsc ond gæst / wuniað in worulde' (597b–8a): 597b–8a thus forms the cornerstone of a four-tier clause structure (object 586b–98a, result 589b–98a, modal 596b–8a and temporal 597b–8a). The Christian-Latin tradition did not supply only the idea of upward and downward movements in spiritual space initiated by the incarnation and ascension; it supplied too the linguistic models for a multi-layered syntax to match the concept. Cynewulf's complex sentence was his artistic response to a universe with perpendicularity (*hydercyme* (587a), *under* (588b), *her* (590a), 'swa helle hienþu swa heofones mærþu' (591 etc.) and *in worulde* (598a)) as well as passing time (*nu* (586a), *eft* (587b), *nu* (589b) and *þendan* (590a and 597b), contrasting with *butan ende* (599b)).

The precise nature of the change this sentence represents is revealed if we set beside it the opening eleven 'lines' of *Beowulf* as a strictly comparable passage composed in the more temporal thought-world of that poem. These 'lines', like those in *Christ II*, extol[53] the virtues of a beneficial exercise of *þrym*, 'power' (*Christ* (*II*) 599a and *Beowulf* 2b):

Hwæt, we Gardena in geardagum,
þeodcyninga þrym gefrunon,
hu ða æþelingas ellen fremedon!

[50] *Christ* (*II*) 586–99, quoted and briefly commented on, above, pp. 313 and 427, n. 35, and in part (591–5) analysed stylistically, pp. 343–4.

[51] That is, repetition of the same connective.

[52] See above, pp. 85–6.

[53] See *Christ* (*II*) 598b–9 and *Beowulf* 11b.

Oft Scyld Scefing sceaþena þreatum,
monegum mægþum meodosetla ofteah,
egsode eorlas, syððan ærest wearð
feasceaft funden; he þæs frofre gebad,
weox under wolcnum weorðmyndum þah,
oð þæt him æghwylc ymbsittendra
ofer hronrade hyran scolde,
gomban gyldan; þæt wæs god cyning!

['Lo, we have learned of the power of the Spear-Danes, of the kings of the people, in days long ago, how those princes put their fighting spirit into action! Often Scyld Scefing deprived companies of harmful enemies, many tribes, of meadseats, struck terror into warriors, after he was first found destitute; he experienced consolation for that, grew under the skies, prospered in honours, until every neighbour across the whaleroad had to obey him, pay tribute; that was a good king!'].

Here narrative statements are linked only temporally (*Oft* (4a), *syððan* (6b) and *oð þæt* (9a)) with a quite different result from that of Cynewulf's more elaborate syntax: 'we', the narrator and his audience (any audience of the poem), are placed in a single time-stream with the exercisers of *þrym*, as against the more distant relationship we have to the *hælubearn* of *Christ II*. 'We' and the Spear-Danes are both assumed to share a temporal experience which needs only to be evoked; 'we' in the ascension poem, as individual members of a spatial system almost too huge to grasp, are in a situation which requires constant restatement (591–6a). The experience 'we' share with the Spear-Danes could progress straightforwardly from *þrym* (2b), through *ellen* (3b), to narrative ('Oft Scyld Scefing . . .' (4–11a)). But Cynewulf's train of thought had to move from *hals*, 'salvation', through a verb-led gloss 'gefreode ond gefreoþade . . .' (588–9a), to a long result clause 'þæt nu monna gehwylc . . .' (589b–98a). For the *Beowulf* poet at 9a it was enough to imply result inwardly by *oð þæt;* Cynewulf was obliged to make explicit the cosmic, systematic connection between *hals* (*Christ* (*II*) 587b) and *monna gehwylc* (589b) and needed all the outward-pointing techniques known to him, whether Latin or vernacular, to give his proclamation of systematic spiritual transfusion a worldly surface of 'universal' language.[54]

The appositional repetition in the initial statement of his object clause,

[54] For Cynewulf's aim, in his preceding narrative of the ascension, to use a language of praise common to the heavenly, eternal, order of existence and the earthly, sequential, one, see above, pp. 332–3. Sedulius's use of the present-tense *datur*, instead of a preterite,

hu þæt hælubearn
þurh his hydercyme hals eft forgeaf,
gefreode ond gefreoþade folc under wolcnum,
mære meotudes sunu (586b–9a),

exemplifies his debts to Latinity. Appositional repetition as such, of course, requires no foreign model, but the native way here would probably have been to set up apposition between *hælubearn* and 'mære meotudes sunu' only, like this:

hu þæt hælubearn
þurh his hydercyme hals eft forgeaf,
mære meotudes sunu;

or, more elaborately, involving *hals* in apposition and including equivalents to 586a and 589b, like this:

Hwæt, we þæs ælmihtgan are gehyrdan,
hu þæt hælubearn hals eft forgeaf,
mære meotudes sunu, monnum under wolcnum.
Nu hæleþa gehwylc, þurh his hydercyme,
cwic . . .

What came from outside native tradition is repetition of a whole statement, 'þæt hælubearn / þurh his hydercyme hals eft forgeaf', by another, matching, whole statement, 'gefreode ond gefreoþade folc under wolcnum, / mære meotudes sunu' and mirroring of the subject–object–verb word order of the first of these units by the verb–object–subject order of the second.[55]

The twice-made statement as such is reminiscent of Hebraic parallelism,[56] but the deliberate syntactic patterning of centralized verbs within the metrical structure of two 'lines', which are themselves enclosed by two symbolic denotations of the subject, the first of them two-element and the second three-, surely belongs with the similar artistry of Latin poets, as

at *Carmen paschale* 28, quoted below, seems to have been intended as a statement of the divine operation rather than as human narrative.

55 An example of the same mirroring, this time on a phrasal scale, occurs later, when the order of 'swa mid dryhten dream swa mid deoflum hream' (594) becomes reversed both semantically and syntactically in 'swa wite mid wraþum swa wuldor mid arum' in the next pair of verses (595).

56 See above, pp. 310–11.

exemplified by these fifth-century hexameters expressing Sedulius's sense of summation in the nativity:

> Tunc prius ignaris pastoribus ille creatus
> Enituit, quia pastor erat, gregibusque refulsit
> Agnus et angelicus cecinit miracula coetus

['Then he, created, shone on previously unknown shepherds because he was shepherd, and the lamb gleamed on flocks and the angelic company praised the marvels in song'].[57]

Two verbs both signifying 'shining' were prominently positioned at either end of the middle line in order to bind *pastoribus* with *pastor* and *gregibusque* with *agnus* respectively, while a link between the shining and angelic celebration of it was effected by bringing side by side the like-sounding (two-syllable) *Agnus* and (three-syllable) *angelicus*. More particularly, Cynewulf's verb-centred word order, SOV, VOS, is reminiscent of the 'golden' symmetry whereby in hexameter poetry two adjectives preceded, and their two related nouns followed, a centrally enclosed verb. Two, alternative, patterns were used, $A^1A^2VN^1N^2$ and $A^1A^2VN^2N^1$, of which the latter had Cynewulf's mirroring arrangement. The 'golden line' was much beloved of Sedulius – nearly one line in ten in the first book of his *Carmen paschale* is golden[58] – and was not much less used by Aldhelm. The latter's line (addressing God as 'you', the creator), 'Pallida purpureo pingis qui flore virecta' ('who paint the pale greensward with the purple flower'),[59] employing the mirroring pattern, $A^1A^2VN^2N^1$, is an example with which Cynewulf might well have been familiar.

Likewise the repetition of the connective *swa* combined with rhyming of the *a* and *b* verses in 591–5 has an analogy in another passage in Sedulius's *Carmen*, which, like Cynewulf's, proclaimed the redemptive mystery of the ascension of the incarnate Christ:

> Nec dubie in caelum substantia peruenit illa,
> Quae Christo conlata datur sub paupere forma,
> Quae damnis augmenta capit, quae spargitur ut sit,
> Quae perit ut maneat, quae uitam mortua praestat

['Undoubtedly there has arrived in heaven that substance which, conferred on

[57] *Carmen paschale*, bk II, lines 70–2 (ed. Huemer, *Opera*, p. 49).

[58] Wright, 'The *Hisperica Famina* and Caelius Sedulius', pp. 75–6.

[59] *Carmen de virginitate*, line 4 (ed. Ehwald, *Aldhelmi Opera*, p. 352).

Christ, is given under the form of poverty, which from losses takes profits, which is scattered so that it may be, which perishes so that it may remain, which shows life when dead', 27–30].

As in Cynewulf's lines,[60] there is in these a five-piece 'envelope' pattern of reference, first moving to good from bad (27–8), then three times from bad to good (29 and the first half of 30) and finally to good from bad once again (in the second half of 30); and, also like Cynewulf's, the pattern was crafted through repetition (of *quae*) and through caesural homoeoteleuton (*capit* : *sit*, *maneat* : *praestat* and perhaps *conlata* : *forma*).[61]

The *Maldon* poet, to return to him, drawing his matter (we may suppose) from survivors' stories and his own knowledge of the participants and of the locality, operated on an altogether different scale from Cynewulf's. The stuff of his poem was no redeeming ascension, but a horse, a hawk, a wood, a ford, a meeting-place, a leader's wealth and patriotism, a grandfather's eminence, some strong-minded villagers and so on. Yet, local as these particulars were, he shared with his universal-minded forerunner a need for explicit techniques to formalize a combination of a 'semi-detached', 'reporter's', view of a whole situation and an underlying unitary moral attitude to what was 'reported'. And his solution was the same. His precise language of public description was a subtle mixture distilled from a Cynewulfian hybrid tradition. For instance, in 96–9[62] the indigenous practice of apposing fundamental symbols was still employed to make *wælwulfas* and 'wicinga werod' provide the initiating narrative thrust in the verbal cluster of 96–8;[63] but all else in these lines had other affinities. The sequence, consisting of a two-staged statement (96–8) and a second, shorter, one (99), was in the manner of Hebraic parallelism,[64] while the technique of following the elaborate word order of 96–8 (beginning with V^1 S^1 and ending, after much else, with O V^3) by a clinching, compact, order in 99 (S prepositional phrase O V) recalls Cynewulf's Latinate artistry.[65] No corresponding 'literary' devices gave

[60] See the analysis above, p. 343.

[61] I am most grateful to Andy Orchard for suggesting the particular parallels I have cited from Sedulius's *Carmen paschale* and Aldhelm's *Carmen de virginitate* and for helpful discussion, both spoken and written.

[62] See above, pp. 426–7.

[63] Formally subdividing, I take it, into 96–7, consisting of V^1 S^1 (adverbial phrase^1 V^2) S^2 adverbial phrase^2, and 98, consisting of adverbial phrase^3 O V^3.

[64] Cf. above, pp. 310–11.

[65] In *Christ II* 591–6a.

Grendel's menacing approach to Heorot (*Beowulf* 702b–21a) any 'picture' quality of this sort. Its four 'atmospheric' *Com* . . ., *Đa com* . . ., *Wod* . . . and *Com þa* . . . statements[66] progressed from *on wanre niht*, 'in the dark night' (702b), by way of *of more*, 'from the moor' (710a), and *under wolcnum*, 'under the clouds' (714a), to *to recede*, 'to the hall' (720a), through incremental psychology (on the one hand, the contrast between the sleeping warriors as a whole and Beowulf alone awake (703–9), and, on the other, Grendel's own developing state of mind[67]). *Maldon*'s language was closer to Cynewulf's than to the *Beowulf* poet's in its movement. However much it appealed to instincts which were standard to ancient past and up-to-date present alike,[68] it had made the grade in Cynewulfian adaptation to a more spatial and less temporal arena than the *Beowulf*ian one.[69] Treating the most traditional of themes, loyalty, *Maldon* had a linguistic surface like the shell of a hatching egg: much of Germanic, antique, oral, culture remained in place, but the eclectic, more recent, 'literary', past of vernacular poetry was breaking it up. Our most satisfactory hypothesis is that this poem was heir to an unbroken tradition of vernacular poetry celebrating the individual courage involved in contemporary secular loyalty and moving with the times not only by adapting to changed social conditions but also by adopting the narrative stance and techniques of expression which we know vernacular Christian narrative poetry had absorbed from its foreign congeners by the ninth century.

The patterned simplicity which was thus at the poet's command articulated the testing of a local community with absolute directness. *Wælwulfas* (96a) was a fancifully dramatic, symbolic, metaphor with more than a hint of riddling,[70] but, as 'wicinga werod' (97a) and finally as *lidmen* (99a), the raiders became more 'ordinarily' menacing the nearer they got to the waiting Byrhtnoth and his followers (100–1a). The social system running through all Germanic time was reduced to a group of men standing apprehensively alert on the bank of an Essex river, but the spirit of that ancient system still validated their situation. Physical surroundings became of little account for the faithful once their leader had been killed (181) and they were left fighting for their lives with honour but without hope: from then on of the ten uses of the temporal adverb, *þa*, 'then', to

[66] 702b–3a, 710–11, 714–16a and 720–1a. [67] 710b–13, 714b–19 and 720b–1a.

[68] See above, p. 424. [69] Cf. above, pp. 85–6.

[70] Cf. the *Andreas* poet's provocatively bizarre conception of the perverted Mermedonians as *wælwulfas* able to write (*Andreas* 149), discussed above, p. 270.

link a structurally independent statement of action to another one preceding it[71] only half were accompanied by an adverbial expression of place (*ðær* (205a) and *æt guðe*, 'in battle' (285b)) and/or direction (*forð* (4×)[72]), even of the most general sort. In the grand manner of traditional vernacular poetry the worth of the loyal still resided ultimately in the absolute dignity of time itself. The courage of diverse local men facing up to circumstances beyond their control has never been more convincingly presented. Making little overt claim on abstract verities, the sheer truthfulness to experience which this poem projected so sharply in its own day has endured to our time as genuinely as it extended back into its past. What is borne in on us, viewing both the present of *Maldon* and its past, is that, whereas Wiglaf, loyal to Beowulf, embodied a social system, the faithful among Byrhtnoth's followers were primarily individuals fulfilling personal obligations publicly declared.

71 202a, 205a, 211a, 225a, 228b, 255a, 260a, 285b, 295a and 297b.
72 205a, 225a, 260a and 297b.

13

This world as part of God's spiritual dominion

Old English poets, traditionally used to treating secular authority, based their system for this world's workings of the divine spirit on a conception of God as the supreme ruler of both heaven and earth. Epithets acknowledging this lordship form by far the largest category of their appellations of the deity, and the items in this 'ruler' group which they used especially often were for the most part adaptations of existing secular social terms. The 'kingship' nouns, which, as self-standing simplexes or as components of compounds or of genitive or adjective combinations, denote God nearly, or over, fifty times apiece, bear this out: *dryhten* 1038× (almost as frequent as *god*), *cyning* 305×, *waldend* (hardly occurring in any other designation) 272× (cf. *alwalda* 23× and *anwalda* 5×), *frea* 112×, *weard* 93×, *þeoden* 87×, *ealdor* 59× and *ælmihtig(a)* (noun) 49× (also with twice this frequency as an adjective).[1] But God's authority was by no means identical to its worldly counterpart. His power, at the heart of an infinite spiritual domain embracing all eternity, emanated from beyond temporal existence. This world's blend of the spiritual and the material was dependent on a purely spiritual external might. Mankind's subordination to its spiritual overlord was partly familiar from traditional social situations and partly *sui generis*.

Starkly polarized options constituted one principle common to the old and the new. The birthright, which Christ's incarnation restored once and for all to every man in this life to choose for eternity, in Cynewulf's pointed words, 'swa lif swa deað',[2] set at the root of all human living a dramatic opposition of the sort warriors in heroic society were used to facing

[1] For a catalogue of the 'kingship' and other epithets, see Crépin, 'Poétique Vieil-Anglaise', pp. 190–313.

[2] *Christ (II)* 596a; see above, p. 313.

whenever they undertook a course of action which could issue only in victory or death. In this vital respect the framework of redemption conformed fundamentally to the narrative tradition of vernacular poetry. Moreover the loyalties basic to that tradition also remained in place, now enshrined in eternity. The culmination of the redemptive cycle, when

liffruma
in monnes hiw ofer mægna þrym
halig from hrusan, ahafen wurde

['the author of life was raised in human form above the glory of the hosts, holy from earth', *Christ (II)* 656b–8],

had instituted a bond between God and man for ever (582b–3):

Wær is ætsomne
godes ond monna, gæsthalig treow,
lufu, lifes hyht, ond ealles leohtes gefea

['There is a covenant of God and men together, a spiritually holy agreement, love, hope of life and joy of complete light', 583b–5].[3]

The spiritual nature of the new ties between Lord and man, however, demanded profound changes.

An essential tool for God's spiritual dominion was a linguistic currency, so to speak, specific to his realm and defining it by serving as its 'legal tender'. By the ninth century the word *gast/gæst* supplied just such a complete coinage. For Cynewulf and poets like him this word had come to signify every kind of spirit of whatever origin, whether that of God, issuing from the father through either Christ[4] or the third person of the trinity,[5] or that of the heavenly host,[6] or that of men,[7] or that of devils.[8] *Gast/gæst*

[3] In *Guthlac B* the adjective *gæsthalig* characterized those who are single-mindedly determined to perform God's will in spite of death's rule (873a, the category to which Guthlac belonged) and the saint himself when close to death (1149a), in *The Panther* it designated those understanding the Old Testament (21a) and Cynewulf himself used it again, in *Elene*, to describe the prophets (562a).

[4] As in Cynewulf's 'godes gæstsunu' ('God's spirit-son', *Christ (II)* 660a and 860a and *Elene* 673a).

[5] As at *Christ (II)* 774b; for this distinction between the second and third persons, see Crépin, 'Poétique Vieil-Anglaise', p. 260.

[6] As in 'gæsta giefstol' (*Christ (II)* 572a).

[7] As in *flæsc ond gæst* (*ibid.*, 597b; cf. *Juliana* 714a and *The Judgement Day I* 102b); see also *Christ (II)* 649a, 707a, 753a, 777a, 816b, 820a and 848a.

[8] As in 'wergan gæstas' (*Christ (I)* 363b; cf. *Beowulf* 1747b and *Guthlac (A)* 25a and 451a).

denoted all these living spirits and more, including, in, for example, *Christ II*, the moon symbolizing God's church ('gæstlic tungol' (699a)) and – seemingly a survival of a pre-Christian sense of active being – fire ('gæsta gifrast' ('greediest of spirits', 813a)).[9] In that 427-'line' poem *gæst* occurs altogether twenty-two times, as a simplex or as the first element of four compounds or as the stem of the adjective *gæstlic*.

In these poets' conception God's all-embracing spirit acting on this world is mighty,[10] creative,[11] bountiful,[12] gracious,[13] helpful[14] and comforting.[15] The spirit of an angel as God's representative and emissary to men is counselling, supportive and protective, whereas a devil's is malevolent to both God and men: the two *weardas*, 'guardians', between whom the youthful Guthlac had to choose in *Guthlac A*, were 'engel dryhtnes ond se atela gæst' ('an angel of the Lord and the horrid spirit', 116), the one inspiring him towards *þa longan god* of heaven, the other urging him towards ruthless worldly greed (117–32). A man's spirit is his eternal entity, with its unending need[16] and capability of everlasting beauty,[17] and is his provider on earth of his potential for faith,[18] wisdom[19] and moral choice.[20] The active spiritual being of God was fully accounted for by this poetry's use of this word, and so was the narrative living of spirits throughout the *mise-en-scène* of earth, heaven and hell, all three. *Gast*/*gæst*, circulating in every part of this vast territory, was used in the course of our extant poems over 400 times, forming in the process no fewer than 124 different symbolic expressions (sixty genitive combinations,

9 Cf. *Christ* (*III*) 972a and *Beowulf* 1123a. Derivation of this set, self-alliterating *a* verse from Germanic tradition seems more likely than influence from the Christian Latin *ignis* analogues involving *spiritus*, which Klaeber proposed (Klaeber, 'Die christlichen Elemente im Beowulf III', p. 468), for these lack any 'greedy' components.

10 As in 'gæstes mægne' in *Christ I*, referring to the manifestation of divine power in the incarnation (319b) and in the Harrowing of Hell (145b); cf. *his gæstes mægen* (*Christ and Satan* 548b) of Christ on the cross.

11 When creating the world (*Christ* (*II*) 659b–60a) and in the incarnation (*Christ* (*I*) 203b).

12 *Christ* (*II*) 660–1.

13 *Ibid.*, 649a.

14 As in 'gæsta geocend' (6× (in *a* verses): *Elene* 682a and 1076a, *Christ* (*I*) 198a, *Guthlac* (*B*) 1133a and *Andreas* 548a and 901a).

15 As in 'frofre gæst' (11×: *Christ* (*II*) 728a, *Juliana*, 724a, *Elene* 1036b and 1105a, *Christ* (*I*) 207b, *Guthlac* (*A*) 136b, *Guthlac* (*B*) 936b, *Andreas* 906b and 1684b, *Judith* 83b and *The Metrical Charms* 11 10b; see Crépin, 'Poétique Vieil-Anglaise', pp. 236–7).

16 'Gæstes þearfe' (*Christ* (*II*) 707a and 816b, *Christ* (*III*) 1057a and *The Gifts of Men* 86b).

17 *Gæstes wlite* (*Christ* (*II*) 848a and *The Order of the World* 33a).

18 *Christ* (*II*) 753a.

19 *Ibid.*, 684a and *Christ* (*I*) 139a.

20 *Christ* (*III*) 1034b and *Bede's Death Song* 4a.

forty-five adjective combinations and nineteen compounds).[21] This was indeed an extensive coinage, which certainly did not come about overnight. Its minting proceeded progressively, involving, among other major factors, a long and gradual convergence of two distinct traditions concerning the nature of personal responsibility, namely the Germanic conviction that this was primarily a duty to fellow members of society and the Christian belief that it was first and foremost an individual obligation to God on behalf of an eternal soul within. We need to trace the main stages in the semantic evolution of this word as the only member of pre-Christian Germanic vocabulary signifying a malevolent spirit to become sufficiently purified to denote the Christian benevolent spirit in all its forms.

The Aryan root from which *gast*/*gæst* derived bore the meaning 'to terrify',[22] and that this sense as well as that of 'spirit' was associated with this stem in the Germanic languages is shown by the Gothic verb **us-gaisjan*, 'to terrify',[23] and the Old Norse verb *geisa*, 'to rage' (as of fire), and noun *geiski*, 'fear, panic'.[24] Dunning and Bliss considered it probable that 'spirit' and 'terror' had been two distinct semantic developments in Germanic,[25] but I think it is more likely that Anglo-Saxons inherited a single tradition to the effect that any spirit which they designated as *gast*/*gæst* was predominantly to be feared, because, in essence, this is how the *Beowulf* poet used this word in combinations, some of which show signs of Germanic derivation, specifically to symbolize Grendel and his kin, the monstrous progeny of Cain and the devil.[26] Unless 'fear' was inherent in

[21] For a full record, see *Concordance to the Anglo-Saxon Poetic Records*, ed. Bessinger.

[22] Skeat, *An Etymological Dictionary of the English Language*, s.v. *ghost*.

[23] Lehmann, *A Gothic Etymological Dictionary*, U52, p. 382, usefully supplementing Skeat.

[24] Dunning and Bliss, in their edition of *The Wanderer* (p. 53, n. 1), dismissed *geisa* as differently derived and therefore 'not relevant'.

[25] In a rather unclear note proposing (correctly in my opinion, for which, see above, p. 404) the meaning 'terrifying' for *gæstlic* at *The Wanderer* 73b (ed. Dunning and Bliss, p. 53).

[26] His only possible non-symbolic use of *gæst* in this group is when Beowulf combined the word with a post-positioned adjective in 'gæst yrre cwom' (2073b), which I have included among the adjective-combinations listed below, n. 28. His single use of *gæst* outside this group, in 'gæsta gifrost', referring to fire consuming the dead on a funeral pyre (1123a), has been mentioned already. Three terms which were applied to the dragon – *gæst* as a simplex without accompanying adjective or genitive (2312a), *inwitgæst* (2670a) and *niðgæst* (2699a) – might be further instances, but they are more likely to represent *gist*, '(hostile) stranger', since the remaining comparable term for the dragon, *gryregiest* (2560a), has an *–ie-* spelling.

gast/gæst itself, none of the nine *gast/gæst* symbolic expressions which he employed for these referents – four compounds,[27] four adjective combinations[28] and one genitive combination[29] – had the 'fear' component which would be expected, seeing that all their contexts suggest that fear was inspired.

Among them a specimen with likely Germanic affiliations is *werga gast*, combining *gast* with an adjective related to the noun *wearg*, 'criminal',[30] 'outlaw', 'outcast',[31] cognate with ON *vargr*, 'wolf' and metaphorically 'outlaw'. *Werga*, used in *Beowulf* in this combination only, seems to have conveyed to the poet two linked connotations, cursing by God for wrongdoing[32] and active hostility on the part of the cursed, for these were the thoughts he coupled explicitly when (at 1265b–7a) identifying Grendel as one of the *geosceaftgastas* descended from Cain, who had been outlawed by God for fratricide, and simultaneously characterizing him as a 'heorowearh hetelic' ('hateful savage outcast' 1267a). Both ideas remain attached to *werga* in the ten further occurrences of the combination of this adjective and *gast/gæst* in other poems,[33] with divine condemnation uppermost in seven of them[34] and savagery in the other three,[35] while, on the evidence of analogues, both ideas were likewise attached to ON *vargr* in pre-Christian and early Christian times: in the first place, 'vargr í véum' ('a

[27] Two applied to Grendel and his mother (*ellorgæst*, 'alien spirit', 5× (counting 86a, on which see above, p. 69 and n. 2) and *wælgæst*, 'slaughter-spirit', 2×), one to Cain's progeny (*geosceaftgastas*, 'fated spirits, 1×) and one to the devil (*gastbona*, 'spirit slayer', 1×).

[28] One designating Grendel and the devil (*werga gæst*, 'accursed spirit', 2×), two just Grendel ('se grimma gæst' ('grim spirit') 1×, and *gæst yrre*, 'angry spirit', 1×) and one his kin (*dyrne gastas*, 'hidden spirits', 1×).

[29] Applied to Grendel (*helle gast*, 'spirit of hell', 1×).

[30] As at *The Dream of the Rood* 31b.

[31] On the probability that *werga* was short-vowelled and to be understood thus rather than long-vowelled and a weak form of *werig*, 'weary' (for which Sievers argued), see *Beowulf*, ed. Klaeber, n. on 133.

[32] Cf. the Gothic verb **ga-wargjan*, 'to damn'; see also **ga-wargeins*, noun, Lehmann, *A Gothic Etymological Dictionary*, G77, p. 153, with Old Saxon and Old High German examples of the verb.

[33] Including two in which *awyrgda* is the adjective.

[34] *Genesis* (*A*) 90b; *Christ and Satan* 125a, 628b and 727b; *Soul and Body I* 115b and *II* 110b; and *The Judgement Day II* 184a.

[35] Devils tempting and tormenting humans are denoted at *Guthlac* (*A*) 25a and 451a and *Christ* (*I*) 363b.

vargr within sanctuary boundaries'), occurring in several sources[36] with the traditional authority which is implied by a self-alliterating phrase, shows *vargr* in customary pagan law already involved in the same association of special guilt with a crime committed in holy circumstances as that which the *Beowulf* poet recognized in Cain's murder of Abel; and, in the second place, the compound *goðvargr*, '*vargr* against the (pagan) gods' (*Kristni saga*, ch. 8), by occurring in a verse which is ascribed to the pagan Thórvaldr inn veili, and by referring to Thangbrandr, the missionary most closely connected with the conversion of Iceland, places in a context of the coming of Christianity the same concept of hostility to God as that expressed by the *Beowulf* poet's genitive combination, 'Godes andsaca'.[37] The probability seems to be that a pre-Christian Germanic tradition antecedently twinning the notions of damnation and savagery in *vargr/wearg/werga*[38] was responsible for the formation in Old English poetry of a combination of this adjective and *gast/gæst* to denote a spirit which struck particular terror because it was both damned and hostile. Accordingly, in my view, we may infer that the *Beowulf* poet was regarding this symbol in this antique perspective when he applied it to the evil threat which both Grendel and the devil represented for society, and thus, by extension, that he basically drew his *gæst* terminology for the evil spirits, which his social-minded hero confronted, from a pagan inheritance which he adapted to Christianity only to the extent of applying it to the devil and descent from Cain.

Analogous evidence, helping rather than hindering this supposition, comes from the six *gæst* symbols employed by the *Guthlac A* poet[39] to denote the evil spirits assailing his spiritual hero.[40] In the first place, the adjectives *grim* and *werga/awyrgda* (in a predominantly 'hostile' sense) figure in both poems, and, in the second place, the *Guthlac A* poet's distinctive use of the adjective *earm* reinforces the likelihood that both repertoires had

[36] See Cleasby and Vigfusson, *An Icelandic–English Dictionary*, s.v. *vargr*, and, for more details, Fritzner, *Ordbog over Det gamle norske Sprog* III, s.v. *vargr*.

[37] 786b and 1862b, referring to Grendel in both of these instances, and occurring eleven times in other poems.

[38] Rather, perhaps, than a mere borrowing from Old Norse by Old English, or the reverse, in view of the evidence concerning the first of these two concepts from Gothic and other Germanic languages, cited above, p. 442, n. 32.

[39] Eight, if *ceargest* and *nyðgist* are counted; see below, p. 445, n. 48, and cf. above, p. 441, n. 26.

[40] Four adjective combinations (the adjectives being *earm* (6×), *grim* and *werga/awyrgda* (2× each) and *atol* (1×)) and two compounds (*gæstcwalu* and *-gewin* (1× each)).

broadly the same derivation, for, whereas throughout its occurrences in extant Old English poetry (including *Guthlac A)* this adjective uniformly means 'wretched, pitiable' whenever it is not combined with *gast/gæst*,[41] in its six instances in combination with this noun in *Guthlac A* and in its one in this combination in *Guthlac B* it has the 'aggressive, hostile' sense which its Old Norse cognate *armr* shows usually, and always in the poetic Edda.[42] Once again there is an agreement with Old Norse usage; but that these two poems should both owe an exceptional debt to poetry in that language for this specialized vocabulary, or that there should be a debt in the opposite direction, is surely probable than that they and Old Norse should be drawing, in this feature, as in others, on a common Germanic past.

The initial vowel alliteration of the adjective in the *earm gæst* symbol was strikingly exploited in all its six occurrences in *Guthlac A*. Employed every time as a complete *b* verse[43] and always in a plural form (especially as the genitive, 'earmra gæsta' (4×)), this combination was used five times to set up an alliterative connection (single or double) between the generic aggression expressed by its adjective and a dramatic sample of that aggression expressed in the corresponding *a* verse – living in hiding places ('eardas onhæle' (297a)), inspiring fear (*egsan* (339a)), grasping painfully and fiercely ('eglum onfengum' (405a) and 'afrum onfengum' (519a)) and tempting relentlessly ('seo æreste . . . / costung' (437a and 438a)) – and once in an impressive double alliterative connection between the aggression and the factor which alone annuls it, fear of the divine ('ufancundne ege' (686a)). The *Beowulf* and *Guthlac A* symbolic exploitation of *gast/gæst* as a powerful expression of spiritual evil exemplifies a tradition which remained in force, with some consolidation and amplification, throughout the fully Christian poems which we have. For instance, the collocation of *helle*, *gast* and *hean*, which was applied so effectively to Grendel departing dejected to hell after Beowulf had defeated him through God's grace,[44] we find established as an elegant, self-alliterating, three-

[41] As in *Beowulf*, where it is never found in this combination.

[42] Cf. Kellogg, *A Concordance of Eddic Poetry*, p. 23, s.v. sense 2. The phrase 'armr er vára vargr' ('the *vargr* of oaths is *armr*', *Sigrdrífumál*, st. 23) is particularly interesting in relation to our present concerns. I am most grateful to Andy Orchard for these references, for those cited above concerning *vargr* and for much helpful advice.

[43] 297b, 339b, 405b, 437b, 519b and 686b.

[44] 'gehnægde helle gast. Þa he hean gewat' ('he [Beowulf] laid low the spirit of hell. Then he [Grendel] went wretched', 1274).

element symbol,[45] 'hean helle gæst', applied twice by Cynewulf to the devil defeated by Juliana;[46] and we find too that, while six of the *Beowulf* poet's nine *gast/gæst* symbols[47] do not occur elsewhere, nineteen others in the same 'doomed and violent' strain of fearful evil do, although happening to have been unused in *Beowulf*.[48]

In another respect, however, *Guthlac A* was a watershed in the semantic development of *gast/gæst*. Its evil *gæstas* were confronted by good *gæst*. They were defeated not by a socially representative hero, as in *Beowulf*, but by a spiritually representative one, *Guðlaces gæst*, violently tempted by hordes of envious devils (188), with God's help firmly unafraid of them (202a), unharmed by them (226), protected (694) and gladdened (722) by St Bartholomew at the door of hell (559b), and finally led by angels lovingly to heaven (781). Six times this heroic *gæst* is collocated alliteratively with *god*, 'God'.[49] A purely spiritual battle is fought and won as one kind of *gæst* triumphs over another. In *Guthlac A*, as not in *Beowulf*, the word *gæst* had escaped from its traditional Germanic confines of frightful wickedness and had come to signify also a human potential for supreme good:

> God wæs Guðlac! He in gæste bær
> heofoncundne hyht, hælu geræhte
> ecan lifes

['Good was Guthlac! He carried in his spirit heavenly hope, attained the salvation of eternal life', 170–2a].

Indeed, this poem could be regarded linguistically as the triumph of the new, good, meaning of *gæst* over the old, bad, meaning of the word.

The exemplary battleground for this contest between good and evil *gæst* was firmly terrestrial. As the *beorg*, 'mound', in *Beowulf*, where long ago a

[45] On these hybrid formations (in this instance a conflation of adjective and genitive combinations), see above, pp. 143–5.

[46] *Juliana* 457a and 615a.

[47] The four compounds and two of the adjective combinations, *dyrne gæst* and *gæst yrre*.

[48] Ten adjective combinations (the adjectives being *earm* (7×), *geomor/geomrende* (6×), *atol* (3×) and *blac*, *gramhydig*, *herm*, *lað*, *sweart*, *unclæne* and *wrað* (1× each)), six genitive combinations (*gastes wund* (2×) and *gastes forwyrd*, *gryre* and *geniðla* (1× each) and *bealowes gast* (2×) and *deofla gastas* (1×)) and three compounds (*gæstcwalu*, *-geniðla* and *-gewin* (1× each); *ceargest* and *nyðgist* (*Guthlac* (*A*) 393a and 540a respectively) could be two more).

[49] 202, 258, 367, 591, 643 and 690.

last survivor had buried his tribe's treasure, provided a courageous but aged king with a symbolic setting for action which was to decide the fate of the entire race of the Geats, so Guthlac's *beorg*, 'hill', in a wasteland which God had left to the devices of demons until he chose the saint to build a holy home there (140b–9 and 206–17), elevated this *Cristes cempa*, 'champion of Christ',[50] into an example (*bysen*) for many in Britain (174b–5) 'usser tidum' ('in our times', 401b): it furnished him with an emblematic location firstly for heroically outfacing the *ealdfeondas*[51] formerly its possessors, and secondly, when it burgeoned with new life in God's safe-keeping, for returning victorious from the door of hell:

> Smolt wæs se sigewong ond sele niwe,
> fæger fugla reord, folde geblowen;
> geacas gear budon. Guþlac moste
> eadig ond onmod eardes brucan.
> Stod se grena wong in godes wære

['Pleasant was that place of victory and new the hall, beautiful the voice of birds, the ground blooming; cuckoos announced the year. Guthlac, blessed and steadfast, was permitted to enjoy the land. The green plain stood in God's protection', 742–6].

In this localized earthly arena Guthlac's spirit received divine support through the mediation of an angelic spirit ('godes ærendu, þa him gæst onwrah / lifes snyttru' ('God's messages, when the spirit revealed to him the wisdom of life', 162–3a)) and through that of a brotherly apostle (714):

> Ða wæs Guðlaces gæst geblissad,
> siþþan Bartholomeus aboden hæfde
> godes ærendu

['Guthlac's spirit was gladdened when Bartholomew had proclaimed God's messages', 722–4a].

And there the saintly warrior provided his own spiritual intermediary too when 'Gyrede hine georne mid gæstlicum / wæpnum' ('he prepared himself eagerly with spiritual weapons', 177–8a) by setting up as his first act the cross of Christ as a marker (179–80a).[52]

God himself, however, remained in the background as an almighty, but

50 153a; cf. 180b, 324b, 345a, 402a, 438b, 513b, 558b, 576a, 643b, 688b and 727b.

51 141b, 203b, 218a, 365a, 390b and 475a.

52 Cf. Clemoes, 'King and Creation at the Crucifixion', p. 33.

mostly undifferentiated, power denoted simply as *God* (40×), *Crist* (8×) or *dryhten* (26×), these words occurring frequently in genitive combinations with nouns which expressed one or another of his agencies in this world (*willa* (4×), *ærende*, *egsa* and *þeow* (3× each), *cempa*, *dom*, *lof* and *wær* (2× each) and *æ*, *ar*, *dream*, *engel*, *leoht*, *lufu*, *mægn*, *meaht*, *milts*, *oretta*, *rod*, *tempel*, *þegn*, *þrowere* and *yrming* (1× each)). The divinity did not operate in this poem as, himself, *gæst*.[53] Guthlac's relationship to him was as *þeow*, 'servant' (5×), and *þegn* (1×) of the creator,[54] saviour[55] and ruler,[56] in whom he dared at the very door of hell to declare his entire trust as 'lifes leohtfruma' (593a and 609a) and *liffruma* (637b), 'nergende Crist' (598b) and 'niðða nergend' (640a), 'þrynnesse þrym' (646a), 'ece onwealda ealra gesceafta' (638), 'weoruda waldend' (594a), 'heofonrices weard' (611b), 'wuldorcyning' (596b) and 'heofoncyning' (617b).

Guthlac personified fulfilment of the bond (*treow*, *wær*) which Cynewulf declared the ascension had instituted between all mankind and this supreme power.[57] He remained faithful to this *treow* in the face of all that evil could do to him (339–40a and 543–4) and accordingly God was true to his part of the covenant by rewarding him with victory:

Treow wæs gecyþed,
þætte Guðlace god leanode
ellen mid arum, þæt he ana gewon

['The covenant was made known that God rewarded Guthlac's resolution with honours so that he conquered alone', 448b–50].

When this glorious warrior's most beloved spirit (688b and 689b–90a) was put to the ultimate test at the door of hell and not found wanting, the divine protection became absolute: he was 'in godes wære' ('in God's safe-keeping', 690b) when St Bartholomew commanded the demons to transport him back unharmed; the *beorg* which sprang to new life on his victorious return (732b–3a) was likewise rendered inviolable (746); and (in an understatement) 'þær he siþþan lyt / wære gewonade' ('there after that he infringed the covenant little', 774b–5a) while he waited, praying humbly to God and grateful for his sufferings (775b–80), until angels led his spirit lovingly into glory,

[53] Though he could be alluded to as *halig gast* by both good (361b) and bad (456b).

[54] *scyppend* (664a).

[55] *hælend* (604b) and *nergend* (658b).

[56] *waldend* (666a, 763a and 800a) and *cyning* (91b and 682b).

[57] See above, p. 439.

þær he symle mot
awo to ealdre eardfæst wesan,
bliðe bidan. Is him bearn godes
milde mundbora, meahtig dryhten,
halig hyrde, heofonrices weard

['where he will be able to stay settled, remain happy, for ever. The son of God is his gentle protector, mighty Lord, holy keeper, guardian of the kingdom of heaven', 785b–9].

The eternal judge (783b) confirmed for him forever in heaven the security he had been granted already on earth.

The reputation for wisdom which Guthlac had won (153b–7a) by heeding his guardian spirit's 'lifes snyttru' to despise the world and by fearing God (160b–9) was, in effect, a living example of the truth of the maxims enunciated by the 'snottor on mode' ('one wise in mind') at the conclusion of *The Wanderer*:

Til biþ se þe his treowe gehealdeþ, . . .
. . . Wel bið þam þe him are seceð,
frofre to fæder on heofonum, þær us eal seo fæstnung stondeð

['Good will it be for him who keeps his faith, . . . Well will it be for him who seeks grace for himself, help from the father in heaven, where all the security for us stands', 112a and 114b–15].[58]

That both parties, good as well as bad, in the territorial rivalry involving Guthlac should be designated *gæst*, whereas the God who rewarded the saint with his unique *fæstnung* (to use *The Wanderer*'s word) was not, seems to rest on the distinction between mutability in this life and the immutability of the next which was drawn intellectually in *The Wanderer* by lauding the divine *fæstnung* in the final maxim, just quoted, after the essential instability of this world had been revealed in another:

Ongietan sceal gleaw hæle hu gæstlic bið,
þonne ealre þisse worulde wela weste stondeð

['The far-seeing man understands how terrifying it will be when the riches of all this world stand desolate', 73–4].[59]

The antithesis between the present ultimately *gæstlic* world and the ultimate *fæstnung* of God in this poem suggests that the *Guthlac A* poet understood *gæst* to apply to any spirit, good or bad, which is subject to the

[58] Cf. above, p. 407. [59] Cf. above, p. 404.

stress endemic to any environment outside the kingdom of heaven itself. Both poems appear to register the same semantic enlargement in this word (in whatever word formation it figures) from signifying a spirit beyond the pale of human society (as it did in *Beowulf*) to signifying any spirit not within the divine communion of heaven itself. The forty-eight occurrences of *gæst* in *Guthlac A*,[60] taken together, seem to reflect a response by this word to a demand in Christian narrative poetry for a term denoting any spirit active in this turbulent sub-celestial sphere.[61] If so, this is about as far as the word could be expected to have developed within its native 'group' tradition. The further stage of conceiving of *gast/gæst* as the individual's means of developing a direct personal relationship with a divine *gast/gæst* would seem to have required some specific pressures from Christian thought, and these requirements must now be looked at.

On the divine level there would have been an ecclesiastical need from the earliest days of conversion to name in the vernacular the third person of the trinity. This want was met, perhaps especially on account of the event of pentecost,[62] by adoption of *halig/se halga gast/gæst* to render *spiritus sanctus*. Doubtless this was the term which Cædmon introduced into poetry when, in Bede's words, he sang 'de Spiritus Sancti aduentu'.[63] Another necessity, this time for instruction at the level of humanity, would have been to

[60] Fifty if *ceargest* (393a) and *nyðgist* (540a) are counted; see above, p. 445, n. 48, and cf. p. 441, n. 26. The average frequency is once every sixteen lines.

[61] That this enlarged denotation had the same semantic range as that of *spiritus* in Felix's *Life of St Guthlac* may imply that this sort of narrative use of this Latin word generated a demand for a vernacular equivalent. This resemblance remains only general, however, for the *Life* was not the direct source of *Guthlac A* as it was of *Guthlac B*, and *Guthlac A*'s confrontation of *gæst* and *gæst* was all its own. The extension may be reflected in the only two occurrences of the verb *gæstan*, which appears to mean 'to persecute, torture' at *Juliana* 17 ('gæston godes cempan gare ond lige' ('persecuted God's soldiers with spear and flame'; see above, p. 355)) and to mean '(repeatedly) to turn over (in the mind)' if the twelfth-century MS form *gastende* (*gastande* with *e* written above the second *a*) is accepted at the beginning of the first book of King Alfred's prose *Soliloquies* ('hys mod foroft gastende and smeagende mislicu and selcuð þing, and ealles swiðust ymbe hyne sylfne – hwæt he sylf wære; . . .' ('his mind very often turning over and pondering various and strange matters, and most strongly of all about himself – what he himself was . . .' (Augustine, 'Volventi mihi'); cf. Hargrove's (1902) and Endter's (1964) texts, the discussion in *King Alfred's Version of St Augustine's 'Soliloquies'*, ed. Carnicelli, at pp. 48–9, and above, p. 381 and n. 42).

[62] As proposed by Betz, 'Die frühdeutschen spiritus-Übersetzungen', p. 55.

[63] Bede, *HE* IV.24 [22] (p. 418).

express in the vernacular the idea that every person in this world, as created by God, consists of a material body and a non-material spirit.[64] That this demand had been met by calling on *gast/gæst* to designate the second, spiritual, component in this combination already in early times is indicated by the cross's statement in *The Dream of the Rood*, 'Eall ic wæs mid blode bestemed, / begoten of þæs guman sidan, siððan he hæfde his gast onsended' ('I was all wet with blood shed from the man's side after he had sent forth his spirit', 48b–9),[65] for the clause including *gast*, quoted here from the Vercelli Book of the second half of the tenth century, probably had a counterpart in the Northumbrian runic inscription on the stone Ruthwell Cross, which was erected perhaps in the second quarter of the eighth century.[66] Indeed, there is firm evidence that application of Latin *spiritus* to both God's and man's spirituality had been responsible for conferring this semantic range on *gast/gæst* among Anglo-Saxon clerics early in that century, for this equivalence which was put into practice in the ninth-century Mercian gloss to the psalms, canticles and hymns in the Vespasian Psalter – where *gast* glosses *spiritus* meaning God's spirit eleven times[67] and men's spirit seventeen times[68] – had been exported to the Continent by eighth-century Anglo-Saxon missionaries.[69] Prior to their influence Old High German *geist* had not been chosen to translate *spiritus*,[70] but thenceforth it was. Accordingly we may infer that Old English poetry's

64 Cynewulf termed this combination *flæsc/lic ond gæst* at *Christ (II)* 597b and 777a and alluded to it again when referring to 'sawel in lice, / in þæm gæsthofe' (819b–20a).

65 Cf. the cross's reference a little later to 'wealdendes hræw' ('the ruler's corpse', 53b) and its statement later again, 'Hræw colode' ('The corpse grew cool', 72b).

66 The surviving part of the inscription, running quite close to the Vercelli text, breaks off at '[*b*]istemi[*d*] bi' with space for a maximum of fifty following characters now lost, enough to suggest that the remainder was equivalent to the rest of Vercelli 49. *Guma* (in the Vercelli text) makes clear that Christ's humanity was at issue here, while *gast onsended* was presumably derived from Matthew XXVII.50 (*emisit spiritum* in the Latin of the seventh/eighth-century Lindisfarne Gospels). Two other occurrences of *gast* in the Vercelli text ('halige gastas' (11b) and 'gasta weorode' (152a)) were never part of the Ruthwell inscription. For recent discussions of the dating of this cross, see Maclean, 'The Date of the Ruthwell Cross', and Meyvaert, 'A New Perspective on the Ruthwell Cross', pp. 147–50.

67 *Spiritus sanctus* (5×) was rendered by *se halga gast* three times and *halig gast* twice.

68 Gneuss, *Lehnbildungen und Lehnbedeutungen im Altenglischen*, pp. 53–4. As Gneuss records (*ibid.*), in this psalter *gast* also glosses *spiritus* in its other meanings of 'breath' (10×) and 'wind, storm' (8×).

69 Betz, 'Die frühdeutschen spiritus-Übersetzungen', p. 49.

70 *Ibid.*, pp. 48–9.

opportunity to use *gast/gæst* to render divine and human spiritual interplay was owed to a modelling of this word on *spiritus* by Anglo-Saxon ecclesiastics which was original as well as early.

For poets, however, this was not the whole story. Following suit in this semantic development involved them in the radical conceptual change of adapting the militaristic, social traditions of their art to the Christian ethos of a divinely oriented individuality. In poetry, as in many other artifacts of the seventh, eighth and ninth centuries, we witness a growing interpenetration of these two ways of thinking. For example, in *Guthlac A*, 'siþþan biorg gestah / eadig oretta, ondwiges heard' ('after the blessed warrior, hardy in resistance, mounted the hill', 175b–6), his initial step was to raise the cross of Christ to mark the ground (179–80a) 'þær se cempa oferwon / frecnessa fela' ('where the champion [i.e. he himself] was to overcome many dangers', 180b–1a), thus displaying the same confidence in an alliance between soldierly strength and spiritually protected victory as that which was proclaimed by the joint presence of a multi-metalled, free-standing, boar crest and a silver cross riveted to the nasal on the mid-seventh-century helmet from Benty Grange, Derbyshire, and now in Sheffield City Museum.[71] A century or so later, however, the copper-alloy strips mounted on the crown of the Coppergate, York, helmet, now in that city's Castle Museum, were proclaiming a belief that spiritual protection in war was more a matter of a personal relationship between the wearer and God's compassion, for they bear Latin inscriptions of a prayer invoking God, Jesus and the holy spirit (*scs. sps.*);[72] and it is likewise this individual spiritual bond which gave Cynewulf, probably in the ninth century, the basis for this advice to us men to arm ourselves for warfare against the devil:

Uton us beorgan þa,
þenden we on eorðan eard weardien;
utan us to fæder freoþa wilnian,
biddan bearn godes ond þone bliðan gæst
þæt he us gescilde wið sceaþan wæpnum,
laþra lygesearwum, se us lif forgeaf,
leomu, lic ond gæst

['Let us then protect ourselves, as long as we defend a habitation on earth; let us beseech the father for defences, pray to the son of God and the compassionate spirit

[71] For a recent description, see *The Making of England*, ed. Webster and Backhouse, pp. 59–60.

[72] See *ibid.*, pp. 60–2.

that he who granted us life, limbs, body and spirit may shield us against the weapons of the injurer, the stratagems of enemies', *Christ* (*II*) 771b–7a].

In *Guthlac A* the portrayal of the saint as a resolute *Cristes cempa* down here on earth had not taken the conception of Christian individuality further than an exemplary fulfilment of God's will in the same mould as Beowulf's fulfilment of the highest expectations of society. Guthlac remained a Christianized warrior without a spiritual personality of his own. A poetic demonstration of the ways the divine *gast/gæst* directly shapes human experience was required if more personalized themes were to develop.[73]

This need Cynewulf met with sensitivity and finesse. In *Christ II* 'godes gæstsunu' who created this world (659b–60a) is celebrated for the manifold 'modes snyttru' ('wisdoms of the mind', 662b) he sends to men 'þurh his muþes gæst' ('through the breath of his mouth', 665b); he came as incarnate saviour 'in ðære godcundan gæstes strengðu' ('in the divine strength of the spirit', 638) and likewise since his ascension repeatedly 'þurh gæstes giefe grundsceat sohte' ('has sought the region of earth through the spirit's gift', 649); in spite of the persecutions which his church has suffered from *synsceaðan*, 'evil injurers' (706a), there has never failed to be 'þurh gæstes giefe godes þegna blæd' ('an abundance of God's servants through the grace of the spirit', 710); and, just as a spirit of comfort was involved in his majestic leap upon the cross ('rodorcyninges ræs, þa he on rode astag, / fæder, frofre gæst' ('the leap of the king of the heavens, when he ascended the cross, father, spirit of consolation', 727–8a)), so too 'se bliða gæst'[74] participates in protecting each one of us from sin now. A loving God has shown his hand and demands an individual response from one and all.

Poetry, however, as was its wont, retained its concern with main themes, main categories of thought, in the face of this multiplicity. After all, divine creation and redemption, initiated in heaven, imposed a system more immutably authoritative than the old social order with its perspective confined to man's own past. God's *gæst* had its essential being in one sphere, but in the ways it was known to men operated in another. The links with which the language of active being had to cope were not between social features of the past and those of the present but between a being who

[73] Cf. discussion of aspects of the individual's development of a spiritual personality, including an eternal thinking self, above, pp. 386–90.

[74] See above, p. 451.

could only be imagined and present-day narrative living. The symbols coupling God's spirit with one of its agents or attributes – such as *gæstsunu*,[75] *gæstes mægen*[76]/*miht*[77]/*strengðu*,[78] *gæstes giefu*,[79] *frofre gæst*,[80] *halig gæst* (26×) and *se bliða gæst*[81] – were called on to straddle this void.[82] But the gap still needed schematic images to structure spiritual narrative living.

The city of Jerusalem was a richly suggestive image of this structural sort, since, according to the standard medieval interpretation of its name, it meant *pacis visio*, 'vision of peace'. In the meditative poet of the Advent lyrics (*Christ I*),[83] for one, it aroused a deeply penitential feeling for the peace of God's pity endlessly conveyed from heaven to earth. Superficially his poem's structure parallels that of the 'O' antiphon which was its starting-point – 'O Hierusalem, civitas Dei summi: leva in circuitu oculos tuos, et vide Dominum tuum, quia iam veniet solvere te a vinculis' ('O Jerusalem, city of the highest God: lift up your eyes round about, and see your Lord, for soon he will come to release you from your chains') – the first nine 'lines' of verse corresponding to the invocation and the rest to the ensuing invitation, or exhortation (the *b* verse of the last 'line' but two and the following *a* verse specifically echoing 'solvere te a vinculis'):

Eala sibbe gesihð,   sancta Hierusalem,
cynestola cyst,   Cristes burglond,
engla eþelstol,   ond þa ane in þe
saule soðfæstra   simle gerestað,
wuldrum hremge.   Næfre wommes tacn
in þam eardgearde   eawed weorþeð,
ac þe firina gehwylc   feor abugeð,
wærgðo ond gewinnes.   Bist to wuldre full
halgan hyhtes,   swa þu gehaten eart.
Sioh nu sylfa þe geond   þas sidan gesceaft,
swylce rodores hrof   rume geondwlitan
ymb healfa gehwone,   hu þec heofones cyning

75 See above, p. 439, n. 4.   76 See above, p. 440, n. 10.

77 *Elene* 1069b and 1099a, *Genesis* (*A*) 2331b and *The Kentish Hymn* 12b.

78 *Christ* (*II*) 638b.

79 *Christ* (*II*) 649a and 710a, *Juliana* 316a, *Elene* 199a, 1057a and 1156a, *Guthlac* (*B*) 1115a, *Christ and Satan* 571a and *Solomon and Saturn* 65a.

80 See above, p. 440, n. 15.   81 *Christ* (*II*) 774b.

82 For a full list, see Crépin, 'Poétique Vieil-Anglaise', pp. 259–61.

83 See above, p. 371.

siðe geseceð,   ond sylf cymeð,
nimeð eard in þe,   swa hit ær gefyrn
witgan wisfæste   wordum sægdon,
cyððon Cristes gebyrd,   cwædon þe to frofre,
burga betlicast.   Nu is þæt bearn cymen,
awæcned to wyrpe   weorcum Ebrea,
bringeð blisse þe,   benda onlyseð
niþum genedde.   Nearoþearfe conn,
hu se earma sceal   are gebidan

['O vision of peace, holy Jerusalem, choicest of royal thrones, native city of Christ, native throne of angels, and in you they alone, the souls of the faithful, rest for ever, exulting in glories. Never is a sign of defilement revealed in that dwelling place, but every sin avoids you afar, every curse and struggle. You are gloriously full of holy hope, as you are named. Look yourself now around, scanning widely this spacious creation and likewise the roof of the heavens on every side, how the king of heaven seeks you on a journey, and comes himself, takes a home in you, as wise prophets have foretold it long ago in their words, have revealed Christ's birth, have spoken as a consolation for you, most excellent of cities. Now that child has come, born as relief from the actions of the Hebrews, brings you joy, releases your bonds, imposed by hostility. He knows the dire need, how the wretched one awaits grace'].

In fact, however, a more complex train of thought has replaced the Latin's relative simplicity. The antiphon addresses the terrestrial Jerusalem throughout, but in the poem the initial invocation does not. Evidently the vernacular poet has treated the city as an image with more than a single significance.

John Cassian, an influential writer living in the area of Marseilles early in the fifth century, had enunciated a framework of the sort which governed the poet's thought. According to this authority, as well as denoting the earthly, historical, city, Jerusalem symbolizes allegorically 'the temporal church of Christ diffused throughout the world', tropologically 'the soul of man' and anagogically 'the heavenly city of God which is mother of us all'.[84] In the poem the *þe/þu*[85] which is first addressed is the celestial city – as 'engla eþelstol' (52a) makes clear – but it is invoked in terms which suggest an earthly point of view: in its heavenly peace the souls of the

[84] *Collationes* XLIX.963–4, cited by Burlin (*The Old English 'Advent'*, p. 83); for a full commentary on the lyric in question, to which I am indebted, see *ibid.*, pp. 82–7.

[85] 52b, 56a and 58b.

faithful enjoy the rest which implicitly contrasts with their preceding struggles in this life, and they rejoice in its glories which they can have earned only by those struggles here and now; likewise the 'hope' usually uppermost in the 'joy' expressed by *hyht* (58a) is a this-worldly motivation. Then, on transition to the exhortation beginning 'Sioh . . .' (59a), direction to a terrestrial *þe*/*þec*[86] starts in earnest. That this too is by no means a simple orientation is indicated by the time sequence within it. The foregoing invocation (50–8) has set the celestial city in an unvarying 'always' (*simle* and *Næfre* (53b and 54b)), but the historical time to which the remainder belongs begins with an exhortation uttered just before the incarnation (like the whole of the Latin antiphon) and then passes into a post-incarnation *Nu*, 'now' (66b), which at first is specific to the narrative statements forming 66b–9a and finally is generalized to an indefinite present in 69b–70. No single reference to the earthly city would account for all this: other meanings must have been blended in as well. Explicit reference to Christ's birth in 65a (which, of course, did not take place in the historical Jerusalem) indicates that by at least this stage the city is being understood figurally as the Virgin Mary, a symbolism which was added to Cassian's list in the course of the Middle Ages on the strength of certain biblical passages,[87] and which the poet may have hinted at already in the spotlessness alluded to in 54b–5;[88] the *þe* (68a) to whom *Nu* the saviour of the new covenant (? 67) is bringing joy and whose bonds he is loosening (68–9a) seems to be his universal church collectively; while the more personalized wretch whose ever-present need for grace the redeemer understands (69b–70) becomes the suffering soul awaiting year by year the season of Advent.

The poet's procedure was certainly not that of the tidy-minded exegete; his musing moves through a series of associations prompted by devotion. An emotional journey is undertaken from the blessings of eternity to historical expectation of universal redemption and then to both the general freedom and the personal yearning which the hope of redemption brings in the present. The imagination, caught by the devotional tone of the invocation and passed imperceptibly from one state of feeling to another, experiences, almost subconsciously, a subtle, unified sense of divine progression from heaven, to earth, through the Virgin Mary and the church and into the individual soul. The poet's vision of peace consists of

[86] 59a, 61b, 63a, 65b and 68a. [87] See *The Christ of Cynewulf*, ed. Cook, p. 81.

[88] Cf. Clayton, *The Cult of the Virgin Mary in Anglo-Saxon England*, pp. 183–4.

the compassion of God everlastingly transmitted from his royal throne in heaven down into the sinful being. At the heart of the poem is an unaffected, trustful dependence on the redeemer.

Cynewulf too showed a lively sense of schematic divine movement in God's spiritual kingdom when he carefully crafted a figure of a Christ-bird, flying to and fro between heaven and earth as an original addition to his paraphrase (*Christ* (*II*) 633–58) of Gregory the Great's Latin prose interpreting *avis* at Job XXVIII.7 as an allusion to the ascending Christ:[89]

Swa se fæla fugel flyges cunnode;
hwilum engla eard up gesohte,
modig meahtum strang, þone mæran ham,
hwilum he to eorþan eft gestylde,
þurh gæstes gife grundsceat sohte,
wende to worulde

['Thus the true bird has essayed flight; at times the bold one, strong in his powers, has sought the dwelling of angels upwards, the glorious[90] home, at times he has sprung again to earth, sought the region of earth through the gift of the spirit, made his way to the world', 645–50a].

The art is more verbal here than in the Advent lyric, though the response to movement is just as strong. The paired *hwilum* . . ., *hwilum* . . ., one for each direction, the frequency of self-alliteration in the *a* verses (in all but one of them), the firmness of alliterative collocations across the paired verses ('fæla fugel flyges', 'engla eard up', 'modig meahtum . . . mæran', 'eorþan eft' and 'gæstes giefe grundsceat'), and a 'line'-long opening statement (645) complemented by a brief, self-alliterating, self-sufficient *a* verse at the end (650a), all these features unify this image into a compact whole, while within it a clearcut contrast is conveyed between a single, driving, action upwards (OVSO, 646–7) and a more progressive movement downwards (a leaping, seeking, coming, OV, OV, VO, 648–50a). Evidently this poet's skill with words was not directed to drawing us into this spiritual process as intimately as the Advent lyric poet involves us in his; rather it turns us into admiring observers of the entirety as a work of art.

In his poems Cynewulf did not demonstrate a one-to-one dependence on God so much as the individual's vulnerability within a cosmic working

[89] See *The Christ of Cynewulf*, ed. Cook, n. on 633–58.

[90] MS and ASPR *maran*.

system. In his four 'signed' epilogues, for instance, his personal grounds for misgiving – loss of youth, need for the prayers of others, prospect of a death with his sins his only certainty, fears for his fate when he is judged – were merged with general principles – of universal dissolution, of the benefit which everyone stands to gain from intercessions, of the terror of punishment all will feel on the day of judgement, of the punishment and reward to be meted out on that great day; and consequently they yielded fruitful advice to others.[91] Characteristically his images depicted grand processes in stylized forms.

Composition of this sort made two radical linguistic demands in addition to straightforward denotation of God's kingdom in all its parts: the expression had to be capable of rendering both terminologically and structurally the spiritual kingdom's vibrancy. Very much in the vein of combining these two potentials was Cynewulf's version of Gregory the Great's figure of Christ's redemption of mankind in a series of great leaps, forming part of the debt to that pope's Latin prose homily for the underlying train of thought of this poet's celebration of the ascension (*Christ II*). Gregory did not invent this figure: it was an ancient topos, going back in patristic thought at least as far as Ambrose in the fourth century and subject to variations in the course of transmission.[92] Gregory's version contained five leaps – *de caelo in uterum*, *de utero in praesepe*, *de praesepe in crucem*, *de cruce in sepulcrum* and *de sepulcro in caelum* ('from the sky into the womb', 'from the womb into the manger', 'from the manger on to the cross', 'from the cross into the tomb' and 'from the tomb into the sky')[93] – and to these Cynewulf added another, between Gregory's fourth and fifth, representing Christ's victory in hell. The poet's way (712–55) was to present each item not as a leap from point to point in the Gregorian manner but as a leap when the saviour did so-and-so – 'Wæs se forma hlyp þa he on fæmne astag' ('The first leap was when he came down into the Virgin', 720), 'Wæs se fifta hlyp / þa he hellwarena heap forbygde' ('The fifth leap was when he brought low the inhabitants of hell', 730b–1) and so on[94] – and he extended the image to the closing moral message to all men

[91] See above, pp. 274–5. [92] See *The Christ of Cynewulf*, ed. Cook, n. on 720.

[93] See *ibid.*, n. on 712–43.

[94] Variations on this basic pattern are: 'Wæs se oþer stiell / bearnes gebyrda, þa . . .'; 'Wæs se þridda hlyp, / rodorcyninges ræs, þa . . .'; 'Wæs se feorða stiell / in byrgenne, þa he þone beam ofgeaf'; and 'Wæs se siexta hlyp, / haliges hyhtplega, þa . . .'

(whereas Gregory had merely exhorted us to 'follow with the heart' where we believe Christ has 'ascended with the body'[95]):

Þus her on grundum godes ece bearn
ofer heahhleoþu hlypum stylde,
modig æfter muntum. Swa we men sculon
heortan gehygdum hlypum styllan
of mægne in mægen, mærþum tilgan

['Thus here on earth God's eternal son sprang in leaps over lofty hills, bold across mountains. So we men in the thoughts of our hearts must spring in leaps from strength to strength, strive after glories', 744–8].

In this coda God and men were bound together in a single spiritual process of two parallel members, each member occupying two-and-a-half pairs of verses (744–6a and 746b–8),[96] and each being centred on the intensified action of 'springing in leaps' (745b and 747b). In the first place the source of the spirituality was marked off in its uniqueness by being designated as 'godes ece bearn', the sole three-element symbol[97] in the passage, while everywhere else pairing was employed, whether to point up unlikeness or likeness. The unlikeness lies in the pairing of the self-alliterating *a* verses (745a with 746a and 747a with 748a) so as to enfold the two verbs of 'leaping' (745b and 747b) with phrases contrasting the spaciousness of the divine action on the one hand with the more concentrated nature of the human one on the other. The likeness consists of the spirituality underlying the verbal pairing in all other respects. The 'lofty hills' and 'mountains' were derived from *montes* and *colles* in the verse of the Song of Solomon which Gregory was expounding, 'Ecce iste venit saliens in montibus, et transiliens colles';[98] 'of mægne in mægen' probably echoed the 'ambulabunt de uirtute in uirtutem' of ps. LXXXIV.7, which was glossed in the Vespasian Psalter 'gongað of mægne in mægen';[99] and the synonyms expressing 'springing in leaps', probably took their cue from Solomon's *saliens* and *transiliens*. To this last pairing, however, Cynewulf assigned a much more extensive rôle. He interlaced his 'leaping' set

[95] Cf. 751b–5 and see *The Christ of Cynewulf*, ed. Cook, n. on 744–55.

[96] The second of these members is then extended by a result clause, with a relative clause subordinate to it (749–51a), and finally there is a sentence paraphrasing Gregory (751b–5; see above, preceding n.).

[97] Cf. above, p. 439 and n. 4.

[98] Cf. 712–19 and see *The Christ of Cynewulf*, ed. Cook, n. on 712–43.

[99] See Clemoes, 'King Alfred's Debt to Vernacular Poetry', p. 224, n. 49.

thus:[100] (introduction, 715–19) *gestylleð*, *gehleapeð*, *styll*; (first leap, 720–3a) *hlyp*; (second leap, 723b–6a) *stiell*; (third leap, 726b–8a) *hlyp*; (fourth leap, 728b–30a) *stiell*; (fifth leap, 730b–6a) *hlyp*; (sixth, final, leap, 736b–43) *hlyp*; and (conclusion, 744–8) 'hlypum stylde', 'hlypum styllan'. In consequence, after signalling the close of the alternating series by repeating in the sixth leap the *hlyp* of the fifth, he could finally underpin an all-embracing parallelism between God and men through a double use of a coupling of these words which had not occurred previously. Cynewulf's verbal artifice presents an analogy between God and men as part – for men the central part – of a system which is structurally composed of active spiritual being.

Plentiful terminology, commonly heightened by self-alliterating *a* verses or three-element symbols, was essential to poetry for fit celebration of God's spiritual kingdom in its variety of action. Such language is noticeable throughout, for instance, the 'leaps' topos just cited. Self-alliterating symbols in *a* verses – such as 'bearnes gebyrda' ('the birth of the child', 724a), 'æþelinga ord' ('the chief of princes', 741a) and 'beorhtra bolda' ('the radiant buildings', 742a) – are relatively common, and there is an unusually high proportion of three-element formations: no fewer than ten of these occur in the forty-four *a* verses concerned – such as 'rodorcyninges ræs' ('the spring of the king of the heavens', 427a) and 'haliges hyhtplega' ('the hope-play of the holy one', 737a).[101] A tripartite formation (with single alliteration) was even used, as we have seen, in a *b* verse ('godes ece bearn' ('the eternal son of God', 744b)). These resources of vocabulary must now claim our attention more generally.

They characterize the whole of *Christ II*, as may be demonstrated by notable differences between this poem's 427 'lines' and the same number of 'lines' at the beginning of *Beowulf* in both quantity and kind of symbolic language. If, as in the discussion of 712–55, we begin with the alliterative treatment of symbols in *a* verses (almost the same number of occurrences of them in *Christ II* (202×) and in *Beowulf* 1–427 (198×)), we find that self-alliteration is more common in the former (91×) than in the latter (72×): in Cynewulf's poem it features in not much less than a half of the instances and in *Beowulf* 1–427 not much more than a third. And there is a more marked statistical difference between the two poems in their *b* verses: in these positions symbols (with single alliteration) were used in *Christ II*

[100] Cf. *The Christ of Cynewulf*, ed. Cook, n. on 723.

[101] The others are at 713a, 714a, 716a, 719a, 723a, 730a, 733a and 751a.

(154×) just over one-and-a-third times as frequently as in *Beowulf* 1–427 (113×), including a much higher increase in the tiny minority of three-element forms (10× in *Christ II* as against 4× in *Beowulf* 1–427). More self-alliterating symbols in *a* verses and more symbols in *b* verses in Cynewulf's poem than in *Beowulf* 1–427 (no plain composition) is part of the greater artistic prominence of symbolic language which, we may infer, was fostered by the most fundamental change of all, the transition from a socially formed vocabulary to a spiritual one.[102]

Comparison of *Christ II* with *Beowulf* provides a fair sample of the wording which made the change from the latter's system of thought to the other and how it became adapted in the process. Some symbols could be applied metaphorically in a more-than-this-worldly sense as they stood, without any formal alteration: for example, 'hyra sincgiefan' ('their treasure-giver', *Christ* (*II*) 460a) exactly matches (*hyra*) *sincgifan* (*Beowulf* 2311a and 1342a), as does 'hyra wilgifan' ('their joy-giver', *Christ* (*II*) 537a) 'wilgeofa Wedra leoda' ('joy-giver of the men of the Weders', *Beowulf* 2900), for in both poems what was at stake was the bond created between close followers and their leader by his bounty, the difference being between the far-reaching debt the apostles owed to Jesus for spiritual revelation and the practical one retainers owed to a warrior chief for material well-being.[103] Other symbols, on the other hand, were produced either by straightforwardly adapting existing models of social terminology in order to take in special features such as the uniqueness of Christ's kingship,[104] or by cleanly departing semantically, but not formally, from existing tradition in order to embrace purely ecclesiastical concepts, for instance by means of epithets such as 'frofre gæst'.[105]

Most interesting of all are those symbols which resulted from both semantic and formal evolution. A case in point, which performed the vital function of building human society into the spiritual, is 'æþelinga ord' ('spiritual originator of princes') used by Cynewulf three times in

[102] Cf. above, pp. 332–3.

[103] *his sincgyfan* at *The Battle of Maldon* 278a shows that in the practical world this symbol lost none of the personal force which it depended on for its spiritual application.

[104] E.g., the self-alliterating 'rodera ryhtend' ('ruler of the heavens', only at *Christ* (*II*) 798a), 'cyning anboren' ('only begotten king', used twice, only by Cynewulf, at *Christ* (*II*) 618a and *Elene* 392a) and 'ece dema' ('eternal judge', *Christ* (*II*) 796b and 836b).

[105] See above, p. 440, n. 15.

Christ II.[106] In our extant poems reflecting the pre-Christian tradition *ord* as a simplex has the meanings 'point (of a weapon)', 'front (of an army)' and 'beginning' and plays a limited part in compound formations, for example in the two three-element self-alliterating symbols 'Ætlan ordwyga' ('Attila's champion [literally 'front-line fighter']', *Waldere* I.6a) and 'æþele ordfruma' (either 'noble front-line chief' or perhaps 'noble originator, begetter', *Beowulf* 263a, used by Beowulf referring to his father). *Frum(a)*, 'origin', 'originator', 'chief', on the other hand, readily forms compounds to do with lineage[107] and leadership.[108] Thus, when Christianity brought in an emphasis on God as the creator and originator of all and on the devil as the origin of all evil, the two words were natural partners and *ordfruma* became frequent in the meaning of 'spiritual originator', especially in three-element symbols forming complete *a* verses, six of them self-alliterating[109] and one with single alliteration.[110] Seemingly, therefore, *ord* came to mean 'spiritual originator', on analogy with symbolic *ordfruma* in this sense, in order to combine with *æþelinga* in the self-alliterating 'æþelinga ord' and thereby provide, semantically and formally, a complement on the human plane to the celestial 'engla ordfruma', a reduction of the compound *ordfruma* to the simplex *ord* being required to compensate for a genitive modifier with a secondary stress (on *-ing-*) and hence rhythmically heavier than *engla* (or *lifes*, *eades*, *yfeles*, *attres*, *ece* or *æþele*).[111]

[106] 515a, 741a and 845a; also once in *Elene* (393a) and once by the poet of *Genesis A* (1278a), always as a complete, self-alliterating, *a* verse.

[107] E.g., *frumcynn* (*Beowulf* 252a).

[108] E.g., *frumgar*, *hildfruma* and *wigfruma*, 'war-chief' (*Beowulf* 2856a, 1678a etc. (3×), and 664a and 2261a, respectively).

[109] 'Engla ordfruma' ('originator of angels', 6×, including Cynewulf's *The Fates of the Apostles* 28a) and *eades* ('of blessedness'), *yfeles* ('of evil'), *attres* ('of venom'), *ece* ('eternal') and *æþele* ('noble', 1× each).

[110] 'Lifes ordfruma' ('originator of life', 1×; cf. *liffruma*, 6× in *b* verses and 2× in *a* verses, in neither of the latter as the whole verse).

[111] Context associates 'æþelinga ord' with *fruma* at *Christ* (*II*) 515–16a, reading 'æþelinga ord, mid þas engla gedryht, / ealra folca fruma' ('originator of princes, with this company of angels, creator of all peoples'), and at *Genesis* (*A*) 1276b–8 reading

Hreaw hine swiðe
þæt he folcmægþa fruman aweahte,
æðelinga ord, þa he Adam sceop

['He, originator of princes, greatly regretted that he had given life to the progenitor of peoples when he created Adam'].

In *The Descent into Hell* Christ is twice termed 'ealles folces fruma' (29a and 41a) and

What at any rate is certain is that by attributing divine origin to human, hereditary, nobility this symbol constituted an imaginative synthesis of the social system traditional to vernacular poetry and the spiritual structure of the Christian universe.

The 356 symbols of all sorts in *Christ II* celebrate an entire social system of the spirit just as the 311 in *Beowulf* 1–427 proffer an earthly one. Like the *gifstol*, 'gift-seat' (*Beowulf* 168a),[112] symbolizing Danish power, a 'fæder eþelstoll' ('native seat of the father', *Christ* (*II*) 516b), a 'gæsta giefstol' ('gift-seat of spirits', 572a), was the centre of the spiritual realm. Heavenly troops surrounded it – a '(heofon)engla þreat' ('company of (heavenly) angels', 492b and 738b), an 'engla gedryht' ('band of angels', 515b), a 'weorud wlitescyne' ('beautiful host', 493a and 554a), a 'geþungen þegnweorud' ('distinguished body of thegns', 751a); it was the focal point of an 'engla eþel' ('native land of angels', 630a), an 'engla eard' ('habitation of angels', 646a). On earth the apostles served 'hyra wilgifan' (537a) faithfully as 'þegnas gecorene' ('picked thegns', 497b), 'þegnas þrymfulle' ('glorious thegns', 541a), 'hæleð hygerofe' ('valiant heroes', 534a). Men at large were bound in allegiance to God by a 'gæsthalig treow' ('spiritually holy agreement', 584b). Divine power manifested itself everywhere – in the 'rodorcyninges ræs' ('leap of the king of the heavens', 727a) when Christ ascended the cross, and in the 'haliges hyhtplega' ('hope-play of the holy one', 737a), 'æþelinges plega' ('play of the prince', 743b), when he ascended into heaven; in despatching angels to earth as 'wuldres aras' ('messengers of glory', 493b), 'aras ufancundne' ('messengers from above', 503a); in fortifying the apostles 'strengðu staþolfæstre' ('with steadfast strength', 490a); in granting to the faithful 'godes þegna blæd' ('the reward of God's thegns', 710b). Men were surrounded by an environment bursting with energy: flame was quick and red (809a); ways stretched far (651a); waves were immoderate (854a); arrows flew flickeringly (676a). The *wrohtbora* ('bearer of strife', 763b, the devil) and his minions assailed mankind with 'eglum earhfarum' ('grievous arrow-flights', 726a), 'gromra

more generally *fruma* makes up several other self-alliterating, mostly three-element, symbols in conjunction with a genitive modifier (including Cynewulf's 'fyrnweorca fruma' ('originator of created things', *Christ* (*II*) 579a)). More often still it formed two- or three-element genitive combinations with single alliteration. For instance, the *Andreas* poet, who used 'engla ordfruma' at 146a, preferred at 226a 'upengla fruma' (occurring only here). *Ord* in 'æþelinga ord' was therefore also following a lead well established by its customary partner.

[112] Cf. *eþelstolas*, 'native seats' (2371b).

garfare' ('spear-flights of enemies', 781a), *færscyte*, 'sudden shooting' (766b), 'feonda færsearo' ('sudden contrivance of foes', 770a), 'laþra lygesearwum' ('lying devices of hostile ones', 776a), 'biter bordgelac' ('sharp attack on shields', 769a). Christ's redeeming spirit revitalized the spiritual cosmos as Beowulf's intervention from across the sea had purified Danish society:

Hæfde þa gefælsod se þe ær feorran com,
snotor ond swyðferhð, sele Hroðgares,
genered wið niðe

['He who had come from afar, wise and strong-minded, had then purged Hrothgar's hall, rescued it from persecution', *Beowulf* 825–7a].

The saviour and his church irradiated the universe like the sun and moon:

He is se soðfæsta sunnan leoma,
englum ond eorðwarum æþele scima.
Ofer middangeard mona lixeð,
gæstlic tungol, swa seo godes circe
þurh gesomninga soðes ond ryhtes
beorhte bliceð

['He is the true light of the sun, noble radiance to angels and dwellers on earth. Over the world the moon shines, spiritual star, as the church of God glitters brightly through unions of truth and justice', *Christ (II)* 696–701a].

Cynewulf's ornate linguistic symbols studded every part of Christ's creation with pulses of interaction like stars in a firmament.

This omnipresent ornate interaction quickened devotion.[113] Whereas in *Beowulf* the interactions which were incorporated in compounds and genitive and adjective combinations were the vital sparks of wisdom carried from past to present, in Cynewulf's poetry they were the flashpoints which brought God and man into living touch and performed this function efficiently to a greater or lesser degree according to the aesthetic quality of the language. Consciously crafted symbolic epithets formed the devotional currency of the spiritual kingdom, as 'sawla nergend' ('saviour of souls') at *Christ (II)* 571b illustrates. This genitive combination attracts attention because it represents Cynewulf's only symbolic use of *sawol* in this poem, and, indeed, is one of only three occurrences of *sawol* of any sort[114] as

[113] Cf. above, p. 452. [114] The other two are at 619a and 819b.

compared with twenty-two of *gæst*.[115] The poet was adopting at 571b a *nergend* combination which is found not infrequently in *b* verses and only in *b* verses (11×[116]). The corresponding *nergend* form in an *a* verse was always the self-alliterating 'nið(ð)a nergend' ('saviour of men', 6×[117]), unless the genitive was in post-position, when 'nergend fira' seems to have been standard (4×[118]). Evidently 'sawla nergend' was an established feature of *b* verses, while 'nið(ð)a nergend', employing a 'poetic' plural word as a genitive which occurs symbolically otherwise only in 'niðða bearn' ('sons of men', 7×, as in *Beowulf* 1005b), gives every sign of having been intended as a 'fancy' *a* verse equivalent. On the other hand 'gæsta nergend' or 'nergend gæsta', which one might expect at least occasionally, never occurs, although 'gæsta geocend' ('helper, saviour, of spirits') does, forming a self-alliterating *a* verse six times[119] by utilizing a 'poetic' word, *geocend*, which otherwise plays no part in symbolic formations.

The symbolic connotations of *sawol* were mainly God's redemption (as expressed in 'sawla nergend') and man's trustworthiness – as shown by the frequency of the word's combination with *soðfæst*[120] or *soðfæstra*[121] – or untrustworthiness.[122] Only three attempts were made, so far as the extant

[115] See above, p. 440.

[116] The ten other references are Cynewulf's *Elene* 461b and 798b, *Andreas* 549b and 921b, *Daniel* 401b, *The Phoenix* 498b, *Maxims I* 134b and *Psalm 50* 16b, 59b and 83b. The only variations are 'folca/es nergend' ('saviour of people(s)', *Christ* (*I*) 426b and *Solomon and Saturn* 80b) and 'weoroda nergend' ('saviour of hosts', *The Fortunes of Men* 93b) and two instances of post-positional genitive, 'nergend fira' ('saviour of men', Cynewulf's *Juliana* 240b) and 'nergend wera' ('saviour of men', *The Lord's Prayer I* 3b); cf. 'nergend ealra / woruldbuendra' ('saviour of all dwellers in the world', *Judith* 81b–2a).

[117] Cynewulf's *Elene* 503a and 1085a, *Guthlac* (*A*) 640a, *Andreas* 1377a, *Daniel* 312a and *The Kentish Hymn* 35a.

[118] Cynewulf's *Elene* 1077a and 1172a and *Andreas* 291a and 1286a.

[119] Including two uses by Cynewulf in *Elene* (682a and 1076a); see above, p. 440, n. 14.

[120] Adjective (5×), as in 'soþfæste sawle' ('righteous soul', *The Death of Edward* 28a). The other references are *The Phoenix* 540a (with the adjective in post-position) and 589, *An Exhortation to Christian Living* 14 and *The Death of Edward* 2.

[121] Nominal, in the genitive plural (6×), as in 'saule soþfæstra' ('souls of the righteous', *Christ* (*I*) 53a). The other references are *Guthlac* (*A*) 22, 567 and 790, *Exodus* 544 and *Andreas* 228.

[122] See, e.g.,

þonne anra gehwylc,
soðfæst ge synnig, sawel mid lice,
from moldgrafum seceð meotudes dom

corpus goes, to exploit the word for self-alliterating *a* verses expressing other aspects of trust in God.[123] Thematic to the poetic use of *sawol*, we may conclude, were the eternal aspects of men's redemption. By contrast the symbolic connotations of human *gast/gæst*, as we would expect from the traditions of this word, were more to do with relationship to God this side of eternity:[124] appellations hailed God as creator,[125] protector[126] and ruler of spirits,[127] besides the 'helper' sense appealed to in 'gæsta geocend' and once in 'helpend gæsta' (*Riddle* 48, 5b). Apart from the six-times-used 'gæsta geocend' only three other self-alliterating genitive combinations occur, and only once each (*gæsta god*, 'God of spirits' (*Christ* (*I*) 130a), 'gæsta god cyning' ('good king of spirits', *Resignation* 40a) and 'gæsta giefstol' ('gift-seat of spirits', *Christ* (*II*) 572a)). The established availability of *gast/gæst* over the whole range of this world's activity in relation to God prompted, we may infer, the creation of 'gæsta geocend' as a decorative *a* verse more complementary to the meaning of the *b* verse 'sawla nergend' than was 'nið(ð)a nergend', with only its general reference to 'men'.

'Sawla nergend', 'nið(ð)a nergend' and 'gæsta geocend' formed a compact, distinctive group of symbols expressing God's unique redemptive force active in this world and the next: 'sawla nergend' probes the everlasting mystery of it, 'gæsta geocend' opens our hearts and minds to the help and succour it affords as we live out our present existence, and 'nið(ð)a nergend' sets a glittering bridge between the two. The fullness of sound in 'gæsta geocund', with its two alliterating long-vowelled stems (both of them back vowels, if that is how the former was pronounced) and a secondary stress on its final syllable, like the deep notes of an organ, made this epithet the ideal component for passionate direct speech both times

['when everyone, righteous and sinful, soul with body, seeks the judgement of God from graves in the earth', *The Phoenix* 522b–4].

123 'Sawle sigesped' ('victorious success of the soul', Cynewulf's *Elene* 1171a), 'sawla symbelgifa' ('feaster of souls', *Andreas* 1417a) and 'sawla soðcyningc' ('true king of souls', *The Metrical Psalms of the Paris Psalter* (ASPR 5), ps. CXX.7, 2a).

124 Mimura [Ono] has commented, 'This [her survey in certain respects] shows that *gast* expresses not just human spirit, but spirit in a wide and general sense, while *sawol* is close to ModE *soul*' (Mimura (Ono), 'The Syntax and Semantics of *gāst* in Old English Poetry' and Mimura (Ono), 'The Syntax and Semantics of *gāst* and *sāwol* in Old English Poetry', p. 240). Cf. Becker, *Geist und Seele im Altsächsischen und im Althochdeutschen*.

125 'Gæsta scyppend' (8×).

126 *Gæsta weard* (5×), *helm* (3×) and *hleo* and *hyrde* (1× each).

127 'Gasta waldend' (2×), and *dryhten*, *ealdor* and *breogo* (1× each).

Cynewulf used it in *Elene*. On the first occasion it provided the climax to three glorifying self-alliterating *a* verses when St Helena was emphasizing with the utmost conviction that God would grant her inmost desire to discover the true cross:

Þæt me halig god
gefylle, frea mihtig, feores ingeþanc,
weoruda wuldorgeofa, willan minne,
gasta geocend

['so that holy God, mighty Lord, may fulfil the inmost thought of my life, giver of the glory of hosts, my desire, helper of spirits', 679b–82a].

The series of *a* verses, centring on the three-member symbol (681a) before coming to a full close with 'gasta geocend', imparts an overwhelming sense of a mighty lordship, bountiful in the next life and redeeming in this. On the second occasion, when Helena was addressing the man who had been the instrument of God's revelation of the cross and was now the ordained bishop of Jerusalem, filled with the holy spirit, 'gasta geocend' introduced three successive symbols celebrating the saviour's divinity at that most sacred of moments, his crucifixion:

Þu me, eorla hleo, þone æðelan beam,
rode rodera cininges ryhte getæhtesð,
on þa ahangen wæs hæðenum folmum
gasta geocend, godes agen bearn,
nerigend fira

['You, protector of men, have correctly shown me the noble tree, the cross of the king of the heavens, on which was hanged by heathen hands the helper of spirits, God's own son, the saviour of men', 1073–7a].

With Christ's celestial majesty already bejewelled in 'rode rodera cininges', the business of 1076–7a was purely his redemptive spirituality. Two epithets lauding the redeemer in action, firstly in this world as 'gasta geocend' and then, summarizing the outcome, as 'nerigend fira', enfold, through a classical application of the appositive technique of vernacular verse, a single three-element appellation, denoting the origin of this process, Christ's uniqueness as 'godes agen bearn'. The more immediate 'gasta geocend' leads to the more general 'nerigend fira' by way of the plainest possible affirmation of the underlying spiritual potential. Our devotional imaginations, engaged by this development, are patterned by the poet's language.

Verbal artistry of this order was to the forefront of Cynewulf's sensibility. For him redemption had implanted as the human heart of the universe a 'gæstes þearf' ('need of the spirit', *Christ* (*II*) 707a and 816b; cf. 847b)

> þæt we gæstes wlite   ær þam gryrebrogan
> on þas gæsnan tid   georne biþencen

['that before the terrible horror we should in this barren time think eagerly about the beauty of the spirit', 848–9].

Beautiful language was designed to intensify the adoration, struggle, fear, hope, which jostle one another in the individual breast, and to channel them creatively.

This poet's exemplary personages were those who worked this spiritual system to the full, whether, like St Juliana, as a virgin renouncing material values altogether, or, like St Helena, ennobling earthly aristocracy by spiritual purpose. The latter, in her own right[128] every inch a powerful,[129] warlike,[130] victorious[131] and blessed queen,[132] grew in spiritual stature as revelation unfolded. Clear-headed gratitude to God for vouchsafing to her both the cross and the faith of the man who had obtained it through miracle and defeat of the devil –

> Gode þancode,
> wuldorcyninge,   þæs hire se willa gelamp
> þurh bearn godes   bega gehwæðres,
> ge æt þære gesyhðe   þæs sigebeames,
> ge ðæs geleafan   þe hio swa leohte oncneow,
> wuldorfæste gife   in þæs weres breostum

['She thanked God, the king of glory, because her desire was fulfilled through the son of God doubly, at the sight of both the tree of victory and of the belief which she so clearly recognized, the glorious grace in the man's breast', 961b–6] –

[128] 'Caseres mæg' ('emperor's kinswoman', *Elene* 330b and 669b) and 'seo æðele cwen' ('the noble queen', 275b, 662a and 1130b).

[129] *Sio rice cwen*, 'the exalted queen' (411b).

[130] *Sio guðcwen*, 'the battle queen' (254a), 'geatolic guðcwen' ('magnificent battle queen', 331a).

[131] *Sigecwen*, 'queen of triumph' (260a and 997a).

[132] *Eadig*, 'fortunate' (619a), *eadhreðig*, 'happy' (266a) and *tireadig*, 'glorious' (605a).

led to an unbearable yearning to find the nails too –

A min hige sorgað,
reonig reoteð, ond geresteð no
ærþan me gefylle fæder ælmihtig,
wereda wealdend, willan minne,
niða nergend, þurh þara nægla cyme,
halig of hiehða

['Always my mind sorrows, weeps, mournful, and never rests until the almighty father, ruler of hosts, fulfils my desire, saviour of men, through advent of the nails, holy from the heights', 1081b–6a] –

and then, when this divine longing was gratified, to an ecstatic joy:

Þa wæs wopes hring,
hat heafodwylm ofer hleor goten,
(nalles for torne tearas feollon
ofer wira gespon), wuldres gefylled
cwene willa. Heo on cneow sette
leohte geleafan, lac weorðode,
blissum hremig, þe hire brungen wæs
gnyrna to geoce. Gode þancode,
sigora dryhtne, þæs þe hio soð gecneow
ondweardlice þæt wæs oft bodod
feor ær beforan fram fruman worulde,
folcum to frofre. Heo gefylled wæs
wisdomes gife, ond þa wic beheold
halig heofonlic gast, hreðer weardode,
æðelne innoð, swa hie ælmihtig
sigebearn godes sioððan freoðode

['Then a ring of weeping, a hot surging from the head, was poured over the cheek (not at all out of grief did the tears fall across the filigree clasp), the queen's desire was gloriously fulfilled. She knelt radiant with belief, blissfully exultant worshipped the gift which was brought to her as a solace for sorrows. She thanked God, the Lord of victories, because she knew at first hand the truth which had been proclaimed often long ago from the beginning of the world as consolation for peoples. She was filled with the grace of wisdom, and the holy heavenly spirit watched over the dwelling, protected her breast, her noble inner heart, as the almighty victorious son of God thenceforth granted her his peace', 1131b–46].[133]

[133] The Latin source stated merely, 'She knelt down, bowed her head and worshipped them [i.e., the nails]. Full of wisdom and much knowledge . . .'; Allen and Calder, *Sources and Analogues*, p. 67.

Weeping with relief, enveloped by the light of faith and kneeling in reverence before the truth which had been at the heart of human life since the world began, she was possessed by the spirit of wisdom and wrapped for ever in the peace which Christ had won for men through his crucifixion. Cynewulf's refined, delicately stylized, language feelingly unifies her rejoicing tears ('hat heafodwylm') and her responding God ('halig heofonlic gast', 'sigebearn godes'). A weeping queen becomes the very figure of this world's faithful sentiment sanctified.

The radiant light, exemplified by this association (in Cynewulf's poem but not in his source) between St Helena's tearful radiance and the triumphant lordship which had been Christ's from the beginning of the world and had given him victory on the cross, was an attribute of active spiritual being which Old English poets regularly invoked. St Helena's manifestation of it represented her elevation to spiritual union with the divine active beings of the 'halig heofonlic gast' (1144a) and the 'sigebearn godes' (1146a). In Old English poetry it was a transcendent image of spiritual being running right through from God the father to his only begotten son and from that son, as creator-king, to all his creatures.[134] In *Christ III*, for instance, an anonymous poet linked the creation of the stars to the response of the heavens when the shining king of all creatures was born:

On þa sylfan tid
heofon hluttre ongeat hwa hine healice
torhtne getremede tungolgimmum;
forþon he his bodan sende, þa wæs geboren ærest
gesceafta scircyning

['At the same time heaven clearly perceived who had arrayed it, glorious on high, with starry gems; for it had sent his herald when the bright king of creatures was first born', 1148b–52a].[135]

In *Andreas* an intimate connection between the incarnate king and his

134 For a recent brief summary of a comparable image of Christ as the sun of salvation, stretching back in the liturgy at least as far as the fourth century, see Lucas, 'Easter, the Death of St Guthlac and the Liturgy for Holy Saturday', p. 9. I am grateful to Peter Lucas for obliging me with a prepublication copy of his article (see further, below, p. 482, nn. 169 and 170).

135 The poet's source, lacking his linking motif of light, was clearly the first of Gregory the Great's six instances of a natural element witnessing to the advent of its creator ('auctorem suum venisse'): 'Deum hunc cœli esse cognoverunt, quia protinus stellam miserunt' ('The skies recognized that he was God because they immediately sent a star', Gregory *Hom. in ev.* I.x.2 (PL 76, col. 1111)).

heavenly father was poignantly expressed when the poet (without any lead from his source) reworded Christ's forlorn cry from the cross thus:

> Ic ðe, fæder engla, frignan wille,
> lifes leohtfruma, hwæt forlætest ðu me

['I wish to ask you, father of angels, author of the light of life, why have you forsaken me', 1412–13],

Christ speaking in this extremity as 'god lifgende', 'fyrnweorca frea', 'cininga wuldor' ('living God, Lord of works of long ago, glory of kings', 1409b–10a and 1411a). In Cynewulf's conception (without prompting in his source), at the resurrection the living Christ arose 'ealles leohtes leoht' ('light of all lights', *Elene* 486a), 'ðeoden engla' ('prince of angels', 487a), to display himself to his disciples as 'soð sigora frea' ('true Lord of victories', 488a). In *Christ II* the same poet introduced into the ascension too the association between light and Christ's victory when angels accompanying the ascending saviour glorified him as *æþeling*, 'noble prince' (503b), and *liffruma*, 'source of life' (504a), and then 'leohte gefegun / þe of þæs hælendes heafelan lixte' ('rejoiced in the light which shone from the saviour's head', 505b–6);[136] and, again in the same poem, as we have seen,[137] Christ's dissemination of post-ascension grace was identified with sunlight shining throughout his creation, when Cynewulf asserted (without equivalent in Gregory's Latin, which was his source):

> He is se soðfæsta sunnan leoma,
> englum ond eorðwarum æþele scima (696–7).

Christ as judge also was conceived of as possessing a brilliance contrasting with sin-stained humanity, when Beowulf declared of Grendel, doomed to death in his den:

> ðær abidan sceal
> maga mane fah miclan domes,
> hu him scir Metod scrifan wille (*Beowulf* 977b–9).[138]

[136] I have suggested that the poet owed this detail to an impression of a nimbed, haloed Christ in the visual arts ('Cynewulf's Image of the Ascension', p. 299).

[137] Above, p. 463.

[138] See above, p. 41. In view of *scir Metod* I prefer here the meaning of 'stained' to that of 'guilty' for *fah*, assumed by Klaeber and others.

Old English poets thus associated light with all Christ's main acts of creation, redemption and judgement and, through the epithet 'lifes leohtfruma' (5 × [139]), with God as preserver or corrector.[140] The section of the Mass Creed concerning the second person, familiar to all Christians, was probably, I would suppose, responsible for the image's connection of father, son and creation, through its associated phrases '. . . God from God, light from light . . . through him all things were made . . .', and for poets' ready recall of the image whenever a function of Christ was in question, through its rehearsal of the redeemer's great acts, finishing 'and his kingdom will have no end'.[141] Vernacular poetry could have reflected this influence early, from its first contacts with Christianity.

In the created, light or darkness constituted a standard measure of merit or demerit. In *Elene* the saint's radiance contrasted with the spiritual blindness of the Jews of which the queen (without equivalent in the Latin source) accused the Jews:

Ge þa sciran miht
deman ongunnon, ond gedweolan lifdon,
þeostrum geþancum, oð þysne dæg

['You began to condemn the bright power and lived with heresy, dark thoughts, until this day', 310b–12].

Human darkness conflicted all too easily with divine brilliance, as in the case of the Jews, when characterized thus in Cynewulf's ascension poem (but not in his source):

þam þe deorc gewit
hæfdon on hreþre, heortan stænne.
Noldan hi þa torhtan tacen oncnawan
þe him beforan fremede freobearn godes,
monig mislicu, geond middangeard

['who had dark understanding in their mind, a heart of stone. They would not acknowledge the bright signs, many and manifold, which he, the noble son of God, performed before them throughout the world', *Christ* (*II*) 640b–4].

[139] At *Genesis* (*A*) 926a, 1410a, 1792a, 1889a and 2423a.

[140] When he expelled Adam from paradise, preserved Noah and his company, showed Abraham the promised land, was thanked for blessings, and sent two angels to Lot at Sodom.

[141] In the 990s Ælfric included a prose translation of this creed in a miscellaneous appendix to his Second Series of *Catholic Homilies*, ed. Thorpe II, 596–8. For the early history of creeds, see Kelly, *Early Christian Creeds*, esp. pp. 297–8.

Light and dark as opposites epitomized even the eternities of heaven and hell in Cynewulf's declaration (not matched in his source) that everyone chooses for ever by what he does in this world

swa þæt leohte leoht   swa ða laþan niht,
swa þrymmes þræce   swa þystra wræce (592–3).[142]

Illumination and darkness polarized human existence in both this world and the next.

Of the utmost complexity as manifestation of the divine nature of the creator-king and of the intrinsic connection between creator and created is the extraordinary interplay of light and darkness in the cross's account of the crucifixion vouchsafed to a visionary in *The Dream of the Rood*:

Feala ic on þam beorge   gebiden hæbbe
wraðra wyrda.   Geseah ic weruda god
þearle þenian.   Þystro hæfdon
bewrigen mid wolcnum   wealdendes hræw,
scirne sciman,   sceadu forðeode,
wann under wolcnum.   Weop eal gesceaft,
cwiðdon cyninges fyll

['Many cruel events have I endured on that hill. I saw the God of hosts stretched severely. Darkness had covered with clouds the ruler's corpse, the bright radiance, shadow advanced, dusky beneath the clouds. All creation wept, lamented the king's death', 50–6a].[143]

Neither the radiance of Christ's corpse nor the weeping of creation was paralleled elsewhere in crucifixion narratives, commentary, liturgy or iconography of the relevant period or earlier, on present knowledge;[144] nor did either have any demonstrable derivation from elsewhere.[145] Both seem to result from the anonymous poet's own imagination working strongly in a devotional spirit within the traditions of native poetry itself.

The origin of the association between the crucifixion and covering clouds was, of course the Bible's statement that 'from the sixth hour there was darkness over all the land'.[146] Patristic thought conceived of this as a

[142] See above, p. 313.

[143] Quoted from the Vercelli text; the Ruthwell inscription may or may not have included an equivalent. For a discussion, see Clemoes, 'King and Creation at the Crucifixion', p. 32, n. 2.

[144] For discussion, see *ibid.*, pp. 33–40.   [145] Again, see *ibid.*, pp. 40–1.

[146] Matthew XXVII.45, Mark XV.33 and Luke XXIII.44, Luke adding 'and the sun was darkened' (XXIII.45).

disruption of systematic nature, and towards the end of the sixth century Gregory the Great introduced the notion that the sun was acting out of deference to God by hiding its rays.[147] This element of refined sensibility attracted devotional attention, and in this vein we find the loss of light singled out and dwelt on intimately in a Latin prayer, *De tenebris*, included in the eighth/ninth-century Book of Nunnaminster (BL, Harley 2965), as an item in a cycle of prayers on the life of Christ, and especially details of his passion, which probably was developed in England in the eighth century:[148]

O misericordia simul et potentia qui es in omnibus honorifice laudandus, Quia in tua passione cuncta commota sunt et euentum dominici uulneris elimenta tremuerunt, Expauit dies non solita nocte et suas tenebras mundus inuenit, Etiam lux ipsa uisa est mori tecum ne a sacrilegis cernere uideris, Clauserat enim suos oculos caelum ne te in cruce aspiceret, Propter ea gratias agendo tuamque pietatem deposco . . . Amen

['O simultaneous mercy and might, you who are to be praised honourably in all things because in your passion all things were disturbed and the elements quaked at the event of their Lord's wound, the day became afraid at the unaccustomed night and the world discovered its shadows, even light itself seemed to die with you lest you should be discerned by the sacrilegious, indeed heaven had closed its eyes lest it should see you on the cross, in rendering thanks on account of those things I earnestly ask for your mercy . . ., amen'].[149]

Instead of Gregory's sun hiding its light, a day is imagined fearful of an unnatural night and the world is supposed finding its shadows. More fancifully still, light is represented as choosing to die itself in order to protect its Lord from shame, and heaven as refraining from looking. Appreciation of such a delicate conceit ('Propter ea gratias agendo') constituted the petitioner's recommendation for entrée to God's mighty presence.

In *The Dream of the Rood*, as in this prayer, the Bible's supervening darkness appears to have been conceived of as the interposition of an unnatural night, but with quite different consequences. In all its other three occurrences in the extant corpus of verse the collocation 'wann under

147 For a somewhat fuller account, and references, see Clemoes, 'King and Creation at the Crucifixion', p. 34.

148 Sims-Williams, *Religion and Literature in Western England*, p. 311.

149 *An Ancient Manuscript of the Eighth or Ninth Century*, ed. Birch, p. 74. For a complete text and translation, see Clemoes, 'King and Creation at the Crucifixion', p. 34–5.

wolcnum' (55a) was applied to night either replacing the sunlight of day (*Beowulf* 651a and *Guthlac* (*B*) 1280a) or giving way to it (*Andreas* 837a). In these contexts the designation of 'night' as *niht* (*Beowulf* 649b, *Guthlac* (*B*) 1281b and *Andreas* 834b) was expanded by reference to its darkness as *þystro* (*Guthlac* (*B*) 1281a), *sceadu* (*Andreas* 836b) or 'scaduhelma gesceapu' ('shapes of shadowy coverings', *Beowulf* 650a), *sceadu* in *Andreas* supplying the nominal modified by 'wonn under wolcnum'.[150] The darkness spreading at the crucifixion seems to have elicited from the poet the language traditionally associated with description of night's coming or going. The wording designating the brilliance which was overcome went further, however. It not merely implied a day, but potentially recalled day, as originally created. The alliterative exploitation of semantic contrast between *sciman* and *sceadu* in the coupling of the *a* and *b* verses of 54 calls to mind the similar device in a self-alliterating *a* verse in the account of the creator's separation of light from darkness ('et divisit lucem a tenebris', Genesis I.4) in *Genesis A*:

Þa gesundrode sigora waldend
ofer laguflode leoht wið þeostrum
sceade wið sciman

['Then the ruler of victories divided over the waters light from dark, shadow from brightness', 126–8a];

and when the *Genesis A* poet went on to describe the transition from day to night he provided our only instance of *scir* and *scima* in combination outside *The Dream of the Rood*:

metod æfter sceaf
scirum sciman, scippend ure,
æfen ærest

['after the bright radiance God, our creator, brought into being first evening', 136b–8a].

The *Dream* poet's verbal cluster of *sceadu*, *þystro*, *scir* and *scima* indicates that he might have been thinking of night at the crucifixion superseding divinely created day.

In fact, he exceeded even that. He imagined that the brilliance which night overcame was not the light of created day but an emanation of the

[150] And in *Beowulf* contributing to it. In *Guthlac B* the nominal is *norðrodor* ('swearc norðrodor / won under wolcnum' ('the northern sky grew dark . . .', 1279b–80a)).

mortal part of the crucified ruler himself, and rightly regarded this as a mystery supremely compelling all creation to weep. Old English poetry could have yielded no more sublime image from its reverence for spiritual light and no more faithful response to this image than universal reverential weeping as an event to be reported by an 'I have experienced, I have seen for myself' witness,[151] whom the prince of glory had appointed to represent living nature, as he had appointed the Virgin Mary to represent humanity (90–4). For this poet light did not die with the creator 'lest he should be discerned by the sacrilegious', as in the Nunnaminster prayer, but to enable the witnessing cross in future generations to be penitentially worshipped, towering in the sky 'leohte bewunden' ('enveloped in light', 5b), a *wuldres treow*, a *wuldres beam* 'tree of glory', 14b and 97b), adored by *eall þeos mære gesceaft*, 'all this glorious creation' (12b).[152]

Poetry's portrayal of tears in reaction to divine power and pity, whether those of St Helena revering the nails of the crucifixion or those of creation revering its dying creator, distilled highly complex feelings which were filtered through the network of religious culture, including its traditions of public liturgy and private devotion, its praying, praising and preaching, its rituals, its meditation, its symbols, its media of words, music, pictures and carvings. The emotions of the speaker of *The Seafarer* by contrast – 'Mæg ic be me sylfum soðgied wrecan' ('I can relate a true report about myself', 1) – issued directly from raw experience of this world as man's environment. His tale was of voyaging through seas that were at their darkest and coldest to the body and their most threatening and savage to the mind. He was recollecting

hu ic geswincdagum
earfoðhwile oft þrowade,
bitre breostceare gebiden hæbbe,
gecunnad in ceole cearselda fela,
atol yþa gewealc, þær mec oft begeat
nearo nihtwaco æt nacan stefnan,
þonne he be clifum cnossað. Calde geþrungen
wæron mine fet, forste gebunden,

[151] See above, p. 169.

[152] For the thematic repetition of *bewrigene*, referring to the covering of the cross by jewels in the dreamer's vision (17a), by *bewrigen*, referring to the covering of the brilliant body of the dead Christ by clouds in the cross's account of the crucifixion (53a), see Smith, 'The Garments that Honour the Cross', p. 30.

caldum clommum, þær þa ceare seofedun
hat ymb heortan; hungor innan slat
merewerges mod

['how in days of toil I often suffered a time of hardship, have experienced fierce anxiety in the breast, explored in my ship many abodes of sorrow, terrible rolling of waves, where an anxious nightwatch often took hold of me at the prow of the ship when it dashes by cliffs. My feet were constricted with cold, gripped by frost, by cold fetters, whereas sorrows sighed hot around the heart; hunger within rent the mind of the one wearied by the sea', 2b–12a].

Anxious sorrow had been the essence of this seafaring ('bitre breostceare', 'cearselda fela', 'nearo nihtwaco', 'þa ceare seofedun / hat ymb heortan'), a recurrent experience (*oft*, *fela*, *oft*) which was already taking on a representative character in the speaker's mind ('þonne he be clifum cnossað', 'merewerges mod'). A 'he who', 'anyone who' figure in an indefinite present,[153] representing a sheltered life on land, typified the opposite state of mind:

Þæt se mon ne wat
þe him on foldan fægrost limpeð,
hu ic earmcearig iscealdne sæ
winter wunade wræccan lastum,
winemægum bidroren,
bihongen hrimgicelum; hægl scurum fleag (12b–17).[154]

Each party, landsman and seafarer, lacked the other's experience ('Þæt se mon ne wat / . . . / hu ic . . .', 'winemægum bidroren'). Points of reference were being established in the speaker's mind for a voyage transcending these limitations.[155]

The God who was to be the lodestar for this venture is sparingly delineated. When dealing with men during this life or the next,[156] he is simply *dryhten*; when expressing his terrible power beyond the grave (101b), beyond the world he has established (103a) or beyond human thought (116a), he is simply *god* (101b) or *meotud*;[157] and when thanked and praised in eternity (122b–4), he is *se halga*, 'wuldres ealdor' and 'ece

[153] See above, pp. 82–5. [154] See above, p. 345.
[155] Cf. the observation that 'in no part of the poem does the speaker's actual "present" play a significant role' (Bately, 'Time and the Passing of Time in *The Wanderer*', p. 11).
[156] 43a, 65a, 106a, 121b and 124a. [157] 103a, 108a and 116a.

dryhten'. The first-person speaker of the poem[158] was the man to follow this lead beyond the bounds of time and space as we know them, for his exposure to nature at its harshest and mightiest, to the exclusion of all else, had given him the clearest sense of utter dependence on God that this life can afford (39–43): his experience had been so drained of everything that makes up normal good living that to his mind it prefigured life after death: his thoughts urged him to journey 'ofer holma gelagu' ('across the expanse of the seas', 64a)

Forþon me hatran sind
dryhtnes dreamas þonne þis deade lif,
læne on londe

['because the joys of the Lord are more alive for me than this dead, brief, life on land', 64b–6a].

Then came the turn of seafaring to become as generalized as the contrasted life on land: '. . . a hafað longunge se þe on lagu fundað' ('he who desires to voyage on the sea always has anxiety',[159] 47), the speaker declared. And next the coming of summer on land was associated with the desire to depart (48–55a), just as winter on the sea had been at the heart of seafaring itself (15a), so that the whole of seasonal, cyclical time and the whole of space seem involved; and through the cuckoo as a heralding image –

Swylce geac monað geomran reorde,
singeð sumeres weard, sorge beodeð
bitter in breostheord

['Likewise the cuckoo urges with its sad voice, the watchman of summer sings, announces keen sorrow to the mind in the breast', 53–5a] –

the suggestion is conveyed that cyclical time itself is essentially passing also. As Janet Bately has aptly commented, 'The cuckoo is a migrant, traditionally appearing in April and departing again in August – a fleeting visitor like Bede's sparrow, temporarily inhabiting the summer countryside just as man temporarily inhabits this world.'[160] One senses that 'each

[158] 1a, 2b, 6b, 9a, 14a, 18a, 20a, 29b, 34b, 36b, 37b, 58a, 59a, 61b, 64b and 66b; cf. *we* 117a, 117b, 118b, 119a and 119b and *usic* 123a.

[159] For a possible admixture of Christian 'yearning' in the meaning of *longunge*, see *The Seafarer*, ed. Gordon, p. 7.

[160] 'Time and the Passing of Time in *The Wanderer*', p. 6.

start to a new cycle of the seasons, each return of the cuckoo, brings the end of the world one year closer'.[161]

Abstraction had reached the point at which the speaker could proclaim a set of observations about all mortal life in the perspective of God's eternal present: each man is subject to intrinsic uncertainty and death (66b–71); everyone should seek the praise on earth and in heaven which outlast death (72–80a); the world is in decline (80b–9), and, just so, every man is subject to decay culminating in physical death (90–6); wealth will be of no avail to the sinful soul before the terrible power of God (97–102); the very earth will turn aside from the presence of God who has established (*gestaþelode*) the depths, the earth and the heights (103–5); he who does not fear God will be unprepared for death but God will secure (*gestaþelað*) the humble heart (106–8); a man must keep his mind fixed on that foundation (*on staþelum healdan*, 109–16); we should concentrate on our eternal destination and thank God that he has done us that honour (117–24). As in *The Wanderer*, so in this poem, God's supreme power over the universe which he has created was recognized as the only source of permanence in this inherently impermanent world, but, whereas the narrator of the other poem gradually comprehended the implications which this impermanence has for us,[162] in this one a speaker's earlier experience of submitting to God's absolute power provoked a transcendent yearning which in its turn gave way to settled belief in the ultimate virtue of labouring

þæt we to moten
in þa ecan eadignesse,
þær is lif gelong in lufan dryhtnes,
hyht in heofonum

['so that we may be allowed into the eternal blessedness, where life belongs to the love of the Lord, joy in heaven', 119b–22a].

For both the authors of these poems the key emanation from God to be looked for in response to the workings of the human mind was *ar*, 'help', 'mercy', 'grace': 'Wel bið þam þe him are seceð, / frofre to fæder on heofonum, þær us eal seo fæstnung stondeð' (114b–15),[163] *The Wanderer* poet declared at the conclusion to the poem which he had begun in a similar vein ('Oft him anhaga are gebideð, / metudes miltse' ('Often a man living alone experiences grace, God's mercy', 1–2a)), and likewise *The Seafarer* poet enunciated towards the end of his poem,

[161] *Ibid.* [162] See above, pp. 399–408. [163] See above, pp. 406–7.

Eadig bið se þe eaþmod leofaþ; cymeð him seo ar of heofonum,
meotod him þæt mod gestaþelað, forþon he in his meahte gelyfeð

['Blessed will he be who lives humble; the grace will come to him from heaven, God will keep his mind steadfast, because he believes in his power', 107–8].

In social tradition, as exemplified in *Beowulf*, the chief blessings of *ar* conferred by secular authority were security, stability, support and prosperity,[164] including the benefits of property and inheritance (2606–8), so that, when the source of true security became the Christian God beyond the confines of time and space (*on heofonum* (*The Wanderer* 115a), *of heofonum* (*The Seafarer* 107b)), it followed that divine *ar* came to be regarded as a strengthening of the mind, as in Beowulf's case when that hero was confronting Grendel –

. . . he gemunde mægenes strenge,
gimfæste gife, ðe him God sealde,
ond him to Anwaldan are gelyfde,
frofre ond fultum; ðy he þone feond ofercwom,
gehnægde helle gast

['he remembered the strength of his power, the liberal gift which God had granted him, and trusted in grace for him from the sole ruler, consolation and help; for that reason he overcame the enemy, laid low the spirit of hell', 1270–4a] –

and as the poet of *The Seafarer* affirmed (107b–8a).

This transfer to the mental level was not, however, the only change brought about: humility before the unqualified power of God (*metudes* (*The Wanderer* 1b), *meotod* (*The Seafarer* 108a)) became in *The Seafarer* specifically the state of mind essential for the reception of *ar* here on earth (*eaþmod* (*ibid.*, 107–8)). In *Guthlac A* too it was precisely the lack of this mental quality which, in the saint's eyes, debarred the previous devilish occupants from the *ar* of retaining possession of the hill which God had granted to him for a holy home:

Ge sind forscadene, on eow scyld siteð!
Ne cunnon ge dryhten duguðe biddan,
ne mid eaðmedum are secan

['You are routed, guilt fills you! You are unable to ask the Lord for benefit, nor seek grace through humility', 478–80].

[164] 293–6a, 1096b–1101, 1181b–3, 1184–7 and 2375–9a.

This humility had been the distinctive contribution of the cross when mediating between the absolute king of the universe who had been crucified (*god ælmihtig* (*The Dream of the Rood* 39b), *weruda god* (51b), (*rice*) *cyning* (44b and 56a), *wealdend* (53b), 'heofona hlaford' (45a) and *frea mancynnes* (33b)) and the humans eager (*fuse* 57a) to receive the body in which this divine power had suffered triumphantly (*ælmihtig god* (60b), *heofenes dryhten* (64a), *sigora wealdend* (67a) and *se mæra þoeden* (69a)):

Sare ic wæs mid sorgum gedrefed, hnag ic hwæðre þam secgum to handa,
eaðmod elne mycle. Genamon hie þær ælmihtigne god,
ahofon hine of ðam hefian wite

['Greviously was I distressed with sorrows, yet I bowed down to those men's hands, humble, very eagerly. They took almighty God there, removed him from the heavy punishment', 59–61a].[165]

And it was this same humility which made perfect the saintly death of Guthlac in *Guthlac B*, although unmentioned in the Latin which was the poet's source:[166]

Ahof þa his honda, husle gereorded,
eaðmod þy æfelan gyfle, swylce he his eagan ontynde,
halge heafdes gimmas, biseah þa to heofona rice,
glædmod to geofona leanum, ond þa his gæst onsende
weorcum wlitigne in wuldres dream

['Then he raised his hands, refreshed by the eucharist, humble because of the noble morsel, likewise he opened his eyes, holy jewels of the head, then looked towards the kingdom of heaven, joyful in mind for the rewards of graces, and then sent his spirit, beautiful through its deeds, into the pleasure of glory', 1300–4].

Spiritual humility called for a poetry of address operating on a radically different scale from that of social exchange. For instance, when Beowulf, newly arrived, appealed to King Hrothgar –

[165] It is uncertain whether an equivalent to 'eaðmod elne mycle' (Vercelli text 60a) ever formed part of the now imperfect Ruthwell inscription; cf. above, p. 472, n. 143.

[166] 'et extendens manus ad altare, munivit se communione corporis et sanguinis Christi, atque elevatis oculis ad caelum extensisque in altum manibus, animam ad gaudia perpetuae exultationis emisit' ('and, stretching his hands towards the altar, he fortified himself by the communion of Christ's body and blood, and, with his eyes raised to heaven and his hands extended aloft, sent forth his spirit to the joys of perpetual bliss', *Felix's 'Life' of St Guthlac*, ch. 50 (ed. Colgrave, p. 158)).

Ic þe nu ða,
brego Beorht-Dena, biddan wille,
eodor Scyldinga, anre bene,
þæt ðu me ne forwyrne, wigendra hleo,
freowine folca, nu ic þus feorran com,
þæt ic mote ana ond minra eorla gedryht,
þes hearda heap, Heorot fælsian

['I now wish to request you, chief of the Bright-Danes, for a particular favour, protector of the Scyldings, that you will not refuse me, protector of warriors, noble friends of peoples, now I have come thus far, that I in particular and the company of my warriors, this brave troop, may be permitted to purge Heorot', *Beowulf* 426b–32] –

his four symbolic epithets for his welcomer (427a, 428a, 429b and 430a), gathering force in meaning and placing, were variations of a homogeneous courtliness assured of a response in like manner.[167] But, when St Juliana, in prison after being savagely tortured and before being confronted by the devil disguised as an angel, praised in her heart God's universal power –

Symle heo wuldorcyning
herede æt heortan, heofonrices god,
in þam nydclafan, nergend fira,
heolstre bihelmad. Hyre wæs halig gæst
singal gesið

['Always she praised the king of glory in her heart, God of the kingdom of heaven, in that forced confinement, the saviour of men, covered with darkness. The holy spirit was her constant companion', *Juliana* 238b–42a] –

her trio of appellations (238b, 239 and 240b), invoking the divine dominion first as a whole, then in all heaven and then on all earth, alternated with evocations of their origin in her heart, in her confinement, and in her encompassing darkness (239a, 240a and 241a). Reference oscillated to and fro between ultimate glory and restrictive local darkness. The social parameters of *Beowulf*ian speech were replaced by the limitlessness of dramatic cosmic contrasts. Christianity created a huge 'space' for movement which was more complex, more unexpected and more flexible: here was room for swirling, curving, darting patterns of human spirituality in unequal contact with the godhead in various 'theatrically' contrived situations; here God could speak; here Christ could appear unrecognized or

167 Cf. the stylistic analysis of 350b–3, above, pp. 130–1.

recognized (as in *Andreas*); here the holy spirit could comfort a human heart with constancy (*Juliana* 241b–2a) steadying zigzagging thoughts (238b–41a); at another it could adopt a subtle pace when entering a penitent's heart, as in the 'Jerusalem' Advent lyric.[168]

This entirety of spiritual 'space' greatly enlarged Old English poetry's traditional scope for dramatic portrayal of the workings of an organically interactive system. The anonymous poet of *Guthlac B*, for one, displayed true native genius when creating out of Felix's separate features of scent, light and angelic song an integrated representation of a model noble soul passing from the cyclical time and space of this world into the constant glory of the next in confident progress from one phase of a consistently spiritual life to another.[169]

In the first place, in this poet's version the saint's attendant, named in the Latin source but not here, receded into the background once he had elicited from his master the explanation that the visitor, whom he had heard conversing spiritually (1220b) with his *fæder* (1211a) morning and evening over a long period (1239b–41a), had been 'gæst haligne, / engel ufancundne' ('a holy spirit, a heavenly angel', 1241b–2a): after this earthly companion had thus prompted the saint, approaching death, to make explicit the celestial dimension of his life in this world, the poet used him only to perform one further, similar, rôle by hearing his master, now on the point of dying, say 'Nu of lice is, / goddreama georn, gæst swiðe fus' ('Now, desirous of the joys of God, the spirit is very eager to leave the body', 1298b–9). From his overarching spiritual perspective the vernacular author did not require this human figure, as Felix had done, to witness authenticatingly a bright light illuminating the place of death the night before the saint died and a tower, as of fire, shining upward from the place the day after. To him these were simply marvels, like the scent and angels' song, signifying as such the celestial intervention, which marked Guthlac's transition from mortality to immortality just as it had his mortal life.[170]

168 See above, pp. 453–6.

169 Several critics have placed *Guthlac B* in the context of large themes in Christian thought, but I have felt able to leave these considerations aside as not essential to my particular purpose of discussing the poet's version in relation to the tradition of Old English poetry itself; for a recent summary of these other concerns, see Lucas, 'Easter, the Death of St Guthlac and the Liturgy for Holy Saturday', p. 2.

170 Lucas (*ibid.*, pp. 3–11), pointing out the ways in which the poet emphasized the connection between the Easter season and the course of the saint's illness culminating in his death on the Wednesday after Easter, argues for special influence from the liturgy for

For the fiery brightness which, according to Felix, the attendant saw lighting up the whole house from midnight until dawn,[171] the poet substituted a holy light from heaven interposing itself in the normal sequence of day and night so as to annul the latter and illuminate the saint while he endured the last pangs of mortality:

Þa se æþela glæm
setlgong sohte, swearc norðrodor
won under wolcnum, woruld miste oferteah,
þystrum beþeahte, þrong niht ofer tiht
londes frætwa. Ða cwom leohta mæst
halig of heofonum hædre scinan,
beorhte ofer burgsalu. Bad se þe sceolde
eadig on elne endedogor,
awrecen wælstrælum. Wuldres scima,
æþele ymb æþelne, ondlonge niht
scan swirwered. Scadu sweþredon,
tolysed under lyfte. Wæs se leohta glæm
ymb þæt halge hus, heofonlic condel,
from æfenglome oþþæt eastan cwom
ofer deop gelad dægredwoma,
wedertacen wearm

['Then the noble radiance sought its setting, the northern sky darkened, dusky beneath the clouds, the world was covered with mist, spread over with gloom, night pressed on across the expanse of the earth's adornments. Then the greatest of lights, holy from heaven, came shining clearly, brightly above the dwellings. He who had to awaited his last day, blessed in endurance, pierced with fatal arrows. The splendour of glory shone clothed with radiance the whole night long, noble around the noble one. Shadows weakened, unloosed beneath the sky. The brilliant light remained round the holy house, a heavenly candle, from twilight until the break of day came from the east up over its deep way, the sign of warm weather', 1278b–93a].

The threefold experience which, in Felix's version, Guthlac's attendant

Holy Saturday. Particularly relevant to my concerns are his opinions that 'heofonlic condel' dispelling the darkness of night (1290b; see below) was a reference to the Paschal candle, that the association in the liturgy between the candle and the Israelites' pillar of fire had some effect on the poet's conception of the tower as of fire and that the music of the choir and the perfume of incense were also influential.

[171] *Felix's 'Life' of St Guthlac*, ch. 50 (ed. Colgrave, p. 158).

had while the saint was dying,[172] likewise changed its character in the poet's treatment. Felix's Beccel suddenly saw a heavenly light filling the house and a tower as of fire stretching from earth to heaven and making the sun in mid-sky grow pale like a lamp in daytime; he heard the whole air thundering with angelic songs; and it seemed to him as though the island were filled with the sweet scents of diverse spices.[173] The poet's version, on the other hand, firstly specified the light's starting-point as the corpse left lifeless when angels led the saint's spirit up to long-lasting bliss, then associated the upward beam with the song of angels in the sky, and lastly attributed to the earthly home left by Guthlac's spirit a joyous blend of sweet smells and heavenly music, which, glorifying God in noise after noise, surpassed anything describable in worldly terms and made the island tremble (whereas in the Latin it had been Beccel who had shaken with terror):

Ða wæs Guðlaces gæst gelæded
eadig on upweg. Englas feredun
to þam longan gefean, lic colode,
belifd under lyfte. Ða þær leoht ascan,
beama beorhtast. Eal þæt beacen wæs
ymb þæt halge hus, heofonlic leoma,
from foldan up swylce fyren tor
ryht aræred oð rodera hrof,
gesewen under swegle, sunnan beorhtra,
æþeltungla wlite. Engla þreatas
sigeleoð sungon, sweg wæs on lyfte
gehyred under heofonum, haligra dream.
Swa se burgstede wæs blissum gefylled,
swetum stencum ond sweglwundrum,
eadges yrfestol, engla hleoðres,
eal innanweard. Þær wæs ænlicra
ond wynsumra þonne hit in worulde mæge
stefn areccan, hu se stenc ond se sweg,
heofonlic hleoþor ond se halga song,
gehyred wæs, heahþrym godes,
breahtem æfter breahtme. Beofode þæt ealond,
foldwong onþrong

['Then Guthlac's spirit was conducted, blessed on its way up. Angels brought it to

[172] For the manner of Guthlac's death, see above, p. 480, n. 166.

[173] *Felix's 'Life' of St Guthlac*, ch. 50 (ed. Colgrave, p. 158).

the long joy, the body grew cool, deprived of life beneath the sky. Then a light shone forth there, the brightest of beams. All the beacon was round the holy house, a heavenly radiance, up from the earth like a fiery tower raised straight to the roof of the heavens, seen under the sky brighter than the sun, the splendour of noble stars. Companies of angels sang a song of victory, music was heard in the sky under heaven, the rejoicing of holy ones. In the same way the dwelling-place was filled with joys, all the inside of the blessed one's home with sweet scents and heavenly wonders of the voice of angels. There it was more splendid and delightful than any voice in the world could relate, how the scent and the music, heavenly voice and the holy song was heard, high praise of God, noise after noise. The island trembled, the earthly plain became unfirm', 1305–26a].'

For the poet the passing of this blessed spirit was an event involving all God's kingdom of heaven and earth. Felix, claiming the authority of Beccel,[174] had already associated with it features usually reserved for the elevation of relics, especially for the discovery of an incorrupt body,[175] and the vernacular author took these hints to their logical conclusion. Guthlac's transition from mortality to immortality was an example of *gæst* transcending the differences between heaven and earth and quickening the whole of the spiritual realm, just as, for the poet of the Advent lyrics, from the mystery of Christ's incarnation 'Eal giofu gæstlic grundsceat geondspreot' ('Every spiritual gift had sprung up throughout the earth', *Christ* (*I*) 42). Both events alike belonged purely to the spiritual plane of God's universal kingdom, and it was to action on this distinct level that the *Guthlac B* poet brought his skills to bear so effectively in passages such as

Ða wæs Guðlaces gæst gelæded
eadig on upweg. Englas feredun
to þam longan gefean, lic colode,
belifd under lyfte. Ða þær leoht ascan (1305–8),

with its thematic series of associative or contrastive alliterative links between *Guðlaces* and *gæst*, between 'eadig on upweg' and *Englas* and between *þam longan gefean*, *lic*, 'belifd under lyfte' and *leoht*. The linear language, especially by enfolding the mortal (1307b–8a) within the immortal (1307a and 1308b) in the four-verse l- alliterating sequence (1307–8), effortlessly organized the elements of individual saintly spirit, blessedness in ascent, angels, eternal joy, body, sub-celestial mortality and supernatural light into a single artistic whole.

[174] *Ibid.* (p. 152).

[175] The sweet odour and the heavenly light; see Colgrave's note, *ibid.*, p. 193.

Old English poetry, traditionally community based, was redirected to the Christian community of the spirit. Because it had habitually focused on actions in the past and the present which demonstrated the analogies underlying social generalization, it was prepared to respect the sequential primacy of the creation and fall, the incarnation, redemption and resurrection and the general judgement ahead, and because its regular treatment of the past and the present as a single organism had already crystallized linear time into a uniform social consensus it was ready to set the sweep of Christian history in the overriding perspective of God's everlasting constancy. Furthermore, because poetry had been the organ of an aristocratic hierarchical society, it could easily conceive of the immensity of God's spiritual kingdom peopled with mighty agents of his power, and, because it was accustomed to the exercise of secular authority across group boundaries in an unbroken drama of alliances and feuds, it brought that familiarity to the continuous narrative of successes and failures in God's dealings with the instability of mortal men and the persistent evil of unredeemed spirits. Most impressive of all is the directness of imagination with which vernacular poets animated the whole spiritual universe, when setting before us unforgettably the awful moment at which the son of God sacrificed himself by crucifixion in the world he had originally created perfect; or when giving us carefully crafted images of a Christ-bird flying to and fro between heaven and earth in matchless strength of spirit and of a Christ-leaper restoring salvation and grace to mankind; or when sharing with us the musing of a reflective, learned mind appreciating from humble devotion the compassion of God subtly moving down from heaven through the Virgin Mary and the church into the individual soul; or when presenting us unequivocally with a seafarer's intense loneliness nurturing belief that the love of God lies everlastingly beyond; or when imparting an uplifting sensation of celestial light, scent and praise of God filling heaven and earth with glory while angels escort a saint's eager spirit to unending joy. In a world of matter infused with spirit a heady mixture of radiance, scent and song, glorifying the departure of Guthlac's spirit to heaven, replaced the sturdy cooperation of beneficent wind and sea and human skill and confidence, constituting Beowulf's victorious return home to Geatland. Poets' instinctive recognition of the quintessential vitality of God's spiritual rule inspired them to adapt the customary resources of their art to the new bearings of this eternal realm and to create exemplary narratives of all its elements – men, nature and supranature – in interaction with one another and, especially, in shared interaction with their divine overlord. They followed Cædmon's precedent (knowingly or not) by expanding traditional conceptions of authority into an all-powerful, eternal figure,[176] as in *Beowulf* and *Guthlac A*; by acknowledging this supreme Lord to be a source of security beyond any in this world,[177] as in *The Wanderer* and *The Seafarer*; and by worshipping this spiritual being as a glorious progenitor,[178] as in the Advent lyrics and Cynewulf's poems.

[176] 'metudæs maecti end his modgidanc' ('the power of God and his thought', *Cædmon's Hymn* 2), 'eci dryctin' ('eternal Lord', 4a and 8a) and 'frea allmectig' ('almighty Lord', 9b).

[177] 'hefaenricaes uard' ('guardian of the kingdom of heaven', *ibid.*, 1b) and 'moncynnæs uard' ('guardian of mankind', 7b).

[178] 'uerc uuldurfadur' ('work of the glorious father', *ibid.*, 3a) and 'haleg scepen' ('holy creator', 6b).

Works cited

Adriaen, M., ed., *Gregorii Magni Moralia in Iob*, 3 vols., CCSL 143, 143A and 143B (Turnhout, 1979–85)

Allen, M.J.B., and D.G. Calder, trans., *Sources and Analogues of Old English Poetry: the Major Latin Texts in Translation* (Cambridge, 1976)

Amos, A.C., *et al.*, ed., *Dictionary of Old English* (Toronto, 1988–)

Anderson, E.R., '"Flyting" in *The Battle of Maldon*', *NM* 71 (1970), 197–202

Andrew, M., 'Grendel in Hell', *ES* 62 (1981), 401–10

Archibald, E., *Apollonius of Tyre: Medieval and Renaissance Themes and Variations* (Cambridge, 1991)

Backhouse, J., D.H. Turner and L. Webster, ed., *The Golden Age of Anglo-Saxon Art 966–1066* (London, 1984)

Bandy, S.C., 'Cain, Grendel, and the Giants of *Beowulf*', *Papers on Language and Literature* 9 (1973), 235–49

Barley, N.F., 'Structural Aspects of the Anglo-Saxon Riddle', *Semiotica* 10 (1974), 143–75

Bassett, S., ed., *The Origins of Anglo-Saxon Kingdoms* (Leicester, 1989)

Bately, J., 'World History in the *Anglo-Saxon Chronicle:* its Sources and its Separateness from the Old English Orosius', *ASE* 8 (1979), 177–94

'Lexical Evidence for the Authorship of the Prose Psalms in the Paris Psalter', *ASE* 10 (1982), 69–95

'Time and the Passing of Time in *The Wanderer* and Related OE Texts', *Essays and Studies* ns 37 (1984), 1–15

'Those Books that are Most Necessary for All Men to Know: the Classics and Late Ninth-Century England, a Reappraisal', in *The Classics in the Middle Ages*, ed. A.S. Bernardo and S. Levin (Binghamton, NY, 1990), pp. 45–78

Bately, J., ed., *The Old English Orosius*, EETS ss 6 (London, 1980)

Bazire, J., and J.E. Cross, ed., *Eleven Old English Rogationtide Homilies* (Toronto, 1982)

Becker, G., *Geist und Seele im Altsächsischen und im Althochdeutschen* (Heidelberg, 1964)

Beckwith, J., *Ivory Carvings in Early Medieval England* (London, 1972)

Beskow, P., *Rex Gloriae: the Kingship of Christ in the Early Church* (Stockholm, 1962)

Bessinger, J.B., Jr, and R.P. Creed, ed., *Medieval and Linguistic Studies in Honor of Francis Peabody Magoun, Jr* (London, 1965)

Bessinger, J.B., Jr, and P.H. Smith, *A Concordance to the Anglo-Saxon Poetic Records* (Ithaca, NY, and London, 1978)

Bethurum, D., 'Stylistic Features of the Old English Laws', *MLR* 27 (1932), 263–79

Bethurum, D., ed., *The Homilies of Wulfstan* (Oxford, 1957)

Betz, W., 'Die frühdeutschen spiritus-Übersetzungen und die Anfänge des Wortes *geist*', *Liturgie und Mönchtum* 20 (1957), 48–55

Biddle, M. and B. Kjølbye-Biddle, 'The Repton Stone', *ASE* 14 (1985), 233–92

Biggs, F.M., *The Sources of 'Christ III': a Revision of Cook's Notes*, OEN Subsidia 12 (1986)

'The Passion of Andreas: *Andreas* 1398–1491', *SP* 85 (1988), 413–27

Birch, W. de Gray, ed., *An Ancient Manuscript of the Eighth or Ninth Century: formerly belonging to St Mary's Abbey, or Nunnaminster, Winchester* (London and Winchester, 1889)

Bischoff, B., M. Budny, G. Harlow, M.B. Parkes and J.D. Pheifer, ed., *The Épinal, Erfurt, Werden, and Corpus Glossaries*, EEMF 22 (Copenhagen, 1988)

Blatt, F., ed., *Die lateinischen Bearbeitungen der Acta Andreae et Matthiae apud anthropophagos* (Giessen, 1930)

Bliss, A.J., ed., *Sir Orfeo*, 2nd ed. (Oxford, 1966)

Bliss, A., and A.J. Frantzen, 'The Integrity of *Resignation*', *RES* ns 27 (1976), 385–402

Bologna, C., ed., *Liber monstrorum de diversis generibus* (Milan, 1977)

Boyd, N., 'Doctrine and Criticism: a Revaluation of *Genesis A*', *NM* 83 (1982), 230–8

Brady, C., 'The Old English Nominal Compounds in *-rád*', *PMLA* 67 (1952), 538–71

'The Synonyms for "Sea" in *Beowulf*, in *Studies in Honor of Albert Morey Sturtevant*, University of Kansas Publications, Humanistic Studies 29 (Lawrence, KA, 1952), 22–46

'"Weapons" in *Beowulf*: an Analysis of the Nominal Compounds and an Evaluation of the Poet's Use of them', *ASE* 8 (1979), 79–141

Breeze, A., 'The Virgin Mary, Daughter of her Son', *Etudes Celtiques* 27 (1990), 267–83

Bright, J.W., 'Cynewulf's *Christ* 495 and 528', *MLN* 13 (1898), 14

Bright, J.W., and R.L Ramsay, ed., *Liber psalmorum: the West-Saxon Psalms, being the Prose Portion, or the 'First Fifty', of the So-Called Paris Psalter* (Boston and London, 1907)

Brockman, B.A., '"Heroic"and "Christian" in *Genesis A*: the Evidence of the Cain and Abel Episode', *MLQ* 35 (1974), 115–28

Brodeur, A.G., *The Art of 'Beowulf'* (Berkeley and Los Angeles, 1959)

'A Study of Diction and Style in Three Anglo-Saxon Narrative Poems', in *Nordica et Anglica: Studies in Honor of Stefán Einarsson*, ed. A.H. Orrick (The Hague and Paris, 1968), pp. 97–114

Brooks, N., 'Weapons and Armour', in *The Battle of Maldon AD 991*, ed. D. Scragg (Oxford, 1991), pp. 208–19

Brown, P.R., G.R. Crampton and F.C. Robinson, ed., *Modes of Interpretation in Old English Literature: Essays in Honour of Stanley B. Greenfield* (Toronto, 1986)

Brown, T.J., *et al.*, ed., *The Durham Ritual*, EEMF 16 (Copenhagen, 1969)

Bruce-Mitford, R., *Aspects of Anglo-Saxon Archaeology: Sutton Hoo and other Discoveries* (London, 1974)

The Sutton Hoo Ship Burial: a Handbook, 3rd ed. (London, 1979)

Bruce-Mitford, R., *et al.*, *The Sutton Hoo Ship-Burial*, 3 vols. in 4 (London, 1975–83)

Bullough, D.A., *Friends, Neighbours and Fellow-Drinkers: Aspects of Community and Conflict in the Early Medieval West*, H.M. Chadwick Memorial Lectures 1 (Cambridge, 1990)

Burlin, R.B., *The Old English 'Advent': a Typological Commentary*, Yale Studies in English 168 (New Haven, CT, 1968)

Burlin, R.B., and E.B. Irving, Jr, ed., *Old English Studies in Honour of John C. Pope* (Toronto and Buffalo, 1974)

Butturff, D., 'The Monsters and the Scholar: an Edition and Critical Study of the *Liber monstrorum*' (unpubl. PhD dissertation, Univ. of Illinois, 1968)

Calder, D.G., *Cynewulf* (Boston, 1981)

'Figurative Language and its Contexts in *Andreas:* a Study in Medieval Expressionism', in *Modes of Interpretation in Old English Literature*, ed. Brown, Crampton and Robinson, pp. 115–36

Calder, D.G., ed., *Old English Poetry: Essays on Style* (Berkeley, CA, 1979)

Cameron, M.L., 'Aldhelm as Naturalist: a Re-examination of some of his *Enigmata*', *Peritia* 4 (1985), 117–33

Campbell, A., 'The Use in *Beowulf* of Earlier Heroic Verse', in *England before the Conquest*, ed. Clemoes and Hughes, pp. 283–92

Campbell, J.J., ed., *The Advent Lyrics of the Exeter Book* (Princeton, NJ, 1959)

'Adaptation of Classical Rhetoric in Old English Literature', in *Medieval Eloquence*, ed. J.J. Murphy (Berkeley, CA, 1978), pp. 173–97

Carney, J., ed. and trans., *The Poems of Blathmac Son of Cú Brettan* (London, 1964)

Carnicelli, T.A., ed., *King Alfred's Version of St Augustine's 'Soliloquies'* (Cambridge, MA, 1969)

Carozzi, C., ed., *Adalbéron de Laon, 'Poème au roi Robert'*, Les classiques de l'histoire de France au moyen âge 32 (Paris, 1979)

Cassidy, B., ed., *The Ruthwell Cross* (Princeton, NJ, 1992)

Cassidy, F.G., 'How Free was the Anglo-Saxon Scop?', in *Medieval and Linguistic Studies*, ed. Bessinger and Creed, pp. 75–85

Chadwick, N.K., 'The Monsters and *Beowulf*', in *The Anglo-Saxons*, ed. Clemoes, pp. 171–203

Chambers, R.W., M. Förster and R. Flower, ed., *The Exeter Book of Old English Poetry* (London, 1933)

Charles-Edwards, T., 'Early Medieval Kingships in the British Isles', in *The Origins of Anglo-Saxon Kingdoms*, ed. Bassett, pp. 28–39 and 245–8

Chase, C., ed., *The Dating of 'Beowulf'* (Toronto, 1981)

Clark, C., 'Onomastics', in *The Cambridge History of the English Language: I. The Beginnings to 1066*, ed. R.M. Hogg (Cambridge, 1992), pp. 452–89

Clayton, M., *The Cult of the Virgin Mary in Anglo-Saxon England*, CSASE 2 (Cambridge, 1990)

Cleasby, R., and G. Vigfusson, *An Icelandic-English Dictionary*, 2nd ed. with supp. by W.A. Craigie (Oxford, 1957)

Clemoes, P., 'Ælfric', in *Continuations and Beginnings: Studies in Old English Literature*, ed. E.G. Stanley (London, 1966), pp. 176–209

'*Mens absentia cogitans* in *The Seafarer* and *The Wanderer*', in *Medieval Literature and Civilization: Studies in Memory of G.N. Garmonsway*, ed. D.A. Pearsall and R.A. Waldron (London, 1969), pp. 62–77

Rhythm and Cosmic Order in Old English Christian Literature (an inaugural lecture, Cambridge, 1970)

'Cynewulf's Image of the Ascension', in *England before the Conquest*, ed. Clemoes and Hughes, pp. 293–304

'Action in *Beowulf* and our Perception of it', in *Old English Poetry*, ed. Calder, pp. 147–68

'Style as the Criterion for Dating the Composition of *Beowulf*', in *The Dating of 'Beowulf'*, ed. Chase, pp. 173–85

The Cult of St Oswald on the Continent, Jarrow Lecture (Jarrow, 1983)

'Language in Context: *her* in the 890 *Anglo-Saxon Chronicle*', in *Sources and Relations: Studies in Honour of J.E. Cross*, ed. M. Collins, J. Price and A. Hamer, *Leeds Studies in English* ns 16 (1985), 27–36

'"Symbolic" Language in Old English Poetry', in *Modes of Interpretation in Old English Literature*, ed. Brown, Crampton, and Robinson, pp. 3–14

'King Alfred's Debt to Vernacular Poetry: the Evidence of *ellen* and *cræft*', in *Words, Texts and Manuscripts*, ed. Korhammer, pp. 213–38

'King and Creation at the Crucifixion: the Contribution of Native Tradition to *The Dream of the Rood* 50–6a', in *Heroes and Heroines in Medieval English Literature: a Festschrift presented to André Crépin on the Occasion of his Sixty-Fifth Birthday*, ed. L. Carruthers, pp. 31–43

Clemoes, P., ed., *The Anglo-Saxons: Studies in some Aspects of their History and Culture presented to Bruce Dickins* (London, 1959)

Clemoes, P., and K. Hughes, ed., *England before the Conquest: Studies in Primary Sources presented to Dorothy Whitelock* (Cambridge, 1971)

Clubb, M.D., ed., *Christ and Satan*, Yale Studies in English 70 (New Haven, CT, 1925)

Colgrave, B., ed., *Two Lives of St Cuthbert* (Cambridge, 1940)

Felix's 'Life' of St Guthlac (Cambridge, 1956)

Colgrave, B., *et al.*, ed., *The Paris Psalter*, EEMF 8 (Copenhagen, 1958)

Colgrave, B. and R.A.B. Mynors, ed., *Bede's Ecclesiastical History of the English People* (Oxford, 1969; cited as Bede, *HE*)

Cook, A.S., ed., *The Christ of Cynewulf* (Boston, 1900)

Cramp, R., *County Durham and Northumberland*, British Academy Corpus of Anglo-Saxon Stone Sculpture in England 1 (Oxford, 1984)

Crawford, S.J., ed., *The Old English Version of the Heptateuch*, EETS os 160 (London, 1922; repr. with additional transcriptions by N.R. Ker, London, 1969)

Crépin, A., 'Poétique Vieil-Anglaise: designations du Dieu Chrétien' (thèse de doctorat ès lettres présentée à l'Université de Paris, Amiens, 1969)

Cross, J.E., '"Ubi Sunt" Passages in Old English – Sources and Relationships', *Vetenskaps-Societetens i Lund Årsbok* (1956), 25–44

'The Ethic of War in Old English', in *England Before the Conquest*, ed. Clemoes and Hughes, pp. 269–82

'The Apostles in the *Old English Martyrology*', *Mediaevalia* 5 (1979), 15–59

'Cynewulf's Traditions about the Apostles in *Fates of the Apostles*', *ASE* 8 (1979), 163–75

'On the Library of the Old English Martyrologist', in *Learning and Literature in Anglo-Saxon England*, ed. Lapidge and Gneuss, pp. 227–49

Cross, J.E., and T.D. Hill, ed., *The 'Prose Solomon and Saturn' and 'Adrian and Ritheus'* (Toronto, 1982)

Cross, J.E., and S.I. Tucker, 'Allegorical Tradition and the OE *Exodus*', *Neophilologus* 44 (1960), 122–7

Day, V., 'The Influence of the Catechetical *Narratio* on some other Medieval Literature', *ASE* 3 (1974), 51–61

Dewick, E.S., and W.H. Frere, ed., *The Leofric Collectar*, 2 vols., HBS 45 and 56 (London, 1914–21)

Doane, A.N., ed., *Genesis A: a New Edition* (Madison, WI, 1978)

The Saxon Genesis (Madison, WI, 1991)

Dodwell, C.R., and P. Clemoes, ed., *The Old English Illustrated Hexateuch (British Museum Cotton Claudius B. iv)*, EEMF 18 (Copenhagen, 1974)

Donoghue, D., *Style in Old English Poetry: the Test of the Auxiliary*, Yale Studies in English 196 (New Haven, CT, 1987)

Dubuisson, D., 'L'Irlande et la théorie médiévale des "trois ordres"', *Revue de l'histoire des religions* 188 (1975), 35–63

Dumville, D.N., 'English Square Minuscule Script: the Background and Earliest Phases', *ASE* 16 (1957), 147–79

'Beowulf Come Lately: some Notes on the Palaeography of the Nowell Codex', *ASNSL* 225 (1988), 51–63

Dunning, T.P., and A.J. Bliss, ed., *The Wanderer* (London, 1969)

Dyer, J., 'The Singing of Psalms in the Early-Medieval Office', *Speculum* 64 (1989), 535–78

Earl, J.W., 'Christian Traditions in the Old English *Exodus*', *NM* 71 (1970), 541–70

'The Typological Structure of *Andreas*', in *Old English Literature in Context: Ten Essays*, ed. J.D. Niles (Woodbridge and Totowa, NJ, 1980), pp. 66–89

Ehwald, R., ed., *Aldhelmi Opera*, MGH, Auctores Antiquissimi 15 (Berlin, 1919)

Endter, W., ed., *König Alfreds des Grossen Bearbeitung der Soliloquien des Augustinus*, Bibliothek der angelsächsischen Prosa 11 (Hamburg, 1922; repr. Darmstadt, 1964)

Evans, D.A.H., ed., *Hávamál* (London, 1986)

Fehr, B., ed., *Die Hirtenbriefe Ælfrics*, Bibliothek der angelsächsischen Prosa 9 (Hamburg, 1914; repr. with a supp. to the introduction by P. Clemoes, Darmstadt, 1966)

Foley, J.M., *Oral-Formulaic Theory and Research: an Introduction and Annotated Bibliography* (New York, 1985)

Frank, R., 'What Kind of Poetry is *Exodus?*' in *Germania: Comparative Studies in the Old Germanic Languages and Literatures*, ed. D.G. Calder and T.C. Christy (Wolfeboro, NH, and Woodbridge, 1988), pp. 191–205

Frankis, P.J., 'The Thematic Significance of *enta geweorc* and Related Imagery in *The Wanderer*', *ASE* 2 (1973), 253–69

Frantzen, A.J., *The Literature of Penance in Anglo-Saxon England* (New Brunswick, NJ, 1983)

Fritzner, J., *Ordbog over Det gamle norske Sprog*, 3 vols. (Kristiania, 1886–96; repr. Oslo, 1954)

Fry, D.K., 'Exeter Book Riddle Solutions', *OEN* 15.1 (1981), 22–31

Gatch, M.McC., *Loyalties and Traditions* (New York, 1971)

'King Alfred's Version of the *Soliloquia*', in *Studies in Earlier Old English Prose*, ed. Szarmach, pp. 17–45

Gattiker, G.L., 'The Syntactic Basis of the Poetic Formula in *Beowulf* (unpubl. PhD dissertation, Wisconsin Univ., 1962)

Gerritsen, J., 'Have With You to Lexington! The *Beowulf* Manuscript and

Beowulf, in *In Other Words: Trans-Cultural Studies in Philology, Translation and Lexicography presented to Prof. dr H.H. Meier*, ed. J.L. Mackenzie and R. Todd (Dordrecht, 1989), pp. 15–34

Glorie, F., ed., *Collectiones aenigmatum Merovingicae aetatis*, 2 vols., CCSL 133–133A (Turnhout, 1968)

Glorieux, P., *Pour revaloriser Migne* (Lille, 1952)

Gneuss, H., *Lehnbildungen und Lehnbedeutungen im Altenglischen* (Berlin, 1955)

Hymnar und Hymnen im englischen Mittelalter (Tübingen, 1968)

'*The Battle of Maldon* 89: Byrhtnoð's *ofermod* Once Again', *SP* 73 (1976), 117–37

Die 'Battle of Maldon' als historisches und literarisches Zeugnis, Bayerische Akademie der Wissenschaften, philosophisch-historische Klasse, Sitzungsberichte 1976.5 (Munich, 1976)

'A Preliminary List of Manuscripts Written or Owned in England up to 1100', *ASE* 9 (1981), 1–60

'King Alfred and the History of Anglo-Saxon Libraries', in *Modes of Interpretation in Old English Literature*, ed. Brown, Crampton and Robinson, pp. 29–49

The Study of Language in Anglo-Saxon England, Toller Lecture (Manchester, 1990; repr. from *BJRL* 72 (1990), 3–32)

Godden, M.R., 'An Old English Penitential Motif', *ASE* 2 (1973), 221–39

'Anglo-Saxons on the Mind', in *Learning and Literature in Anglo-Saxon England*, ed. Lapidge and Gneuss, pp. 271–98

'Money, Power and Morality in Late Anglo-Saxon England', *ASE* 19 (1990), 41–65

Godden, M.R., ed., *Ælfric's Catholic Homilies. The Second Series: Text*, EETS ss 5 (Oxford, 1979)

Gollancz, I., ed., *The Cædmon Manuscript of Anglo-Saxon Biblical Poetry, Junius XI in the Bodleian Library* (Oxford, 1927)

Goolden, P., ed., *The Old English 'Apollonius of Tyre'* (Oxford, 1958)

Gordon, I.L., ed., *The Seafarer* (London, 1960)

Gradon, P.O.E., ed., *Cynewulf's 'Elene'* (London, 1958; rev. ed., Exeter, 1977)

Green, M., 'Man, Time and Apocalypse in *The Wanderer*, *The Seafarer*, and *Beowulf*, *JEGP* 74 (1975), 502–18

Greenfield, S.B., 'The Formulaic Expression of the Theme of "Exile" in Anglo-Saxon Poetry', *Speculum* 30 (1955), 200–6 (repr. in his *Hero and Exile: the Art of Old English Poetry*, ed. G.H. Brown (London and Ronceverte, NC, 1989), pp. 125–31)

'*Beowulf* 207b–228: Narrative and Descriptive Art', *N&Q* ns 13 (1966), 86–90 (repr. in his *Hero and Exile*, pp. 27–32)

'The Authenticating Voice in *Beowulf*, *ASE* 5 (1976), 51–62 (repr. in his *Hero and Exile*, pp. 43–54)

'A Touch of the Monstrous in the Hero or Beowulf Re-Marvellized', *ES* 63 (1982), 294–300 (repr. in his *Hero and Exile*, pp. 67–73)

'*Wulf and Eadwacer:* All Passion Pent', *ASE* 15 (1986), 5–14 (repr. in his *Hero and Exile*, pp. 185–94)

Grierson, P., and M. Blackburn, *Medieval European Coinage, with a Catalogue of the Coins in the Fitzwilliam Museum, Cambridge: I. The Early Middle Ages (5th to 10th Centuries)* (Cambridge, 1986)

Grimm, J., and W. Grimm, *Deutsches Wörterbuch*, 16 vols. in 32 (Leipzig, 1854–1960)

Hamilton, N.E.S.A., ed., *Willelmi Malmesbiriensis Monachi Gesta Pontificum Anglorum*, RS 52 (London, 1870; cited as WM, *GP*)

Hansen, E.T., *The Solomon Complex: Reading Wisdom in Old English Poetry* (Toronto, 1988)

Hargrove, H.L., ed., *King Alfred's Old English Version of St Augustine's Soliloquies*, Yale Studies in English 13 (New Haven, CT, 1902)

Healey, A. di Paolo, ed., *The Old English Vision of St Paul*, Speculum Anniversary Monographs 2 (Cambridge, MA, 1978)

Healey., A. di Paolo, and R.L. Venezky, *A Microfiche Concordance to Old English* (Toronto, 1980)

Henel, H., ed., *Ælfric's 'De temporibus anni'*, EETS os 213 (London, 1942)

Hilberg, I., ed., *Sancti Eusebii Hieronymi Opera*, 3 vols, CSEL 54–6 (Vienna, 1910–18)

Hill, J., 'A Sequence of Associations in the Composition of *Christ* 275–347', *RES* ns 27 (1976), 296–9

'The Soldier of Christ in Old English Prose and Poetry', in *Essays in Honour of A.C. Cawley*, ed. P. Meredith, *Leeds Studies in English* ns 12 (1981), 57–80

'On the Semantics of Old English *cempa* and *campian*', *Neophilologus* 67 (1983), 273–6

'"Þæt wæs geomuru ides!" A Female Stereotype Examined', in *New Readings on Women in Old English Literature*, ed. H. Damico and A.H. Olsen (Bloomington and Indianapolis, IN, 1990), pp. 235–47

Hill, T.D., 'Figural Narrative in *Andreas:* the Conversion of the Mermedonians', *Neophilologus* 70 (1969), 261–73

'Satan's Fiery Speech: *Christ and Satan* 78–9', *N&Q* ns 19 (1972), 2–4

Hinton, D.A., *A Catalogue of the Anglo-Saxon Ornamental Metalwork 700–1100 in the Department of Antiquities Ashmolean Museum* (Oxford, 1974)

Hollis, S., 'The Thematic Structure of the *Sermo Lupi*', *ASE* 6 (1977), 175–95

Hoover, D.L., 'Evidence for Primacy of Alliteration in Old English Metre', *ASE* 14 (1985), 75–96

A New Theory of Old English Meter, American University Studies ser. IV, English Language and Literature 14 (New York, 1985)

Howlett, D.R., 'Biblical Style in Early Insular Latin', in *Sources of Anglo-Saxon Culture*, ed. P.E. Szarmach (Kalamazoo, MI, 1986), pp. 127–47

Huemer, J., ed., *Sedulii Opera Omnia*, CSEL 10 (Vienna, 1885)

Hughes, A., ed., *The Portiforium of Saint Wulstan: Corpus Christi College, Cambridge, MS. 391*, 2 vols., HBS 89–90 (London, 1958–60)

Hume, K., 'The Concept of the Hall in Old English Poetry', *ASE* 3 (1974), 63–74

Hunter Blair, P., *The World of Bede*, 2nd ed. (Cambridge, 1990)

Irving, E.B., Jr, 'Latin Prose Sources for Old English Verse', *JEGP* 56 (1957), 588–95

'The Heroic Style in *The Battle of Maldon*', *SP* 58 (1961), 457–67

'New Notes on the Old English *Exodus*', *Anglia* 90 (1972), 289–324

'A Reading of *Andreas:* the Poem as Poem', *ASE* 12 (1983), 215–37

'*Exodus* Retraced', in *Old English Studies*, ed. Burlin and Irving, pp. 203–23

Irving, E.B., Jr, ed., *The Old English 'Exodus'*, Yale Studies in English 122 (New Haven, CT, 1953)

Jabbour, A., 'Memorial Transmission in Old English Poetry', *Chaucer Review* 3 (1968–9), 174–90

Jespersen, O., *Language: its Nature, Development and Origin* (London, 1954)

Jónsson, F., ed., *Den norsk-islandske Skjaldedigtning*, 4 vols. (Copenhagen, 1912–15)

Jost, K., ed., *Die 'Institutes of Polity, Civil and Ecclesiastical'*, Swiss Studies in English 47 (Bern, 1959)

Keary, C.F., *A Catalogue of English Coins in the British Museum: I. Anglo-Saxon Series* (London, 1887)

Keenan, H.T., 'Satan Speaks in Sparks: *Christ and Satan* 78–79a, 161b–162b, and the *Life of St Anthony*', *N&Q* 21 (1974), 283–4

Keller, W., *Angelsächsische Palaeographie*, 2 vols., Palaestra 43 (Berlin, 1906)

Kellogg, R.L., *A Concordance of Eddic Poetry* (Woodbridge, 1988)

Kelly, B., 'The Formative Stages of *Beowulf* Textual Scholarship: Part II', *ASE* 12 (1983), 239–75

Kelly, J.N.D., *Early Christian Creeds*, 3rd ed. (London, 1972)

Kendall, C.B., 'The Prefix *un-* and the Metrical Grammar of *Beowulf*', *ASE* 10 (1982), 39–52

The Metrical Grammar of 'Beowulf', CSASE 5 (Cambridge, 1991)

Keynes, S., 'A Tale of Two Kings: Alfred the Great and Æthelred the Unready', *TRHS* 5th ser. 36 (1986), 195–217

Anglo-Saxon Manuscripts in the Library of Trinity College, Cambridge, OEN Subsidia 18 (1992)

'A Lost Cartulary of St Albans Abbey', *ASE* 22 (1993), 253–79

Keynes, S., and M. Blackburn, *Anglo-Saxon Coins: an Exhibition*, ed. T.R. Volk (Cambridge, 1985)

Keynes, S., and M. Lapidge, trans., *Alfred the Great: Asser's 'Life of King Alfred' and other Contemporary Sources* (Harmondsworth, 1983)

Kiernan, K.S., *'Beowulf' and the 'Beowulf' Manuscript* (New Brunswick, NJ, 1981)

'Reading Cædmon's "Hymn" with Someone Else's Glosses', *Representations* 32 (1990), 157–70

Klaeber, F., 'Die christlichen Elemente im Beowulf III', *Anglia* 35 (1911), 453–82

Klaeber, F., ed., *Beowulf and the Finnsburh Fragment*, 3rd ed. (Boston, 1950)

Korhammer, M., ed., *Words, Texts and Manuscripts: Studies in Anglo-Saxon Culture presented to Helmut Gneuss on the Occasion of his Sixty-Fifth Birthday* (Woodbridge, 1992),

Koskenniemi, I., *Repetitive Word Pairs in Old and Early Middle English Prose* (Turku, 1968)

Kotzor, G., ed., *Das altenglische Martyrologium*, 2 vols. (Munich, 1981)

Krapp, G.P., and E.V.K. Dobbie, ed., ASPR, 6 vols. (New York, 1931–42)

Kretzschmar, Jr, W.A., 'Adaptation and *anweald* in the Old English Orosius', *ASE* 16 (1987), 127–45

Kuhn, S.M., 'Old English *aglæca* – Middle Irish *óclach*', in *Linguistic Method: Essays in Honor of Herbert Penzl*, ed. I. Rauch and G.F. Carr (The Hague, 1979), pp. 213–30

Lagenpusch, E., *Das germanische Recht im 'Heliand'* (Breslau, 1894)

Laistner, M.L.W., 'Some Early Medieval Commentaries on the Old Testament', *Harvard Theological Review* 46 (1953), 27–46

Laistner, M.L.W., ed., *Bedae Venerabilis Expositio Actuum Apostolorum et Retractatio*, Mediaeval Academy of America Publications 35 (Cambridge, MA, 1939)

Lapidge, M., 'The Hermeneutic Style in Tenth-Century Anglo-Latin Literature', *ASE* 4 (1975), 67–111 (repr. in his *Anglo-Latin Literature 900–1066* (London and Rio Grande, OH, 1993), pp. 105–49)

'Aldhelm's Latin Poetry and Old English Verse', *Comparative Literature* 31 (1979), 209–31

'Some Latin Poems as Evidence for the Reign of Athelstan', *ASE* 9 (1981), 61–98 (repr. in his *Anglo-Latin Literature 900–1066*, pp. 49–86)

'*Beowulf*, Aldhelm, the *Liber monstrorum* and Wessex', *SM* 23 (1982), 151–92

'The School of Theodore and Hadrian', *ASE* 15 (1986), 45–72

'*Beowulf* and the Psychology of Terror', in *Heroic Poetry in the Anglo-Saxon Period. Studies in Honor of Jess B. Bessinger, Jr*, ed. H. Damico and J. Leyerle, Studies in Medieval Culture 32 (Kalamazoo, MI, 1993), 373–402

Lapidge, M., and H. Gneuss, ed., *Learning and Literature in Anglo-Saxon England: Studies presented to Peter Clemoes on the Occasion of his Sixty-Fifth Birthday* (Cambridge, 1985)

Lapidge, M., and M. Herren, trans., *Aldhelm: the Prose Works* (Cambridge and Totowa, NJ, 1979)

Lapidge, M., and J.L. Rosier, trans., *Aldhelm: the Poetic Works* (Cambridge, 1985)

Larrington, C., '*Hávamál* and Sources outside Scandinavia', *SBVS* 23 (1991), 141–57

Lehmann, W.P., *A Gothic Etymological Dictionary* (Leiden, 1986)

Leigh, D., 'Ambiguity in Anglo-Saxon Style I Art', *AntJ* 64 (1984), 34–42

Liebermann, F., ed., *Die Heiligen Englands* (Hannover, 1889)

Die Gesetze der Angelsachsen, 3 vols. (Halle a. S., 1903–16)

Lindsay, W.M., ed., *Isidori Hispalensis Episcopi Etymologiarum sive originum libri xx*, 2 vols. (Oxford, 1911)

Loyn, H.R., *The Governance of Anglo-Saxon England 500–1087* (London, 1984)

Lucas, P.J., 'Easter, the Death of St Guthlac and the Liturgy for Holy Saturday in Felix's *Vita* and the Old English *Guthlac B*', *MÆ* 61 (1992), 1–16

Lucas, P.J., ed., *Exodus* (London, 1977)

Maclean, D., 'The Date of the Ruthwell Cross', in *The Ruthwell Cross*, ed. Cassidy, pp. 49–70

Malmberg, L., ed., *Resignation*, Durham and St Andrews Medieval Texts 2 (Durham, 1979)

Malone, K., 'The Old English Period (to 1100)', in *A Literary History of England*, ed. A.C. Baugh (New York, 1948), pp. 3–105

Malone, K., ed., *The Nowell Codex: British Museum Cotton Vitellius A. xv*, EEMF 12 (Copenhagen, 1963)

Mayer, A., 'Mater et Filia: ein Versuch zur stilgeschichtlichen Entwicklung eines Gebetsausdrucks', *Jahrbuch für Liturgiewissenschaft* 7 (1927), 60–82

Mayr-Harting, H., *The Coming of Christianity to Anglo-Saxon England*, 3rd ed. (London, 1991)

Meissner, R., *Die Kenningar der Skalden: ein Beitrag zur skaldischen Poetik* (Bonn and Leipzig, 1921)

Mellinkoff, R., 'Cain's Monstrous Progeny in *Beowulf*: Part I, Noachic Tradition', *ASE* 8 (1979), 143–62

'Cain's Monstrous Progeny in *Beowulf*: Part II, Post-Diluvian Survival', *ASE* 9 (1980), 183–97

Meyvaert, P., 'A New Perspective on the Ruthwell Cross: Ecclesia and Vita Monastica', in *The Ruthwell Cross*, ed. Cassidy, pp. 95–166

Miller, T., ed., *The Old English Version of Bede's Ecclesiastical History of the English People*, 4 vols., EETS os 95, 96, 110 and 111 (London, 1890–8)

Mimura (Ono), E. 'The Syntax and Semantics of *gāst* in Old English Poetry', *Annual Collection of Essays and Studies, Faculty of Letters, Gakushurin University* 33 (1986), 103–37

'The Syntax and Semantics of *gāst* and *sāwol* in Old English Poetry', *Annual Collection of Essays and Studies, Faculty of Letters, Gakushurin University* 34 (1987), 201–45

Mincoff, M.K., *Die Bedeutungsentwicklung der ags. Ausdrücke für 'Kraft' und 'Macht'*, Palaestra 188 (Berlin, 1933)

Mitchell, B., 'Some Syntactical Problems in *The Wanderer*', *NM* 69 (1968), 172–98 (repr. in his *On Old English: Selected Papers* (Oxford, 1988), pp. 99–117)

Old English Syntax, 2 vols. (Oxford, 1985)

Moffat, D., ed., *The Old English 'Soul and Body'* (Woodbridge, 1990)

Morin, G., ed., *Caesarii Arelatensis Opera*, 2 vols., CCSL 103–4 (Turnhout, 1953)

Morison, S., 'OE *cempa* in Cynewulf's *Juliana* and the Figure of the *Miles Christi*', *ELN* 17 (1979), 81–4

Morris, R., ed., *The Blickling Homilies*, EETS os 58, 63 and 73 (London, 1874–80; repr. in 1 vol., 1967)

Morrish, J., 'King Alfred's Letter as a Source on Learning in England in the Ninth Century', in *Studies in Earlier Old English Prose*, ed. Szarmach, pp. 87–107

Mostert, M., *The Political Theology of Abbo of Fleury* (Hilversum, 1987)

Napier, A., ed., *Wulfstan, Sammlung der ihm zugeschriebenen Homilien* (Berlin, 1883; repr. with an app. by K. Ostheeren, Berlin, 1966)

Neckel, G., ed., *Edda. Die Lieder des Codex Regius nebst verwandten Denkmälern*, 2 vols., 3rd ed. rev. H. Kuhn (Heidelberg, 1962–8)

Niles, J.D., *'Beowulf': the Poem and its Tradition* (Cambridge, MA, and London, 1983)

Nöth, W., 'Semiotics of the Old English Charm', *Semiotica* 19 (1977), 59–83

Oakeshott, W., *The Mosaics of Rome* (London, 1967)

Ohlgren, T.H., *Anglo-Saxon Art: Texts and Contexts*, OEN Subsidia 17 (1991)

O'Keeffe, K.O'B., 'Orality and the Developing Text of Cædmon's *Hymn*', *Speculum* 62 (1987), 1–20

Visible Song: Transitional Literacy in Old English Verse, CSASE 4 (Cambridge, 1990)

Olsen, A.H., 'Oral-Formulaic Research in Old English Studies: I', *Oral Tradition* 1 (1986), 548–606

'Oral-Formulaic Research in Old English Studies: II', *Oral Tradition* 3 (1988), 138–90

O'Neil, W.A., 'Oral-Formulaic Structure in Old English Elegiac Poetry' (unpubl. PhD dissertation, Wisconsin Univ., 1960)

O'Neill, P.P., 'The Old English Introductions to the Prose Psalms of the Paris Psalter: Sources, Structure, and Composition', *SP* 78 (1981), 20–38

Ono, see Mimura (Ono)

Ono, S., *On Early English Syntax and Vocabulary* (Tokyo, 1989)

Opland, J., 'A *Beowulf*-Analogue in *Njáls saga*', *Scandinavian Studies* 45 (1973), 54–8

Orchard, A.P.McD., 'Some Aspects of Seventh-Century Hiberno-Latin Syntax: a Statistical Approach', *Peritia* 6–7 (1987–8), 158–201

The Poetic Art of Aldhelm, CSASE 8 (Cambridge, 1994)

Page, R.I., *An Introduction to English Runes* (London, 1973)

Parkes, M.B., 'The Manuscript of the Leiden Riddle', *ASE* 1 (1972), 207–17

Parks, W., 'The Traditional Narrator and the "I Heard" Formulas in Old English Poetry', *ASE* 16 (1987), 45–66

Parry, M., 'Studies in the Epic Technique of Oral Verse-Making. 1: Homer and Homeric Style', *Harvard Studies in Classical Philology* 41 (1930), 73–147

Plummer, C., ed., *Venerabilis Baedae Opera Historica*, 2 vols. (Oxford, 1896)

Pope, J.C., 'The Lacuna in the Text of Cynewulf's *Ascension* (*Christ II*, 556b)', in *Studies in Language, Literature, and Culture of the Middle Ages and Later*, ed. E.B. Atwood and A.A. Hill (Austin, TX, 1969), pp. 210–19

'Beowulf's Old Age', in *Philological Essays: Studies in Old and Middle English Language and Literature in Honour of Herbert Dean Meritt*, ed. J.L. Rosier (The Hague and Paris, 1970), pp. 55–64

'Palaeography and Poetry: some Solved and Unsolved Problems of the Exeter Book', in *Medieval Scribes, Manuscripts and Libraries: Essays presented to N.R. Ker*, ed. M.B. Parkes and A.G. Watson (London, 1978), pp. 25–65

Pope, J.C., ed., *Homilies of Ælfric: a Supplementary Collection*, 2 vols., EETS os 259–60 (London, 1967–8)

Porsia, F., ed., *Liber monstrorum* (Bari, 1976)

Quirk, R., 'Poetic Language and Old English Metre', in *Early English and Norse Studies presented to Hugh Smith in Honour of his Sixtieth Birthday*, ed. A. Brown and P. Foote (London, 1963), pp. 150–71

Rankin, S., 'The Liturgical Background of the Old English Advent Lyrics: a Reappraisal', in *Learning and Literature in Anglo-Saxon England*, ed. Lapidge and Gneuss, pp. 317–40

Reinhard, M., *On the Semantic Relevance of the Alliterative Collocations in 'Beowulf'*, Swiss Studies in English 92 (Bern, 1976)

Remley, P.G., 'The Latin Textual Basis of *Genesis A*', *ASE* 17 (1988), 163–89

Renoir, A., '*Wulf and Eadwacer:* a Noninterpretation', in *Medieval and Linguistic Studies*, ed. Bessinger and Creed, pp. 147–63

Rice, R.C., 'The Penitential Motif in Cynewulf's *Fates of the Apostles* and in his Epilogues', *ASE* 6 (1977), 105–19

Richman, G., 'Speaker and Speech Boundaries in *The Wanderer*', *JEGP* 81 (1982), 469–79

Ridyard, S.J., *The Royal Saints of Anglo-Saxon England*, Cambridge Studies in Medieval Life and Thought, 4th ser. 9 (Cambridge, 1988)

Robertson, A.J., ed., *Anglo-Saxon Charters* (Cambridge, 1939)

Robinson, F.C., 'The Significance of Names in Old English Literature', *Anglia* 86 (1968), 14–58

'Elements of the Marvellous in the Characterization of Beowulf', in *Old English Studies*, ed. Burlin and Irving, pp. 119–37

Rollason, D.W., 'Lists of Saints' Resting-Places in Anglo-Saxon England', *ASE* 7 (1978), 61–93

The Mildrith Legend: a Study in Early Medieval Hagiography in England (Leicester, 1982)

Rosier, J.L., '*Instructions for Christians:* a Poem in Old English', *Anglia* 82 (1964), 4–22

Rypins, S.I., ed., *Three Old English Prose Texts*, EETS os 161 (London, 1924)

Sawyer, P.H., *Anglo-Saxon Charters: an Annotated List* (London, 1968)

Schaar, C., *Critical Studies in the Cynewulf Group*, Lund Studies in English 17 (Lund, 1949)

Schapiro, M., 'The Image of the Disappearing Christ', *Gazette des Beaux-Arts*, 6th ser. 23 (1943), 135–52 (repr. in his *Late Antique, Early Christian and Mediaeval Art* (London, 1980), pp. 266–87)

Scharer, A., 'Die Intitulationes der angelsächsischen Könige im 7. und 8. Jahrhundert', in *Intitulatio: III. Lateinische Herrschertitel und Herrschertitulaturen von 7. bis zum 13. Jahrhundert*, ed. H. Wolfram and A. Scharer (Vienna, 1988), pp. 9–74

Scragg, D.G., 'The Compilation of the Vercelli Book', *ASE* 2 (1973), 189–207

'The Corpus of Vernacular Homilies and Prose Saints' Lives before Ælfric', *ASE* 8 (1979), 223–77

Scragg, D.G., ed., *The Battle of Maldon* (Manchester, 1981)

The Battle of Maldon A.D. 991 (Oxford, 1991)

The Vercelli Homilies and Related Texts, EETS os 300 (London, 1992)

Sedgefield, W.J., ed., *King Alfred's Old English Version of Boethius 'De consolatione Philosophiae'* (Oxford, 1899)

Shippey, T.A., *Old English Verse* (London, 1972)

Silverstein, T., *'Visio Sancti Pauli': the History of the Apocalypse in Latin together with Nine Texts*, Studies and Documents 4 (London, 1935)

Sims-Williams, P., 'Cuthswith, Seventh-Century Abbess of Inkberrow, near Worcester, and the Würzburg Manuscript of Jerome on Ecclesiastes', *ASE* 5 (1976), 1–21

'Thought, Word and Deed: an Irish Triad', *Ériu* 29 (1978), 78–111

Religion and Literature in Western England 600–800, CSASE 3 (Cambridge, 1990)

Sisam, C., ed., *The Vercelli Book*, EEMF 19 (Copenhagen, 1976)

Sisam, K., 'Anglo-Saxon Royal Genealogies', *PBA* 39 (1953), 287–348

Studies in the History of Old English Literature (Oxford, 1953)

The Structure of 'Beowulf' (Oxford, 1965)

Skeat, W.W., *An Etymological Dictionary of the English Language* (Oxford, 1882)

Skeat, W.W., ed., *Ælfric's Lives of Saints*, 4 vols., EETS os 76, 82, 94 and 114 (London, 1881–1900)

Sleeth, C.R., *Studies in 'Christ and Satan'* (Toronto, 1982)

Smith, J., 'The Garments that Honour the Cross in *The Dream of the Rood*', *ASE* 4 (1975), 29–35

Speake, G., *Anglo-Saxon Animal Art and its Germanic Background* (Oxford, 1980)

Stanley, E.G., 'Old English Poetic Diction and the Interpretation of *The Wanderer*, *The Seafarer* and *The Penitent's Prayer*', *Anglia* 73 (1955), 413–66 (repr. in his *A Collection of Papers with Emphasis on Old English Literature* (Toronto, 1987), pp. 234–80)

'Studies in the Prosaic Vocabulary of Old English Verse', *Neuphilologische Mitteilungen* 72 (1971), 385–418

'Two Old English Poetic Phrases Insufficiently Understood for Literary Criticism: *þing gehegan* and *seonoþ gehegan*', in *Old English Poetry*, ed. Calder, pp. 67–90 (repr. in his *A Collection of Papers*, pp. 298–317)

'*The Judgement of the Damned* (from Cambridge, Corpus Christi College 201 and other Manuscripts) and the Definition of Old English Verse', in *Learning and Literature in Anglo-Saxon England*, ed. Lapidge and Gneuss, pp. 363–91 (repr. in his *A Collection of Papers*, pp. 352–83)

Stenton, F.M., *Anglo-Saxon England*, 3rd ed. (Oxford, 1971)

Storms, G., *Anglo-Saxon Magic* (The Hague, 1948)

Sveinbjorn Egilsson, S., *Lexicon Poeticum Antiquae Linguae Septentrionalis*, rev. F. Jónsson (Copenhagen, 1966)

Sweet, H., ed., *King Alfred's West-Saxon Version of 'Gregory's Pastoral Care'*, 2 vols. EETS os 45 and 50 (London, 1871)

Szarmach, P.E., ed., *Studies in Earlier Old English Prose* (Albany, NY, 1986)

Tangl, M., ed., *S. Bonifacii et Lullii Epistolae*, MGH Epistolae selectae 1 (Berlin, 1916)

Taylor, H.M., *Repton Studies 2: the Anglo-Saxon Crypt and Church* (Cambridge, 1979)

St Wystan's Church Repton: a Guide and History (Repton, 1989)

Taylor, H.M., and J. Taylor, *Anglo-Saxon Architecture*, 3 vols. (Cambridge, 1965–78), vol. III by H.M.T. only

Þórólfsson, B.K., and G. Jónsson, ed., *Fóstbræðra saga*, Islenzk Fornrit 6 (Reykjavik, 1943)

Thorpe, B., ed., *The Homilies of the Anglo-Saxon Church: the First Part containing the Sermones Catholici, or Homilies of Ælfric*, 2 vols. (London, 1844–6)

Timmer, B.J., ed., *The Later Genesis*, rev. ed. (Oxford, 1954)

Trahern, Jr, J.B., 'Caesarius of Arles and Old English Literature: some Contributions and a Recapitulation', *ASE* 5 (1976), 105–19

Tripp, Jr, R.P., 'Did Beowulf have an "Inglorious Youth"?', *Studia Neophilologica* 61 (1989), 129–43

Vries, J. de, *Altnordisches etymologisches Wörterbuch* (Leiden, 1961)

Walker, A., trans., *Apocryphal Gospels, Acts, and Revelations*, Ante-Nicene Christian Library 16 (Edinburgh, 1870)

Wallace-Hadrill, J.M., *Early Germanic Kingship in England and on the Continent* (Oxford, 1971)

Waterhouse, R., 'Spatial Perception and Conceptions in the (Re-)Presenting and (Re-)Constructing of Old English Texts', *Parergon* ns 9 (1991), 87–102

Watts, A.C., *The Lyre and the Harp: a Comparative Reconsideration of Oral Tradition in Homer and Old English Epic Poetry* (New Haven, CT, 1969)

Webster, L., and J. Backhouse, *The Making of England: Anglo-Saxon Art and Culture AD 600–900* (London, 1991)

Weman, B., *Old English Semantic Theory with Special Reference to Verbs Denoting Locomotion* (Lund, 1933)

Whallon, W., *Formula, Character, and Context* (Cambridge, MA, 1969)

Whitelock, D., 'Wulfstan and the So-Called Laws of Edward and Guthrum', *EHR* 56 (1941), 1–21 (repr. in her *History, Law and Literature in Tenth-Eleventh Century England* (London, 1981), item IX)

'The Numismatic Interest of an Old English Version of the Legend of the Seven Sleepers', in *Anglo-Saxon Coins: Studies presented to F.M. Stenton on the Occasion of his Eightieth Birthday*, ed. R.H.M. Dolley (London, 1961), pp. 188–94

Whitelock, D., ed., *Sermo Lupi ad Anglos*, 3rd ed. (London, 1963; repr. with additional bibliography, Exeter, 1976)

English Historical Documents, c. 500–1042, 2nd ed. (London, 1979)

Anglo-Saxon Wills (Cambridge, 1930)

Whitelock, D., with D.C. Douglas and S.I. Tucker, *The Anglo-Saxon Chronicle: a Revised Translation* (London, 1961)

Williamson, C., ed., *The Old English Riddles of the 'Exeter Book'* (Chapel Hill, NC, 1977)

Williamson, C., trans., *A Feast of Creatures: Anglo-Saxon Riddle-Songs* (Philadelphia, PA, 1982)

Wilson, A., trans., *Apocryphal Gospels, Acts, and Revelations*, Alexander Ante-Nicene Christian Library 16 (Edinburgh, 1870)

Wilson, D.M., *Anglo-Saxon Art from the Seventh Century to the Norman Conquest* (London, 1984)

Wilson, D.M., ed., *The Bayeux Tapestry* (London, 1985)

Winterbottom, M., ed., *Three Lives of English Saints* (Toronto, 1972)

Wormald, P., 'Bede, *Beowulf* and the Conversion of the Anglo-Saxon Aristocracy', in *Bede and Anglo-Saxon England*, ed. R.T. Farrell, BAR 46 (1978), 32–95

Wright, C.D., 'The Irish "Enumerative Style" in Old English Homiletic Literature, Especially Vercelli Homily IX', *CMCS* 18 (1989), 27–74

The Irish Tradition in Old English Literature, CSASE 6 (Cambridge, 1993)

Wright, C.E., *The Cultivation of Saga in Anglo-Saxon England* (Edinburgh, 1939)

Wright, N., 'The *Hisperica Famina* and Caelius Sedulius', *CMCS* 4 (1982), 61–76

Appendix to *Aldhelm: the Poetic Works*, trans. Lapidge and Rosier, pp. 181–219

Index I

Quotations of two or more 'lines' of Old English poetry

The italicized reference before a colon is to 'lines'; the reference after a colon is to page.

Index II

A representative selection of the symbols and word pairs cited in discussion

Symbols

Under a headword I have not included a form which is in a passage listed in Index I without featuring in discussion accompanying the passage (e.g., *swegles gæst* (*Christ* (*I*) 203b) at p. 374); nor under a form have I registered an occurrence in these circumstances (e.g., 'fela feorhcynna' (*Beowulf* 2266a) at p. 198).

[*a*] = compounds [*b*] = genitive combinations
[*c*] = adjective combinations [*d*] = three-element symbols
— = inclusion of the headword in a compound
~ = use of the headword in a genitive or adjective combination
X = various words compounded with the headword or a derivative of it and discussed collectively
Round brackets indicate variables and hyphens indicate variant spellings.

Bold type indicates substantial discussion. Reference is to page.

Word pairs

Bold type indicates substantial discussion. Reference is to page.

Index III

General